VIRGINIA

KATIE GITHENS

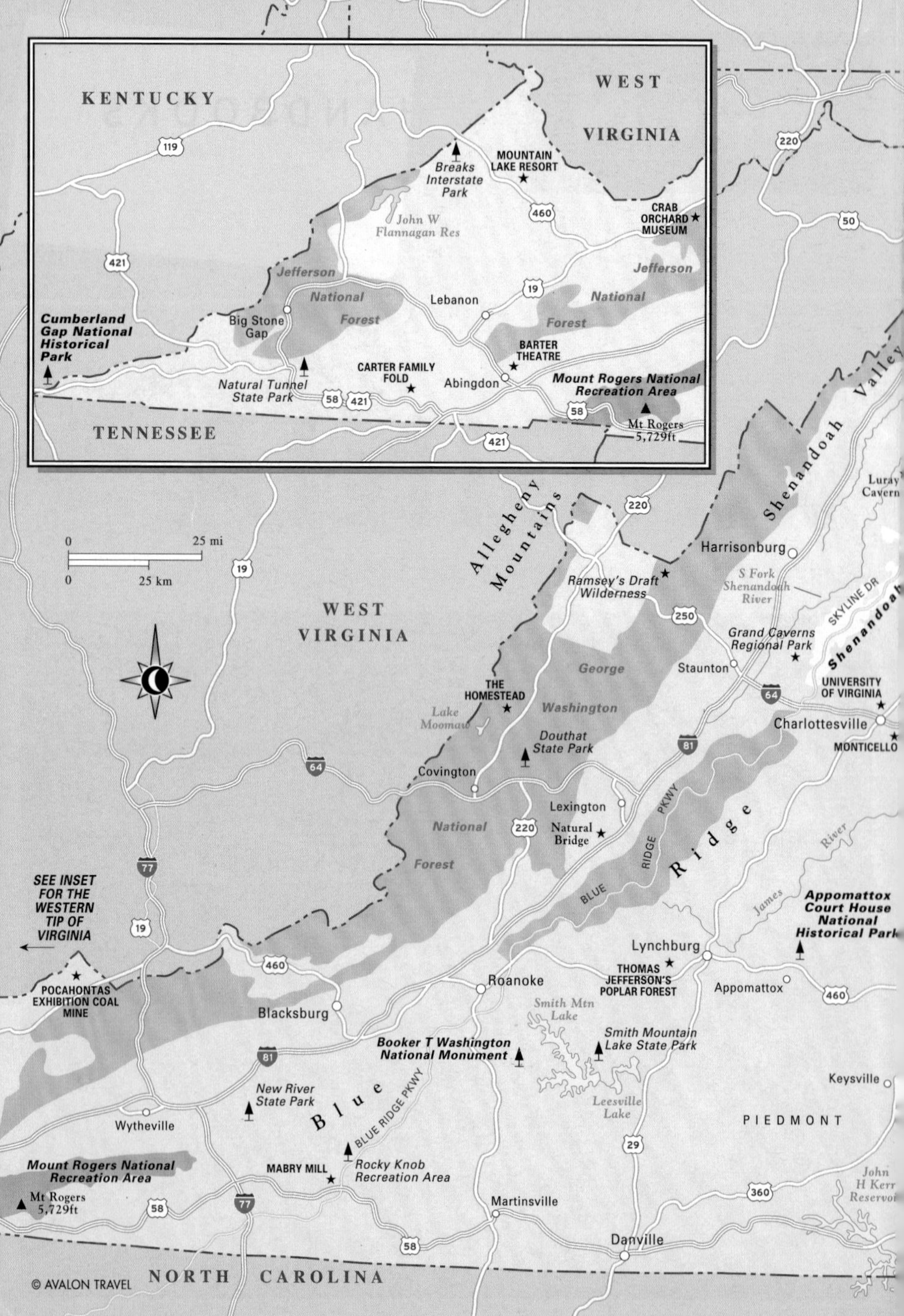

KENTUCKY
WEST VIRGINIA
TENNESSEE
Breaks Interstate Park
MOUNTAIN LAKE RESORT
CRAB ORCHARD MUSEUM
John W Flannagan Res
Jefferson National Forest
Lebanon
Big Stone Gap
Cumberland Gap National Historical Park
BARTER THEATRE
CARTER FAMILY FOLD
Abingdon
Natural Tunnel State Park
Mount Rogers National Recreation Area
Mt Rogers 5,729ft
119
421
460
19
58
220
50
0 25 mi
0 25 km
WEST VIRGINIA
Allegheny Mountains
Shenandoah Valley
Luray Caverns
Harrisonburg
Ramsey's Draft Wilderness
S Fork Shenandoah River
SKYLINE DR
Shenandoah
250
Grand Caverns Regional Park
Staunton
George Washington National Forest
THE HOMESTEAD
Lake Moomaw
Douthat State Park
UNIVERSITY OF VIRGINIA
Charlottesville
MONTICELLO
64
81
Covington
Lexington
Natural Bridge
BLUE RIDGE PKWY
Blue Ridge
James River
77
SEE INSET FOR THE WESTERN TIP OF VIRGINIA
Appomattox Court House National Historical Park
POCAHONTAS EXHIBITION COAL MINE
Lynchburg
THOMAS JEFFERSON'S POPLAR FOREST
Roanoke
Appomattox
Blacksburg
Smith Mtn Lake
Smith Mountain Lake State Park
Booker T Washington National Monument
Keysville
New River State Park
Leesville Lake
Wytheville
PIEDMONT
29
Mount Rogers National Recreation Area
MABRY MILL
Rocky Knob Recreation Area
360
John H Kerr Reservoir
Martinsville
Danville
NORTH CAROLINA

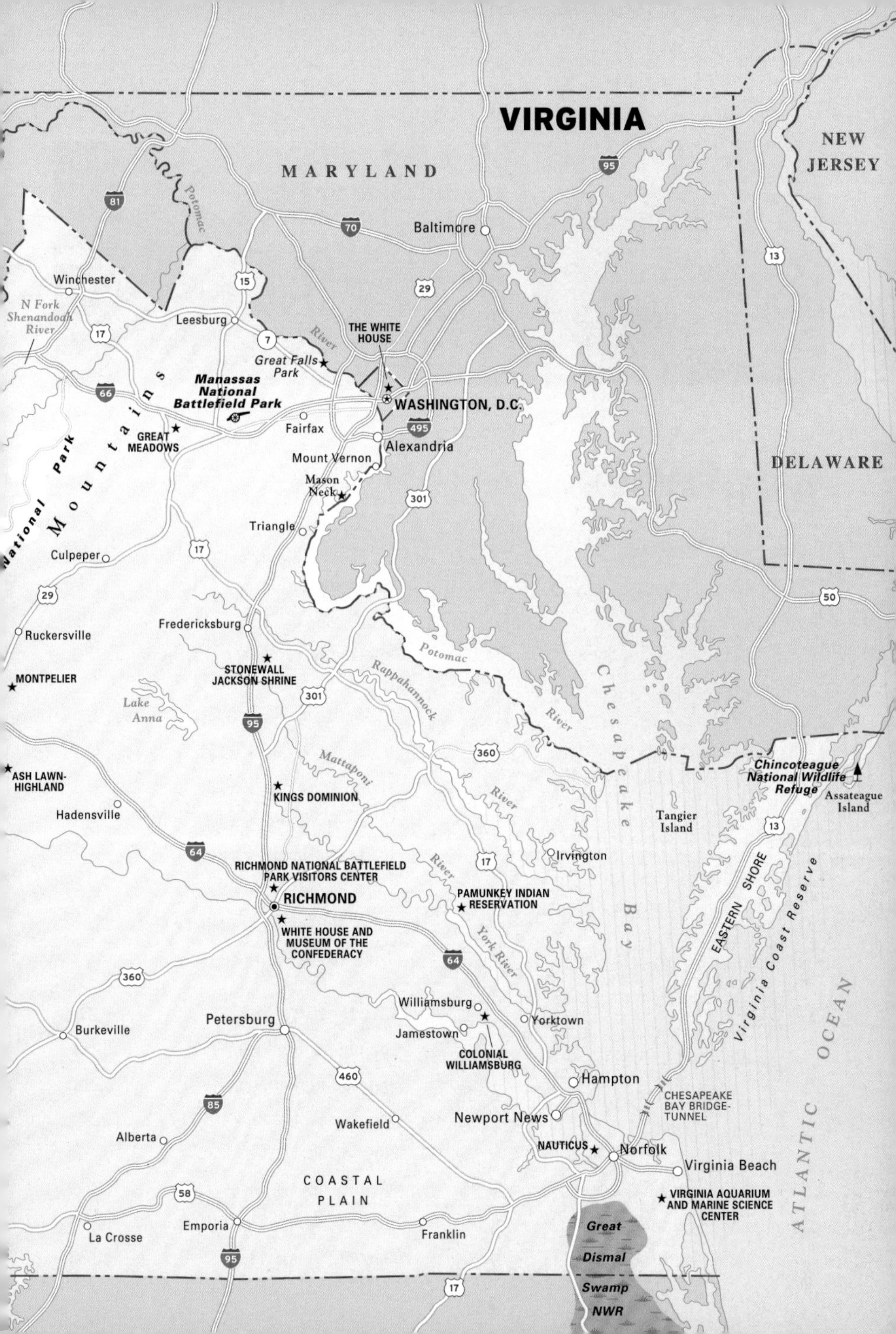

VIRGINIA
MARYLAND
NEW JERSEY
DELAWARE
Baltimore
Winchester
N Fork Shenandoah River
Leesburg
Potomac
River
THE WHITE HOUSE
Great Falls Park
Manassas National Battlefield Park
WASHINGTON, D.C.
GREAT MEADOWS
Fairfax
Alexandria
Mount Vernon
Mason Neck
Triangle
National Park
Mountains
Culpeper
Fredericksburg
Ruckersville
STONEWALL JACKSON SHRINE
MONTPELIER
Lake Anna
Potomac River
Rappahannock River
Chesapeake Bay
Mattaponi River
ASH LAWN-HIGHLAND
KINGS DOMINION
Hadensville
Chincoteague National Wildlife Refuge
Assateague Island
Tangier Island
Irvington
RICHMOND NATIONAL BATTLEFIELD PARK VISITORS CENTER
RICHMOND
WHITE HOUSE AND MUSEUM OF THE CONFEDERACY
PAMUNKEY INDIAN RESERVATION
York River
EASTERN SHORE
Virginia Coast Reserve
ATLANTIC OCEAN
Williamsburg
Jamestown
Yorktown
COLONIAL WILLIAMSBURG
Petersburg
Burkeville
Hampton
CHESAPEAKE BAY BRIDGE-TUNNEL
Newport News
Wakefield
Alberta
NAUTICUS
Norfolk
Virginia Beach
VIRGINIA AQUARIUM AND MARINE SCIENCE CENTER
COASTAL PLAIN
La Crosse
Emporia
Franklin
Great Dismal Swamp NWR
95
81
70
15
29
17
7
66
495
301
50
13
360
64
460
85
58

Contents

STONEWALL
JACKSON

Discover Virginia

President John F. Kennedy, in a moment of irritation at life inside the Beltway, once described Washington, D.C., as a city of "northern charm and southern efficiency." Just across the Potomac spreads a state that's just the opposite, and justifiably proud of it. From the banking towers of Richmond to the most remote Blue Ridge farm, Virginia incorporates the best of the two worlds it bridges. The result is one of the most fascinating and appealing states in the country.

Any American who's sat through the eighth grade knows that Virginia embodies history like few other states in the Union. From the first English colonists to settle in the New World at Jamestown and the heady days of the founding fathers in Williamsburg through the end of the American Revolution at Yorktown and the tragedy and heroism of the Civil War, many of the major events that shaped this country happened in the Old Dominion.

The state's gorgeous scenery is only one reason it has always been such a magnetic lure, first for settlers and now for millions of visitors every year. They're drawn to world-famous places such as Mount Vernon, Monticello, Colonial Williamsburg, and more Civil War battlefields than any other state. Lovers of the outdoors are drawn to Virginia's incredible diversity of landscapes, from sandy coastal plains to rugged Appalachian peaks, lazy rivers to white water, barrier islands to hidden mountain

coves. You can find hiking, biking, rafting, climbing, fishing, and skiing from one end of the state to the other.

Best of all, though – in this state of 50-cent-soda machines and billion-dollar aircraft carriers, urban sprawl and wild ponies – are the Virginians themselves. Anyone who ventures beyond the interstates and the parking-lot hordes of tourists will quickly discover the Old Dominion's true treasure: her inhabitants, who embody the opposite of Kennedy's assessment – southern warmth, northern know-how – along with a generous helping of that unique ingredient summed up in this popular quotation of unknown origin: "To be a Virginian, either by birth, marriage, or adoption, or even on one's mother's side, is an introduction to any state in the union, a passport to any foreign country, and a benediction from Almighty God."

Virginia clings to her roots as she careens toward the future, but luckily most Virginians don't give this potentially schizophrenic situation much mind. Lucky for you and me, the result is the best of both worlds – and then some.

Planning Your Trip

▸ WHERE TO GO

Northern Virginia

Northern Virginia is an intriguing mix of fast-forward and rewind, with some of the nation's quickest-growing counties only a short drive from quaint horse-country towns such as Middleburg and Waterford. Arlington County is home to the Pentagon and the sobering Arlington National Cemetery—a before-and-after of war, if you will—as well as a spillover of ethnic restaurants and nightlife from the capital. The Potomac roars over rocks at Great Falls Park. Old Town Alexandria has kept its cobblestone Colonial past alive, and George Washington retired to Mount Vernon just downriver. To the west are the Civil War battlefields of Manassas, the equestrian estates of Loudoun County, and a number of Virginia's best wineries.

IF YOU HAVE...

- **A WEEKEND:** Visit Old Town Alexandria, Mount Vernon, and the Hunt Country.
- **FIVE DAYS:** Take Skyline Drive through Shenandoah National Park to Charlottesville.
- **ONE WEEK:** Add Richmond and Colonial Williamsburg, driving Route 5 between the two.
- **TWO WEEKS:** Add the coastal loop and Washington, D.C., or a meandering trip through southwest Virginia.

Washington, D.C.

The nation's capital draws visitors from around the world with monuments to the ideals that accompanied the founding of the country. From the Washington, Jefferson, and Lincoln Monuments to the White House, the U.S. Capitol to the Vietnam Veterans Memorial, it's as much a symbol as a city. There aren't many places with so

cherry blossoms in Washington, D.C.

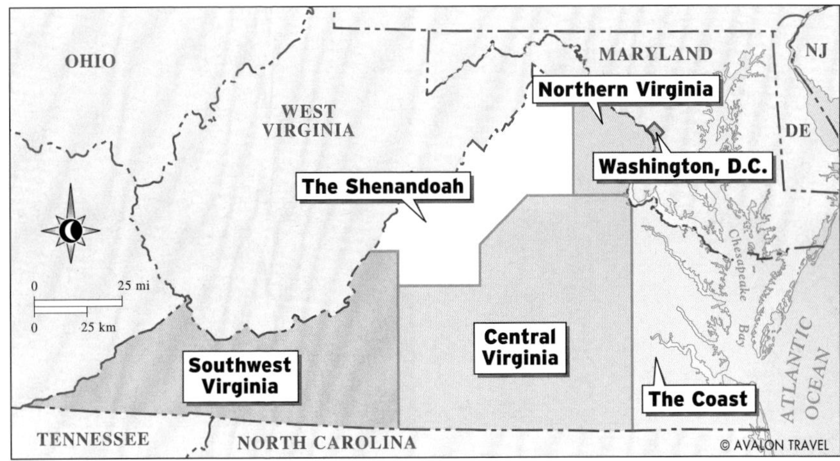

many world-class museums open for free, mostly thanks to a forward-thinking scientist named Smithson. On a sunny spring afternoon, the National Mall really does become America's front yard. Thanks to its international status, D.C. boasts an array of restaurants rivaling anywhere in the country, and even a little nightlife. It's a surprisingly outdoorsy city, too, full of joggers, bikers, and paddlers on the Potomac River.

The Coast

Virginia's thousands of miles of Atlantic coastline have several distinct faces. First are the beautiful sandy beaches and boardwalk of Virginia Beach. Only a short distance away is the Historic Peninsula, home to world-famous Colonial Williamsburg; Jamestown, site of the first English settlement in the New World; and Yorktown, where the American Revolution ended. One of the largest estuaries on the planet, the Chesapeake Bay harbors sleepy fishing villages and wildlife-rich marshlands. Chincoteague National Wildlife Refuge, on Assateague Island at the northern end of the Eastern Shore, is famous for its herds of wild ponies, and Tangier Island is a unique cultural microcosm in the middle of the bay.

Central Virginia

It's probably dangerous to pick the "most Virginian" part of the state, but the

D.C.'s Vietnam Veterans Memorial

Assateague Island

Colonial Williamsburg

Richmond's Museum of the Confederacy

Luray Caverns

Piedmont is in the running. The capital city of Richmond is a lively metropolis saturated with Civil War history and has some of the best urban white water in the country. Bucolic Charlottesville is home to Jefferson's twin legacy of Monticello and the University of Virginia. Lynchburg embodies the legacy of the tobacco trade, and nearby are monuments to the end of the Civil War at Appomattox Court House and D-Day's most affected community at Bedford. Boating and fishing are popular at Smith Mountain Lake, and the various rivers that wind through the countryside—the James in particular—are perfect for a summer afternoon float or fly cast.

The Shenandoah

Witness to some of the Civil War's most dramatic fighting, the legendary valley between the Blue Ridge and the Alleghenies is celebrated in song and story. Moderate-size cities strung along I-81 each have their own brand of charm, from Winchester's apple-mania to Lexington's historic reverence. Shenandoah National Park covers a good portion of Virginia's Blue Ridge Mountains, threaded by Skyline Drive and the Appalachian Trail and replete with trails, waterfalls, and peaks to climb. Back down in the valley there's rafting, tubing, and angling on the Shenandoah River's broad bends. Luray Caverns are the finest in this part of the country. In the rugged Allegheny Highlands you'll find peaceful Monterey and the Homestead, Virginia's leading all-season resort.

Southwest Virginia

Not as many visitors make it down to the state's most distant corner (meaning farthest from Washington, D.C.), but those who do find a unique array of cultural diversions and just as many outdoor options as in the Shenandoah. The "Star City" of Roanoke is the largest along the Blue Ridge Parkway and has several excellent museums. Farther down I-81 is Blacksburg, home to Virginia Tech and one of the best-situated outdoorsy cities in the state. The Mount Rogers National Recreation Area contains Virginia's highest peak and a wealth of trails. In tiny Abingdon, you'll find the outstanding Martha Washington Inn and the Barter Theatre. Fans of roots music head to Floyd, Galax, and Maces Spring, home to the celebrated Carter Family.

summertime in Virginia, as painted by Richard Houser at the Harvest Table Restaurant in Meadowview

WHEN TO GO

If you're lucky enough to choose the time of year you can visit Virginia, then seasonal weather will be one of your prime concerns. Overall, spring and fall are probably the best times to visit. In April, May, and September you'll find lulls in the tourist season *and* great weather.

In the spring, equestrian events such as races and fox hunts thunder through northern Virginia, and crowds aren't yet a problem. Be warned, though, that many attractions don't open until April or May. Summer is high tourist season, even though high temperatures and humidity send most visitors to the mountains or the beaches, historic sites, and theme parks along the coast.

Fall colors typically arrive earliest in the mountains, starting in mid-October.

(Washington, D.C., is infamous for emptying out in August.) Fall's famous colors bring a second high season, although a smaller one than in the summer. In the winter, the least crowded season, you can have entire days to yourself. Many sights close, especially in the mountains and the coast. Local festivals happen throughout the year.

▸ BEFORE YOU GO

Transportation

Virginia is a smallish state by U.S. standards, but driving times can still add up: It can take a full day or more to get from one end to the other. And driving is by far the easiest way to do it: Public transportation by bus or rail is limited at best, and nonexistent at worst. Before you hit the road, arm yourself with a detailed road map or a GPS. Virginia roads—at least in northern Virginia—are notoriously convoluted and often have multiple names and/or numbers that make it easy to miss a turn.

What to Take

It's wise to dress for the weather. Temperature averages are similar throughout the state, making it easier to pack. In the spring and fall, average highs of 60–70°F, dropping to the 40s at night, mean short sleeves in the daytime and a light jacket or sweater at night. Summer highs in the 80s and 90s, amplified by high humidity levels in the Piedmont and coast, dictate shorts and short sleeves. Bring warm clothing (don't forget hats and gloves) for winter lows in the 30s and 40s, particularly up high. In terms of style, most of the state falls somewhere between Laura Ashley and J. Crew (which has one of its two distribution centers in Lynchburg): Think mild, conservative, stylish. Beachwear is OK at the beach, but no cutoff jeans at dinner.

From spring to fall, insect repellent is a must, especially along the coast, as is an umbrella. This is Lyme disease territory, so watch for ticks too. Don't forget sunscreen in the summer. It's good to bring some snacks and water in the car for long drives. Most hotels and bed-and-breakfasts supply towels and bathing accessories.

fall colors

wintertime

daffodils in spring

Explore Virginia

▶ THE BEST OF VIRGINIA

Virginia's story is really the story of the United States. From the archaeological digs of Jamestown to the Civil War battlefields in Manassas, this itinerary through the state's highlights will take you on a clockwise loop. Starting in Washington, D.C., head south to Richmond and the coast, then west through Charlottesville to the Blue Ridge Mountains. Arc back to the nation's capital through northern Virginia. While it's possible to tour the state's highlights in a week, it's better to take 10 days to do them justice.

Old Town Alexandria

Day 1

Starting in Washington, D.C., drive across the Potomac to Old Town Alexandria and George Washington's Mount Vernon. Spend the night in Fredericksburg.

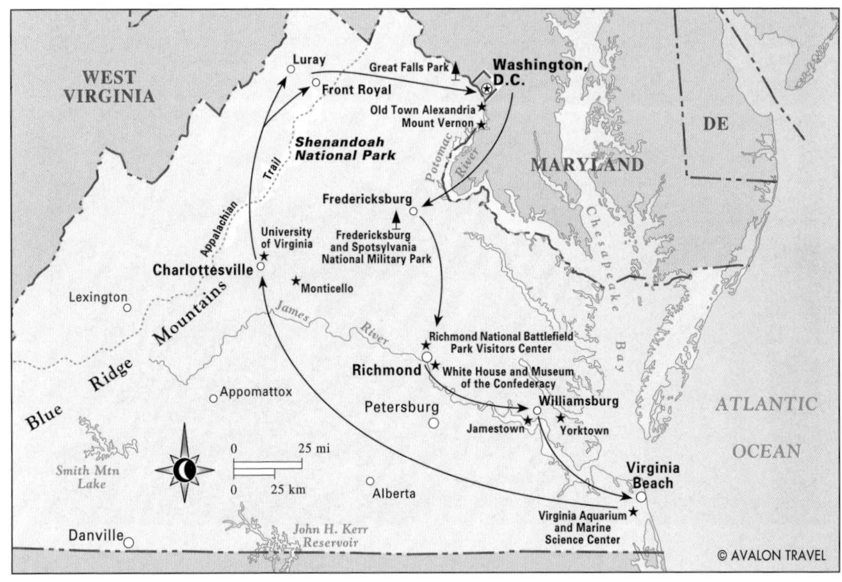

ROMANTIC GETAWAYS

With a slogan like "Virginia is for Lovers," the state sets a high bar for romantic getaways. The Old Dominion can treat you and your love to a grand tour of country inns that cater to your every romantic whim. Stone fireplace? Check. Virginia vintages? Check. Canopy beds, secluded cottages, and claw-foot tubs? Triple-check. Heck, one hideaway even has a private bathtub outdoors for soaking under the moon. Use this list, and you'll be treated to English gardens, sumptuous three-course Provençal breakfasts, and distinguished inn quarters older than America itself. Enjoy.

- **Hope and Glory Inn,** Irvington (Coast): A former schoolhouse with a (private) bath out back in the English cottage garden.
- **Inn at Little Washington,** Washington (Central): The granddaddy of them all – five stars in food and lodging.
- **L'Auberge Provençale,** White Post (Shenandoah): A charming French country inn with gourmet cooking.
- **Liberty Rose B&B,** Williamsburg (Coast): Designer fabrics and old-time hospitality in a historic setting.
- **The Red Fox Inn,** Middleburg (Northern): A cozy 18th-century inn in the heart of Hunt Country.

Other Ideas

- Grab a bottle of wine and enjoy Shakespeare and a picnic among the historic ruins at the **Barboursville Vineyards** near Charlottesville.
- Catch a movie – or the beginning of one, at least – at **Hull's Drive-In Theater** near Lexington.
- Soar in a **hot-air balloon** over the Hunt Country at dawn, and land to a champagne toast.
- Take a Thermos of coffee to the top of **Humpback Rocks,** on the northern end of the Blue Ridge Parkway, for a 360-degree sunrise view.

candlelit dinner at the 18th-century Red Fox Inn

wagon ride in Colonial Williamsburg

Day 2

Tour the Civil War battlefields of Fredericksburg and Spotsylvania National Military Park and Richmond National Battlefield Park. Sleep in Richmond.

Day 3

Take your pick of the many museums, art galleries, and restaurants in Richmond. Don't miss the White House and Museum of the Confederacy and the Richmond National Battlefield Park Visitors Center at Tredegar Ironworks. Head out for a jog, bike, or walk on Belle Isle in the James River Park for fresh air after all the museum hopping.

Day 4

Catch anything you missed in Richmond yesterday. Then take your time heading east on Route 5, visiting the historic plantation homes along the James River. Spend the night in Williamsburg.

Day 5

Spend a day in the 18th century at Colonial Williamsburg, perhaps with a side trip to Busch Gardens Europe.

Day 6

More history today: See the first English settlement in the New World at Jamestown and the decisive battle of the American Revolution at Yorktown, both part of Colonial National Historical Park. Drive to Virginia Beach in the evening to spend the night.

Day 7

You've earned a break—enjoy Virginia Beach for the day, with some sun, sand, seafood, and

Berkeley Plantation, along the James River

BEAT-THE-HEAT WEEKENDS

one of Chincoteague's wild ponies

Come August, many Virginian cities (and Washington, D.C.) start to feel like muggy terrariums. The kudzu vines love it, but just about everyone else starts daydreaming about a refreshing weekend getaway.

THE BEACH

- **Chincoteague National Wildlife Refuge and Assateague Island** (Coast): Wild ponies and stretching horizons of surf and sand. Mind the mosquitoes, though.
- **Virginia Beach** (Coast): Home to the first waves ever surfed on the East Coast.

THE LAKE

- **Mountain Lake** (Southwest): The classic family lake resort where *Dirty Dancing* was filmed is right here in Virginia.
- **Lake Anna** (Central): Man-made but great for fishing, boating, and taking a dip.
- **Smith Mountain Lake:** (Central): This lake's 500 miles of gorgeous shoreline made a cameo in *What About Bob?* with Bill Murray.

THE RIVER

- **The James** (Central): Raft Class III and IV rapids right through Richmond, or if the river is too low in August, tube 'em.
- **The Shenandoah** (Shenandoah): Another lazy tubing destination.
- **The Potomac** (Northern): Board a party barge or rent kayaks near Arlington – just don't fall in.

THE MOUNTAINS

- **Mount Rogers National Recreation Area** (Southwest): At a mile above sea level, the air is guaranteed to be cooler on Virginia's tallest peak.
- **Shenandoah National Park** (Shenandoah): Shady hollows, waterfalls, swimming holes...and hiking trails to connect them all.

sunset reflecting on the Potomac River near Mount Vernon

the Virginia Aquarium and Marine Science Center in Virginia Beach

a stop at the Virginia Aquarium and Marine Science Center.

Day 8

Drive west on I-64 through Richmond to Charlottesville. Stop by Thomas Jefferson's Monticello in the afternoon and enjoy an evening stroll on the Lawn at his University of Virginia. Sleep in Charlottesville.

Day 9

Head for the green hills of Shenandoah National Park, further west on I-64. Just driving down Skyline Drive is a pleasure, but make sure you at least step into the woods on a portion of the Appalachian Trail. Spend the night in Luray or Front Royal.

Day 10

Enjoy your last day driving back to D.C. through northern Virginia, stopping at Great Falls on the Potomac for a last impressive view of nature.

▸ THE APPALACHIAN TRAIL

One of the best ways to explore Virginia is the way its first inhabitants did—on foot. The state has some of the best and most accessible trail networks on the East Coast, ranging from flat coastal promenades to rugged Appalachian backcountry.

North America's most famous footpath, the Appalachian Trail (AT) winds over 2,170 miles from Maine to Georgia, connecting Appalachian ridges and river valleys, pristine wilderness, and stoplight suburbia like an enormous green zipper. Almost all of the greenway is on government-owned land; the U.S. Forest Service administers 850 miles, and 14 states oversee another 420 miles.

Virginia contains a quarter of the AT's 14-state path and some of its most breathtaking scenery. Winding down around the Skyline Drive through Shenandoah National Park, the trail then steers west to touch the West Virginia line. It crosses the Blue Ridge Parkway nine times on its way through some of the state's most beautiful wilderness, including the Mount Rogers National Recreation Area. South of Virginia, the AT follows the state line between Tennessee and North Carolina on its way through the rugged undulations of the Great Smoky Mountains National Park.

Thru-hiking, as difficult and expensive as it is (about six months and thousands of dollars in either direction), has become a way of life for some people ever since Early Shaffer first hiked the entire length of the trail in 1948. Hikers ranging from a six-year-old to octogenarians have completed the journey, including a blind man led by his seeing-eye dog. Bill Bryson's humorous bestseller *A Walk in the Woods,* published in 1998, has brought the trail even more fame.

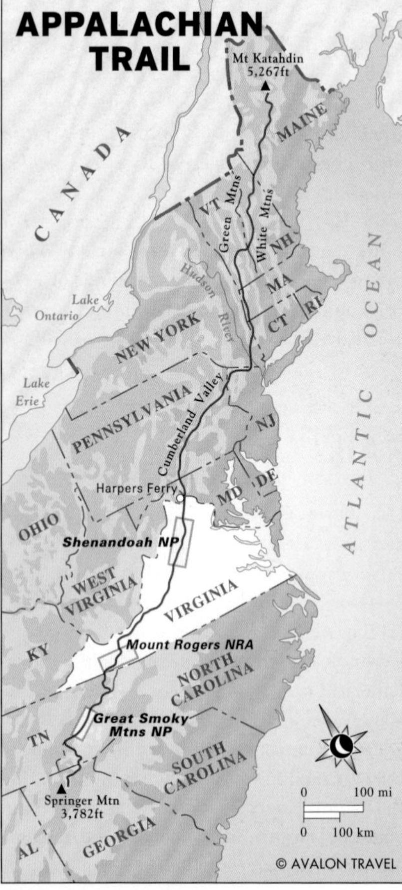

Hitting the Trail

There are almost 500 miles of hiking trails lacing **Shenandoah National Park,** led by what many consider to be **the most scenic portion** of the Appalachian Trail. You can access short portions of this for **day hikes** all along the Skyline Drive inside the park. Shorter hikes like **Dark Hollow Falls** and **White Oak Canyon** are still stunningly beautiful, while climbs up **Old Rag Mountain** and **Hawksbill Mountain** challenge even veteran trekkers.

Decades of experience in regulating the Appalachian Trail have resulted in a time-proven set of regulations and strong suggestions. No motorized traffic, horses, or pack animals are allowed on the trail, and dogs must be on a leash. (They're prohibited in the Smokies and discouraged in general.) **Stay on the trail,** since much of the surrounding land is private, and follow **Leave No Trace** principles (see www.lnt.org); camp at established sites and build no campfires. **Overnight camping permits** are necessary in the two national parks. Hiking with a partner or group is recommended to increase your safety. White painted blazes mark the path the entire way, doubled at turns and junctions.

Thru-hiking requires extensive planning (the resources listed here will help get you started). Of the thousand-plus who start each year in Georgia, only about 200 make it to the end of the trail in Maine. But don't let that stop you from trying.

Researching the Trail

The **Appalachian Trail Conservancy** (304/535-6331, www.appalachiantrail.org) in Harpers Ferry, West Virginia, works to maintain the trail and to preserve the natural habitats and inhabitants of the surrounding buffer zone. Membership is $35 per person per year and comes with a year's subscription to *A.T. Journeys* and discounts in its Ultimate Trail Store. Its booklist includes guidebooks and maps for different sections of the trail.

Old Rag Mountain

autumn in Shenandoah

The 7,000-member Potomac Appalachian Trail Club (PATC, 703/242-0693 www.potomacappalachian.org), one of the largest of dozens of clubs that maintain sections of the trail, concentrates on the Virginia portion from Pennsylvania to Rockfish Gap at the southern end of Shenandoah National Park. The PATC maintains 80 percent of the trails in the park, along with huts and cabins along the trail. Membership is $35 per year for individuals, $40 per couple, and includes a subscription to the monthly newsletter. Dozens of maps and guidebooks are also available.

The *AT Thru-hikers' Companion* and the *AT Data Book* are updated yearly. Other volumes cover natural history, hikers' memoirs, geology, and history of the trail.

A standout memoir about hiking the Appalachian Trail is the aforementioned *A Walk in the Woods* by Bill Bryson, though he "only" completed 870 miles of the trek, and his book is an amusing account of his misadventures on the trail.

▶ FUN FOR THE FAMILY

There's as much or more for the kids in Virginia as there is for their parents. Whether you're here to learn or play—or a bit of both, ideally—you'll find Virginia is as "edu-taining" as any place in the United States. And some of the best family-friendly destinations will make anyone feel like a kid.

Parks

Shenandoah National Park can look like one big playground to children, who can ramble down trails, clamber over rocks, and splash in creeks the length of the park. Amusement parks like Paramount's Kings Dominion and Busch Gardens Europe are obvious first choices. Both have water parks attached for cooling off in the summer. The Virginia Beach boardwalk also has a small amusement park, not to mention acres of sand and waves to play in.

History

You may be surprised at how quickly children

Notes scribbled and posted outside the town tavern lend authenticity to the colonial reproduction of Williamsburg.

warm up to history when it's brought to life at places like Colonial Williamsburg and the Frontier Culture Museum near Staunton. Nothing sparks Junior's interest like a mountain man in full buckskin explaining how to hunt bears or a blacksmith pounding red-hot iron over a forge. You can even "experience" Colonial cooking at places like the Michie Tavern near Monticello. Civil War sites, which could easily bore young minds to tears, offer frequent battle reenactments and fascinating museums. Richmond's Richmond National Battlefield Park Visitors Center has animated battle maps—neato!

Science

Many hands-on exhibitions statewide are designed with kids in mind. The Children's Museum of Richmond lets visitors crawl through a giant digestive tract and play inventor or checkout clerk. Next door, the Science Museum of Virginia explains electricity, aeronautics, and computers in easy-to-understand displays. Roanoke's Science Museum of Western Virginia is similar, and there are many smaller local versions, such as Charlottesville's Virginia Discovery Museum and the Shenandoah Valley Discovery Museum in Winchester. The Virginia Air and Space Center in Hampton holds moon rocks and an Apollo command module, and Norfolk's NAUTICUS (and its adjacent battleship) will leave them begging to join the navy.

Animals

The Virginia Living Museum in Newport News features indoor and outdoor displays on dozens of critters and their habitats. Outstanding zoos include the Virginia Zoo in Norfolk, the Metro Richmond Zoo, and the Mill Mountain Zoo above Roanoke. In Virginia Beach, the Virginia Aquarium and Marine Science Center brings denizens of the deep up close and personal, and Chincoteague's wild ponies roam free but are rounded up every summer in a very popular festival.

The Arts

Art museums and theaters such as the Taubman Museum of Art in Roanoke, the Barter Theatre in Abingdon, and the Wolf Trap National Park for the Performing Arts often host children's plays and special programs. Storytellers, musicians, face-painters, and puppeteers frequent regional festivals. (Not to mention the glut of free museums in D.C.)

THE COASTAL LOOP

A true tour of the coast obviously has to leave the pavement at some point, but even if you don't want to get your feet wet, you can still see a substantial portion of Virginia's shoreside highlights in a little more than a week. Starting in Washington, D.C., make a rough counterclockwise loop down through the Necks, Richmond, and Hampton Roads, followed by an unhurried transect of the Eastern Shore. Tack on a day or two anywhere along the way if you're inspired to actually get out on—or in—the water.

Day 1

Drive down to Fredericksburg and east on Route 33 onto the Northern Neck. Stop at George Washington Birthplace National Monument and Stratford Hall Plantation. Swing by Reedville to admire the historic architecture. Stay there or, even better, in Irvington, where you can dine at the Trick Dog Cafe.

Day 2

Pick up a picnic lunch in White Stone and head south across the tip of the Middle Neck.

VIRGINIA IS FOR FOODIES

While best known for country ham and Southern cooking, the Old Dominion has a wine and dining scene that's far from old-fashioned. These country byways can lead to culinary gems where you least expect to find them. As a *New York Post* reporter once said about Shenandoah's Skyline Drive: "Come to think of it, you can eat better along this route than just about any U.S. road trip that doesn't go through major cities or, say, the Napa Valley."

WINERIES

Pack a picnic basket for your winery tour; you have many choices. Sip and sup amidst ruins and a Shakespeare festival at the **Barboursville Vineyards** near Charlottesville, or choose from numerous wine festivals. One of the biggest, the **Virginia Wine Festival,** takes place in September at Bull Run Regional Park in Centreville. A great resource for Virginia wine tours is www.virginiawine.org.

METRO DINING

While Norfolk and Washington, D.C., have the big-name celebrity chefs, **Richmond**'s sheer variety of quality mid-range restaurants is hard to beat. Work up an appetite with a walk along the James River, and then head to **Millie's Diner, Edo's Squid, The White Dog,** or any of dozens of other neighborhood favorites.

SEAFOOD

Chincoteague oysters are the most famous; no wonder the small island town is home to the world's only oyster museum. Raw bars and seafood fests pepper other coastal towns as well, serving the bivalves steamed, fried, and on the half-shell. The **Urbanna Oyster Festival** in November is among the oldest and largest in Virginia.

FARM TO TABLE

Both the **Shenandoah Valley** and **Charlottesville** are ground zero for Virginia's resurging farm-to-table cuisine. Try **The Red Hen** in Lexington; **Zynodoa, Staunton Grocery,** or **Cranberry's** in Staunton; and more restaurants than can fit in print in Charlottesville. On the farming end of the equation, take a tour of "beyond organic" **Polyface Farms** near Staunton, harvest apples in **Winchester,** or pick strawberries at the **Westmoreland Berry Farm** in Oak Grove.

OFFBEAT MENUS

You won't find Swiss chocolate in Highland County, known as Virginia's Switzerland, but you will find the **Highland Maple Festival** in March. This ode to all things maple syrup includes an all-you-can-eat pancake breakfast. Visit the **Route 11 Potato Chip Factory** in Mount Jackson near I-81 for a sample of the hand-cooked chips.

Replicas of the ships *Godspeed, Discovery,* and *Susan Constant* are moored at Jamestown Settlement's pier.

Visit Urbanna and then take either Route 360 or Route 33 and I-64 back toward Richmond. Spend the night there.

Day 3

Take Route 5 east down the Historic Peninsula, stopping at the plantations along the way. Depending on what time you arrive, explore as much of Colonial Williamsburg as you fancy. Dine and lodge in Williamsburg.

Day 4

Finish up your tour of Colonial Williamsburg in the morning. After lunch, visit Jamestown and Yorktown and the Colonial National Historical Parkway connecting them. Sleep in Newport News or Hampton.

Days 5 and 6

Explore the rich cultural offerings of Hampton Roads, both north and south of the James River. Newport News, Hampton, Portsmouth, and Norfolk have a wealth of parks, museums, and historic neighborhoods.

Day 7

Head to Virginia Beach and hit the boardwalk (and the ocean, if it's summer). Other options here include the Virginia Aquarium and Marine Science Center, Cape Henry, and First Landing State Park. Eat seafood at least once.

Day 8

Cross the Chesapeake Bay Bridge-Tunnel to the Eastern Shore. Spend a leisurely day driving north along Route 13, stopping in pleasant historic towns like Cape Charles and Onancock for chowder and some window-shopping. Spend the night in Chincoteague.

Day 9

Look for wild ponies at the Chincoteague National Wildlife Refuge or just stare out at the seemingly endless beach of Assateague Island. When you're ready, head back north and west through Maryland to Washington, D.C.

▸ DOWN-HOME VIRGINIA: MUSIC AND MOUNTAIN BIKING

Virginia's lumpy tail is out of the way and a little out of the ordinary, home to a high concentration of unusual attractions that set it apart from the rest of the Old Dominion. From *real* country music performances to a tour of an old coal mine, the southwestern part of the state just begs you to leave the interstate and explore its nooks and crannies. Starting in Roanoke (where Miniature Graceland, sadly, is no more), take a week to roam the back roads of this slice of Appalachia for a truly unique travel experience. Ideally, start on a Friday to catch the Flatfoot Jamboree in Floyd and then the Saturday night show at the Carter Family Fold.

Day 1

Begin your tour in Roanoke by exploring the striking Taubman Museum of Art, designed by architect Randall Stout, a protégé of Frank Gehry. Then cross the railroad tracks to the O. Winston Link Museum, which displays the New York shutterbug's famous photographic obsession with locomotives. Head south along the Blue Ridge Parkway to spend the night in or near Floyd, where the Floyd Country Store thrums with bluegrass and dancing feet on Friday evenings.

Day 2

Head southwest toward Galax, World Capital of Old Time Mountain Music. Here the Jeff Matthews Museum is not to be missed (dig that grizzly!), and local luthiers Tom Barr and Wayne Henderson craft exquisite fiddles, guitars, and other country music instruments. Keep going past Mt. Rogers to Abingdon and the Carter Family Fold in Maces Spring, where large crowds gather on Saturday evenings to honor the famous family's legacy with great down-home music and dancing. Spend the night in Abingdon.

memorabilia at the Carter Family Fold in Maces Spring

Day 3

From Abingdon, drive the short jaunt to Damascus. Fat-tire fans can rent a full-suspension bike and test their mettle on the heart-thumping single-track of the Iron Mountain Trail. For a mellower ride take a shuttle to the top of the Virginia Creeper Trail, a converted rail-to-trail, then watch the views roll past as you descend. Route 76, part of the TransAmerica Trail for road cyclists, also zips through town. Nearby Mount Rogers National Recreation Area has the highest peak in the state and trails galore to occupy hikers, including the AT.

Day 4

Make a clockwise loop west and north on Routes 23 and 19. At Natural Tunnel State Park, you can ride a chairlift down into an 850-foot passageway carved by Stock Creek. Keep going to Big Stone Gap, home to the excellent Southwest Virginia Museum and *The Trail of the Lonesome Pine* melodrama on summer weekends.

Day 5

Head northeast on Route 19 through undulating country to Tazewell and its Crab Orchard Museum and Pioneer Park, which combines living history with archaeology. To the north, almost on the West Virginia line, is the Pocahontas Exhibition Coal Mine, now open to the public through tours led by former miners. East of town is Burke's Garden, a small, serene valley. If you have the time, take a few extra days to enjoy the area.

Day 6

After a quick nip up into West Virginia at Bluefield (grab a free lemonade if it's over 90°F!), head back down I-77 toward the New River Valley. Take a detour to the Big Walker Lookout, near the tunnel through Big Walker Mountain. Stop at the Wolf Creek Indian Village and Museum near Wytheville for a look at life in the 12th century, and if there's time, make a detour south to Shot Tower Historical State Park, where molten lead was once dropped 150 feet into water to make round bullets.

Day 7

From Wytheville, opt for the more scenic Route 11 as an alternative to I-81 back to Roanoke. Take the Route 100/460 detour north to Mountain Lake, where the movie *Dirty Dancing* was filmed, for a hike in the Cascades Recreation Area within Jefferson National Forest (the trail up Little Stony Creek Gorge to a 60-foot waterfall is particularly pretty). Return to Roanoke by nightfall.

a view of the Blue Ridge Mountains from Mount Rogers National Recreation Area

NORTHERN VIRGINIA

Virginians usually have one name for their cousins in the northern part of the state: Yankees. It's true that the hustle and bustle of Washington, D.C., blows across the Potomac, quickening the clip of northern Virginians' speech and daily life. And there is no question that the electoral map changes from red to a bluer hue. But while northern Virginia politics, geography, and society tend to play second fiddle to the nation's capital, in history, the region takes a starring role in the Commonwealth's coming-of-age story. Retracing the Civil War brings you back and doubled-back through the rolling hills of Manassas National Battlefield. The Mother of Presidents, so nicknamed for the eight commanders-in-chief born on Virginia soil, holds the final resting place for her favorite son, George Washington, in these northern reaches, on the banks of the Potomac.

For visitors, the region can be a springboard into D.C. or a destination in its own right. Arlington County has come to be synonymous with the national cemetery that shares its name, but its restaurants and nightlife are also worth a look. Upriver, from the serene Riverbend Park to the tumultuous Great Falls, outdoor escapes are easy to find, while downriver, Old Town Alexandria's cobblestone streets and Colonial aura are nothing short of charming. Further downriver still you'll find Washington's stately Mount Vernon estate and the view that kept him pining for the life of a gentleman farmer rather than first president. Off the river and beyond the Capital Beltway, once you press through gridlocked suburbia,

© KATIE GITHENS

HIGHLIGHTS

Arlington National Cemetery: Here Robert E. Lee's mansion overlooks rows of thousands of headstones. The changing of the guard at the Tomb of the Unknown Soldier and the eternal flame at John F. Kennedy's gravesite are not to be missed (page 30).

Great Falls Park: Hiking, climbing, kayaking, or just enjoying the view – you can do it all within earshot of the thundering roar of the Potomac tumbling 77 feet (page 52).

Wolf Trap National Park for the Performing Arts: Enjoy a picnic on the lawn and an outdoor concert at the nation's only national park dedicated to the performing arts (page 54).

Manassas National Battlefield Park: The Civil War began in earnest at this site of two major battles (page 56).

Mount Vernon: George Washington's enviable riverside getaway still retains its Revolutionary allure in spite of the crowds (page 73).

Mason Neck: Here you can sit in a sea kayak and spot the country's national bird nesting only a short drive from the Capitol (page 76).

LOOK FOR TO FIND RECOMMENDED SIGHTS, ACTIVITIES, DINING, AND LODGING.

Virginia's distinctive horse and hunt country still shines through.

PLANNING YOUR TIME

As the smallest region of the state, northern Virginia can be covered in a jam-packed long weekend, but four or five days will leave you more time to do it justice. Washington, D.C., is the obvious home base, but if you want to stay in the Old Dominion then head to Alexandria or Arlington. Just about anything in this part of the state can be visited in a day trip from the capital. Consider taking public transportation when possible.

More than 4,000 buildings in Old Town Alexandria reside within two National Historic Districts. In the vicinity of Arlington are **Arlington National Cemetery,** presided over by Robert E. Lee's mansion; George Washington's home at **Mount Vernon;** and, further to the south, the outdoors offerings of **Mason Neck.** Each are worth half a day's visit at least. Heading west brings you to **Manassas National Battlefield Park,** where the Civil War started, the stage and picnic lawn of the **Wolf Trap National Park,** and **Great Falls Park** along the Potomac. A visit to horse-happy Hunt Country, centered on Leesburg, will show you why the American foxhound is the Virginia state dog. It's a choice our first president would approve; George Washington created the breed. With plenty of interesting battlefields, plantations, town, and parks nearby, Leesburg and Middleburg make a good weekend trip in themselves for tourists and D.C. residents alike.

Access

Northern Virginia does prove one sprawl theory true: Driving can be a nightmare, especially on major highways during the weekday rush hours of 6–9 A.M. and 4:30–7 P.M., starting even earlier on Friday afternoons. The Washington metropolitan area has consistently rated in the top five worst cities for traffic congestion in the country. Ouch. The maze of highways and swarms of traffic lights sometimes seem designed solely to slow things down, and simply turning around can be a chore. Don't get caught driving alone in a high-occupancy vehicle (HOV) lane, marked with white diamonds, or you'll get a hefty fine.

Inside the Beltway (the loop of I-495 and I-95 around the nation's capital), the **Metrorail** (202/637-7000, www.wmata.com) provides a clean, quiet, and (usually) quick way to get around. Three lines enter northern Virginia from Washington. The orange and blue lines cross the Potomac together into northern Arlington; from there the orange line heads west as far as Vienna, while the blue line turns south past Arlington National Cemetery to join with the yellow line (spanning the river next to I-395) at the Pentagon. This pair continues south to the King Street Station before splitting for a final stop or two.

Ronald Reagan Washington National Airport (703/417-8000, www.metwashairports.com/reagan) officially acquired the former president's name in the late 1990s, but most people ignore the Gipper and still just call it "National." The blue and yellow Metro lines both stop at the airport, located in Arlington.

Washington-Dulles International Airport (703/572-2700, www.metwashairports.com/dulles) is a 40-minute drive, depending on

Manassas National Battlefield Park has views of rolling hills nearly unchanged since the Civil War.

traffic, from Arlington National Cemetery via I-66 to the free Dulles Access Road (Rte. 267). You can catch a **Washington Flyer** (888/927-4359, www.washfly.com) transfer bus with service to the airport every half hour on the quarter hour from the West Falls Church station on the Metro orange line. The trip takes about 20 minutes and costs $10 each way or $18 round-trip.

Super Shuttle (202/296-6662 or 800/258-3826, www.supershuttle.com) runs to downtown D.C. from National airport starting at $14 per person and from Dulles at $29 per person. For the thriftiest travelers, the municipal bus (Metrobus route 5A) takes an hour from L'Enfant Plaza Metro station in D.C. to Dulles airport in Virginia, and it's cheap: $3.20 (exact change required). On the way to the airport, the 5A stops at the Rosslyn Metro station in Arlington. This is a common place for travelers to board the 5A.

Passengers exit the train at the Rosslyn Metro station, home to the fourth longest escalator in the world, in Arlington.

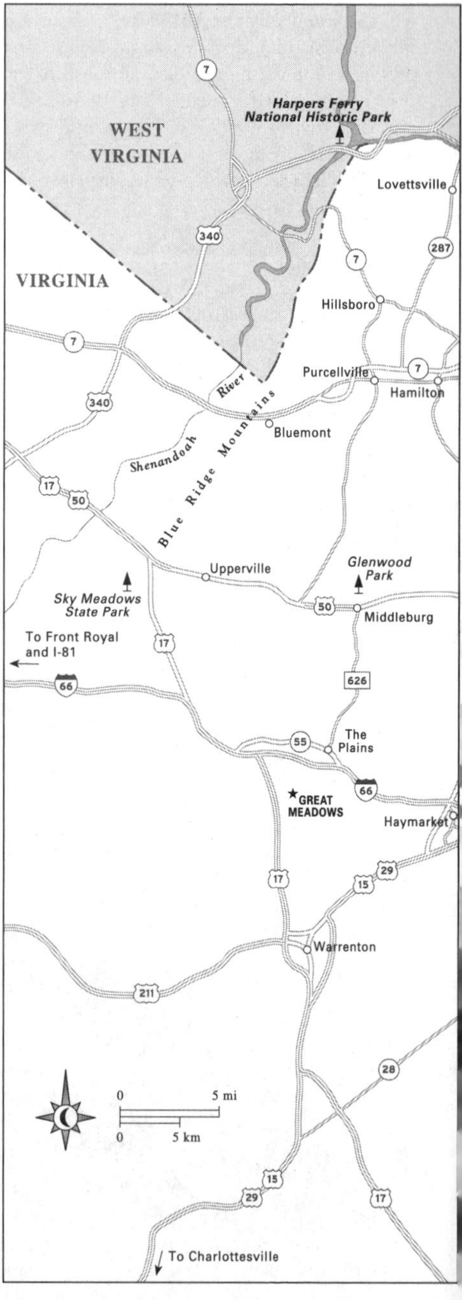

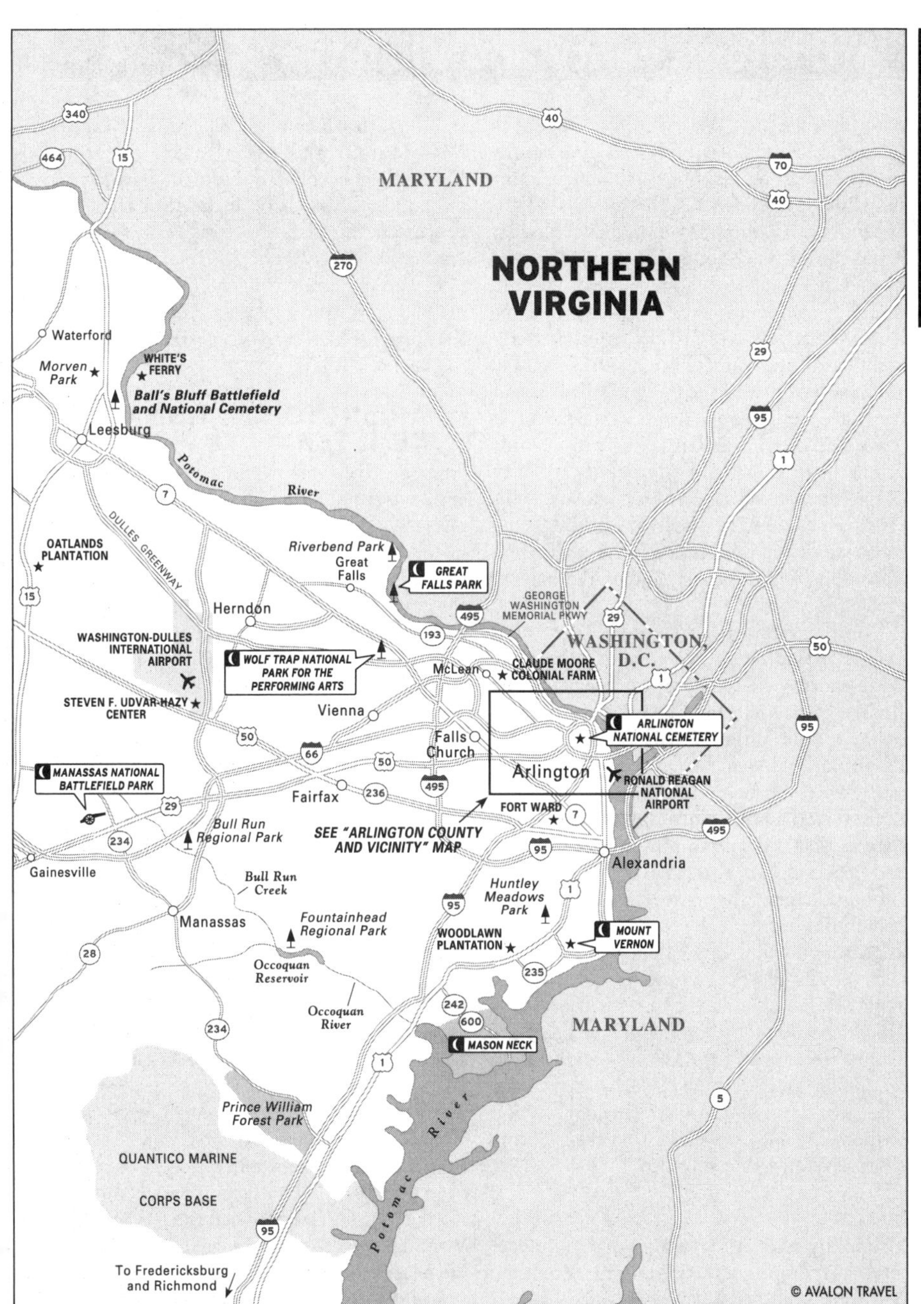

NORTHERN VIRGINIA
MARYLAND
340
40
464
15
70
40
270
Waterford
Morven Park
WHITE'S FERRY
Ball's Bluff Battlefield and National Cemetery
Leesburg
29
95
1
Potomac River
7
DULLES GREENWAY
OATLANDS PLANTATION
15
Riverbend Park
Great Falls
GREAT FALLS PARK
Herndon
495
GEORGE WASHINGTON MEMORIAL PKWY
29
193
WASHINGTON, D.C.
50
WASHINGTON-DULLES INTERNATIONAL AIRPORT
WOLF TRAP NATIONAL PARK FOR THE PERFORMING ARTS
McLean
CLAUDE MOORE COLONIAL FARM
1
STEVEN F. UDVAR-HAZY CENTER
Vienna
50
Falls Church
ARLINGTON NATIONAL CEMETERY
95
66
MANASSAS NATIONAL BATTLEFIELD PARK
50
Arlington
RONALD REAGAN NATIONAL AIRPORT
495
Fairfax
236
29
Bull Run Regional Park
FORT WARD
7
495
234
SEE "ARLINGTON COUNTY AND VICINITY" MAP
95
Alexandria
Gainesville
Bull Run Creek
Huntley Meadows Park
1
Manassas
Fountainhead Regional Park
95
WOODLAWN PLANTATION
MOUNT VERNON
28
Occoquan Reservoir
235
Occoquan River
242
600
MARYLAND
234
MASON NECK
1
5
Prince William Forest Park
Potomac River
QUANTICO MARINE CORPS BASE
95
To Fredericksburg and Richmond
© AVALON TRAVEL

Arlington County and Vicinity

At just under 26 square miles, Arlington County is the smallest self-governing county in the United States, but it is home to more than 200,000 residents. Although once a D.C. appendix of "bedroom communities" that lay empty during office hours, Arlington has grown up and these days rush-hour traffic drives both directions across the four bridges connecting it to the nation's capital. The federal government is still the county's largest employer, but computer, defense, and communications industries have set up shop in neighborhoods such as Rosslyn, Ballston, and Crystal City (the county has no incorporated cities), sparking the birth of the Internet and sparing local employees the cross-river commute. Federal buildings and monuments still concentrate in the eastern portion, along with high-rise condos and most of the county's hotels.

Together with Fairfax County, Arlington is part of a region many Virginians consider almost another state. Closer in demeanor and skyline to the nation's capital than to most of the rest of Virginia, this part of the Old Dominion is one of the few areas that consistently votes Democratic in presidential elections. It is part of Virginia, though, and a tasty slice at that. Be sure to sample from the kaleidoscope of bars and eateries in Arlington's "urban villages," the more densely populated neighborhoods near the Metro stations, such as Shirlington and Clarendon.

To find out what's going on here, as well as in D.C., pick up a copy of the *Washington Post*'s "Weekend" section (out on Fri.); the *Post*'s free *Express* (see "Express Night Out" section on Thurs.); the *Washington City Paper,* a free weekly; or look at the "Calendar" section of the *Arlington Connection* (also check online editions of all publications).

History

Originally part of the arbitrary diamond of land that comprised the District of Columbia, Arlington County was returned to Virginia in 1847. Both the Custis (as in Martha Washington) and Lee (Robert E.) families, which eventually merged, had extensive landholdings here in the 18th and 19th centuries; the Lee family mansion gave the county its name. By the 20th century, war offices and commuter homes for capital workers had started to replace farmlands, setting the stage for high-tech businesses and defense industries.

ARLINGTON NATIONAL CEMETERY

The country's most famous burial grounds embrace hundreds of acres of hills, grass, and endless mesmerizing rows of white marble headstones. More than 300,000 American veterans from every war are buried here, and the graves are visited by four million mourners and sightseers every year. If predictions hold true, all plots in Arlington Cemetery may be filled by 2020.

Even with the crowds and circling Tourmobiles, Arlington National Cemetery is a somber place. Most visitors respectfully heed the numerous signs for quiet, leaving a silence punctuated only by birdcalls, the infrequent crack of a rifle salute, and the plaintive notes of "Taps" played during the hundred or so services held every week.

History

The cemetery land began as an estate surrounding Arlington House, built 1802–1817 by George Washington Parke Custis, grandson of Martha Washington (née Custis). In 1831, the house and property changed owners when Mary Custis, George's daughter, married Robert E. Lee, who had often come to visit from his home in Alexandria. Robert and Mary lived in Arlington House for 30 years until, on April 22, 1861, Lee accepted the command of Virginia's forces in the war against the Union. He never returned.

In 1864 the 1,100-acre estate was confiscated

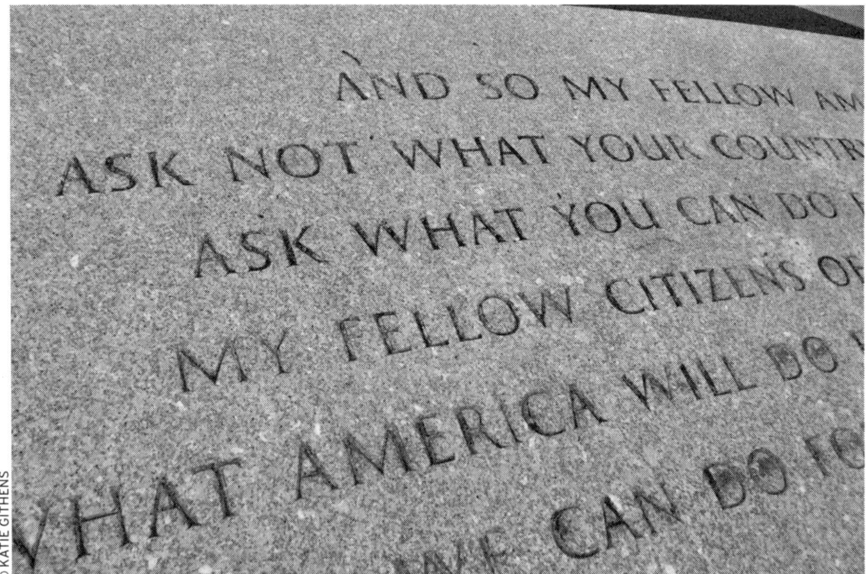

John F. Kennedy's grave is the most visited in Arlington National Cemetery. It bears engravings of his "Ask not" speech.

by the federal government when Martha couldn't appear in person to pay the property taxes. Quartermaster Gen. Montgomery Meigs, a Georgian who had remained loyal to the Union, considered Lee the worst kind of traitor and came up with a scathing revenge: the burial of Union dead, literally, in Lee's backyard. Meigs crossed the Potomac to personally oversee the interment of the first Union soldiers in Martha's rose garden. Eventually, 16,000 soldiers were buried in the fields around Arlington House.

After the war, Lee's grandson, George Washington Custis Lee, sued the U.S. government for possession of the estate and won after taking the case to the Supreme Court. In 1883, he sold it back to the government for $150,000. Two hundred surrounding acres were set aside to start the cemetery.

Sights

At the main entrance gate, the **Women in Military Service for America Memorial** (703/533-1155 or 800/222-2294, www.womensmemorial.org, 8 A.M.–7 P.M. daily Apr.–Sept., to 5 P.M. Oct.–Mar., free) contains an education center and theater dedicated to all women serving in the armed forces in war and peace. A short uphill walk brings you to the eternal flame at the final resting place of former president **John F. Kennedy,** the most visited grave at Arlington. A low marble wall engraved with quotes from his famous "Ask not" speech offers a view of the Potomac and the capital. The resting places of **Jacqueline Kennedy Onassis** and her two infant sons lie nearby, as does that of **Robert F. Kennedy,** whose grave, as requested in his will, is marked only by a single white wooden cross and excerpts from two of his speeches on civil rights. Sadly, the Kennedy family's plot has expanded yet again. In 2009, senator **Edward Kennedy** succumbed to cancer and joined his brothers, buried beneath a simple white cross and stone, like Robert's—a quiet end to his roaring 46-year political career.

On the hilltop above the Kennedys presides **Arlington House** (703/235-1530, www.nps

.gov/arho, 9:30 A.M.–4:30 P.M. daily, free), the Greek Revival mansion that Robert E. Lee described as the spot "where my affection and attachments are more strongly placed than at any other place in the world." In 1824 the Marquis de Lafayette proclaimed the panorama of the Potomac and the capital "the finest view in the world." The house was transferred to the care of the National Park Service in 1933 and filled almost to its 12-foot ceilings with Lee-era antiques and reproductions. Today the Memorial Bridge draws a visual line between Arlington House and the Lincoln Memorial, creating a symbolic link between the two former adversaries. Pierre Charles L'Enfant, Revolutionary War veteran and designer of the capital, was reburied in front of the house in 1909.

Look for the white marble **Memorial Amphitheater** and pass behind it to reach the **Tomb of the Unknown Soldier,** where unidentified bodies from World War I, World War II, and the Korean War are guarded around the clock. (DNA testing revealed the identity of the unknown soldier from Vietnam, and in 1998 the body was exhumed and reburied elsewhere; that crypt remains symbolically empty.)

The U.S. Third Infantry watches over the site in an amazing display of discipline and precision. Even their physique must meet exacting specifications, down to height (between 5'11" and 6'4") and waist size (a precise 30 inches around). Each guard paces back and forth in 21 unerring steps, snapping his or her heels at every turn, often under the gaze of hundreds of people. Three people take part in the changing of the guard (every 30 minutes Apr.–Sept., every hour otherwise), in which one gives the orders as two others march in step, inspect weapons, and transfer orders.

In addition to this solemn duty, the Third Infantry participates in more than 6,000 military ceremonies per year throughout the capital region. Formed in 1784, the "Old Guard" is the Army's official ceremonial unit and is the oldest active-duty infantry unit in the Army. They are the only unit allowed to pass in review with fixed bayonets, in remembrance of a

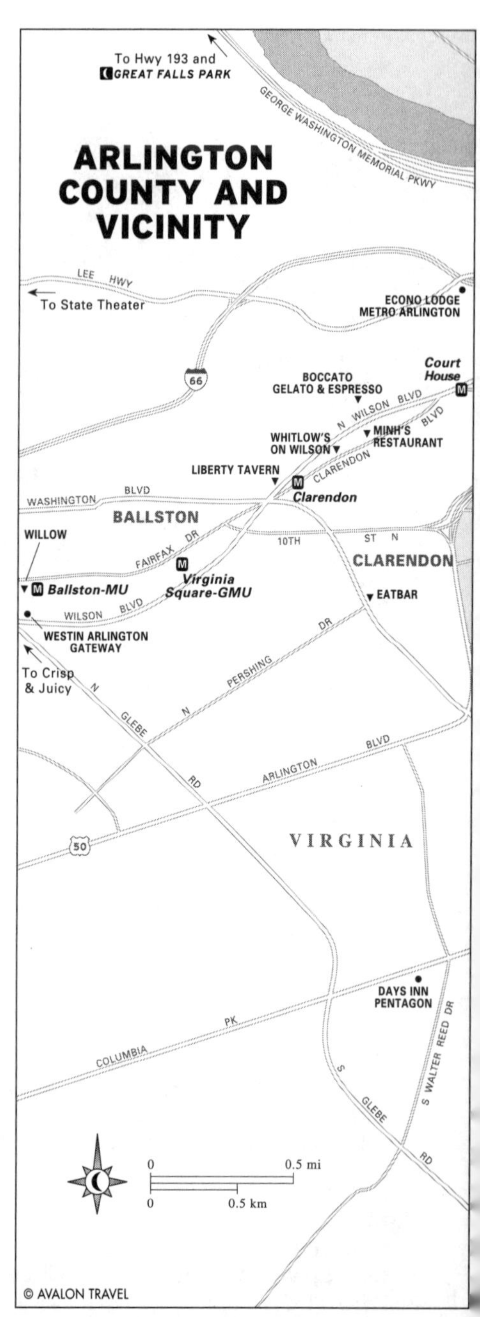

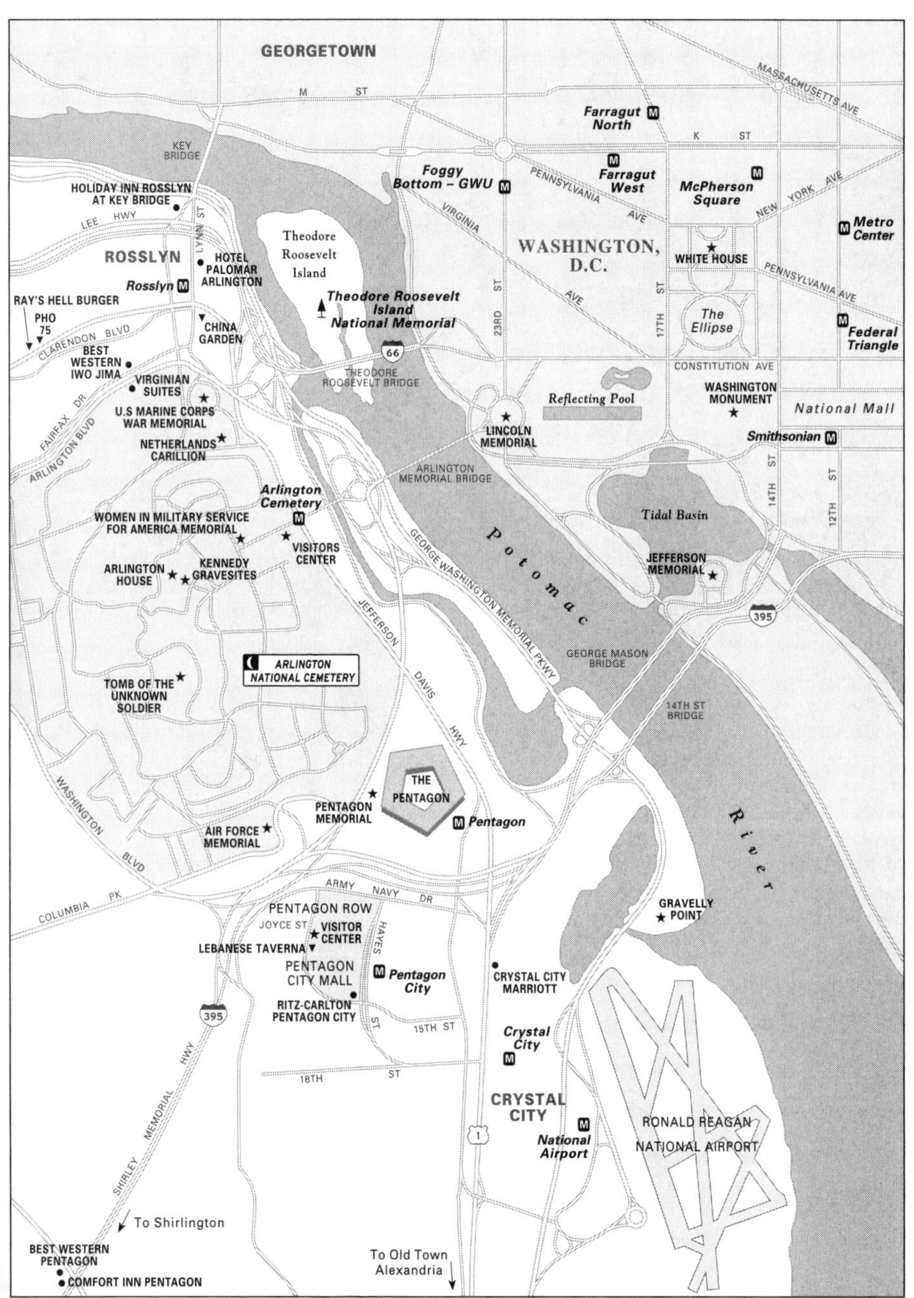
GEORGETOWN
M ST
MASSACHUSETTS AVE
Farragut North
K ST
KEY BRIDGE
Foggy Bottom – GWU
Farragut West
McPherson Square
PENNSYLVANIA AVE
NEW YORK AVE
HOLIDAY INN ROSSLYN AT KEY BRIDGE
LEE HWY
LYNN ST
VIRGINIA
Metro Center
Theodore Roosevelt Island
WASHINGTON, D.C.
ROSSLYN
HOTEL PALOMAR ARLINGTON
WHITE HOUSE
Rosslyn
PENNSYLVANIA AVE
RAY'S HELL BURGER
Theodore Roosevelt Island National Memorial
23RD ST
17TH ST
The Ellipse
PHO 75
CHINA GARDEN
Federal Triangle
CLARENDON BLVD
66
BEST WESTERN IWO JIMA
THEODORE ROOSEVELT BRIDGE
CONSTITUTION AVE
VIRGINIAN SUITES
WASHINGTON MONUMENT
Reflecting Pool
National Mall
U.S MARINE CORPS WAR MEMORIAL
FAIRFAX DR
ARLINGTON BLVD
LINCOLN MEMORIAL
NETHERLANDS CARILLION
Smithsonian
ARLINGTON MEMORIAL BRIDGE
14TH ST
12TH ST
Arlington Cemetery
Tidal Basin
WOMEN IN MILITARY SERVICE FOR AMERICA MEMORIAL
Potomac
VISITORS CENTER
GEORGE WASHINGTON MEMORIAL PKWY
JEFFERSON MEMORIAL
ARLINGTON HOUSE
KENNEDY GRAVESITES
395
JEFFERSON DAVIS HWY
GEORGE MASON BRIDGE
ARLINGTON NATIONAL CEMETERY
TOMB OF THE UNKNOWN SOLDIER
14TH ST BRIDGE
WASHINGTON BLVD
THE PENTAGON
PENTAGON MEMORIAL
Pentagon
River
AIR FORCE MEMORIAL
ARMY NAVY DR
COLUMBIA PK
GRAVELLY POINT
PENTAGON ROW
JOYCE ST
VISITOR CENTER
HAYES ST
LEBANESE TAVERNA
PENTAGON CITY MALL
Pentagon City
CRYSTAL CITY MARRIOTT
RITZ-CARLTON PENTAGON CITY
395
15TH ST
Crystal City
18TH ST
SHIRLEY MEMORIAL HWY
CRYSTAL CITY
RONALD REAGAN NATIONAL AIRPORT
National Airport
1
To Shirlington
BEST WESTERN PENTAGON
COMFORT INN PENTAGON
To Old Town Alexandria

© KATIE GITHENS

the changing of the guard at the Tomb of the Unknown Soldier

successful bayonet charge in the Mexican War in 1847.

Dozens of other memorials are scattered about Arlington, including the **Mast of the Battleship *Maine*,** whose mysterious explosion on February 15, 1898, in Havana Harbor sparked the Spanish-American War; the **Tomb of the Unknown Dead of the Civil War** (guarding 2,111 bodies); and the ***Challenger* Memorial** for the crew of the downed space shuttle.

Visiting Arlington National Cemetery

The **visitors center** (703/607-8000, www.arlingtoncemetery.org, 8 A.M.–7 P.M. daily Apr.–Sept., to 5 P.M. Oct.–Mar.) is free to visitors. It has its own Metro stop on the blue line, and paid parking is available in a garage off Memorial Drive for $1.75 the first three hours, $2/hour thereafter (private vehicles may not enter the cemetery). Narrated shuttle tours aboard the **Tourmobile** (202/554-5100, www.tourmobile.com) visit the John F. Kennedy gravesite, the Tomb of the Unknowns, and Arlington House in about two hours for $7.50 adults, $6.50 seniors, $3.75 children 3–11. Tickets must be purchased from the booth inside the Arlington National Cemetery Visitors Center and passengers may then get on and off different buses all day. Contact Tourmobile for information on optional extensions to Mount Vernon and Washington, D.C.

NEAR ARLINGTON NATIONAL CEMETERY

On the cemetery's northern border stands the 50-bell **Netherlands Carillon** (703/289-2500, www.nps.gov/gwmp/nethcarillon.htm), a 1960 gift from the people of Holland in gratitude for American help against the Nazis in World War II. Concerts are given by outstanding carillonneurs in the afternoon or evening on Saturdays and national holidays May–September; call or visit the website for a schedule. In view of the National Mall, this location is an ideal perch for watching the Fourth of July fireworks and the sunrise in any season.

© KATIE GITHENS

The U.S. Marine Corps War Memorial is the largest cast bronze statue in the world and a tribute to fallen Marines.

Just to the north, the **U.S. Marine Corps War Memorial** (703/289-2500, www.nps.gov/gwmp/usmc.htm) depicts Joe Rosenthal's Pulitzer Prize–winning photograph of Marines raising the U.S. flag over Iwo Jima during the Battle for the Pacific in 1945. The memorial is the largest cast bronze statue in the world, erected in memory of all Marines who have died serving their country since 1775. In summertime, join the packed crowd for the Marine Corps Sunset Parade, a concert and silent drill platoon performed in tribute to fallen comrades (7–8 P.M. Tues.; 202/433-6060).

A footbridge connects the Virginia side of the Potomac with **Theodore Roosevelt Island** (703/289-2500, www.nps.gov/this, dawn–dusk daily). Those proposing a memorial for the nation's 26th president decided nothing less than an entire island would do, and choose 88 wilderness acres in the middle of the Potomac. Popular with joggers, walkers, and dog lovers (and surprisingly abundant with wildlife), the park's three miles of flat, easy trails wander through a swampy, wooded expanse of willow and ash, mud and muskrat. Rocky beaches with D.C. city views compete for visitors' attention with Paul Manship's 17-foot-tall bronze statue of the conservation-minded Roosevelt.

Theodore Roosevelt Island can only be reached via northbound George Washington Parkway. The easiest way to get to the island memorial from D.C. is to drive into Virginia across the Theodore Roosevelt Bridge, and veer right onto the northbound lanes of the George Washington Parkway. From the parkway, pull into the poorly marked Roosevelt Island lot, and walk across the pedestrian footbridge that provides access to the island.

Not far downriver at **Gravelly Point,** you can watch planes take off and land at National airport from startlingly close range. Visit at night for the most dramatic effect, though watch the clock—the gates close at 10 P.M. Like Theodore Roosevelt Island, Gravelly Point can only be reached via northbound George Washington Parkway.

The Pentagon

The headquarters of the U.S. Department of Defense (703/697-1776, http://pentagon.afis.osd.mil) occupies the largest office building in the world, just south of Arlington National Cemetery. Designed in one weekend in 1941 by the U.S. Army Corps of Engineers, it was built over a filled-in swamp in only 16 months. The building covers 6.5 million square feet spread over five floors. Each of the five sides is longer than the U.S. Capitol, and the whole thing is covered by 7.1 acres of glass. About 23,000 employees (half military and half civilian) tell time by 4,200 clocks, drink from 691 water fountains, and navigate 17.5 miles of corridors planned so well it supposedly takes only seven minutes to walk between any two points in the building.

Tours are free and are once again offered to the public (they were suspended in the years immediately following the terrorist attacks of September 11, 2001). Offered 9 A.M.–3 P.M. Monday–Friday, tours last 60 minutes and follow a 1.5-mile route. They must be reserved well in advance. Non-U.S. citizens must contact their embassy in Washington, D.C., to reserve a tour.

The Pentagon Memorial

Full of understated symbolism, the Pentagon Memorial (703/693-8935, www.whs.mil/memorial, www.pentagonmemorial.net) honors the 184 victims killed in the 9/11 terrorist attacks with 184 aluminum benches oriented in the flight pattern of American Airlines Flight 77, moments before it nosedived into the southwestern wall of the Pentagon. The 1.9-acre site opened in 2008 and stays open 24 hours a day, year-round. It is located on the Pentagon grounds, between the western face of the Pentagon building and Route 27/Washington Boulevard.

A quiet memorial designed to give grieving families a place to sit and reflect, it can appear stark at first glance. The gravel crunches loudly underfoot and the angular benches and maple saplings look small against the Pentagon's expanse, but perhaps as the maples mature and spread out their leafy branches, the site will feel less new and raw—likewise with the nation's wounds.

Air Force Memorial

It's impossible to miss the 270-foot stainless-steel spires of this memorial (1 Air Force Memorial Dr., 703/247-5808, www.airforcememorial.org) near Arlington National Cemetery and the Pentagon. The soaring monument was erected in 2006 in honor of the Air Force and its predecessor organizations, the only branch of the Armed Forces that didn't yet have a memorial in the capital. It was designed by the late James Ingo Freed, who also designed the U.S. Holocaust Memorial Museum. The Air Force Memorial includes an eight-foot bronze Honor Guard statue and a glass Contemplation Wall depicting the "missing man formation." For an audio tour, dial 800/217-7740, ext. 11, from your cell phone or download it from www.mobiletours.org. The entrance is off Columbia Pike/Route 244.

ENTERTAINMENT AND RECREATION

Nightlife

The tiny little **Galaxy Hut** (2711 Wilson Blvd., 703/525-8646, www.galaxyhut.com) has a long list of beers on tap and features live local bands, often unusual and up-and-coming, with a hipster streak. It charges a cover, as does the nearby **Iota Club and Café** (2832 Wilson Blvd., 703/522-8340, www.iotaclubandcafe.com), which hosts everything from folk and alternative rock to poetry readings. For jazz and blues, try **Whitlow's on Wilson** (2854 Wilson Blvd., 703/276-9693, www.whitlows.com), which combines a restaurant, bar, and pool hall—and also has one of the most popular Sunday brunches in Arlington (with a Bloody Mary bar to nurse your previous evening here).

Built in nearby Falls Church in 1936, the **State Theater** (220 N. Washington St., 703/237-0300, www.thestatetheater.com)

© KATIE GITHENS

Arlington Cinema 'N' Drafthouse, a favorite for beer and a movie

underwent a multimillion-dollar restoration in the late 1990s. It's now a great place to see live music, hosting a diverse lineup of bands.

Arlington Cinema 'N' Drafthouse (2903 Columbia Pike, 703/486-2345, www.arlingtondrafthouse.com) is a second-run theater, meaning it shows films at a discount a few months after they premiere ($5.50 admission, $1 Monday nights). The 1930s art deco theater serves food and drink tableside, and frequently hosts live comedy shows, wine tastings, and film festivals. Annual crowd favorites include the Biannual TPS Report Managers Meeting (*Office Space* flair encouraged).

Outdoor Recreation

Bikers, joggers, strollers, and stroller-pushers flock to the **Mount Vernon Trail,** which runs for 18 miles along the George Washington Memorial Parkway and the Potomac River from Memorial Bridge south to Mount Vernon. As you pass Gravelly Point and Old Town Alexandria, you can stop to watch jets taking off from National airport, boaters sliding their crafts into the river, and the city lights as they start to sparkle in the evening.

AIRBORNE

Not all the fun in northern Virginia is on the ground. Learn how to soar with John Middleton's **Silver Wings Hang Gliding** (703/533-1965, www.silverwingshanggliding.com) in Arlington. Mandatory ground school is $10, and after that lessons cost $85. Most people attain a novice rating after 10 to 20 lessons, allowing you to launch from a mountainside – with supervision. Must be at least 18 years old.

The **Flying Circus Air Show** (540/439-8661, www.flyingcircusairshow.com) in Bealeton is a flight enthusiast's dream. Every Sunday from May to September, barnstorming pilots thrill crowds with their airborne acrobatics, with the assistance of wing walkers, sky divers, and the tongue-in-cheek drama of the Red Baron and Fifi LaBombshell. Admission is $10 for adults, $3 for children. While you're there you can take an open-cockpit ride in an antique biplane starting at $70 per person (aerobatic rides are $130).

Balloons Unlimited (41153 John Mosby Hwy., Aldie, 703/327-0444, www.balloonsunlimited.com) is based midway between Dulles airport and Middleburg. It operates hot-air balloon flights in the Middleburg area as well as the Shenandoah Valley, with sunrise and sunset flights for $200 per person ($100 children).

An October fundraiser for Special Olympics Virginia, the **Dulles Day Plane Pull** (www.planepull.com) pits teams against each other to see who can pull a 164,000-pound Airbus across 12 feet of tarmac the fastest. Kids will gravitate to the aircraft displays and smaller-scale school bus-pull contest.

To the north, the **Potomac Heritage Trail** continues along the Virginia side of the river for 10 miles from the west end of the Theodore Roosevelt Island parking lot to the west end of the I-495 bridge. This path sees much less traffic, even though it passes through a riverside wilderness, along cliff tops, and across countless streams gurgling toward the Potomac. It's blazed in blue, and you can reach it from eight access points, including Potomac Overlook Park, Fort Marcy, and Turkey Run Park. The trail running is excellent for stretches, especially from Windy Run to Teddy Roosevelt Island. You can connect with the C&O Canal Towpath on the other side of the river by crossing the Key Bridge into Georgetown, or the Chain Bridge. Also popular, the **Washington & Old Dominion Trail** begins in Shirlington and runs west to Purcellsville.

For maps and more information, contact the **Northern Virginia Regional Park Authority** (703/352-5900, www.nvrpa.org) or the **Arlington County Department of Parks and Recreation** (703/228-3323).

EVENTS

In May, the D.C. Blues Society co-sponsors the **Columbia Pike Blues Festival** at Columbia Pike and Walter Reed Street. The outdoor festival takes place noon–6 P.M., rain or shine.

Every summer Friday, the Rosslyn Business Improvement District sponsors the free **Rosslyn Outdoor Film Festival** in Gateway Park near Key Bridge (1300 Lee Hwy., 703/522-6628, www.rosslynva.org). Past themes have included James Bond and '80s flicks.

August brings 60,000 people or more to enjoy the rides, music, crafts, and international food of the **Arlington County Fair** (www.arlingtoncountyfair.org) at the Thomas Jefferson Community Center (3501 S. 2nd St.). Shuttle bus service is available from nearby Metro stations.

The free **Rosslyn Jazz Festival** swings through Gateway Park at the Virginia end of the Key Bridge in early September, followed by the **Marine Corps Marathon** (800/786-8762, www.marinemarathon.com) in late October. Some 21,000 runners huff through Arlington, Georgetown, and Washington, D.C., in the country's fourth-largest marathon, which begins and ends at the U.S. Marine Corps War Memorial.

ACCOMMODATIONS

Lodgings in Arlington are often a cheaper alternative to staying across the river, with the Metro providing a quick and easy link to the capital.

Under $100

The **Days Inn Pentagon** (3030 Columbia Pike, 703/521-5570, $90–100), near the big five-sided building, is the most reliable sub-$100 lodging option on this side of the Potomac. Another to try is the **Econo Lodge Metro Arlington** (6800 Lee Hwy., 703/538-5300, $80–100) is off I-66 exit 69, on U.S. 29 (Lee Hwy.).

$100-150

Midrange accommodations are concentrated to the south in Crystal City and Pentagon City. All offer complimentary shuttle service to National airport. The **Best Western Pentagon** (2480 S. Glebe Rd., 703/979-4400, $100–170) sits near the intersection of South Glebe Road and I-395 (Shirley Hwy.).

$150-200

The **Virginian Suites** (1500 Arlington Blvd., 703/522-9600) is a smaller place with one- and two-bedroom units for $100–190, including continental breakfast. Convenient to Arlington National Cemetery is the **Best Western Iwo Jima** (1501 Arlington Blvd., 703/524-5000, $130–200). In this price range is also **Comfort Inn Pentagon** (2480 S. Glebe Rd., 703/682-5500, $100–210).

For great views overlooking the river, try the sleek **Hotel Palomar** (1121 N. 19th St., 703/351-9170, www.hotelpalomar-arlington.com, $140–300) or the **Holiday Inn Rosslyn at Key Bridge** (1900 N. Fort Myer Dr., 703/807-2000, $150–200).

Over $200

At the **Crystal City Marriott** (1999 Jefferson Davis Hwy., 703/413-5500, $160–410), guests can enjoy a heated pool, saunas, and an exercise room. A short passage connects the hotel with a shopping mall and the Crystal City Metro stop. The **Westin Arlington Gateway** (801 N. Glebe Rd., 703/717-6200, $140–360) is convenient to the Ballston Metro stop.

Tops in the area is the **Ritz-Carlton Pentagon City** (1250 S. Hayes St., 703/415-5000, $400–500), located in the Fashion Centre complex and laden with antiques, paintings, and every amenity you could ask for. The elegant fyve Restaurant Lounge serves all meals daily, and the Pentagon City Metro station is minutes away.

FOOD

The ethnic diversity of the city across the river spills over into a diverse plethora of great eateries in Arlington. Swankier bistros have also begun lining the streets of neighborhoods such as Clarendon, augmenting the array of inexpensive ethnic restaurants. Here's a sampling of both.

Snacks and Cafés

At **Boccato Gelato & Espresso** (2719 Wilson Blvd., 703/869-6522, all meals daily), scoops are tasty but pricey, so savor each Italian-inspired spoonful. Some of the unusual flavors (pineapple basil, banana biscotti) are divine, others only so-so. Scoopers are usually generous with samples, so try before buying.

On the border between south Arlington and Alexandria, **Buzz** (901 Slaters Ln., 703/600-2899, all meals daily) hints at its target vices: sugar, caffeine, and drink. You'll find options for satisfying all three in this cute cupcakery, coffee shop, and lounge.

Casual

Rocketed into prime time by a surprise visit from President Obama and Vice President Biden, **Ray's Hell Burger** (1713 Wilson Blvd., 703/841-0001, lunch and dinner Tues.–Sun., dinner only Mon.) had a cult following even before then. Condiments and rolls of paper towels top each metal table, and a few B horror flick posters adorn the walls, but otherwise it's all about the beef. A 10-ounce freshly ground, hand-trimmed burger, served on a toasted brioche bun with toppings from gruyere to dill pickle chips, will cost you $6.95 ($1.50 extra for the cheese).

Devotees of Peruvian *pollo a la brasa,* or rotisserie chicken, should head to **Crisp & Juicy** (4540 Lee Hwy., 703/243-4222, lunch and dinner daily), a small take-out joint on Lee Highway. A whole chicken costs $9.75; a half goes for $5.95. If feeding more than one mouth, get one of the platters. Make sure to order the fried yucca, rice and beans, and delectable hot sauce.

Two excellent choices for Vietnamese food are **Minh's Restaurant** (2500 Wilson Blvd., 703/525-2828, lunch and dinner daily) and **Pho 75** (1721 Wilson Blvd., 703/525-7355, all meals until 8 P.M. daily). Both serve up a hearty bowl of *pho* that goes well with an iced lemonade or Vietnamese coffee. Dinner ranges $10–16 at Minh's; credit cards accepted. Dishes are $6–8 at Pho 75; cash only.

A family atmosphere—in this case, that of the Abi-Najm family—pervades the **Lebanese Taverna** (1101 S. Joyce St., 703/415-8681, lunch and dinner daily) in Pentagon Row. The assortment of small dishes (mezes) is always a good bet, with a sample of everything from hummus to baba ghanoush. You can also opt for a larger entrée like shawarma or roast chicken ($14–25 for dinner).

Occupying the former front bar of Tallula's restaurant next door, **EatBar** (2761 Washington Blvd., 703/778-9951, lunch Tues.–Fri., dinner daily) is spearheading the trend of "gastropubs," or bars that also offer quality food for a reasonable price. Very few things on the menu are over $10, including the pork belly BLT ($9). Pair with a selection off the extensive list of craft beer and wine, which includes over 50 bottles available by the glass.

Upscale

Come for the upscale munchies at chef Tracy

O'Grady's American bistro **Willow** (4301 N. Fairfax Dr., 703/465-8800, lunch and dinner daily), such as prosciutto-fontina fritters, and stay for the big plates of seared scallops and bacon-crusted salmon ($7–20 lunch, $18–33 dinner). Don't skip dessert; pastry chef Kate Jansen was named the best in the D.C. region in 2009.

The Liberty Tavern (3195 Wilson Blvd., 703/465-9360, lunch and dinner daily) turns out seasonally influenced American cuisine and Neapolitan-style pizza from its wood-fired ovens. The tavern prides itself in making nearly everything in-house—from the bread, to the butternut gnocchi, to the bratwurst and grain mustard, to the heirloom apple strudel and brown butter ice cream. Lunch runs $9–15, and dinner $10–23. Happy hour at the downstairs bar gets packed.

INFORMATION

The **Arlington Convention & Visitors Service** staffs a helpline 9 A.M.–5 P.M. daily (800/677-6267, www.stayarlington.com).

Old Town Alexandria

Less than half an hour from downtown D.C., one of the country's oldest port cities (pop. 143,000) preserves a core that is little changed, at least cosmetically, from the days when George Washington and a young Robert E. Lee called it home. Tall, narrow houses in brick or pastel clapboard line cobblestone streets, embellished by ivy escaping over the walls of small front gardens. The majority of the 4,750 buildings within the two National Historic Districts in Old Town date from the 18th and 19th centuries. These have been lovingly preserved and restored to give Old Town a dignified Colonial aura, from the smallest "spite" or "mother-in-law" house to the redbrick mansions of Captain's Row along Prince Street.

an Old Town home with a nautical flair

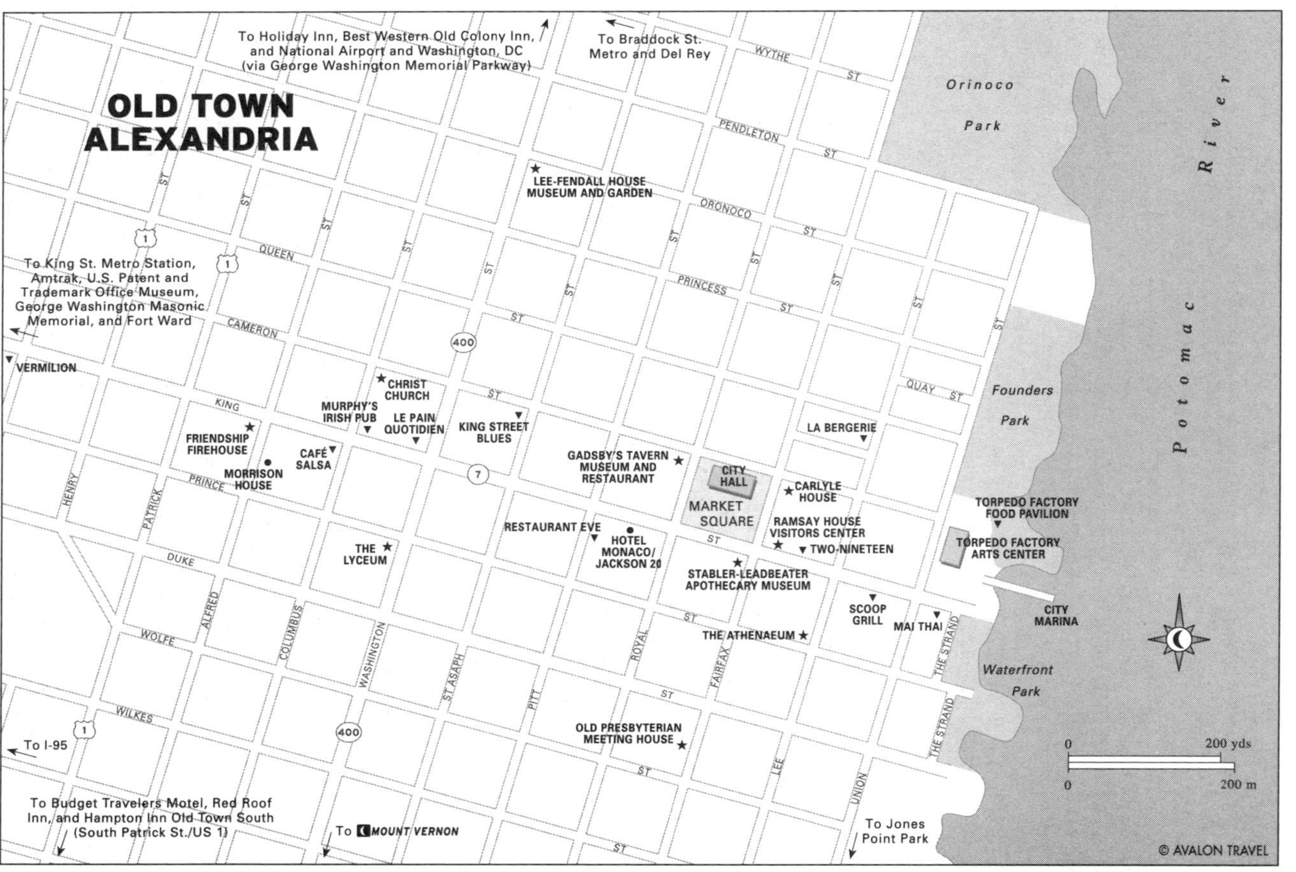
OLD TOWN ALEXANDRIA
To Holiday Inn, Best Western Old Colony Inn, and National Airport and Washington, DC (via George Washington Memorial Parkway)
To Braddock St. Metro and Del Rey
Orinoco Park
Potomac River
WYTHE
PENDLETON
ORONOCO
PRINCESS
QUEEN
CAMERON
KING
PRINCE
DUKE
WOLFE
WILKES
QUAY
ST
HENRY
PATRICK
ALFRED
COLUMBUS
WASHINGTON
ST ASAPH
PITT
ROYAL
FAIRFAX
LEE
UNION
THE STRAND
LEE-FENDALL HOUSE MUSEUM AND GARDEN
To King St. Metro Station, Amtrak, U.S. Patent and Trademark Office Museum, George Washington Masonic Memorial, and Fort Ward
VERMILION
CHRIST CHURCH
MURPHY'S IRISH PUB
LE PAIN QUOTIDIEN
KING STREET BLUES
FRIENDSHIP FIREHOUSE
CAFÉ SALSA
MORRISON HOUSE
GADSBY'S TAVERN MUSEUM AND RESTAURANT
CITY HALL
MARKET SQUARE
LA BERGERIE
CARLYLE HOUSE
Founders Park
TORPEDO FACTORY FOOD PAVILION
TORPEDO FACTORY ARTS CENTER
RAMSAY HOUSE VISITORS CENTER
TWO-NINETEEN
RESTAURANT EVE
HOTEL MONACO/JACKSON 20
THE LYCEUM
STABLER-LEADBEATER APOTHECARY MUSEUM
SCOOP GRILL
MAI THAI
CITY MARINA
THE ATHENAEUM
Waterfront Park
OLD PRESBYTERIAN MEETING HOUSE
To I-95
To Budget Travelers Motel, Red Roof Inn, and Hampton Inn Old Town South (South Patrick St./US 1)
To MOUNT VERNON
To Jones Point Park
1
7
400
0 200 yds
0 200 m
© AVALON TRAVEL

District residents escape to Old Town for more than a history lesson, though—scores of shops and restaurants keep the sidewalks crowded and the parking spaces filled on most weekend evenings. The restored waterfront area along the Potomac, which once echoed with the hammers of shipbuilders and the cries of tobacco merchants and slave auctioneers, now features the famous Torpedo Factory Art Center, riverside parks, and the occasional America's Cup contender, paddle wheeler, or old-style sailboat. Old Town prides itself on its dog friendliness, so don't be surprised to see a wagging tail on every street corner—or in every upscale boutique.

History

In 1669, British Gov. Sir William Berkeley granted 6,000 acres along the Potomac to English ship captain Robert Howsing, as a reward for bringing 120 settlers to the area. Less than one month later, Howsing sold the land to John Alexander, a Scottish captain, for "six thousand pounds of Tobacco and Cask." In 1748, the town of Alexandria, organized by Scottish merchants William Ramsay and John Carlyle, was named in his honor. One year later, the 60-acre plot was surveyed by John West Jr., and, according to local tradition, a 17-year-old George Washington. Washington liked the location so much that he returned to buy a house and a pew in Christ Church, and later he drilled troops in Market Square and served as Worshipful Master of the local Masonic Lodge.

Plantations flourished into the 18th century, turning Indian trails into "rolling roads" on which horse and ox teams rolled hogsheads of tobacco to public warehouses along the water. As the last good anchorage before the falls upriver, Alexandria grew into an important shipping port complete with taverns, shipyards, and a public ferry. Soon hemp and wheat became exports as important as tobacco, drawing caravans of "flour wagons" from as far as Winchester for shipment to England. A French visitor in 1796 called Alexandria

a cobblestoned block in Old Town

"beyond all comparison the handsomest town in Virginia—indeed...among the finest in the United States."

Henry "Light-Horse Harry" Lee, Robert E. Lee's father, brought his family to Alexandria in 1810. By the mid-19th century, so many of Robert E. Lee's relatives lived near the corner of Oronoco and Washington Streets that it became known as "Lee Corners." The future general spent the first few decades of his life in his father's house in the heart of town.

Soon after receiving city status in 1852, Alexandria saw much of its oceangoing trade lured away by Baltimore and its clipper ships. Old Town's prosperity began anew ironically in the 1930s, with an influx of out-of-towners (once called the "Foreign Legion"—even if they hailed from D.C.) drawn by old houses just dying for renovation.

Orientation

The George Washington Memorial Parkway becomes Washington Street as it passes through downtown, intersecting with the major east–west thoroughfare of King Street. Route 1 splits into one-way northbound (Patrick Street), and southbound (Henry Street) stretches a few blocks west. Traffic and parking can be tough, especially at night, so it's usually best to park your car in a lot or on the street (the visitors center has free passes) and walk. The City of Alexandria website (www.alexandriava.gov/parking) has a useful map of Old Town parking garage locations.

SIGHTS

Old Town

In fair weather, Old Town visitors and locals descend on the **City Marina** and **Founders Park,** a stretch of riverfront along Union Street that's dear to picnickers, street performers, joggers, and dog walkers (703/838-4340, www.alexandriava.gov/recreation). Called West Point in the early 1700s, it harbors a darker past: Here African slaves were unloaded from ships for the auction block at **Market Square,** in the center of town. Alexandria was one of the largest slave trading ports in the South.

If you visit in foul weather, at least it's a good excuse to head to the closest bar. George Washington, Thomas Jefferson, and the Marquis de Lafayette were among the many patrons of **Gadsby's Tavern** (134 N. Royal St., 703/838-4242, www.gadsbystavern.org, 10 A.M.–5 P.M. Tues.–Sat., 1–5 P.M. Sun.–Mon., Apr.–Oct, shorter hours in winter, $5 adults, $3 children) since it opened at the end of the 18th century. The tavern and the adjacent City Hotel have been restored and converted into a museum on dining, drinking, and dozing in the heart of Colonial America. While you're in the mood, stop by the Colonial restaurant of the same name next door. A lavish ball and banquet commemorating the first president's birthday has been held in the upstairs ballroom since 1797.

Established in 1792, the **Stabler-Leadbeater Apothecary Museum** (105–107 S. Fairfax St., 703/838-3852, www.apothecarymuseum.org, 10 A.M.–5 P.M. Tues.–Sat., 1–5 P.M. Sun.–Mon., shorter winter hours, $5 adults, $3 children) operated for almost 150 years, making it the second-oldest shop of its kind in the country. George and Martha Washington shopped here, as did Robert E. Lee, who bought paint for his house. A five-minute taped tour points out the finest collection of medicinal bottles in America, pill machines, original cash registers, and jars filled with native cures such as dandelion, sassafras, and snakeroot. Colored water fills a pair of two-foot show globes in the windows, which are said to have served as an early version of Open/Closed signs. Red indicated "stay away: plague"; blue or green meant "all clear, come on in."

Scottish merchant John Carlyle built **Carlyle House** (121 N. Fairfax St., 703/549-2997, www.carlylehouse.org, 10 A.M.–4 P.M. Tues.–Sat., noon–4 P.M. Sun., $5 adults, $3 children) for his blushing bride, Sarah Fairfax, in 1753. Two years later, Maj. Gen. Edward Braddock met here with five Colonial governors to organize a tax on the colonies to pay for Britain's role in the French and Indian War. Local governments refused to pay, marking one of the first serious rifts between England and America. Today the property remains an outstanding 18th-century manor home, furnished with period furniture and sheltering a small but radiant garden out back. Tours are given every half hour until closing.

The Northern Virginia Fine Arts Association has found a home in the Greek Revival **Athenaeum** (201 Prince St. at Lee St., 703/548-0035, www.nvfaa.org, call for hours), built in 1850 as a banking house. National and local art exhibits are free and open to the public.

Head toward the croak of gulls perched on riverfront pilings to find the **Torpedo Factory Arts Center** (105 N. Union St., 703/838-4565, www.torpedofactory.org, 10 A.M.–6 P.M. daily, free; closes at 5 P.M. on evenings with private events). The name is no hyperbole: Shell casings for torpedoes were built here during the first part of the 20th century. The factory was reopened in 1983 as one of Virginia's first and best artistic cooperatives. More than 165 painters, potters, sculptors, glassmakers, photographers, and fiber artists turn out artwork both fine and fun. The artists occupy 82 studios and six galleries in exchange for opening their creative processes and workspaces to the public. Thursday is the best time to visit, especially the second Thursday of each month; the studios stay open until 9 P.M. and local musicians perform.

Alexandria Archaeology (703/746-4399, http://oha.alexandriava.gov/archaeology) maintains a museum (10 A.M.–3 P.M. Tues.–Fri., 10 A.M.–5 P.M. Sat., 1–5 P.M. Sun., free) and research lab on the 3rd floor dedicated to unearthing the town's long history.

Learn about inventors and their innovative, offbeat, and sometimes indispensable creations at the **U.S. Patent & Trademark Office Museum** (600 Dulany St., 571/272-0095, www.uspto.gov/web/offices/ac/ahrpa/opa/museum, 9 A.M.–5 P.M. Mon.–Fri., noon–4 P.M. Sat.). It's run by the National Inventors Hall of Fame and includes permanent and changing exhibits on everything from Thomas Edison's lightbulbs to Michael Jackson's patent on the gravity-defying "Smooth Criminal" dance shoes.

The **Old Presbyterian Meeting House** (321 S. Fairfax St., 703/549-6670, www.opmh.org, 9 A.M.–4 P.M. Mon.–Fri., free) has been in use for all but 60 years since it was built in 1774. George Washington attended services here in 1798, one year before ministers preached at his memorial service. Twin balconies bracket the plain, almost severe interior, and many of the stones in the graveyard behind it have weathered into near illegibility. Several of Washington's friends and local luminaries, including William Ramsay and John Carlyle, are buried near the Tomb of the Unknown Soldier of the American Revolution.

About six blocks south on Royal Street, **Jones Point Park** (703/746-4343, www.alexandriava.gov/recreation) hides away a small lighthouse that from 1826 to 1926 guided ships through the Potomac's dangerous shoals. If you scout the riverbank in front of the diminutive lighthouse, you'll find the original southern cornerstone of the District of Columbia locked in the seawall, as well as views of the National Harbor and Woodrow Wilson Memorial Bridge.

Built in 1839 in the style of a Doric temple, **The Lyceum** (201 S. Washington St., 703/746-4994, www.alexandriahistory.org, 10 A.M.–5 P.M. Mon.–Sat., 1–5 P.M. Sun., $2) served as a hall for meetings, debates, and lectures on literature, history, and science. Today the imposing two-story columns flank the entrance of a museum, which covers Alexandria's history from Native Americans to the 20th century.

Friendship Firehouse (107 S. Alfred St., 703/746-3891, 10 A.M.–4 P.M. Fri.–Sat., 1–4 P.M. Sun., $2) commemorates the city's first organization to battle blazes, founded in 1774. Washington's involvement is debated by historians, but around here it's taken for granted. During opening hours you can view the collection of antique fire-fighting equipment, including an engine.

Historians do agree that the first president and his wife attended services beneath the distinctive octagonal tower of **Christ Church** (118 N. Washington St. at Cameron St.,

703/549-1450, www.historicchristchurch.org, 9 A.M.–4 P.M. Mon.–Sat., 2–4:30 P.M. Sun., free). Established in 1773, the church served as the place for Robert E. Lee's confirmation, and it still holds Episcopal services. Both the Washington and Lee family pews remain inside. Grave markers in the surrounding burial ground (the only one in town until 1805) don't necessarily mark actual gravesites; many were moved by Union soldiers during the Civil War to make room for campfires and grazing horses. The restored Old Parish Hall next door contains a gift shop and small historical museum.

At the intersection of Oronoco and Washington Streets stands the **Lee-Fendall House Museum and Garden** (614 Oronoco St., 703/548-1789, www.leefendallhouse.org, 10 A.M.–4 P.M. Wed.–Sat., 1–4 P.M. Sun., $5 adults, $3 children), built in 1785 by a relative of Henry "Light-Horse Harry" Lee. It was renovated in 1850 in the Greek Revival style and remained in the Lee family until 1903.

Nearby you'll find **Alexandria's skinniest house,** only seven feet wide with 345 feet of living space, on Queen Street at North St. Asaph Street. The structure was originally built in 1830 as a "spite house," a dwelling constructed to keep pesky neighbors out of an alleyway.

Head west on King Street past the Metro stop to reach the monumental neoclassic spire of the **George Washington Masonic National Memorial** (101 Callahan Dr., 703/683-2007, www.gwmemorial.org, 9 A.M.–4 P.M. Mon.–Sat., noon–4 P.M. Sun. Apr.–Sept., shorter hours in winter, free). Towering atop Shuter's Hill—considered as a potential site for the U.S. Capitol when Alexandria was part of the District of Columbia—the memorial encloses a 17-foot bronze statue of the first Worshipful Master of Alexandria Lodge No. 22 gazing over the city and the Potomac. Three-story marble columns and heroic murals on either side make this a monument on the D.C. scale. A museum on the 4th floor contains Washington memorabilia such as the clock stopped by his physician at 10:20 P.M., the moment of his passing, along with an

the skinniest house in Alexandria

18-by-25-foot Persian carpet that dates to 1540. Keep going to the 9th-floor observatory for a spectacular view clear across the river. Guided tours are given daily until 4 P.M.

Beyond Old Town

During the Civil War, Washington, D.C., was one of the most heavily defended cites in the nation. Thirty-six guns and 162 earthwork forts and batteries bristled from hillsides around the capital, awaiting the all-out Confederate assault that never came. Today, the best-preserved part of those fortifications are in the **Fort Ward Museum and Historic Site** (4301 W. Braddock Rd., 703/838-4848, www.fortward.org, 9 A.M.–5 P.M. Tues.–Sat., noon–5 P.M. Sun., park 9 A.M.–sunset daily, free), a 45-acre park enclosing restored earthwork bastions, six guns, and a Civil War–era museum patterned after a Union headquarters building. Call for information on living-history events. To get there, take King Street west, then bear left onto West Braddock, and it's on the right near I-395 exit 4.

A quick detour from Old Town lands you in what could be mistaken for Pleasantville. The small neighborhood of **Del Ray** (www.delraycitizen.org) has an astonishing number of enticing restaurants and specialty shops for its size. Mount Vernon Avenue has the old-fashioned feel of a 1920s Main Street, complete with a Wisconsin-style frozen custard shop. Del Ray is north of Old Town; heading west on King Street, turn right on West Street, left on Braddock Road, cross the train tracks, and turn right on Mount Vernon Avenue. For those on foot, the Braddock Metro station is the closest, about a 15-minute walk to the best eats.

HOME BREW

For those who have ever daydreamed about opening a brewpub, here's the next best thing. **Shenandoah Brewing Company** (652 S. Pickett St., Alexandria, 703/823-9508, www.shenandoahbrewing.com) is a brew-on-premises establishment – in other words, a do-it-yourself brewery. It provides the crucial equipment, ingredients, expertise, and more than 80 recipes, from a honey maibock to an India pale ale.

To avoid accidents – and losing precious future beer – read the directions carefully and don't partake too freely in Shenandoah's drafts on tap until you successfully finish your batch. Fermentation takes 3-12 weeks, then you return to bottle it and add labels if you choose. Prices start at $190; a batch makes between four and five cases of 12-ounce bottles (96-120 bottles).

Aspiring enologists can join in the fun too; contact **Carafe Wines** (111 S. Alfred St., Alexandria, 703/739-5850, www.carafewines.com) for prices and details.

ENTERTAINMENT AND RECREATION

Nightlife

The Two-Nineteen restaurant's **Basin Street Lounge** (219 King St., 703/549-1141) hops with live jazz and blues on weekends, and **King Street Blues** (112 N. St. Asaph St., 703/836-8800) hosts live music in its 1st-floor bar on Thursday evenings. **Café Salsa** (808 King St., 703/684-4100) is the hottest salsa club in town, with lessons Tuesday evenings and live music Thursday–Saturday.

If two-stepping is more your style, try **Nick's Night Club** (642 S. Pickett St., 703/751-8900, www.nicksnightclub.com), located in a strip mall in west Alexandria near the Landmark Mall. **Jackson 20** (480 King St., 703/842-2790, www.jackson20.com) and **Vermilion** (1120 King St., 703/684-9669, www.vermilionrestaurant.com) are both hip Old Town happy hour destinations. Local musicians showcase their tunes at the latter every Tuesday and Wednesday around 9:30 P.M.

For a pint of Old Country stout, try **Murphy's Irish Pub** (713 King St., 703/548-1717), voted one of the 50 best bars in the D.C. area thanks to its roaring fireplace, generous pub fare, and nightly Irish and Welsh singalongs. Check the website (www.murphyspub.com) for an entertainment calendar.

The **Birchmere** (3701 Mount Vernon

Ave., 703/549-7500, www.birchmere.com) features nationally known bluegrass, folk, rock, and country acts in an intimate, informal "music hall" setting. To get there, head west on Pendleton to West Street, turn right, then quickly left onto Braddock, and finally right onto Mount Vernon. It's just south of Glebe Road.

Tours

Guided **walking tours** (703/329-1122) focusing on the history and architecture of Old Town leave from the Ramsay House Visitors Center at 10:30 A.M. Monday–Saturday and 2 P.M. Sunday, April–November ($15 pp). **Old Town Experience** (703/836-0694, oldtwntour@aol.com) also offers daily guided walking tours of major sites in Old Town, with tidbits of legends and folklore along the way. Call for prices and reservations.

For ghost tours, try **Alexandria Colonial Tours** (703/519-1749, www.alexcolonialtours.com), which offers hour-long lantern-lit walks Wednesday–Sunday in summer (Fri.–Sun. spring through fall) for $10 adults and $5 children. At the end your guide will abandon you in a graveyard—and that's a selling point. **Footsteps to the Past** (703/683-3451, www.footstepstothepast.com) also does ghost tours daily, as well as black history and Civil War–themed tours by appointment.

The **Potomac Riverboat Company** (703/684-0580 or 877/511-2628, www.potomacriverboatco.com) offers a variety of floating tours from the city marina near the Torpedo Factory April–October. A 40-minute narrated tour of Alexandria from the water aboard the *Admiral Tilp* is $14 adults, $8 children. The company also sends boats to the Washington, D.C., monuments ($26/$13 round-trip), and Mount Vernon ($38/$20 round-trip). ***Nina's Dandy*** (757/683-6076, www.dandydinnerboat.com) is a 100-ton restaurant cruise ship that leaves from Waterfront Park at the end of Prince Street. Three-course lunches ($45–55) and five-course dinners ($86–96) compete with the D.C. monuments for your attention on three-hour cruises up to the capital. There's dancing in the main salon, and a sister ship, the *Dandy,* does private events.

Outdoor Recreation

With the **Mount Vernon Trail** ending just to the north, Alexandria sees plenty of foot and bike traffic in the sunny months. Only a block from the trail, **Wheel Nuts** (302 Montgomery St., 703/548-5116, www.wheelnuts.net) is a full-service bike shop that rents hybrid bikes

WASHINGTON & OLD DOMINION TRAIL

Sometimes called "Virginia's Skinniest Park," the Washington & Old Dominion Trail links northern Virginia's split personalities in a 100-foot-wide 45-mile-long stretch from the suburbs of Arlington County to Loudoun County's rural reaches. A train ran this route 1859–1968, but today all you'll encounter on the way from condos to meadows, or vice versa, are other walkers, bikers, and riders on horseback.

The asphalt path, technically the **W&OD Railroad Regional Park** (703/729-0596, www.nvrpa.org/parks/wod), begins at the intersection of Shirlington Road and Four Mile Run Drive in Arlington County, two blocks north of I-395 exit 6. From here it noses west through Falls Church in Fairfax County, roughly paralleling Route 7. A bridle path joins in Vienna, and the double trail continues through Reston, Herndon, and Leesburg before ending at Purcellsville west of Leesburg, on 21st Street (Rte. 690) one block off Main Street (Rte. 7).

Camping isn't allowed along the trail, but plenty of hotels and motels on the way make it possible to spend a few days making the whole trip. For more information, contact the **Friends of the W&OD Trail** (703/729-0596, www.wodfriends.org). The group also sells a 56-page guide and REI map. The trail itself is owned and operated by the Northern Virginia Regional Park Authority.

for $25 and tandem bikes for $28 per day. Pedal down to George Washington's estate on the eponymous bike trail or cross the Woodrow Wilson Memorial Bridge in the wide pedestrian lane to visit the giant *Awakening* statue in his new home among the shops and restaurants of **National Harbor** (877/628-5427, www.nationalharbor.com).

Rent kayaks, canoes, or sailboats from the **Belle Haven Marina** (703/768-0018, www.saildc.com, see website for rates), just south of Old Town on the George Washington Parkway. Or mosey over to the **Dyke Marsh Wildlife Preserve,** located next to the Belle Haven Marina, for bird-watching or a pleasant stroll along the river.

SHOPPING

Alexandria abounds with places to shop, so serious browsers will want to start at the **Torpedo Factory** and simply work their way west.

Treat (103 S. St. Asaph St., 703/535-3294, www.shoptreat.com) is the first and—thus far—only "sample sale boutique" in the D.C. metro area, meaning it sells overstocked, discounted, and end-of-season merchandise from higher-end labels. It's open five days a week (11 A.M.–7 P.M. Wed.–Sat., noon–6 P.M. Sun.). Fashionistas will also enjoy **Diva** (116 S. Pitt St., 703/683-1022, www.divaboutiqueva.com, 11 A.M.–6 P.M. Tues.–Sat., 1–5 P.M. Sun.), a designer consignment boutique.

For home furnishings, **Decorium** (116 King St., 703/739-4662, www.decoriumhome.com) has a whimsical touch with interior design expertise. **Ten Thousand Villages** (915 King St., 703/684-1435, www.tenthousandvillages.com) is northern Virginia's oldest fair-trade retailer, selling handcrafted jewelry, home decor, and gifts from more than 130 artisan groups hailing from 38 countries. **Why Not?** (200 King St., 703/548-4420) sells children's clothing, toys, books, and puzzles, and has done so for more than four decades.

Gallery West (1213 King St., 703/549-6007) is the oldest artist-owned and -operated gallery in northern Virginia, and displays paintings, photography, and sculpture works that are constantly rotating. Everything Irish—from Celtic crosses to shamrock ties—can be found at **The Irish Walk** (415 King St., 703/548-0118).

The southern section of Market Square is home to the Alexandria Saturday-morning **farmers market** (703/838-4770). It's been going since 1753, making it one of the oldest continuously operating markets in the country. Early morning is the best time to go.

EVENTS

For details on any of the following events, contact the Alexandria Convention and Visitors Association. Most charge a small admission fee.

Both Henry "Light-Horse Harry" Lee and his son Robert are honored during the **Lee Birthday Celebrations** on the third Sunday in January with special tours, refreshments, and period music at the Lee-Fendall House. The third weekend in February brings another party, this time for **George Washington's Birthday** (703/991-4474, www.washingtonbirthday.net). On Saturday, a black-tie/Colonial-costume Birthnight Banquet & Ball at Gadsby's Tavern commemorates George and Martha's attendance there in 1798 and 1799. A Revolutionary War encampment at Fort Ward follows on Sunday, including a mock skirmish between British and Revolutionary troops. On Monday, a gigantic parade snakes through town, honoring Alexandria's favorite son with Colonial drums and bugle musters. As you might guess, there's a lot going on at Mount Vernon this weekend, too.

At the end of May, the **Memorial Day Jazz Festival** arrives at Fort Ward Park (4301 W. Braddock Rd., 703/883-4686), and in June the **Alexandria Red Cross Waterfront Festival** (703/549-8300, www.waterfrontfestival.org) brings tall ships, live music, living history, and amusement rides to Oronoco Bay Park at Union and Madison Streets. The Juneteenth Commemoration (703/838-4000, www.alexblackhistory.org), also known as Emancipation Day, celebrates African American freedom and community with live music, hands-on crafts, storytelling, and a marketplace.

Over the second weekend of September is the **Alexandria Festival of the Arts,** during which five blocks of King Street are closed and turned into an outdoor art gallery with works by hundreds of artists on display.

In early December, Old Town wraps the Christmas spirit in tartan for the **Scottish Christmas Walk** (703/548-0111, www.scottishchristmaswalk.com). The rousing parade of bagpipers, drummers, Scottish Highland dancers, representatives from over 100 clans, and sweater-wearing Scottie dogs pay tribute to the town's Scottish heritage. That evening, stay for the **Holiday Parade of Lights** (703/746-3301), when sailing and motorboats troll past the waterfront decorated in festive lights. The self-guided **Historic Alexandria Candlelight Tours** (703/838-4242), also in early December, pass through Gadsby's Tavern, Christ Church, and other historic buildings for a holiday tour at your own pace.

ACCOMMODATIONS

$50-100

Most of Alexandria's less-expensive lodgings are outside of Old Town. Head south along Route 1 (first called the Jefferson Davis Highway, then Richmond Highway) to find the **Budget Host Travelers Motel** (5916 Richmond Hwy., 703/329-1310, $65–90), near I-95 and U.S. 1 South, and the **Red Roof Inn – Alexandria** (5975 Richmond Hwy., 703/960-5200, $85–110).

$100-150

Both the **Comfort Inn Alexandria** (5716 S. Van Dorn St., 703/922-9200, $100–160) and the **Hawthorne Suites** (420 N. Van Dorn St., 703/370-1000, $130–220) are west of Old Town on Van Dorn Street, which runs perpendicular to Duke Street between I-95 and I-395. Most of the rooms at the latter fall within this price range, and all are efficiencies or suites with kitchens.

$150-250

The **Hampton Inn Old Town South** (5821 Richmond Hwy., 703/329-1400, $100–250) is on the border of Alexandria proper just south of the I-95/I-495 intersection. The small-scale **Holiday Inn Hotel & Suites** (625 1st St., 703/548-6300) off the George Washington Memorial Parkway just east of the intersection of 1st and Washington Streets. Rooms start at $130 and climb toward $300, but most are between $150 and $250.

Just north of Old Town is the **Best Western Old Colony Inn** (1101 N. Washington St., 703/739-2222, $130–260), which offers suites, some with whirlpool bath. Located in the heart of Old Town, **Hotel Monaco** (480 King St., 703/549-6080, $140–270) is a luxury hotel under the Kimpton brand that features 241 stylish rooms and suites, a health club, pool, and the Jackson 20 restaurant, and is a popular happy hour destination with people and pets (the hotel hosts a doggie happy hour twice a week).

Over $250

Kimpton has also taken the reins of the small but luxurious **Morrison House** (116 S. Alfred St., 703/838-8000 or 866/834-6628, www.morrisonhouse.com); it combines Federal Period reproductions and a pet-friendly policy in its 45 rooms and suites. Deluxe guest rooms have Italian marble baths, mahogany armoires, and four-poster beds. The Grille restaurant (all meals daily) serves American classics like diver scallops and rack of lamb for $20–30 at dinner. A pianist graces the 1st-floor Parlor on Thursday, Friday, and Saturday nights. Room rates start at $200.

Services

The **Alexandria and Arlington Bed & Breakfast Network** (888/549-3415, www.aabbn.com) can help with bed-and-breakfast lodgings in Old Town.

FOOD

Old Town

SNACKS AND CAFÉS

For rich café au lait and chewy, artisanal breads and breakfast pastries, try **Le Pain Quotidien** (701 King St., 703/683-2273, all meals daily). Enjoy homemade ice cream and frozen yogurt beneath stained-glass lampshades at **The Scoop Grill** (110 King St., 703/549-4527, lunch and dinner daily), which also offers breakfast specials. A handful of inexpensive lunch options fill the glass-walled **Torpedo Factory Food Pavilion** by the river.

CASUAL

Cross a roadhouse with a funhouse, add neon, and you'll end up with something like **King Street Blues** (112 N. St. Asaph St., 703/836-8800, lunch and dinner daily). Voted the best barbecue, burger, and cheap eats in town, this art bar serves up "comfort food with a Southern accent" amid riotous paintings and sculptures. Try sammies, po' boys, and blue-plate specials ($8–15) like the Eastern Shore Chicken Pie, baked with oysters. In a similar vein, culinarily speaking, is the **Hard Times Cafe** (1404 King St., 703/837-0050, lunch and dinner daily), whose chili is ambrosial, whether you pick the Texas, Cincinnati, or vegetarian version. Also on the menu are microbrews, root beer floats, and an authentic Frito chili pie, with dishes in the $5–8 range. Near the riverfront, **Mai Thai** (6 King St., 703/548-0600, lunch and dinner daily, $11–15) is popular for pad thai, *panang* curry, and cocktails.

UPSCALE

Occupying the 2nd floor of an old warehouse, **La Bergerie** (218 N. Lee St., 703/683-1007, lunch Mon.–Sat., dinner daily) is known for dependable high-quality French cooking in a cozy bare-brick ambience. Appetizers such as foie gras and escargot are a great lead-in to main courses ($27–42 for dinner) such as roasted sea scallops and veal chops. The dessert soufflés are outstanding. They also offer changing prix-fixe menus for lunch ($22) and dinner (three courses for $45, four courses for $65).

Gadsby's Tavern Restaurant (138 N. Royal St. at Cameron St., 703/548-1288, lunch daily, dinner Mon.–Sat.) re-creates the 18th century in its pewter plates, creaking wood floor, and costumed waiters. The food is just as authentic, with entrées for $9–15 at lunch and $22–30 at dinner, and strolling minstrels providing entertainment. Try the George Washington duck.

Dublin native Cathal Armstrong, voted one of America's Best New Chefs by *Food & Wine* magazine in 2006, created **Restaurant Eve** (110 S. Pitt St., 703/706-0450) with his wife, Meshelle Armstrong, and named it after their first child. It's really two restaurants in one restored warehouse building. The Bistro is the less formal half, with New American dishes such as bouillabaisse and pan-roasted sweetbreads with wild mushrooms served for lunch Monday–Friday ($19–25) and dinner Monday–Saturday ($35–40). In the 34-seat Chef's Tasting Room, Armstrong shows his skills with five- and nine-course prix-fixe tasting menus ($105 and $145). For shoestring gourmets, try the Lickity Split Lunches, served only in the bar and lounge 11:30 A.M.–4 P.M. Monday–Friday for $13.50. Ingredients change with the seasons and are local and sustainable when possible.

Del Ray

Old Town has enough restaurants to keep a diner busy for months, let alone a short trip. Straying off the beaten path a bit can be rewarding, though. In the front-porch neighborhood of Del Ray, about two miles northwest of Old Town, eclectic restaurants and cute shops line Mount Vernon Avenue. The cozy **Bombay Curry Company** (3110 Mount Vernon Ave., 703/836-6363, lunch Sun.–Fri., dinner daily, $6–14) rewards those who venture this far with unusually tasty tandoori and curries for excellent prices. Sunday afternoon buffets ($10) include a little of everything.

Del Merie Grille (3106 Mount Vernon Ave., 703/739-4335, lunch Tues.–Fri., dinner daily, $13–26) is known for its Southern-inspired comfort foods such as collard greens, chicken pot pie, and a heart-stopping starter known simply as "The Plate." For a pre-dinner drink or a nightcap, head to **Cheesetique** (2411 Mount Vernon Ave., 703/706-5300, lunch Tues.–Sun., dinner Tues.–Sat.), a specialty cheese shop and wine bar—for cheese lovers, it's close to nirvana. Entrées cost around $10 and wine flights start at $18.

The neighborhood favorite **Evening Star Café** (2000 Mount Vernon Ave., 703/549-5051, all meals daily, $19–27) is a cozy place with creative American cuisine like Alaskan halibut with Moroccan couscous. Its wine selection is top-notch thanks to Planet Wine, the wine store under the same management next door. You can purchase any vintage from the selection of more than 1,000 bottles at retail and the café will pour it for a modest service fee.

No trip to Del Ray is complete without a stop at **The Dairy Godmother** (2310 Mount Vernon Ave., 703/683-7767) for Wisconsin-style frozen custard. On muggy summer evenings, you'll know it by the line of patrons on the sidewalk.

INFORMATION

Alexandria's Convention and Visitors Association runs a **visitors center** in the Ramsay House (221 King St. at Fairfax St., 703/746-3301 or 800/388-9119, www.visitalexandriava.com). The building, the oldest in town, was built in 1749 by Scottish merchant William Ramsay, a friend of George Washington and one of the founders of Alexandria. Over the years it served as a tavern, grocery store, cigar factory, and rooming house and is thought to have been brought here on a barge from its original location some 30 miles downriver.

Along with brochures, walking-tour maps, and lists of hotels, restaurants, and shops, the visitors center hands out free 24-hour parking permits for two-hour metered street zones, which can be renewed. It also sells a "Key to the City" coupon book for $12 that includes admission to the Carlyle House, Gadsby's Tavern Museum, Lee-Fendall House, Stabler-Leadbeater Apothecary Museum, and numerous other sites within Alexandria.

GETTING THERE AND AROUND

The yellow and blue Metro lines converge at the **King Street station,** which is west on King Street just before the George Washington Masonic Memorial. From here you can hop on the free **King Street Trolley** (703/838-4966, www.alexandriava.gov/trolley) that runs to the Potomac River waterfront via the 1.5-mile stretch of King Street from 11:30 A.M. to 10 P.M. daily, with trolleys departing every 20 minutes.

Across the street is the Alexandria **Amtrak** station (703/836-4339). There's another yellow/blue Metro stop at **Braddock Road;** to reach it, head west on Wythe Street, jog right on West Street, and then left on Braddock Road.

The **Potomac Riverboat Company**'s D.C. monuments tour (703/684-0580 or 877/511-2628, www.potomacriverboatco.com) will get you to Georgetown in 45 minutes for $14 adults, $7 children (more for round-trip), or to the National Harbor on the Maryland side of the river for $8 one-way, $16 round-trip.

Near the Beltway

McLEAN

The Claude Moore Colonial Farm at Turkey Run

The 18th-century homestead of a family of tenant farmers is brought to life inside the Beltway at this small but respectable living-history enclave. A one-room log farmhouse anchors the 100-acre site, surrounded by a barn and fields of tobacco, wheat, flax, corn, and rye. Split-rail "worm fencing" keeps the turkeys, hogs, and chickens out of the kitchen gardens and the quarterhorse out of the orchard. Costumed historical interpreters are on hand to explain the care and feeding of the Devon cattle and the use and manufacture of antique tools and clothing.

The best times to stop by are during **market fairs** in mid-May, July, and October, when visitors can buy homegrown produce, bob for apples, taste period food, and see a puppet show. Other special events include the **wheat harvest** in June, the **tobacco harvest** in August, and **wassail** in late December to assure a "howling crop." Old-time skills are taught in workshops throughout the year.

To reach the farm (6310 Georgetown Pike, 703/442-7557, www.1771.org or www.nps.gov/clmo, 10 A.M.–4:30 P.M. Wed.–Sun. Apr.–Dec., $3 adults, $2 children 3–12), take Route 738 off Old Dominion Drive (Rte. 309) into McLean, turn north onto Chain Bridge Road for 0.5 mile, then east on Dolley Madison Boulevard (Rte. 123). After two miles, turn north on Georgetown Pike (Rte. 193), and make an immediate right on Colonial Farm Road. It's on the left.

GREAT FALLS PARK

The Potomac would have been the perfect transport route for goods between the ocean and the heart of the colonies, except for one small detail: the river drops 77 feet in just a quarter mile as it seethes over the unyielding shelf of the fall line. Now this source of historical headaches is one of the most exciting natural places close to the capital, combining trails, historic ruins, rugged rocks, and white water.

History

Great Falls stood as a barrier between the open water and important Maryland ports until 1802, when a firm founded by George Washington (is there anything that guy *didn't* do?) opened the Patowmack Canal parallel to the river on the Virginia side. Elevator locks were hewn from solid rock, and a small settlement sprang up around the steady trade. In 1828, the Chesapeake & Ohio (C&O) Canal took over on the opposite bank, from downtown D.C. to Cumberland, Maryland. By the mid-19th century, one million tons of goods per year flowed through the C&O's 75 locks, but the opening of the Baltimore & Ohio Railroad in 1924 spelled the end of water transport on both sides.

Visiting Great Falls

Start at the **visitors center,** which has exhibits on the geology and human and natural history of the area. There's a snack bar downstairs and picnic tables nearby. Many trails wind along the edge of the steep cliffs above the river. Be careful on the slippery rocks near the edge—fatal falls happen with frightening regularity. Notice the posts indicating high-water marks of floods that cover the falls completely about once a decade, occasionally reaching as high as the visitors center.

The park has 15 miles of **hiking trails,**

Great Falls as seen from the Maryland side of the Potomac, gazing at the Virginia banks

mostly easy rambles. The 1.5-mile River Trail skirts the cliffs, where you might spot a red-shouldered hawk, osprey, or great blue heron, and joins the 1.5-mile Ridge Trail that runs between Old Dominion Drive and the river. Take the 0.75-mile Patowmack Canal Trail along the remains of the old canal past the ruins of the canal town of Matildaville, and the one-mile Swamp Trail runs above an old terrace of the Potomac, where you'll likely see skunk cabbage and jewelweed in the swampy former riverbed. Five miles of trails, including the Old Carriage Road, Ridge, and Difficult Run Trails, are open to horseback riders and mountain bikers.

Fishing and cross-country skiing after the rare snowfall are other seasonal possibilities. Great Falls is the most popular spot in the state for **rock climbing,** with more than 100 climbs up to 5.12 in difficulty. It's almost all top-roping and you'll need at least three 50-foot lengths of webbing to set the anchors.

Needless to say, swimming is prohibited and will bring the rescue personnel (and attendant fines) surprisingly quickly. White-water boaters, though, can run the Class V+ rapids, and you'll often see kayakers out spinning in the eddies. Maryland-based **Liquid Adventures** (301/229-0428, www.liquidadventures.org) teaches white-water kayaking and roll classes in the milder riffles of these waters.

On the Maryland bank, the **C&O Canal National Historical Park** (301/739-4200, www.nps.gov/choh) contains the historic Great Falls Tavern and a footbridge to an island in the middle of the torrent. Mule-drawn barge trips are offered on *The Canal Clipper.*

To reach the park (703/285-2965, www.nps.gov/grfa, dawn–dusk daily, visitors center 10 A.M.–4, 5, or 6 P.M. depending on season, $5 per car, $3 per pedestrian or cyclist, May–Oct.), take I-495 exit 13 to Georgetown Pike (Rte. 193). Follow this four miles west to Route 738, and take a right into the park.

RIVERBEND PARK

Adjoining Great Falls to the north, this small reserve encloses a calmer section of river inhabited by animals rare for the area, such as foxes, minks, river otters, and the infrequent bald eagle. Ten miles of hiking, biking, and equestrian trails explore the park's 400 acres of meadows and forest, including two miles along the river and a short paved trail for disabled visitors. Huge beech, elm, birch, and poplars grow along the 1.7-mile Potomac Heritage Trail (which shares its name with another trail farther south).

To reach the park (703/759-9018, www.fairfaxcounty.gov/parks/riverbend), keep going west past the Great Falls entrance to Riverbend Road, take a right, and then go right on Jeffrey Road. Another right after two miles brings you to the riverbank and the **visitors center** with small museum displays, trail maps, and brochures (9 A.M.–5 P.M. Wed.–Mon.). The wide deck with Adirondack chairs at the visitors center is reason enough to visit. Outside are picnic areas, fishing spots, and a boat ramp, and a **Nature Center** is just down Jeffrey Road. Over 10 miles of hiking trails include the Potomac Heritage Trail along the river, which connects with Great Falls Park downriver in 1.75 miles.

Kayak tours are given May–August for small groups (1–6 people $330, $55 for each add'l person, max. 11), and you can rent kayaks and Jon boats for $25 per day ($15 half day). Be careful not to pass the white buoys that indicate a dangerous dam one mile downriver from the boat ramp.

In early September the park hosts the **Virginia Indian Festival,** which draws thousands of visitors. An entrance fee of $4 per car is charged on summer weekends and holidays; otherwise, entrance is free.

GREAT FALLS TOWN

A few special eateries make this otherwise unassuming town, centered at the intersection of Georgetown Pike (Rte. 193) and Walker Road (Rte. 681), an appetizing place to stop before or after visiting the falls. The **Serbian Crown Restaurant** (1141 Walker Rd., 703/759-4150, www.serbiancrown.com, lunch Tues.–Fri., dinner daily) serves authentic Russian/French fare, along with a wide selection of iced vodka to top things off. Start with beluga caviar and some borscht, then move on to Sole Vladimir or *kulibiaka* (Russian salmon with lobster sauce) to the strains of live gypsy music. Reservations are recommended on weekends. Walker Road runs between Georgetown Pike and Leesburg Pike.

Jacques Haeringer's **L'Auberge Chez François** (332 Springvale Rd., 703/759-3800, www.laubergechezfrancois.com, from 5:30 P.M. Tues.–Sat., from 1:30 P.M. Sun.) holds a special place in the heart of Washingtonians, who vie for reservations weeks ahead of time. An *auberge* is a small local restaurant traditionally run by a chef-owner and his family, and this Alsace-meets-Virginia version measures up well. Six-course prix-fixe dinners include entrées like rack of lamb and, in winter, game dishes such as antelope, pheasant, and rabbit. Outdoor tables under the trees are first-come, first-served, and the wine list draws from France and Virginia, naturally. Two seatings are offered on Friday and Saturday and three on Sunday. Expect to pay upward of $100 for dinner for two. To get there, head west of the main intersection about one mile to Springvale Road. Turn right, and it is on the left after 2.5 miles.

Continuing in the international vein, **Moby Dick's House of Kabob** (6854 Old Dominion Dr., 703/448-8448, lunch and dinner daily) is a local chain and favorite in the D.C. metro region. Entrées such as lamb kabobs and gyro sandwiches come with yogurt cucumber sauce or *shirazi* salad and your choice of flat bread or saffron rice ($7–15).

WOLF TRAP NATIONAL PARK FOR THE PERFORMING ARTS

The country's only national park dedicated to the performing arts, Wolf Trap (703/255-1900 or 877/965-3872, ticket information 703/255-1868, www.wolftrap.org) offers a wide array of performances throughout the year, amid 130 acres of hills and woodlands. Jazz, opera, folk,

the Filene Center at the Wolf Trap National Park for the Performing Arts

country, and popular music concerts are held in the **Filene Center,** a partially outdoor amphitheater, during the summer, and inside at **The Barns at Wolf Trap** October–May. The two 18th-century barns, relocated from upstate New York, are half a mile down Trap Road from the Filene Center. The **Wolf Trap Opera Company** performs in both venues. Children's programs, from mime to storytelling, happen in the **Theater-in-the-Woods** in June, July, and August, and an International Children's Festival spans Labor Day weekend.

Dining options include the casual open-air **Ovations Restaurant** (703/255-4017, www.mealsbeneaththemoon.com), serving à la carte or buffet meals daily two hours before evening Filene Center performances. They'll also pack you a picnic, or you're welcome to bring your own wine and picnic to enjoy on the lawn during a concert—a wonderful way to pass a summer evening.

Tickets are available at the park box office, through the park's website, or from various outlets of Tickets.com (703/218-6500 or 800/955-5566, www.tickets.com). Prices range from about $10 for lawn space to $70 and up for orchestra seats. The park is on Trap Road between Route 7 and the Dulles Toll Road, north of Tysons Corner, and parking is free. For Filene Center performances (except operas and the Children's Festival), the **Wolf Trap Metro Shuttle Bus Express** runs to and from the West Falls Church Metro station (on the orange line) for $3 per person round-trip (exact change). For more information, see the National Park Service website (www.nps.gov/wotr).

Hunt Country

Some of Virginia's choicest acres pick up where the Beltway sprawl ends, stretching all the way to the Shenandoah. From the banks of the upper Potomac—one of the wildest urban rivers in the East—to the foothills of the Blue Ridge, Hunt Country is a mix of tiny villages and huge estates, with a few modest farms still holding on in between. Old stone walls crawling with honeysuckle curve into neat lines of black-and-white fences along dirt lanes sunken with centuries of use. Cows and horses speckle emerald fields among silver silos, red barns, and white farmhouses.

Ever since Lord Fairfax first rode off behind a braying pack of hounds, both Loudoun (LOUD-un) and Faquier (fah-KEER) Counties have been known as Virginia's Hunt Country. Presidents from Washington to Kennedy have fled the bustle of the capital to chase foxes through the early-morning tranquility of the countryside. Some of the richest people in the world breed, show, train, and race thoroughbreds on multimillion-dollar estates, popping into towns like Middleburg and Upperville to repair a harness or pick up a quart of oil for the Mercedes.

The development juggernaut, though, rolls slowly closer. High-tech industries moving west from Arlington and Fairfax have made Loudoun one of the fastest-developing counties in the country. Huge tracts of land not yet swallowed up by office parks and housing developments stand on the brink, not yet urbanized but no longer rural. Hunt Country holds its future in its hands, and if its performance with Disney in the 1990s is any indication, it will be a while before these farmlands are paved. The Mouse (aka the Walt Disney Co.) wanted to build a $650 million history theme park on 3,000 acres of Fairfax and Loudoun Counties. Concerns surfaced over visitor impact—the complex would have been only four miles from the Manassas Civil War battlefields—and good taste (how would Disney portray slavery?). Despite governor George Allen's support, the plan fell to an organized opposition led by an unlikely coalition of Ralph Nader and Old Money.

HUNT COUNTRY FUN

Get a taste of the equine world during Loudoun County's annual **Hunt Country Stable Tour** on Memorial Day weekend. During the self-driven auto tour, you can visit barns, stables, and training facilities on exquisite country estates where thoroughbreds are raised and ridden. Chat with a historical reenactor along the way and become familiar with various breeds of horses, foxhounds, and livestock in hands-on demonstrations at the historic estate of the late Mr. Jack Kent Cooke. Tickets are $20 per person (all proceeds go to charity), and you can grab a bite at half a dozen places along the way. Order tickets ahead of time from the Trinity Episcopal Church in Upperville (540/592-3711, www.middleburgonline.com/stabletour).

MANASSAS NATIONAL BATTLEFIELD PARK

The gently rippled hills north of Manassas—still almost as rural as they were 150 years ago—saw two major Civil War battles. The first opened the war with a horrific bang, and the second set the stage for Lee's abortive invasion of the North three years later.

First Battle of Bull Run (First Manassas)

In 1861, Manassas was a vital railroad junction only 30 miles from Washington, D.C. The war had just begun, and both sides were equally untried. On July 18, Union Gen. Irvin McDowell, under pressure from a populace flush with patriotism and the romance of a clean, quick war, led 35,000 troops against 22,000 Confederates under Brig. Gen. P. G. T. Beauregard, his West Point classmate. Then 10,000 more Rebels fresh from the Shenandoah Valley under Gen. Joseph E. Johnston joined the fray, which climaxed on Henry House Hill, where 85-year-old Judith Henry refused to leave her home despite Confederate sharpshooters firing from her windows.

Union gunfire had killed Ms. Henry and begun to crumble the Rebel lines when Gen. Thomas Jackson incited his men to hold the hill, earning him his nickname "Stonewall" and turning the tide of battle. (As the story goes, Confederate general Bernard Bee exhorted his own troops, "There stands Jackson like a stone wall! Rally behind the Virginians!") Reinforcements arrived, and the Confederate army was able to send the Federals into retreat even though they were too exhausted to pursue. Three-fifths of the 4,900 casualties were members of the Union Army, which by July 22 was back in Washington, D.C. George McClellan soon replaced McDowell as general, and the war had begun in earnest.

Second Battle of Bull Run (Second Manassas)

A little more than a year later, Robert E. Lee, having pushed McClellan back from the gates of Richmond, attacked 62,000 Union soldiers under Gen. John Pope in hopes of crushing the Federals before McClellan could arrive with reinforcements. Together with Stonewall Jackson and Gen. James Longstreet, Lee had 55,000 men, plus the advantage of Pope's poor judgment. On August 30, the Union general ordered a pursuit when the Rebels weren't retreating, and watched his line crumble under Longstreet's counterattack. During hand-to-hand fighting in an unfinished railroad bed, Confederate soldiers threw rocks when they ran out of ammunition. A nighttime retreat avoided a complete Union rout, but the army still lost half again as many men as the Confederates. Pope blamed his officers for conspiring against him but was relieved of command in any case, and Lee rode the momentum of victory as far north as Antietam, Maryland.

Visiting the Park

Any visit to the Manassas Battlefield (703/361-1339, www.nps.gov/mana, dawn–dusk daily) should start at the **Henry Hill Visitors Center** (6511 Sudley Rd., 8:30 A.M.–5 P.M. daily, $3 adults), on Route 234 south of its intersection with Route 29. The park movie, *Manassas: End*

© KATIE GITHENS

Gen. Thomas "Stonewall" Jackson overlooks the First Manassas battlefield, where he earned his famous nickname.

of Innocence, is another $3 per person. Slide programs are shown every half hour, and you can pick up tour maps of the battlefields. Walk the loop trail of First Manassas in about 45 minutes, passing reconstructed houses and a muscular statue of Jackson commemorating his bold stand. Runners may prefer to jog through history; a convenient 10-mile trail loops around First Manassas. Nine sites of Second Manassas are linked by a driving tour. For more information, contact the **Friends of Manassas National Battlefield Park** (www.fmnbp.org).

BULL RUN REGIONAL PARK

One thousand wooded acres along Bull Run Creek include the northern end of the **Bull Run-Occoquan Trail,** which traverses four regional parks in 17.5 rural miles along the river and Occoquan Reservoir. Wood thrushes, scarlet tanagers, hooded warblers, and red-eyed vireos all make an appearance along the blue-blazed trail. It's moderately strenuous and open to hikers and horses. Inside the park, the 1.5-mile **Bluebell Nature Loop** erupts with countless Virginia bluebells in mid-April—a nice alternative to the crushing throngs at D.C.'s Cherry Blossom Festival.

Numerous events are staged in the sweeping grass fields of the park's special events center, including the **Virginia Wine Festival** (703/823-1868 or 866/877-3343, www.atwproductions.com) in mid-September. Dozens of wineries and hundreds of vendors gather for the state's oldest celebration of the grape. Food, rides, and music of all kinds round out the fun.

The park (7700 Bull Run Dr., Centreville, 703/631-0550, www.nvrpa.org/parks/bullrun, $7 per vehicle) has a camp store, pool, miniature golf and disc golf courses, a playground, a public shooting center, and picnic areas open March–October. There are also 150 campsites for $23–42.

FOUNTAINHEAD REGIONAL PARK

Farther south along the Occoquan Reservoir is this mountain bikers' favorite. You can fish or paddle on the water (rent Jon boats and canoes at the Marina Building) and hike on the southern end of the Bull Run–Occoquan Trail, but what brings most people to Fountainhead (10875 Hampton Rd., Fairfax Station, 703/250-9124, www.nvrpa.org/park/fountainhead, dawn–dusk daily, free) is a great trail designed by and for mountain bikers. Tight turns, steep climbs, log hops, rocky stream crossings, and Shock-A-Billy Hill—this one has everything, and it continues to grow (18 miles at last count). It's one of the most fun trails within an hour of D.C. and challenging enough for experienced riders. Shorter and easier loop options are possible. For trail conditions, call 703/250-9124.

STEVEN F. UDVAR-HAZY CENTER

Opened in 2003 on the 100th anniversary of the Wright brothers' first powered flight, this branch of the Smithsonian Institution's National Air and Space Museum provides greatly expanded display space for historic planes and spacecraft. More than 80 aircraft and space artifacts are parked or suspended in two hangars, including an SR-71 Blackbird reconnaissance plane, the B-29 Superfortress *Enola Gay* that dropped the atomic bomb, and the massive Space Shuttle *Enterprise.* Visitors can climb the observation tower to watch takeoffs and landings at Dulles, and watch aviation films in the IMAX theater. There's also a large food court and a museum store.

The center (202/633-1000, www.nasm.si.edu/museum/udvarhazy, 10 A.M.–5:30 P.M. daily, free) is south of the main terminal at Dulles airport, near the intersection of Routes 28 and 50. Parking is $15, and a Virginia Regional Transit (540/338-1610, www.vatransit.org) bus links the center to Dulles airport and Dulles Town Center.

LEESBURG

Poised between the weight of the past and modern development pushing from the east, the largest city in Hunt Country noses up against the Potomac at the far horizon of D.C.'s suburban spread. One of northern Virginia's oldest cities, Leesburg (pop. 37,000) began as a cluster of log houses at the intersection of two settler's roads. It served as an outfitting post during the French and Indian War and was eventually named for Robert E. Lee's ancestors. During the War of 1812, 22 wagonloads of government documents, including the Declaration of Independence and the Constitution, were brought here for safekeeping as the British torched the capital.

Leesburg's Historic District, enclosed by the original 1878 boundaries, is chock-full of antiques stores and rows of narrow 18th- and 19th-century buildings, usually with one or two residential levels over a ground-floor shop or apartment. Here's a place where each building has reinvented itself more times than Madonna. Ask proprietors; they'll tell you. There's the antiques shop that used to manufacture and sell electroshock therapy machines around the world. The local museum that once belonged to the first black doctor in town, and the bank turned bistro and cobbler turned coffee shop. A trip to historic Leesburg is a charming weekend outing or a nice addition to a tour of one of the many vineyards nearby.

Sights

Stop by the **Loudoun Museum** (16 Loudoun St., 703/777-7427, www.loudounmuseum.org, 10 A.M.–5 P.M. Mon. and Wed.–Sat., 1–5 P.M. Sun., $3 adults, $1 children) for a walking-tour brochure and tips from the knowledgeable docents. While you're there, look over the collection of artifacts spanning Leesburg's three centuries of history, including a kids' discovery room and garden. A restored 1767 log cabin across the street houses a gift shop.

Other notable buildings include the Classical Revival **Thomas Balch Library** (208 Market St.), built in 1922, and the **Loudoun County Courthouse** at the corner of Market and King Streets, dating to 1894. The courthouse, topped by an octagonal tower, was the third built on this site. Gen. George C. Marshall, author of the plan to reconstruct Europe after World War II, owned and occupied the late 19th-century

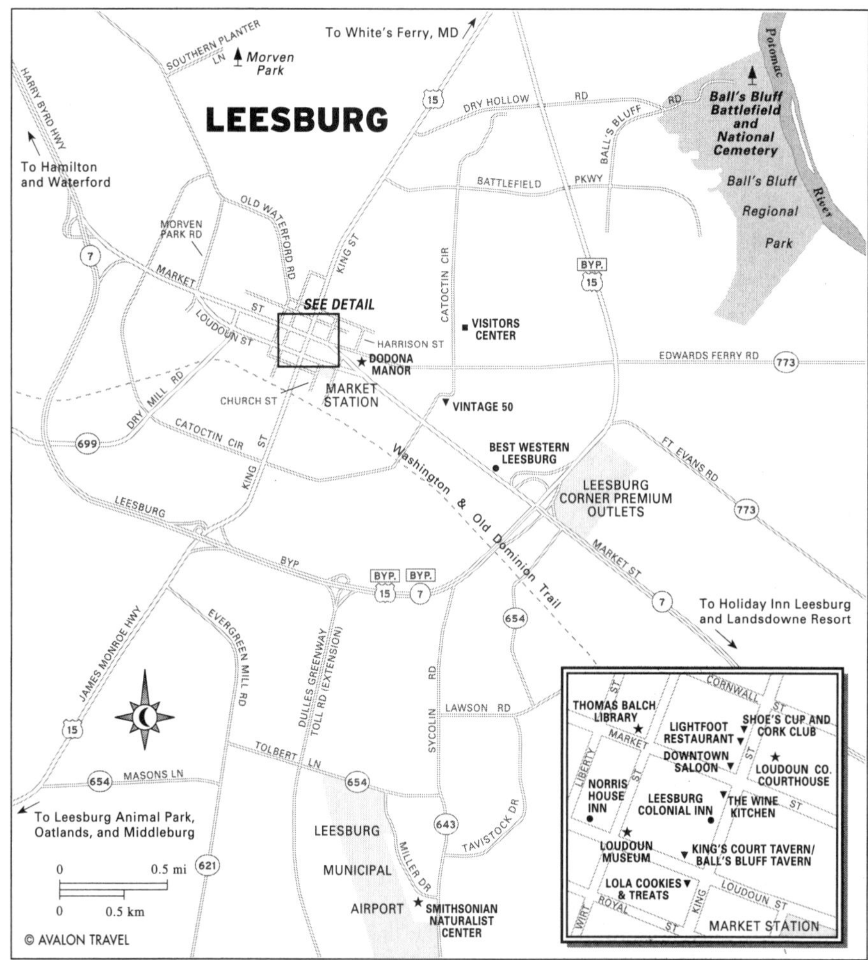

Federal-style **Dodona Manor** (217 Edward's Ferry Rd., 703/777-1880, www.georgecmarshall.org) from 1941 to 1959. Tours are offered on the hour 10 A.M.–5 P.M. Saturday and 1–5 P.M. Sunday, also Monday in June–August ($10 adults, $8 seniors, $5 children).

Follow Route 15 south of town a few miles to find the **Leesburg Animal Park** (19270 James Monroe Hwy., 703/433-0002, www.leesburganimalpark.com, 10 A.M.–6 P.M. daily, until 5 P.M. after daylight savings, $8.50 weekdays, $12.50 weekends, children under 2 free), a petting zoo with animals ranging from the mundane (sheep, donkeys) to the exotic (ring-tailed lemurs, giant tortoises). Call for information on pony and wagon rides and the Pumpkinville fall celebration.

Budding zoologists, along with anyone interested in the natural world, should stop by the **Smithsonian Naturalist Center** (741 Miller Dr. SE., Ste. G2, 703/779-9712 or 800/729-7725, 10:30 A.M.–4 P.M. Tues.–Sat., free) in the

© KATIE GITHENS

Dodona Manor, estate of George C. Marshall, chief military officer to Franklin Delano Roosevelt during World War II

Leesburg Airpark Business Center. It's a small branch of the National Museum of Natural History and houses a great study collection of 30,000 items, from mounted bugs to a horse skeleton and the biggest polar bear you've ever seen. Lab equipment and a reference library are also available.

Entertainment

Both **King's Court Tavern** (2C Loudoun St. SW, 703/777-7747) and **Ball's Bluff Tavern** (downstairs from King's Court, 703/777-7757) host live music and dancing nightly; Ball's Bluff has been voted best live entertainment in the county. Having survived a fire in 1998 and a renaming in 2001, the **Downtown Saloon** (7 N. King St., 703/669-3090) is as real a biker bar as you're likely to find in Loudoun County. It faces the courthouse (a neon sign reads Better Off Here Than Across the Street) and has pool tables, a jukebox, a bar menu, and karaoke on Friday nights.

Vintage 50 (50 Catoctin Ct. NE #100, 703/777-2169, www.vintage50.com, 11:30 A.M.–1 A.M. Mon.–Sat., 11 A.M.–10 P.M. Sun.) injects a dose of modern lounge culture to staid Leesburg. Craft-brewed beers, a contemporary tapas menu, and a wine bar with over 200 selections will make you feel like you're in D.C. or L.A. instead of the middle of Virginia horse country.

Shopping

With dozens of shops in town—most of them selling antiques—Leesburg has plenty of options for browsing and buying. **Glenfiddich Farm Pottery** (17642 Canby Rd., 703/771-3329, www.glenfarmpottery.com) sells Richard Busch's handmade salt-fired stoneware out of a 160-year-old dairy barn west of town on Catoctin Mountain. It's a good idea to call ahead before arriving.

Antiques stores have taken over Leesburg's historic center like an occupying army. Start at the **Leesburg Court of Shoppes Antique Mall** (19487 James Monroe Hwy., 703/777-7799, www.leesburgantiques.com). The **Black Shutter Antique Center** (1 Loudoun St. SE,

703/443-9579, www.blackshutterantiques.com) also has a large selection spread throughout more than 20 rooms. **Old House Antiques & Upscale Consignments** (209 Loudon St., 703/771-7890, www.theoldhouseonmarket.com) merits a browse for those in search of shabby-chic decor.

And, truth be told, most D.C. metro residents drive to Leesburg for the **Leesburg Corner Premium Outlets** (241 Fort Evans Rd. NE, 703/737-3071, www.premiumoutlets.com), which are vast as far as outlet malls go. A free shuttle is available between the mall and the town's historic center.

Events

Just north of Leesburg, the Tarara Vineyard and Winery (13648 Tarara Ln., 703/771-1000) holds a **summer concert series** on Saturdays July–September at Shadow Lake. It also hosts **wine festivals** in early August and late September. Hundreds of classic autos cruise into downtown in mid-June during the annual **Leesburg Classic Car Show.** Businesses stay open late and DJs play music from the 1950s and '60s.

Accommodations

The **Best Western Leesburg** (726 E. Market St., 703/777-9400, $90–140) is a short way east of the town center on Route 7. Keep going to reach the **Holiday Inn Leesburg** (1500 E. Market St., 703/771-9200, $100–180), with 126 rooms and five suites ($180–280) in a former 18th-century mansion surrounded by rolling lawns. The spread includes the Mansion House Restaurant, open for all meals daily, and the Lighthorse Tavern.

Rooms at the **Leesburg Colonial Inn** (19 S. King St., 703/777-5000 or 800/392-1332) are appointed with 18th-century decor, including antique poster beds and Persian rugs, as well as working fireplaces and whirlpool baths. It's conveniently located in the heart of the city. Rates (rooms $110–150, suites $125–175) include full gourmet breakfast on weekends.

From the sunny upstairs sitting room to the fireplace in the library, **The Norris House Inn** (108 Loudoun St. SW, 703/777-1806 or 800/644-1806, www.norrishouse.com, $145–200 weekend, $130–160 weekday) offers top-notch lodgings right downtown. Rooms in the 1760 Federal home have brass and feather beds and there's a veranda overlooking the lovingly tended gardens.

Four miles east of Leesburg on Route 7, the **Lansdowne Resort** (44050 Woodridge Pkwy., 703/729-8400 or 877/509-8400, www.lansdowneresort.com, $180 and up) has 305 deluxe guest rooms and 14 suites styled after Frank Lloyd Wright overlooking the Potomac River valley. Amenities include a Robert Trent Jones Jr. championship golf course, a full-service spa and salon, a health club, tennis courts, and indoor and outdoor pools. For dining there's the elegant On the Potomac restaurant (703/729-4073, dinner Tues.–Sat.), specializing in steaks; the Riverside Hearth (703/729-4105, all meals daily), with buffet and à la carte service with a view of Sugarloaf Mountain; casual Stonewalls Tavern off the lobby; and two eateries on the golf course for guests only.

For a listing of bed-and-breakfasts in Loudoun County, see www.loudounbandb.com or call 866/771-2597.

Food

An unpretentious wine bar (yes, truly) with a farm-to-table menu, **The Wine Kitchen** (7 S. King St., 703/777-9463, lunch and dinner Tues.–Sun.) serves seasonal American fare at reasonable prices. Lunch and dinner prices range $9–17 for small plates such as "chicken and waffles" (with quail instead) and panzanella salad. One plate suffices for a light lunch; plan to share three or four for a dinner for two. Flights of wine arrive with playful descriptions on placards—for example, a cabernet sauvignon has "a quiet reserved power; like a bear that wears a necktie." Arrive early; the slim 1860s-era building seats only about 35 people.

First built in 1888 as the Peoples National Bank, the **Lightfoot Restaurant** (2 W. Market St., 703/771-2233, lunch and dinner

NORTHERN VIRGINIA WINERIES

Bluemont Vineyard
18755 Foggy Bottom Rd., Bluemont
540/554-8439
www.bluemontvineyard.com

Boxwood Winery
2042 Burrland Rd., Middleburg
540/687-8778
www.boxwoodwinery.com

Breaux Vineyards
36888 Breaux Vineyard Ln., Purcellville
540/668-6299 or 800/492-9961
www.breauxvineyards.com

Casanel Vineyards
17952 Canby Rd., Leesburg
540/751-1776
www.casanelvineyards.com

Chateau O'Brien at Northpoint
3238 Rail Stop Rd., Markham
540/364-6441
www.chateauobrien.com

Chester Gap Cellars
4615 Remount Road, Front Royal
540/636-8086
www.chestergapcellars.com

Chrysalis Vineyards
23876 Champe Ford Rd., Middleburg
540/687-8222
www.chrysaliswine.com

Corcoran Vineyard
14635 Corkys Farm Ln., Waterford
540/882-9073
www.corcoranvineyards.com

Doukénie Winery
14727 Mountain Rd. (Rte. 690), Purcellville
540/668-6464
www.doukeniewinery.com

Dry Mill Vineyards
18195 Dry Mill Rd., Leesburg
703/737-3930
www.drymillwine.com

Fabbioli Cellars
15669 Limestone School Rd., Leesburg
703/771-1197
www.fabbioliwines.com

Fox Meadow Vineyards
3310 Freezeland Rd., Linden
540/636-6777
www.foxmeadowwinery.com

Glen Manor Vineyards
2244 Browntown Rd., Front Royal
540/635-6324
www.glenmanorvineyards.com

Gray Ghost Vineyards
14706 Lee Hwy., Amissville
540/937-4869
www.grayghostvineyards.com

Hidden Brook Winery
43301 Spinks Ferry Rd., Leesburg
703/737-3935
www.hiddenbrookwinery.com

Hiddencroft Vineyards
12202 Axline Rd., Lovettsville
540/535-5367
www.hiddencroftvineyards.com

Hillsborough Vineyards
36716 Charles Town Pike, Purcellville
540/668-6216
www.hillsboroughwine.com

Linden Vineyards
3708 Harrels Corner Rd., Linden
540/364-1997
www.lindenvineyards.com

Lost Creek Winery
43277 Spinks Ferry Rd., Leesburg
703/443-9836
www.lostcreekwinery.com

Loudoun Valley Vineyard
38516 Charles Town Pike, Waterford
540/882-3375
www.loudounvalleyvineyards.com

Mediterranean Cellars
8295 Falcon Glen Rd., Warrenton
540/428-1984
www.mediterraneancellars.com

Naked Mountain Vineyard
2747 Leeds Manor Rd., Markham
540/364-1609
www.nakedmtnwinery.com

Notaviva Vineyards
13274 Sagle Rd., Purcellville
540/668-6756
www.notavivavineyards.com

The Oasis Winery
14141 Hume Rd. (Rte. 635), Hume
540/635-3103
www.oasiswine.com

Pearmund Cellars
6190 Georgetown Rd., Broad Run
540/347-3475
www.pearmundcellars.com

Piedmont Vineyards & Winery
2546-D Halfway Rd., The Plains
540/687-5528
www.piedmontwines.com

Quattro Goomba's Winery
22860 James Monroe Hwy., Aldie
703/327-6052
www.goombawine.com

Rappahannock Cellars
14437 Hume Rd., Huntly
540/635-9398
www.rappahannockcellars.com

Rogers Ford Farm Winery
14674 Rogers Ford Rd., Sumerduck
540/439-3707
www.rogersfordwine.com

Sharp Rock Vineyards
5 Sharp Rock Rd,. Sperryville
540/987-8020
www.sharprockvineyards.com

Stillhouse Vineyards
4366 Stillhouse Rd., Hume
540/364-1203
www.stillhousevineyards.com

Sunset Hills Vineyard
38295 Fremont Overlook Ln., Purcellville
540/882-4560
www.sunsethillsvineyard.com

Swedenburg Estate Vineyard
23595 Winery Lane, Middleburg
540/687-5219
www.swedenburgwines.com

Tarara Vineyard & Winery
13648 Tarara Ln., Leesburg
703/771-7100
www.tarara.com

Three Fox Vineyards
10100 Three Fox Ln., Delaplane
540/364-6073
www.threefoxvineyards.com

Unicorn Winery
489 Old Bridge Rd., Amissville
540/349-5885
www.unicornwinery.com

Village Winery
40405 Browns Ln., Waterford
540/882-3780
www.villagewineryandvineyards.com

Willowcroft Farm Vineyards
38906 Mt. Gilead Rd., Leesburg
703/777-8161
www.willowcroftwine.com

Winery at La Grange
4970 Antioch Rd., Haymarket
703/753-9360
www.wineryatlagrange.com

Zephaniah Farm Vineyards
19381 Dunlop Mill Rd., Leesburg
703/431-2016
www.zephwine.com

daily) is an upscale bistro in a colorful, elegant setting. Note the original vaults behind the bar as you enjoy artichoke gratin crusted salmon and other entrées ranging $8–19 for lunch and $22 and up for dinner.

A few doors down, **Shoe's Cup and Cork Club** (17 N. King St., 571/291-9535) is a quirky stop for a quick bite and a cup of joe. This time the former Arthur's Shoe Repair has been repurposed as a fair-trade coffee shop that serves sandwiches and smoothies, with plans to add a wine and beer menu. Donate new and gently used children's footwear for the Walk in My Shoes Global Project, and receive a free cup of coffee or tea.

Those with a sweet tooth will want to swing by **Lola Cookies & Treats** (109 S. King St., 703/669-6970, lunch Mon.–Sat.).

Another popular option is the **Tuscarora Mill Restaurant** (203 Harrison St., 703/771-9300, lunch and dinner daily). Called "Tuskies" by locals, it's housed in an 1899 mill building in Market Station. Moved here and restored in 1985, the structure still feels like an antique with its bare wood beams adorned with plants and quilts. Delicious, varied entrées like Portuguese seafood pasta start at $10 for lunch and $16 for dinner, served in the café and dining room.

Run by the owners of next-door Tuskies, **Fireworks** (201 Harrison St. SE, 703/779-8400) serves wood-fired gourmet pizza and an excellent beer selection—eight drafts on tap and an assortment of domestic and European brews.

Information

The **Loudoun Convention and Visitors Association** has a visitors center on the 2nd floor of the Market Station complex south of Loudoun Street (112G South St., 703/771-2617 or 800/752-6118, www.visitloudoun.org, 9 A.M.–6 P.M. daily). Parking at the garage at Market and Wirt Streets is free for the first three hours.

VICINITY OF LEESBURG

Ball's Bluff Battlefield and National Cemetery

On the evening of October 20, 1861, a Union reconnaissance force of 1,000 mistook a row of haystacks lit by moonlight on a foggy night for Confederate tents, and in their confusion ended up revealing themselves to an actual enemy force. The next day, the Federals crossed the Potomac into disaster. Finding themselves trapped between the water and a row of high bluffs, they floundered as Confederate rifle fire

emblem on the gate to the Ball's Bluff National Cemetery

mowed them down from above. Nine hundred Union troops died in the fighting, including their commander, Gen. Edward Baker, a U.S. senator and friend of Lincoln. Bodies that floated downriver to Washington galvanized the U.S. government into organizing its forces in earnest.

A one-mile self-guided interpretive trail loops to the top of the bluff and back, passing a tiny cemetery ringed by Virginia bluebells and white trout lilies in the spring. The adjacent **Ball's Bluff Regional Park** (703/737-7800, www.nvrpa.org/parks/ballsbluff, dawn–dusk daily, free) claims a mile-long stretch of riverbank. Volunteers give guided tours of the battlefield on weekends at 11 A.M. and 1 P.M. April–October.

White's Ferry, Maryland

The only cable-guided ferry on the East Coast has been hauling people and cargo across the Potomac since the 1820s. Today the *General Jubal A. Early* carries cars and bicycles across the 0.25-mile stretch from Route 655 to Maryland, averaging 1,200 cars per day. On the opposite bank, the C&O Towpath runs downriver toward the capital, and a snack bar and souvenir store has fishing supplies and boats for rent. White's Ferry (301/349-5200, 5 A.M.–11 P.M. daily, $4 cars one-way, $7 round-trip, $3 motorcycles one-way, $1 bicycles one-way) runs even on holidays but is out of service occasionally due to high water or ice.

Morven Park

The 1,000-acre estate of Gov. Westmoreland Davis, who was elected in 1918, centers on a Greek Revival mansion where lavish parties once filled the Renaissance Great Hall with laughter, music, and candlelight. Paintings, tapestries, and sculptures acquired by Mrs. Davis in her travels throughout Europe and Asia adorn the Jacobean dining room and French drawing room.

In the north wing, the **Museum of Hounds and Hunting** (www.mhhna.org) displays art, photos, clothes, and artifacts from centuries of fox chasing, including a 1731 hunting horn

White's Ferry, the only wire-cable ferry on the East Coast, averages 85 trips daily.

carried by a Colonial governor. The estate's **Winmill Carriage Collection** contains more than 100 antique coaches, one of the largest personal collections in the world. Wrought-iron gates and a reflecting pool set off the impressive boxwood gardens surrounded by the original brick walls.

Morven's International Equestrian Center has a full calendar of events, including horse shows, trials, competitions, schools, and steeplechase races throughout the year. In mid-June, the **Potomac Celtic Festival** (866/771-7786, www.potomacceltic fest.org), one of the country's best, brings Highland games, music, artisans, and a historical reenactment of life in 200 B.C. Kids' activities include storytelling and games, and for the adults there's single-malt whiskey tastings and the caber toss. **Steeplechase races** are held in October.

Morven Park (703/777-2414, www.morvenpark.org, 11 A.M.–4 P.M. Fri.–Mon., from 1 P.M. Sun., Apr.–Dec.) is northwest of Leesburg. Take Route 7 west one mile from the town

© KATIE GITHENS

a barn along Route 662 en route to Waterford

center, make a right onto Morven Park Road, then a left onto Old Waterford Road. Guided tours of the mansion, the hunting museum, the carriage collection, and the grounds ($7 adults, $1 children) leave on the hour from the Coach House Visitor Center.

Oatlands Plantation

George Carter, the great-grandson of planter baron Robert "King" Carter, built a boxy Greek Revival mansion here in 1803. Refugees, both black and white, sought shelter on the 3,000-acre plantation during the Civil War, which was later operated as a guest retreat until mounting debt forced its sale in 1897. William Corcoran and Edith Morton, a pair of affluent Washingtonians, bought the place and restored it as an English country house to entertain weekend guests from the capital. The formal gardens, designed by Carter, are so lavish that Morton was said to have bought the place after one look without even seeing the house. Don't miss the 1920s teahouse, reflecting pool, and boxwood bowling allée. You'll be in good company; this is the most visited estate in Loudon County.

Oatlands (703/777-3174, www.oatlands.org, 10 A.M.–5 P.M. Mon.–Sat., 1–5 P.M. Sun., Apr.–Dec., $10 adults, $7 gardens and grounds only) is six miles south of Leesburg on Route 15. Guided house tours take 30–45 minutes, and you can show yourself around the grounds. Traditional afternoon tea ($25 pp) is offered frequently; see the website for a schedule.

Waterford

A gorgeous drive along Route 662 from Leesburg deposits you in this village on the bank of Catoctin Creek, where most of this historic town has been declared a National Historic Landmark. Almost painfully pretty, Waterford is a diametric opposite to the suburbs near the capital. Mossy stone walls, gravel lanes, big trees, and sloping lawns set off dozens of 18th- and 19th-century homes in a smorgasbord of architectural styles.

Founded by Quakers, Waterford staunchly opposed slavery during the Civil War, a rarity in Confederate Virginia. After the war ended, animosity from neighboring towns did not, and when the railroad extended into Loudoun County it purposefully bypassed Waterford, drawing business away from the village. The buildings and pastures languished and Waterford became a snapshot in time.

Give credit to the **Waterford Foundation** (540/882-3018, www.waterfordva.org) for preserving the town, most of which was falling into ruin by the 1930s. Contact the foundation for information on guided walking tours sometimes given on summer and fall weekends.

The first weekend in October brings the **Waterford Homes Tour & Crafts Exhibit,** where artisans dress in period costume à la Colonial Williamsburg and demonstrate their craft, inviting kids and grown-ups to try their hand at turn-of-the-19th-century basket weaving or earthenware. Craft traditions dating from 200 years ago have one thing in common: durability. As such, this fair has none of the chintz that the term "arts and crafts" can sometimes conjure up. Military reenactments, food, music, and tours of historic homes in the community round out the bustling weekend.

Otherwise, things are pretty quiet in Waterford. You can get a sandwich at the **Waterford Market** (15487 2nd St., 540/882-3631, 10 A.M.–7 P.M. Mon.–Fri., 10 A.M.–5 P.M. Sat. "unless the sheep need attending"), but that's about it.

Bluemont

Previously (and unenviably) known as Pumpkintown and Snickersville, Bluemont is home to the **Bear's Den Lodge** (540/554-8708, www.bearsdencenter.org), half a mile south of Route 7 on Route 601/Blueridge Mountain Road. The snug stone building, only minutes from the Appalachian Trail, was originally built in true castle style (notice the turrets) in 1933 by Washington physician Huron Lawson as a place for his opera singer wife to practice. It has dorm rooms from $21 per person, a full kitchen, dining room, laundry facilities, and a camp store. Private rooms are $55, and a separate cabin with a wood-burning

© KATIE GITHENS

artisans in Colonial dress at the Waterford Homes Tour & Crafts Exhibit in early October

stove, deck, and outdoor privy is $75 per night for up to 10 people. Camping spots ($8) are also available.

With the Blue Ridge in your backyard, hiking is an obvious choice of activity, especially to the panoramic Bear's Den Rock Overlook, but the nearby country roads and C&O Canal should appeal to cyclists too. Day parking costs $3.

The **Bluemont Fair** (540/554-2367, www.bluemontfair.com), held on the third weekend of September, features plenty of old-fashioned fun such as stagecoach rides, farmers markets, crafts, food, and music.

Harpers Ferry, West Virginia

Made infamous by abolitionist John Brown's failed insurrection against slavery more than 150 years ago, Harpers Ferry is a picturesque, if bloody, corner of the nation's history. On October 16, 1859, Brown stormed and took possession of the United States Armory and Arsenal with his makeshift militia of 21 men, including freed slaves and two of his sons. He believed that if they could seize the 100,000 weapons in storage and then wage guerrilla warfare from the Blue Ridge Mountains, they could go from town to town freeing slaves and causing an uprising against the institution he saw as a moral evil.

For 36 tense hours, hope remained in his "Provisional Army of the United States," but Marines knocked down the doors of the Armory on October 18. While John Brown's raid failed and he was soon hanged for treason, his actions succeeded in polarizing the nation over the issue of slavery—North vs. South—thus hastening the onset of the Civil War.

Today the town is small and tidy, with its white church steeple and smattering of brick buildings tucked in a crook of land at the confluence of the Potomac and Shenandoah Rivers where West Virginia, Maryland, and Virginia converge. A day trip to Harpers Ferry, located just over a half-hour drive from Leesburg, can revolve around both history and outdoor pursuits. The steep, strenuous hike up to the Maryland Heights overlook rewards you with a bird's eye view of town, or the C&O Canal provides a more leisurely stroll. Refer to the National Park Service website for hiking trail descriptions or contact the visitors center in Harpers Ferry (171 Shoreline Dr., 304/535-6029, www.nps.gov/hafe). The Maryland Heights trailhead is on the Maryland side of the Potomac River north on U.S. 340 and then right on Sandy Hook Road. The C&O Canal towpath runs parallel to the Potomac River and Sandy Hook Road, so you can access it here, too.

Also popular are float trips by raft, kayak, or inner tube; **River & Trail Outfitters** can make the arrangements (604 Valley Rd., Knoxville, MD, 888/446-7529, www.rivertrail.com). Tube trips start at $25 per person, raft trips at $55 per person. Full-day kayak rentals cost $55 per boat, canoe rentals $60 per boat.

For those without a car, Harpers Ferry can also be reached by train; contact Amtrak (800/872-7245, www.amtrak.com) for details. The wooden Victorian-style train station is located at Potomac and Shenandoah Streets.

MIDDLEBURG AND VICINITY

Leesburg may be the commercial center of Hunt Country, but Middleburg captures its essence. Established in 1787, it began as a local commercial center halfway along the stagecoach route from Alexandria to Winchester (hence the name). Today Middleburg is still a one-stoplight place with only about 600 residents, but it's sure worth more than the original $2.50 an acre. This is barn jacket and Range Rover territory, surrounded by huge estates whose owners pay well to live in one of northern Virginia's quaintest small towns. Upscale shops sell fine cigars, antique jewelry, and everything horse-related right next to the big Safeway stuck incongruously in the center of town.

Sights

The National Sporting Library (102 The Plains Rd., 540/687-6542, www.nsl.org), located on the outskirts of downtown Middleburg, establishes itself at the center of the world of horse and field sports. It is free and

THE GRAY GHOST OF LOUDOUN COUNTY

Born on December 6, 1833, in Edgemont, Virginia, John Singleton Mosby was raised near Charlottesville and entered the University of Virginia in 1849. During his stay he shot and wounded a few other students, for which he had to serve a short jail term before graduating in 1852. His imprisonment sparked an interest in the law; three years later, he was admitted to the bar and practiced law in Bristol until the start of the Civil War.

Mosby saw action as a scout with J. E. B. Stuart's Confederate cavalry in First Bull Run and the Seven Days Campaign, where he came up with the bold idea to ride completely around McClellan's Union Army. In January 1863, with nine men, he began the guerrilla attacks that would make him famous. Under the Partisan Ranger Law, Mosby's Rangers began to attack isolated Union posts in Maryland and northern Virginia. Dressed in his trademark ostrich-plumed hat and red-lined cape, the dashing horseman led lightning-quick cavalry strikes to disrupt communication and supply lines. Anywhere from 20 to 80 volunteers, convalescents, and civilians made up the Rangers, whose officers were chosen by merit and dismissed when ineffective. Men furnished their own uniforms, weapons, food, and horses and divided captured goods evenly among themselves. When danger threatened, they melted into the night, staying with private families or living in the hills near Middleburg. At any moment, bragged Mosby, he could gather his band at a predetermined time and place "like Children of the Mist," ready for their next raid.

As a result, Mosby estimated that he kept at least 30,000 Union soldiers on his tail instead of at the front. Loudoun County became known as Mosby's Confederacy, and Union generals were livid at the guerrillas' audacious exploits and rising fame. Ulysses S. Grant ordered all supplies and forage in Loudoun County destroyed and all men younger than age 50 arrested to prevent them from joining the Rangers. Federal officials regarded the cavaliers as criminals rather than soldiers – for their habit of keeping captured spoils – and put a price on their heads. (When the Rangers also started hanging prisoners without trial, the order was rescinded.) Grant even considered taking the families of known Rangers hostage.

On March 9, 1863, Mosby led 29 men through the Federal lines at Fairfax Court House, where corpulent Union Brig. Gen. Edwin Stoughton sat surrounded by mountains of food and wine. The Confederates captured Stoughton, 33 men, and 58 horses ("For that I am sorry," Lincoln said, "for I can make brigadier generals, but I can't make horses"). They also made off with a canvas sack holding $350,000 worth of gold and silver coins and jewelry, which Mosby and a companion were forced to bury during hot pursuit by Union troops. Mosby was never able to return for the loot, which by his recall was stashed somewhere between Haymarket and New Baltimore in a shallow hole between two tall pine trees. His partner was eventually captured and hanged, and the treasure has never been found.

The "leather-bed soldiers" were mustered into the regular army on June 10, 1863, and the "Gray Ghost" continued to attract followers and earn praise from Stuart and Robert E. Lee. In late 1864, Maj. Gen. Philip Sheridan sent Capt. Richard Blazer and 100 men armed with Spencer repeating rifles to hunt down the marauding band at all costs. The Rangers suffered 18 casualties before killing or wounding all but two of Blazer's party and capturing their rifles. By April 1865, Mosby had been promoted to colonel, wounded seven times, and sat in command of eight well-trained companies. His last raid came on April 10, the day after Robert E. Lee surrendered at Appomattox. He disbanded his men soon after, urging them to turn themselves in and seek individual pardons – as he did himself two months later.

After the war, Mosby returned to practicing private law in Warrenton. His legendary status followed, dimmed only slightly by his support of Republican candidate Ulysses S. Grant, who had become an admirer himself, for president. Mosby wrote two books during terms as U.S. Consul to Hong Kong and assistant attorney in the Justice Department: *Mosby's War Reminiscences and Stuart's Cavalry Campaigns* (1887), and *Stuart's Cavalry in the Gettysburg Campaign* (1908). He died in Washington, D.C., on May 30, 1916.

open to the public 10 A.M.–4 P.M. Tuesday–Friday, 1–4 P.M. Saturday. Peek inside at the nearly 200 stately oil paintings and other art enshrining horse, hound, and hunt among the 17,000-book collection. A National Sporting Art Museum will open next door in 2011.

Shopping

Middleburg has to have one of the state's highest ratios of antiques stores to residents. Try **Hastening Antiques** (1 W. Washington St., 540/687-5664) or the two-story **Middleburg Antique Emporium** (105 W. Washington St., 540/687-8680). **The Shaggy Ram** (3 E. Washington St., 540/687-3546) sells English and French antiques. **Books & Crannies** (19 E. Washington St., 540/687-6677, www.booksandcrannies.com) is a good local bookstore with a telling look at Middleburg's interests (need a copy of *The Horse Show Mom's Survival Guide*?).

Outfit your filly at **The Tack Box** (7 W. Federal St., 540/687-3231), with riding equipment, clothing, and gifts. And should your dog or cat get jealous, you'd best stop at **Wylie Wagg** (5B E. Washington St., 540/687-8727, www.wyliewagg.com) too.

© KATIE GITHENS

An early snow blankets the countryside outside Middleburg.

Events

Several **Point-to-Point** horse races gallop through town in March, April, and May, followed by the **Virginia Hunt Country Stable Tour** with wine tastings, food, and crafts on the second weekend in May. The **Middleburg Garden Tour** happens in May, **polo** is played June–August, and more races, trials, and horse shows occur in September and October.

GLENWOOD PARK

A long list of annual equestrian events at the Glenwood Park track, a few miles north of Middleburg off Foxcroft Road (Rte. 626), is capped by the Middleburg Spring Races (540/687-6545, www.middleburgspringraces.com), the state's oldest steeplechase event. On the third Saturday in April, thousands of race fans watch riders compete for purses totaling hundreds of thousands of dollars. Autumn brings—what else?—the Middleburg Fall Races (540/687-5662, www.vafallraces.com), with more steeplechase racing, fox hunting, and canine field trials.

GREAT MEADOWS

Hunt Country's premier horse-racing venue, Great Meadows, lies in the opposite direction of Middleburg near a village called The Plains. On the first Saturday in May, everyone puts on their country best and packs the tailgate with gourmet munchies for the **Virginia Gold Cup Races** (540/347-2612, www.vagoldcup.com). Seven races, held since 1925, draw more than 40,000 spectators, including a good bit of Capitol Hill. Order your ticket well ahead of time and arrive early. The **Middleburg Classic Horse Show** arrives in mid-September, followed by the **International Gold Cup Races,** another steeplechase event, in October.

Accommodations

The **Red Fox Inn** (2 E. Washington St. at Madison St., 540/687-6301 or 800/223-1728, www.redfox.com) began as Mr. Chinn's

© KATIE GITHENS

The Red Fox Inn is the second-oldest tavern in the country.

Ordinary in 1728, making it the second-oldest tavern in the country. A young George Washington stopped by on a surveying trip, and on June 17, 1863, John Mosby met here with J. E. B. Stuart to discuss the upcoming Gettysburg campaign. The latter left his name on a room where JFK occasionally held press conferences. The tavern's bar even took a turn as a surgeon's operating table in the Civil War. It's been known as the Red Fox since 1937 and houses 20 rooms in three buildings. Six of the seven dining rooms offer stone fireplaces and thick wood beams overhead, and the kitchen serves contemporary American dishes ($22–30). Room rates start at $175 and include hot or cold breakfast.

An old carriage stands in front of the **Middleburg Country Inn** (209 E. Washington St., 540/687-6082 or 800/262-6082, www.midcountryinn.com, $150–230, $70 surcharge on Sat.), a former Episcopal rectory. A night in one of eight period rooms comes with access to the outdoor hot tub in back and a full country breakfast. Fireplaces and four-poster beds are included, too.

Further outside town, **The Ashby Inn & Restaurant** (692 Federal St., Paris, 540/592-3900, www.ashbyinn.com) has a reputation as a dignified getaway with fine French-American dining. Six rooms furnished in antiques and handmade quilts ($155–195) sit above the inn's restaurant and four dining rooms. A one-room schoolhouse two doors down has been converted into four private guest suites ($275). This is not a good spot for small children.

Food

Tutti Perricone's **Back Street Cafe** (4 E. Federal St., 540/687-3122, lunch and dinner Mon.–Sat., sandwiches $7–8.50, dinner entrées $13–18) is a local favorite for its zesty cooking and live jazz on weekend evenings. Pizzas, salads, sandwiches, and pasta are served inside and on the outdoor deck. One block away, the **Hidden Horse Tavern** (7 W. Washington St., 540/687-3828, lunch and dinner daily, $7–11) occupies a 200-year-old building. Seafood and other Hunt Country standbys, including crab cake sandwiches, are offered.

For a smoothie or a dose of caffeine, drop by **Cuppa Giddy Up** (8 E. Washington St., 540/687-8122, breakfast and lunch daily). **Mello Out** (2 E. Federal St., 540/687-8635, lunch and dinner daily) serves up coffee drinks, teas, five varieties of hot chocolate, and assorted nibbles in the basement of one of Middleburg's oldest buildings. Try one of the Cosmic Cupcakes or a homemade marshmallow. The **Upper Crust Bakery** (2 N. Pendleton St., 540/687-5666, breakfast and lunch daily) is a local favorite named with just a hint of irony, offering cookies and sandwiches among the usual array of baked goods. Stop by for a mutton button or cow puddles. (You'll have to ask.)

Information

For details on events and anything else about the area, pop in the **Pink Box Visitors Information Center** (12 Madison St., 540/687-8888, www.middleburg.org, 11 A.M.–3 P.M. Mon.–Fri., 11 A.M.–4 P.M. Sat.–Sun.). It really is a pink-hued stone building, surrounded by a white picket fence.

SKY MEADOWS STATE PARK

Almost 2,000 acres of clover-dotted fields and wildflower pastures were once part of a 7,883-acre tract purchased from Lord Fairfax in 1713. Thirteen miles of bridle trail and footpaths, including 3.6 miles of the Appalachian Trail, head across open meadows ringing with birdcalls and into the forested hills beyond. Nestled at the base of Shenandoah National Park, Sky Meadows delivers the sweeping views of pastureland that are anticipated but sometimes obscured by trees within the national park. The North and South Ridge Trails in particular ascend quickly and afford airy glimpses of farmhouses and red barns.

Take the Gap Run Trail to a primitive campground with 12 sites ($13 per site, $5 pet fee). Note that the water from the campsite pump is non-potable and must be boiled or treated before drinking. The **Mount Bleak visitors center** occupies an early-19th-century farmhouse on a hilltop near a picnic area and fishing pond. You can take tours of the house and learn about the night sky during **public sky watches** on Saturday nights April–October. On Memorial Day, the park hosts the **Delaplane Strawberry Festival,** with arts and crafts, music, children's games, a petting zoo, wagon rides, and lots of fresh strawberries ($20 per car).

To get to Sky Meadows (540/592-3556, www.dcr.virginia.gov/state_parks/sky.shtml, 8 A.M.–dusk daily, $3 per car, $4 on weekends), take U.S. 17 south from U.S. 50 for 1.2 miles to the park entrance on Route 710. You can also reach U.S. 17 from I-66 exit 18.

PEACHY KEEN

Located near Sky Meadows State Park, Virginia's "Peach Way" is a seven-mile stretch of winding country road that is home to four of the largest peach orchards in northern Virginia. Many of these u-pick peach orchards grow apples and other fruits and vegetables too (contact farms for details).

Hartland Farms
3064 Hartland Ln., Markham
540/364-2316
www.hartlandorchard.com

Hollin Farms
1524 Snowden Rd., Delaplane
540/592-3574
www.hollinfarms.com

Stribling Orchard
(Owned by the same family for nearly 200 years!)
11587 Poverty Hollow Ln., Markham
540/364-3040
www.striblingorchard.com

Virginia Perfection Farm
1562 Leeds Manor Rd., Delaplane
540/592-3730

© KATIE GITHENS
vista from Sky Meadows State Park

Down the Potomac

HUNTLEY MEADOWS PARK

Fairfax County's Hybla Valley hides 1,425 acres of wetlands, meadows, and forests. The Potomac flowed here long ago, leaving behind freshwater marshes dotted by beaver ponds and teeming with birdlife. Local bird-watchers know the wildlife-viewing tower is one of the best places in the Washington area to spot yellow-crowned night herons, woodpeckers, and any one of 200 other resident species.

In the spring, park naturalists lead evening hikes along the quarter-mile interpretive boardwalk trail to the sounds of a frog chorus in the wetland. Bicycles are allowed on another two-mile trail. The park entrance and visitors center (3701 Lockheed Blvd., 703/768-2525, www.fairfaxcounty.gov/parks/huntley, dawn–dusk daily, free) is reached from Lockheed Boulevard off U.S. 1, south of Alexandria. While bird-watching is a good solitary activity, for safety reasons bring a buddy along if visiting here early or late in the day.

MOUNT VERNON

More than one million people visit the home of America's first president every year, making it second in popularity only to the current president's house. If you can avoid or ignore the crowds, though, it's still possible to glimpse those things that made Mount Vernon so dear to George Washington's heart: the view of the Potomac on a misty morning, the wind through the gardens in the evening, and all of the smells and sounds of a practical, prosperous farm estate far from the public eye.

History

In 1726, George's father, Augustine Washington, obtained half of a 5,000-acre property called Little Hunting Creek

© MOUNT VERNON LADIES' ASSOCIATION

George Washington once said of his plantation home Mount Vernon, "No estate in United America is more pleasantly situated than this."

Plantation. Nine years later he moved his family, including three-year-old George, into a cottage he had built on a bluff overlooking the Potomac. The Washingtons soon moved away again, but George returned at age 16, after his half-brother Lawrence had inherited the property and managed it for a few years. Washington began renting the estate in 1754, after Lawrence's death, and assumed ownership in 1761 after the death of his brother's daughter and widow.

Washington began expanding the mansion in the late 1750s. He continually added to the house and property until he owned 8,000 acres surrounding one of Virginia's finest plantations. George's vision of a quiet farming life had to wait through a few interruptions—the Revolutionary War, the Philadelphia Constitutional Convention, becoming the first president of the United States—but by 1797, he was finally able to retire to Mount Vernon for two quiet years, which he spent with his wife, Martha, until his death from a throat infection on December 14, 1799, at age 67. By the dictates of his will, he was buried in a tomb on his beloved estate and was joined there by his wife in 1802. Between 1858 and 1860, the newly formed Mount Vernon Ladies' Association of the Union raised enough money to purchase the crumbling estate and begin to restore it to its former glory.

Visiting Mount Vernon

A wide bowling green leads to the main house, which is flanked by two curved colonnades leading to nearby outbuildings. The 19-room mansion mixes the original Georgian style with the feel of an English Palladian villa, thanks to its owner's later remodelings. As they were in Washington's time, the outer pine boards have been beveled and coated with alternating layers of paint and sand to resemble masonry. The view from the columned riverfront facade, 126 feet over the Potomac, rivals even hilltop Monticello's view.

Many original pieces have been tracked down and returned to rooms painted their original eye-catching shades of Prussian blue and bright green. Lafayette sent Washington the key to the Bastille that's displayed in the main hall, and the English harpsichord once played by Martha's granddaughter Nelly Custis sits silent in the "little parlor." Notice the agricultural motifs—wheat, shovel, and scythe—worked into the molded plaster on the ceiling of the two-story dining room, and the globe in the study that's missing the then-unknown continent of Antarctica. Upstairs are the bedroom where French nobleman Lafayette slept on three visits and Washington's bedroom, containing the bed in which he died.

The half-moon of outbuildings includes a kitchen, smokehouse, slaves' quarters, stable, and reconstructed working blacksmith shop. Don't miss the outhouses (known in George's day as "necessaries"), the rebuilt 16-sided barn, and the farm animals. Mount Vernon is still a working farm, as it was when Washington kept detailed records of his experiments with crop rotation and different strains of plants. A squad of hard-working employees tends flourishing heirloom herb and vegetable gardens and a barnyard of horses, sheep, and pigs, including heritage breeds such as the rare Milking Red Devon Cattle and Ossabaw Island Hogs that date back to Washington's day. Imported English deer once mingled with native species in the deer park, an area between the east lawn of the mansion and the river. George and Martha's tombs are found south of the orchard, marked with simple inscriptions: "Washington," and "Martha, consort of Washington."

In 2007 Mount Vernon opened the doors to a host of new interpretive buildings to the tune of $110 million. The high-tech education center includes videos, recordings, lighted maps, and eerily lifelike reconstructions of Washington at various ages (as well as everything about his hippo ivory teeth you ever wanted to know). It's followed by a more traditional museum whose collections are just as impressive.

Another thing you might not have known about Washington is that at one time he was probably distilling more whiskey than anyone else in the country—11,000 gallons in 1799 alone. Washington's distillery was excavated and reconstructed starting in 2000, and it was reopened to the public in 2007. You can even buy a potent re-creation of the man's own firewater. The **distillery** (10 A.M.–5 P.M. daily Apr.–Oct., $2 adults, $1.50 children with Mount Vernon ticket, otherwise $4 for adults and $2 for kids) is three miles west of Mount Vernon, next to Washington's reconstructed **gristmill.**

Mount Vernon (703/780-2000, www.mountvernon.org, 8 A.M.–5 P.M. daily Apr.–Aug., from 9 A.M. Mar., Sept., and Oct., 9 A.M.–4 P.M. Nov.–Feb., $15 adults, $7 children 6–11) is eight miles south of Old Town Alexandria via U.S. 1 or the George Washington Memorial Parkway (Rte. 235). On Washington's Birthday (also a national holiday), visits are free and a wreath-laying ceremony takes place at his tomb. Tours are self-guided, but interpreters are ready to explain details of the house and grounds. At the gift shop in front of the gate you can rent an audio tour ($6) that you can take at your own pace (kid-friendly versions are available, too) or buy a guidebook. Special annual events include an Independence Day celebration, craft fair, and candlelit tours during the holidays (call for a schedule). Costumed waiters serve Colonial food and Virginia wine by the glass at the elegant **Mount Vernon Inn** (703/780-0011, lunch daily, dinner Mon.–Sat.), which has six dining rooms and three fireplaces. Lunch entrées like a pulled pork barbecue sandwich run $9–12, and dinner plates such as a venison mixed grill are $21–25. The food court at Mount Vernon offers less-expensive quick bites.

If you can't drive to Mount Vernon, don't worry—there are plenty of other ways to get there. One option is to take the **Metro** yellow line to the Huntington station and catch the Fairfax Connector Bus No. 101 (703/339-7200) to the estate for $1.35.

Gray Line Tours (202/289-1995, www.grayline.com) sends buses from Union Station in Washington at 8 A.M. daily for a four-hour tour of Mount Vernon ($55 adults, $30 children, including admission). Free pickups are possible from major hotels. Motorcoaches operated by **Tourmobile Sightseeing Tours** (202/289-1995, www.tourmobile.com) depart from Arlington National Cemetery at 11 A.M. mid-June through Labor Day for a five-hour tour through Old Town Alexandria and Mount Vernon ($32 adults, $16 children).

The **Spirit Cruise Line** (866/211-3811, www.cruisetomountvernon.com) offers day-trip cruises on the *Spirit of Washington II* Tuesday–Sunday mid-March–August and Friday–Sunday in September and October. It leaves Pier 4 at 6th and Water Streets SW in Washington, D.C., at 8:30 A.M., arriving in Mount Vernon at 10 A.M., and returns to D.C. at 1:30 P.M. for $42 adults, $34 children round-trip, including admission.

From the City Marina behind the Torpedo Factory in Old Town Alexandria, the **Potomac Riverboat Company** (703/684-0580, www.potomacriverboatco.com) runs the *Miss Christin* to Mount Vernon at 11 A.M. Tuesday–Sunday, returning at 4 P.M., April–August for $38 adults, $20 children round-trip, including admission and a narrated tour.

The **Mount Vernon Trail** parallels the George Washington Memorial Parkway from here to north of Alexandria.

Near Mount Vernon

A pair of homes reflecting very different eras share a part of the original Mount Vernon estate grounds to the west. **Woodlawn Mansion** (703/780-4000, www.woodlawn1805.org) was presented to Washington's nephew Lawrence Lewis on his marriage to Eleanor "Nelly" Custis, Martha's granddaughter by her first marriage. Built 1800–1805, the brick building was designed in part by William Thornton, one of the architects of the U.S. Capitol. The gardens include an exceptional collection of 19th-century roses.

Frank Lloyd Wright designed the low, angular **Pope-Leighey House** (www.popeleighey1940.org) in 1914 as an example of his "Usonian" style, meant to be an affordable, tasteful home for middle-income families. Originally near Falls Church, the L-shaped building was rescued from destruction in 1964, dismantled, and rebuilt here. Inside it's snug but comfortable thanks to high ceilings, warm cypress walls, and strategically placed windows (some in corners!).

Both buildings, at the intersection of the Mount Vernon Memorial Parkway (Rte. 235) and U.S. 1, are open 10 A.M.–5 P.M. daily March–December. Admission to Woodlawn only is $8.50 adults, $4 children, and a ticket to both is $15/$5. Tours of both homes are included. The mansion hosts the country's oldest and largest **Needlework Show** in March.

MASON NECK

This stubby peninsula, less than an hour's drive from the capital, is a great natural getaway and a haven for bald eagles. There's enough here to easily fill an entire day, whether you want to learn, recreate, or just relax.

Pohick Bay Regional Park

The first stop is named for the Algonquin word for "water place." Besides the quiet marshes of Pohick Bay, it offers a huge water park that gets packed during muggy summers, a campground with hookups ($25–42), a camp store, boat access, an 18-hole golf course, mini putt-putt and a disc golf course, picnic areas, and nature trails. The park (703/339-6104, www.nvrpa.org/parks/pohickbay, sunrise–sunset daily, $7 per car) has canoes, sailboats, Jon boats, and pedalboats for rent starting at $13 per day, and the pool is open Memorial Day to Labor Day for separate admission. Naturalists lead guided canoe and kayak trips to spot osprey, eagles, and great blue herons. Take Route 242 from U.S. 1, and the entrance is on the left.

Gunston Hall Plantation

A short distance farther down Route 242 sits an 18th-century plantation built for George Mason, one of the nation's unsung founding fathers. Mason was a friend of George Washington and the author of the Virginia Declaration of Rights, whose words Thomas Jefferson borrowed for the Declaration of Independence. Even though he helped write the U.S. Constitution, Mason refused to sign the document because it didn't abolish slavery or include a bill of rights.

A certain serenity pervades the Georgian mansion and 550 acres of grounds, all that's left of the original 5,500-acre tobacco and wheat plantation. Stop by the **visitors center** to see a short film on Mason before taking a tour of the house, built 1755–1760. Many of the furnishings are original, as are the remarkable decorative wood carvings done by a young British indentured servant named William Buckland. Mason designed the formal boxwood gardens. Visitors can follow the nature trail through the wooded deer park to the Potomac and visit the grave of Mason and his wife, Ann.

Gunston Hall (703/550-9220, www.gunstonhall.org, 9:30 A.M.–5 P.M. daily, $9 adults, $5 children) has a museum, a gift shop, and a cafeteria serving an inexpensive lunch. Call ahead for information on interpretive activities such as cooking and harvest demonstrations and candlelit tours.

Mason Neck National Wildlife Refuge

Six miles of shoreline, 2,000 acres of hardwood forest, and northern Virginia's largest marsh fall within the first national wildlife refuge created specifically to protect the habitat of bald eagles. It's perhaps the best place to see our national bird within range of the capital. Along with the Occoquan Bay and Featherstone refuges, the refuge (703/490-4979, dawn–dusk, free) is part of the Potomac River National Wildlife Refuge Complex, which encompasses a sizable chunk of the Chesapeake Bay–Susquehanna River ecosystem. The majestic raptors feed in the 245-acre Great Marsh alongside a 1,000-pair colony of great blue herons, ducks, and 200 varieties of songbirds. Trails lead through fern-filled glades and over streams to the marsh edge. Winter is arguably the best time of year to visit because it's easier to spot the birds of prey when there aren't any leaves on the trees.

Mason Neck State Park

In 1969, the state of Virginia purchased 1,800 acres from The Nature Conservancy, leaving the national wildlife refuge split into two sections on either side of Belmont Bay. The Dogue Indian tribe once hunted and fished here among the oak, ash, and maples. Today you can view ospreys, great blue herons, and many of the Chesapeake Bay's nesting pairs of bald eagles from several short trails and walkways over marshy areas. The **visitors center** (703/339-2380) includes a museum and can provide information on guided activities such as canoe trips and hikes. The park (703/339-2385, www.dcr.state.va.us/parks/masonnec.htm, dawn–dusk daily, $3 per car, $4 on weekends) is five miles east on Route 242 from U.S. 1.

PRINCE WILLIAM FOREST PARK

Inhabited as early as 4,500 B.C., the watershed of Quantico Creek was home to Potomac Indian villages from A.D. 700 until the arrival of English colonists. After centuries of severe erosion from overfarming, in 1948 it was turned over to the National Park Service, which kept it a wooded sanctuary sandwiched between the Marine Corps Base Quantico and the metropolitan sprawl of northern Virginia. Hardwoods and pines dominate the 18,500 acres, which makes it the largest parcel of piedmont forest protected by the National Park Service. Because it spans both the Piedmont and the Coastal Plain physiographic provinces, it shelters a wide variety of plants and animals, including great horned owls and the rare whorled pogonia orchid. It's also one of the cheapest places to stay, and best places to camp, close to Washington, D.C.

Start at the **Pine Grove visitors center** (703/221-7181, www.nps.gov/prwi, 9 A.M.–5 P.M. daily, $5 per vehicle) on Route 619 from I-95 exit 150. Ask here for directions to the fishing ponds and picnic areas, and for information on interpretive programs and the 37 miles of hiking trails. A four-mile geology trail covers 570 million years of history. Mountain bikers can choose from 21 miles of paved and fire roads that span the two main creeks and the intervening ridges and valleys.

Campers have several choices. The Oak

Ridge tent and RV campground charges $15 per night for up to six people. The Chopawamsic Backcountry Camp, three miles west of the town of Triangle on Route 619, is undeveloped but free with a permit from the visitors center, open mid-March–mid-October. You can rent cabins in Camp Orenda, one of five cabin camps (the other four are for groups and families) built by the Civilian Conservation Corps in the 1930s. Each one has beds, a picnic table, a grill, and electric lights, and they're arranged around a central bathhouse with hot showers. They range $30–50 per night and can sleep 4–10 people. For RV hookups, steer toward the **Prince William Travel Trailer Village** (16058 Dumfries Rd., 703/221-2474, www.traveltrailervillage.com), off Route 234 a few miles west of I-95 exit 152, with sites for $27–30.

QUANTICO

Practically a military outpost on its own, this 500-person town is completely encircled by the Potomac River and the Marine Corps Base Quantico, one of the largest in the world. It's also home to the training academies of the U.S. Drug Enforcement Administration (DEA) and the Federal Bureau of Investigation (FBI); the latter includes the most active crime scene investigation lab in the country.

Quantico is also home to the **National Museum of the Marine Corps** (18900 Jefferson Davis Hwy., Triangle, 800/397-7585, www.usmcmuseum.org, 9 A.M.–5 P.M. daily, free). The building's soaring spear shape, easily visible from I-95, echoes the famous flag-raising photo on top of Mount Suribachi on Iwo Jima, and you can see those very flags inside. You can also see everything related to the United States Marine Corps, from rifles to helicopters, along with exhibits on World War II, the Korean War, Vietnam, and the ongoing fight against terrorism. There's a mess hall (with much better food than your average leatherneck sees in the field) and the Tun Tavern, a working re-creation of the 18th-century tavern in Philadelphia where the first Colonial Marines were recruited in 1775.

A few sporting events will get you invited onto base too. Run Amuck (www.marinecorpshistorichalf.com) is a four-mile race in August that pits runners against obstacles, mud pits, a water challenge, and their own coordination. The EX2 Adventures Cranky Monkey mountain bike races, also in August (www.ex2adventures.com), take advantage of the Quantico single-track that used to be a favorite of president George W. Bush and his Secret Service detail.

WASHINGTON, D.C.

Each year millions of tourists—from families to foreign dignitaries to legions of 8th graders and their supervisors—take pilgrimages to the nation's capital for a simple reason: American history is far more impressive in person than in textbooks. White marble punctuates the District of Columbia from the Lincoln Memorial to the White House to the U.S. Capitol to the Supreme Court, lending an added sense of gravity to this center of power.

The capital of the United States is inspiring, depressing, exciting, frustrating, and more—often in equal measure and simultaneously. D.C. can easily overwhelm with the sheer range of its offerings, from the babble of languages in Dupont Circle to the no-nonsense bustle of Capitol Hill, the leafy line of Rock Creek Park to the echoing halls of the National Gallery of Art. At the same time, slums sprawl next to wealthy neighborhoods and homeless people sleep in the shadows of the halls of power. Living conditions in some parts of the city are appalling, and even the wealthiest of residents don't yet have true representation in Congress.

Nonetheless, Washington, D.C., is a great place to visit, and the tourist center is wonderfully accessible to visitors. Once-sketchy neighborhoods are rapidly gentrifying and sprouting bars, restaurants, and spiffed-up row houses. Rowing sculls skimming the Potomac at dawn, majestic monuments lit at night, Georgetown's aristocratic pedigree, Congressional staffers gossiping over cocktails on U Street—it all combines into one of the world's great cities. Our most monumental, symbolic, and international city serves as a reminder of all that is

HIGHLIGHTS

Lincoln Memorial: Pay a visit to the preserver of the Union, and glance over your shoulder at the sweeping view of the Reflecting Pool (page 84).

Vietnam Veterans Memorial: This monument is a lesson in minimalist design – it's hard to imagine a more effective way to convey the terrible cost of war than a simple wall bearing the names of the dead (page 87).

National Museum of American History: From Dorothy's red shoes to the Star-Spangled Banner, there's a slice of Americana in every room (page 89).

Jefferson Memorial: From inside the memorial, a fur-robed statue of the founding father gazes out over the Tidal Basin, which in spring is lined with the delicate blooms of Japanese cherry trees (page 96).

U.S. Capitol: Take a guided tour to check up on our elected officials at work and gaze upon some interesting art in the building (page 98).

The White House: No trip to Washington, D.C., would be complete without a visit to the president's house (page 100).

Donald W. Reynolds Center for American Art and Portraiture: Combined under one roof with the Smithsonian American Art Museum, the faces portrayed in the **National Portrait Gallery** are as endlessly fascinating as they are candid (page 102).

Newseum: Washington's most interactive museum has all the headlines, from historic front-page blunders ("Dewey Defeats Truman!") to the tragedy of 9/11. Don't miss the gallery of Pulitzer photographs (page 104).

Washington National Cathedral: An Old World cathedral built with New World flair – look for moon stone in the stained glass and Darth Vader in the gargoyles (page 110).

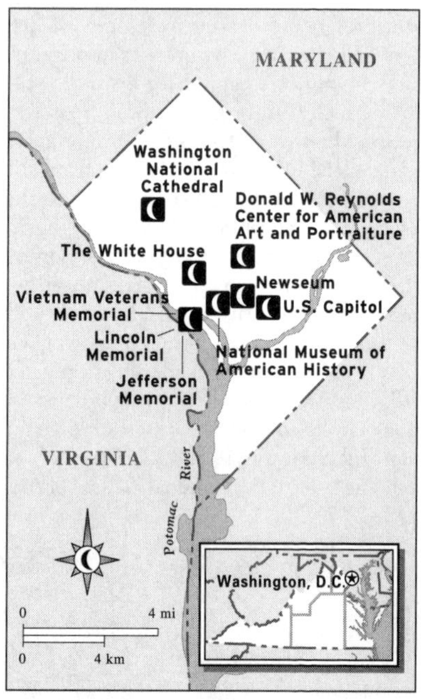

LOOK FOR TO FIND RECOMMENDED SIGHTS, ACTIVITIES, DINING, AND LODGING.

desirable—and some that is not—in the country it embodies.

HISTORY

With the dust still settling from the American Revolution, a nervous Congress knew that the fledgling United States needed a federal city where its lawmakers could govern in relative peace. Creating one would be no easy task: The 13 colonies were united in freedom but divergent in interests, there was no president yet, and the war had left the national coffers nearly empty.

The location for the country's new capital was decided by a combination of political compromise and pragmatism. After considering many locations in both North and South,

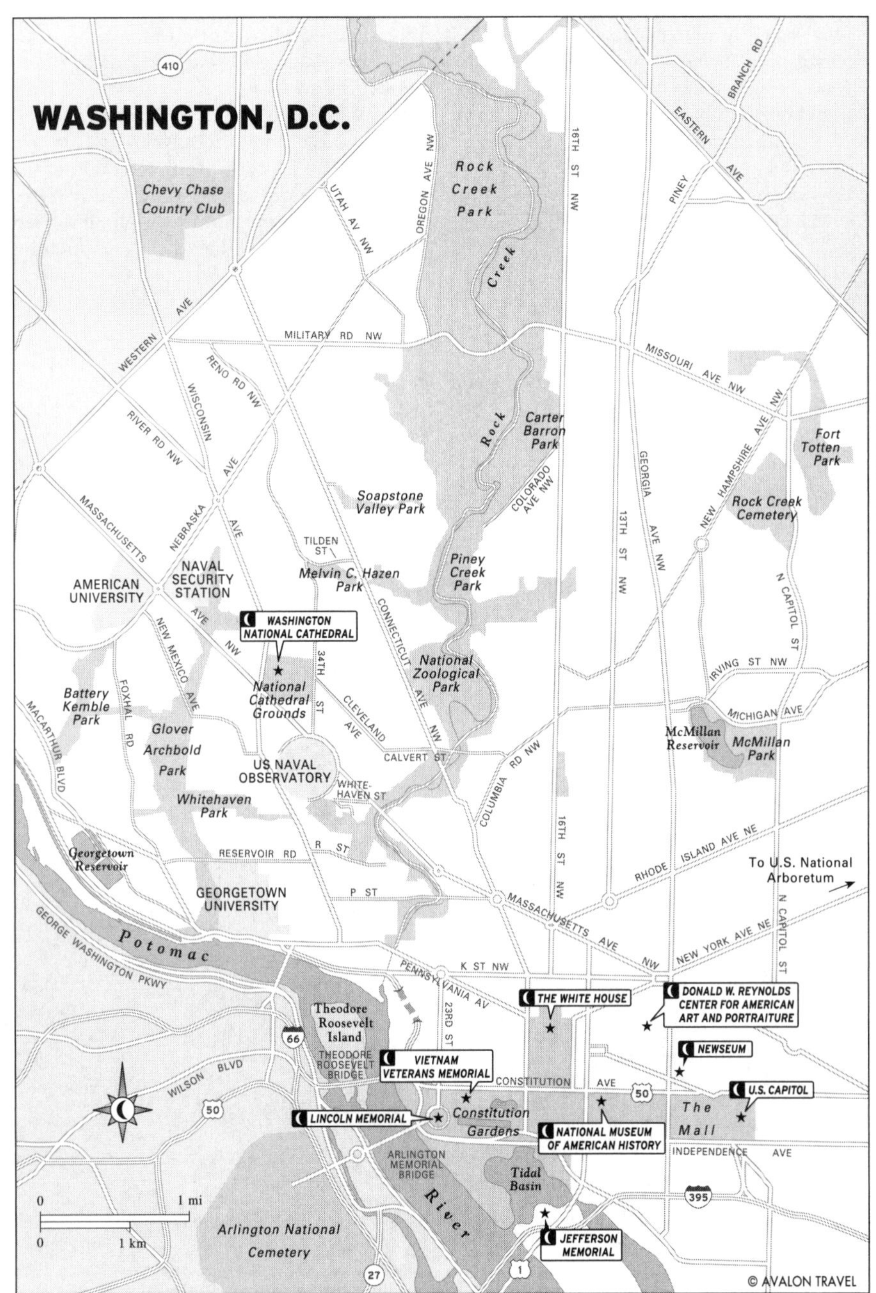
WASHINGTON, D.C.
Chevy Chase Country Club
Rock Creek Park
Rock Creek
Carter Barron Park
Soapstone Valley Park
Melvin C. Hazen Park
Piney Creek Park
Fort Totten Park
Rock Creek Cemetery
AMERICAN UNIVERSITY
NAVAL SECURITY STATION
WASHINGTON NATIONAL CATHEDRAL
National Cathedral Grounds
National Zoological Park
Battery Kemble Park
Glover Archbold Park
US NAVAL OBSERVATORY
Whitehaven Park
McMillan Reservoir
McMillan Park
Georgetown Reservoir
GEORGETOWN UNIVERSITY
Potomac River
To U.S. National Arboretum
Theodore Roosevelt Island
THEODORE ROOSEVELT BRIDGE
THE WHITE HOUSE
DONALD W. REYNOLDS CENTER FOR AMERICAN ART AND PORTRAITURE
NEWSEUM
VIETNAM VETERANS MEMORIAL
U.S. CAPITOL
LINCOLN MEMORIAL
Constitution Gardens
NATIONAL MUSEUM OF AMERICAN HISTORY
The Mall
ARLINGTON MEMORIAL BRIDGE
Tidal Basin
JEFFERSON MEMORIAL
Arlington National Cemetery
0 1 mi
0 1 km
WESTERN AVE
MILITARY RD NW
MISSOURI AVE NW
EASTERN AVE
BRANCH RD
PINEY
16TH ST NW
OREGON AVE NW
UTAH AV NW
RENO RD NW
WISCONSIN AVE
RIVER RD NW
MASSACHUSETTS AVE NW
NEBRASKA AVE
TILDEN ST
CONNECTICUT AVE NW
COLORADO AVE NW
GEORGIA AVE NW
13TH ST NW
NEW HAMPSHIRE AVE NW
N CAPITOL ST
IRVING ST NW
MICHIGAN AVE
NEW MEXICO AVE
FOXHALL RD
MACARTHUR BLVD
34TH ST
CLEVELAND AVE
CALVERT ST
COLUMBIA RD NW
WHITE-HAVEN ST
RESERVOIR RD
R ST
P ST
RHODE ISLAND AVE NE
NEW YORK AVE NE
GEORGE WASHINGTON PKWY
K ST NW
PENNSYLVANIA AV
23RD ST
CONSTITUTION AVE
INDEPENDENCE AVE
WILSON BLVD
410
66
50
395
27
1
© AVALON TRAVEL

newly elected president George Washington decided on a spot near where the Anacostia River meets the Potomac, for its economic potential near the tobacco market of Georgetown and a planned canal across the Cumberland Gap to the western frontier.

French engineer and revolutionary volunteer Pierre L'Enfant was given the task of designing the nation's capital, which he planned on a grand scale in the spirit of his beloved Paris. A bold grid pattern, anchored by great parks and monumental squares, was overlaid with diagonal avenues named for the states and radiating outward from the White House and the Capitol building, both of which were begun in 1793. In October 1800, the governmental archives and general offices were shifted to Washington from Philadelphia. That same year, president John Adams moved into the White House, and Congress met for the first time in the Capitol.

Critics soon began to attack D.C.'s seemingly arbitrary location. What was conceived as a "city of magnificent distances" was derided as the "capital of miserable huts," and members of both Congress and the national press tried to have the capital moved to a more accessible—and, in the summertime heat, bearable—location. National outrage over the British invasion in 1814, however, firmly seated Washington, D.C., as America's capital in the minds of her citizens. The city's key role in the Civil War, as the heart and brain of the victorious Union, further solidified its symbolic image. A sudden influx of 40,000 freed slaves more than doubled D.C.'s population and set it on a course of racial diversity that eventually would embrace immigrants from every country in the world.

PLANNING YOUR TIME

Bedraggled families rushing from one place to another, trying to "do it all" in a day or two, is an all-too-familiar sight in D.C. Avoid that fate by being realistic about how much ground you can cover and how much culture you (and your kids, if applicable) can absorb at one go. If you have a weekend, stick to Capitol Hill and the National Mall, where 2–4 museums and monuments per day is more than enough. The **U.S. Capitol** and **The White House** are both must-sees, as are the **Washington Monument** (if only

© KATIE GITHENS

the U.S. Capitol

© KATIE GITHENS

the Vietnam Veterans Memorial

© KATIE GITHENS

The Newseum is Washington's "most interactive museum" and has seven floors of news history on display.

from below) and the **Jefferson Memorial.** New in 2009, the **Newseum** brings to life history's biggest events and headlines with seven floors of theaters and galleries. The **Vietnam Veterans Memorial** and the **National Air and Space Museum** are both also popular—one poignant, the other uplifting. Farther off the well-beaten path, shaded **Rock Creek Park** and the **U.S. National Arboretum** can be great antidotes to the museum-overdosed.

Venture to **Dupont Circle, Adams-Morgan, U Street,** or **Georgetown** for drinks, dinner, and entertainment, including shopping. If you have more time or want to avoid the crowds and take things at a slower pace, these neighborhoods each have worthwhile sights of their own. For a slightly more offbeat experience—remember, here "offbeat" means not wearing a power suit to work—see the pandas at the **National Zoological Park** or look for Darth Vader's likeness lurking in the gargoyles of the **Washington National Cathedral.**

Spring, and then fall, are the city's loveliest seasons, but each month has its benefits—even swampy August, when the city empties out and traffic lightens.

Sights on the National Mall

The area between Constitution Avenue NW and Independence Avenue SW is truly America's backyard. The grassy expanse, wide as a football field, stretches 2.5 miles from the Capitol at the east end to the Lincoln Memorial at the west. Along both sides stand many of the Smithsonian museums, and just to the north is the White House. The Mall encompasses monuments to George Washington and veterans of four wars, outdoor sculpture gardens, and the Reflecting Pool—all in all, more iconic American sights per square mile than anywhere else in the country.

For information on any of the free attractions on the Mall, contact the National Parks superintendent (900 Ohio Dr. SW, 202/426-6841, www.nps.gov/nama). Unless otherwise noted, all National Park Service sights on the Mall are open 24 hours a day, with rangers available between 9:30 A.M. and 11:30 P.M. Be aware that access to some sites in the D.C. area may be limited because of security concerns.

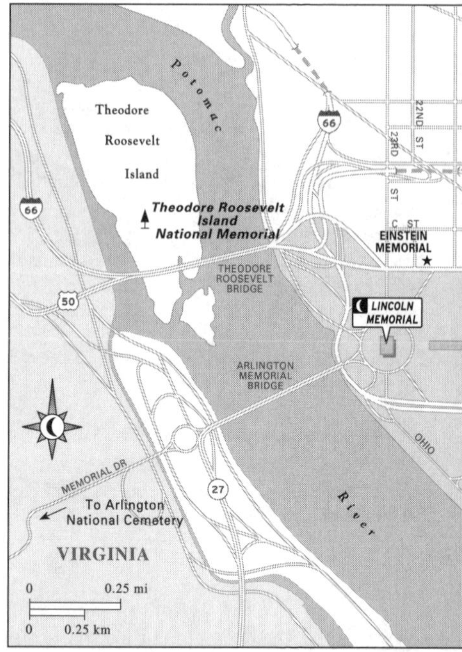

Lincoln Memorial

Although more than a century elapsed before the Washington Monument moved from contemplation to completion, the Lincoln Memorial (www.nps.gov/linc) was built in 60 years. Henry Bacon's white marble temple is another D.C. testimonial to the Greeks, while the 19-foot statue of Lincoln by Daniel French that sits inside the temple bears signs of Roman influence, especially in the chair arms bearing *fasces,* symbols of Roman imperial power. The statue of the Great Emancipator has a watchful intensity, bordering on sternness.

Although the 1922 unveiling ceremonies were segregated, the site began a long association with the civil rights movement 17 years

While impressive by day, late evening is really the best time to visit the Lincoln Memorial.

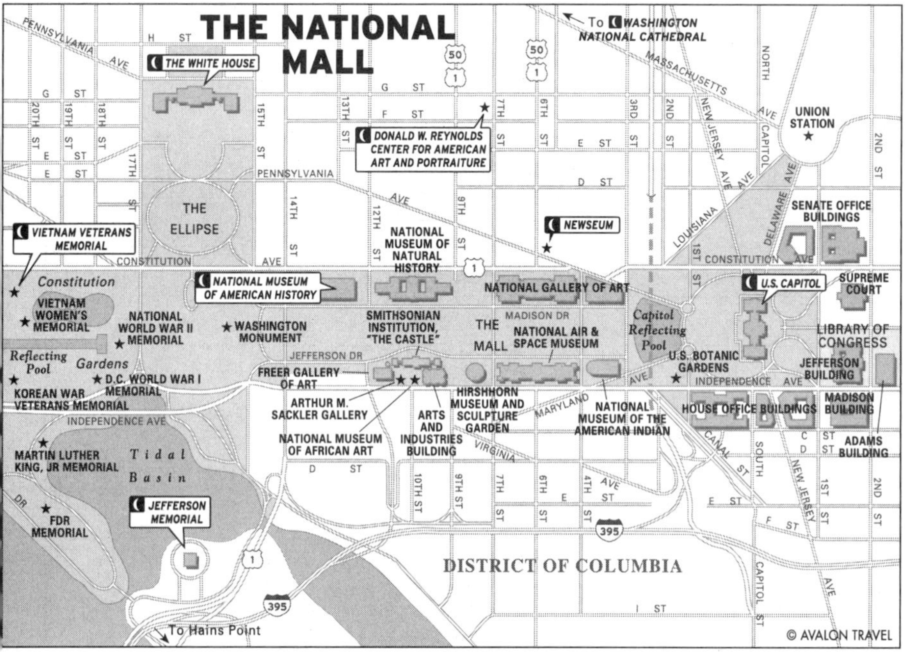

later when contralto Marian Anderson sang from the steps after she was barred from performing at nearby Constitution Hall. Anderson ascended the steps again in 1963, preceding the Reverend Martin Luther King Jr.'s momentous "I have a dream" speech.

Located at the west end of the Mall, the memorial is best visited at night, when the spirit of the place is most alive.

Korean War Veterans Memorial

The centerpiece of the Korean War Veterans Memorial (www.nps.gov/kowa), dedicated in 1995, is the triangular "field of service" depicting a wedge of soldiers slogging through the countryside. Sculpted by Frank Chalfant Gaylord II, this symbolic patrol of 19 stainless-steel figures is made up of members from each of the four main branches of the armed services. The memorial is most haunting at night, when the seven-foot statues are softly illuminated from below. It's just south of the Reflecting Pool near the FDR Memorial Park.

© KATIE GITHENS

The anguished faces of the 19 stainless-steel figures of the Korean War Veterans Memorial can feel haunting late at night.

USING THE METRO IN D.C.

Destination	Metro Station/Line
Botanic Garden	Federal Center SW/Blue or Orange
FBI Building	Archives-Navy Memorial/Yellow or Green
Federal Triangle	Federal Triangle/Blue or Orange
Ford's Theatre	Metro Center/Blue, Orange, or Red
Georgetown	Rosslyn/Blue or Orange (walk north across Francis Scott Key Bridge)
Kennedy Center	Foggy Bottom/Blue or Orange (walk south along New Hampshire Avenue)
Library of Congress	Capitol South/Blue or Orange
National Aquarium	Federal Triangle/Blue or Orange
National Archives	Archives-Navy Memorial/Yellow or Green
National Building Museum	Judiciary Square/Red
National Mall	Smithsonian/Blue or Orange
National Portrait Gallery (Reynolds Center)	Gallery Place/Green, Red, or Yellow
Shakespeare Theatre	Archives/Green or Yellow
Smithsonian American Art Museum (Reynolds Center)	Gallery Place/Green, Red, or Yellow
Union Station	Union Station/Red
Verizon Center	Gallery Place/Green, Red, or Yellow
Washington National Cathedral	Woodley Park-Zoo/Red (walk west along Woodley Road)
White House	Metro Center/Blue, Orange, or Red
Zoological Park	Woodley Park-Zoo/Red

Metro transfer stations include L'Enfant Plaza, Gallery Place, King Street, Metro Center, Pentagon, Rosslyn, and Stadium-Armory.

Vietnam Veterans Memorial

The revolutionary work that designer Maya Lin described simply as "a rift in the earth" doesn't trumpet the glory of struggle or the legacy of some lauded general. Instead it lists, in neat, simple seemingly endless columns, the name of every person killed in America's longest war. More than 58,000 names are carved into the 492-foot wall of black granite whose polished surface reflects the faces of those who visit to pay homage. The names are listed chronologically in the order of death as the wall descends into and then ascends out of the earth. At each end of the memorial (www.nps.gov/vive) are registers listing the names alphabetically, with a key to their location on the wall.

Vietnam veteran Jan Scruggs raised the funds to construct the memorial through a nonprofit organization, and today it is America's most potent shrine, a place of grief and cleansing where every year tens of thousands of people bring offerings of poems and rings, harmonicas, and sardines for lost friends, lost sons, or the parent they never knew.

The memorial also includes two bronze sculptures, additions to appease critics of Lin's nontraditional memorial design. The first depicts three weary but alert servicemen, and the other portrays three women tending an injured soldier, communicating the emotional bond that formed between the male soldiers and women who served primarily as nurses and support staff. Congress approved plans for an underground visitors center in 2003, but the design process remained embroiled in debate in 2010.

© KATIE GITHENS

Names are listed chronologically in the order of death on the simple yet powerful Vietnam Veterans Memorial.

Constitution Gardens

The last of the unsightly "temporary" buildings marring the Mall was finally removed in the mid-1970s and replaced by this tranquil 50-acre oasis of landscaped gardens, meandering footpaths, and a duck pond (www.nps.gov/coga). A willow-shrouded island at the center of the pond contains a roster of the signers of the Declaration of Independence, inscribed on a granite-and-gold plate.

Einstein Memorial

Fitting for one of the 20th century's intellectual giants, Einstein is immortalized in a larger-than-life bronze statue on 22nd Street NW, across from Constitution Gardens. From unruly hair to big toe, the statue measures 21 feet and weighs 7,000 pounds; sculptor Robert Berks cast the bronze in 19 sections, which were later shipped and welded together. His statue sits in an elm and holly grove on the grounds of the National Academies of Science, which Einstein joined in 1942 after arriving from Berlin the decade prior. Though he was politically involved in his later years, Einstein once said, "Politics is for the present, but an equation...is...for eternity." Look for his most famous equation, $E = mc^2$, carved for perpetuity in the papers held by the statue.

National World War II Memorial

Dedicated on Memorial Day 2004, this monument to the 16 million Americans who took part in history's most devastating conflict came none too soon; according to some estimates, over 1,000 WWII veterans die every day. The oval structure (800/639-4992, www.wwiimemorial.com), which was

© KATIE GITHENS

The National World War II Memorial is one of the newest on the Mall, completed in 2004.

funded mostly by private donations, sits at the east end of the Reflecting Pool and contains a smaller pool. Fifty-six pillars inscribed with the names of states, territories, and the District of Columbia are linked by a bronze rope, and two arches at either end symbolize the war's Atlantic and Pacific fronts. Bas-relief sculpture recalls scenes from the war, and the Freedom Wall displays 4,053 gold stars in remembrance of the over 400,000 service members who were killed.

D.C. World War I Memorial

If you find yourself on the edge of Independence Avenue, pay a quick visit to the lonesome D.C. World War I Memorial. The Doric temple, 40 feet in diameter, is a tribute to local residents who lost their lives in World War I, the only D.C. memorial on the National Mall and the first to list all D.C. residents regardless of their race, class, or gender. The weathered white marble illustrates the confusion between the National Park Service and the District of Columbia over who is responsible for the caretaking of the memorial, but it's beautifully dignified even in its neglect.

Washington Monument

Contrary to popular belief, no federal law requires buildings in the capital to be shorter than the 555-foot tapered shaft of the Washington Monument. The truth is more mundane: D.C.'s building height restriction law was implemented in reaction to an over-reaching apartment building in Dupont Circle in 1899. Nonetheless, the Washington Monument towers above the District and is an instant landmark.

In 1783, the Continental Congress first suggested a monument honoring the nation's inaugural president, but more than a century passed before the idea became reality; from cornerstone to completion took 40 years. During one embarrassing interlude from 1854 to 1876, the obelisk languished as an unsightly stump of 150 feet, described by Mark Twain as "a factory chimney with the top broken off."

When work began again, the marble

© KATIE GITHENS

the oft-overlooked D.C. World War I Memorial

© KATIE GITHENS

the Washington Monument

originally drawn from a Maryland quarry had been exhausted; thus the noticeable change in shade of the remaining 400 feet. The monument finally opened in 1888 with women and children dutifully trudging up the 898 steps (the elevator was considered patently dangerous, braved only by men). Today everyone rides the elevator, ascending to 360-degree views of the capital's historic heart through narrow windows.

Tickets to visit the monument (www.nps.gov/wamo, 9 A.M.–5 P.M. daily except Christmas and July 4) are free, available each day from the kiosk at 15th Street and Madison Drive on a first-come, first-served basis. Since they tend to go quickly, get there early—as in 7 A.M.—or reserve them well in advance for a small fee by calling 877/444-6777 or visiting www.recreation.gov.

SMITHSONIAN INSTITUTION

In 1829, eccentric British mineralogist and chemist James Smithson passed on, leaving to the United States—a country he had never seen—105 bags of gold sovereigns "to found an establishment for the increase and diffusion of knowledge." After no small amount of puzzlement and a fair amount of wrangling, Congress decided in 1846 to spend Smithson's largesse on an institute of scientific research, which has evolved into the peerless Smithsonian (202/633-1000, www.si.edu/visit).

Most of the 15 Smithsonian buildings and attractions are on the Mall, although the National Portrait Gallery, the Renwick Gallery, the Anacostia Museum, the Postal Museum, and the National Zoological Park are elsewhere in the city. All are free and open 10 A.M.–5:30 P.M. daily except Christmas. Extended summer hours are determined annually, but generally the biggies—the Natural History Museum, the American History Museum, the Air and Space Museum, and the Zoo—stay open until 7:30 P.M.

National Museum of American History

Living up to the nickname "America's attic,"

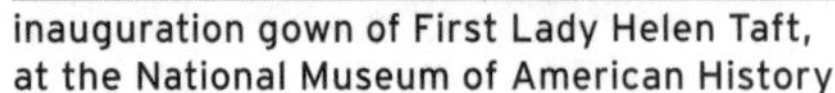

inauguration gown of First Lady Helen Taft, at the National Museum of American History

life-size model of a 45-foot North Atlantic right whale, at the National Museum of Natural History

this museum (14th St. and Constitution Ave. NW, 202/633-1000, http://americanhistory.si.edu) is as big, rich, and sprawling as the country whose past it collects. The sheer quantity of material is staggering; it would require several hours to appreciate the intricate, painstaking, exhaustively informative lightbulb display alone. See the tattered fabric Francis Scott Key immortalized as "The Star-Spangled Banner," proof the flag *is* still there; say hello to Kermit the Frog; admire the inauguration gowns of First Ladies from Helen Taft to Laura Bush—and soon Michelle Obama; and step into Julia Child's kitchen, complete with all of her utensils and a TV showing episodes of her PBS show *The French Chef.*

Plans are underway to break ground in the grassy field next door in 2012 for the National Museum of African American History and Culture, with plans to complete construction by 2015. In the meantime, the 2nd floor of the American History Museum houses items in the collection. Look for the Woolworth's lunch counter where one of the first nonviolent sit-ins took place in Greensboro, North Carolina, spurring forward the civil rights movement.

National Museum of Natural History

Here you'll find an endless amalgamation of artifacts—animal, vegetable, and mineral—from the jaws of a prehistoric shark large enough to swallow entire automobiles to the Hope diamond, the most famous in the 7,500 gemstone collection. A 13-foot-tall stuffed African elephant and a great stone head from Easter Island round out the gigantic collection. The exhibits aren't limited to fossils and rocks, though; children will delight (or freak out) in the Live Butterfly Pavilion, where 400 tropical butterflies take flight around visitors. Special tickets are required and best purchased in advance (202/633-4629, http://butterflies.si.edu, $6 adults, $5 children, free Tues.).

The museum (10th St. and Constitution Ave. NW, 202/633-1000, www.mnh.si.edu) is often packed with raucous school groups and has a café downstairs, as well as an IMAX theater showing 40-minute films during the day ($8.75 adults, $7.25 children 2–12) and a full-length feature in the evening ($10).

Mall Carousel

On the grounds of the south side of the Mall, a small merry-go-round offers a pleasant respite from the solemnity of its monumental surroundings. A circular journey or two aboard gaily painted horses, serenaded by cheery carnival tunes, can serve as a bracing antidote to historic dates and endless museum rounds. The carousel (202/633-1000, 10 A.M.–5:30 P.M. daily, $2.50) spins just east of the Smithsonian Castle.

Smithsonian Castle

In 1855, James Renwick completed the fairytale red sandstone structure popularly known as the Castle. The institution quickly outgrew these grand confines, so today the building serves simply as an information center guiding visitors to the Smithsonian's scattered holdings. It has an exhibit hall, interactive touch-screen stations with information in six languages, and a short video orientation to the institution's offerings. Smithson's dusty remains arrived in 1904 and rest in a crypt beneath the castle. Beautifully landscaped gardens await behind the building between the entrances to the Sackler Gallery and the National Museum of African Art.

The castle (1000 Jefferson Dr. SW, 202/633-1000, www.si.edu/visit/infocenter/sicastle.htm, 8:30 A.M.–5:30 P.M. daily) is unmistakable on the south side of the Mall.

Freer and Sackler Galleries

Charles Lang Freer raked in millions designing railroad cars and then began to spend his accumulated wealth on fine art. Freer first became enamored of the prints, pastels, oils, and watercolors of James Whistler and then, at the artist's urging, began accumulating Asian art. When Freer died in 1919, his entire collection went to the Smithsonian; the **Freer Gallery of Art** (Jefferson Dr. at 12th St. SW, 202/633-1000, www.asia.si.edu) opened four years later.

Kids who need a break from museum-hopping will appreciate the carousel on the Mall, just east of the Smithsonian Castle.

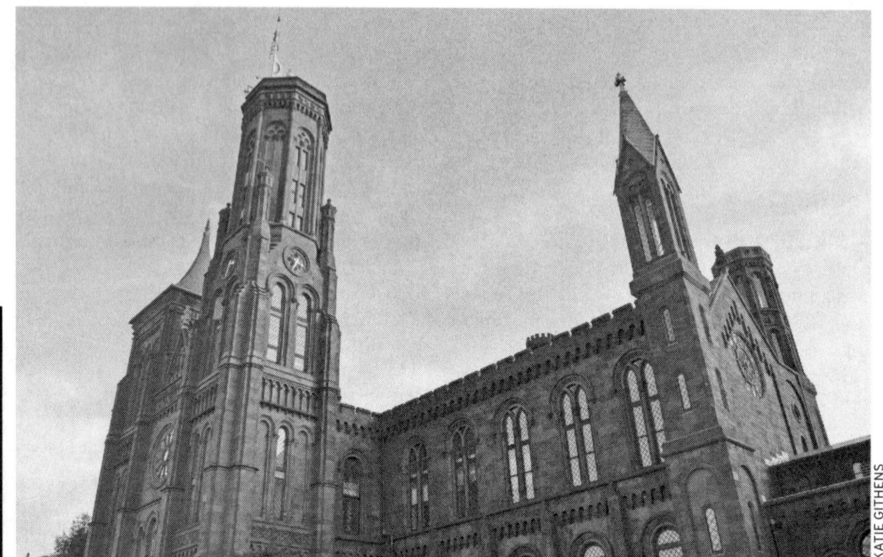
© KATIE GITHENS

The "Castle" was the Smithsonian's first exhibit hall; British scientist and founder James Smithson is buried here.

Today the Freer houses more than 26,000 objects, including more than 1,200 works by Whistler—the largest collection of the artist's work found anywhere.

Most impressive is Whistler's **Peacock Room,** a London dining room he lavishly decorated though his patron only requested tips on paint colors. Ask curators about the fight—and painting of squabbling peacocks—that ensued. The gallery is connected to the Sackler Gallery by an underground passage.

The eye-boggling three-tiered subterranean **Arthur M. Sackler Gallery** (1050 Independence Ave. SW, 202/633-1000) houses 5,000 years of Asian art. Highlights of the Sackler's unequaled permanent collection include Chinese bronze, jade, and lacquerware; delicate Persian paintings; Near Eastern works in silver, gold, bronze, and clay; and a pantheon of Buddhist and Hindu deities executed in stone and bronze.

National Museum of African Art

Founded as a private institution in 1964 and absorbed by the Smithsonian in 1979, this underground museum (950 Independence Ave. SW, 202/633-4600, www.nmafa.si.edu) focuses primarily on the traditional arts of sub-Saharan Africa. Permanent exhibits include pieces from the royal court of the kingdom of Benin as it was before British colonial rule, traditional and modern ceramic works from many regions of the continent, and a display of utilitarian objects illustrating daily African life. Its entrance is behind the Castle facing the Sackler Gallery.

Arts and Industries Building

At the conclusion of the 1876 U.S. International Exposition in Philadelphia, most exhibiting nations and many U.S. states craftily donated their exhibits to the U.S. government, thus saving the costs of shipping them home. It took 60 trains to transport all of these objects to the Smithsonian, increasing its holdings fourfold and requiring the construction of this Victorian edifice to house it all. In 2010, the Arts and Industries Building (900 Jefferson Dr.

SW, 202/633-1000, www.si.edu/ai) was closed for a full renovation with no immediate plans to reopen. Call for the latest news and opening hours.

Hirshhorn Museum and Sculpture Garden

Created to quiet critics who complained that the Smithsonian cared only for classic art, the Hirshhorn is built around the extensive 11,000-piece modern art collection of uranium tycoon Joseph Hirshhorn. The museum (Independence Ave. and 7th St. SW, 202/633-4674, http://hirshhorn.si.edu) holds revolving exhibitions dedicated to promulgating appreciation for "the art of our time." The building itself is evocative of a UFO and is as much a part of the artistic experience as the collection inside. Outside, the sculpture garden (7:30 A.M.–dusk daily) is set down into the ground and filled with a diverse array of pieces.

National Gallery of Art

One of the finest collections in the world is housed in two separate facilities. In the 1930s, the museum's west wing sprang full-grown from the wallet of rapacious banker Andrew Mellon, who wisely declined to append his name to the edifice. I. M. Pei designed the angular east wing, which was built in 1978 and boasts one of the sharpest corners you'll ever see on a building. Both wings are constructed of pink Tennessee marble, but there the similarity ends: the east displays 20th-century works by the likes of Miró, Magritte, and Matisse, while the homier, more crowded west wing is the domain of classic art by masters such as Raphael, Rembrandt, and Renoir. An underground passage connects the two wings, with a skylight-lit café and gift shop in the middle.

Across 7th Street from the west wing is a pleasant sculpture garden full of whimsical works. In winter, a festive ice-skating rink opens here (10 A.M.–9 P.M. Mon.–Thurs., until 11 P.M. Fri.–Sat., 11 A.M.–9 P.M. Sun., $7 adults, $6 children, skate rental $3 for two hours). In summer, free jazz concerts—and a buzzing picnic and happy hour crowd—grace the gardens Fridays 5–8 P.M.

The gallery (600 Constitution Ave. NW, 202/737-4215, www.nga.gov, 10 A.M.–5 P.M. Mon.–Sat., 11 A.M.–6 P.M. Sun., free) is open every day except Christmas and New Year's Day.

National Air and Space Museum

Year after year, this is the most visited attraction in the city. People just can't get enough of the model of *Sputnik,* the 1903 Wright Brothers' *Flyer,* Charles Lindbergh's *Spirit of St. Louis,* a knockoff of the Hubble space telescope, and a walk through a full-scale reproduction of the Skylab space station. Perhaps the most popular item on display is the four-billion-year-old shard of lunar rock brought back by the astronauts of *Apollo 17;* hardly anyone can resist running fingers over this chunk of another world.

The museum (Independence Ave. and 6th St. SW, 202/633-1000, www.nasm.si.edu) charges only for IMAX and planetarium shows. (The massive Steven F. Udvar-Hazy Center, a side branch of this impressive tree, is located near Dulles airport in northern Virginia.)

National Museum of the American Indian

In stark contrast to the orderly lines of architecture surrounding it, the Mall's newest museum (4th St. and Independence Ave. SW, 202/633-1000, www.nmai.si.edu) boasts a billowing silhouette sculpted in sandstone. Opened in September 2004, it holds a collection spanning the native cultures of North, Central, and South America. Artworks, textiles, sculptures, baskets, carvings, and hundreds of thousands of other artifacts make up the extensive collection. The presentation is less strictly linear than in other museums, making for a very different experience than your typical D.C. collection. The building includes two theaters, a café serving excellent food based on native recipes, and a 120-foot central dome, lined with glass prisms sited to catch the sun at particular times of the day and year.

Sights Beyond the Mall

TIDAL BASIN AREA

Tidal Basin

Separating West Potomac Park from East Potomac Park, the Tidal Basin was originally dredged as a reservoir but soon proved popular as a recreational area. From 1917 to 1925, white Washingtonians flocked to a segregated beach located where the Jefferson Memorial now stands. Today the basin is famous worldwide for the 1,300 cherry trees along its banks. The first batch, a peace offering from Japan, arrived in 1909, but the trees were contaminated with insects and were immediately destroyed. In 1912, a second shipment fared better and thrived through World War II, notwithstanding occasional efforts by enraged citizens to fell them. These days you can cruise the basin on pedalboats rented from the boathouse (202/479-2426, www.tidalbasinpaddleboats.com, 10 A.M.–6 P.M. daily Mar. 15–Labor Day, Wed.–Sat. Labor Day–Columbus Day, $10–18 per hour). This is an understandably popular activity during the cherry blossom festival in the spring, when advance reservations are a must.

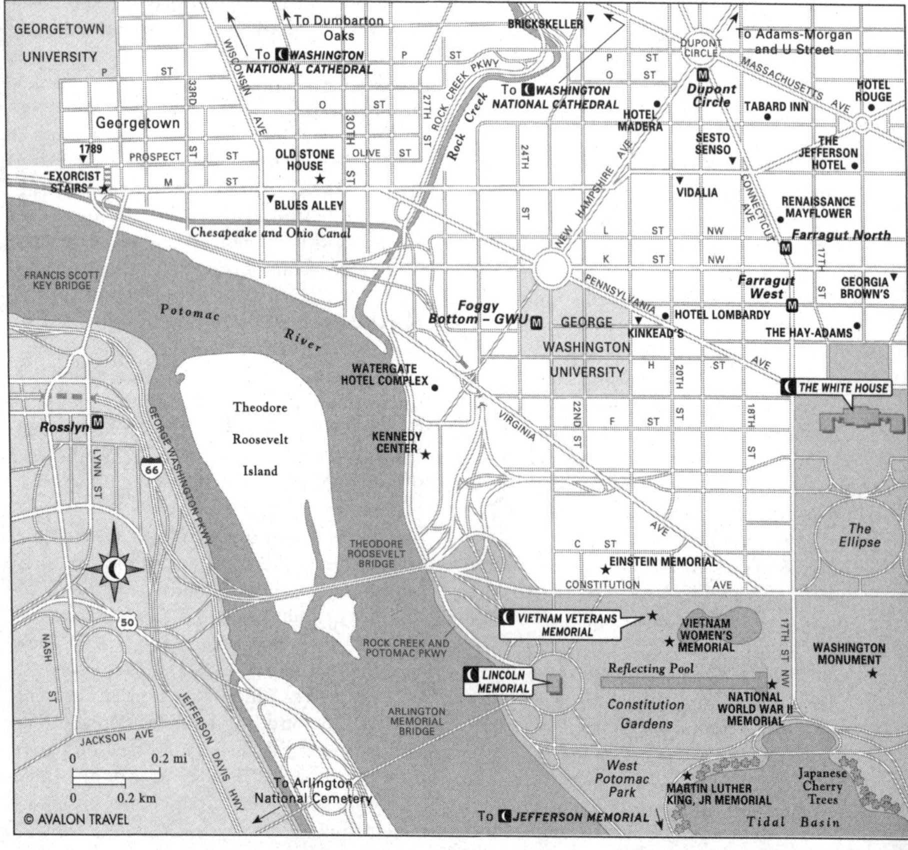

A public area, the Tidal Basin is officially open 8 A.M.–midnight daily.

Franklin Delano Roosevelt Memorial

Composed of four outdoor rooms, one for each of Franklin Delano Roosevelt's terms in office, this granite structure, designed by Lawrence Halprin, spreads along the west shore of the Tidal Basin in West Potomac Park. Visitors to the memorial enter past an inscribed FDR quote—"This generation of Americans has a rendezvous with destiny"—and a bronze bas-relief of the presidential seal as it appeared at FDR's first inauguration in 1933. The interiors of each room include waterfalls, plants, shrubs, and trees, as well as sculpture and inscriptions highlighting FDR's accomplishments as president, from bringing the nation out of the Great Depression to leading the United States during World War II. The fourth room includes FDR's "four freedoms": Freedom of Speech, Freedom of Worship, Freedom from Want, Freedom from Fear—symbolizing what the United States was fighting for during the war. It also presents the contributions of First Lady Eleanor Roosevelt as U.N. ambassador after her husband's death.

There was some controversy over the memorial (202/426-6841, www.nps.gov/fdrm, 24 hours daily except Christmas, interpretive rangers

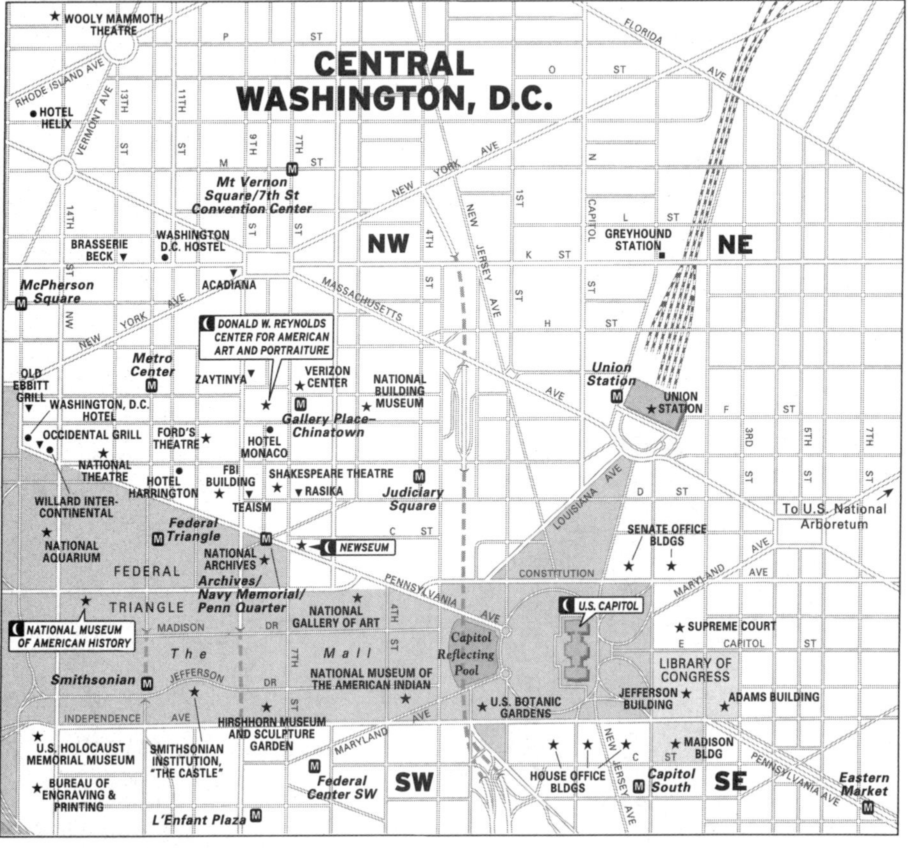

© KATIE GITHENS

A statue of FDR in his wheelchair was added to the FDR Memorial only after protests from historians and the disabled community.

© KATIE GITHENS

The Great Depression features prominently in the FDR Memorial.

on duty 8 A.M.–11:45 P.M. daily, free) at its unveiling. Initially it completely neglected the fact that Roosevelt used a wheelchair for most of his life because of the polio he contracted as a child. After protests by historians and the disabled community, the memorial's designers agreed to include a statue of FDR in his wheelchair.

Jefferson Memorial

Although it has stood on the south shore of the Tidal Basin only since 1942, the Jefferson Memorial (202/426-6841, www.nps.gov/thje, 24 hours daily, rangers on duty 9 A.M.–11:30 P.M. daily) is frequently under repair, its columns cracked by the effects of auto exhaust and acid rain. Nevertheless, the 19-foot-tall hollow bronze statue of Thomas Jefferson in furs is undeniably impressive, centered in an open-air rotunda surrounded by massive Ionic columns, an architectural copy of Jefferson's own rejected plans for the White House. The interior walls are crammed with quotes from Jefferson's voluminous writings, although not all of them are accurate. This monument is particularly nice to visit at night.

Washington D.C. National Martin Luther King Jr. Memorial

On the northwest shore of the Tidal Basin, nearly within earshot of his 1963 "I have a dream" speech, a memorial will soon pay tribute to this civil rights pioneer (888/484-3373, www.mlkmemorial.org). Progress on the memorial began in earnest after the U.S. Department of the Interior signed the construction permit in October 2009. When finished, as early as 2011, the four-acre crescent-shaped memorial will be the first on the National Mall honoring an African American. In a nod to Dr. King's call "to hew out of the mountain of despair a stone of hope," at the memorial's center will be a statue of the reverend emerging from a two-and-a-half-story granite boulder, surrounded by water, stones, and cherry trees.

Bureau of Engraving and Printing

Here thousands of people labor around the clock to produce more than $100 billion in paper currency each year, along with stamps, White

© KATIE GITHENS

Starting in 2009, millions of dollars in repairs were slated for the scenic, but sinking, seawall of the Jefferson Memorial along the Tidal Basin.

House invitations, and other U.S. securities. Through plates of thick glass, visitors can watch workers inking, stacking, cutting, and examining millions of dollars a day. There's also an interesting exhibit on the curious history of money and, yes, bags of shredded bills are for sale in the gift shop (*everyone* considers trying to glue them back together, but it's futile). Another facility was opened in Fort Worth, Texas, in 1991 to handle increased currency demand.

The Bureau (14th St. and C St. SW, 202/874-2330 or 866/874-2330, www.moneyfactory.com, Mon.–Fri.) offers free tours every 15 minutes 9 A.M.–11 A.M. and 12:15–2 P.M., with extended hours (2–7 P.M.) March–August. During these busy months you'll have to wait in line for a ticket at the ticket booth, which opens at 8 A.M. (Get there early, as in *hours* early.) The rest of the year you can just show up and wait for the next tour, which takes about an hour all told.

THE LIFE SPAN OF MONEY

U.S. currency is ubiquitous – the dollar bill is one of the best-known images in the world, right up there with Mickey Mouse and Bugs Bunny. But just how long, literally, does a U.S. bill last? According to the U.S. Treasury, it depends on how often it changes hands, which in turn depends on how big it is. Hundred-dollar bills usually last around nine years, twenties four years, tens three years, and fives two years. The lowly but ever-useful one-dollar bill has an average life span of just 22 months.

United States Holocaust Memorial Museum

A visit to the Holocaust Museum (100 Raoul Wallenberg Place SW and Independence Ave., 202/488-0400, www.ushmm.org, 10 A.M.–5:30 P.M. daily except Yom Kippur and Christmas, free) is a truly wrenching experience, but also one of the most moving sights you'll see in this or any other city. From the outside, the building intentionally resembles the high brick ovens used to dispose of the bodies of millions of European Jews. Inside, exhibits methodically trace the rise of Nazi Germany and its systematic implementation of its policy of genocide. The displays make clear that government officials in the United States and elsewhere were well aware of Hitler's implementation of the "Final Solution" but chose to do nothing. Visitors will witness many depictions of horrific atrocities, but perhaps the most affecting items are the heaps of personal effects collected by the Nazis from those they murdered: mute piles of shoes, brushes, and hair.

You'll need a timed pass to visit the permanent collection. A limited number are distributed at the museum each morning, and another quantity is made available for advance purchase online (see museum website) for a $1 service fee or by calling 877/80-USHMM. Allow at least 4–5 hours to visit. Not recommended for children under age 11.

CAPITOL HILL

U.S. Capitol

Any first-time visitor to D.C. should take advantage of the opportunity to peek at our elected congressional officials at work, if only to ensure they're earning the salaries paid by your tax dollars. The small but well-appointed Senate chamber offers each senator a private desk, whereas House representatives are jammed together in long, curved pews. The rest of the building presents its own peculiar charms: halls and rotundas stuffed with statues, and the frenzied frescoes of Constantino Brumidi, whose work was incisively described by Mark Twain as "the delirium tremens of art." A word of warning: Much of the Capitol is off-limits to non-officeholders, and visitors must heed the guidance of Capitol police, especially since the events of 9/11.

You can only visit the Capitol on a guided tour, given 8:30 A.M.–4:30 P.M. Monday–Saturday. Book a tour in advance online (www.visitthecapitol.gov) or through the offices of your senator or representative. Or show up extra early to get a free ticket from the tour kiosks on the east and west fronts of the Capitol or on the lower level of the Capitol Visitors Center.

© KATIE GITHENS

A guided tour must be scheduled to see the inside of the U.S. Capitol, but the impressive view from the outside is open any time day or night.

The visitors center, opened in December 2008, extends three floors underground and is three-quarters as large as the Capitol itself with an exhibition gallery, theaters, and a cafeteria. Backpacks and large bags are not permitted in the Capitol, nor are food and drink.

To observe the House and Senate in session, U.S. citizens must obtain passes from the office of their senator or representative. International tickets are available in the Capitol for visitors from foreign countries (picture ID is required for visits to the House gallery). The Senate buildings are to the north, on Constitution Avenue, and the House buildings are south of the Capitol on Independence Avenue. Check the *Washington Post* to see what's on the Congressional docket for each day.

Library of Congress

In 1800, the nation's legislators allocated a modest $5,000 "for the purchase of such books as may be necessary for the use of Congress." The collection was contained in a single room and was consulted as much to settle bets as to determine fine points of law. In 1814 the British put a torch to the entire nascent library. Fortunately for the nation, Thomas Jefferson was suffering through one of his periodic spasms of acute financial distress around the same time and sold to Congress his entire personal library of 6,500 volumes to rebuild the collection after the fire.

Today "Mr. Jefferson's library" consists of more than 28 million books, with an additional 90 million holdings of film, photographs, music, other media, and splendid exhibitions. The library complex consists of three structures and 532 miles of shelves. Start, appropriately, at the Jefferson Building (1st St. SE between Independence Ave. and E. Capitol St.), completed in 1897 and offering a feast of mosaics and murals, sculptures and bas-reliefs. The main reading room, with 236 desks arranged in a circular pattern beneath a 160-foot dome, is one of the most beautiful sights in the city. Inside the west front entrance is the **visitors center** (202/707-9779, www.loc.gov, 8:30 A.M.–4:30 P.M. Mon.–Sat.), where you can join free guided tours given at 10:30 A.M., 11:30 A.M., 1:30 P.M., and 2:30 P.M. (also 3:30 P.M. Mon.–Fri.).

The library's other two buildings are the James Madison Building (101 Independence Ave. SE) and the John Adams Building (2nd St. SE between Independence Ave. and E. Capitol St.). The Library of Congress is not a lending library—materials must be perused on-site.

U.S. Supreme Court

Completed in 1935, this structure is undeniably opulent, with lush curtains, grandiose statues, and portentous inscriptions at every turn. The main chamber is particularly impressive, with the seats of the nine justices placed high above the rest of the court.

Check the schedule in advance to find out when the Court (202/479-3211, www.supremecourtus.gov, 9 A.M.–4:30 P.M. Mon.–Fri.) hears oral arguments. The public is welcome to attend, but there is limited seating, allocated on a first-come, first-served basis to those willing to line up outside the building. When the Court is not in session, visitors can view exhibits, watch a film about the Supremes (no, not the singing group), and attend courtroom lectures on the half hour 9:30 A.M.–3:30 P.M.

Union Station

When it was completed in 1907, Union Station, modeled after the Baths of Caracalla in Rome, was the largest train station in the world. For the next 50 years, most visitors to the city first set foot in D.C. on the station's elegant marble floors. By the 1970s, however, the place had become a national embarrassment: The floors buckled, torrential rains caved in portions of the roof, and a runaway train had slammed into the station, scattering spiraling shards of cars.

In 1981, Union Station was shut and sealed, until a business–government consortium invested $160 million to restore it to its former beaux arts grandeur. Today visitors revel in acres of white marble flooring, bronze grilles, coffered ceilings, gold leaf, Honduran mahogany, and a plethora of stone carvings and statues. Once again a working train station, Union Station (50 Massachusetts Ave. NE, 202/289-1908, www.unionstationdc.com) is open all day, every day, and there is no admission charge. There are more than 100 places to eat and shop (most 10 A.M.–9 P.M. Mon.–Sat., noon–6 P.M. Sun.), and the catacomb-like lower level has a food court.

U.S. Botanic Garden

Another lovely idea of Thomas Jefferson's, this humid haven has enchanted visitors since 1820. Wander the unmistakable glass-domed conservatory amid a wealth of tropical, subtropical, and desert plants. Guide dinosaur-entranced young ones to the garden of the Jurassic, or picnic on a flowery terrace overlooking the Capitol Reflecting Pool. The conservatory (100 Maryland Ave. SW, 202/225-8333, www.usbg.gov, 10 A.M.–5 P.M. daily) sits southwest of the Capitol. It's a great place to go just for a big gulp of fragrant, oxygen-rich air. Before you go, check the website to see what's in bloom.

West of the conservatory on Independence Avenue is the three-acre National Garden (10 A.M.–5 P.M. daily), opened in 2006. It was planned to highlight "unusual, useful, and ornamental" plants from the mid-Atlantic and includes a butterfly garden, rose garden, and water garden. South across Independence Avenue is the more formal Bartholdi Park (dawn–dusk daily), named after the sculptor of the ornate fountain at its center.

Eastern Market

Opened in 1873 in a sky-lit redbrick hall, this local touchstone is the oldest continuously operating market in D.C. (225 7th St. SE, www.easternmarketdc.com, 7 A.M.–7 P.M. Tues.–Fri., 7 A.M.–6 P.M. Sat., 9 A.M.–5 P.M. Sun.). A fire gutted the building in 2007, but the market reopened in 2009 after $22 million in repairs; it's now back to selling fresh meats, seafood, cheese, flowers, and baked goods—and fresh produce at the farmers' line along 7th Street on Saturdays. If all the grocery shopping stirs up your appetite, grab a bite at a café under the same roof, **Market Lunch,** famous for its crab cakes and blueberry pancakes called "bluebucks" (202/547-8444, breakfast and lunch Tues.–Sat., lunch only on Sun.).

On Sunday, the flea market comes to life in the chain-linked schoolyard across the street (7th and C St. SE, www.easternmarket.net). Peruse the wares of more than 175 exhibitors, selling everything from vintage posters to handmade furniture. For arts and crafts, check out the stalls along North Carolina Avenue and 7th Street SE, open on Saturday too.

WHITE HOUSE AREA

The White House

First occupied by John Adams, the mansion at 1600 Pennsylvania Avenue NW was known as the President's House until it was whitewashed to cover smoke damage from the 1814 British burning of the city. It's not nearly as accessible today as it was during Jefferson's time, when the president examined mastodon fossils in the East Room and enthusiastic dairymen would bustle in to deposit huge cheeses. Nevertheless, it's the only chief executive's abode in the world that is open to tourists. When visiting the White House, don't step across the boundary ropes or make other foolish moves—those friendly men patrolling the halls can quickly turn serious.

Self-guided group tours of the White House (202/456-7041, www.whitehouse.gov) for groups of 10 or more are free, although you'll have to secure tickets through your congressperson up to six months in advance. Tours are scheduled about one month ahead of time and take place 7:30 A.M.–11 A.M. Tuesday–Thursday, until noon Friday, and until 1 P.M. Saturday. Stop by the White House Visitors Center at the southeast corner of 15th and E Streets NW (7:30 A.M.–4 P.M. daily) before or after to view a 20-minute video and displays on the famous abode's architecture, furnishings, and other interesting details.

Corcoran Gallery of Art

A block southwest of the White House, the Corcoran (17th St. NW and New York Ave. NW, 202/639-1700, www.corcoran.org,

10 A.M.–5 P.M. Wed.–Sun., $10) is at once a prestigious arts school and the largest museum in D.C. outside the Smithsonian. With lectures and traveling exhibits ranging from photography by Annie Leibovitz and Ansel Adams to advice from the reigning fashionista on *Project Runway,* it adds a fresh edge to the District's art museum scene. The permanent collection includes works from Renoir and other European masters, as well as American artists such as Winslow Homer, Thomas Cole, and Aaron Douglas.

OLD DOWNTOWN AND THE FEDERAL TRIANGLE

The area enclosed by Pennsylvania Avenue, Constitution Avenue, and 15th Street is home to such stern, solemn edifices as the Internal Revenue Service (IRS) and Justice Department buildings. It has a somewhat sordid history; for many years, the area was the most notorious neighborhood in D.C., popularly known as "Murder Bay," and during the Civil War it was called "Hooker's Division" in honor of the Union general and the prostitutes encamped there. (Etymology can be a fascinating subject.) The place didn't get straightened out until the U.S. government bought the land in the 1930s, razing the shacks and replacing them with grim granite.

The area north of Federal Triangle, between the White House and the Capitol Building, and bordered to the north by New York and Massachusetts Avenues, was the city's original downtown area. Popular restaurants and theaters, fashionable tailors' shops, and other more practical businesses kept those in office from having to stray too far from their seats of power for dining, entertainment, and life's necessities. Between the time the buildings of the Federal Triangle were built and the late 1960s, the area became run-down again, gaining the name "Old Downtown" to separate it from "New Downtown"—the area north of the White House, where new businesses opened shop next door to vendors fleeing run-down Old Downtown. The entire Old Downtown area, especially Pennsylvania Avenue, underwent a major face-lift in the 1980s. Today, the area again boasts popular restaurants and galleries, as well as landscaped plazas and memorials.

doors of the U.S. Department of Justice in Federal Triangle

WHERE IS J STREET?

If you look at a map of D.C.'s spider web of roads, you'll notice that I Street and K Street are right next to each other. Some people have said that this was an intentional slight by designer Pierre L'Enfant against John Jay, the first chief justice of the Supreme Court, for an offense that has been lost to history. The truth, though, is more prosaic. In 18th-century English, the letters *I* and *J* were often written the same way and used interchangeably. To avoid confusion, designers decided to leave one out on the street plan, and *I* won out. (It's still often written as Eye Street to distinguish it from the number *1*.)

National Building Museum

In 1885, the general-cum-architect Montgomery Meigs erected the Pension Building. Damned at its dedication as an "unsightly monstrosity," the structure is recognized today as a masterpiece. Built of more than 15 million bricks, it features a 1,200-foot-long terra-cotta frieze of Union soldiers forever filing for pensions. Eight central Corinthian columns, some of the largest in the world, dominate a great hall large enough to contain a 15-story building.

Today the eccentric old edifice is home to the National Building Museum (401 F St. NW, 202/272-2448, www.nbm.org, 10 A.M.–5 P.M. Mon.–Sat., 11 A.M.–5 P.M. Sun., $5 suggested donation), the only institution in the United States dedicated to architectural achievements. On permanent display are exhibits dedicated to D.C. and the Pension Building. Past temporary shows have covered the classic American barn, architectural plans in New Orleans after Hurricane Katrina, and design proposals for the new World Trade Center. Free 45-minute building tours are given at 11:30 A.M., 12:30 P.M., and 1:30 P.M. daily. It also offers family programs and a Lego Building Zone area for kids, as well as films, lectures, music, and other special programs.

Donald W. Reynolds Center for American Art and Portraiture

After a six-year renovation, the former **Smithsonian American Art Museum** and **National Portrait Gallery** were combined into one entity, known as the Reynolds Center (8th and F Sts. NW, 202/633-1000, www.reynoldscenter.org, 11:30 A.M.–7 P.M. daily, free) for short. Housed in an imposing edifice Philip Johnson once adjudged "the greatest building in the world," the American Art Museum's eclectic collection includes truly marvelous works in the folk and ethnic traditions. Don't miss Albert Bierstadt's landscape painting and D.C. janitor James Hampton's *The Throne of the Third Heaven of the Nations' Millennium General* sculpture, the fruit of some 15 years of cementing together found objects such as lightbulbs, electrical cables, and aluminum foil.

On the site where D.C. designer Pierre L'Enfant once wished to build a national cathedral is a fascinating collection of America's heroes and villains portrayed in sculptures, paintings, and photographs. Highlights of the National Portrait Gallery include Gilbert Stuart's famous "Lansdowne" image of George Washington; a treasury of 19th-century black-and-white photography; and a dizzying diversity of portraiture saluting American athletes, politicians, and artists—comedian Stephen Colbert even got permission to hang his portrait above a drinking fountain...for about six weeks.

The Reynolds Center also has two cafés and an art conservation lab on-site.

The National Aquarium

The nation's oldest public aquarium (202/482-2825, www.nationalaquarium.com, 9 A.M.–5 P.M. daily, $9 adults, $4 children 3–11, cash or check only) is stuck unexpectedly (and unfortunately) in the basement of the Commerce Building. Besides the usual collection of fish-tank fare, it offers belligerent fiddler crabs banging on the glass, sleepy alligators, gape-mouthed eels exuding yellow slime, and pale axolotl salamanders. A touch pool allows young ones to stroke horseshoe crabs.

Animals are fed daily at 2 P.M. The entrance

to the museum is on the west side of 14th Street between Pennsylvania and Constitution Avenues NW.

J. Edgar Hoover FBI Building

The free guided tour of the FBI headquarters (935 Pennsylvania Ave. NW, 202/324-3447, www.fbi.gov) offers an extremely selective history of the Bureau, including Dillinger, drugs, and a firearms demonstration by an FBI sharpshooter. As of 2010, tours were suspended pending the completion of extensive renovations. Contact the Bureau for an update.

Old Post Office

When it was completed in 1899, this former home of the U.S. Postal Service was described as "a cross between a cathedral and a cotton mill." These days, surrounded by the abominations of modern architecture, the old joint looks pretty good, one of the last remaining examples of Richardsonian Romanesque architecture in the city.

The Old Post Office (1100 Pennsylvania Ave. NW, 202/289-4224, www.oldpostofficedc.com, free) houses federal workers for such agencies as the National Endowment for the Arts (NEA) and the National Endowment for the Humanities (NEH). Downstairs are dozens of eateries and shops, and you can take a tour up the 315-foot granite clock tower, the second-highest point in the city after the Washington Monument and one of the finest aerial views in D.C. Contact the National Park Service (202/606-8691) for information.

National Archives

Preservationists of "the nation's memory," archivists here determine the worth of billions of documents generated annually by the world's busiest government. Pride of place goes to the Declaration of Independence, the Constitution, and the Bill of Rights, which are displayed daily and then mechanically lowered into a vault to shield them from vandals and nuclear attack. Famous primarily as a center

© KATIE GITHENS

The Old Post Office has views to rival the Washington Monument, with a much shorter wait in line.

© KATIE GITHENS

The Declaration of Independence, the Constitution, and the Bill of Rights are on display at the National Archives.

of genealogical research, the Archives (700 Pennsylvania Ave. NW, 866/272-6272, www.archives.gov, free) have in recent years become a pilgrimage site for those wishing to listen to Nixon's Watergate tapes.

The entrance to the Rotunda (10 A.M.–7 P.M. daily in spring and summer, to 5:30 P.M. in fall and winter) is on Constitution Avenue between 9th and 7th Streets NW. Opening hours of the Research Center vary; that entrance is on the north side of the building on Pennsylvania Avenue. For more information see the online National Archives Experience (www.archives.gov/nae).

Ford's Theatre National Historic Site

In one of history's tragic events, president Abraham Lincoln was shot in Ford's Theatre just five days after Confederate general Robert E. Lee surrendered at Appomattox. Today the basement of the theater is a museum to the president's martyrdom (511 10th St. NW, 202/426-6924, www.nps.gov/foth, 9 A.M.–5 P.M. daily, free), where you can see the bronze of a slumping, exhausted Lincoln, the simple contents of his pockets at the time of his death, and the .44 single-shot derringer used by assassin John Wilkes Booth, a famous actor at the time.

Upstairs the show still goes on in the active theater, renovated in 2009 (202/347-4833, www.fordstheatre.org); check its website for a performance schedule and buy tickets from Ticketmaster (202/397-7328, www.ticketmaster.com). You'll also need a free, timed ticket to tour Ford's Theatre and the museum, available first-come, first-served at the box office starting at 8:30 A.M. or in advance from Ticketmaster for $1.50 per ticket. The Ford's Theatre website lists daily talks scheduled and closures for visitors (during rehearsals and matinees, usually Thursdays and weekends).

Newseum

If the *New York Times'* slogan is "All the news that's fit to print," the mammoth Newseum's (555 Pennsylvania Ave. NW, 888/639-7386, www.newseum.org, 9 A.M.–5 P.M. daily, $20 adults, $13 children) could be "All the news that fits in 250,000 square feet."

The powerful 9/11 exhibit at the Newseum is a must-see.

© KATIE GITHENS

From the concourse level of the museum, opened in spring 2009, pass by a graffitied section of the Berlin Wall and board a large glass elevator. You'll rise up, up seven floors to the terrace and one of the best views of the U.S. Capitol. Then descend your way through five centuries of journalism displayed in 14 interactive galleries, 15 theaters, and hundreds of historical front pages, from Lincoln's assassination to the *Apollo* moon landing.

Must-sees include a powerfully moving 9/11 exhibit beneath the twisted Twin Towers broadcast antennae, and the most complete collection of Pulitzer Prize photographs assembled anywhere. Footage of interviews with the photojournalists responsible for these iconic images—the Kent State shooting, the napalmed girl in Vietnam—tells the backstory.

While some exhibits may be too intense for children (they're noted accordingly), others are great for budding news reporters. Kids and grown-ups can go on camera to tape their own newscast or take a seat in the 3-D *I-Witness!* movie.

GEORGETOWN

President Kennedy lived in this classy neighborhood sandwiched between Rock Creek and the Potomac River 1957–1961 during his pre-presidential term as a U.S. Senator. No one is certain who named the quarter: Some say it was named after one of the King Georges or one or another of the area's founders. Regardless, Georgetown didn't become part of the District of Columbia until after the Civil War.

Since then, it has had ups and downs, but the present moment is decidedly up. Between the peaceful towpaths of the old C&O Canal to the south and what has come to be known as "the most civilized square mile in America" to the north abides some of the most expensive real estate on earth. An average-sized house in Georgetown runs into the millions of dollars. Like Beverly Hills in Los Angeles, the homes in Georgetown are pedigreed, known by their former famous owners, like the house at 3017 N Street where Jacqueline Kennedy lived for a time.

Despite being 20 minutes by foot from

Visitors walk the sidewalk labyrinth at Georgetown's waterfront park.

the nearest Metro station, Georgetown definitely deserves, and can easily consume, a day or more of touring. Walk the historic homes, idle at Dumbarton Oaks, and dine in town. History and personality blend in Georgetown's streets. Many great authors, such as Katherine Anne Porter and Sinclair Lewis, have called the neighborhood home. Historical figures such as Alexander Graham Bell lived in Georgetown, as did Dr. Walter Reed, the American army surgeon who proved yellow fever was carried by mosquitoes. Georgetown's main crossroads is at M Street and Wisconsin Avenue, a bustling area of jazz clubs, good restaurants, and boutiques.

One block south of M Street toward the Potomac, you'll find a byway with a much slower pace: the **Chesapeake and Ohio Canal.** Lock number 4 of this 184-mile-long National Historical Park (202/653-5190, www.nps.gov/choh) is in Georgetown and features a working barge operated by rangers in 19th-century costumes that takes visitors under the bridge and through the locks in a mule-towed journey through the past.

A bit farther south is **Washington Harbor,** a terraced riverfront extravaganza of condominiums, shops, and restaurants. Once something of a joke, the Harbor has grown into a delightful and popular setting for weekend brunch and happy hours. There's great people-watching—or regatta-watching when the summertime rowing and dragon-boat races begin. Georgetown has continued to spiff up its waterfront by converting a former parking lot just upriver in front of Whitehurst Freeway into a landscaped park popular with well-coiffed dogs and their people. Be sure to do a loop around the sidewalk labyrinth.

Movie buffs will recognize the ***"Exorcist* stairs"** that climb steeply from the gas station at the west end of M Street past Key Bridge up to Prospect Street. This dark, narrow staircase was made famous in the climactic scene of the 1973 horror movie, based on the book by Georgetown alumnus William Peter Blatty. Local sports teams do the five-story climb on training runs.

Dumbarton Oaks

The crown jewel of Georgetown is Dumbarton Oaks (1703 32nd St. NW, 202/339-6401, www.doaks.org), a former estate that is now a museum and outstanding garden spot. In

Rowers and scullers are a frequent sight on the Potomac River.

1944, as World War II moved into its final phase, the leaders of the United States, Britain, China, and the Soviet Union met here to lay the groundwork for what was to become the United Nations.

It's easiest to think of the estate in three parts. The first is the 16-acre compound owned by Harvard University and known as the Dumbarton Oaks Research Library and Collection. Here, one block east of Wisconsin Avenue between R and S Streets, you'll find the estate's renowned collection of some 1,500 eastern Mediterranean artifacts dating from A.D. 330–1453. The library holds more than 12,000 Byzantine coins, one of the most complete collections in the world. The museum entrance is on 32nd Street between R and S Streets NW.

Next comes Dumbarton Oaks Park (2–6 P.M. Tues.–Sun. mid-Mar.–Oct., $8 adults, $5 children; 2–5 P.M. Tues.–Sun. Nov.–mid-Mar., free). Ten acres are given over to one of the finest examples of European-style formal gardens in America, boasting nearly 1,000 rose bushes, 10 pools, and 9 fountains. The garden entrance is at R and 31st Streets NW. The remaining 17 acres of the estate are covered by well-groomed parkland.

Georgetown University

Another cornerstone of the community is the 104-acre main campus of Georgetown University (202/687-0100, www.georgetown.edu), one of the nation's premier schools for law and international affairs. Just over 3,000 students (who cheer on the Hoyas during the electrifying basketball season) attend the oldest Catholic and Jesuit university in the nation, founded in 1789. Free maps and brochures on the gorgeous campus and its environs are available at the main gate at 37th and O Streets NW.

Old Stone House

One of the oldest standing structures in the city, the Old Stone House (3051 M St. NW, 202/895-6070, www.nps.gov/olst, noon–5 P.M. daily, free) was built in 1765 by cabinetmaker Christopher Layman in what was then the Town of George. Over the years the dwelling also served as boardinghouse, tavern, bordello, and artists' studio. Today its low doorways and lumpy beds are preserved as a relic of working-class life in pre-Revolutionary times. Rumors that Pierre L'Enfant worked here while designing D.C. helped secure congressional protection for the structure in the 1950s. It's said that children are those most likely to encounter the many ghosts inhabiting the structure. The garden is open from dawn to dusk daily.

NORTHWEST D.C.

A successive series of residential neighborhoods interspersed with lively streets full of restaurants and nightspots gives this part of the city its own distinct character and allure.

Dupont

Arguably, **Dupont Circle** marks the center of the area that fills the district's borders between Adams-Morgan and the Maryland state line. On one side of the circle, popular with chess players, bike messengers, and office workers on their lunch breaks, sits some of the city's great think tanks, such as the **Brookings Institution,** established in 1927. Along Connecticut Avenue near the circle you'll find good restaurants in a variety of price ranges. To the north, **Kramerbooks & Afterwords Café** (1517 Connecticut Ave. NW, 202/387-1400, www.kramers.com, 7:30 A.M.–1 A.M. daily) is a D.C. institution, "Serving Latte to the Literati Since 1976." The bookstore has a café in back, where, after browsing the aisles, you can hear live music Wednesday–Saturday. On Friday and Saturday, Kramerbooks stays open 24 hours for late-night literary binges and flirtation.

Opened in 1921 in a private home, the **Phillips Collection** (1600 21st St. NW, 202/387-2151, www.phillipscollection.org, 10 A.M.–5 P.M. Tues.–Sat., to 8:30 P.M. Thurs., 11 A.M.–6 P.M. Sun., free Tues.–Fri., $10 adults Sat.–Sun.) was America's first modern art museum. The permanent collection of close to 3,000 pieces includes Renoir's *Luncheon* *of the Boating Party* and works by Van Gogh, Degas, Rothko, O'Keeffe, Picasso, and Klee. Admission is $10 for visitors over 18 during exhibitions. Indoor concerts are offered at 4 P.M. on Sundays October–May (included in the ticket price).

Embassy Row

Along the two-mile stretch of Massachusetts Avenue between Scott Circle and Observatory Circle, you'll find the greatest concentration of D.C.'s more than 170 embassies (for a complete list, see www.embassy.org). Embassy Row came to be after the stock market collapse of 1929 forced out once-wealthy District socialites. By the 1960s foreign governments began buying up the real estate. Look for the countries' flags or plaques in front of the palatial residences to find out who lives inside.

Adams-Morgan

North of Dupont, Adams-Morgan is D.C.'s version of New York City's East Village, only smaller and with fewer tattoos. Most of this teeming quarter's nightlife takes place along two main drags, Columbia Road and 18th Street, which meet in a *V* at their northern apex. A little bit tony, a little bit tawdry, Adams-Morgan is a place where Washingtonians feel free to step outside the bars of their pin-striped suits. This is an immigrant neighborhood, a largely Hispanic enclave that is also home to wealthy Anglos and a veritable United Nations of other ethnicities. Once a row of tired Ethiopian restaurants scrunched cheek-by-jowl into redbrick townhouses, Adams-Morgan has hip-hopped into its own over the last decade, as Washington discovered that there was life after legislation. The streets actually become more crowded after 6 P.M., while the rest of D.C. rolls up its sidewalks.

Along with delightfully leafy lanes lined with elegant (and expensive) townhouses, Adams-Morgan offers a wide variety of good restaurants and entertainment—the neighborhood's name is synonymous with its bar scene. Stroll up the block to a club to close the night, unwind with some dancing, or just relax and listen to good music.

A big problem is that there are no convenient Metro stops near Adams-Morgan. It's a long walk from the two nearest stations, Dupont Circle and Woodley Park–Zoo, to the heart of the quarter. It's best to pay for taxis or, better yet, let a friend drive; finding a parking spot in Adams-Morgan has been known to reduce would-be visitors to tears. The No. 42 bus connects Dupont to Adams-Morgan and Mount Pleasant.

National Zoological Park

Under the auspices of the Smithsonian Institution, the National Zoo is one of the nation's preeminent animal parks. More than three miles of trails wander past more than 2,700 animals caged on 163 hilly acres at the edge of Rock Creek. Visitors will find no class hierarchy here: paramecia and leafcutter ants are displayed as proudly as lions, tigers, and bears. An enclave of naked mole rats even gets exposure via the Internet with the zoo's live Naked Mole Rat Webcam.

Visitors can view such rarities as Komodo dragons, watch the cuttlefish transform from a mass of transparent jelly into a voracious predator, or ponder the ways animals use their brains, described in the "Think Tank" exhibit. The rainforest environment of the Amazonia exhibit approaches D.C.'s own August heat and humidity. Orangutans occasionally swing overhead along a specially built network of platforms and cables. The biggest news is always the most recent darling animal baby. While D.C. tends to be panda-crazy, the baby gorilla Kibibi (meaning "little lady" in Swahili) held the spotlight in 2010.

Although the zoo (3001 Connecticut Ave. NW, 202/673-4800, www.nationalzoo.si.edu) is free, you'll have to pay for parking. The grounds are open 6 A.M.–8 P.M. daily April–October, to 6 P.M. November–March, buildings 10 A.M.–6 P.M. daily April–October, to 4:30 P.M. November–March. It's best to come during the week, early in the morning or late in the afternoon, to avoid the crowds and to find the animals up and about. Enter off Rock

Creek Parkway or from Connecticut Avenue in Woodley Park.

Rock Creek Park

These 1,750 acres were purchased in 1890 by Congress for the "pleasant valleys and ravines, primeval forests and open fields, its running waters, its rocks clothed with rich ferns and mosses, its repose and tranquility, its light and shade, its ever-varying shrubbery, its beautiful and extensive views." Rock Creek Park still offers all that, as well as more than one million wildflowers at the right time of year.

Bordering the Upper Northwest to the east, the city's largest park (202/895-6070, www.nps.gov/rocr) is a magical finger of green pointing toward the apex of the D.C. diamond. Hikers, horseback riders, cyclists, and joggers have the right of way, and on Sunday, with long sections of the park's roads, including Rock Creek Parkway, closed to cars, they take control. The park offers some 15 miles of **hiking trails,** from toddler-friendly to quite rugged. Trail maps are available at both the park headquarters and the nature center. The park is generally safe, but hiking alone (especially for women) or after dark is unwise.

An 11-mile **bike path** from the Lincoln Memorial to the Maryland border runs the full length of the park; it's paved the entire distance and closed to vehicular traffic on weekends and holidays. Numerous access points make visiting the park on bike or on foot an easy day's outing. Trail **horseback rides** ($38 per hour) are available Tuesday–Thursday evenings and twice a day on weekends at the **Rock Creek Park Horse Center** (5100 Glover Rd. NW, 202/362-0117, www.rockcreekhorsecenter.com), located next to the nature center.

Next door, the park's **nature center** (5200 Glover Rd. NW, 202/895-6070, 9 A.M.–5 P.M. Wed.–Sun.) includes a planetarium. **Peirce Mill** (Tilden St. NW at Beach Dr., 202/895-6070) was originally built in 1820 and is the last existing gristmill in the District. Next to a springhouse and barn, it is awaiting fundraising efforts to restore it to working condition.

The Rock Creek Park **cemetery** (Rock Creek Church Rd. NW, 8 A.M.–6 P.M. daily) is the oldest in the city and home to one of the most arresting statues in D.C. In 1883 Marian Adams, wife of historian Henry Adams, downed enough photographic chemicals to end her life. Her husband interred her in Rock Creek Cemetery, then commissioned sculptor Augustus Saint-Gaudens to create a monument in bronze, adding "no attempt is to be made to make it intelligible to the average mind." When the work was ready, the grave-keepers were horrified, saying they wanted no part of it. But Adams persisted, and the cloaked, hooded lady was set among holly and ivy in section E. The sculptor called it *"The Peace of God or The Mystery of the Hereafter...beyond pain and beyond joy,"* but most visitors agree with Mark Twain that the most appropriate designation is simply *Grief.*

North of Adams-Morgan

Just north of Adams-Morgan is **Mount Pleasant,** an up-and-coming but still funky little community with a strong Hispanic presence. Centered on Mount Pleasant Street west of 16th Street, the neighborhood enjoys a choice location close to the zoo, Rock Creek Park, and Adams-Morgan. Because rents haven't skyrocketed here quite like they have elsewhere—yet—it's popular with the twenty- and thirtysomethings who congregate at local cafés and watering holes.

Northwest from Dupont Circle across Rock Creek Park is **Woodley Park,** known principally for its entrance to the National Zoo. The area also claims to be home to more international restaurants than anywhere in D.C., which is saying a lot in this international metropolis. Beyond Woodley Park is exclusive **Cleveland Park,** where former President Grover Cleveland built his "summer White House," and consequently lent his name to the neighborhood. If you find yourself here, try to catch a movie at the opulent **Uptown Theater** (3426 Connecticut Ave. NW, 202/966-5400), a 1936 art deco palace with a large balcony and a 40-by-70-foot screen.

Heading farther north, the campus of

American University (4400 Massachusetts Ave. NW, 202/885-1000, www.american.edu), alma mater of Willard Scott and novelist Anne Beattie, covers 84 acres in the area known as **Tenleytown.** The final reaches of Northwest D.C. extend out to Friendship Heights and Chevy Chase at the border with Maryland.

Washington National Cathedral

Medieval cathedrals often required centuries to complete, so perhaps it's not so embarrassing that 199 years passed before this one was considered finished. In 1791 D.C. designer Pierre L'Enfant envisioned a "church intended for national purposes, and assigned to the special use of no particular Sect or denomination, but equally open to all." In 1893 Congress finally allocated funds for the edifice, and in 1990 the last stone was placed atop a west front pinnacle.

The cathedral (3101 Wisconsin Ave. NW, 202/537-6200, www.cathedral.org/cathedral, 10 A.M.–5:30 P.M. Mon.–Fri., 10 A.M.–4:30 P.M. Sat., 8 A.M.–5 P.M. Sun., free) is a truly magnificent structure, and its stone and wood carvings, stained glass, and metalwork are unsurpassed on these shores. The Gothic wonderment is constructed of Indiana limestone, with all details carved from the walls by hand. High above dwell angels, gargoyles, and grotesques; one carving (you'll have to use binoculars to see it) is of Darth Vader's mask. Outside, visitors to the 57-acre grounds can stroll a medieval walled garden of roses and herbs.

Sunday sermons are at 11:15 A.M. Evensong (or evening prayer) is held at 5:30 P.M. Monday–Friday; call for other service times. Guided tours are offered at varying hours.

NORTHEAST D.C.

While the heart of Washington's tourist attractions is squarely centered on the National Mall, the unassuming Northeast quadrant of D.C. has a few tricks up its sleeve. Returning visitors and locals especially will appreciate seeing the city from a new perspective and exploring Northeast D.C.'s parks and sights.

© KATIE GITHENS

Begun in 1907, the Washington National Cathedral was not completed until 1990.

© KATIE GITHENS

The National Cathedral has 231 stained-glass windows, even one with a piece of moon rock.

D.C.'S MISSING PIECE

The District of Columbia used to be a perfect diamond shape, its land extending as far south as Alexandria, which was donated by Virginia along with part of Fairfax County to form the newly organized capital district in 1789. Residents welcomed the honor at first but started to grumble when the government prohibited the construction of public buildings south of the Potomac and denied District residents congressional representation and the right to vote for president (the former grievance, amazingly, is still an issue). The threat of a ban on slavery in the District was the final straw. Several petitions later, in 1847, the region was given back to Virginia, leaving a ragged bite out of D.C.'s southern border.

You can still see most of the 40 boundary stones laid out every mile around the perimeter in 1791 and 1792 by Andrew Ellicott and his surveying team. See the website www.boundarystones.org for details and directions.

U.S. National Arboretum

Don't be fooled by the rickety appearance of the New York Avenue entrance. The U.S. National Arboretum (3501 New York Ave. NE, 202/245-2726, www.usna.usda.gov, 8 A.M.–5 P.M. daily, free) is a gem for walkers, botanists, backyard gardeners, and lovers of fresh air. The expansive 446 acres of gardens are crisscrossed with hiking trails and 9.5 miles of roadways. Besides a grove of state trees, an herb garden, and, in spring, the jubilantly blooming Azalea Hill, the arboretum inherited the original marble columns from the east face of the Capitol building when it was expanded in the 1950s. Arranged in a semicircle on a hill, the Capitol Columns look almost mythical, especially during one of the arboretum's popular **moonlight tours** ($22, registration required).

Be sure to stop at the **National Bonsai and Penjing Museum** (10 A.M.–4 P.M. daily, free), which has specimens of living bonsai trees that are centuries older than the United States of America.

Basilica of the National Shrine of the Immaculate Conception

You can't miss the gold-and-blue dome of the basilica, one of the 10 largest church edifices in the world (400 Michigan Ave., 202/526-8300, www.nationalshrine.com, 7 A.M.–7 P.M. daily Apr.–Oct., until 6 P.M. Nov.–Mar.)—it often astonishes D.C. residents who infrequently venture into this part of the District. Come to tour the basilica (see website for details), or attend one of the six masses held daily.

Entertainment and Nightlife

CLUBS

In Adams-Morgan, **Habana Village** (1834 Columbia Rd. NW, 202/462-6310) offers a different activity for each of its three levels: food, entertainment, and dancing. The restaurant ambience is wicker and white wine—and *mojitos,* of course. Live music groups play by the bar, but there's not much space to dance. Upstairs there's plenty more, and a Latin-flavored singles scene gyrates to the strains of merengue, salsa, cumbia, reggae, flamenco, and tango. It can get crowded, but the atmosphere is more fun than claustrophobic. Grab a drink and join in!

Over on 18th Street, redheads get half-price drinks at **Madam's Organ** (2461 18th St. NW, 202/667-5370). This blues/reggae bar has survived being named one of the country's best by *Playboy* magazine and features live bands, stuffed animal heads, and Southern cooking under the motto, "Where the beautiful people go to get ugly." Look for the unmistakably voluptuous painting on the wall outside. There's also a rooftop deck.

Oenophiles would be wise to visit wine bars **Proof** (775 G St. NW, 202/737-7663) in Penn Quarter and **Cork** (1720 14th St. NW, 202/265-2675) in Logan Circle. The latter has 50 wines by the glass and 160 bottles to explore, along with bimonthly wine tastings. Both serve delicious small bites to pair with their whites and reds.

Anchoring the U Street nightlife scene, **Bohemian Caverns** (2001 11th St. NW, 202/299-0800, www.bohemiancaverns.com) has hosted every jazz legend imaginable: Duke Ellington, Billie Holiday, Louis Armstrong, John Coltrane...the show goes on Tuesday–Saturday evenings in a three-level club, including the original underground venue that opened in 1926.

A few blocks away, comfy velvet couches and Peruvian appetizers are the signatures of the **Chi-Cha Lounge** (1624 U St. NW, 202/234-8400). It's often crowded, with semi-regular live jazz and Latin music, but it's still dimly lit enough for intimate conversation.

Farther east down U Street, the **9:30 Club** (815 V St. NW, 202/265-0930, www.930.com) is a midsized venue that has hosted the likes of Ziggy Marley, the Beastie Boys, and Smashing Pumpkins for more than 30 years. It's one of the best places to see live music in the city, if not the country, and can hold up to 1,200 dancing, drinking guests on two levels. Head to the far downstairs bar to escape the crush, and visit the club's website for up-to-the-minute concert information.

Down 14th Street is another great (albeit smaller) live music venue, **The Black Cat** (1811 14th St. NW, 202/667-4490, www.blackcatdc.com), which hosts more cacophonous, up-and-coming groups. The red bar on the 1st floor also has music in back. Nearby is **HR-57** (1610 14th St. NW, 202/667-3700, www.hr57.org), subtitled the Center for the Preservation of Jazz and Blues. This zero-frills place, named after a Congressional resolution that declared jazz a national treasure, offers live performances by amateurs and professionals on Wednesday–Sunday evenings. Tickets are usually $8–12 and you can bring your own wine for a $3 corkage fee. Order a plate of soul food and settle back in the garage-like space; places this authentic are rare.

A Georgetown landmark (assuming you can find it), **Blues Alley** (1073 Wisconsin Ave. NW, 202/337-4141, www.bluesalley.com) is a side-street success. The 40-table club attracts top jazz and blues acts to the town that gave birth to Duke Ellington. Cover charges are high, and there's a drink minimum, but you get what you pay for. Part of the tab goes toward the Blues Alley Music Society, which promotes jazz performance and education in the city.

THEATERS AND CONCERTS

John F. Kennedy Center for the Performing Arts

This D.C. landmark (2700 F St. NW, 202/467-4600 or 800/444-1324, www.kennedy-center.org) is home to the **Washington Ballet** (www.washingtonballet.org), the **National Symphony Orchestra (NSO)** (www.kennedy-center.org/nso), and the **Washington National Opera** (202/295-2400 or 800/876-7372, www.dc-opera.org).

The Nutcracker has a local twist when the Washington Ballet performs it. George Washington is the Nutcracker Prince, King George III is the Rat King, and dancing cherry blossoms twirl across the stage. Contemporary and modern pieces from choreographers such as Twyla Tharp and Mark Morris revolve through the company's repertoire as well.

Founded in 1931, the NSO has enjoyed a succession of brilliant musical directors: Antal Dorati, Mstislav Rostropovich, and, today, Leonard Slatkin. The NSO has promised to visit all 50 states, but don't miss them while you're in Washington.

General director Plácido Domingo gives the Washington National Opera the sex appeal and gravitas it so deserves, making D.C. one of the world's centers for song. The Kennedy Center

Opera House offers a prolific schedule of performances September–June.

The center also presents repertory theater, jazz, Shakespeare, and more. Free performances featuring performers from the local area and around the world are held every day at 6 P.M. on the Millennium Stage. Tours of the center's main theaters and selected art holdings are offered 10 A.M.–5 P.M. during the week (to 1 P.M. on weekends). Call 202/416-8340 for details.

Other Venues

The elegant **National Theatre** (1321 Pennsylvania Ave. NW, 202/628-6161, www.nationaltheatre.org) is Washington's only Broadway-style theater and the city's oldest cultural institution. *West Side Story* had its world premiere here, as did *Hello, Dolly!* The theater's acoustics are excellent, but watch out for the distant seats in Balcony Two. The Helen Hayes Gallery (a workshop-sized auditorium) hosts free events on Monday evenings.

The classical and Shakespearean adaptations for which the **Shakespeare Theatre** (450 7th St. NW, 202/547-1122 or 877/487-8849, www.shakespearedc.org) is known are vivid and nontraditional productions, attracting big-name actors. The company regularly returns to more traditional presentations, such as Tennessee Williams's *Sweet Bird of Youth.*

From repertory classics to musicals, performances at the **Arena Stage** (1101 6th St. SW, 202/488-3300, www.arenastage.org) have won more than 50 prestigious Helen Hayes theater awards. The Arena was the first theater outside of New York to capture a coveted Tony Award. James Earl Jones, Dianne Wiest, Kevin Kline, James Woods, and many other notable actors have graced its stages. The theater will open the 2010–2011 season under the roof of the Mead Center for American Theater, a dramatic $125 million renovation of the existing venue that adds a third stage.

The **Woolly Mammoth Theatre Company** (641 D St. NW, 202/393-3939, www.woollymammoth.net) is Washington's off-Broadway-style troupe for experimental cutting-edge works. Finally, the **Studio Theatre** (1501 14th St. NW, 202/332-3300, www.studiotheatre.org) has grown more ambitious each year. The contemporary productions are first-rate.

OTHER ENTERTAINMENT

Spectator Sports

Located in the heart of Chinatown, the **Verizon Center** (601 F St. NW, 202/628-3200, www.verizoncenter.com) is not your typical sports venue. Home to the NHL's Washington Capitals, the NBA's Wizards, and the WNBA's Mystics, the arena features a video center showcasing historic moments in athletics, a sportscasters' hall of fame, and plenty of shopping.

The Washington Nationals baseball team (1500 S. Capitol St. SE, 202/675-6287, http://nationals.mlb.com/was/ballpark) moved into the 41,000-seat **Nationals Park** along the Anacostia River in Southeast Washington in 2008, transforming the neighborhood in the process. At the leading edge of D.C.'s green building trend, it's the first Major League Baseball stadium to earn Leadership in Energy and Environmental Design (LEED) certification.

Robert F. Kennedy Memorial Stadium (2400 E. Capitol St. SE, 202/547-9077, www.dcunited.com), known locally as RFK, was once home to the Washington Redskins, but it now hosts the city's pro soccer team, D.C. United, as well as rock concerts and the occasional outdoor convention.

The Washington Redskins (301/276-6050, www.redskins.com) moved out of town in 1996 and now play at **FedEx Field** in Landover, Maryland. Parking at the stadium is pricey, but extra Metro buses and trains (202/637-7000, www.wmata.com) make the journey to and from Maryland much more convenient.

The 4,200-seat **Carter Barron Amphitheatre** (16th St. and Colorado Ave. NW, 202/426-0486, www.nps.gov/rocr/cbarron) can host major tennis tournaments but more often offers free concerts. Located along

16th Street north of Adams-Morgan, it's also easily accessible.

Comedy

People say Washington's a funny town, but they're not usually talking about the sort of humor on display at the **D.C. Improv** (1140 Connecticut Ave. NW, 202/296-7008, www.dcimprov.com, Tues.–Sun., showtimes at 8, 8:30, or 10:30 P.M.). Tickets start around $15, and food and drinks are reasonably priced. For musical skits laced with political satire, try the **Capitol Steps** (202/397-7328, www.capsteps.com), a group of former Capitol Hill staffers who are "putting the mock back in democracy." Performances take place in the Ronald Reagan Building and International Trade Center (1300 Pennsylvania Ave. NW) every Friday and Saturday at 7:30 P.M. for $35.

Tours

The **Tourmobile** shuttle bus fleet (202/554-5100 or 888/868-7707, www.tourmobile.com) is a common sight on the Mall and a convenient way to see the major sights in D.C. and northern Virginia. They stop at 40 different monuments, memorials, and other attractions, with narration along the way, and you can get on and off at your leisure. Buy tickets from kiosks at the Washington Monument, Union Station, or Arlington National Cemetery, or from Ticketmaster (800/551-7328, www.ticketmaster.com). One-day tickets including Arlington National Cemetery are $27 adults, $13 children.

The **Potomac Riverboat Company** (703/684-0580 or 877/511-2628, www.potomacriverboatco.com) has a small fleet that plies the waters around the capital. A 40-minute narrated sightseeing tour to Alexandria ($14 adults, $8 children) runs hourly during the day May–August and on weekends April and September–October. Another boat runs between the Alexandria and Georgetown docks every 1–2 hours daily March–September and on weekends in October. This costs $26 adults, $14 children round-trip, with half-price one-way tickets also available.

© KATIE GITHENS

Four wheels, two wheels, or no wheels, it's easy to tour around D.C.

There's also a boat from Alexandria to Mount Vernon ($38 adults, $20 children round-trip).

Zip around the city on a Segway—those high-tech two-wheeled people-movers that somehow stay upright—with **City Segway Tours** (202/626-0017 or 877/734-8687, www.citysegwaytours.com). Three-hour guided jaunts during the day and evening are $70 per person.

If you'd rather get around under your own power, try **Bike the Sites** (202/842-2453, www.bikethesites.com), which operates out of the Old Post Office pavilion at 1100 Pennsylvania Avenue NW downtown. This company offers tours of the city's museums, sculpture gardens, and historic bridges, as well as the expected Mount Vernon and monument sightseeing. Tours of varying difficulty range 2–6 hours and run about $30–42 per person (children $22–35). Bike the Sites also rents cruiser bikes ($10 for two hours, $35 per day) as well as child trailers, tandem bikes, and mobility scooters.

Accommodations

For the most part, accommodations in the District are pricey. There are exceptions to that rule, though, and your options increase dramatically if you consider staying outside of D.C. in Maryland or Virginia. This is a business town, so hotel rates are usually lower on weekends and in the winter and summer, when there are fewer legislative sessions. Rates can also fluctuate dramatically if big conventions or events are in town. Planning ahead and shopping around will help you find the best accommodations deal.

UNDER $100

Reservations are a good idea for both of D.C.'s hostels. Hostelling International's **HI-Washington, D.C. Hostel** (1009 11th St. NW, 202/737-2333, www.hiwashingtondc.org, dorm rooms $25–45 pp, more for private rooms, $3 fee for non-HI members) is centrally located downtown near the Smithsonian Museums, the White House, and other attractions. Only a three-block walk from Metro Center station, the renovated eight-story hotel offers 250 beds, shared bathrooms, kitchen and laundry facilities, high-speed Internet access, and wheelchair accessibility. Dorm beds are available in single-sex or coed dorms. For night owls, the hostel offers 24-hour access; there are also tours, movies, and other special programs. The D.C. Hostel is open year-round, and the environmentally minded will be happy to know it is the first hostel in the world to be Energy Star rated, a designation of the building's energy efficiency.

On the main strip of Adams-Morgan's nightlife and ethnic eateries, the **Washington D.C. International Student Center** (2451 18th St. NW, 202/667-7681 or 800/567-4150, www.dchostel.com) offers a free continental breakfast, free pick-up from Greyhound or Amtrak stations, Internet, and 24-hour access. Shared dorm rooms are $25 per person ($28 pp if you book online), and some private rooms are available. Children are not permitted.

$100–150

The venerable, friendly **Hotel Harrington** (436 11th St. NW, 202/628-8140 or 800/424-8532, www.hotel-harrington.com, $145–190) is downtown, only two blocks from the Smithsonian. The excellent location makes the Harrington a particular favorite of international travelers. The Harrington also offers a restaurant and is wheelchair accessible. The 242 rooms and 26 suites must be booked in advance. Parking is available for $15 per night. The rooms range in size depending on price and are clean and comfortable.

Adam's Inn (1746 Lanier Place NW, 202/745-3600 or 800/578-6807, www.adamsinn.com, $110–170) consists of three brick townhouses and a carriage house hidden away on a leafy residential street two blocks from the heart of Adams-Morgan. Built around 1913, the inn has a definite Victorian feel, with some modern touches. The common rooms are equipped with TV and computers for Internet access. A lavish continental breakfast is included in the price of your stay. A total of 26 rooms are available. As elsewhere in Adams-Morgan, parking is limited.

The charming, inexpensive **Kalorama Guest House** in Adams-Morgan (1854 Mintwood Pl. NW, 202/667-6369 or 800/974-6450, www.kaloramaguesthouse.com, $120 with shared bath, $140 with private bath) consists of two Victorian townhouses filled with creative antique furnishings, such as brass beds and oriental rugs, set off by fresh flowers. Enjoy a sherry in front of the fire or lemonade on the patio, then take a short walk to many of the finest restaurants in the city. Parking is $15 per day and must be reserved when you book the room. The same owners actually run two guesthouses of the same name; the other is in Woodley Park (2700 Cathedral Ave. NW, 202/328-0860).

The **Savoy Suites Georgetown** (2505 Wisconsin Ave. NW, 202/337-9700 or 800/944-5377, www.savoysuites.com, $120–200) features 150 fine large suites, some with excellent views of the D.C. skyline. The hotel restaurant offers outdoor dining in season and serves as gallery space for area artists. Area transportation services are available at the Savoy, including a D.C. Metro shuttle.

$150-250

Only five blocks west of the White House, the **Hotel Lombardy** (2019 Pennsylvania Ave. NW, 202/828-2600 or 800/424-5486, www.hotellombardy.com, $180–380) provides sumptuous accommodations including cherry-wood furnishings, dusty rose carpeting, and fine art on the walls. Most of the 140 rooms offer fully equipped kitchens, but the fine restaurant Café Lombardy is on the premises as well. Rates at the low end of the range can be had in the off-season, and multiple-night stays are often required in high season.

Ideally located between Dupont Circle and Embassy Row, the **Beacon Hotel** (1615 Rhode Island Ave. NW, 202/296-2100, www.beaconhotelwdc.com, $245) is quickly becoming a favorite for business travelers, thanks to high-tech rooms with flat-screen TVs and Wi-Fi everywhere. Panoramic views of the city make the rooftop deck a favorite summertime hangout.

Located close to Dupont Circle, the cozy **Tabard Inn** (1739 N St. NW, 202/785-1277, www.tabardinn.com, $128–158 with shared bath, starting at $173 with private bath) is an unspoiled mark of good taste. This country inn in the heart of Washington offers live jazz and eclectic continental cuisine and an indoor-outdoor restaurant, which is without peer in its business-class price range.

Another good Dupont option is the friendly 10-story **Hotel Madera** (1310 New Hampshire Ave. NW, 202/296-7600 or 800/430-1202, www.hotelmadera.com, $210–290), with 82 spacious rooms. This boutique hotel, part of the Kimpton family, also has seven "specialty rooms" that offer amenities varying from in-room exercise equipment to DVD libraries and free Internet access. The on-site Firefly Bistro serves contemporary American cuisine.

In Logan Circle, Hollywood swank meets mid-century pop art in the glamorous **Hotel Helix** (1430 Rhode Island Ave. NW, 202/462-

COURTESY TABARD PHOTO COLLECTION

the Tabard Inn

9001, www.hotelhelix.com, $150–330). From your grand entrance through gold-lamé curtains, this 178-room Kimpton hotel transports you into a den of psychedelic lighting, funky furniture, and a martini lounge to make Andy Warhol proud. In summertime, the pet-friendly hotel often hosts "yappy hours" (dog happy hours) on its sparkly light-strewn patio. Parking is $33/night, with a $10 eco-discount for hybrids.

The **Carlyle Suites** (1731 New Hampshire Ave. NW, 202/234-3200 or 800/964-5377, www.carlylesuites.com, $130–280) is simply a wonder. The bold exterior and accompanying interior frills are pure art deco. Located on a pleasant residential street near Dupont Circle, the eight-story hotel features 170 guest suites with sitting areas, kitchenettes, and limited free parking, and offers guests complimentary use of the nearby Washington Sports Club. Twist, its on-site restaurant, has a Mediterranean flair and serves all meals daily, most notably its Sunday jazz brunch.

The hanging ferns and welcoming porch of the **Swann House Bed & Breakfast** (1808 New Hampshire Ave. NW, 202/265-4414, www.swannhouse.com, $169–369) await in Dupont Circle. Situated in a circa-1883 mansion of red bricks and Victorian turrets, this is the only bed-and-breakfast in D.C. to earn membership in the Select Registry of the Distinguished Inns of North America. It has nine guest rooms, each with private bathrooms and free Wi-Fi, and a few with fireplaces, private balconies, and whirlpool tubs. Don't miss the homemade granola, part of the continental breakfast included with your stay.

The **Hotel Rouge** (1315 16th St., 202/232-8000 or 800/738-1202 reservations, www.rougehotel.com, $199–369) is a hip, modern boutique hotel. Leopard-print hallway carpet leads to artistically decorated rooms that carry on the hotel's vampish red motif. Special options include "Chill" rooms with all the modern technology you could want and "Chow" rooms with stainless-steel kitchenettes. Chic Bar Rouge on the premises serves breakfast, dinner, and late-night cocktails. Amenities at this Kimpton hotel include a state-of-the-art fitness center, high-speed Internet, and hosted red wine, red beer, Bloody Mary, and cold pizza bars at various times of the week.

OVER $250

The 150-year-old **Willard InterContinental Hotel** (1401 Pennsylvania Ave. NW, 202/628-9100 or 800/827-1747, www.washington.intercontinental.com, $600 and up during high season, $350 and up during summer weekends) is the grande dame of Pennsylvania Avenue, located just around the corner from the White House. Its architect, H. J. Hardenberg, designed New York's prestigious Plaza, but did his best work in Washington. The hotel features the fine-dining Occidental Grill as well as the European-style Café du Parc and the Round Robin bar, where Washington, D.C., was introduced to the pleasures of the mint julep.

When it's time to inaugurate a president, no hotel offers better views of the parade than the 90-year-old, 344-room **W Washington D.C.** (515 15th St. NW at Pennsylvania Ave., 202/661-2400, $290–400), a Starwood property that started as the Hotel Washington. You can't get much closer to the Treasury Building and the White House. It offers the refined J&G Steakhouse and the POV Lounge and Rooftop Terrace, which afford spectacular vistas of the White House, the Ellipse, and the Washington Monument. Woodrow Wilson reviewed U.S. troops marching off to war from here.

With its grand European lobby, plush decor, and ultra-customized guest rooms, the **Hotel Monaco** (700 F St. NW, 202/628-7177 or 800/649-1202, www.monaco-dc.com, $250–490) combines whimsical downtown charms with specialized service. Lanky patrons can request "tall rooms," and even your pooch can get pampered with gourmet doggy snacks.

The venerable **Renaissance Mayflower Hotel** (1127 Connecticut Ave. NW, 202/347-3000 or 800/228-7697, www.marriott.com/hotels/travel/wassh-renaissance-mayflower-hotel, $190–400) is now owned by the Marriott chain. It underwent an $11 million restoration, revitalizing ballrooms and meeting rooms. Formerly the haunt of political stalwarts such as Huey P. Long and J. Edgar Hoover, the stately Mayflower is Washington's largest luxury hotel and its answer to New York City's Waldorf-Astoria. Lines of black limos parked around the hotel signal that government dignitaries have dropped by for a meal or are staying for the night in one of the 660 rooms. The Mayflower is rich in history: Hoover arrived at the Mayflower Grille Room every day of the last 20 years of his life for his regular meal of chicken soup, grapefruit, and cottage cheese, and Franklin Delano Roosevelt wrote "The only thing we have to fear is fear itself" in Suite 776.

If not for a king, the **Hay-Adams Hotel** (16th and H St. NW, 202/638-6600, www.hayadams.com, $400 and up) is certainly fit for a president—and located right across the park from one. Barack Obama and his family stayed here in the weeks preceding the 2008 inauguration, no doubt enjoying the direct views of the White House from the penthouse suite with anticipation. The 144-room Italian-Renaissance luxury hotel opened its doors in 1928 on Lafayette Square, and has earned the AAA Four Diamond award for—get this—24 consecutive years. It's named for the dignified residents who lived on the site: John Hay, secretary of state, and Henry Adams, author and relative of presidents John Adams and John Quincy Adams. The Lafayette Room restaurant serves contemporary American cuisine, and downstairs the Off the Record bar dishes the latest Washington gossip.

SERVICES

Washington D.C. Area Bed & Breakfast Accommodations Ltd. (877/893-3233, www.bedandbreakfastdc.com) can arrange stays in private homes, guesthouses, inns, and small hotels in the nation's capital and surrounding metropolitan area.

Food

Obviously these listings provide just a sampling of D.C.'s incredible variety of eating options—one of the city's best features. With so many great eats, it's almost painful to have to choose. Most restaurants of interest to visitors are concentrated downtown and in the Northwest quadrant, with a few exceptions.

SNACKS AND CAFÉS

In Adams-Morgan, **Tryst** (2459 18th St. NW, 202/232-5500, all meals daily) is a cozy combination of a coffee bar, liquor bar, and lounge filled with couches, artwork, and patrons from all walks of life. It's a great place for people-watching at any time of day or night (open to 2 or 3 A.M. Thurs.–Sat.) and serves a light menu of soups, sandwiches ($3–10), and all sorts of drinks. It offers free Wi-Fi and operates under the motto, "No corporate coffee, no matching silverware."

Teaism (2009 R St. NW, 202/667-3827, all meals daily) in Dupont is a quiet two-story nook with delicious Asian dishes and dozens of varieties of tea. Try the bento box ($8–9), and be patient—the upstairs tables free up eventually. The Penn Quarter location (400 8th St. NW, 202/638-6010) has the same great menu, but with ample seating downstairs. Another good place to curl up with a good read and some caffeine is the basement coffee shop in the **Politics & Prose Bookstore** (5015 Connecticut Ave. NW, 202/364-2408, all meals daily). It offers vegetarian-leaning bites including pastas and excellent soups, with bagels and giant cookies to boot.

In Dupont Circle is **Kramerbooks** (1517 Connecticut Ave. NW, 202/387-3825, all meals daily), a great bookstore-café that's open 24 hours on Fridays and Saturdays.

Ah, beer! Miles of beer. The **Brickskeller** (1523 22nd St. NW, 202/293-1885, lunch Wed.–Fri., dinner daily) is Washington's monument to the mighty brew, packing in more than

1,000 varieties from 50 countries, including 400 from the United States alone. Be forewarned that availability for some of the more exotic beers can sometimes be hit-or-miss—with everything from civil wars to natural disasters tying up the supply chain—but the owners claim to have served 5,000 different styles of suds since opening in 1957. The burgers are excellent, too.

Many a late-night prowl down the U St. corridor has ended up at **Ben's Chili Bowl** (1213 U St. NW, 202/667-0909, all meals Mon.–Sat., lunch and dinner Sun.), and for good reason—bite into one of their legendary chili dogs, burgers, or fries and you're munching on history. This Formica-countered place opened in 1958 and has not only weathered a half-century of neighborhood upheavals but has thrived. Today it's an icon of black culture and cuisine in the District, with friendly service, cheap prices, and even the occasional celebrity sighting (Bill Cosby has a chili dog named after him). Ben's is open almost around the clock and has old Motown and Stax-Volt tunes on the jukebox—what more could you ask for?

CASUAL

Star chef José Andrés guides you through the eastern Mediterranean flavors of Greece, Lebanon, and Turkey at **Zaytinya** (701 9th St. NW, 202/638-0800, lunch and dinner daily). The bustling high-decibel restaurant is airy and white-walled, good for a quick bite or drink before heading to a Georgetown Hoyas basketball game at the Verizon Center. The menu offers mezes, small plates ranging from sumptuous roasted lamb shoulder to seared scallops in a yogurt-dill sauce. Order at least a couple each ($6–12).

Relaxed but stately, the **Old Ebbitt Grill** (675 15th St. NW, 202/347-4800, all meals daily) offers wonderful service and dependable food in an old-school Victorian atmosphere next to the Treasury Building and the White House. The bar is long on character, and the Kumamoto oysters are magnificent. Call for reservations and ask for the main room to catch the power-lunch scene. Lunch dishes start at $10 and dinner plates range $13–24.

With the highest population of Ethiopians outside the country itself, D.C. offers a feast of the African nation's vegetarian-friendly food. Try **Etete Ethiopian Cuisine** (1942 9th St. NW, 202/232-7600, lunch and dinner daily). Be ready to eat with your hands, specifically your right hand, tearing off bits of *injera* (a sourdough-tasting crepe made from fermented tef grain) to scoop up delicious stewed cabbage and savory lentil dishes and *doro wat,* the spicy chicken stew that is Ethiopia's national dish. Entrées cost $10–14.50. Finish your meal with some coffee—the ubiquitous caffeinated beverage originated in Ethiopia.

Georgia Brown's (950 15th St. NW, 202/393-4499, lunch and dinner Mon.–Sat., brunch and dinner Sun.) is unique in Washington for its soul-food version of haute cuisine—collard greens and black-eyed peas never looked this fancy. Enjoy the handsome crowds (keep one eye open for the Secret Service, as the Obamas are said to dine here frequently), smashing ambience, and tantalizing menu descriptions here at McPherson Square. Lunch and dinner entrées run upward of $18, and live jazz enhances Sunday brunch.

Belgian cuisine isn't tough to find in Washington—the hardest part is choosing *which* Belgian restaurant. Try the intimate **Belga Café** (514 8th St. SE, 202/544-0100, lunch and dinner daily, entrées $19–27) on Capitol Hill for asparagus and bacon-flecked mussels steamed in red ale, *pommes frites* and hand-whipped mayo, and a stein of Belgian's finest Abbey ales. Waffles and Nutella headline the weekend brunch. Downtown, the flashier **Brasserie Beck** (1101 K St. NW, 202/408-1717, lunch Mon.–Fri., dinner daily, $23–32) is also excellent, as is the grittier **Granville Moore's** (1238 H St. NW, 202/399-2546, dinner daily, $12–17) on up-and-coming H Street. Take a cab or the free shuttle to H Street (www.atlasarts.org/plan_shuttle.php); don't walk.

UPSCALE

When White House staff members take a break to celebrate a political victory, the courtly

Occidental Grill (1475 Pennsylvania Ave. NW, 202/783-1475, lunch and dinner Mon.–Sat., $12–28 lunch, $28–39 dinner) is their destination. Straighten your tie, make your reservations, and admire the century-old trophy wall of 3,000 photographs of famous Washington faces. The menu is contemporary American, and the helpings are generous; the fish dishes are particularly good. It's part of the Willard Hotel complex and popular for power lunches.

Rasika (633 D St. NW, 202/637-1222, lunch Mon.–Fri., dinner Mon.–Sat.) is Sanskrit for "flavors," and there are plenty of them here. John Mariani of *Esquire* magazine called this modern Penn Quarter restaurant "one of America's best restaurants, period." The glowing dining room is awash in red and orange, and the food from Bombay-bred chef Vikram Sunderam's kitchen is equally colorful: scallops brightened with a tingling red pepper sauce, a deep amber vindaloo that's complex without being overpowering (entrées range $17–28).

At **Acadiana** (901 New York Ave. NW, 202/408-8848), chef Jeff Tunks takes guests down South with his dignified riff on po' boys, jambalaya, and étouffée. The space is more boardroom than Bourbon Street—though the bar offers a few dozen bourbons!—but that hasn't stopped the crowds of politicos and conventioneers from lining up. Try the "twelve-napkin" roast beef po' boy and the amazing biscuits; dinner entrées range $21–33.

Makoto (4822 MacArthur Blvd. NW, 202/298-6866, lunch Tues.–Sat., dinner Tues.–Sun.) is Washington's most exclusive Japanese restaurant. There are only four tables, with just 10 seats at the sushi bar. The presentation and service are both exquisite. Try the tasting menu ($60 pp) for a bit of everything. If the tables at Makoto are full, or if your wallet is empty, try **Kotobuki Sushi** (202/281-6679, lunch Mon.–Sat., dinner Mon.–Sun.) upstairs instead. With $1.25 apiece sushi, it's a good value and surprisingly good quality.

Vidalia (1990 M St. NW, 202/659-1990, lunch Mon.–Fri., dinner daily) is a Southern belle of a restaurant known for its roasted Vidalia onion appetizer and manicured Southern cooking. But don't be misled; the food here is elegant and imaginative—specialties include the shrimp and grits and Sallie Buben's church tea—and the menu is a palette for the palate. It all happens in a tastefully decorated two-level underground dining room. Lunch entrées are in the teens and dinner entrées run $30–46; save room for the lemon chess pie for dessert.

The setting for **1789** (1226 36th St. NW, 202/965-1789, dinner daily) is a Federal-style townhouse overlooking Georgetown. The oak-walled bar serves perfect silver bullets, while chef Nathan Beauchamp conspires to fuse East and West with soys, peanut flavors, and lime marinades. It's a classy place; dress is semi-formal, and don't be surprised if you catch a wedding proposal while you're here. You're also likely to spot Georgetown students taking advantage of a parental visit to eat the excellent crab cakes or rack of lamb. Dinner is $15–38.

Information and Transportation

VISITOR INFORMATION

The D.C. Chamber of Commerce runs the **D.C. Visitor Information Center** (1213 K St. NW, 866/324-7386, www.dcchamber.org, 9 A.M.–4:30 P.M. Mon.–Fri.) near the McPherson Square Metro stop. Here you can book a hotel, grab a map, ask a question, or buy tour and event tickets.

Two other helpful organizations are **Destination DC,** which has a great website with sample itineraries (202/789-7000 or 800/422-8644, www.washington.org), and **Cultural Tourism D.C.** (202/661-7581, www.culturaltourismdc.org), a nonprofit intent on linking you to Washington's heritage and arts; they have a dependable events calendar. For half-price tickets, stop by **TicketPlace** (www.ticketplace.org) at 7th and D Streets

DAY TRIPS FROM D.C.

© KATIE GITHENS
Arlington National Cemetery

So you have just one extra day before or after your Washington, D.C., visit to explore the Old Dominion? Don't despair – there's plenty to see and do within day-trip distance of the capital. Luckily, you'll probably be going in reverse of the rush-hour crowds: outbound in the morning and back into the city in the afternoon. You can also hop aboard a bus tour or D.C.'s public rail system to visit nearby tourist favorites like **Arlington National Cemetery** – just across the Potomac from the Lincoln Memorial – George Washington's **Mount Vernon** estate, and **Old Town Alexandria,** which is also accessible by Metro.

DAY TRIP 1

At the **Claude Moore Colonial Farm** in McLean, 12 miles west of the capital, the life of tenant farmers in the 18th century is re-created. This isn't far from **Great Falls Park,** where the Potomac River plunges 77 feet in a booming froth of white water. Stop by Moby Dick's House of Kabob in McLean for perfectly seasoned lamb kabobs and falafel. If you still have energy come evening, see who's playing at the **Wolf Trap National Park for the Performing Arts,** north of Tysons Corner.

DAY TRIP 2

Two major Civil War battles tore through Manassas, 37 miles from D.C., including the first of the war. Now the contested fields are preserved within the **Manassas National Battlefield Park.** Even more scenic acres fall within the **Bull Run** and **Fountainhead Regional Parks** nearby, which offer great nature-watching, hiking, and mountain biking. For a dose of air and space minus the National Mall crowds, say hi to the Space Shuttle and dozens of other planes at the Smithsonian's **Steven F. Udvar-Hazy Center** near Dulles International Airport. (There are many places to eat along Route 50.)

DAY TRIP 3

Things get rural quickly as you continue west toward **Leesburg,** a little over 40 miles west, in the center of an area that is well worth a quick visit. Here you'll find upscale horse-country shopping and dining – see what's cooking in The Wine Kitchen restaurant – along with **Morven Park, Ball's Bluff Battlefield,** and the quaint historic towns of **Waterford** and **Middleburg.** Several **wineries** are located nearby if you want to visit the vineyards yourself, perfect for a picnic lunch and a chilled bottle or two.

DAY TRIP 4

Head south past Alexandria to arrive at George Washington's **Mount Vernon,** 20 miles south of D.C. You can get here by car on the George Washington Memorial Parkway or by bicycle on the 18-mile Mount Vernon Trail along the water. For a full day of historic homes, swing by **Woodlawn Mansion** as well, where you'll also find Frank Lloyd Wright's 1914 **Pope-Leighey House.** Grab lunch at the Mount Vernon Inn or pack a picnic for **Mason Neck,** a small peninsula that can easily fill an afternoon by itself with two parks, a National Wildlife Refuge, and Gunston Hall Plantation.

NW near the Gallery Place–Chinatown Metro station.

For the latest news and events in Washington, and a little inside-the-Beltway gossip, visit DCist.com.

GETTING THERE AND AROUND

Most of the major sightseeing highlights in central Washington—the Mall, the White House, the Tidal Basin area—are within walking distance of each other, so using public transportation is only an option (but usually the best one for tired feet). If you want to see anything away from these areas or need to travel to any of the outlying neighborhoods, you'll be happy to know that Washington has one of the best subway systems of any major city in the world. The related bus service is usually reliable (except when more than half an inch of snow falls), and there are always plenty of taxis and rental car options, not to mention rental bikes, rickshaws, and Segways. Driving around downtown should always be your last choice: Parking is scarce and expensive, and with its many narrow and/or one-way streets, diagonal avenues, and roundabouts, D.C. was definitely not designed with modern automobiles in mind. Let's just say it can make New York City traffic look reasonable in comparison.

By Air

The Washington area is served by three major airports. **Dulles International Airport** (703/572-2700, www.metwashairports.com/dulles) receives both international and domestic arrivals, and **Ronald Reagan Washington National Airport** (703/417-8000, www.metwashairports.com/reagan) primarily takes domestic arrivals. **Baltimore-Washington International Airport (BWI)** (301/261-1000, www.bwiairport.com), 35 miles northeast in Maryland, also receives international and domestic flights, which are often cheaper than flights to either of the other airports. It's a 30-to-45-minute drive to downtown from any of the airports—much longer at rush hour—although National airport is accessible by Metro, making it a very convenient choice if you have the option.

Taxis run to each airport (National is $20 one-way from downtown; Dulles $50; BWI $60). The **Washington Flyer** bus (888/927-4359, www.washfly.com) runs every 30 minutes to Dulles from the West Falls Church Metro station ($10 one-way, $18 round-trip). **SuperShuttle** (202/296-6662 or 800/258-3826, www.supershuttle.com) runs to all three airports (to Dulles starts at $29 pp).

By Rail

Amtrak (800/872-7245, www.amtrak.com) trains pull into Washington, D.C., at opulent Union Station. The Amtrak line connects directly to the **Maryland Area Rail Commuter (MARC)** system (410/539-5000 or 866/743-3682, www.mtamaryland.com/services/marc), a Monday–Friday commuter service with dozens of trains connecting the Baltimore–Washington corridor, southern Maryland counties, and northeastern West Virginia. It also connects to **Virginia Railway Express** (703/684-1001, www.vre.org), which runs to Manassas and Fredericksburg.

By Metro

The **Washington Metropolitan Area Transit Authority (WMATA)** operates the D.C. subway system called the **Metrorail,** or simply "the Metro" (202/637-7000, www.wmata.com). It covers the downtown area and the suburbs (except Georgetown), but plans are always underway to expand. Metro stations are identified by a large letter *M* atop a brown pylon. For as chaotic as D.C. can get, the Metro system is surprisingly fast, clean, and efficient.

To use the system, purchase a magnetic fare card from a vending machine at your departure station. Simply insert the card into the turnstile, grab it again as you pass through, and when you get where you're going, put the card into the exit turnstile to pay the fare. Don't forget to grab it again; you can use any remaining balance on your next trip. Should your card not have enough credit for you to exit the station, use one of the special exit-fare machines to add more money to the card and try the turnstile again.

Fares range from $1.45 to $4.60 depending on how far you go and whether it's during peak commuting times. Trains run every 5–6 minutes during peak times and every 10–15 minutes at other times, 5 A.M.–midnight Monday–Thursday, 7 A.M.–3 A.M. Friday–Saturday, and 7 A.M.–midnight Sunday. One-day passes are $8.30, and seven-day passes are $26.40–40.50. Up to two children under the age of five ride free when accompanied by a paying adult. Make sure you get on the correct side of the tracks for your destination (look at the maps located by the fare machines and at the digital displays on the various platforms to see which trains are coming and how soon).

By Bus

Also run by WMATA, **Metrobuses** connect with Metrorail stations for travel to outlying areas. Fares are $1.45 per trip (exact change only). Express routes, such as L'Enfant Plaza to Dulles airport, cost $3.20, and one-week passes are $12. Buses run on roughly the same schedule as trains.

The **DC Circulator** (202/962-1423, www.dccirculator.com) bus system runs five loops between the Convention Center and the SW Waterfront (7 A.M.–9 P.M. daily), Georgetown and Union Station (7 A.M.–9 P.M. daily, later on weekends), Woodley Park and Adams-Morgan and McPherson Square (7 A.M.–midnight Sun.–Thurs., until 3:30 A.M. Fri.–Sat.), Union Station and the Navy Yard on Capitol Hill (6 A.M.–7 P.M. daily), and around the National Mall (10 A.M.–6 P.M. weekends only). Buses pass every 10 minutes, and tickets are $1 (exact change only).

Washington's **Greyhound** station (1005 1st St. NE, 202/289-5154, www.greyhound.com) is a 10-minute walk north of Union Station. This area can be a little dicey at night, so taking a taxi is a good idea.

By Taxi

Because some D.C. neighborhoods are not served by the Metro (most notably Georgetown and Adams-Morgan), the capital's taxicabs are a nice complement to the subway and bus systems.

Fares are metered by distance traveled, a long-awaited change that occurred in 2008 to replace an often-cryptic zone system. Fare costs $3 for the first one-sixth of a mile, and $0.25 every sixth of a mile thereafter. There are extra charges for additional passengers ($1.50 each), radio-dispatched taxis ($2), and luggage. For a list of cab companies, see the website of the **D.C. Taxicab Commission** (202/645-6018, http://dctaxi.dc.gov). A few reliable taxi companies include **Capitol Cab** (202/545-8900) and **Yellow Cab** (202/546-7900).

By Rickshaw

Yes, rickshaw. The District is in a rickshaw renaissance, with at least three of these bicycle-powered companies at work. You'll often see "drivers" of rickshaws, also called pedicabs, pedaling around the Mall pulling a cart with room for two or three passengers. While it's not the fastest ride in town (7 mph is more or less top speed), it is fun, and downtown at rush hour rickshaws can scoot around the gridlock faster than motorized vehicles. Hail them from the sidewalk or call ahead for service. Try **Capitol Pedicabs** (202/232-6086, www.capitolpedicabs.com), **DC Pedicab** (202/345-8065, www.dcpedicab.com), or **National Pedicabs** (202/269-9090, www.nationalpedicabs.com).

By Rental Car

Most rental car agencies have offices at Dulles airport, National airport, and Union Station, although you probably won't need a car if you're planning on staying within the city limits.

THE COAST

A simple concept—Virginia meets the ocean—is quite complex in reality. Comprising both the state's largest city and towns where the whole population could fit in a school bus, the coast embraces some of Virginia's greatest diversity in both its landscape and its people. Aside from the Atlantic Ocean, its major defining natural feature is the Chesapeake Bay, whose gaping mouth opens onto one of the finest, largest, and busiest natural ports in the world. Around this harbor spreads Hampton Roads, which counts some 1.6 million residents—more than a fifth of Virginia's population.

Rivers divide the inner shore of the Chesapeake Bay into three large "necks" of land. The southernmost one, called the Historic Peninsula, is home to three of the state's most exceptional sites, each within a short drive of the others: Jamestown became the first permanent English settlement in the New World in 1607 when three ships full of settlers sailed up the bay; Yorktown was the site of the decisive final battle of the American Revolution; and a visit to Colonial Williamsburg can make you think the 18th century never really ended.

In stark contrast to all this history is Hampton Roads, officially the Norfolk–Virginia Beach–Newport News Metropolitan Statistical Area. It boasts the world's largest coal-shipping port, privately owned shipyard, and naval facility, and one-third of its workers are employed by the Department of Defense or private defense contractors. Yet around this megalopolis—close enough, in parts, to see its glow at night—are some of the state's most pristine natural acres, covering miles of

HIGHLIGHTS

Irvington: This tiny town on the Northern Neck is great for a weekend getaway, with the outstanding trio of the Hope and Glory Inn, the Trick Dog Cafe, and historic Christ Church (page 132).

Historical Sights of Colonial Williamsburg: Here, at one of America's most popular family destinations, life in the 18th century is re-created down to bootstraps and belt buckles (page 139).

Jamestown Island (Colonial National Historical Park): Jamestown, Yorktown, and the connecting parkway make up this historical park, which spans centuries of history, from the first lasting English settlement in the New World to the final battle of the American Revolution (page 149).

James River Plantations: The impressive lineup along the James River includes Shirley Plantation, America's oldest, and Berkeley Plantation, site of one of the first Thanksgivings by European settlers (page 153).

The Mariners' Museum: In Newport News, this museum plays host to all things nautical, from scrimshaw to pieces of the famous ironclad, the *Monitor* (page 157).

NAUTICUS: The National Maritime Center in Norfolk is a high-tech museum that's as impressive as the 887-foot USS *Wisconsin* berthed next door (page 167).

Virginia Beach Boardwalk: This is a scrubbed-up version of the classic beach boardwalk, with lots to do and people to watch (page 179).

Virginia Aquarium and Marine Science Center: Check out sharks, turtles, and gentle stingrays at this outstanding aquarium, one of the best of its kind in the country (page 180).

Chincoteague National Wildlife Refuge and Assateague Island: At the northern end of the Eastern Shore, this refuge at one end of wild Assateague Island is home to the world-famous wild ponies, rounded up every year by volunteer firemen (page 203).

Tangier Island: A boat trip to Tangier Island, isolated in the middle of the Chesapeake Bay, is a unique cultural experience and almost a trip back in time – life here hasn't changed much in decades (page 206).

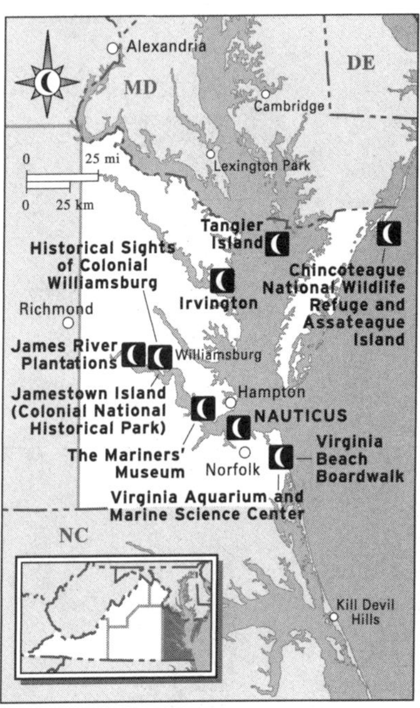

LOOK FOR TO FIND RECOMMENDED SIGHTS, ACTIVITIES, DINING, AND LODGING.

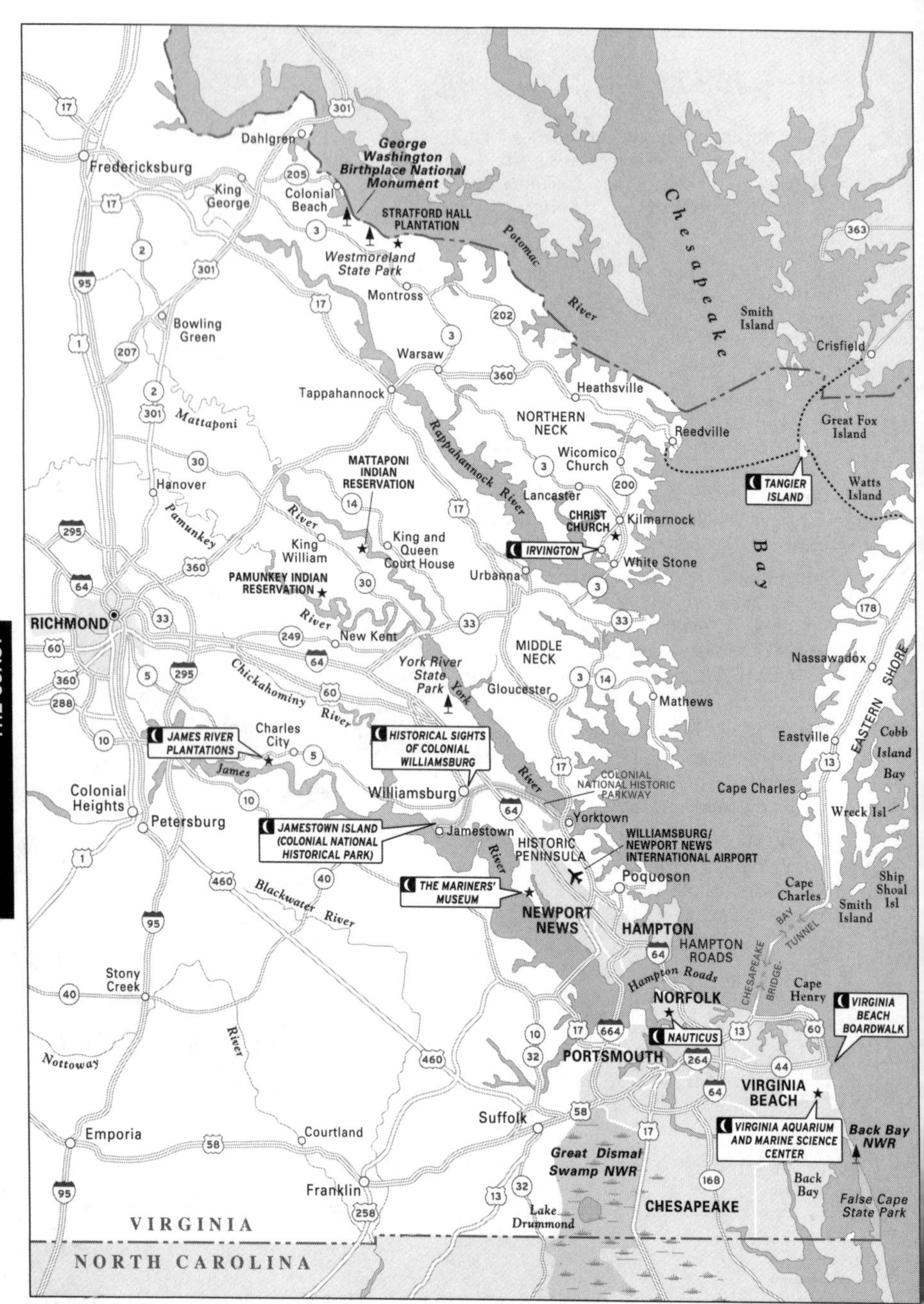
Fredericksburg
Dahlgren
King George
Colonial Beach
George Washington Birthplace National Monument
STRATFORD HALL PLANTATION
Westmoreland State Park
Montross
Potomac River
Chesapeake Bay
Bowling Green
Warsaw
Tappahannock
Mattaponi
Heathsville
NORTHERN NECK
Reedville
Smith Island
Crisfield
Great Fox Island
TANGIER ISLAND
Watts Island
Wicomico Church
Lancaster
Rappahannock River
MATTAPONI INDIAN RESERVATION
Hanover
Pamunkey River
King William
King and Queen Court House
CHRIST CHURCH
Kilmarnock
IRVINGTON
White Stone
Urbanna
PAMUNKEY INDIAN RESERVATION
RICHMOND
New Kent
MIDDLE NECK
York River State Park
York River
Gloucester
Mathews
Nassawadox
EASTERN SHORE
Chickahominy River
JAMES RIVER PLANTATIONS
Charles City
HISTORICAL SIGHTS OF COLONIAL WILLIAMSBURG
Eastville
Cobb Island Bay
James
Colonial Heights
Williamsburg
COLONIAL NATIONAL HISTORIC PARKWAY
Cape Charles
Petersburg
Yorktown
Wreck Isl
JAMESTOWN ISLAND (COLONIAL NATIONAL HISTORICAL PARK)
Jamestown
HISTORIC PENINSULA
WILLIAMSBURG/ NEWPORT NEWS INTERNATIONAL AIRPORT
Blackwater River
THE MARINERS' MUSEUM
Poquoson
Cape Charles
Ship Shoal Isl
Smith Island
NEWPORT NEWS
HAMPTON
HAMPTON ROADS
Hampton Roads
CHESAPEAKE BAY BRIDGE-TUNNEL
Stony Creek
NORFOLK
Cape Henry
VIRGINIA BEACH BOARDWALK
NAUTICUS
Nottoway River
PORTSMOUTH
VIRGINIA BEACH
Suffolk
Emporia
Courtland
VIRGINIA AQUARIUM AND MARINE SCIENCE CENTER
Back Bay NWR
Great Dismal Swamp NWR
Franklin
Back Bay
False Cape State Park
Lake Drummond
CHESAPEAKE
VIRGINIA
NORTH CAROLINA
17
301
205
3
2
95
1
207
202
360
30
14
200
295
64
33
178
60
249
5
288
10
13
460
40
664
264
44
58
168
32
258
363

THE COAST

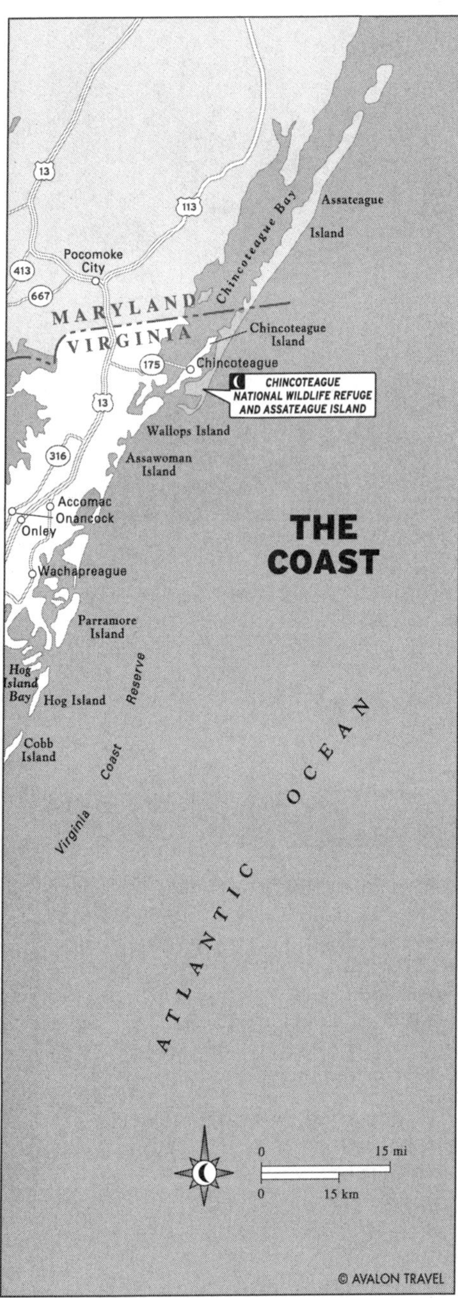

undisturbed shoreline, barrier islands, swamps, marshes, and estuaries.

PLANNING YOUR TIME

Because it's a little less convenient to get around by car, what with all the rivers and bays and estuaries everywhere you turn, Virginia's coast really takes a week or more to explore thoroughly. If you have less time than that you should head down the Historic Peninsula to Hampton Roads, but be warned that most of the millions of people who visit this part of the state every year will be doing the same. Heading out the peninsula from Richmond, don't miss the **historic plantations** along the James River and all the fun stuff in and near Williamsburg, including **Busch Gardens Europe, Colonial Williamsburg,** and the **Colonial National Historical Park,** which encompasses Jamestown and Yorktown. Each deserves a full day.

Along with plentiful nightlife, restaurants, and hotels, the Hampton Roads area offers some of Virginia's most outstanding museums, including **The Mariners' Museum** in Newport News, **NAUTICUS** in Norfolk, and the **Virginia Aquarium and Marine Science Center** in Virginia Beach. (The latter also boasts dozens of miles of beaches and a classic boardwalk.) Any of these cities can serve as a home base for exploring the area. A few out-of-the-way destinations worth a stop are the charming town of **Irvington** on the Northern Neck and culturally unique **Tangier Island** out in the bay. In a weekend you can visit Tangier and the wild ponies at the **Chincoteague National Wildlife Refuge** at the northern end of the pastoral Eastern Shore.

Access

The only Virginia interstate that heads seaward is I-64 from Richmond, threading the Historic Peninsula as it runs east to Williamsburg and the Hampton Roads area. U.S. 17 leaves Fredericksburg for the Middle Neck, where it crosses U.S. 360 before crossing the York River at Yorktown. The Northern and Middle Necks each have their own backbone: Route 3 runs the length of the former, and U.S. 17 skewers

© KATIE GITHENS

The Virginia Aquarium in Virginia Beach draws 620,000 visitors per year.

the latter. U.S. 360 runs from Richmond across both to Reedville.

Farther south, U.S. 460 connects Petersburg with Suffolk near Hampton Roads, and U.S. 58 rolls east from Emporia more or less along the North Carolina state line toward Portsmouth. Two of the most scenic ways to reach the coast are Route 5, which passes half a dozen James River plantations southeast of Richmond, and U.S. 13 down the length of the Eastern Shore from Maryland.

Northern Neck

Reaching bayward between broad, patient rivers, the Necks evoke the Piedmont, but with a shoreside twist. A hazy light filters across the flat farmland, where the odor of freshly mown fields mixes with the brackish breeze off the Chesapeake Bay. Talk at the local store is as likely to be about fixing outboards as about keeping a Chevy running. Full of local color, it's more rural than much of central Virginia. Visitors come for quiet walks, fishing, boating, and shopping from spring to fall. In the off-season, many towns shut down much of their tourist facilities, so calling ahead is always a good idea.

Information and Tours

For more information on this part of the coast, contact the **Northern Neck Tourism Council** in Warsaw (804/333-1919 or 800/393-6180, www.northernneck.org). **Northern Neck Heritage Tours** (804/580-5179, www.nnht.com) offers guided, customizable historical and ecological tours of the area and can help set up accommodations and food, as well as logistical support for paddlers and bird-watchers.

GEORGE WASHINGTON BIRTHPLACE NATIONAL MONUMENT

The father of this country squalled into the light on February 22, 1732, on Pope's Creek Plantation, on the southern bank of the Potomac. It doesn't seem like a bad place to spend the first three and a half years of one's life, here among the trees where a meandering creek empties into the river. Although the building in which Washington was born is gone, an outline in crushed oyster shells shows where it stood, next to a reconstructed farm complete with outbuildings and animal pens.

Pleasant paths lead from the visitors center to the Memorial House, which contains an original tea table. George's father, grandfather, and great-grandfather lie in the family cemetery nearby. Rangers offer talks on the hour, and costumed interpreters manage the working farm in season, providing a window into 18th-century life in the Tidewater. A nature trail continues to a picnic area, and at the end of the road a beach on the Potomac. The monument (804/224-1732, www.nps.gov/gewa, 9 A.M.–5 P.M. daily, $4 pp) is on Route 204 off Route 3.

WESTMORELAND STATE PARK

Ancient marine fossils trapped in Horsehead Cliffs attest to the age (more than 127 million years) of the sediments that make up this peninsula between the Rappahannock and Potomac Rivers. It was set aside in 1936 as one of Virginia's first six state parks. Behind the beach and steep riverside bluffs stretch 1,299 acres of meadows and forest populated by beavers, hawks, and turkeys. Six miles of easy and moderate hiking trails lead to Rock Spring Pond and an observation tower over Fossil Beach.

The park (804/493-8821, www.dcr.virginia.gov/state_parks/wes.shtml, dawn–dusk daily, $3 weekdays, $4 weekends) is on Route 347 off Route 3 and has seven miles of hiking trails, a swimming pool, picnic areas, and a playground. You can spend the night in one of 26 camping cabins ($57–112), open year-round, or at one of the park's 133 campsites ($20–25), open March–December. The Potomac River Retreat can hold 16 people in two fully contained living areas and has deck areas facing the Potomac River ($250–360). A seasonal camp store sells supplies and rents kayaks and pedalboats. The visitors center (noon–5 P.M. Wed.–Sun. in season, weekends only May and

kayaks at Westmoreland State Park

WESTMORELAND BERRY FARM AND ORCHARD

You can pick your own raspberries, blackberries, blueberries, and strawberries at this 80-acre farm along the Rappahannock. Or you can just stop by to sample more than a dozen seasonal fruits, including apricots, peaches, cherries, apples, plums, and pumpkins. The plump red strawberries grown at Westmoreland have been known to draw lines dozens deep at northern Virginia farmers markets in early summer, so why not beat the crowds and pick them yourself? A snack bar serves fruit sundaes, frozen yogurt, and other toothsome mouthfuls. (Look for goats clambering about the raised platforms and ramps of the aerial "goat walk.")

The **farm** (804/224-9171 or 800/997-2377, www.westmorelandberryfarm.com) is southwest of Oak Grove on Route 638, reached from Route 3 via Route 634. It's open during growing season (May-Oct.) 9 A.M.-5 P.M. Monday-Saturday, 10 A.M.-5 P.M. Sunday. Check out its website for a harvest schedule and a list of annual events.

Sept.–Oct.) has exhibits on the natural history of the area, including shark's teeth. Ask about kayak trips along the Horsehead Cliffs on weekends May–October ($16–22).

STRATFORD HALL PLANTATION

Robert E. Lee, the Northern Neck's other famous son, was born on an estate his family had occupied for almost a century. In the late 1730s on a bluff near the Potomac, Thomas Lee built a huge mansion shaped like an *H* in honor of his wife, Hanna. In 1782 his nephew, Henry, moved in and married Annie Hill Carter of Shirley Plantation. Henry went on to make a name for himself in the Revolutionary War as Harry "Light-Horse" Lee. But on January 19, 1807, just four years before Henry lost his fortune in land speculation and moved the family to Alexandria, Annie gave birth to a son who was destined for even greater fame: Robert Edward.

The Great House, one of the most majestic buildings in the state, looks like a brick castle set back a short distance from the river. Sixteen fireplaces and numerous 17th- and 18th-century furnishings fill the cavernous interior. These include many Lee heirlooms, such as a 1660 clock and the crib in which Robert slept as a baby. Notice the 17-foot "inverted tray" ceiling in the Great Hall, and ask about the fireplace angels to which Robert bid good-bye as the family was packing to move. Downstairs are servants' quarters, the original kitchen, bedrooms, and a schoolroom where the teacher slept.

Stratford Hall (804/493-8038, www.stratfordhall.org, 9:30 A.M.–4 P.M. daily, $10 adults, $5 children) is on Route 214 off Route 3. A reception center houses a museum, where you can learn about things like estimating the age of clay pipes by the diameter of their stems, and a gift shop selling fresh-ground corn and oats from the estate's fully functional mill. Stratford has two guesthouses, each with a full kitchen, with 20 rooms between them for $132 d. There's also a log-cabin dining room serving a hearty plantation lunch daily. Three miles of nature trails explore the working plantation's 1,700 rural acres. Annual events include Robert E. Lee's birthday (January 19), African-American Heritage Day (usually the last weekend in February), and a traditional Thanksgiving feast.

REEDVILLE

Founded in 1867 ("by Northerners," grumbles one pamphlet), this small city was reportedly the richest per capita in the country around World War I, thanks to the abundant menhaden fishing in Chesapeake Bay. Today, boats sit in the driveways of tidy houses along Main Street (Rte. 360), which dead-ends at the water along Millionaires' Row, named for a succession of gorgeous Victorian mansions. Reedville is also one gateway to Tangier Island in the Chesapeake Bay.

Sights

The **Reedville Fisherman's Museum** (504 Main St., 804/453-6529, www.rfmuseum.org, 10:30 A.M.–4:30 P.M. daily May–Oct., by appt. only Jan.–Mar., otherwise weekends only in off-season, $5 adults) has been set up in the 1875 Walker House along Main Street just before Millionaires' Row. Displays of ship models, photos, tools, and artwork lead visitors to traditional boats such as a crabbing skiff moored to the rear dock.

Recreation

Captain Billy's Charters (804/580-7292, www.captbillyscharters.com) runs fishing trips aboard the 46-foot *Liquid Assets II* out of the Ingram Bay Marina, near Wicomico Church, for $650 for up to six people. Fishing trips for rockfish, striped bass, and tuna cost more. Other fishing charter options include Capt. Jim Hardy's *Ranger II* (804/453-6635) and Jim Conner's *Jeannie C* (804/453-4021). All outfits provide gear and will even clean your fish for you.

Events

The opening of the fishing season is celebrated during the **Blessing of the Fleet** the first weekend in May. In mid-September, the **Antique Boat Parade** floats down Reedville's Cockrells Creek. The traditional **RFM Oyster Roast** takes place the second Saturday in November and packs tiny Reedville with crowds hankering for tons of seafood. The Reedville Fisherman's Museum also hosts a **family boatbuilding weekend** each year, though dates vary. Contact the museum for information on all events.

Accommodations

The Gables (804/453-5209, www.thegablesbb.com) occupies the unmistakable brick mansion at the end of Main Street, built in the late 1800s by a local captain who brought the bricks by schooner from New England. (The boat's three masts were used in the construction.) One room in the mansion and four in the nearby Coach House Inn (where you'll find the ice cream parlor) are $90–175. Two luxury suites in the well-named Waterside Cottage, built in 2006, run $195–235. In the nearby village of Fleeton is the **Fleeton Fields B&B** (2783 Fleeton Rd., 804/453-5014 or 800/497-8215, www.fleetonfields.com), with three suites with a view of rose-filled gardens and the bay for $150–195.

The **Chesapeake Bay Camp-Resort** (382 Campground Rd., 804/453-3430) is located 2.5 miles northeast of the intersection of Route 652 and U.S. 360 and has 82 campsites for $40–50, as well as cabins for $55–110. Rowboats and canoes are rented here, of course.

Food

Down at the end of Main Street by the marina is **The Crazy Crab** (902 Main St., 804/453-6789, dinner Tues.–Fri., lunch and dinner Sat.–Sun., weekends only in off-season, $14–26), with an outdoor deck, plenty of wine, and daily chef specials of seafood, steak, and chicken. The deli counter at **Cockrell's Creek Seafood Deli** (south on Seaboard Rd. off Fleeton Rd., 804/453-6326, 10 A.M.–5 P.M. Mon.–Sat. in season) sells scallops, shrimp, crabs, and other marine delicacies to go or to eat at its picnic area. Sandwiches are $5–6, and full dinners are $10–15.

Tours and Transportation

Smith Island Cruise (804/453-3430, www.cruisetosmithisland.com) offers narrated day tours to Smith Island, Maryland, in the Chesapeake Bay aboard the 150-person *Spirit of the Chesapeake.* Departing at 10 A.M. from the Chesapeake Bay Camp-Resort in Reedville (daily May–Oct.), the tours allow time to explore Ewell Island, one of three fishing villages, each on its own island, that make up Smith Island. The trip returns at 3:45 P.M. and costs $25 adults, $13 children. Reservations are required.

Day trips to Tangier Island and lunch cruises up the Rappahannock to the Ingleside Plantation Winery are only two of the trips offered by **Tangier & Rappahannock Cruises** (804/453-2628, www.tangiercruise.com). The

Chesapeake Breeze leaves daily at 10 A.M. for Tangier Island, returning about 4 P.M., for $25 adults, $13 children, with an optional lunch. Reservations are recommended during the summer. Narrated lunch and dinner tours aboard a paddle wheeler in Fredericksburg are also offered ($26–45 adults, $16.50–27 children), with onboard dancing on Friday and Saturday. Boats leave May–October from the Buzzard's Point Marina, reached by taking a right before Reedville onto Fairport Road (Rte. 626), followed by a left onto Buzzard Point Road.

IRVINGTON

Christ Church

The showpiece of this small fishing town is a monolithic house of worship completed in 1735 by Robert "King" Carter. One of the few unaltered Colonial churches in the country, it features a high arching ceiling, shoulder-high walls between family-sized pew "boxes," and a three-level pulpit, although it has no bell tower. Services are still held here from June to Labor Day, and the church building (804/438-6855, www.christchurch1735.org) is open 8:30 A.M.–4 P.M. Monday–Friday year-round, and 10 A.M.–4 P.M. Saturday and 2–5 P.M. Sunday April–November. A reception center with a small museum is open 10 A.M.–4 P.M. Monday–Saturday and 2–5 P.M. Sunday April–November. Suggested donation is $5. The church is on Christ Church Road (Rte. 646) off Route 200 just north of town.

Events

Come by the first Saturday in September for the **Irvington Stomp** (www.irvingtonstomp.com), celebrating the annual grape harvest at the White Fences Vineyard with music and the crowning of the King and Queen of the Stomp. Tickets are $10 for adults, $5 for children 6–16.

Accommodations and Food

In 1890, a schoolhouse opened in an old Methodist church near the center of Irvington. Today the building houses **The Hope and Glory Inn** (65 Tavern Rd., 804/438-5362 or 800/497-8228, www.hopeandglory.com). This award-winning place is decked out with folk art and a large central lobby where classrooms once echoed with children's voices. If the seven bedrooms in the schoolhouse ($175–245 weekdays, $195–290 weekends) are full, there are also six charming guest cottages ($240–430) out back, near an enclosed outdoor bath with claw-foot tub, shower, and sink. The English cottage garden features a moon patch that blooms in the evening. They've also opened a handful of "tents" (read: super-cute cottages) at the nearby White Fences Vineyard. These three-bedroom places have screened porches and outdoor showers, and start at $310–385 for one-bedroom usage.

The chic little **Trick Dog Cafe** (4357 Irvington Rd., 804/438-6363) was named for a dog statue in the entrance that was rescued, blackened but unhurt, from the great town fire of 1917. (Petting it is supposed to bring good luck.) They serve tasty bites like tuna tartare and excellent crab cakes ($18–25) for dinner Tuesday–Saturday. Irvington has been called a place "where Mayberry meets Manhattan," a reputation no doubt cultivated by the Trick Dog—though it could just be the green apple martinis going to a travel writer's head.

Along Carter's Creek you'll find the first-class **Tides Inn** (480 King Carter Dr., 804/438-5000 or 800/843-3746, www.tidesinn.com). This all-inclusive getaway has been rated among the top 50 in the country by *Travel + Leisure* magazine. It features two restaurants, a spa, the top-rated Golden Eagle golf course, a sandy beach, a saltwater pool, and a marina. Rooms start at $260. If all the water in every direction has you itching to learn to sail, contact its certified sailing school (804/438-9300, www.sailingschool.net).

Information

Contact the town of Irvington (804/438-6230, www.irvingtonva.org) for more information.

White Stone

Just minutes from Irvington, this village is home to the **White Stone Wine and Cheese Co.** (572

Rappahannock Dr., 804/435-2000) on Route 3, offering the largest local wine selection and gourmet soups and sandwiches in a small café. Another nearby option for a gourmet breakfast or lunch is **Willaby's** (453 Rappahannock Dr., 804/435-0000), serving fancy burgers and tasty desserts for lunch ($5–10) Monday–Saturday. **Rocket Billy's** (851 Rappahannock Dr., 804/435-7040, 6 A.M.–3 P.M. Mon.–Sat.) serves excellent seafood, including crab cakes, soft-shell-crab sandwiches, and bisque, from a red, white, and blue trailer.

Middle Neck

URBANNA

One of 20 port towns established by a 1680 Act of Assembly, Urbanna was named for England's Queen Anne (as was Annapolis, Maryland). The town has weathered pirate attacks and three wars during its centuries as a tobacco export center and fishing village. Watermen still unload their day's catch on wharves shared by recreational boaters and anglers, only a short walk from Victorian homes on the National Register of Historic Places.

Sights

Opened in 1876, the **R. S. Bristow Store** (Virginia St. at Cross St., 804/758-2210) once sold patent medicines, live chickens, and wood by the cord. More than 125 years later it's still in business, selling clothes, gifts, and household goods. There's a shoe section where the post office used to be and an old-fashioned rolling ladder to reach the higher shelves. The nearby **courthouse building** dates to 1748, making it the oldest structure in Urbanna. It has served various functions over the years, shifting from a church to Confederate Civil War barracks to its present role as a women's club headquarters.

Events

Held on the first weekend in November, the **Urbanna Oyster Festival** (804/758-0368, www.urbannaoysterfestival.com) draws nearly 75,000 people with a firemen's parade, food and crafts, oyster-shucking contest, and the crowning of the Oyster Festival Queen and Little Miss Spat. It's been going strong for more than 50 years.

Accommodations

The **Atherston Hall B&B** (250 Prince George St., 804/758-2809, www.atherstonhall.com, $115–150) was originally the home of a 19th-century schooner captain. It offers three rooms, a suite, homemade granola and other breakfast offerings, afternoon tea, and day sailing trips aboard the *Victorious, Tregony,* or *Harry.*

A pair of former restaurateurs have turned an 1870s Victorian mansion into the **Inn at Urbanna Creek** (210 Watling St., 804/758-4661, www.innaturbannacreek.com, $95–160). Choose from three rooms and a separate cottage with vaulted ceilings and a private deck and garden. Rates include a full breakfast.

Waterfront campsites at the **Bethpage Camp Resort** (804/758-4349, www.bethpagecamp.com), about 15 miles west near the intersection of Routes 17 and 684, are $40–55 with full hookups. This huge place has two pools, a tennis court, a grocery store, and a marina. Open April–mid-November.

Seven miles away in Church View, at the intersection of Routes 17 and 602, is the **Dragon Run Inn** (35 Ware Bridge Rd., 804/758-5719, www.dragon-run-inn.com). The former farmhouse was built in 1913 with cypress from a nearby swamp. The four rooms (whimsically named Dog, Cow, Pig, and Sheep) are each $100–150 per night, and meals can be arranged with advance reservations.

Food

For such a small town, Urbanna has no shortage of cafés. **Marshall's Drug Store** (50 Cross St., 804/758-5344) offers an authentic old-fashioned lunch counter with real milk shakes, and the **Virginia Street Café** (201 Virginia St., 804/758-3798, all meals daily) serves simple but satisfying food.

Café Mojo (230 Virginia St., 804/758-4141, dinner Thurs.–Sat.) is more upscale, serving up eclectic surf, turf, and pasta entrées ($12–16) with European and Mexican influences and a funky bar with live music.

Two miles north of town is **Something Different** (3617 Old Virginia St., 804/758-8004, 10 A.M.–6 P.M. Wed.–Fri., 8 A.M.–6 P.M. Sat., 8 A.M.–3 P.M. Sun.), a country store and deli serving up fresh-ground coffee, homemade ice cream, and some of the best North Carolina–style barbecue around.

Information

For more on Urbanna, contact the town offices at 45 Cross Street (804/758-2613, www.urbanna.com).

INDIAN RESERVATIONS

A museum on the 1,200-acre **Pamunkey Indian Reservation** (804/843-4792, www.pamunkey.net, 10 A.M.–4 P.M. Tues.–Sat., 1–5 P.M. Sun., $2.50 adults, $1.25 children) traces the history of the largest chiefdom of the Powhatan confederacy, established in 1607. Extensive displays include beautiful ceremonial garments and a collection of mean-looking weapons, including a huge collection of handmade flint points. Several local potters have formed a guild to begin reviving traditional methods, and their wares are for sale in the museum shop. To find it, take Route 633 or Route 626 south from Route 30, then follow the signs.

Officially designated in 1658, the **Mattaponi Reservation** (http://indians.vipnet.org/tribes/mattaponi.cfm) has been whittled down to only 150 acres. It's located off Route 30 opposite the Pamunkey Reservation via Route 626 or Route 640 and hosts an annual powwow in mid-June, with dancing, drumming, food, and crafts ($5 pp). Every year the tribal chief presents the governor of Virginia with a gift of peace in accordance with original treaties.

Colonial Williamsburg

America's largest and most popular living-history museum re-creates the Colonial capital as it was on November 11, 1775, the tense eve of the Revolutionary War. One of the most ambitious historical projects ever, this isn't just a few restored farms or households—this is an entire town brought back to life and inhabited by people portraying a cadre of craftspeople, slaves, merchants, and aristocrats.

It may not be everyone's cup of tea (or ale), but Colonial Williamsburg is a remarkable feat, the product of decades of research, experimentation, and refinement. The realism—aside from the hordes of tourists—is amazing. Horse-drawn carriages clop past a merchant arguing with his neighbor over the best course of political action, while nonplussed ducks wander down a dusty lane where a smith stands sweating over his forge. Best of all, you can even take part in it yourself. Join a tipsy Colonial gentleman in singing tavern songs, learn the finer points of baking apple fritters from his wife, immerse yourself in the latest findings at an archaeological dig, or sit on a courthouse jury to decide whether a pig thief deserves a flogging or just a day in the stocks.

Children especially love the "living" aspect of Williamsburg, and get a kick out of rolling hoops across the Palace Green in three-cornered hats or taking lessons from the Dancing Master in the Governor's Palace. Colonial Williamsburg has done an enviable job of marketing itself as the ultimate family destination, covering both the educational and entertainment angles—and a million visitors a year would argue it has been successful.

Costumed interpreters in Colonial Williamsburg dress the part and often present their characters in the first person.

HISTORY

Rural acreage known as Middle Plantation got a rude awakening when it was picked as the site for the new Colonial capital in 1699. The planter aristocracy of the day had decided it needed a more sophisticated spot for the business of governing and socializing than damp Jamestown, and this site, near the newly established Royal College of William and Mary, seemed suitable.

Plans were immediately set in motion to transform a scattering of plantation buildings into a capital fit for one of Britain's oldest colonies. First to be laid out was Duke of Gloucester Street, 100 feet wide and almost one mile long, from William and Mary's Wren Building at one end to the capitol building at the other. A grassy mall led to the Governor's Palace.

The town quickly became the cultural and political center of Virginia and the focus of Colonial America's most fashionable social scene. As a ceremonial city with little manufacturing base, Williamsburg swelled during "Public Times" in April and October. Rural gentry rode in from their plantations to attend sessions of the House of Burgesses and Governor's Council, delighting in a social whirl that, they said, rivaled London's. Countless balls, races, and a fair competed for attention with performances by English actors and musicians in one of the earliest theaters in America.

Williamsburg welcomed some impressive names during its heyday, including George Washington, George Mason, and Patrick Henry. Thomas Jefferson first arrived in the early 1760s as a student at William and Mary and returned later as a member of the House of Burgesses. In 1719, 13 pirates from the ship of the notorious Edward Teach (Blackbeard) were tried and condemned to death in the General Court chamber in the capitol building. A decade later, Williamsburg boasted the first successful printing press in the colony, followed soon after by its first newspaper and paper mill.

Patrick Henry defied the British Stamp Act

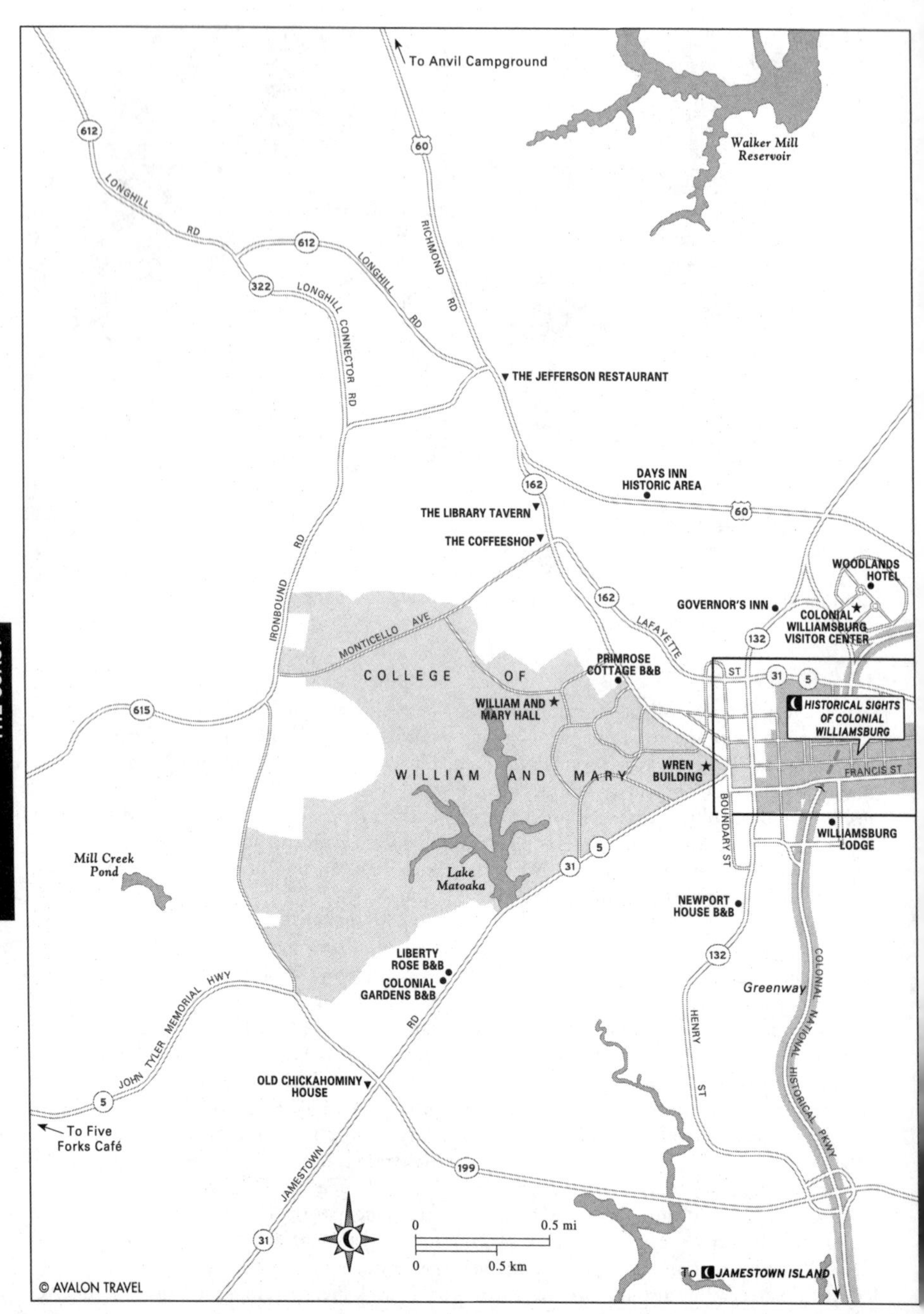
To Anvil Campground
Walker Mill Reservoir
612
60
LONGHILL RD
612
LONGHILL RD
RICHMOND RD
322
LONGHILL CONNECTOR RD
THE JEFFERSON RESTAURANT
DAYS INN HISTORIC AREA
162
60
THE LIBRARY TAVERN
THE COFFEESHOP
IRONBOUND RD
162
WOODLANDS HOTEL
GOVERNOR'S INN
COLONIAL WILLIAMSBURG VISITOR CENTER
MONTICELLO AVE
LAFAYETTE ST
132
COLLEGE OF WILLIAM AND MARY
PRIMROSE COTTAGE B&B
31
5
615
WILLIAM AND MARY HALL
HISTORICAL SIGHTS OF COLONIAL WILLIAMSBURG
WREN BUILDING
FRANCIS ST
BOUNDARY ST
WILLIAMSBURG LODGE
Mill Creek Pond
Lake Matoaka
NEWPORT HOUSE B&B
132
LIBERTY ROSE B&B
COLONIAL GARDENS B&B
Greenway
JOHN TYLER MEMORIAL HWY
HENRY ST
COLONIAL NATIONAL HISTORICAL PKWY
OLD CHICKAHOMINY HOUSE
JAMESTOWN RD
To Five Forks Café
199
0 0.5 mi
0 0.5 km
31
To JAMESTOWN ISLAND

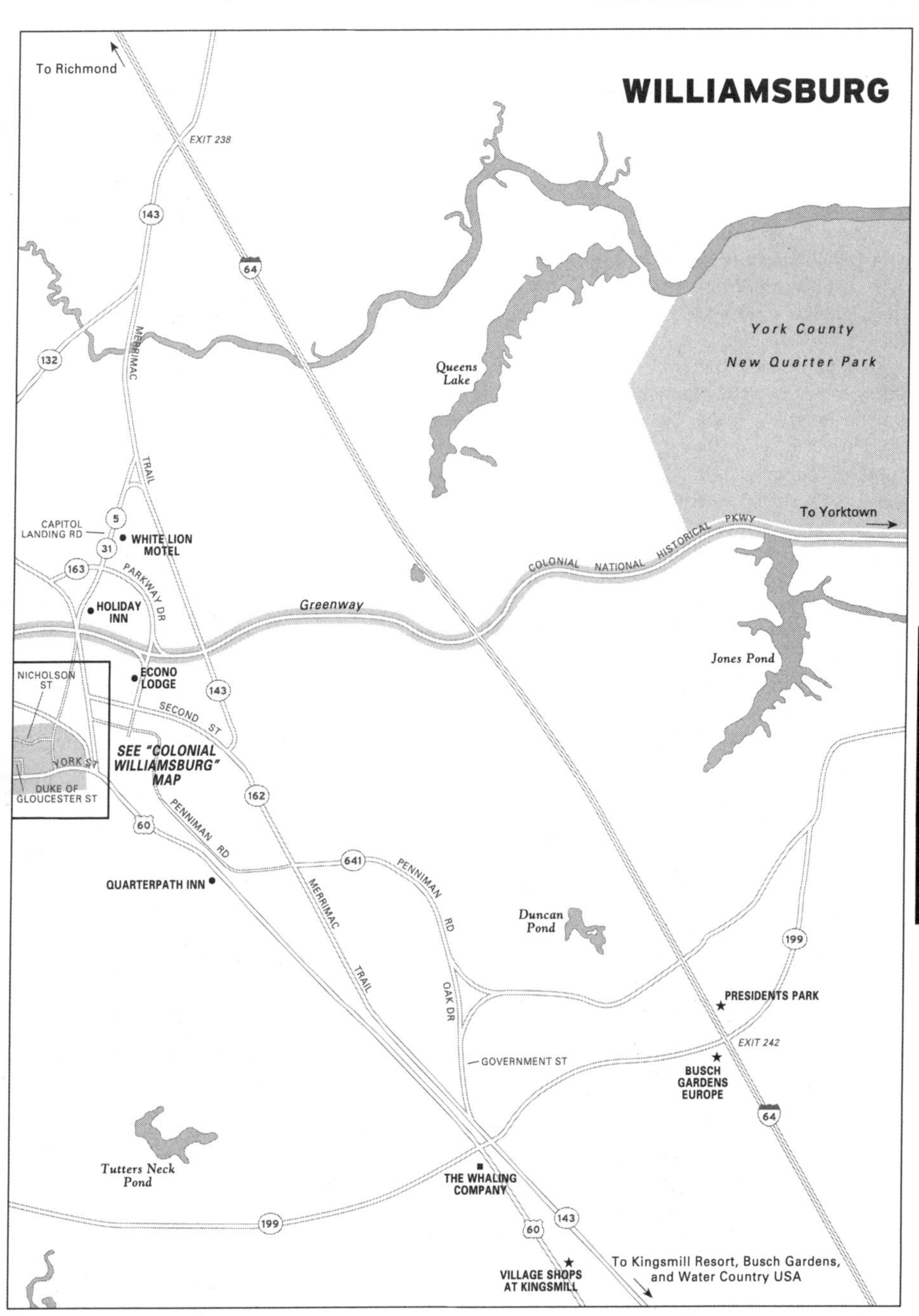
WILLIAMSBURG
To Richmond
EXIT 238
143
64
132
MERRIMAC
TRAIL
Queens Lake
York County
New Quarter Park
To Yorktown
COLONIAL NATIONAL HISTORICAL PKWY
5
CAPITOL LANDING RD
WHITE LION MOTEL
31
163
PARKWAY DR
HOLIDAY INN
Greenway
Jones Pond
NICHOLSON ST
ECONO LODGE
143
SECOND ST
SEE "COLONIAL WILLIAMSBURG" MAP
YORK ST
DUKE OF GLOUCESTER ST
162
60
PENNIMAN RD
641
PENNIMAN RD
QUARTERPATH INN
MERRIMAC TRAIL
Duncan Pond
199
OAK DR
PRESIDENTS PARK
EXIT 242
GOVERNMENT ST
BUSCH GARDENS EUROPE
64
Tutters Neck Pond
THE WHALING COMPANY
199
143
60
VILLAGE SHOPS AT KINGSMILL
To Kingsmill Resort, Busch Gardens, and Water Country USA

in his "Caesar-Brutus" speech to the House of Burgesses on May 30, 1765, throwing sparks ever closer to the fuse of revolution. When Royal Governor Botetourt dissolved the House of Burgesses as it was about to vote to boycott British goods in 1769, its members simply reassembled at the Raleigh tavern and voted there. On May 6, 1776, the fifth Virginia Convention met in Williamsburg to declare Virginia an independent commonwealth, and four years later the capital was moved to Richmond to escape the invading British.

British, Continental, and French forces all billeted on the city's grassy lawns during the Revolutionary War, buying goods from local merchants and providing temporary relief from an economic slump that continued into the 19th century. Restoration began in the 1920s at the instigation of Rev. Dr. W. A. R. Goodwin, rector of the historic Bruton Parish Church. Bankrolled by no less than John D. Rockefeller Jr. (who signed documents anonymously as "David's father"), the plan met with some local resistance until residents realized it was probably the best thing to happen to the city in 150 years.

Exhaustive research in libraries and museums in Europe and America uncovered documents, drawings, and maps detailing Williamsburg's faded glory. More than 450 buildings were torn down, 91 were built, and 67 Colonial structures restored (with their inhabitants allowed to stay on for life).

Eighty-eight original buildings have been meticulously restored on 301 acres. More than 500 other structures have been rebuilt as closely as possible to their original specifications, surrounded by 90 acres of greens and gardens and a 2,800-acre buffer zone against further development. Restoration is constantly being refined as new archaeological information comes to light, from hearth-stone material to hand-painted wallpaper designs.

VISITING COLONIAL WILLIAMSBURG

If you don't plan ahead, visiting Colonial Williamsburg can be an exercise in patience. Reservations for hotels and special events are essential during peak periods (April, May, July, August, October, late November, and December), and early morning is always the best time to visit the more popular stops, such as the Governor's Palace and capitol building.

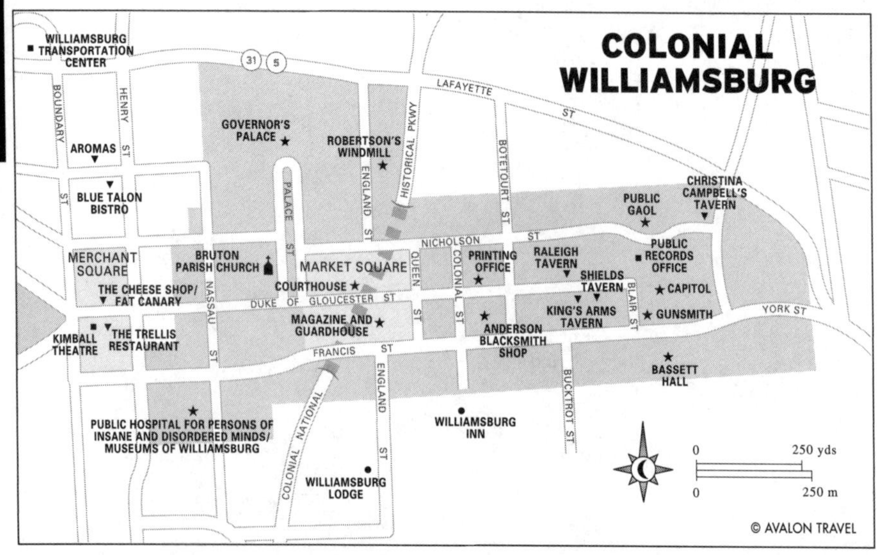

© KATIE GITHENS

weather vane on a home in Colonial Williamsburg

You can do the highlights in one day, even a single tiring morning, but a much better plan is to leave yourself a few days to wander the back lanes, chat with the interpreters, and linger over a pint at one of the taverns.

Williamsburg is open 365 days a year, and hours are generally 9 A.M.–5 P.M. daily, but vary with the season. Restaurants and taverns bustle until after dark, and the streets are always free to wander, but you'll need to buy passes to enter the historic buildings. Get information, buy tickets, and make reservations for dining and lodging through the **Colonial Williamsburg Foundation** (800/447-8679, www.history.org).

First stop is the **visitors center** off U.S. 60 bypass and the Colonial Parkway just east of Route 132. Ticket lines can take a while, so you might want to designate a volunteer to wait while everyone else in your party catches the 35-minute orientation film, *Williamsburg—The Story of a Patriot.*

Admission passes come in a few different versions. You can always upgrade to the next level by paying the price difference, and all tickets can be purchased online though the foundation's website. The **1-Day Basic Pass** ($36 adults, $18 children 6–17) gives admission to the town core, including the Capitol, trade shops, and more (it excludes the Governor's Palace Tour). The **1-Day Plus Pass** ($46 adults, $23 children 6–17) adds admission to the Governor's Palace. The **Annual Pass** ($58 adults, $29 children 6–17) provides year-round access and a 25 percent discount on most Colonial Evening Programs. If you stay at one of the Colonial Williamsburg hotels, you can get a **hotel guest ticket** for $30 adults/$15 children, which covers general admission to the historic area. Some evening programs, including music, dancing, and theater performances, require advance reservations and separate admission. With any ticket, you'll receive a copy of the brochure *This Week,* which contains a map and details on the week's events.

The Colonial Williamsburg Foundation has concocted several discount **vacation packages** involving food, lodging, seasonal events, and admission to certain attractions. Contact the foundation for details.

HISTORICAL SIGHTS

The mammoth **Governor's Palace** building was constructed 1708–1722 to symbolize the power of the Crown in the colonies. Thomas Jefferson and Patrick Henry stepped through the door as the capital's first two governors, shortly before it burned to its foundation in 1781. The restored building is the single most popular in Colonial Williamsburg, receiving 650,000 visitors annually, so try to get there early in the day.

Shaped like a bulbous *H,* the brick **Capitol** is a reconstruction of the original structure finished in 1705 and burned in 1747. George Washington, among other notables, polished his oratory in the House of Burgesses, the lower elected body that sent proposed laws to the Council for consideration. Interpreters explain how jury duty today is a garden party compared to what it was in the 18th century, when juries were denied heat, food, and water in order to encourage a speedy verdict.

Speaking of verdicts, many a criminal quaked at the sight of the cupola and weather vane atop Williamsburg's **Courthouse,** where severe punishment followed quick judgment. Visitors can take part in the dispensation of Colonial justice on either side of the docket—as a member of the jury or a defendant. Punishments are optional. Across the street, weapons and 60,000 pounds of gunpowder were once stored in the octagonal **Magazine and Guardhouse,** built in 1715 on Duke of Gloucester Street.

One of the country's oldest Episcopal houses of worship, **Bruton Parish Church** (757/229-2891, www.brutonparish.org) stands at the foot of Palace Green, built in 1715. The walls and windows are original. It's not officially part of Colonial Williamsburg, and services are still held here; contact the church for visiting hours.

Offenders and the merely offensive, from pirates and runaway slaves to Tory sympathizers and the insane, all enjoyed the hospitality of Williamsburg's **Public Gaol,** or jail, as we call it today. Built in 1704, it was used until 1910 and has been restored to its 1720s appearance. Miserable barred cells still hold the little extras—manacles, leg irons, and the like—that made every stay special.

© KATIE GITHENS

steeple of the Bruton Parish Church, circa 1715

Those with mental disorders found themselves in the unfortunate care of Williamsburg's **Public Hospital for Persons of Insane and Disordered Minds** (11 A.M.–6 P.M. daily), the first facility in the country to care for the mentally ill. In the 18th century, insanity was considered a conscious choice, so along with the progressive therapies like sports and music, patients were also kept in cages, dunked in water, and held in manacles to "convince" them to mend their mindset.

Master craftspeople, many of whom have served multiyear apprenticeships, practice Colonial-era crafts at dozens of shops and exhibits throughout the historic area. At the **gunsmith** house, an armorer explains the intricacies of a flintlock musket. You can watch handbills and newspapers being printed on an 18th-century press in the **Printing Office.** One of the best areas to watch demonstrations is near **Robertson's Windmill** (between the Governor's Palace and Randolph House), where coopers build casks and carpenters plane boards for the latest restoration. A shoemaker, silversmith, saddlemaker, and wigmaker operate along **Duke of Gloucester Street** (and elsewhere you can catch a milliner, wheelwright, and blacksmith at work). Stop by the **Pasteur and Galt Apothecary Shop** for a disquieting display of the medical knowledge (or ignorance) of the time. Then visit **R. Charlton's Coffeeshop** for a sip of steaming coffee or hot chocolate.

College of William and Mary

America's second-oldest college (757/221-400, www.wm.edu) was chartered on February 8, 1693, by King William III and Queen Mary II, consisting of three buildings in the angle formed by Richmond and Jamestown

Roads. The **Wren Building** was named for Sir Christopher Wren, though he probably didn't design it, and is the oldest academic building in the country still in use (1695). It's been restored to its 1776 appearance. To either side stand the **President's House,** still in use, and the **Brafferton,** originally built as an Indian School.

The college severed ties with Great Britain in 1776 and soon became the first school in the United States to have branches of law and modern languages and operate under an honor system. Thomas Jefferson, James Monroe, and John Tyler are among its more prestigious alumni. The school became state-supported in 1906 and went coeducational in 1918. Today it counts close to 8,000 students, most of whom take advantage of one of the top undergraduate programs in the country taught by more than 667 faculty.

Some 3,000 works of art dating to 1732 are displayed in the **Muscarelle Museum of Art** (757/221-2700, www.wm.edu/muscarelle, 10 A.M.–5 P.M. Tues.–Fri., noon–4 P.M. Sat.–Sun., $5) in Lamberson Hall on Jamestown Road.

OTHER SIGHTS

The Museums of Colonial Williamsburg

A gift of $14 million (the largest in Williamsburg's history) from DeWitt Wallace, the owner of *Reader's Digest,* funded construction of the modern **Wallace Decorative Arts Museum** (325 W. Francis St., 757/229-1000, 10 A.M.–7 P.M. daily, until 5 P.M. in off-season). Entered through the Public Hospital at Francis and North Henry Streets, the museum houses an astonishing collection of 10,000 objects from England and America. Furniture, paintings, ceramics, textiles, silver, and glass on display date to the 17th and 18th centuries. Highlights in the Masterworks Gallery upstairs include a Charles Wilson Peale portrait of George Washington and a case clock made for King William III in 1699. The **Museum Cafe** serves light sandwiches, salads, soups, and wine for lunch.

The world-class **Abby Aldrich Rockefeller Folk Art Museum** (10 A.M.–7 P.M. daily, until 5 P.M. in off-season) houses everything from toys and weather vanes to painted furniture and tinware, ranging in age from the 1730s to the present. The 10,400-square-foot museum was the passion of John D. Rockefeller's wife, one of the first collectors to search out untutored rural artists in the 1920s and 1930s. Her collection shows that true inspiration can have the most humble beginnings. Notice the ship carvings and embroidered mourning pictures.

Presidents Park

A more unusual way to absorb history awaits at this 10-acre park near Water Country USA. Opened in 2004, Presidents Park (211 Water Country Pkwy., 800/588-4327, www.presidentspark.org, 10 A.M.–4 P.M. daily, to 5 P.M. Mar.–May, to 7 P.M. June–Aug., $12.75 adults, $8 children) displays white concrete busts of 43 U.S. presidents. These aren't your everyday busts—each is 18–20 feet tall and weighs around 7,000 pounds. Signs near each one list biographical details, and the overall effect is entertainingly quirky, with educational overtones.

ENTERTAINMENT AND RECREATION

Historical Diversions

Colonial Williamsburg offers a full roster of activities by day and night, from guided walking tours of the historic area to an evening of Vivaldi at the Palace of the Governors. Some events, such as a candlelit walk around the city's haunted spots, are scheduled. Others just happen—as when wandering reenactors allow you to debate the rights of man with Thomas Jefferson or gossip with Martha Washington about her husband's snoring.

Theater, Music, and Other Nightlife

J. M. Randall's Restaurant and Lounge (4854 Longhill Rd. in the Olde Towne Square, 757/259-0406) features acoustic rock and blues. **The Corner Pocket** (4805 Courthouse

COAST AREA WINERIES

Belle Mount Vineyards
2570 Newland Rd., Warsaw
804/333-4700
www.bellemount.com

Bloxom Vineyards
26130 Mason Rd., Bloxom
757/665-5670
www.bloxomwinery.com

Ingleside Plantation Vineyards
5872 Leedstown Rd., Oak Grove
804/224-8687
www.inglesidevineyards.com

James River Cellars
11008 Washington Hwy., Glen Allen
804/550-7516
www.jamesrivercellars.com

Lake Anna Winery
5621 Courthouse Rd., Spotsylvania
540/895-5085
www.lawinery.com

Oak Crest Vineyard & Winery
8215 Oak Crest Dr., King George
540/663-2813
www.oakcrestwinery.com

Williamsburg Winery
5800 Wessex Hundred, Williamsburg
757/229-0999
www.williamsburgwinery.com

St., 757/220-0808), in the Williamsburg Crossing Shopping Center at Routes 5 and 199, is an upscale 18-and-over pool hall with high-quality tables and occasional live music.

The coziest place to see a movie in town is the **Kimball Theatre** (428 Duke of Gloucester, 757/565-8588 or 800/447-8679, www.kimballtheatre.com). Even though it's right smack in the center of Colonial Williamsburg (in Merchants Square), the 410-seat theater is far from traditional. This is the go-to venue for foreign and indie films, classic cinema, and documentaries, making it a popular choice with William and Mary students and faculty. In fact, the college's Global Film Festival is held here in mid-February. The Kimball also has a 35-seat screening room on the 2nd floor. Tickets ($7) can be purchased at the box office (open 4–9 P.M. daily) or any Colonial Williamsburg ticket location. See the website for current programming.

The Williamsburg Players (200 Hubbard Ln., 757/229-0431, www.williamsburgplayers.org) is the city's oldest continuously operating community theater, in operation since 1957. Performances are held in an intimate venue where you're never far from the stage.

Outdoor Recreation

You can rent bicycles from **Bikes Unlimited** (141 Monticello Ave., 757/229-4620), which sponsors William and Mary's cycling team. Comfort bikes with big cushy seats cost $20/day, and road and mountain bikes go for $40/day.

Tours

The darker side of Williamsburg's history is the focus of the **Ghosts of Williamsburg Tours** (757/253-1058 or 877/624-4678, www.theghosttour.com). Historical interpreters lead candlelit tours of town, weaving tales of history, ghosts, and other interesting tidbits. Tours ($11 pp age 7 and up) leave nightly at 8 P.M. and also at 8:45 P.M. June–August.

SHOPPING

Williamsburg has droves of shops, so the trick is figuring out what you want to buy, not where to buy it. Outlets galore fill malls and shopping centers in every direction from the historic center, but the most distinctive souvenirs come from specialty shops in and around Colonial Williamsburg.

Most of the items you can see being made by Williamsburg craftspeople are for sale in several **craft houses** run by the Colonial Williamsburg Foundation in Merchants Square, which is also home to various upscale shops. **The Peanut Shop** (414 Prince George

St., 757/229-3908) has dozens of sweet and salty snacks to sample, and there's plenty to peruse in **The Toymaker of Williamsburg** (415 Duke of Gloucester St., 757/229-5660) and the **Shirley Pewter Shop** (417 Duke of Gloucester St., 757/229-5356) next door. For something different, head to **Mermaid Books** (421-A Prince George St., 757/229-3603), a hole-in-the-wall new-and-used bookseller under Smithfield Ham Shoppe that, besides stacks of literature, sells vintage crockery and quirky mermaid paraphernalia. The **Williamsburg Farmers Market** (www.williamsburgfarmers market.com) is a real charmer too. It sets up in Merchants Square 8 A.M.–noon on Saturdays year-round, as well as 10 A.M.–2 P.M. Tuesdays in June–August.

Farther afield, **Williamsburg Pottery** (6692 Richmond Rd., 757/564-3326, www.williams burgpottery.com) has grown so large since it opened in 1938 that it now has its own campground. It's been called "the greatest assemblage of kitsch in America," with items from over 20 countries.

EVENTS

In early October, the **Williamsburg Scottish Festival and Celtic Celebration** (www .wsfonline.org) brings bagpipes, brogues, and a Balmoral reception to the Rockahock Campgrounds (www.rockahock.com). Celtic dancing, clan tents, and a ceilidh (Scottish musical party) round out the festivities.

The Christmas holiday season is one of Colonial Williamsburg's busiest times, beginning with the **Grand Illumination** in early December, when the entire historic area flickers with candlelight. Homes are hung with natural decorations such as pinecones and evergreen boughs, and the streets echo with concerts and carols. Special holiday programs, concerts, feasts, fireworks, and military salutes continue through New Year's Eve, when there's a **First Night** celebration.

ACCOMMODATIONS

With more than 10,000 hotel rooms, Williamsburg has no shortage of places to stay. Still, this is such a popular destination that reservations are always helpful—and essential during the peak periods of April, May, July, August, October, late November, and December.

Colonial Williamsburg Foundation Hotels

For information and reservations for these accommodations in the historic area, contact the Colonial Williamsburg Foundation (800/447-8679, www.history.org).

What could be more authentic after a long day in the 18th century than curling up in an actual Colonial home? The foundation operates 26 **Colonial houses,** each with its own unique history and anywhere from one to 16 rooms. The **Market Square Tavern** is where Thomas Jefferson lodged as a student at William and Mary; the **Quarter** was a favorite of Cary Grant in the 1940s. Some of the buildings, including the **Bracken Tenement** and **Ewing House,** are original, whereas others are reconstructed. Many have canopied beds, fireplaces, period antiques, and views of Duke of Gloucester Street. Prices range $150–460; see the foundation's website for details and reservations.

The **Williamsburg Inn** (136 E. Francis St., 757/253-2277) is probably the finest hotel in the city, if not the entire Historic Peninsula. Renovations completed in 2001 enlarged the hotel to 62 rooms and upped its AAA category to four diamonds. No two rooms in this posh place are alike, but all are lavishly decorated with antiques. The inn's formal Regency Dining Room is justly famous for its elegant setting and extensive wine list; the Regency Lounge provides a more casual option. English tea is served several days a week. Guests have access to full sports facilities and three golf courses, including the nationally known Golden Horseshoe. Rates are $300 and up.

The **Williamsburg Lodge** (310 S. England St., 757/220-7976) is a resort hotel popular with conference groups. Three hundred rooms and 24 suites alternate between Colonial and modern decor, and the sunken garden is perfect for an after-dinner ramble. Dining choices include the Bay Room Restaurant and the relaxed Lodge Cafe. Prices start at around $130.

The **Woodlands Hotel** (105 Visitors Center Dr., 757/220-7690) offers 204 contemporary rooms and 96 suites in comfortably wooded surroundings next door to the Colonial Williamsburg visitors center. It's one of the foundation's less expensive lodging options, with rooms for $70–160.

The **Governor's Inn** (506 N. Henry St., 757/220-7940, $60–100) began its career as a Sheraton a short walk from the visitors center and the historic area. It has 200 rooms and a pool that's open seasonally. The Governor's Inn is usually closed January–mid-March.

$50-100

The **White Lion Motel** (912 Capitol Landing Rd., 757/229-3931, www.whitelionmotel.com) has rooms for $52–78 and efficiency suites for up to $100. The **Days Inn Historic Area** (331 Bypass Rd., 757/253-1166, $70–100) goes for a country-inn atmosphere in its 120 rooms, including some suites. Two other inexpensive lodging options near the historic area are the **Quarterpath Inn** (620 York St., 757/220-0960, www.quarterpathinn.com, $55–100) and the **Econo Lodge** (216 Parkway Dr., 757/253-6450, $55–90).

$100-150

German-born Inge Curtis opened **Primrose Cottage at Two Rivers** (16538 Chickahominy Bluff Rd., 800/522-1901, www.primrose-cottage.com, $195) as an outlet for her interests in cooking, gardening, and carpentry, and it shows in the beds of pansies and primroses in the front yard.

The **Colonial Capital Bed & Breakfast** (501 Richmond Rd., 757/229-0233 or 800/776-0570, www.ccbb.com, $145–160) occupies a 1926 Colonial Revival home across the street from the College of William and Mary. Oriental rugs and family heirlooms fill the three-story house, whose large plantation parlor is warmed by a roaring fire in the winter.

$150-200

At the **Colonial Gardens Bed & Breakfast** (1109 Jamestown Rd., 800/886-9715, www.colonial-gardens.com, $155–185), rocking chairs sit on the front porch and plush robes wait in the bedrooms, named after the rhododendrons and azaleas that bloom in the gardens. Breakfast is served on fine china in the formal dining room, and over the holidays a Christmas tree brightens each room.

The **Newport House B&B** (710 S. Henry St., 757/229-1775 or 877/565-1775, www.newporthousebb.com, $150–225) is Williamsburg's most historically themed bed-and-breakfast. It's a 1998 museum-standard reconstruction of a 1756 home designed by Colonial architect Peter Harrison, with wood siding carved to look like cut stone (Harrison's solution for a client who couldn't afford a stone house). The two rooms are furnished with top-notch English and American antiques, accurate down to the bedspread patterns. Hosts John and Cathy Millar teach English country dancing in the ballroom and often include a historic recipe or two for breakfast. Josephine Bunnyparts is the resident rabbit.

Over $200

Century-old beech, oak, and poplar trees welcome you to the **Liberty Rose B&B** (1025 Jamestown Rd., 757/253-1260 or 800/545-1825, www.libertyrose.com, $195–245), called the most romantic bed-and-breakfast in Williamsburg. Set on a hilltop, the two-story home features rooms with names like Magnolias Peach and Savannah Lace, decorated with designer wall coverings and vintage fabrics. Soak in an antique claw-foot tub or savor a gourmet breakfast on the sunny porch.

Five miles east of Colonial Williamsburg on U.S. 60 is **Kingsmill Resort** (757/253-1703 or 800/832-5665, www.kingsmill.com), the state's largest golf and spa resort. Three 18-hole championship golf courses on the banks of the James River include the difficult River Course, site of the Michelob Championship at Kingsmill for 22 years and currently part of the LPGA tour. Fifteen tennis courts, a marina, nature trails, and a full fitness center–spa round out the amenities, and there are six restaurants and lounges to choose from for meals. More than 400 guest rooms and suites with 1–3 bedrooms and kitchens cost from $170 upward. Call for information on various package deals, including admission to Colonial Williamsburg and nearby attractions.

Camping

The **Anvil Campground** (5243 Mooretown Rd., 757/565-2300 or 800/633-4442, www.anvilcampground.com, open year-round) is the closest to central Williamsburg. A laundry, TV room, three playgrounds, and basketball courts are just some of the services offered. Sites are $35–50, and there are cottages for $120–130.

Take Route 646 north from I-64 exit 234 (Lightfoot) to reach the **Williamsburg KOA Resort** (4000 Newman Rd., 800/562-1733, www.williamsburgkoa.com, open Mar.–Dec.), a hefty 180-acre 370-site campground. Campsites ($35–58) and one- and two-room cabins ($60–90) are available.

FOOD

Snacks and Cafés

Savor the smells of **Aromas** (431 Prince George St., 757/221-6676, all meals daily), a coffeehouse and then some where you can find gourmet coffees and teas along with smoothies, fresh pastries, sandwiches, and a full breakfast and dinner menu. Wine and beer are also on the menu, and live music happens on weekend nights. More excellent coffee drinks await at **The Coffeehouse** (5251-6 John Tyler Hwy., 757/229-9791, breakfast and lunch daily) in the Williamsburg Crossing Shopping Center. Sandwiches, muffins, and bagels from scratch round things out, and there's an outdoor terrace for sunny weather. Both are good meeting places—or refuges from historic overload.

Casual

Half restaurant, half antiques shop, the **Old Chickahominy House** (1211 Jamestown Rd., 757/229-4689, breakfast and lunch daily) resembles an old farmhouse and serves food to match. Plantation meals in the 18th-century dining room include chicken and dumplings and homemade pie; hearty country breakfasts of Virginia ham, bacon, sausage, eggs, grits, and biscuits are around $7–8. (The pancakes are excellent.)

Inexpensive pizzas, subs, sandwiches, and steamed seafood are the standard favorites at **The Library Tavern** (1330 Richmond Rd., 757/229-1012, lunch and dinner daily, open until 2 A.M., $7–16), "where silence isn't golden." There's a full bar and pool tables in the back.

For a greasy-spoon diner with a friendly waitstaff, you can't beat **Five Forks Café** (4456 John Tyler Hwy., 757/221-0484, all meals Tues.–Sat., breakfast and lunch Sun.). At breakfast, mix and match fillings for a three-egg omelet, or fill up on blueberry pancakes or biscuits and gravy. For dinner, the most expensive item on the menu is also the most traditional: roasted turkey with cranberry sauce for $11. Active duty military get a 25 percent discount with their military identification card.

The Cheese Shop (410 Duke of Gloucester St., 757/220-0298, 10 A.M.–9 P.M. Mon.–Sat., 11 A.M.–6 P.M. Sun.) offers over 200 types of cheese (and samples!) along with fresh-baked bread, sandwiches, and a wine cellar with thousands of bottles on offer. It's next to Fat Canary on Merchant Square and run by the same folks.

Fresh seafood is the specialty, naturally, of **The Whaling Company** (494 McLaws Circle, 757/229-0275, dinner daily), on Route 60 East near Busch Gardens. Plates like shrimp scampi linguine run $13–38, and the hand-carved steaks are also worth a mention.

Take a lunch stop at the **Jamestown Pie Company** (1804 Jamestown Rd., 757/229-7775, lunch and dinner daily), where "round food is good food"—namely pizzas ($15–23 for a 16-inch), pot pies ($9–11 individual pie), and dessert pies ($14–18). This pizzeria and pie company is a convenient stop en route to Jamestown from Williamsburg on Route 31. It's take-out only, but there are a few tables on the patio.

Upscale

Billing itself as "serious comfort food," the **Blue Talon Bistro** (420 Prince George St., 757/476-2583, all meals daily) dresses up classics like mac-and-cheese and meatloaf in their Sunday best ($16–26). Check out the plate of the day for specials such as shrimp and polenta or braised goat with a yellow curry sauce. Blue Talon is located on the perimeter of Merchants Square in Colonial Williamsburg. You can watch the chefs in their starched white jackets and hats whipping up delicious entrées from a window on the sidewalk along Prince George Street.

The confections of original owner Marcel Desaulniers, author of the popular dessert manual *Death by Chocolate,* are reason enough to visit **The Trellis Restaurant** (403 Duke of Gloucester St., 757/229-8610, lunch and dinner daily). In early 2010, the Trellis came under the wing of Blue Talon Bistro's management and underwent a $1 million renovation. After choosing a new look and a new menu for the Trellis emphasizing local cuisine such as rockfish and pan-roasted chicken and Virginia wines, new executive chef David Everett has left one thing unchanged: Desserts continue to be lethal. While Desaulniers is no longer in the kitchen, many of his original recipes endure.

Overlooking Merchants Square is **Fat Canary** (410 Duke of Gloucester St., 757/229-3333, dinner daily), a modern gourmet dining room with an open kitchen and a stylish bar. The food is pricey but fantastic—Fat Canary has earned the prestigious AAA Four Diamond award every year since it opened in 2003 (at least as of 2010). Chef Thomas Power draws on the seasons for the freshest ingredients, concocting plates such as pan-seared monkfish with lemon and fennel risotto for $26–38.

Historic Dining

Colonial Williamsburg's four reconstructed taverns carry on the tradition of "savory victuals." Low-beamed ceilings, roaring fireplaces, and pewter plates evoke the days when wealthy planters gathered to dine on classic dishes such as peanut soup, Sally Lund bread, and Brunswick stew. All of the taverns have garden seating in cooperative weather, and some have roving balladeers and costumed servers. Reservations are required (757/229-2141) unless noted otherwise, and most of these establishments operate seasonally (Apr.–Dec.).

Christiana Campbell's Tavern (101 S. Waller St., dinner daily, Tues.–Sat. off-season) specializes in seafood; Mrs. Campbell's gumbo and Carolina fish muddle were favorites of George Washington ($20–34).

Grilled poultry, seafood, and Colonial game pie are served in candlelit elegance at the **King's Arms Tavern** (416 E. Duke of Gloucester St., lunch and dinner daily). Top it off with a slice of pecan pie and goblet of Colonial punch. Lunch entrées such as fried chicken and sandwiches cost $12–14; dinner entrées cost $27–34.

The **Shields Tavern** (422 E. Duke of Gloucester St., lunch and dinner daily) next door is the oldest and largest tavern in Williamsburg, re-creating a rustic eatery of the late 1740s. Eleven dining rooms fill with the smell of pork chops baking and beef roasting on a specially designed spit. Other tempting choices, including the catch of the day and filet mignon (around $25), go well with a mug of sparkling cider.

Adjacent to the Courthouse is **Josiah Chowning's Tavern** (109 E. Duke of Gloucester St., lunch and dinner daily), opened in 1766. Mr. Chowning's black walnut ice cream is a standout after a heaping plateful of baked stuffed pork chops. After 9 P.M., you can knock back a tankard or two in a setting rich with 18th-century music and games in Gambol's pub. Reservations are not required here.

INFORMATION

The best sources of information are the **Colonial Williamsburg Foundation** (800/447-8679, www.history.org) and the **Greater Williamsburg Area Chamber & Tourism Alliance** (421 N. Boundary St., 757/229-6511 or 800/368-6511, www.williamsburgcc.com).

GETTING THERE AND AROUND

Getting There

The **Williamsburg Transportation Center** (468 N. Boundary St. at Lafayette) houses the terminals of Greyhound (757/229-1460) and Amtrak (757/229-8750). Here you can also catch a ride with Yellow Cab of Williamsburg (757/722-1111).

Fourteen miles east of Williamsburg, at I-64 exit 255 in Newport News, is the **Newport News-Williamsburg International Airport** (900 Bland Blvd., 757/877-0221, www.nnwairport.com), served by AirTran, U.S. Airways Express, Frontier, and Delta Connections. Both the transportation center and the airport have a handful of car rental agencies.

Getting Around

Public buses are managed by **Williamsburg Area Transport** (757/220-5493 or 757/259-4093, www.williamsburgtransport.com). Buses ($1.25–1.50 one way, exact fare required) run 6 A.M.–8 or 10 P.M. Monday–Saturday, 8 A.M.–5 P.M. Sunday. Call or see the website for routes and times.

The same agency operates the jaunty red-and-green **Williamsburg Trolley** on a loop around Merchants Square, the Williamsburg Shopping Center, High Street, and New Town. Rides cost $0.50 (exact change required) and the trolley runs 3–10 P.M. Monday–Thursday, 3–11 P.M. Saturday, and noon–8 P.M. Sunday.

Colonial Williamsburg's own **shuttle buses** are the easiest way to get around the historic area, stopping at the visitors center, Merchants Square, the Magazine, Governor's Palace, and capitol building.

NEAR WILLIAMSBURG

York River State Park

A rugged landscape of gorge, forest, marsh, and bluff covers 2,500 brackish acres where Taskinas Creek meets the York River. The site of public tobacco warehouses in the 17th and 18th centuries, when it was known as Taskinas Plantation, this park has a much longer history than that: Fossilized whale vertebrae, sharks' teeth, and coral up to five million years old have all been found nearby.

More than 25 miles of trails connect the river, creek, and freshwater ponds plied by anglers during fishing season (boat rentals are available). Guided canoe trips—including moonlight trips—up the tidal waters of Taskinas Creek (May–Oct.) leave from the **Taskinas Point Visitors Center** (757/566-3036, www.dcr.virginia.gov/state_parks/yor.shtml, $3), and interpretive programs explore the park's fossils and natural offerings. The visitors center is off I-64 exit 231 to Route 507 north; continue to Route 606; within one mile, take a right, continue 1.5 miles, and take a left onto Route 696.

Busch Gardens Europe

Historic recreation takes on a slightly different meaning in Virginia's largest amusement park, repeatedly voted America's most beautiful for its Old World theme. Roller coasters are the stars, beginning with Griffon, the world's tallest and first "floorless dive coaster," which hauls riders 205 feet before sending them down the track at 75 mph. On the Alpengeist, passengers hang from the track as if on a ski lift, although the similarity ends when the ride hits 3.7 Gs during the "cobra roll."

Get an up-close look at the gray wolves at Jack Hanna's Wild Reserve or Big Bird and Elmo from *Sesame Street,* and you won't believe how big and beautiful the Clydesdales in the Highland Stables are. If you get hungry (tip: wait until *after* you ride the Alpengeist), you'll find wurst, beer, and an oompah band in the 2,000-seat Festhaus.

Busch Gardens (800/343-7946, www.buschgardens.com, $62 adults, $52 children, $12 parking, opens 10 A.M. daily June–Aug., weekends only Apr.–May, Sept.–Oct., and Dec., closing hours vary) is off U.S. 60 three miles southeast of Williamsburg. Various family packages are available.

Water Country USA

Busch Gardens' sister park is the mid-Atlantic's largest water park, which offers more than 30 ways to escape the summer swelter. Splash through the darkened tunnels of the Aquazoid; team up for the Meltdown, a three-person water toboggan; or hit escape velocity on the super-speed 320-foot Nitro Racer waterslide. The H2O UFO and Cow-a-Bunga areas are geared toward kids, and whole families can enjoy the wave pools and dive shows.

Water Country USA (800/343-7946, www.watercountryusa.com, $43 adults, $36 children 3–9, $12 parking, opens 10 A.M. daily Memorial Day–Labor Day, closing times vary) is on Water Country Parkway (Rte. 199) near Busch Gardens.

JAMESTOWN

The first "successful" permanent English colony in America began as James Fort, hastily erected in 1607 by a handful of nervous settlers who had traded three cramped sailboats for an endless, untamed wilderness. A combination of sickness, inexperience, hostile natives, and bad management almost spelled the colony's doom in the first few years, but the leadership of Capt. John Smith and a series of fragile truces with the local tribes allowed 5,000 inhabitants to survive to 1634.

It all fell to ruins after the Colonial capital was moved to Williamsburg in 1699. A Confederate fort took the place of the original wooden stockade in 1861, a year before Jamestown Island was occupied by Union troops. In 1933, the island became part of the Colonial National Historical Park. In the late 1980s, an archaeological reassessment led to the discovery of the original settlement (part of which had been hidden by the shifting currents of the James River). Further excavations uncovered the triangular footprint of the Jamestown fort in 1994.

Two separate locations provide contrasting interpretations of the site. First comes Jamestown Settlement, a re-creation of life on the pitiless frontier run by the Commonwealth of Virginia. Across the bridge is the real thing, on Jamestown Island, a much more low-key but equally affecting spot maintained by the National Park Service. In both locations, major enhancements coincided with the celebrations in 2007 of the 400th anniversary of the settlers' landing.

Jamestown Settlement

Hardy colonists and their native counterparts come to life in this living-history museum of life in 17th-century Virginia—albeit a somewhat sanitized and user-friendly version—down to the smell of cooking fires and the roar of gunpowder muskets. Start at the museum, packed with artifacts and information on the English pioneers and their alternating allies and enemies, the Powhatan Indians, as well as Africans who arrived in Virginia in the 1600s. Catch the film *1607: A Nation Takes Root* before you step outside for the real attractions.

First comes the **Powhatan Indian village,** half a dozen domed houses made of woven reeds over sapling frames. Here, interpreters costumed in animal skins show you how to make stone and bone tools, scrape hides, and weave plant fibers into cordage. Kids will enjoy grinding corn (at least for a while) and will probably ask about the ceremonial circle of wooden poles carved with faces.

A short walk down the path brings you to the river pier, where three life-size **ship reproductions** of the vessels that brought the European settlers are tied up. Cormorants fish in the water next to the *Discovery,* the *Godspeed,* and the *Susan Constant.* Climb aboard and imagine crossing 6,000 miles of open ocean in quarters this cramped—the smallest craft is only 66 feet long, with roughly as much space as a school bus. The *Susan Constant,* the largest, is 116 feet long with a brightly painted hull. Reenactors will point out the brick hearth (surprising on a wooden ship) and demonstrate various shipboard activities, including furling sails and handling cargo. These are fully functioning ships, and they occasionally sail away to participate in nautical events.

The colonists must have breathed a sigh of relief to step out into the safety and relative spaciousness of **James Fort,** which has been carefully re-created as it was in 1610–1614. Tall wooden palisades connect three raised circular

COURTESY JAMESTOWN-YORKTOWN FOUNDATION

Reproductions of the 1607 English ships – *Godspeed, Discovery,* and *Susan Constant* – are moored at Jamestown Settlement's pier.

platforms at each corner. Farm fields stretch beyond the walls, while inside stand wattle-and-daub homes, a church, a guardhouse, and storehouses. Try your hand at ninepins (an early version of bowling), and cover your ears for the periodic firing of matchlock muskets.

Yearly events start in mid-March with **Military through the Ages,** with reenactors demonstrating weapons, tactics, and camp life; **Jamestown Landing Day** in mid-May brings more living-history demonstrations. **Virginia Indian Heritage Day** in June celebrates the importance of the Powhatan Indians, complete with drumming and dancing from multiple tribes in the region. In late November, Jamestown hosts **Foods & Feasts of Colonial Virginia,** a three-day Thanksgiving event focusing on Colonial and native food, followed by **A Colonial Christmas,** showcasing 17th- and 18th-century holiday decorations and traditional activities.

Jamestown Settlement (9 A.M.–5 P.M. daily, until 6 P.M. mid-June–mid-Aug., $14 adults, $6.50 children 6–12) has a gift shop and café and is managed by the **Jamestown-Yorktown Foundation** (757/253-4838 or 888/593-4682, www.historyisfun.org). A combination ticket including the Yorktown Victory Center is available for $19.25 adults, $9.25 children.

Jamestown Island (Colonial National Historical Park)

The earlier end of this elongated park begins with the **Jamestown Glasshouse of 1608,** next to the ruins of the original brick and riverstone furnaces. The first factory industry in the colonies folded after one shipment to England, but artisans in the reconstructed workshop still sell lovely handblown glassware made from the same mixture of ash and sand.

Keep driving across a narrow spit of land into the island to reach the National Park Service **visitors center,** which shows an 18-minute orientation video. You can explore Olde Towne and New Towne on your own or join the ranger-led walks. Part of the original town

© KATIE GITHENS

English colonists hastily built James Fort to protect against the Spanish, who never attacked.

site has been inundated as the James River shoreline shifted, but brick outlines mark where certain buildings once stood. The oldest standing structure is the 1639 tower of the Memorial Church, near statues of Pocahontas and Capt. John Smith. A memorial cross marks 300 shallow graves dug during the Starving Time of 1609–1610. Standing on the edge of the windswept beach with the sparse logs of the reconstructed fort behind you, life as a colonist suddenly seems startlingly real—and lonesome.

Queen Elizabeth II showed up for Jamestown's 400th anniversary celebrations in 2007, which heralded a number of improvements to this part of the park, including a monument commemorating the four centuries since the English arrived and a café (open seasonally). A glass-walled "archaerium" now displays archaeological findings, and virtual viewers let you see what things looked like four centuries ago using computerized videos. This museum houses one of the largest collections of 17th-century artifacts in the country. Everyday utensils including hairpins, buckles, and candlesticks invoke the real people who suffered, survived, and died on this swampy island an ocean away from anything safe and familiar.

Along the five-mile wilderness loop drive, which can be shortened to three, you'll stand a good chance of spotting descendants of the same deer, muskrats, and water birds hunted by the Jamestown settlers.

Living-history programs and children's activities are held in June and July. Annual events include **Jamestown Day,** celebrating the founding of the colony, in mid-May; the **First Assembly Day Commemoration** in late July; **Arrival of the First Africans,** examining slavery's start in Jamestown and the contributions of early African Americans in Virginia in mid-August; and an evening walking tour and symbolic torching of the town in late September near the anniversary of **Bacon's Rebellion** in 1676.

Admission to Jamestown Island (757/229-1733, www.nps.gov/jame, 9 A.M.–5 P.M. daily, $10 adults, free for children 15 and

During the "Starving Time," the winter of 1609-1610, only 60 of the 400-500 settlers living at Jamestown survived.

under) is good for a week and includes the Yorktown Battlefield. For more information on the archaeological angle, see the website of Preservation Virginia's Jamestown Rediscovery project (www.historicjamestowne.org).

YORKTOWN

One of Virginia's major ports in the 18th century, Yorktown rivaled Williamsburg with its thriving waterfront at the base of a bluff beneath Main Street's regal homes. Almost 2,000 people lived here when Lord Cornwallis arrived in 1781, pursued by the American army and the French navy just offshore during the Revolutionary War. Days of bombardment convinced the British general to request a meeting on October 17 and to surrender officially two days later. The 225th anniversary of the battle was celebrated in 2006.

Yorktown Visitors Center (Colonial National Historical Park)

The earth ramparts erected by George Washington's troops now defend this museum, filled with various relics saved from the final confrontation of the Revolutionary War. George Washington's field tents are displayed next to surrendered flags and a rifle stock broken by a British soldier in disgust. Walk through a partial reconstruction of a British warship (watch your head), and get your bearings through a narrated map presentation.

Walking tours, led by rangers or interpreters in costume and character, leave from here for the British Inner Defensive Line and the town of Yorktown, exploring Surrender Field, George Washington's headquarters, and earthworks reconstructed through archaeological excavations and detailed studies of 18th-century military maps.

Like Jamestown Island, the Yorktown Visitors Center (757/898-2410, www.nps.gov/colo, 9 A.M.–5 P.M. daily, $10) is administered by the National Park Service. Tickets are good for a week and include admission to Jamestown Island as well. A free trolley runs down into town and back every half hour or so during summer.

Yorktown Victory Center

This well-done museum and living-history center sits across U.S. 17 from Yorktown. Brush up on your background knowledge along the outdoor timeline that leads inside the main building, where exhibits on people affected by the war—from slaves to common women to soldiers—are told through narrated recordings, films, relics, and documents. Don't miss the Declaration of Independence on display; it's a rare broadside printing that dates back to July 18, 1776—not the original handwritten parchment version signed by members of Congress that's today on display at the National Archives in Washington, D.C., but nearly as old.

Outside, at the Continental Army encampment, you can try on a soldier's coat, learn about medicine, food, and music in Colonial armies, and become one of the 17 people needed to fire a cannon (unloaded, of course). A short distance away is a reconstructed farm site typical of a lower- to middle-class family of the late 18th century. A tobacco barn, kitchen building, and modest home stand next to vegetable and herb gardens and animal pens, managed by costumed interpreters who demonstrate Colonial cooking, farming, and games.

The center (9 A.M.–5 P.M. daily, until 6 P.M. mid-June–mid-Aug., $9.50 adults, $5.25 children 6–12) operates under the auspices of the state-run **Jamestown-Yorktown Foundation** (757/253-4838 or 888/593-4682, www.historyisfun.org). A combination ticket including the Jamestown Settlement is available for $19.25 adults, $9.25 children. There's also a large gift shop with a beverage and snack vending area.

As you can imagine, the Fourth of July is a big deal around here, and it's saluted with the **Liberty Celebration,** a blitz of 18th-century military drills and reenactments to honor America's independence. More skirmishes with Redcoats fire away in October during the **Yorktown Victory Celebration,** commemorating the game-changing Revolutionary War victory on October 19, 1781. Holiday celebrations for Thanksgiving and Christmas also find their way into the Yorktown Victory Center's educational programming.

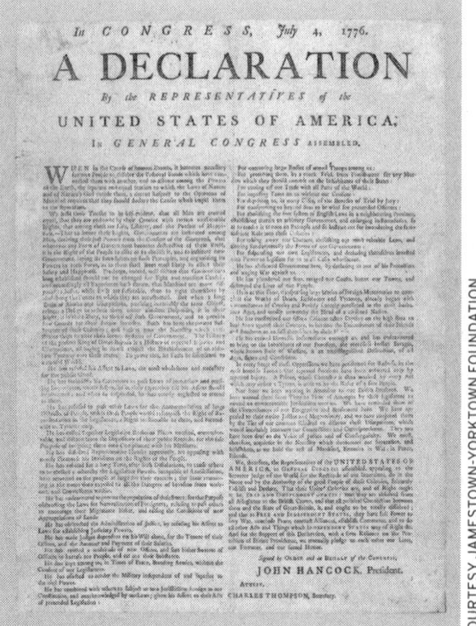

In CONGRESS, July 4, 1776.

A DECLARATION

By the REPRESENTATIVES of the

UNITED STATES OF AMERICA,

In GENERAL CONGRESS assembled.

JOHN HANCOCK, President.

Attest.

CHARLES THOMSON, Secretary.

COURTESY JAMESTOWN-YORKTOWN FOUNDATION

A rare broadside printing of the Declaration of Independence is on display at the Yorktown Victory Center.

Historic Yorktown

Still a sparse but working village, Yorktown counts dozens of homes more than two centuries old, many of which occupy their own "lots" (blocks) on the fringes. A path from the visitors center takes you past the 84-foot **Victory Monument,** topped by a winged statue of Liberty, to **Cornwallis's Cave** on the riverbank, a dank hole where the British general is said to have made his headquarters during the shelling. The **Nelson House** was once home to Thomas Nelson Jr., a signer of the Declaration of Independence. It still bears scars from cannonballs directed by Nelson, who suspected Cornwallis was inside. The terms of surrender were drafted in the **Moore House.**

Yorktown's military past tends to be what's on display. **Civil War Weekend** in late May observes Memorial Day and includes musical performances on the waterfront. In mid-October, Yorktown's better-known **Revolutionary War**

weekend features fife and drum players on parade, encampments, and demonstrations.

History of a different sort is remembered in the **Watermen's Museum** (309 Water St., 757/887-2641, www.watermens.org, 10 A.M.–5 P.M. Tues.–Sat., 1–5 P.M. Sun. in season, weekends only Thanksgiving–Mar., $3). Boat models, marine life, and a boat-building area out back honor the "iron men and wooden boats" who have fished the local waters since the first Indians ventured out in dugout canoes. A gift shop sells work by local artists. It's near the U.S. 17 bridge by the water.

Activities

The Colonial-themed **Riverwalk Landing** development (www.riverwalklanding.com) features a year-round performance area, a beach, two floating piers, and a mile-long pedestrian walkway by the York River. Sail aboard the 105-foot schooner ***Alliance*** (757/639-1233, www.schooneralliance.com), home ported in Yorktown from May through October (and in the Caribbean the rest of the year). Daily sails leave from Riverwalk Landing at 11 A.M. and 2 P.M. (May–Oct., $30 adults, $18 children), and sunset sails (call for departure times) are $35 per person. Try to buy tickets online ahead of time; both the daily sails and the sunset sails sell out.

Accommodations and Food

The **Duke of York Hotel** (508 Water St., 757/898-3232, www.dukeofyorkmotel.com, $75–180) offers beachfront and river-view rooms as well as an outdoor pool. Set on a high bluff above the Watermen's Museum, the **York River Inn** (209 Ambler St., 757/887-8800 or 800/884-7003, www.yorkriverinn.com) is an elegant little bed-and-breakfast with two rooms and a suite ($115–140). The **Marl Inn Bed & Breakfast** (220 Church St., 757/898-3859, www.marlinnbandb.com, $110 d, $130–150 suite) is only a few blocks away—but then again, so is everything in this tiny town.

You can grab a bite along the water at the **Yorktown Pub** (112 Water St., 757/886-9964, lunch and dinner daily, $5–11 lunch, $19–22 dinner), with hearty food, homemade desserts, and live music on weekend nights. It accepts cash only.

The Dining Room at **Nick's Riverwalk Restaurant** (323 Water St., 757/875-1522, lunch and dinner daily) is one of the more upscale places to eat along the Riverwalk Landing strip, with seafood-centric main dishes such as Chesapeake stew or seared scallops wrapped in prosciutto ($11–15 lunch, $17–30 dinner). Sandwiches, salads, and pizzas are also served on the sunny patio of the restaurant's more casual **Rivah Café.**

The **Carrot Tree** (411 Main St., 757/988-1999, lunch daily, dinner Thurs.–Sat.) in the Cole Digges House, Yorktown's oldest home, features soups, salads, and sandwiches from scratch ($6–14)—and a carrot cake you'll wish could grow on trees. High tea is served at 4 P.M. on Wednesdays, often with a literary theme and readings. Dinner turns more savory, with stuffed pork tenderloin, tomato tarts, and Battlefield Beef Stroganoff ($14–15). There's a kids menu with familiar favorites like PB&J.

Information

Find information on the town and its environs in **The Gallery at York Hall** (Main and Ballard Sts., 757/890-4490, 10 A.M.–4 P.M. Tues.–Sat., 1–4 P.M. Sun., open seasonally Apr.–Dec.). Otherwise contact Historic Yorktown at 757/890-3500, www.yorkcounty.gov/tourism.

JAMES RIVER PLANTATIONS

The fertile banks of the lower James have been prime real estate ever since the days of the Powhatan capital at Sandy Point. During the 18th and 19th centuries, lavish mansions served as business and social centers for huge tobacco plantations. Carriages no longer clatter down long, tree-shaded gravel lanes, with servants waiting to escort visitors into the parlor for tea and talk of planting, but the area is still mostly forest and farmland with no major town center. (There is no city in Charles City County.)

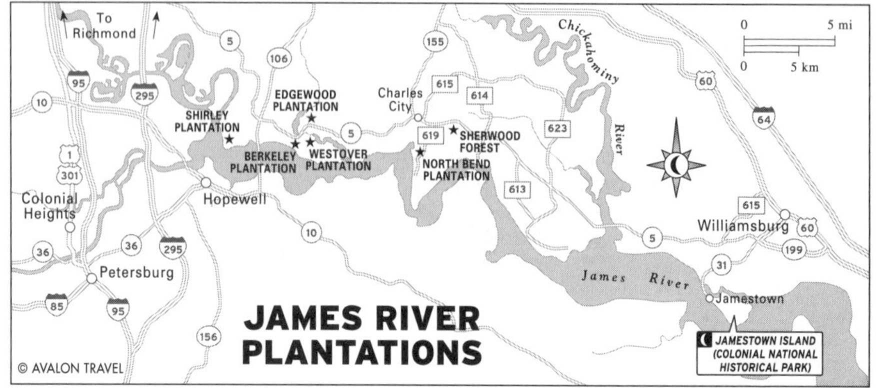

Route 5, also called the John Tyler Highway, leads straight from Richmond to six major plantations along the river's north bank. Annual events such as garden tours, special teas, birthday celebrations, and progressive luncheons happen almost every month of the year. Best of all, the drive is gorgeous. If you're traveling between Richmond and the Historic Peninsula, skip I-64 and its pell-mell traffic and take to this leafy country byway instead. It adds very little driving time and is worth the peace of mind.

Shirley Plantation

Virginia's oldest plantation sits on land settled in 1613 by Sir Thomas West. Begun in 1723 and finished in 1738, the house survived both the Revolutionary and Civil Wars and is the

© KATIE GITHENS

Berkeley Plantation

birthplace of Anne Hill Carter Lee, mother of Robert E., who married Light-Horse Harry in the parlor. Today, Shirley Plantation (804/829-5121 or 800/232-1613, www.shirleyplantation.com, 9:30 A.M.–4:30 P.M. daily, $11 adults, $7.50 children 6–18) is home to the 11th and 12th generations of the Hill-Carter family, plenty of heirlooms, and centuries of stories. Guided house tours run throughout the day.

Berkeley Plantation

On December 4, 1619, 38 English settlers kissed the earth and thanked the heavens upon landing partway up the James River after three months at sea. A monument marks the spot where many scholars believe the first Thanksgiving took place—followed two years later by the first batch of bourbon whiskey distilled in the New World. While the Thanksgiving memorial—an understated stone arch on the banks of the James—is anticlimactic, it's a peaceful spot and the plantation has its own charms.

The Harrison family bought this property in 1691. Benjamin Harrison IV built the manor house in 1726, leaving a stone bearing the date and his and his wife's initials over a side door. His son Benjamin V signed the Declaration of Independence and served three terms as governor of Virginia. *His* son William Henry became the ninth president of the United States after making his name on the western frontier. George Washington stopped by from time to time, the first in a string of 10 presidents to enjoy the Harrisons' hospitality. Although he didn't live at Berkeley, William Henry's grandson Benjamin Harrison did the family name proud yet again by becoming the 23rd president of the United States.

During Union occupation in 1862, Gen. Dan Butterfield composed the haunting melody of "Taps" here shortly before Lincoln visited to review McClellan's army. In the 20th century, the property was lovingly restored through the efforts of Malcolm Jamieson, whose father was a Federal drummer boy. Worth a stop in themselves are Berkeley's terraced boxwood gardens, spread between the

The grounds of Berkeley Plantation witnessed the first Thanksgiving celebrated by English colonists.

house and wide lawns leading down to the river, where geese and sheep wander. The view of the James is unparalleled.

Berkeley (804/829-6018 or 888/466-6018, www.berkeleyplantation.com, 9 A.M.–5 P.M. daily, $11 adults, $7 children 13–16, $6 children 6–12) also hosts a **First Thanksgiving Festival** on the first Sunday in November, commemorating the original ceremony of gratitude with Colonial and native reenactors.

Westover Plantation

William Byrd III, founder of Richmond and Petersburg, built this Georgian manor house in the 1730s. It's famous for its elegant proportions, its view of the James, and the ancient tulip poplars around the lawn. Westover is also known as one home of the ghost of Byrd's daughter Evelyn, who pined to death at age 18 after her Catholic parents forbade her to marry a Protestant. She told friends she would come back from the beyond, and her glowing ghost has since been reported here and at Evelynton (witnesses describe it as nonthreatening).

Westover (804/829-2882, www.jamesriverplantations.org/westover.html) shares an access road off Route 5 with Berkeley Plantation. The house is open only during Historic Garden Week in April, but the grounds and garden are open to visitors 9 A.M.–6 P.M. daily for $2 adults, $0.50 children.

Sherwood Forest

The only home owned by two U.S. presidents was begun in 1730 under the name Smith's Hundred. William Henry Harrison inherited it in the 1790s but never lived here, in part because he died one month after his inaugural speech. Harrison's vice president, John Tyler, took over both the presidency and ownership of this white clapboard house, where he retired in 1845. Tyler's grandson still lives upstairs.

Additions to the original building have made Sherwood Forest the longest wooden-frame house in the country at more than 300 feet. A 68-foot ballroom was designed to accommodate guests dancing the Virginia reel. Scars in the woodwork bear witness to Civil War action, and many of the furnishings and decorations belonged to President Tyler. Original outbuildings, terraced gardens, and more than 80 varieties of trees brighten the grounds. Sherwood Forest (804/829-5377, www.sherwoodforest.org, 9 A.M.–5 P.M. daily) is also home to a ghost called the Gray Lady, whose rocking has been heard in the Gray Room for more than two centuries. Access to the grounds is $10 adults, free children under 15, and admission to the house, open only by prior appointment, is $35 per person.

Accommodations and Food

Edgewood Plantation (4800 John Tyler Hwy., 804/829-2962, www.edgewoodplantation.com) hosts guests in a Gothic Revival home built in 1849 that has since served as post office, church, and Confederate signal post. Fireplaces and a two-story freestanding spiral staircase wait inside, while a 1725 gristmill, formal gardens, and pool surround the house. (Look for the "Lizzie" etched in an upstairs window by a woman who supposedly died of a broken heart waiting for her lover to return from the Civil War.) Eight guest rooms—six in the house and two in the former slaves' quarters—are $140–200.

Across Route 5 is the **North Bend Plantation** (12200 Weyanoke Rd., 804/829-5176, www.northbendplantation.com), built in 1819 for William Henry Harrison's sister Sarah. Union Gen. Philip Sheridan made his headquarters here in 1864 and dug trenches that still exist at the eastern edge of the property. The owners, the fifth generation of the Copland family to own North Bend, are happy to point out Sheridan's plantation desk, the 1914 billiard table, and a library full of rare and old books. Rates ($145–175) include a full country breakfast and use of the swimming pool.

Northern Hampton Roads

NEWPORT NEWS

Virginia's fifth-largest city (pop. 180,000), Newport News was named for Capt. Christopher Newport, pilot of the three-ship fleet that landed at Jamestown in 1607, whose "news" was word sent back to England that the settlers had arrived safely. Newport News stretches along I-64 and U.S. 60 toward the largest privately owned shipyard in the country, the massive Northrop Grumman Newport News facility.

The shipyard employs about one-tenth of the city's population, churning out nuclear attack submarines and aircraft carriers for the U.S. Navy; according to its founder's 19th-century credo: "We shall build good ships here at a profit—if we can—at a loss—if we must—but always good ships."

On their way to the largest coal-shipping port in the country, trains rattle south past one of the country's largest municipal parks and the outstanding Mariners' Museum, well worth a day's detour in itself.

The Mariners' Museum

A 3,200-pound, 18-foot golden eagle figurehead ushers you into one of the best nautical collections in the world. The congressionally delegated National Maritime Museum (100 Museum Dr., 757/596-2222 or 800/581-7245, www.marinersmuseum.org, 10 A.M.–5 P.M. Wed.–Sat., noon–5 P.M. Sun., $12 adults, $7 children 6–12) displays gleaming Chris Crafts from the 1920s and 1930s, but also a handmade boat used by Cuban refugees to cross the Caribbean and an outrigger sailing canoe from Micronesia. The $30 million USS *Monitor* Center, opened with the help of the National Oceanic & Atmospheric Administration (NOAA) in 2007, draws the most fanfare. The Civil War ironclad, finally found off the coast of North Carolina in 1973, is memorialized in this state-of-the-art permanent exhibit, with two full-scale replicas, interactive displays, videos, and re-creations of the surprisingly civilized-looking officers' quarters. The original engine, turret, and propeller are on display in huge desalinization tanks.

YOU CAN'T DRIVE THE HAMPTON ROADS

Spend a little time near the mouth of the Chesapeake Bay and you'll probably start to get confused by a fair amount of the local terminology. Most important, and least distinct, is the term Hampton Roads itself.

In sea-faring lingo, "roadstead" means a safe anchorage for ships, usually in a sheltered natural harbor, which the lower Chesapeake Bay has in abundance. "Hampton" comes from the English nobleman Henry Wriothesley (RIZ-lee), the third Earl of Southampton, who financed early colonizing expeditions. What was originally the "Earl of Southampton's Roadstead," then, has been shortened over the years to "Hampton Roads."

You'll also hear Hampton Roads used to refer not only to where the James, Nansemond, and Elizabeth Rivers flow into the Chesapeake Bay, but to the entire metropolitan area surrounding it, from Newport News to Virginia Beach. Hampton Roads itself is usually divided further into the "South Side" (of the James River) – including Norfolk, Virginia Beach, Chesapeake, Portsmouth, and Suffolk – and "the Peninsula" (as in the Historic Peninsula) to the north, the setting of Newport News and Hampton itself.

Even though "Tidewater" technically refers to the entire region affected by the ebb and flow of the ocean (basically all of Virginia east of the fall line), it's often used the same way South Side is – to refer to everything south of the James River.

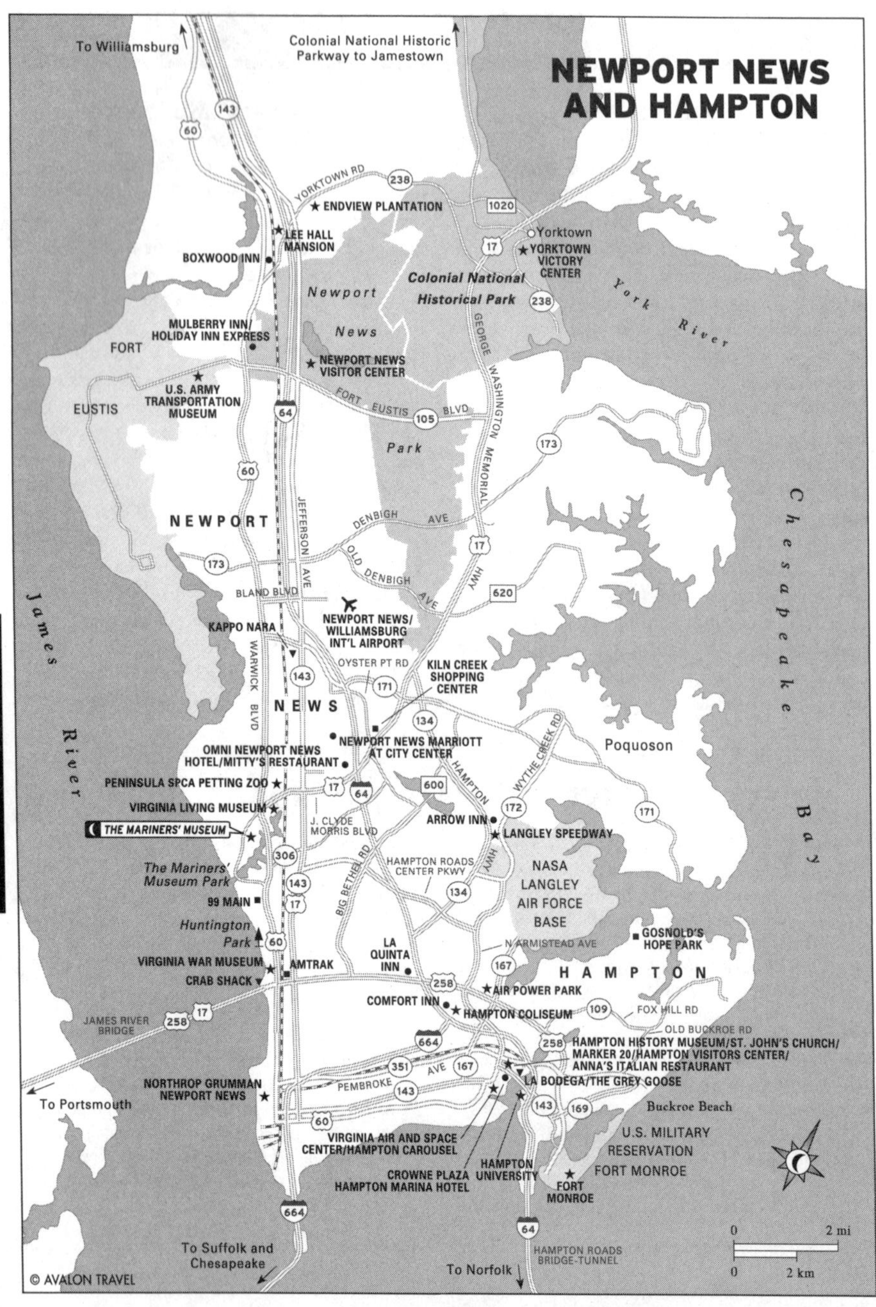
NEWPORT NEWS AND HAMPTON
To Williamsburg
Colonial National Historic Parkway to Jamestown
YORKTOWN RD
ENDVIEW PLANTATION
LEE HALL MANSION
BOXWOOD INN
Yorktown
YORKTOWN VICTORY CENTER
Colonial National Historical Park
Newport News Park
York River
MULBERRY INN/ HOLIDAY INN EXPRESS
FORT EUSTIS
NEWPORT NEWS VISITOR CENTER
U.S. ARMY TRANSPORTATION MUSEUM
FORT EUSTIS BLVD
GEORGE WASHINGTON MEMORIAL HWY
NEWPORT NEWS
JEFFERSON AVE
DENBIGH AVE
OLD DENBIGH AVE
BLAND BLVD
Chesapeake Bay
James River
KAPPO NARA
NEWPORT NEWS/ WILLIAMSBURG INT'L AIRPORT
WARWICK BLVD
OYSTER PT RD
KILN CREEK SHOPPING CENTER
WYTHE CREEK RD
Poquoson
OMNI NEWPORT NEWS HOTEL/MITTY'S RESTAURANT
NEWPORT NEWS MARRIOTT AT CITY CENTER
HAMPTON HWY
PENINSULA SPCA PETTING ZOO
VIRGINIA LIVING MUSEUM
J. CLYDE MORRIS BLVD
ARROW INN
THE MARINERS' MUSEUM
LANGLEY SPEEDWAY
The Mariners' Museum Park
HAMPTON ROADS CENTER PKWY
BIG BETHEL RD
NASA LANGLEY AIR FORCE BASE
99 MAIN
Huntington Park
N ARMISTEAD AVE
GOSNOLD'S HOPE PARK
LA QUINTA INN
VIRGINIA WAR MUSEUM
AMTRAK
HAMPTON
CRAB SHACK
AIR POWER PARK
COMFORT INN
HAMPTON COLISEUM
FOX HILL RD
JAMES RIVER BRIDGE
OLD BUCKROE RD
HAMPTON HISTORY MUSEUM/ST. JOHN'S CHURCH/ MARKER 20/HAMPTON VISITORS CENTER/ ANNA'S ITALIAN RESTAURANT
PEMBROKE AVE
NORTHROP GRUMMAN NEWPORT NEWS
LA BODEGA/THE GREY GOOSE
To Portsmouth
Buckroe Beach
U.S. MILITARY RESERVATION FORT MONROE
VIRGINIA AIR AND SPACE CENTER/HAMPTON CAROUSEL
CROWNE PLAZA HAMPTON MARINA HOTEL
HAMPTON UNIVERSITY
FORT MONROE
HAMPTON ROADS BRIDGE-TUNNEL
To Suffolk and Chesapeake
To Norfolk
0 2 mi
0 2 km
© AVALON TRAVEL

This hefty eagle figurehead greets you at the Mariners' Museum.

Especially remarkable are the 16 miniature model ships made over two decades by August and Winnifred Crabtree. Magnifying glasses built into the display cases let you appreciate the stunning detail, down to inch-tall figureheads carved with modified dental tools. It's a wonder the Crabtrees didn't go blind during the 20 years it took to finish the collection, which comprises everything from Indian dugouts to Columbus's ships.

You can learn how to navigate using interactive video displays in the Chesapeake Bay gallery. Other displays include knot-tying lessons, the evolution of the U.S. Navy, well-worn boat-building tools, and changing exhibits covering topics such as pirates, the slave trade, and the *Titanic.*

The same turn off U.S. 60 leads to the 550-acre **Mariners' Museum Park.** A five-mile trail circles Lake Maury, where you can rent pedalboats (757/596-2222 or 800/581-7245).

Newport News Park

Covering more than 8,000 acres, the largest city park east of the Mississippi (13560 Jefferson Ave., 757/886-7912, www.nnparks.com) is a patchwork of meadows, swamps, lakes, and hardwood forest threaded by mountain-bike, horse, and nature trails. There's an 18-hole disc golf course, a five-star archery range, and the kaleidoscopic azaleas and Japanese teahouse of the Peace Garden. Visitors can rent bikes to explore 10 miles of Civil War fortifications or take out a canoe or pedalboat to fish on Lee Hall Reservoir. The **Newport News Golf Club at Deer Run** (757/886-7925, www.nngolfclub.com) has two full courses and a driving range. You can even spend the night at one of 188 campsites (757/888-3333 or 800/203-8322), with full hookups for $28.50–31. From I-64, take exit 250B to reach the park.

At the Mariners' Museum, August and Winnifred Crabtree's miniature model ships are astonishing in their detail and beauty.

Virginia Living Museum

It doesn't have statues that walk or paintings that talk, but this place does boast a bevy of wild animals in outdoor pens modeled after their natural habitats. Start in the exhibition building, where different sections of the

James River—complete with plants, catfish, and bass—have been reproduced in a series of aquariums. At the touch tank, find out why horseshoe crab blood sells for $30,000 an ounce, and try not to wake the screech owl in the World of Darkness. Many different Virginia ecosystems have been re-created here, from mountain streams to a southeastern cypress swamp.

Step outside onto the elevated boardwalk to reach open-air enclosures where raccoons scurry, bobcats pace, and otters zoom away from an underwater window in streams of bubbles. Past the raucous coastal plain aviary, home to great blue herons and snake-necked cattle egrets, are more pens containing animals native to Virginia in natural habitats. The Virginia Garden, a permanent exhibit on Virginia's botanical history from 1607 to the present, includes the native species that were present when the first settlers arrived at Jamestown and shows how Indians employed plants for food and medicine and how the colonists learned to use them in their struggle for survival.

A $22.6 million expansion added a raised outdoor aviary, housing birds from Virginia's coastal plains such as ibis, herons, and egrets. The gift shop is full of neat stuff along the lines of ant farms and glowing, floating plastic jellyfish. Also glowing are Virginia's starry night skies, projected in the Abbitt Planetarium onto a 30-foot dome above 71 specially designed seats. See the website for stargazing times as well as laser shows.

The museum (524 J. Clyde Morris Blvd., 757/595-1900, www.thevlm.org, 9 A.M.–5 P.M. Mon.–Sat., noon–5 P.M. Sun., extended hours Memorial Day to Labor Day, $15 adults, $12 children 3–12, with admission to planetarium $19 adults, $16 children) also offers various educational programs and outings, including Chesapeake Bay eco-safaris.

Huntington Park

At the east end of the James River Bridge (Rte. 258), Huntington Park (757/886-7912, www.nnparks.com) is a good spot for lazing around—sunbathers can catch some rays on the lifeguarded beach, open Memorial Day through Labor Day—or running around. Kids can wear themselves out splashing in the river or playing in **Fort Fun,** a 15,000-square-foot wooden playground overlooking the water. There's even a kids' fishing pier.

The grown-up version is the **James River Bridge Fishing Pier** (757/247-0364, 9 A.M.–11:30 P.M. Sun.–Tues., 24 hours a day Wed.–Sat., Apr.–Nov., $8.50 adults, $6 children, including fishing license), which sells bait and supplies and rents poles. At 0.6 mile, this is one of the longest piers on the East Coast.

Also within the park, the **Virginia War Museum** (9285 Warwick Blvd., 757/247-8523, www.warmuseum.org, 9 A.M.–5 P.M. Mon.–Sat., 1–5 P.M. Sun., $6 adults, $4 children 7–18) displays hundreds of artifacts from centuries of combat. From flintlock pistols to M-16s, sabers to WWII Japanese officers' samurai swords, anything and everything having to do with conflict in all its forms is displayed next to actual pieces of the Dachau concentration camp and the Berlin Wall.

Other Sights

Even more animals live across J. Clyde Morris Boulevard at the **Peninsula SPCA Exotic Sanctuary and Petting Zoo** (757/595-1399, www.peninsulaspca.com/gallery.html, 11 A.M.–5:30 P.M. Mon.–Fri., 10 A.M.–4:30 P.M. Sat., noon–3:30 P.M. Sun., $2 adults, $1 children). A surprising collection of exotic animals, including a Siberian tiger, a jaguar, and an African mandrill (a type of baboon), shares a rear lot with a petting barnyard, home to goats, ducks, sheep, peacocks, and a few nervous llamas. You can't take any of these animals home with you, but you might be inspired to adopt a dog or cat inside.

The history of the transport wing of the U.S. Army (motto: "Nothing happens until something moves") is the subject of the **U.S. Army Transportation Museum** (757/878-1115, www.transchool.eustis.army.mil/museum/museum.html, 9 A.M.–4:30 P.M. Tues.–Sun., free), located on the grounds of Fort Eustis off I-64 exit 250A. If it ever carried men or equipment, it's here, from a Conestoga wagon to Desert Storm Humvees. (Visitors must show a valid ID and vehicle registration to get a visitor pass just inside the gate.)

Accommodations

The **Omni Newport News Hotel** (1000 Omni Blvd., 757/873-6664) has rooms for $110–160, an indoor heated pool, a nightclub, and Mitty's Ristorante, one of the better Italian eateries this side of Hampton Roads. In the growing City Center at Oyster Point development is the 256-room **Newport News Marriott at City Center** (740 Town Center Dr., 757/873-9299), with rooms ranging $140–200.

The smaller-scale **Mulberry Inn** (16890 Warwick Blvd., 757/887-3000 or 800/223-0404, www.mulberryinnva.com) has a total of 101 rooms and efficiencies for $90–140. In the same complex, there's a **Holiday Inn Express** (16890 Warwick Blvd., 757/887-3300) offering 57 rooms for $90–130.

The **Boxwood Inn** (10 Elmhurst St., 757/888-8854, www.boxwood-inn.com) began as the early-1900s home of Simon Curtis, railroad baron and unofficial "boss man" of Warwick County. Set along the train tracks that made Curtis his fortune, the building was gradually expanded and altered into a general store, boardinghouse, post office, and county hall of records, until its latest turn as a bed-and-breakfast with four rooms for $105–145. In addition to breakfast, innkeepers Kathy and Derek Hulick serve Friday dinners by reservation only. If you're lucky, you might catch one of their themed dinners for larger groups, which run the gamut from a 1950s sock hop to an antebellum plantation dinner.

Food

Swing by the historic Hilton Village neighborhood to find **99 Main** (99 Main St., 757/599-9885, dinner Tues.–Sat.), voted one of the top fine-dining eateries in Hampton Roads. Whether you sit in the formal dining room or the smaller bar room, entrées like grilled tuna and sea scallops and truffles ($15–30) are always terrific.

On the James River Fishing Pier sits the **Crab Shack** (7601 River Rd., 757/245-2722, lunch and dinner daily), with a window-lined dining room and outdoor deck overlooking the James River. Fresh soft-shell crabs and the catch of the day come in sandwiches ($7–10) and on platters ($17–20). If you think it can't get any fresher, try the sushi and sashimi ($2–4) at **Kappo Nara** (550 Oyster Point Rd., 757/249-5396, dinner daily).

Al Fresco (11710 Jefferson Ave., 757/873-0644, lunch Mon.–Fri., dinner Mon.–Sat.) comes recommended for authentic Italian fare (especially the lobster ravioli), with dinner entrées in the $12–22 range.

Information

The **Newport News Visitor Center** (13560 Jefferson Ave., 757/886-7777 or 888/493-7386, www.newport-news.org, 9 A.M.–5 P.M. daily) is at the entrance to Newport News Park at I-64 exit 250B.

Getting There

Newport News is connected to Hampton, Norfolk, Virginia Beach, Portsmouth, and Chesapeake by **Hampton Roads Transit** (757/222-6100, www.gohrt.com). Call or check the website for routes, hours, and fares. **Amtrak** (9304 Warwick Blvd., 757/245-3589) is in Huntington Park, the closest station to Hampton Roads, and has shuttle bus service to Norfolk and Virginia Beach. To reach the terminal of the **Newport News-Williamsburg International Airport** (757/877-0221, www.nnwairport.com), turn onto Bland Boulevard off Jefferson Avenue (Rte. 143) near I-64 exit 255.

HAMPTON

The oldest English-speaking community in America leapt into the modern age with the seven *Mercury* astronauts, who trained at Langley Air Force Base on gear supplied by NASA's Langley Research Center. Hampton (pop. 145,000) overflows with history, especially African American history. The city boasts an attractive modern waterfront jammed with masts and fishing boats.

History

A settlement of Kecoughtan (KICK-o-tan) Indians was overrun on July 9, 1610, by a band of settlers sent by Capt. John Smith to build a fort at the mouth of the James River. (The city recognizes the date of this skirmish as its official Founders Day, and in 2010 celebrated its 400th anniversary.) While Jamestown was founded first, Hampton's population stayed put, thus it wins the title of the nation's oldest continuously settled English community.

Fort Henry and Fort Charles both came in handy when relations with the native tribe went downhill. Formally established and named in 1680, Hampton was plagued by pirates during its early years. In 1718, Lt. Robert Maynard is said to have captured and killed Edward Teach, aka Blackbeard, and displayed his head at the entrance to the bay as a warning to other pirates.

Hampton was spared during the Revolutionary War but attacked and occupied by the British in 1813. The Civil War ironclads *Monitor* and *Virginia* battled within sight of Fort Story in March 1862, eight months after Hampton's inhabitants had burned most of the city to the ground to prevent its falling into Federal hands.

A rich vein of African American history in the area began in August 1619 with the arrival of British America's first shipment of "20 and odd" Africans to Old Point Comfort and continued with the founding of the Hampton Normal and Agricultural Institute (now Hampton University) in 1868.

Hampton Carousel

This ornate merry-go-round ($2 pp) graced an amusement park on Buckroe Beach 1921–1985. Now located on Hampton's downtown waterfront, it's been fully restored and enclosed from the elements, with all the original paintings, mirrors, and organ music intact. From Memorial Day to Labor Day, the carousel is open 11 A.M.–5 P.M. daily, until 7 P.M. Thursday–Sunday. During the off-season, it's open weekends noon–5 P.M. Call the Virginia Air and Space Center (757/727-0900) for more details.

Virginia Air and Space Center

Imagine an airplane hangar opening like a beetle's wings and you'll have a good picture of Hampton Roads' temple of aeronautics, full to its curving roof with jets, spacecraft, and all the high-tech gizmos that keep them in the air. The *Apollo 12* command module and a three-billion-year-old moon rock commemorate the Space Race, and dozens of hands-on displays explain the principles of flight and space travel. You can have your height scanned electronically, try to keep lunch down in the tri-axis astronaut trainer, or catch a movie in the five-story IMAX theater. The **Hampton Roads History Center** upstairs traces the area's past and includes what archaeologists believe is a pirate's skeleton.

The Air and Space Center (600 Settlers Landing Rd., 757/727-0900, www.vasc.org, 10 A.M.–5 P.M. daily, to 7 P.M. Thurs.–Sun., Memorial Day to Labor Day, shorter hours off-season, $9.50 adults, $7.50 children) offers combination admission with an IMAX movie ($15 adults, $12 children).

Air Power Park

If you're still hungry for more planes, this outdoor park (413 W. Mercury Blvd., 757/727-8311, 9 A.M.–4:30 P.M. daily, free) should do the trick: It's one of the largest privately owned collections of aircraft in the country. Plenty of airborne lethality is on display, from a Nike surface-to-air missile to supersonic jets.

Hampton History Museum

Hampton's story of place is told through 7,000 square feet of exhibits, including two interactive galleries, the Kecoughtan Indian Gallery and the Port Hampton Gallery, unveiled since the doors opened in 2003. The museum (120 Old Hampton Ln., 757/727-1610, www.hampton.gov/history_museum, 10 A.M.–5 P.M. Mon.–Sat., 1–5 P.M. Sun., $5 adults, $4 children 4–12) focuses on the Civil War and the periods before and after, including the Battle of Big Bethel and the burning of Hampton.

St. John's Church

Elizabeth City Parish, the oldest continuous

English-speaking parish in the country, was established in the same year Europeans arrived at Hampton. This small cruciform church (100 W. Queens Way, 757/722-2567, 9 A.M.–3 P.M. Mon.–Fri., 9 A.M.–noon Sat., free) is the congregation's fourth, erected in 1728. Eight-foot-thick walls are graced by stained-glass windows dating to 1883, one of which portrays the baptism of Pocahontas. Take a minute to wander the surrounding graveyard, with its ornate monuments and Confederate tombstones.

Hampton University

The story of America's foremost black university (757/727-5000, www.hamptonu.edu) goes back to the Civil War, when escaped slaves sought refuge at Union-held Fort Monroe. Federal officers declared the runaways "contraband of war" to ensure their safety, and in 1868 Gen. Samuel Chapman Armstrong answered their pleas for education by opening the Hampton Normal and Agricultural Institute in the center of the city. Initially consisting of only three teachers and 15 students, Hampton University has grown to 5,700 students, counting Booker T. Washington among its many distinguished alumni. Still standing near the entrance is Emancipation Oak, under whose branches slaves once labored over the alphabet and the Emancipation Proclamation was first read to the local populace.

The galleries of the **Hampton University Museum** (757/727-5308, http://museum.hamptonu.edu, 8 A.M.–5 P.M. Mon.–Fri., noon–4 P.M. Sat., free) hold 9,000 pieces of African American, Native American, Asian, and Pacific art, including works by John T. Biggers, Elizabeth Catlett, and Henry O. Tanner's *The Banjo Lesson.* The museum store sells handcrafted ethnic art. In 1997 the collection was moved to the Huntington Building on Frissell Avenue, a former beaux arts library renovated to the tune of $5 million.

Fort Monroe

Fort Monroe is the largest stone fortification ever built in the United States, constructed in 1819–1834 at Old Point Comfort to protect the strategic entrance to Chesapeake Bay. Edgar Allan Poe was stationed here 1828–1829, and Robert E. Lee was here 1831–1834 as a second lieutenant and engineer. Manned by 6,000 soldiers, Monroe was the only fort in the upper South that remained in Union hands during the Civil War. In May 1862, Abraham Lincoln visited "Fort Freedom," two months after Federal troops watched the *Monitor* and the *Virginia* shell it out from the ramparts.

Today—well, at least until 2011—the fort is headquarters for the U.S. Army Training and Doctrine Command. It's still surrounded by a moat with a bridge wide enough for only a single car. But change is coming to Fort Monroe. Due to Department of Defense recommendations for moving or closing bases, which Congress approved in 2005, the army will vacate the property by September 2011. What next? Many locals wonder the same thing. At the time of writing the National Park Service had committed to overseeing a portion of the historic fort, and museums from Richmond to Martinsville were eyeing the property.

In the meantime, visitors can still walk around the walls for the view of Norfolk across the water and visit the **Casemate Museum** (757/727-3391, 10:30 A.M.–4:30 P.M. daily, free), in whose cool, dank chambers Jefferson Davis was imprisoned for six months after the end of the war. Displays on the history of the fort and coastal artillery include relics of Davis's stay, including his intricate meerschaum pipe. Unquestionably the oldest witness to history on base, and all its comings and goings, is the Algernourne Oak, a nearly 500-year-old tree growing on the parade field.

Entertainment and Recreation

Buckroe Beach (757/850-5134) is a wide, clean stretch of sand on the Chesapeake Bay. Outdoor movies are held at the waterfront pavilion on Tuesdays in the summer; beach-music favorites are on the bill every Sunday. You can rent watercraft in the summer.

Racing vehicles of every stripe roar through **Langley Speedway** (3165 N. Armistead Ave.,

757/865-7223, www.langley-speedway.com) during its yearly schedule of races.

Head down to the public piers near the visitors center to find the ***Miss Hampton II*** (757/722-9102 or 888/757-2628, www.misshamptoncruises.com), a double-decker motor boat that explores the Chesapeake Bay on sightseeing cruises Tuesday–Sunday April–October ($22.50 adults, $11.50 children). On sunny days, it passes the Norfolk Naval Base and stops at Fort Wool, a pre–Civil War citadel built on a 15-acre man-made island.

For an evening out, it's hard to beat the **Hampton Coliseum** (757/838-4230, www.hamptoncoliseum.org), which has welcomed everyone from the Rolling Stones to Metallica over the years. (The Coliseum's "Elvis Door" was cut into the side of the arena in the 1970s so the King could escape straight to his limo after the show.) **Marker 20** (21 E. Queens Way, 757/726-9410) often hosts live music.

Events

Hampton's big yearly event is the **Hampton Jazz Festival** (www.hamptonjazzfestival.com) at the Coliseum in late June, boasting some of the world's best musicians. It's shifting toward more soul, blues, and pop; performers in previous years included Aretha Franklin, Ray Charles, and B. B. King. Hotel rooms fill up months ahead of the three-day festival, so plan accordingly.

Street Fest brings local music, eats, and kids' events to Queens Way near the visitors center on Saturday evenings throughout the summer. The **Hampton Cup Regatta** (www.hamptoncupregatta.org) in mid-August is the oldest ongoing race of its kind in the country. Numerous classes of hydroplane boats hit up to 170 mph on their way from the Mercury Boulevard Bridge to Fort Monroe. In early September, the Chesapeake Bay is cause for celebration during **Hampton Bay Days** (www.baydays.com), the city's biggest event. Held the weekend after Labor Day, it includes carnivals, seafood, sports, music, crab races, water events, and fireworks.

Accommodations

The **Arrow Inn** (3361 Commander Shepard Blvd.—which used to be 7 Semple Farm Rd., 757/865-0300 or 800/833-2520, www.arrowinn.com) is a motel near the Langley Speedway with rooms for $40–60. Only a few blocks away from the Hampton Coliseum, the **La Quinta Inn** (2138 W. Mercury Blvd., 757/827-8680) has rooms for $85–135. Nearby you'll find a **Comfort Inn** (1916 Coliseum Dr., 757/827-5052) with rooms for $70–160. The **Crowne Plaza Hampton Marina** (700 Settlers Landing Rd., 757/727-9700, www.hamptonmarinahotel.com) offers waterfront accommodations for $120–160, with suites for twice that. The Crowne Plaza's dining options include an upscale grill, a sports bar, and a casual waterside bistro.

RVs can camp at **Gosnold's Hope Park** (757/850-5116) for $11 per night with water and electric hookups. It's north of downtown Hampton off Little Back River Road, and open year-round, but can get a bit rowdy on game days at the nearby sports fields or the Hampton Supertrack, a BMX racecourse.

Food

Look for the Dionysian painting on the outer wall of **La Bodega** (22 Wine St., 757/722-8466, breakfast and lunch Mon.–Sat., $5–8). Homemade bread and signature sandwiches around $7 are among the edible offerings at this gourmet deli and espresso bar. **Anna's Italian Pizza** (1979 E. Pembroke Ave., 757/723-3593, lunch and dinner Tues.–Sun.) serves dependable Italian fare—subs, pastas, seafood, salads, and the obvious pizza. Prices range $7–18.

For fresh seafood, you could do much worse than **Marker 20** (21 E. Queens Way, 757/726-9410, lunch and dinner daily). All the fruits of the Chesapeake Bay range $10–19, and there are special late-night and Sunday brunch menus as well. (Make your own mimosas and Bloody Marys for brunch.) Live music, microbrews, and covered outdoor dining make this a favorite local place to take guests. **The Grey Goose** (101 W. Queens Way, 757/723-7978, breakfast Mon.–Fri., lunch Mon.–Sat.) is a continental-style restaurant with homemade soups, salads, sandwiches, biscuits, and desserts ($6–9).

Information

Hampton's **visitors center** (120 Old Hampton Ln., 757/727-1102, 9 A.M.–5 P.M. daily) is located under the same roof as the Hampton History Museum. The Hampton Convention & Visitors Bureau is another good resource (757/722-1222, www.visithampton.com).

Getting There

Hampton is connected to Norfolk, Newport News, Virginia Beach, Portsmouth, and Chesapeake by **Hampton Roads Transit** (757/222-6100, www.gohrt.com). Call or check HRT's website for routes, hours, and fares. There's a **Greyhound/Trailways** terminal (757/722-9861) located at 2 West Pembroke Avenue and Jefferson Avenue (Rte. 143).

Norfolk and Vicinity

Norfolk (pop. 234,000), Virginia's second-largest city and the unofficial hub of Hampton Roads, is more than home to the world's largest naval base. The city also gives the region a "real" downtown and city-style skyline, and it is home to a galaxy of great restaurants, outstanding museums, five colleges and universities, and enough nightlife and shopping to keep even visiting sailors happy—now that most of the off-color waterfront joints have closed.

Norfolk is a surprisingly pleasant city, with a walkable waterfront marketplace, a $36 million cruise terminal, and plenty of green parks and blue water in every direction. (By the way, it's pronounced NOR-fik—or NAW-fik if you want to sound like a true old-time local.)

History

The original town site of about 500 acres was bought near the turn of the 18th century for 10,000 pounds of tobacco. It quickly became one of Colonial Virginia's largest trade centers, sending out tobacco, flour, meat, and lumber to be exchanged for sugar and molasses in the West Indies. With a spring at Main and Church Streets the only source of drinking water, visiting sailors naturally steered for the taverns (and have been doing so, more or less, ever since).

With a little more than 1,000 residents by the latter part of the 18th century, Norfolk almost ceased to exist on New Year's Day 1776, when an 11-hour British bombardment leveled two-thirds of the city. Within two months, colonists had destroyed the rest to prevent it from sheltering Lord Dunmore's soldiers. Only a few brick structures were left standing in "chimney town," including the cannon-scarred walls of St. Paul's Church.

Such a great location couldn't go to waste, though, and Norfolk soon rebuilt itself into the largest town in Virginia. Many of its 7,000 inhabitants worked on the docks and in the warehouses that exchanged produce from the Piedmont for goods from abroad. Some historians blame the economic jealousy of upriver cities for Norfolk's failure to become a great ocean port akin to Boston or New York.

Tens of thousands of Confederate troops stationed nearby couldn't keep Norfolk, along with Portsmouth and Suffolk, from falling into the hands of the Federals in March 1862. The first steps to becoming the world's largest coal port came with the first load, which arrived in 1882 on the Norfolk & Western Railroad. In 1907, the Jamestown Exhibition drew national attention to Norfolk and planted the seeds of the naval base in a few abandoned buildings used for offices and barracks. Three years later, Eugene Ely made the first airplane flight from a ship (an honor turned down by the Wright brothers).

A friendly force of soldiers, sailors, and officers invaded Norfolk during World War I, prompting

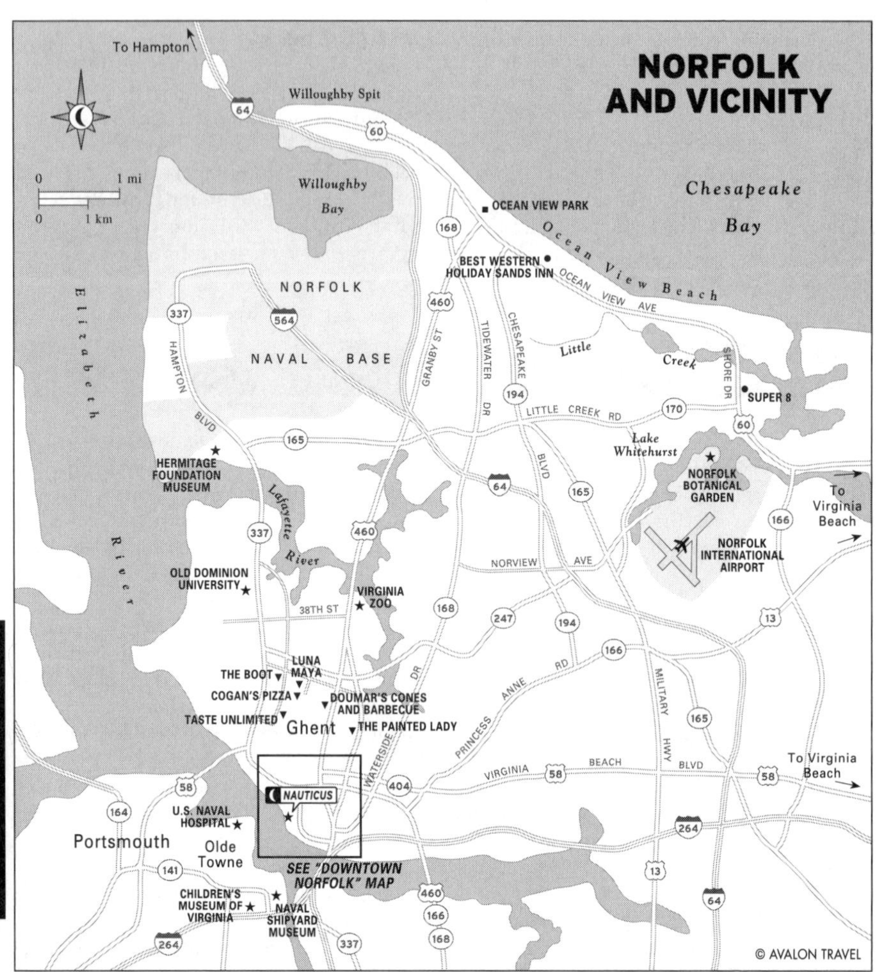

construction of a working base in 1917. Huge ships steamed in and out of Hampton Roads, dropping off men for training and R&R and picking up munitions turned out by the thousands. By the end of the war, Norfolk counted 34,000 enlisted residents and was well on its way to becoming synonymous with the U.S. Navy. East Main Street was famous worldwide for its bars, burlesque halls, and tattoo parlors. (The last were banned from 1950 to 2006.)

Even with the base closings of the 1990s, Norfolk is still the world's largest naval center. A recent downtown renaissance cleaned up seedy sections of the waterfront and saw the creation of a 12,000-seat baseball stadium for the AAA Norfolk Tides and the futuristic NAUTICUS maritime center. A 260-foot whale mural gracing a parking garage on Waterside Drive illustrates the revival. The Ghent neighborhood, once one of Norfolk's classiest zip codes, has been rescued from a mid-century decline and turned into a hot spot of boutiques, fine restaurants, and historic homes within walking distance of Old Dominion University.

SIGHTS

NAUTICUS

The $52 million maritime-themed science center was opened in 1994 to much fanfare (and some controversy over the price tag). Designed to resemble an aircraft carrier—down to a Blue Angel fighter landing on top—this high-tech gallery offers children and adults a plethora of interactive displays on all things nautical, from ship design to cleaning up after an oil spill.

Experience warfare at sea in the AEGIS theater, which simulates the bridge of a destroyer. Beautiful tropical fish and moray eels flit through aquariums near a touch tank and working aquatic laboratories. On the 2nd floor, the **Hampton Roads Naval Museum** covers two centuries of local naval history through archaeology, models, and photographs.

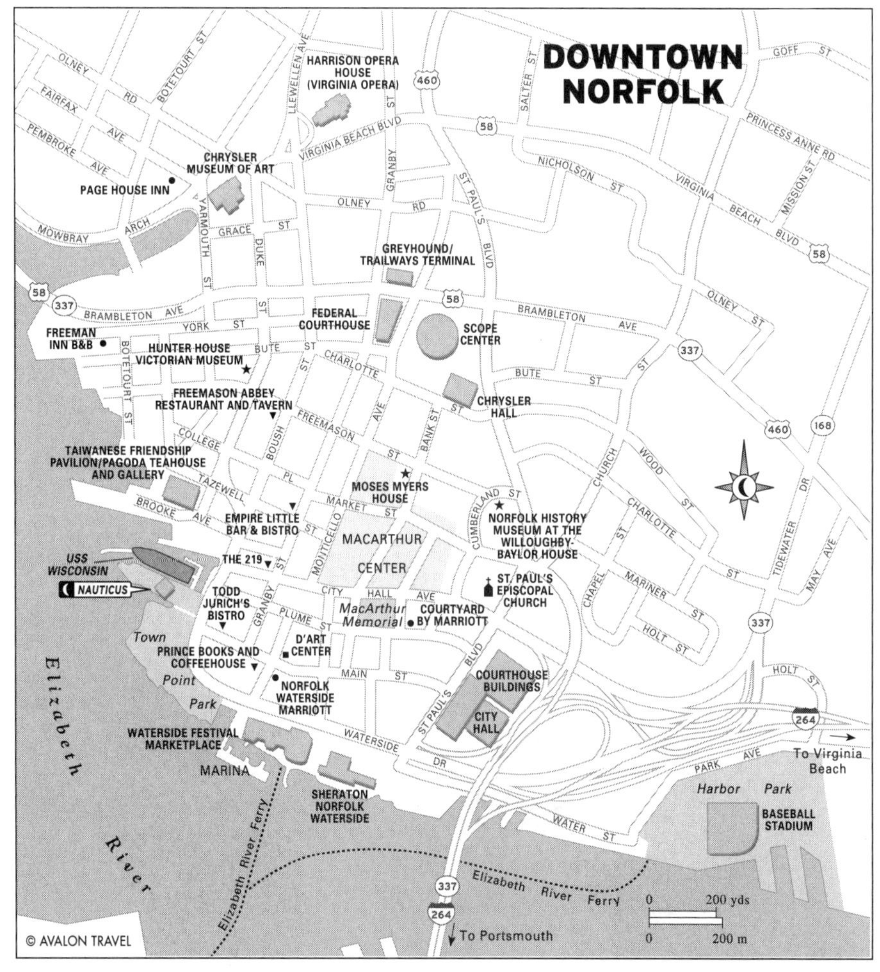

The latest addition to the Naval Museum is parked next door and easily as big as the center itself. The 887-foot **USS *Wisconsin*** is one of four Iowa-class battleships in the U.S. Navy, and it's almost unbelievably big. Nine 16-inch guns saw action in World War II, Korea, and the Persian Gulf. Some 2,700 men served onboard during World War II—1,000 more than there were room for, leading to such crowding that one sailor searched for a friend for three days, then ended up sending him a postcard in frustration. Because the navy has to have two battleships on call at all times (currently this one and the USS *Iowa*), the *Wisconsin* could technically be called into service at any time, thus the lower decks remain sealed off to visitors.

NAUTICUS (1 Waterside Dr., 757/664-1000 or 800/664-1080, www.nauticus.org, 10 A.M.–5 P.M. daily, $19 adults, $15 children 4–12) has a gift shop and a cafeteria on its 1st floor, open to anyone who crosses the "gangplank" entrance ramp.

MacArthur Memorial

Norfolk's 19th-century City Hall, a neoclassic monolith designed by the same architect as the U.S. Capitol, was chosen as the final resting place for General Douglas MacArthur (1880–1964), one of the past century's most intriguing military figures, who is buried in the building's rotunda (757/441-2965, www.macarthurmemorial.org, 10 A.M.–5 P.M. Mon.–Sat., 11 A.M.–5 P.M. Sun., free).

St. Paul's Episcopal Church

The only building to survive the leveling of Norfolk in 1776 stands in an island of trees and ancient gravestones amid the clutter and clamor of downtown. The first church on this site was built in 1639; this one dates to 1739 and still has a British cannonball embedded in its south wall. The church (St. Paul's Blvd. and City Hall Ave., 757/627-4353, www.saintpaulsnorfolk.com, 9 A.M.–4 P.M. Mon.–Sat., Sun. services, free) still supports an active Episcopal parish.

Chrysler Museum of Art

Named one of the 20 best art museums in the country by the *Wall Street Journal,* the Chrysler houses the personal collection of Walter Chrysler, who ran one of the "big three" car companies and built New York's Chrysler Building. The collection ranges from pre-Columbian to modern, touching on Greco-

© KATIE GITHENS

You have to see the USS *Wisconsin*, parked next to the NAUTICUS maritime center, to grasp its size.

© KATIE GITHENS

The Torch Bearers, **by sculptor Anna Hyatt Huntington, dramatically marks the entrance to the Chrysler Museum of Art.**

Roman, Asian, Islamic, Egyptian, and Indian along the way. Works by Mary Cassatt, Paul Gauguin, and Edward Hopper hang alongside an outstanding collection of decorative glass, including dozens of gorgeous Tiffany lamps, windows, and the famous flower-form vase.

The museum (245 W. Olney Rd., 757/664-6200, www.chrysler.org, 10 A.M.–5 P.M. Thurs.–Sat., 10 A.M.–9 P.M. Wed., noon–5 P.M. Sun., permanent exhibit is free) also administers the Moses Myers and Willoughby-Baylor historic houses. **Cuisine and Company** (757/333-6291, lunch Wed.–Sun., dinner Wed.) serves light lunch fare, coffee, and dessert—and on Wednesday, dinner specials.

Historic Houses

The **Moses Myers House** (Freemason and Bank Sts., 757/441-1526, 10 A.M.–4 P.M. Wed.–Sat., noon–4 P.M. Sun., free) was built 1789–1791 by one of Norfolk's first Jewish residents, a consul and merchant originally from New York. His family lived here until 1931, when the house was opened as a museum concentrating on the lifestyle and traditions of Virginia's early Jewish immigrants. Most of the furniture, including a beautiful tall case clock, is original.

The furnishings and medical paraphernalia collected by the family of James Wilson Hunter fill the **Hunter House Victorian Museum** (240 W. Freemason St., 757/623-9814, www.hunterhousemuseum.org, 10 A.M.–3:30 P.M. Wed.–Sat., 12:30–3:30 P.M. Sun., Apr.–Dec., $5 adults, $1 children). Guided tours leave every half hour. Don't miss the stained-glass windows and the turn-of-the-20th-century EKG machine.

A blend of Georgian and Federal styles characterizes the structure that now holds the **Norfolk History Museum at the Willoughby-Baylor House** (601 E. Freemason St., 757/441-1526, 10 A.M.–4 P.M. Wed.–Sat., noon–4 P.M. Sun., free), restored to reflect the middle-class 18th-century life of Capt. William Willoughby's family. Cooking and medicinal herbs have been replanted in the kitchen garden. Tours are given on the hour until 3 or 4 P.M. depending on the season.

Hermitage Foundation Museum

The 12-acre summer retreat of William and Florence Sloane, built 1908–1932 on the shore of the Lafayette River, now houses one of the largest private collections of Asian art in the country. The mock Tudor house is a wonder, filled with hidden doors and stairways and incredible wood carvings by Charles Woodsend. Then there's the collection: 1,400-year-old Chinese marble Buddhas, unique Persian prayer rugs, and minutely detailed Chinese and Japanese snuffboxes. Other ancient cultures are represented by glass vials to catch the tears of Roman mourners, intricately carved Spanish *varqueños* (traveling desks), Bronze Age burial containers for food, and more.

The museum (7637 North Shore Rd., 757/423-2052, www.hermitagefoundation.org, 10 A.M.–5 P.M. Mon.–Tues. and Fri.–Sat., 1–5 P.M. Sun., $5 adults, $2 children 6–18) offers mandatory tours that last one hour. The lush, wooded grounds are free.

Norfolk Naval Base

The home of NATO's Atlantic operations and the U.S. Atlantic Fleet—all 150 ships and 100,000 workers—the Norfolk Naval Base stretches for 15 miles along the Elizabeth River and Willoughby Bay. Visitors can ogle monstrous aircraft carriers, amphibious assault vessels, submarines, cruisers, and destroyers on narrated bus tours ($10 adults, $5 children), which leave on a seasonally varying schedule from the Waterside; call the Naval Base Tour Office (757/444-7955) for details. Two-hour harbor boat tours leave from NAUTICUS aboard the *Victory Rover* (1 Waterside Dr., 757/627-7406, www.navalbasecruises.com) for $18 adults and $10 children.

Virginia Zoo

A century old, this is the state's largest zoo, with 350 animals in its collection. Most popular is a special 10-acre African exhibit, with African elephants, white rhinos, lions, zebras, giraffes, meerkats, and warthogs displayed in natural surroundings near a replica of an African village. The zoo (3500 Granby St., 757/441-2374, www.virginiazoo.org, 10 A.M.–5 P.M. daily, $7 adults, $5 children) offers special children's events, including summer safaris, crafts, and games. Changing exhibits pass through regularly.

Norfolk Botanical Garden

This is the perfect antidote to Hampton Roads' urban sprawl—155 acres of trees, shrubs, and flowering plants covering the area between the Norfolk International Airport and Lake Whitehurst. It's easy to spend a whole day wandering among beds brimming with so many varieties of plants that something's almost always in bloom. Every known variety of azalea—250 in all—blooms March–May, followed by the 4,000 plants in the Bicentennial Rose Garden. Add 500 camellias and one of the largest collections of rhododendrons east of the Mississippi, and you have a flower lover's nirvana. More than 30 special gardens include a tropical plant pavilion, Colonial herb garden, and a unique garden in a bog, where unfortunate Confederate POWs were held during the Civil War.

The gardens (6700 Azalea Garden Rd., 757/441-5830, www.norfolkbotanicalgarden.org, 9 A.M.–7 P.M. daily, to 5 P.M. Oct.–Apr., $7 adults, $5 children 3–18) offer 12 miles of trails winding through the greenery, including the Fragrance Garden Trail for visitors with impaired vision. You can walk or drive the paths (no bikes) or take a tram tour for free. A boat tour on the lake costs $4 adults, $2 children. In the main building, you'll find a horticultural gift shop and the **Garden House Café,** with a patio over the Japanese garden. Kids love the "children's adventure garden," called the World of Wonders, with fountains, herbs from around the world, and the "dirt factory."

It's no surprise that the gardens are popular with wedding parties and, especially in late April, with picnickers, who flock for the azalea-themed **Norfolk NATO Festival.** The four-day event celebrates Norfolk's role in NATO, honoring a different country every year and ending with the coronation of an Azalea Queen in a special garden pavilion. (The only thing to disturb the peace of the place are the airplanes taking off overhead from the airport next door, but at least there's an overlook to get a good view.)

ENTERTAINMENT AND RECREATION

To find out what's going on around Norfolk, pick up a free copy of the *Port Folio* entertainment weekly or the Friday *Preview* section of the *Virginian Pilot.*

Nightlife

The **Tap House Grill** (931 W. 21st St., 757/627-9172) has a young crowd and a long list of microbrews to go with live music most evenings. **The Banque** (1849 E. Little Creek Rd., 757/480-3600) has been voted Club of the Year by the Virginia Country Music Association several times for its huge dance floor and quality bookings. The **NorVa** (317 Monticello Ave., 757/627-4547, www.thenorva.com) is a mid-sized concert venue with room for 1,500 people and a great sound system.

The beautiful people are reported to congregate at **Havana** (255 Granby St., 757/627-5800). In Ghent, the **Naro Expanded Cinema** (1507 Colley Ave., 757/625-6276, www.narocinema.com, $8) shows independent flicks and the cult classic *Rocky Horror Picture Show.*

Performing Arts

Norfolk's eye-catching **Scope** arena (201 E. Brambleton Ave., 757/664-6464, www.sevenvenues.com) can seat more than 12,000 for concerts, ice shows, and circuses. The more intimate **Chrysler Hall** (215 St. Paul's Blvd., 757/664-6464) is reminiscent of D.C.'s Kennedy Center and hosts the **Virginia Symphony** (757/892-6366, www.virginiasymphony.org) as well as Broadway shows and an annual pops series. The symphony has been performing since the 1920s and gives more than 140 concerts per year.

The **Virginia Opera** (866/673-7282, www.vaopera.org) is the official company of the Commonwealth, performing at the 1,600-seat Harrison Opera House (160 E. Virginia Beach Blvd.), as well as in Richmond and Fairfax. Six productions per year are on the schedule for the **Virginia Stage Company** (757/627-1234, www.vastage.com) September–April at the cozy Wells Theater on Monticello Avenue. Contact **Ballet Virginia** (757/446-1401, www.balletvirginia.org) for its current schedule.

Spectator Sports

The AAA **Norfolk Tides** (757/622-2222, www.norfolktides.com) aren't the only ones enjoying the Harbor Park stadium. The **Hits at the Park** restaurant helped earn the park a reputation as one of the best minor-league ballparks in the country—perfect for this farm team for the Baltimore Orioles, and before that the New York Mets. (The Tides have already produced stars such as Dwight Gooden and Darryl Strawberry.) Partners with the Washington Capitols, the **Norfolk Admirals** hockey team (757/640-1212, www.norfolkadmirals.com) competes in the East Coast Hockey League in the Scope arena October–March.

On the Water

Vacation homes and inexpensive apartment-hotels line the seven miles of **Ocean View Beach** on the Chesapeake Bay, with public bathrooms, picnic facilities, and a 1,600-foot pier where you can rent fishing and crabbing gear. It's a quieter alternative to Virginia Beach's crowds, and lifeguards keep an eye out during the summer, even though there's no undertow. Ocean View Beach Park hosts free movies, concerts, and food festivals May–August; contact Norfolk Festevents (757/441-2345, www.festeventsva.org) for a schedule.

Certified instructor Randy Gore runs **Kayak Nature Tours** (757/480-1999 or 888/669-8368, www.kayaknaturetours.net), which offers beginning and intermediate kayak classes, as well as rolling clinics. The focus is on 2.5-hour local trips ($50–55 pp), but he also does longer trips to the Back Bay, the Eastern Shore, and the Great Dismal Swamp ($75–115).

Cruises and Tours

Sightseeing, dining, and fun-time cruises

aboard the sleek ***Spirit of Norfolk*** (866/304-2469, www.spiritofnorfolk.com) leave from the Waterside year-round. Choices range from moonlight cruises to lunch and dinner trips ($60–80). Call for information on tours of the Naval Base.

Standing 135 feet tall, the red-sailed ***American Rover*** (757/627-7245, www.americanrover.com) is the largest topsail passenger schooner flying the stars and stripes. Daily tours of Hampton Roads nautical landmarks past and present run April–October from the Waterside dock for $16 adults, $10 children under 12. There are also sunset ($25/$15) cruises and party cruises ($12) after dark with a full bar and music.

Hampton Roads Transit (757/222-6100, www.gohrt.com) operates a Paddlewheel Ferry that runs between the Norfolk and Portsmouth waterfronts. It's a quick way to port-hop and a cheap way to see the waterfront ($1.50 one-way).

SHOPPING

Designed by the same architectural team responsible for Baltimore's Harborplace and Richmond's Sixth Street Marketplace, Norfolk's **Waterside Festival Marketplace** (333 Waterside Dr., www.watersidemarketplace.com) has dozens of shops selling African art, Southwestern jewelry, clothes, herbs, and Virginiana. Art exhibits and music performances pass through various public spaces, and there are plenty of places to stop for a bite. The complex also has bars, restaurants, and a visitors center. In a similar vein, smack in the center of downtown is the gargantuan **MacArthur Center,** a shopping mall with 140 well-known chain stores and eateries and an 18-screen multiplex.

Prince Books and Coffeehouse (109 E. Main St., 757/622-9223) has an excellent selection and friendly service, along with a coffee shop for sipping while perusing your latest find. Also downtown is the **d'Art Center** (208 E. Main St., 757/625-4211, www.d-artcenter.org, 10 A.M.–5 P.M. Tues.–Sat., 1–5 P.M. Sun.) in the Selden Arcade, home to 40 artists laboring over everything from ceramics to calligraphy. You can stop by to chat or browse; call the center for information on art classes and changing exhibits.

Norfolk's trendiest shopping neighborhood is historic Ghent, centered on Colley Avenue and 21st Street. Here you'll find antiques stores such as **Merlo's** (810 Granby St., 757/622-2699) and upscale consignment stores like **2nd Act Consignment** (110-A W. 21st St., 757/622-1533).

EVENTS

With as many annual celebrations as any city in the state, Norfolk takes its festivals seriously. It even has an office devoted just to scheduling and information, called **Festevents** (120 W. Main St., 757/441-2345, www.festeventsva.org). Unless indicated otherwise, all events are held among the trees in the pleasant Town Point Park on the Waterfront. Along with those listed here, the park hosts free **Big Bands on the Bay** concerts and dancing May–August. Sailing fans will want to keep an eye out for regular **tall-ship visitations,** when ships from as far away as South America dock at the park. When you climb aboard you'll find the crews are happy to show you around.

March brings the **ShamRock 'N Roll** party over St. Patrick's Day. In early May, the **Norfolk NATO Festival,** formerly the International Azalea Festival, ends with an air show featuring the Blue Angels, barnstormers, and free-fall teams celebrating Norfolk's importance to NATO. The festival culminates in the coronation of an Azalea Queen. From late April to late May, the **Virginia Arts Festival** (www.virginiaartsfest.com) attracts world-class performers such as Itzhak Perlman and the Russian National Ballet for a series of concerts in Norfolk, Hampton, Portsmouth, and Virginia Beach.

Early June's **Harborfest** is Norfolk's biggest celebration, attracting 100,000 people for water and air shows, live entertainment, fireworks, and seafood the first weekend of the month. A highlight is the Parade of Sails, a procession of fully rigged sailboats through the harbor.

Zydeco and crawdads arrive in late June

during the **Bayou Boogaloo,** followed by the **Norfolk Jazz Festival** in late July. Giant puppets, costumed characters, and theater shows mark the **Virginia Children's Festival** in early October.

In mid-October 25 Virginia wineries are featured during the **Town Point Virginia Wine Festival,** which sets the stage for the Halloween **Masquerade in Ghent.**

ACCOMMODATIONS

$50-100

Only a short walk from the Chesapeake Bay and Ocean View Beach is a **Super 8** (7940 Shore Dr., 757/588-7888, $90–100). The beachfront **Best Western Holiday Sands Inn** (1330 E. Ocean View Ave., 757/583-2621, $80–140) also has an outdoor pool and fitness center.

$100-150

The **America's Best Value Inn** (235 N. Military Hwy., 757/461-6600, $90–150) near I-264 has a pool, sauna, and gym. There's also the **Crowne Plaza Norfolk** (700 Monticello Ave., 757/627-5555) with 204 rooms starting at $140.

$150-200

Carl Albero runs the restored 1899 Georgian Revival mansion near the Chrysler Museum now known as the **Page House Inn** (323 Fairfax Ave., 757/625-5033 or 800/599-7659, www.pagehouseinn.com). It's furnished with four-poster beds, claw-foot tubs, and 19th-century artwork. Four rooms ($150–170) and three suites ($175–230), including the Bathe Suite with its gas-log fireplace and sunken hot tub, are available in the house. Guests can enjoy the basement billiard room and yard games on the lawn.

The **Courtyard by Marriott** (520 Plume St., 757/963-6000, $140–170) is centrally located downtown, offering a heated indoor pool and valet parking.

$200-250

The elegant rooms at the **Freemason Inn Bed and Breakfast** (411 W. York St., 757/963-7000 or 866/388-1897, www.freemasoninn.com, $145–245) have names like Sir York and East India Tea Co. and come with accoutrements like plush bathrobes and claw-foot tubs. This narrow place was opened by the lawyer whose office is next door, and the 19th-century building has been beautifully restored. It's known for its three-course gourmet candlelight breakfasts. (When's the last time you had dessert before noon?)

Some of the rooms at the 24-story **Norfolk Waterside Marriott** (235 E. Main St., 757/627-4200, $150–220) have views of the Elizabeth River just outside. It offers all the amenities business travelers expect—concierge service, exercise rooms, valet service—and its steak house serves lunch and dinner.

Over $250

Also downtown near the water is the **Sheraton Norfolk Waterside** (777 Waterside Dr., 757/622-6664, $170–200), with 468 rooms and nine suites. It's near the Waterside Marketplace, with great views and an outdoor pool.

FOOD

From cones made on the world's first ice cream–cone machine to dinner in a restored abbey, the city has it covered—and with the headquarters of People for the Ethical Treatment of Animals (PETA) in town, you can be sure there are plenty of vegetarian options.

Snacks and Cafés

Next to NAUTICUS and the USS *Wisconsin* in the ornate Taiwanese Pavilion is the **Pagoda Teahouse and Gallery** (265 Tazewell St., 757/622-0506, lunch Mon.–Sat., dinner Tues.–Sat.), selling tea, coffee, snacks, soups, salads, and sandwiches for $5–7. Heartier entrées like fried tempura shrimp cost up to $14. There are an Asian art gallery and a shop, and an upstairs balcony overlooks the surrounding fountains and flowers. The coffee shop at **Prince Books and Coffeehouse** (109 E. Main St., 757/622-9223, lunch daily) serves pastries, panini, salads, and desserts.

Afternoon tea with scones at **The Painted Lady** (112 E. 17th St., 757/622-5239, lunch and dinner Tues.–Sat., brunch Sun.), a pair of restored Victorian homes painted pink and purple and full of odds and ends, is always fun. Tea is served 2–4 P.M., and there's Teddy Bear Tea for kids.

For healthy gourmet sandwiches for $5–9, look no further than **Taste Unlimited** (1619 Colley Ave., 757/623-7770, lunch daily). This is one of several locations in the Hampton Roads area. It also stocks snacks, chocolates, and wines and will make you a box lunch if you order ahead.

Casual

Thanks in part to the opening of the million-square-foot shopper's paradise called the MacArthur Center nearby, Granby Street has undergone a culinary renaissance of sorts. Case in point is the **Empire Little Bar & Bistro** (245 Granby St., 757/626-3100, dinner daily), which offers bite-sized tapas ($5–12) and more than 30 kinds of martinis and cocktails in a snug, elbow-rubbing setting.

Ghent is the current hot spot outside of downtown for fun, creative dining options. **Cogan's Pizza** (1901 Colonial Ave., 757/627-6428, lunch and dinner daily) serves, unsurprisingly, pizza ($15–20)—it's been voted the best in Hampton Roads—and has dozens of beers on tap. It's an art-filled, tattooed-bartender type of place with a young clientele and an outdoor patio (dogs welcome). It also serves subs and pastas. Along similar lines is **The Boot** (123 W. 21st St., 757/627-2668, dinner Tues.–Sat.). Italian dishes using fresh local ingredients go well with local art on the walls and live music in the evenings. Main dishes are $15–25, with plenty of vegetarian options.

Another good choice in Ghent is **Luna Maya** (2000 Colonial Ave., 757/622-6986, dinner Tues.–Sat.), run by Bolivian sisters in the Corner Shoppes complex. The menu ranges across Latin America, the atmosphere is vibrant, and the prices are reasonable ($11–18 for dinner entrées).

You can munch a bit of history at **Doumar's Cones and Barbecue** (Monticello Ave. and 20th St., 757/627-4163, all meals Mon.–Sat.). "Uncle" Abe Doumar invented the ice cream cone at the 1904 World's Fair, and his original hand-rolling machine is still in use at this true-as-they-come drive-in with famous limeade and curb service (flash your headlights for a server). Even the prices haven't changed in decades: burgers, hot dogs, and barbecue sandwiches are all under $5.

Upscale

A high arched ceiling and stained-glass windows show that the **Freemason Abbey Restaurant & Tavern** (209 W. Freemason St., 757/622-3966, lunch and dinner daily) occupies a real late-19th-century abbey. Daily specials such as lobster, prime rib, and tempura shrimp are $8–18 for lunch and up to $30 for dinner. Lighter choices such as seafood quiche and house sandwiches are also available.

Produce from small, ecologically sound farms goes into the food at **Todd Jurich's Bistro** (150 W. Main St., Ste. 100, 757/622-3210, lunch Mon.–Fri., dinner Mon.–Sat.). Jurich, one of the best chefs in the area, mixes the innovative with the down-home in dishes such as bouillabaisse and Kobe beef short ribs. Entrées range $18–32.

INFORMATION

The **Norfolk Convention & Visitors Bureau** (232 E. Main St., 757/664-6620 or 800/368-3097, www.visitnorfolktoday.com) operates visitors centers in the Waterside complex and at 9401 4th View Street at Ocean View, both open 9 A.M.–5 P.M. daily.

GETTING THERE AND AROUND

Getting There

You can catch a Thruway bus to the Amtrak station at Newport News at Norfolk's **Greyhound/Trailways** terminal (701 Monticello Ave., 757/625-7500). Reach the **Norfolk International Airport** (757/857-3351, www.norfolkairport.com) from I-64 exit 279 to Norview Avenue. **Airport Express** (877/455-7462) will take you there.

Getting Around

Norfolk Electric Transit (NET) (www.norfolk.va.us/visitors/net.asp) runs free buses from Harbor Park to the Harrison Opera House, stopping at Waterside and NAUTICUS along the way. They operate 6:30 A.M.–11 P.M. Monday–Friday, noon–midnight Saturday, and noon–8 P.M. Sunday. Norfolk is connected to Newport News, Hampton, Virginia Beach, Portsmouth, and Chesapeake by **Hampton Roads Transit** (757/222-6100, www.gohrt.com). Call or check its website for routes, hours, and fares. HRT also runs the **Paddle Wheel Ferry** ($1.50) between Waterside in Norfolk and North Landing and High Street in Portsmouth.

PORTSMOUTH

About 100,000 people live in this centuries-old seaport across the Elizabeth River from Norfolk. The nation's oldest naval shipyard bristles with cranes and girders south of the narrow tree-lined brick sidewalks of the Olde Towne district, with more historic buildings than any other city between Alexandria, Virginia, and Charleston, South Carolina.

History

Portsmouth was established in 1752 on the land of a colonist who was executed for participating in Bacon's Rebellion. The Gosport Navy Yard arrived 15 years later, quickly becoming the busiest in the colonies during the Revolutionary War. British soldiers ransacked Portsmouth in 1779 and burned ships in the harbor, but by 1798 the city was again so busy that, according to a witness, "one might walk...to Norfolk on the decks of vessels at anchor." In 1799, the shipyard turned out the *Chesapeake,* the first ship built for the new U.S. government. The British paid another visit during the War of 1812, when 2,600 men landed here only to be beaten back by American troops at forts Norfolk and Nelson (today home to the Navy Medical Center Portsmouth).

Federal forces evacuated the city and burned the naval yard soon after Virginia's entry into the Civil War, allowing Confederate shipbuilders to raise the sunken frigate *Merrimac* and turn her into the CSS *Virginia* in time to battle the Union ironclad *Monitor.* In May 1862, it was the Confederates' turn to torch the city as Union troops moved back in. The country's first battleship, the USS *Texas,* rolled off the docks in 1892, followed by the first American aircraft carrier, the USS *Langley,* in 1922. Portsmouth's docks, well on their way to becoming the largest in the country, were renamed the Norfolk Naval Shipyard in 1945.

Sights

All of Portsmouth's attractions are within easy walking distance of each other. The city's central **Olde Towne** area includes many period homes and cafés and restaurants, especially along High and Court Streets.

A Key Pass ($9 adults, $6 children) gives admission to the following four attractions, all within easy walking distance. At the water end of London Street, the retired Coast Guard vessel *Portsmouth* houses the **Lightship Museum** (757/393-8591, 10 A.M.–5 P.M. Tues.–Sat., 1–5 P.M. Sun., www.portsnavalmuseums.com, $3 adults, $1 children 2–17, admission includes Naval Shipyard Museum). Commissioned in 1915 and anchored offshore, the ship guided vessels into the tricky Hampton Roads harbor for decades before being restored as a floating museum and National Historic Landmark. Tour the captain's quarters, boiler room, and crew's mess.

Ship models, artifacts, and uniforms fill the **Naval Shipyard Museum** (757/393-8591, 10 A.M.–5 P.M. Tues.–Sat., 1–5 P.M. Sun., www.portsnavalmuseums.com, $3 adults, $1 children 2–17, admission includes Lightship Museum). The collection, dating to the 1700s, includes antique diving helmets.

A bubble-making station, rock-climbing wall, and an antique toy and model train collection to please Thomas the Tank Engine fans are only a few of the diversions at the **Children's Museum of Virginia** (221 High St., 757/393-5258, 9 A.M.–5 P.M. Tues.–Sat., 11 A.M.–5 P.M. Sun., www.childrensmuseumva.com, $5). In 2009, major renovations began to add 12,000 square feet and new exhibits, with the museum's reopening expected for early 2011. In the interim the museum has opened **Andalo's Clubhouse** at 420 High Street. It's next to the Courthouse Galleries and continues to focus on science, the arts, and fun.

Portmouth's **Courthouse Galleries** (High and Court St., 757/393-8543, 9 A.M.–5 P.M. Tues.–Sat., 11–5 P.M. Sun., www.courthousegalleries.com, $5) fill a restored 1846 courthouse with works by international and regional artists.

Immerse yourself in the athletic world, from dribbling a basketball to driving a stock car on a (simulated) professional track, at the **Virginia Sports Hall of Fame & Museum** (206 High St., 757/393-8031, 10 A.M.–5 P.M. Mon.–Sat., 1–5 P.M. Sun. Memorial Day to Labor Day, shorter off-season hours, www.vshfm.com, $7).

Entertainment and Recreation

One of the best sound systems in Hampton Roads makes a movie at the **Commodore Theatre** (421 High St., 757/393-6962, www.commodoretheatre.com, $8) an experience not to be missed. Built in 1945, the art deco theater underwent a two-year $800,000 restoration that brought back 40-foot canvas murals and Italian lead crystal chandeliers. You can enjoy appetizers and light meals during the show in the 200-person dining area downstairs, but up in the balcony you'll have to be content with the usual movie snacks.

Lantern Tours of Olde Towne are led by a guide in period attire on Tuesday and Sunday evenings June–September (757/393-5111, $5). Check at the visitors center for information. Portsmouth's **Memorial Day Parade** is a big local event, and the oldest in the country.

Information

Portsmouth's **visitors center** is near the riverfront just past the corner of Crawford and High Streets (6 Crawford St., 757/393-5111, www.visitportsva.com, 9 A.M.–5 P.M. daily). For details on Portsmouth festivals and events, visit www.portsvaevents.com.

Getting There

Portsmouth is connected to Newport News, Hampton, Norfolk, Virginia Beach, and Chesapeake by **Hampton Roads Transit** (757/222-6100, www.gohrt.com). HRT also runs the **Paddlewheel Ferry,** leaving regularly from North Landing and High Street for Norfolk's Waterside daily for $1.50; call or see the website for a current schedule.

GREAT DISMAL SWAMP NATIONAL WILDLIFE REFUGE

Steeped in mystery, legend, and dread, this sodden corner of the state is actually more beautiful than it is dreary, and it still bursts with life despite multiple attempts to tame its wildness. Deep peat bogs echo with the strange cries of concealed animals down long, straight canals that contrast against the seething disorder of the bog.

History

Estimates put the age of the swamp at close to 10,000 years, when the rivers flowing through it began to slow and accumulate peat. An Indian legend of a great fireball falling from the sky has led some to believe that 3,100-acre Lake Drummond—one of only two natural lakes in the state—was formed by a meteorite. Early colonists saw the swamp as an ugly hindrance rather than a wildlife haven and tried their best to "improve" it. In 1728, after nearly losing his life surveying the state line, Col. William Byrd gave the area its name and called it a "vast body of dirt and nastiness [that] not even a Turkey Buzzard will venture to fly over."

George Washington organized a logging company in 1763, building roads and digging drainage ditches through what he considered a "glorious paradise." One 22-mile canal bearing his name is the oldest artificial waterway in the country. Eventually most of the timber was cut, leaving the swamp a shadow of its former self. In 1973, the Nature Conservancy transferred 49,100 acres to the Department of the Interior to make into a National Wildlife Refuge. Today, the Great Dismal Swamp covers over 112,000 acres in Virginia and North Carolina, primarily in Virginia.

Habitats and Residents

Ironically, human interference has left a greater variety of habitats than if the swamp had been left alone. Mixed forest, brier thickets, pine barrens, and shrub bogs now surround the original cypress swamps, whose peaty depths can reach 18 feet. Vines, including the tree-strangling supplejack, colorful hydrangea, and fast-growing Virginia creeper, festoon the branches of maples, black gums, and bald cypress, with their knobby mud-level "knees" and swollen lower trunks. Poison ivy vines as thick as your arm and a sharp-spined shrub called the devil's walking stick will make you want to hew to the trails. Venture out at night and you'll probably see the ghostly glow of foxfire (a type of fungus) in the distance. The swamp is home to declining bird species such as the bright yellow prothonotary warbler, and millions of blackbirds roost here in the winter.

In among the greenery live otters, raccoons, foxes, mink, and white-tailed deer, along with the rare bobcat and black bear. Snakes, including copperheads, rattlers, and cottonmouth moccasins, are all found here, albeit infrequently, as well as 22 species of amphibians and dozens of kinds of birds. The tannic acid is too much for most fish to live in Lake Drummond, whose position in an unusual "perched bog" makes it the highest point in the swamp.

Visiting the Swamp

One hundred forty miles of hiking and biking trails follow old drainage ditches from one end of the swamp to the other. Boating on Lake Drummond, accessed via a feeder ditch from the Dismal Swamp Canal, is also popular (there's a public boat ramp north of the feeder ditch). Bring water, good shoes, and above all insect repellent—the mosquitoes are merciless. Spring is the best time to catch migrating birds and the tiny blooms of dwarf trillium. The main **Washington Ditch entrance,** off Route 32 south of Suffolk via U.S. 13, is open sunrise to sunset daily year-round, and offers access to a one-mile **Boardwalk Trail** over the swamp. On this day-use path, you'll see bald cypress draped with Spanish moss standing over dark water. (The Jericho Lane entrance is open the same hours.) The 8.5-mile **Dismal Swamp Canal Trail,** once part of Route 17, is now a multiuse trail along the canal open to walkers, horseback riders, bicyclists, and boaters (who use it for water access, of course). Find the northern trailhead where Dominion Boulevard meets Old Route 17 in Chesapeake.

For more information, contact the refuge office in Suffolk (3100 Desert Rd., 757/986-3705, www.fws.gov/northeast/greatdismalswamp, 8 A.M.–4 P.M. Mon.–Fri.).

Virginia Beach and Vicinity

With 35 miles of beaches, surf, sand, and sun, Virginia's premier seaside resort has it all, along with gloriously tacky gift shops and more than 433,000 people in residence. While Virginia Beach has suffered an over-commercialized fate similar to places like Ocean City, Maryland, from the beach it's hard to question the pleasures of sunshine and crashing waves, no matter what's on the boardwalk behind you. And you can't argue with the variety: Be it miniature golf, family festivals, wide beaches, or a world-class aquarium, you can probably find it in Virginia Beach, although you might have to share it with a few thousand new friends.

Tourism, obviously, is one of the top local industries, ever since the first beachfront hotel went up in 1884. The boardwalk was built four years later, and the landmark Cavalier hotel arrived in 1927—both are still going strong. Virginia's most populous city didn't really become a national resort, though, until recently. The population doubled between 1980 and 1990, and it currently welcomes nearly three million visitors annually.

The municipality has invested hundreds

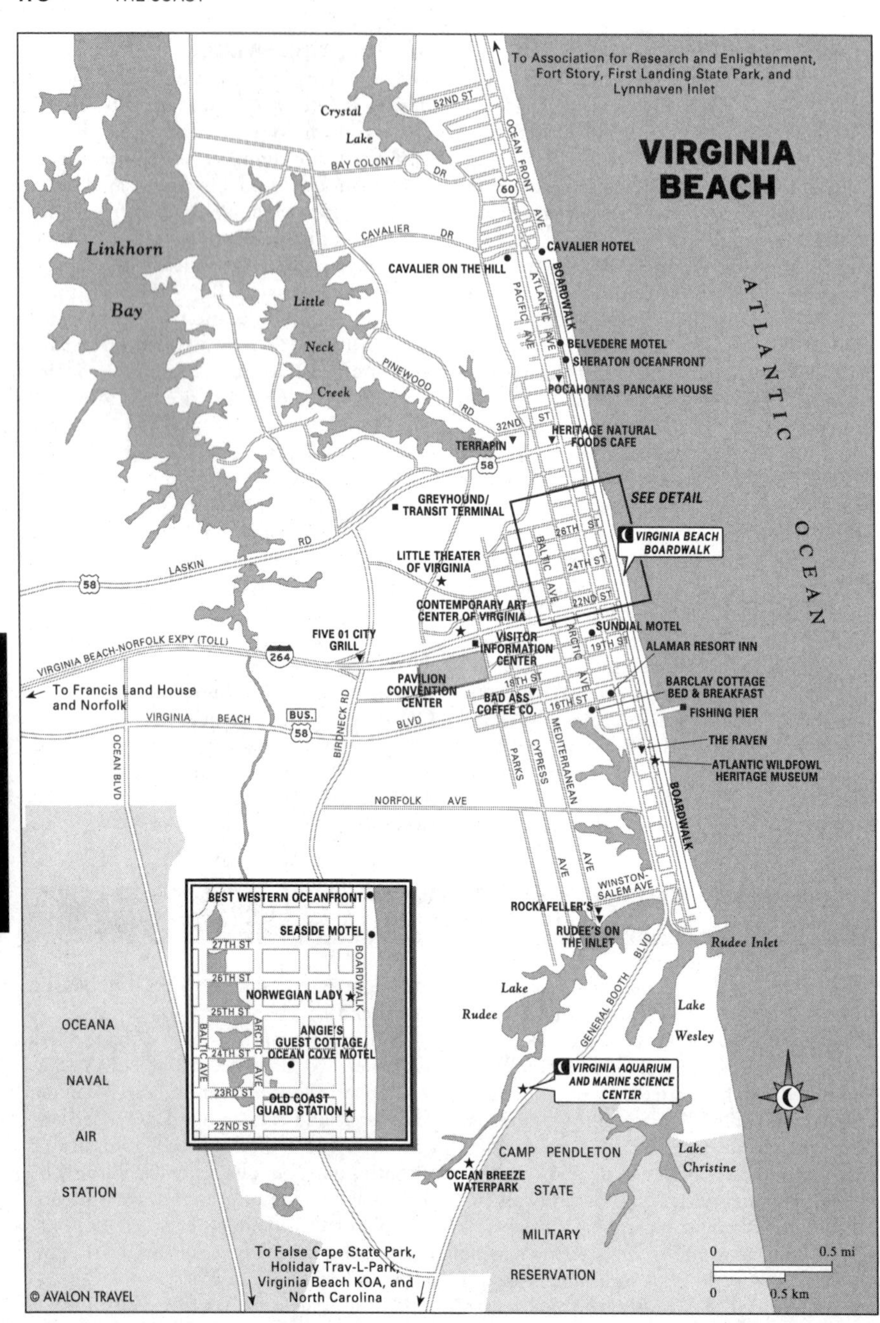
VIRGINIA BEACH
To Association for Research and Enlightenment, Fort Story, First Landing State Park, and Lynnhaven Inlet
Crystal Lake
52ND ST
BAY COLONY DR
OCEAN FRONT AVE
60
Linkhorn Bay
Little Neck Creek
CAVALIER DR
CAVALIER HOTEL
CAVALIER ON THE HILL
BOARDWALK
ATLANTIC AVE
PACIFIC AVE
BELVEDERE MOTEL
SHERATON OCEANFRONT
POCAHONTAS PANCAKE HOUSE
PINEWOOD RD
32ND ST
HERITAGE NATURAL FOODS CAFE
TERRAPIN
58
ATLANTIC OCEAN
SEE DETAIL
GREYHOUND/ TRANSIT TERMINAL
LASKIN RD
26TH ST
24TH ST
22ND ST
BALTIC AVE
VIRGINIA BEACH BOARDWALK
LITTLE THEATER OF VIRGINIA
CONTEMPORARY ART CENTER OF VIRGINIA
SUNDIAL MOTEL
FIVE 01 CITY GRILL
VISITOR INFORMATION CENTER
ARCTIC AVE
19TH ST
ALAMAR RESORT INN
VIRGINIA BEACH-NORFOLK EXPY (TOLL)
264
To Francis Land House and Norfolk
PAVILION CONVENTION CENTER
18TH ST
BAD ASS COFFEE CO.
16TH ST
BARCLAY COTTAGE BED & BREAKFAST
FISHING PIER
VIRGINIA BEACH BLVD
BUS. 58
BIRDNECK RD
OCEAN BLVD
PARKS
CYPRESS
MEDITERRANEAN
THE RAVEN
ATLANTIC WILDFOWL HERITAGE MUSEUM
NORFOLK AVE
AVE
AVE
WINSTON-SALEM AVE
BEST WESTERN OCEANFRONT
SEASIDE MOTEL
27TH ST
26TH ST
NORWEGIAN LADY
25TH ST
ANGIE'S GUEST COTTAGE/ OCEAN COVE MOTEL
24TH ST
BALTIC AVE
ARCTIC AVE
23RD ST
OLD COAST GUARD STATION
22ND ST
ROCKAFELLER'S
RUDEE'S ON THE INLET
Rudee Inlet
GENERAL BOOTH BLVD
Lake Rudee
Lake Wesley
OCEANA NAVAL AIR STATION
VIRGINIA AQUARIUM AND MARINE SCIENCE CENTER
CAMP PENDLETON STATE MILITARY RESERVATION
Lake Christine
OCEAN BREEZE WATERPARK
To False Cape State Park, Holiday Trav-L-Park, Virginia Beach KOA, and North Carolina
0 0.5 mi
0 0.5 km
© AVALON TRAVEL

THE COAST

© KATIE GITHENS / PAUL DIPASQUALE, RICHMOND, VA

Richmond artist and sculptor Paul DiPasquale's statue of King Neptune greets you on the Virginia Beach boardwalk.

of millions of dollars to make its beachside resort area more welcoming and family oriented, from boutique shops to high-end hotels and restaurants to high-profile PR campaigns canvassing metropolises such as Washington, D.C., nearby. New benches and lighting, wider sidewalks, buried power lines, and a boardwalk bicycle trail have all transformed Pacific and Atlantic Avenues.

The effort seems to have paid off: The Clean Beaches Council has officially recognized Virginia Beach as a Blue Wave beach, for excellence in public safety and environmental health. Numerous awards for livability, mostly revolving around fitness—Best Walking City, Most Stroller-Friendly City, and so on—attest to the high value locals and visitors place on getting out and about. Further testimony to this sporty streak is the perennially popular Virginia Beach Rock 'n' Roll Half Marathon; more than 15,000 runners descend on the boardwalk for the Labor Day weekend race. Any time of year, navy jets roar overhead regularly, reminders of the strong military presence in Hampton Roads.

Orientation

The resort area of Virginia Beach stretches north and south along the main beach area, lined by the boardwalk from 1st Street through 42nd Street. This is where most of the hotels, restaurants, and tourist shops are, as well as the oceanfront amusement park. Locals call the beach from 43rd Street to 86th Street "the North End"—you can rent homes here at any time of year, and there are bike paths and a wide feeder road. Sandbridge, south of Camp Pendleton toward Back Bay, offers more seclusion and rustic beach homes for rent. Chick's Beach is a calm beach area along the bay north of the resort area that includes Lynnhaven Inlet. Here you can charter a boat for sportfishing and then pull right up to a dockside restaurant for dinner when you return.

SIGHTS

Virginia Beach Boardwalk

Virginia Beach's pride and joy, a wide expanse of pure white sand facing the Atlantic, stretches along "the Strip" from 1st Street to 42nd Street. The city's sandy heart has been significantly spruced up by a $125 million erosion control and hurricane protection project. In 2001, the beach was widened by the length of a football field using 3.2 million cubic yards of imported sand—enough to fill 15,000 residential swimming pools. There are information kiosks open in the summer at 17th and 24th Streets, and public restrooms at 17th, 24th, and 30th Streets open year-round. You can rent beach umbrellas and chairs from vendors on the beach.

From Memorial Day through Labor Day, certified lifeguards are stationed every block 9:30 A.M.–6 P.M. daily (and at various stations along the beach until dusk), keeping an eye out for wayward vacationers and anyone drinking alcohol without a special-event permit. Surfing is allowed in designated areas on the north end and in Sandbridge, as well as in the main resort area during certain times (it's forbidden 10 A.M.–4 P.M. weekdays and to 6 P.M. weekends). Wave-riders congregate near Rudee Inlet and the 14th Street pier.

The **Norwegian Lady** faces the sea at 25th Street, where the bark *Dictator* sank in 1891. A twin of the nine-foot bronze figurehead stands in Moss, Norway, a sister city to Virginia Beach. The sand becomes less crowded as you head north into Fort Story or south to Croatan.

Disabled visitors can borrow all-terrain wheelchairs for free on the boardwalk (they'll lock up your standard wheelchair for you until you return; call 757/385-5659 for details). For more information on beach regulations, visit www.vbgov.com.

Virginia Aquarium and Marine Science Center

You'll find yourself eye-to-eye with a harbor seal before you're even inside this place, the most popular aquarium in the state and one of the best of its kind in the country. From the seal pool at the entrance to a drift through a kelp forest in the three-dimensional IMAX theater, the aquarium draws 620,000 visitors per year (from the sound of it sometimes, mostly schoolchildren), with a collection that's the next best thing to strapping on a scuba tank and getting wet yourself.

More than 300 exhibits include aquariums galore containing more than 800,000 gallons of fresh and saltwater. Starting with the 300,000-gallon Norfolk Canyon Aquarium, these pools are the highlight of any visit. See if you can count five varieties of sharks, and don't miss the sea-turtle hatchling laboratory next to the aquarium holding the youngsters' cat-eyed

It's easy to imagine yourself underwater while visiting the Virginia Aquarium.

parents. The Ray Touch Pool is full of harmless stingrays that are so eager to be petted that they pop halfway out of the water. Just down the hall are exhibits on deep-sea diving and beach ecology. Try your hand at oyster tonging before taking a walk down the nature trail to the marsh pavilion, where you can watch river otters cavorting and ospreys nesting on specially built platforms near their brethren enclosed in the outdoor aviary.

Be sure to visit Restless Planet, a multimillion-dollar 12,000-square-foot renovation that opened in 2009 and doubled the aquarium's animal collection, adding species that could surprise you—among them, Komodo dragons, cobras, and impossibly cute hedgehogs. The newest exhibit features four diverse habitats (a Malaysian peat swamp, coastal Sahara Desert, the Red Sea, and Indonesia's Flores Island) that resemble ecosystems that existed in Virginia millions of years ago, but are now only found in more remote corners of the globe.

The aquarium (717 General Booth Blvd., 757/385-3474, www.vmsm.com, 9 A.M.–5 P.M. daily, extended summer hours, $17 adults, $12 children 3–11) has various IMAX combination tickets available and also organizes various day trips.

Old Coast Guard Station

From 1875 to 1915, more than 600 ships foundered and sank off the Virginia coast, prompting the creation of 11 life-saving stations from the North Carolina border to the Eastern Shore. This 1903 building is the only one left of five along the southern Virginia shore. Formerly called the Life-Saving Museum, the Old Coast Guard Station (24th St. and Boardwalk, 757/422-1587, www.oldcoastguardstation.com, 10 A.M.–5 P.M. Mon.–Sat., noon–5 P.M. Sun., closed Mon. off-season, $4 adults, $2 children 6–18) still traces the history of early rescue efforts, which is really the history of Virginia Beach because the town grew up around the five nearby stations.

Among other exhibits, a roof-mounted "Towercam" allows guests to identify far-off ships, and the museum's archives hold over 1,800 photographs. Knowledgeable volunteers tell you how the attic is said to be haunted, ever since the bodies of wreck victims were stored there.

Atlantic Wildfowl Heritage Museum

The long history of bird hunting is told in the centuries-old DeWitt Cottage (1113 Atlantic Ave., 757/437-8432, www.awhm.org, 10 A.M.–5 P.M. Mon.–Sat., noon–5 P.M. Sun., closed Mon. off-season, free, donations welcome) in prints, decoys, and marvelously detailed sculptures.

Contemporary Art Center of Virginia

The only museum of its kind in the state, the Contemporary Art Center (2200 Parks Ave., 757/425-0000, www.cacv.org, 10 A.M.–5 P.M. Tues.–Fri., 10 A.M.–4 P.M. Sat., noon–4 P.M. Sun., $7 adults, $3 children 4–14) is a nonprofit institution founded in 1952. An airy main atrium filled with trees and windows leads to galleries full of paintings, sculptures, photographs, and works in glass, video, and other media. Studio art classes and outdoor shows are part of the schedule of regularly changing exhibits, which have included the likes of Maurice Sendak's *Where the Wild Things Are* illustrations.

Association for Research and Enlightenment (A.R.E.)

The work of Edgar Cayce, the 20th-century American psychic known as the father of holistic medicine, is the basis for this institution and museum. After entering a self-induced trance, Cayce would deliver predictions on the future and surprisingly accurate diagnoses of patients from just their names and addresses. Opened in 1931, the A.R.E. has some 14,000 transcripts of the sessions, called "readings," including the one that convinced Cayce to move to Virginia Beach and open the center. It's one of the largest metaphysical libraries in the world—second only to the Vatican.

The A.R.E. (67th St. and Atlantic Ave., 757/428-3588 or 800/333-4499, www.edgarcayce.org, 9 A.M.–8 P.M. Mon.–Sat.,

11 A.M.–8 P.M. Sun.) has a daily list of free activities including group meditations, extrasensory perception (ESP) classes, and lectures on Cayce's work. You'll have to pay extra for yoga, meditation instruction, and evening lectures. The **A.R.E. Health Services Center** next door offers massage, hydrotherapy, Reiki, and various other spa treatments.

Fort Story

In the middle of this U.S. Army base, north of the boardwalk on Atlantic Avenue, stands the **Battle Off the Capes Monument,** replacing one erected by Jamestown colonists under Capt. Christopher Newport on April 29, 1607, in gratitude for a safe arrival on solid ground. Part of Colonial National Historical Park, the memorial describes the naval battle that raged offshore on September 5, 1781, between 24 French ships commanded by Adm. Comte de Grasse and 19 British vessels under Rear Adm. Charles Graves. After surprising the French at anchor, the British hesitated long enough for the colonists' allies to line up in battle formation and win after a brief fight. Cornwallis was thus denied reinforcements, and the American Revolution was brought one step closer to success.

© CINDY HAGGERTY / 123RF.COM

Old Cape Henry Lighthouse in Fort Story

The official symbol of Virginia Beach, the **Old Cape Henry Lighthouse** (757/422-9421, www.apva.org/capehenry, 10 A.M.–5 P.M. daily mid-Mar.–Oct., to 4 P.M. Nov.–mid-Mar., $4 adults, $2 children 3–12) was built in 1791, the first building authorized by the first Congress. Stones from the same quarry that supplied the U.S. Capitol, the White House, and Mount Vernon went into the 90-foot octagonal tower set on the tallest sand hill in the area. In use until 1881, the lighthouse is now open to the public. The ascent—up a steep spiral staircase, two ladders, and through a small hole in the floor of the upper room—is not for the weak of heart or wide of midsection, but the view from the top is outstanding.

Remember that all visitors over 16 years old must show valid ID at the security gates of Fort Story, as it's still an active military base.

First Landing State Park

The inner half of Cape Henry manages to hide 2,900 acres of dunes, marshes, and cypress forest within sight of Virginia Beach's seaside strip. It's the most visited state park in Virginia, drawing more than one million sightseers annually, yet it remains an amazingly unspoiled nugget of nature considering its location within the state's most populous city. It also happens to be where the first permanent English settlers landed in America before settling in Jamestown.

First Landing protects mostly maritime forest, one of the most endangered habitat types in the world. The park ranges from tidal cordgrass salt marshes to live oak and loblolly pine scrub atop 75-foot dunes—the highest point in this part of the state—and shelters prothonotary warblers (also called swamp canaries) and wading birds such as green herons. Spring peepers, bullfrogs, and kingfishers ply the tannin-browned waters of gothic flooded forests in the center, one of the northernmost stands of Spanish moss and bald cypress in North America.

Stop at the **visitors center,** off Seashore Drive (U.S. 60) at the west end of the park

© KATIE GITHENS

First Landing State Park is a nice place for a stroll.

(757/412-2300, www.dcr.virginia.gov/state_parks/fir.shtml, $4 weekdays, $5 weekends), for a map of 20 miles of **hiking** trails. The six-mile Cape Henry trail runs the length of the park and is popular with mountain bikers, and the Bald Cypress Nature Trail leads into the heart of the swamp. The park's **Chesapeake Bay Center,** developed in cooperation with the Virginia Aquarium and Marine Science Center, houses displays on the aquatic life of the region and its human history. At the **Cape Henry Memorial,** part of Colonial National Historical Park, a cross erected in 1935 marks the approximate spot where the Jamestown settlers first landed. This park can get crowded, especially with trail runners, so come early and on weekdays to avoid the herds—and bring insect repellent. Primitive campsites near this entrance are $24–30 (Mar.–Dec.) and require advance reservations in the summer and on weekends year-round. Two-bedroom cabins ($88–132) are also available. The gates are open 8 A.M.–dusk daily, and parking is free.

Mount Trashmore Park

This aptly named park, on your right as you drive on I-264 from Norfolk to Virginia Beach, is the first above-ground solid-waste landfill to become a municipal park. It's over 60 feet high and 800 feet long and covers 165 acres. You'd never guess that underneath two lakes and a skateboard park lie 650,000 tons of garbage. The park includes Kids' Cove, a huge nautical-themed playground designed by children.

Historic Houses

Virginia Beach's three historic homes are each a substantial drive from the Boardwalk area. The **Adam Thoroughgood House** (1636 Parish Rd., 757/460-7588, 9 A.M.–5 P.M. Tues.–Sat., $7.50 adults, $4 children) is a 17th-century English cottage built of brick and oyster-shell mortar. Formal gardens and four rooms of antiques reflect the English ancestry of its builder, whose grandfather had come to Virginia as an indentured servant around 1620. The house, one of the oldest brick homes in the country, is on the Lynnhaven River directly east of the intersection of Northampton Boulevard (U.S. 13) and Independence Boulevard (Rte. 225).

A modest but elegant example of early Virginia architecture, **Lynnhaven House** (4401 Wishart Rd., 757/460-7109, 10 A.M.–4 P.M. Tues.–Sun., $7.50 adults, $4 children) dates to 1725. Costumed interpreters give tours of the home and demonstrate 18th-century skills and crafts. It's east of Independence Boulevard and south of the Adam Thoroughgood House.

Period attire–clad interpreters also lead tours of the **Francis Land House** (3131 Virginia Beach Blvd., 757/385-5100, 9 A.M.–5 P.M. Tues.–Sat., $7.50 adults, $4 children), a 200-year-old plantation home built by a wealthy local planter.

ENTERTAINMENT

Nightlife

Beach towns always have hopping after-hours activities going on, and Virginia Beach is no exception. Summer crowds tend toward the young, tanned, and beautiful, but whatever your stripe, you'll probably be able to find some place that's your speed. If you'd like a bite to eat with your music, try a restaurant-nightclub such as **Hot Tuna Bar & Grill** (2817 Shore Dr., 757/481-2888, www.hottunavb.com).

The Jewish Mother (3108 Pacific Ave., 757/422-5430, www.jewishmother.com) is a bit of a dive but is a dependable live music spot, featuring jazz, folk, and blues most nights. It serves deli-style sandwiches to boot. You can catch acoustic performances at the **Abbey Road Restaurant** (203 22nd St., 757/425-6330, www.abbeyroadpub.com) and **Smackwater Jack's** (3333 Virginia Beach Blvd., 757/340-6638). **Peabody's** (209 21st St., 757/422-6212) has the biggest dance floor in town.

For a game of pool, stop by **Q-Master II Billiards** (5612 Princess Anne Rd., 757/499-8900, www.q-masters.com). For a chuckle, try the **Funny Bone Comedy Club & Restaurant** (217 Central Park Ave., 757/213-5555, www.vabeachfunnybone.com) at Town Center, which has hosted high-caliber comics such as Mark Curry and D. L. Hughley.

The **Verizon Wireless Virginia Beach Amphitheater** (3550 Cellar Door Way, 757/368-3000, www.vwvba.com) presents 40 or so concerts per season. Performers include the likes of John Mayer, Kenny Chesney, Aerosmith, and Sting. There's space for 12,500 people on the lawn in addition to 7,500 covered seats. It's off Princess Anne Road near Princess Anne Park.

Performing Arts

Not all of Virginia Beach's nighttime entertainment involves booze and shaking your booty. Both the **Virginia Beach Symphony Orchestra** (291 Independence Blvd., Ste. 421, 757/671-8611, www.symphonicity.org) and the **Virginia Beach Ballet** (4716 Larkspur Square Shopping Center, 757/495-0989) perform locally. The **Little Theater of Virginia Beach** (550 Barberton Dr. at 24th St., 757/428-9233, www.ltvb.com) showcases local thespian talent. These acts sometimes take to the stage at the Sandler Center for the Performing Arts (201 Market St., 757/385-2787, www.sandlercenter.org), which features local, regional, and national performing artists, with 1,200 seats and an outdoor performance plaza.

Virginia Beach has no shortage of outdoor venues. Six outdoor stages grace the boardwalk at 7th, 13th, 17th, 24th, 25th, and 31st Streets; contact Beach Street USA for details on free concerts and movies in the summer months (757/425-3111, www.beachstreetusa.com).

RECREATION

Fishing

A boatload of places offer half-day, full-day, and overnight **charters** in pursuit of the marlin, dolphin, tuna, rockfish (aka striped bass), tautog, sailfish, and wahoo that teem offshore at the right times of year. At Rudee Inlet, at the south end of Pacific Avenue at the bridge, the **Virginia Beach Fishing Center** (200 Winston-Salem Ave., 757/491-8000 or 800/725-0509, www.virginiafishing.com) runs half- and full-day on- and off-shore trips starting at $600. It also rents personal watercraft and offers parasailing.

If all you want is to get a hook in the water, you can rent rods, reels, and crab cages May–October at the **Virginia Beach Fishing Pier** (15th St. at Oceanfront, 757/428-2333), near the small amusement park, and the **Lynnhaven Fishing Pier** (2350 Starfish Rd. off Shore Dr., 757/481-7071). In November 2009 a wicked nor'easter knocked down portions of the Lynnhaven Pier, but through a fundraiser that sold boards for $100 apiece, it's scheduled to reopen in May 2010. Look for the new wooden planks engraved with the names of donors who helped to restore the local landmark. No fishing license is required at the piers, but you do have to pay a small entrance fee.

Scuba Diving

Explore centuries of shipwrecks for $75–150 per dive ($350 for overnighters) with the **Lynnhaven Dive Center** (1413 N. Great Neck Rd., 757/481-7949, www.ldcscuba.com), which offers certification courses in its heated indoor pool. Visibility is usually 40–50 feet, and many wrecks have some coral growth.

Surfing

When James Jordan stood up on a 110-pound redwood board off Virginia Beach around 1912, he became the first person to surf the East Coast. Virginia Beach is now home to the East Coast Surfing Championships, North America's oldest running surfing competition, held each summer. For board sales, rentals, and advice, try the **17th Street Surf Shop** (1612 Pacific Ave., 757/422-6105, www.17thstsurfshop.com). **Ocean Rentals** (577 Sandbridge Rd., 757/721-6210, www.oceanrentalsltd.com) also offers surfboard rentals and lessons for all ages and experience levels. Former East Coast surf champion Jason Borte teaches surfing at the **Billabong Surf Camp** (757/965-9659, www.thesurfschool.com).

Natural History Excursions

Guided kayak tours on Virginia Beach's 120 miles of waterways are only one way to get up close and personal with the amazing variety of life in the surrounding ecosystems. Dolphin kayak trips start at $49 per person for three hours with outfits like **Wild River Outfitters** (3636 Virginia Beach Blvd., Ste. 108, 757/431-8566, www.wildriveroutfitters.com) and **Kayak Nature Tours** (757/480-1999 or 888/669-8368, www.tidewateradventures.com). They both also offer sunset and overnight trips and paddling instruction, and the latter rents kayaks.

The **Virginia Aquarium and Marine Science Center** (717 General Booth Blvd., 757/385-3474, www.vmsm.com) offers 90-minute and two-hour trips year-round that explore different facets of Virginia Beach's rich waters. Whale-watching excursions (Dec.–Mar., $28 adults, $24 children) go after humpbacks and fin whales with cameras instead of harpoons. In spring and summer, the mid-Atlantic's largest population of bottlenose dolphins can often be seen offshore on the museum's dolphin-watching trips (Apr.–Oct., $19 adults, $14 children). Check the city's visitors website (www.vbfun.com) for a list of operators offering dolphin-watching trips, which run 1–2 hours.

Chesapean Outdoors (313 Laskin Rd., 757/961-0447, www.chesapean.com) is an eco-tour company that offers guided dolphin tours in the summer months ($55 pp), along with kayaking, surfing, fishing, and sailing charters. **Back Bay Getaways** (3713 S. Sandpiper Rd., 757/721-4484, www.backbaygetaways.com) runs guided kayak and mountain bike tours at the southern end of Sandbridge Beach.

Other Activities

The three-mile bike trail along the boardwalk will make you glad you brought your wheels or soon have you looking for some to rent. **Cherie's Bicycle and Blade Rentals** (757/437-8888, www.cheriesbikes.com) rents bikes, in-line skates, and safety gear from its 12 locations along the boardwalk. Innumerable beach-supply places also rent bikes and in-line skates along with boogie boards, beach chairs, strollers, and umbrellas. Try your hand (and heart) at parasailing in the one- and two-person Skyriders operated by the **Virginia Beach Fishing Center.**

The **Ocean Breeze Waterpark** (849 General Booth Blvd., 757/422-4444, www.oceanbreezewaterpark.com, daily Memorial Day–Labor Day, $24 adults, $17 children under 10) has a million-gallon wave pool, water flume, and 16 slides. You'll have to buy individual passes for miniature golf, batting cages, and rides such as the Grand Prix cars in Motorworld Thrill Park.

Another popular (and free) diversion in Virginia Beach is to watch **navy jets** take off from the Oceana Naval Air Station along Oceana Boulevard and London Bridge Road. There's an observation park at the POW/MIA Memorial Park on Oceana Boulevard, near the F/A18 Super Hornet runways. Tours of the base are available from early June through August. Call 757/433-3131 for a schedule and details.

SHOPPING

If your tastes don't run to seashell fishermen and sunset ashtrays, a few places in town sell souvenirs of a more memorable kind. **Echoes of Time** (600 N. Witchduck Rd., 757/428-2332, www.echoes-of-time.com) offers vintage clothing and books, along with well-used furniture.

At the corner of Dam Neck and Princess Anne Roads, the **Virginia Beach Farmers Market** (3640 Dam Neck Rd., 757/385-4395, www.vbgov.com/farmersmarket) is open year-round with a litany of shops that sounds like a nursery rhyme: the grocer, the dairy, the butcher, the baker, the candy maker. Farmers sell produce in the partially enclosed public market during the growing season, and most merchants are open 10 A.M.–5 P.M. Monday–Saturday, noon–4 P.M. Sunday.

EVENTS

Most Virginia Beach festivals involve music or sports in proximity to the ocean. For more information, contact the visitors center or **Beach Street USA** (757/425-3111, www.beachstreetusa.com).

In April, the **Atlantic Coast Kite Festival** takes flight on the beach between 16th and 18th Streets. Early summer brings several options: in **Monsters on the Beach,** cult-classic monster trucks like Grave Digger and Monster Mutt do battle on the sand; **Beach Music Weekend** in mid-May has performances on the 29th Street stages; and bring your *djembe* for the drum circles at the **World Music Drum Festival** at 17th Street Park in late May.

In early June, the **North American Sand Soccer Championships** (www.sandsoccer.com) are sponsored by the Hampton Roads Soccer Council. They are followed by the **Boardwalk Art Show and Festival** (www.cacv.org), held since 1955, between 17th and 32nd Streets along the beach. That same month the sounds of merengue and mambo mingle with the smells of spicy cuisine and vibrant works of art during the **Latin Fest.**

In July, the **Mid-Atlantic Hermit Crab Challenge** begins with a Most Curvaceous Crustacean pageant and continues with racing heats that culminate in the championship Crustacean 500 race. The fastest hermit crab scuttles away with the coveted Order of the Mercury Claw trophy.

Since 1963, the **East Coast Surfing Championships** (www.surfecsc.com) have determined the best North Atlantic rider in professional and amateur categories. Held in August, the second-oldest continuously run surfing competition in the world draws hundreds of surfers and viewers with live music, a 5K race, and volleyball, skateboarding, and swimsuit competitions. The **Verizon Wireless American Music Festival** in early September welcomes 30 bands, including national acts from pop to country. Performances are held along the oceanfront from 5th to 31st Streets. Labor Day weekend kicks off the **Virginia Beach Rock 'n' Roll Half Marathon** (800/311-1255, www.virginia-beach.competitor.com).

September also brings Virginia Beach's biggest blowout, the **Neptune Festival** (www.neptunefestival.com). Parades, surfing, sailing, and the North American Sand Sculpting Competitions alternate with the Sandman Triathlon, a U.S. Navy Air Show, and the formal King Neptune's Ball. The **Oktober Brewfest,** held in the 24th Street park, celebrates all things German with food, drink, oompah bands, and a dachshund beauty pageant. From mid-November through the end of

December, the boardwalk is illuminated with surfing Santas and glowing sea creatures during **Holiday Lights at the Beach,** with over half a million sparkling lights. (It's the only time you're allowed to drive on the boardwalk.) Virginia Beach's historic homes are also decorated around the holidays, and play host to candlelit tours, tavern nights, and Yule log celebrations.

Various fishing tournaments are held throughout the year, including the **Virginia Saltwater Fishing Tournament** year-round and the **Virginia Beach Billfish Tournament** in August.

ACCOMMODATIONS

At last count, some 12,000 rooms, 1,800 campsites, and hundreds of rental cottages were available in Virginia Beach. Many offer bay or ocean views. Keep in mind that rates can vary wildly from one season to the next. High season is loosely defined as May to mid-September, plus a week in March for spring break. From November to February or March is the low season, leaving March–May and September–November in between. The same room can cost three times as much in June as it does in January. (Prices listed here are for high season.)

Many hotels require a minimum stay and offer good deals midweek and during shoulder season. Call the visitors center for help finding accommodations.

Under $100

Angie's Guest Cottage (302 24th St., 757/491-1830, www.angiescottage.com) is a comfy house in the center of the strip with six air-conditioned private rooms for $65–100. Angie's HI-USA Hostel (Apr.–Oct.) has five dorm-style rooms with a total of 34 bunk beds for $20–32 per bed per night. There's a porch, library, and full kitchen.

Most of the rooms at the **Seaside Motel** (2705 Atlantic Ave., 757/428-9341 or 800/348-7263, www.seasidehotel.net) are in this price range, and some are efficiencies. There's a sun deck and a heated indoor pool.

$100-150

Next door to Angie's and under the same management is the **Ocean Cove Motel** (300 24th St., 757/491-1830, www.oceancovemotel.com), with three-bedroom, two-bath cottages. Call for daily rates, though in summer season reservations are only taken for weekly bookings ($950–1,350/week). Also in this price range is the **Belvedere Motel** (3603 Atlantic Ave., 757/425-0612), which offers good rates for being right on the ocean: $100–156 in season, along with an outdoor pool and bicycles for guests.

The **Alamar Resort Inn** (311 16th St., 757/428-7582 or 800/346-5681, www.alamarresortinn.net) has 22 units (half one-bedroom, half suites with kitchens) set around a courtyard and heated pool for $72–210 in season. Sixty-seven rooms (half efficiencies) at the **Sundial Motel & Efficiencies** (308 21st St., 757/428-2922, www.sundialvirginiabeach.com) run $50–230.

$150-250

Opened in 1927, the original **Cavalier Hotel** (42nd St. at Oceanfront, 757/425-8555 or 800/446-8199, www.cavalierhotel.com) was *the* place to stay in Virginia Beach between the wars. Chauffeured limos and Pullman coaches brought seven presidents and celebrities including Jean Harlow, Fatty Arbuckle, and Johnny Weissmuller (Olympic swimmer and the original Tarzan) to enjoy the indoor seawater pool and swing at the Cavalier Beach Club. During the 1930s, 1940s, and 1950s it was the largest booker of big bands in the world; everyone from Frank Sinatra to Glenn Miller played at the Cavalier Beach Club. The hotel on the hill became a radar training school in the 1940s. Today it has undergone renovations and is open May–September, with rooms for $100–230. Suites are also available.

The newer **Cavalier Oceanfront,** open year-round, sits across Pacific Avenue on the beach. Guests can dine at tables favored by presidents in the Hunt Room. Guests can enjoy two Olympic-size pools, two clay tennis courts, shuffleboard, and a croquet lawn. The Cavalier Oceanfront has a health club and Camp Cavalier for kids. Rooms for the Cavalier, both the original and the newer hotel, range $180–480 in season. Contact information is the same for both.

An 1895 summer cottage, one of Virginia Beach's more distinguished houses, has become the **Barclay Cottage Bed & Breakfast** (400 16th St., 757/422-1956 or 866/466-1895, www.barclaycottage.com). It once served as a boarding school where Ms. Lillian Barclay taught until age 80. Double-covered balconies run all the way around the building, decorated with antiques such as an 1810 sleigh bed and items donated by former students. It's open year-round, with five rooms (two with shared bathrooms) for $155–225.

At the two-part **Best Western Oceanfront** (2809 Atlantic Ave., 757/428-5370 or 800/344-3342, www.col-inn.com), rates range $100–225 for oceanfront accommodations and slightly less for other rooms.

The **Sheraton Oceanfront** (3501 Atlantic Ave., 757/425-9000, www.sheratonvirginia beach.com) has close to 200 rooms right on the beach, along with two outdoor pools (one with a swim-up bar) and the Mediterranean-themed Aqua Vi restaurant. Rooms start around $200 in season.

Long-Term Rentals

Usually rented by the week, fully furnished houses and condominiums offer a comfortable alternative for extended stays. Prices range $700–2,200 per week during peak season for a two-bedroom apartment with full bath, kitchen, and dining room near the beach, with lower off-season rates. As an example, **Oceanfront Rentals** (314 26th St., 757/428-7473, www.oceanfrontrentals.homestead.com) has accommodations with one ($1,050 per week), two ($1,200), three ($1,775–1,995), or four bedrooms ($1,995–2,395). Virginia Beach Convention & Visitors Bureau has many more listings (www.vbfun.com).

For more information and options on vacation house rentals, contact **Siebert Realty** (601 Sandbridge Rd., 757/426-6200 or 877/422-2200, www.siebertrealty.com) or **Atkinson Realty** (5307 Atlantic Ave., 757/428-4441, www.atkinsonrealty.com).

Camping

The **Holiday Trav-L-Park** (1075 General Booth Blvd., 757/425-0249 or 866/849-8860, www.campingvb.com, open year-round) is the size of a small city, with more than 800 sites, four pools, sports courts, a restaurant, a miniature golf course, and a one-acre fenced dog park. Campsites are $39–77, and 44 cabins are $80–95.

Just down the road, the **Virginia Beach KOA** (1240 General Booth Blvd., 757/428-1444 or 800/562-4150, www.koavirginiabeach.com) has nearly 500 sites for $45–75 and cabins for $75–200. Campsites are also available in First Landing State Park. Primitive campsites are $24–30 (Mar.–Dec.) and require advance reservations in the summer and on weekends year-round. Two-bedroom cabins ($88–132) are also available.

FOOD

As you might expect, Virginia Beach has plenty of places to eat, with seafood spots leading the pack (about 300 at last count). Many restaurants add gratuities automatically—ask or check your bill.

Snacks and Cafés

Bad Ass Coffee Co. (619 18th St., 757/233-4007, breakfast and lunch daily) will kick-start your day with Kona coffee in a Hawaiian-style coffee shop near the oceanfront.

The **Pocahontas Pancake House** (Atlantic Ave. and 35th St., 757/428-6352) serves breakfast and lunch daily in its kitschy dining hall with wall-to-wall murals of Pocahontas, Capt. John Smith, and crew. Besides a dozen kinds of pancakes, you'll find Belgian waffles, French toast, and omelets galore. The **Heritage Natural Foods Cafe** (314 Laskin Rd., 757/428-0500, late breakfast and lunch daily) specializes in vegetarian entrées, sandwiches, and organic salads next to a natural foods market and New Age bookstore.

Casual

The Raven (Atlantic Ave. at 12th St., 757/425-1200, lunch and dinner daily) pulls off the usual beach-strip steaks, seafood, and poultry ($6–24) with a little more friendly flair than most.

An urban chic pervades the **Five 01 City Grill** (501 N. Birdneck, 757/425-7195, dinner daily) in the Birdneck Shoppes. Try the Southwest tuna tacos or trademark Michelob shrimp appetizers for around $10, followed by a Cajun bourbon penne pasta, pizza from the wood oven, or grilled rib-eye steak ($14–26), with a cappuccino or something from the long wine list to top it off.

In a big old three-story house on Rudee Inlet, **Rockafeller's** (308 Mediterranean Ave., 757/442-5654, lunch and dinner daily) is one of Virginia Beach's most popular standbys. Sit inside or out on two levels of covered balcony seating, it doesn't matter—the Caesar salads, crab cakes, steaks, and pasta are dependable favorites. Entrées range $15–30, but less expensive early-bird specials, kids' plates, and a moderately priced Sunday brunch are also offered. **Rudee's on the Inlet** (227 Mediterranean Ave., 757/425-1777, lunch and dinner daily, $15–30) is another popular choice nearby for fresh seafood, with a raw bar, an outdoor deck, and the requisite nautical decor.

Near the southern end of the Chesapeake Bay Bridge-Tunnel is **Alexander's on the Bay** (4536 Ocean View Ave., 757/464-4999, dinner daily), with fine dining in a weathered-wood setting or on an open-air beach deck. Escargot and baked brie appetizers ($8–11) lead to lobster, duck, and steak as well as pasta entrées for $18–32.

If the Mediterranean-style fresh fish of the day is any indication, the **Lynnhaven Fish House** (2350 Starfish Rd., 757/481-0003, lunch and dinner daily) serves seafood as good as any in Virginia Beach in front of picture windows overlooking the oceanfront. They claim to boast the largest fresh fish selection in Hampton Roads, with dinner entrées ($14–40) such as Chesapeake Bay crabs and pan-roasted mahimahi. Lunch dishes like seafood omelets, sandwiches, and quiches start at $8.

The best sushi in town belongs to **Kyushu Japanese Restaurant** (400 Newton Rd., 757/490-1177, lunch Mon.–Fri., dinner Mon.–Sat.), with rolls starting at $3.50 and various sushi and sashimi platters ranging $7.50–18. Traditional Japanese dishes like *yakisoba* (noodles sautéed with vegetables) and beef teriyaki are also on the menu.

For a switch from seafood, try **Jade Villa** (353 Independence Blvd., 757/473-2228, dinner daily, lunch and dim sum Sat.–Sun.), whose weekend dim sum selection, available 11 A.M.–2 P.M., comes highly recommended. Entrees range $9 to more than $20 for seafood and whole fish specials.

Upscale

Oddly enough, a number of fine-dining establishments in Hampton Roads are located in unassuming strip malls—so in this region especially you can't judge a restaurant by its storefront. Leading this argument is the **Cobalt Grille** (1624 Laskin Rd., Ste. 762, 757/333-3334, lunch and dinner Mon.–Sat.), located in the Hilltop North Shopping Center. English-born, Jamaican-bred chef Alvin Williams infuses many flavors into his contemporary American dishes, evident in the chicken penne pasta with sliced leeks and shallots. New York strip and Chesapeake jumbo lump crab cakes make it onto the menu both as entrées ($18–30) and tapas ($7.50–12), a choice at the trendy bar.

One Fish Two Fish (2109 W. Great Neck Rd., 757/496-4350, dinner daily) near the Lynnhaven Inlet bills itself as "upscale without the uppity," and this energetic waterside place feels like California with its open-air patio and exhibition kitchen. The seafood is imaginatively prepared (entrées $23–32), and the wine list is excellent.

Coastal Grill (1427 N. Great Neck Rd., 757/496-3348, dinner daily) is arguably the most consistent gourmet meal in Virginia Beach, and has been since it opened its doors in 1989. Seafood is delicious here, but so are the lamb chops served in a cilantro sauce with a side of the restaurant's signature acorn squash basted in butter and brown sugar (entrées $17–24). They go through 600 bushels of squash each year! Live music, like classical guitar strummed in the corner, adds atmosphere to the cozy 65-seat restaurant on Sunday, Monday, and Wednesday evenings. Reservations recommended.

Three blocks away from the boardwalk, **Terrapin** (3102 Holly Rd., 757/321-6688, dinner Tues.–Sun.) is the current Virginia Beach mecca for a special occasion meal. From truffle mac-and-cheese to martinis at the zebrawood bar, this fine-dining establishment strikes the right balance between classy and comfortable, and chef Rodney Einhorn continues to draw praise for his creative dishes. Farm-fresh ingredients, many of them organic, go into dinner entrées such as beef tenderloin with truffle carrot purée and pan-roasted rockfish with Israeli couscous ($18–38).

INFORMATION

The **Virginia Beach Visitors Center** (2100 Parks Ave., 757/437-4888 or 800/822-3224, www.vbfun.com, 9 A.M.–7 P.M. daily Memorial Day to Labor Day, to 5 P.M. rest of year) is near 21st Street. There are information kiosks along Atlantic Avenue at 17th and 24th Streets.

GETTING THERE AND AROUND

Getting There

Greyhound/Trailways has a terminal at 1017 Laskin Road (757/422-2998 or 800/231-2222). The nearest **Amtrak** station is in Newport News. A Thruway bus connects the terminal to the Amtrak shelter at 19th Street and Pacific Avenue.

If you're driving to North Carolina, try this neat route: Take Pacific Avenue south to Princess Anne Road (Rte. 615), which ends at Knott's Island at the southern end of Back Bay. From here a car ferry heads to Currituck, North Carolina. Call the North Carolina Department of Transportation Ferry Information Line (800/293-3779, www.ncdot.org/ferry) for up-to-the-minute ferry information.

Getting Around

Virginia Beach is connected to Newport News, Hampton, Norfolk, Portsmouth, and Chesapeake by **Hampton Roads Transit** (757/222-6100, www.gohrt.com). Call or check the website for routes, hours, and fares to these cities. **VB Wave Trolleys** run up and down Atlantic Avenue every 15 minutes 8 A.M.–2 A.M. daily May–September on route 30. The connecting Aquarium & Campground Shuttle (route 31) runs to the Virginia Aquarium and Marine Science Center, and the Shoppers' Shuttle (route 32) heads to the Hilltop area and the Lynnhaven Mall hourly 8 A.M.–2 A.M. Fares are $1.50 for adults (kids under 38 inches ride free), or you can buy five-day passes ($10).

BACK BAY NATIONAL WILDLIFE REFUGE

A thin strip of shoreline and a set of islands in Back Bay make up this sanctuary, which preserves 9,000 unspoiled acres of Virginia's southern Atlantic coast as it was before the high-rises and personal watercraft arrived. Once the haunt of wealthy duck hunters from New England, Back Bay National Wildlife Refuge was established in 1938 as an important stop along the Atlantic Flyway for migrating waterbirds, especially greater snow geese. Some 10,000 of these birds visit during their fall migration, usually around December.

A wide range of habitats starts among the sea oats on the mile-wide Atlantic strip, a constantly shifting stretch of sand that is predicted to eventually break free from the northern headland near Sandbridge. Maritime forests of scrub oak and loblolly pine cover the higher elevations, interspersed with wax myrtle shrubs and bayberry and blueberry bushes.

Three-quarters of the refuge is marsh, covering the bay side of the strip and Long and Ragged Islands at the north end of Back Bay.

Three hundred species of birds sighted here includes 30 kinds of waterfowl, among them the bald eagle and peregrine falcon. Spring is the peak migration time of songbirds and shorebirds, while hawks arrive in the fall. Tens of thousands of greater snow geese swing through November–March on their way south from Greenland and Canada's Northwest Territories. Snow goose migration peaks in December, accompanied by Canada geese and tundra swans. The mammal list includes gray foxes, river otters, mink, muskrats, and nutria (a large rodent), which compete with feral horses and pigs introduced by settlers. Back Bay is also one of the northernmost nesting spots for endangered loggerhead sea turtles, who drag themselves ashore in the summer to lay clutches of leathery eggs under the watchful eyes of refuge staff.

Visiting Back Bay

Take Sandbridge Road south to reach the entrance gate, open dawn–dusk daily ($5 per car or $2 per hiker). A **visitors center** (8 A.M.–4 P.M. Mon.–Fri., from 9 A.M. Sat.–Sun., closed Sat. Dec.–Mar.) has displays and films on the ecology of the refuge. Boardwalk trails cross the beach, while others along interior dikes are open to mountain bikes. Surf and freshwater fishing is permitted from land or small boats, which many visitors use to explore the bay and islands.

Camping is permitted only in False Cape State Park to the south, reached by a five-mile hike after parking outside the refuge gate. The fat-tire **Terra-Gator** (800/933-7275; reservations required), designed for minimal beach impact, runs to False Cape State Park through the refuge on weekends November–March ($8 pp, minimum 10 people). December and January are the best times to go to see peregrine falcons and bald eagles. The **Back Bay Restoration Foundation** (757/721-7666, www.bbrf.org) runs three-hour guided **tram rides** through Back Bay and False Cape daily Memorial Day–Labor Day, and on a limited schedule the rest of the year, for $8 adults, $6 children under 12. For more information on Back Bay, contact the refuge office in Virginia Beach (757/721-2412, www.fws.gov/backbay).

FALSE CAPE STATE PARK

This mile-wide park—the least visited in the state—encloses six miles of pristine beaches, shore forest, and marsh at the primitive southern end of a barrier spit between the ocean and Back Bay. It earned its name—and its reputation as a ship graveyard—because 19th-century sea captains commonly confused it with Cape Henry at the entrance to the Chesapeake Bay. Halfway down lie the brick foundations and old cemetery of the town of Wash Woods, moved because of shifting dunes that threatened to inundate it. False Cape is home to an abundance of wildlife, including 54 rare and endangered species.

False Cape State Park prohibits private vehicles, so the general public can reach the park only by a six-mile hike or bike ride though Back Bay National Wildlife Refuge, via the tram through Back Bay National Wildlife Refuge, or by boat. Primitive **camping** is $11 per night. During the winter, the entrance may be closed; check with the **park office** (4001 Sandpiper Rd., Virginia Beach, 757/426-7128, www.dcr.virginia.gov/state_parks/fal.shtml) for details and information on various guided hikes and programs. The fat-tire **Terra-Gator** runs to False Cape State Park through the Back Bay National Wildlife Refuge on weekends November–March ($8 pp, minimum 10 people). It usually departs Little Island City Park in Virginia Beach at 9 A.M. and returns at 1 P.M.; reservations are required by calling 800/933-7275. This is the same number you should call for permits and information on using the 12 primitive campsites.

The Eastern Shore

"Junk & Good Stuff" reads a sign outside a store on U.S. 13, inadvertently but rather neatly summing up Virginia's Eastern Shore. The long, flat neck of the Delmarva Peninsula, dividing the Chesapeake Bay from the Atlantic from Maryland to Cape Charles, is something of a throwback, an often-forgotten corner of crusty watermen, rusty pickups, and salt breezes. It's also one of the most subtly enticing parts of Virginia.

They say that when you cross the Chesapeake Bay Bridge-Tunnel from Virginia Beach you step back in time, and it's not all hyperbole. A rural 1950s feeling pervades all 70 miles of the Eastern Shore, so after a while it's the modern cars on U.S. 13 that start to look out of place, not the vine-covered buildings slowly being reclaimed by the earth on either side. Fewer than 50,000 residents—more than in Charlottesville, fewer than in Lynchburg—are divided into "born-heres" (occasionally "stuck-heres") and recently arrived "come-heres," many of whom have opened bed-and-breakfasts in small historic towns.

Agriculture is the biggest money-maker on this peninsula, and most of the low-lying fields are covered with acres of potatoes, soy beans, and other crops. Seafood comes next, from netfuls of finfish to oyster beds and crab pots seeded the length of the bay. Pockets of poverty evidence the recent slipping of both industries.

Visiting the Eastern Shore

A slower pace of life means that it might take a little longer to get your crab cakes on the table, but use the time to savor your surroundings. Roadside stands selling produce, shrimp, fireworks, and flowers line U.S. 13, running the length of the Eastern Shore along a historic railroad route. (Route 600, running parallel, is a good back-road alternative.) Countless "creeks"—wide, shallow estuaries—perforate the "bayside" and "seaside," just waiting to be explored by boat. A few public beaches on the bay and ocean are open for swimming and fishing, and trails through miles of marshland are gold mines for bird-watchers.

Fans of historic architecture will have a field day with hundreds of buildings in continual use since before the Civil War. Many fit the classic country-house design of the 19th century, consisting of four connected structures—"big house," "little house," "colonnade," and "kitchen"—with a roofline like a descending bar graph. Towns like Eastville, Accomac, and Cape Charles brim with centuries-old churches, courthouses, schools, and homes.

Local transportation is provided by **Star Transit** (757/787-7332, www.mystartransit.com), whose bus routes run from Cape Charles to Chincoteague every few hours from early morning to midafternoon, Monday–Friday. Fares are $1.50–3, and the buses have bike racks and wheelchair ramps.

For more information on the Eastern Shore, contact the **Eastern Shore of Virginia Chamber of Commerce** (757/787-2460, www.esvachamber.org), which runs a visitors center on U.S. 13 just south of Melfa (19056 Industrial Pkwy., 8:30 A.M.–5 P.M. Mon.–Fri.). **Eastern Shore of Virginia Tourism** (757/787-8246, www.esvatourism.org) is another helpful organization.

EASTERN SHORE OF VIRGINIA NATIONAL WILDLIFE REFUGE

The southernmost tip of the Eastern Shore was set aside in 1984 as a sanctuary for migratory birds. Most of the 1,220 protected acres are saltwater marsh, with some maritime forest, grasslands, and thickets of myrtle and bayberry. The refuge includes most of Fisherman Island, the northernmost island crossed by the Chesapeake Bay Bridge-Tunnel, as well as Skidmore Island to the east.

Bird-watching is excellent from late August to early November due to the "funneling effect" that occurs as birds migrate down the Delmarva Peninsula and gather to wait until wind and weather conditions are right to cross the bay. Shorebirds including cattle egrets,

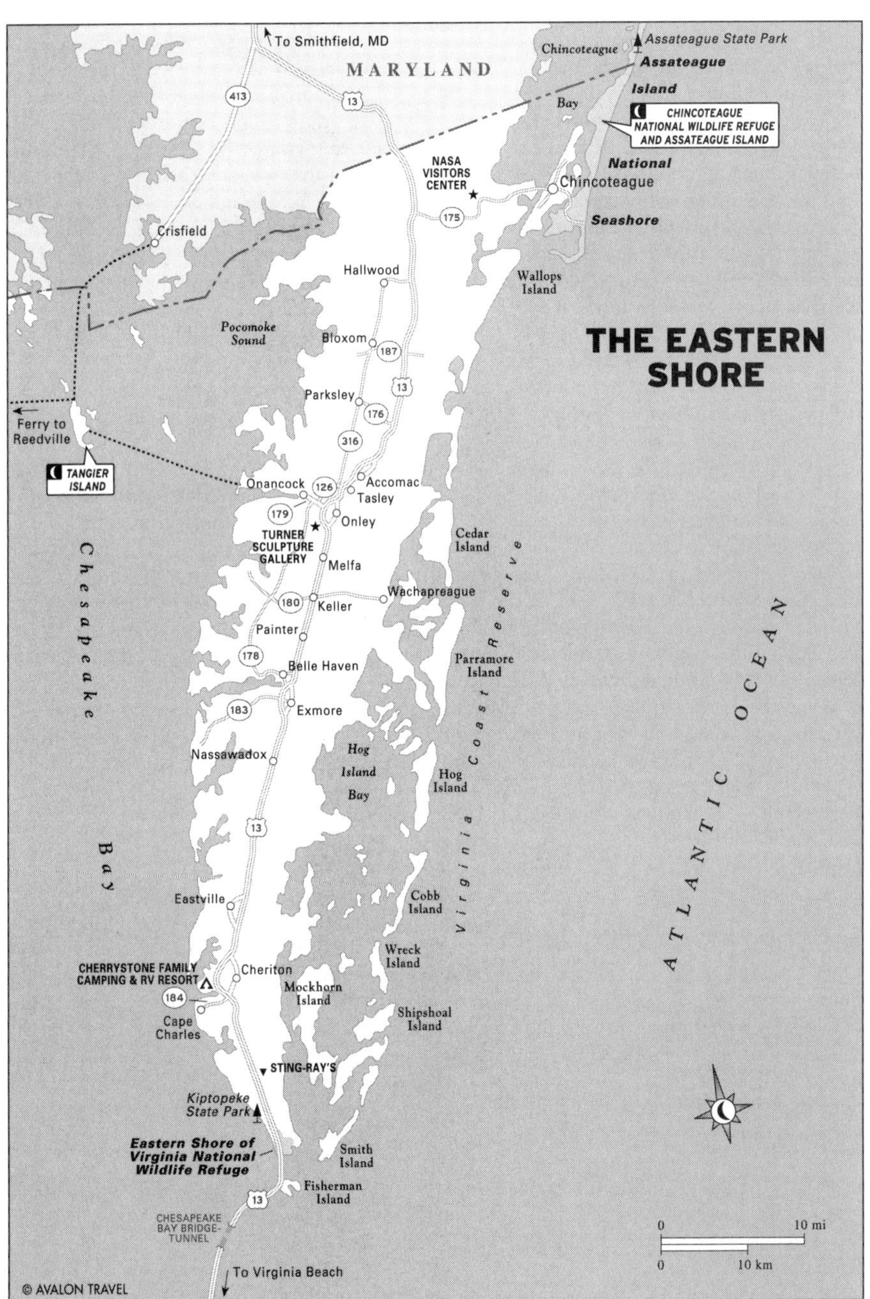
THE EASTERN SHORE
To Smithfield, MD
MARYLAND
Chincoteague
Assateague State Park
Assateague Island
Bay
CHINCOTEAGUE NATIONAL WILDLIFE REFUGE AND ASSATEAGUE ISLAND
National
Chincoteague
Seashore
NASA VISITORS CENTER
Crisfield
Hallwood
Wallops Island
Pocomoke Sound
Bloxom
Parksley
Ferry to Reedville
TANGIER ISLAND
Onancock
Accomac
Tasley
Onley
TURNER SCULPTURE GALLERY
Melfa
Cedar Island
Wachapreague
Keller
Painter
Belle Haven
Parramore Island
Exmore
Nassawadox
Hog Island Bay
Hog Island
Virginia Coast Reserve
Chesapeake Bay
ATLANTIC OCEAN
Eastville
Cobb Island
Wreck Island
CHERRYSTONE FAMILY CAMPING & RV RESORT
Cheriton
Mockhorn Island
Shipshoal Island
Cape Charles
STING-RAY'S
Kiptopeke State Park
Eastern Shore of Virginia National Wildlife Refuge
Smith Island
Fisherman Island
CHESAPEAKE BAY BRIDGE-TUNNEL
To Virginia Beach
0 10 mi
0 10 km
© AVALON TRAVEL

glossy ibis, and willets pass through in the spring, but the major migration takes place from late summer to early fall, when large groups of songbirds and raptors wait at the south side of the bay until weather conditions permit a crossing. Ospreys nest on special platforms in the spring and fall, and in the winter you have a good chance of spotting American kestrels, northern harriers, and snow geese. Bird species resident year-round include great blue herons, great horned owls, woodpeckers, and black ducks.

The refuge **visitors center** (9 A.M.–4 P.M. daily Apr.–Nov., reduced hours off-season) is beyond the northern end of the bridge. It has hands-on displays on the refuge's natural history and a viewing room over a marsh complete with binoculars and spotting scopes. A half-mile interpretive loop trail passes a 60-foot observation tower and old concrete gun emplacements that protected Norfolk's Naval Base during World War II. You can canoe or hike on your own from dawn to dusk, and free half-day guided tours of **Fisherman Island** leave Saturday mornings October–March (reservations required). Kayakers and canoeists can launch from the neighboring county boat ramp during daylight hours year-round. During the winter, staff lead tours on Fisherman Island (reservations also required). Contact the U.S. Fish and Wildlife Service in Cape Charles (5003 Hallett Circle, 757/331-2760, http://easternshore.fws.gov) for more information.

KIPTOPEKE STATE PARK

One of the few public beaches on the Eastern Shore started out as the northern terminus of the ferry to Virginia Beach, which moved to Cape Charles in 1949. Kiptopeke, which means "Big Water" in the Accawmack Indian language, now protects a half mile of sand with a swimming beach Memorial Day to Labor Day, as well as trails, a fishing pier, a boat launching ramp, and a full-service campground. Entrance is $4 per car on weekends ($3 weekdays), and naturalist programs are offered during the summer.

In addition to the 147 campsites ($24–35), guests can rent a bunkhouse that sleeps 14 (call for rates), one of seven RV trailers (each sleeps six people), or a wood-frame yurt (sleeps six). The trailers cost $88–98 per night and are available March–November. It's the same pricing for the yurt, but it's only available until Labor Day. Five lodges were added in 2007, with full cooking and sleeping facilities and room for up to 16 people. They're open year-round for $249–371 per night. In general, the park requires a two-night stay minimum; in high season, Memorial Day through Labor Day, it's often a week.

The Virginia Society of Ornithology maintains a bird-banding station and raised observation platform to take advantage of the park's location on the Atlantic Flyway. Some 80,000 raptors pass through in early September and October, including sharp-shinned and Cooper's hawks, ospreys, bald eagles, and peregrine falcons. Kiptopeke's hawk observatory is considered one of the best in the country. The tours, presentations, and workshops of the **Eastern Shore Birding Festival** (757/787-2460) coincide with the peak fall migration in early October. Contact the park office in Cape Charles (757/331-2267, www.dcr.virginia.gov/state_parks/kip.shtml) for information on guided canoe tours through the park's marshes during the hawk migration.

CAPE CHARLES

This quiet town sprang up in 1884 as the southern terminus for the New York, Philadelphia, and Norfolk Railroad. Ferries carried automobiles and freight trains across the Chesapeake Bay to Norfolk and Hampton until the 1950s, when the freight business faded and the newly opened Chesapeake Bay Bridge-Tunnel killed the auto ferry. Today Cape Charles offers only hints that it was once the busiest town on the Eastern Shore, but its appeal hasn't faded completely.

Most of Cape Charles is a historic district. With more than 500 buildings erected between 1885 and 1940, this is one of the largest collections on the East Coast. Colonial Revival, neoclassic, and Victorian homes decorated with gingerbread woodwork line residential streets named after famous Virginians, fruits, and trees. Keep an eye out for several Sears Roebuck mail-order houses from the 1920s.

Sights

The **Cape Charles Museum and Welcome Center** (814 Randolph Ave., 757/331-1008, 10 A.M.–2 P.M. Mon.–Fri., 10 A.M.–5 P.M. Sat., 1–5 P.M. Sun., Apr.–Nov., free) occupies a building that used to be a generator house for Delmarva Power and still has one gigantic generator (which still turns over) embedded in the floor. Old photos, decoys, and boat models trace the history of Cape Charles.

Recreation

Operating out of an old service station next to the

THE CHESAPEAKE BAY BRIDGE-TUNNEL

Stretching across the mouth of the Chesapeake Bay like a gap-toothed smile, this engineering wonder lets thousands of drivers a day save a hundred-mile detour between Hampton Roads and the Eastern Shore. Officially named the Lucius J. Kellam Jr. Bridge-Tunnel, after the Eastern Shore businessman who conceived of it, the longest bridge-tunnel system in the world comprises 17.65 miles of U.S. 13 from Virginia Beach to Cape Charles.

Construction began in 1958 to replace ferry service that had operated since the 1930s. Over the following six years, some 825,000 tons of concrete and 55,000 tons of steel were cast into pilings and sections of roadway on shore, hauled out on barges, and fit together like the world's biggest Lego project. The most impressive feat was the raising of four man-made islands in water averaging 40 feet deep. Each one, large enough to hold Yankee Stadium, serves as one end to two mile-long tunnels sunk beneath the main shipping channels.

Two hundred million dollars later the bridge opened, allowing the first ceremonial vehicle to cross 12 miles of trestled roadway, dip under the bay twice, and pass over two high-clearance bridges near Fisherman Island off Cape Charles. (The idea of one long bridge was scrapped by navy strategists, who said it would be too easy for enemies to destroy and block the navigable lanes with debris during wartime.) In 1965 it was declared one of the Seven Engineering Wonders of the Modern World. In the 1990s, a parallel bridge was constructed to handle future traffic demands. Today, one bridge carries northbound traffic while the other handles southbound traffic. Total cost: $450 million. In 2006, the bridge-tunnel was destroyed – fictionally – in the movie *Mission: Impossible 3.*

Sea Gull Island, the southernmost of the man-made islands, is home to a simple, inexpensive **restaurant** (serving all meals), **gift shop,** and **625-foot fishing pier** (757/331-2960) with bait and tackle for sale and rent. Fish-cleaning stations and a certified scale are available and no fishing license is needed. It's a great way to go deep-sea fishing without a boat.

Even though you might not believe that all this thundering traffic is conducive to wildlife viewing, the artificial islands are among the best places in Virginia to watch migratory seabirds in the winter. Scooters, ruddy turnstones, scaup, eiders, and other duck species, including buffleheads, gadwalls, and common goldeneyes, all make appearances in the winter, especially after a hard freeze. Be advised, though, that increased bridge security measures begun in 2005 mean you'll have to arrange for the bird-watching session well ahead of time by submitting $50 and a permit (www.cbbt.com/birding.html). The fee goes to cover the police escort required to accompany your group of no more than 15 people while you're on the island. Another, easier option is to head to the wildlife viewing area north of the Bridge-Tunnel toll plaza on Virginia's Eastern Shore.

The bridge-tunnel, by the way, is a private enterprise, as permitted by Virginia law. A hefty $12 toll is charged each way, with a $17 round-trip option within 24 hours. Contact the bridge authority (757/331-2960, www.cbbt.com) for more information.

Sunset Beach Resort, **SouthEast Expeditions** (32218 Lankford Hwy., 757/331-2680, www.southeastexpeditions.net) runs kayak trips as well as sunset excursions and clamming junkets. Two-hour tours start at $45 per person, half-day tours are $85 per person, and full-day trips are $125 and include lunch. It also rents kayaks by the hour or day and was the first place in the state to offer instruction in the hair-raising sport of kiteboarding (www.gogetlit.com). Imagine strapping your feet onto a floating surfboard and grabbing the reins of an inflatable kite that's big enough to yank you dozens of feet into the air (not to mention pull you along at a swift clip in between jumps), and you have the general idea.

Events

In May, July, and September, Cape Charles holds an **Applaud the Sun Harbor Party** the first Saturday evening of each month June–September to celebrate its location on the largest harbor between Norfolk and Maryland.

Accommodations and Food

The **Sea Gate Bed & Breakfast** (9 Tazewell Ave., 757/331-2206, www.bbhost.com/Seagate, $120–130) is in a lovingly restored 1912 house with four guest rooms. A curving porch wraps around the entire front of the building, which was once split into a duplex. The Peach and Rose Rooms share a balcony with wicker chairs. Corinthian columns flank the foyer of the **Cape Charles House** (645 Tazewell Ave., 757/331-4920, www.capecharleshouse.com), set in a 1912 Colonial Revival frame house with high ceilings and maple plank floors. Five rooms range in price $120–200.

The **Sunset Beach Resort** (32246 Lankford Hwy., 757/331-4786 or 800/899-4786, www.sunsetbeachresortva.com) has 73 rooms ($160–180) and an outdoor pool along with a beachfront café by a small stretch of private beach. In winter, the resort also opens 52 RV campsites for $40 per night. It's located a few miles north of the Bridge-Tunnel entrance on U.S. 13. Approximately 1.5 miles west of U.S. 13 on Route 680, you'll find the **Cherrystone Family Camping & RV Resort** (757/331-3063, www.cherrystoneva.com), with three pools, a beach, sports courts, and a playground spread over more than 300 acres. They rent sea kayaks, pedalboats, and bikes and have more than 300 campsites for $37–63, plus cabins for $390–975 a night in high season. Sites with a water view cost $5 extra.

There aren't many service stations where you can get a hand-pulled pork barbecue plate and a glass of merlot, but Cape Charles has one. Head back out to U.S. 13 and a little more than four miles south, where **Sting-Ray's** (26507 Lankford Hwy., 757/331-2505, from 6 A.M. daily) is a local gathering place serving gourmet seafood platters in the back of a big red Exxon station. It may not look like much, but wait until you try the soft-shells and crab imperial, maybe accompanied by a bottle from one of the best wine selections on the Eastern Shore. It also serves inexpensive sandwiches, breakfasts, and the usual ribs and chili ($5–27).

Information

For details on anything else about the town, contact the **Northhampton County Chamber of Commerce** (757/678-0010, www.ccncchamber.com).

EASTVILLE

In 1766, 10 years before the signing of the Declaration of Independence, the county court of this tiny village—then called Peachburg—declared the Stamp Act of Parliament unconstitutional. By the early 19th century, it boasted 217 inhabitants who, in the words of one visitor, were "not to be surpassed for their morality and hospitality to strangers."

The **Old Courthouse** on Courthouse Square guards the oldest continuous court records in America, which have escaped fire, rot, and rats since they were begun in 1632. The building dates to the turn of the 20th century. Next door, the **Clerk's Office** has a small museum inside, with items including leg irons and a device for measuring slaves' heights. Barred windows mark the **Debtors' Prison,** on Courthouse Road (U.S. 13 Business), built around 1814, with an old whipping post

OFFSHORE EDEN

The Nature Conservancy oversees the outermost fringe of Virginia's Eastern Shore, the largest stretch of unspoiled coastal wilderness in the country. With 38,000 acres spread over 14 barrier islands, the Virginia Coast Reserve has been designated one of the 10 Last Great Places in America by its custodians and an International Biosphere Reserve by the United Nations.

Beaches, lagoons, pine forests, marshes, and scrub woodlands shelter as many as 80,000 pairs of nesting birds at a time, including every species found along Virginia's coast. Visiting is limited to day use, but the boating, bird-watching, and picnicking are unsurpassed. Getting there is the only catch; it requires a boat or canoe. Parramore, Shipshoal, and Revel Islands are closed to the public, and much of Cedar Island remains in private hands.

Check with **The Nature Conservancy** (757/442-3049) for regulations and information. Captain Rick Kellam's **Broadwater Bay Ecotours** (757/442-4363, www.broadwaterbayecotour.com) can be customized to focus on history, nature, or sightseeing. Kellam is a former waterman and marine law enforcement officer (five generations of Kellams lived on Hog Island before the hurricane of 1933 persuaded them to pack up), and he worked for The Nature Conservancy before starting his own tour business – his tours are excellent (half-day $90 pp, full-day $180 pp, half-price for kids under 12).

in front that may make you grateful for the comparatively civilized techniques of modern collection agencies. Ask in the modern Northampton Administration Building (757/678-0440) for keys to these three buildings during business hours.

WACHAPREAGUE

Two hundred folks live in the Flounder Capital of the World, whose name means "Little City by the Sea" in an Indian tongue. Wachapreague (WAH-cha-preeg) is a good base for charter fishing or exploring the islands and marshes of the Eastern Shore's Atlantic edge.

Three brothers named Powell established a wharf and shipping firm here in 1872. Weekly freight and passenger steamers left for points north around the turn of the 20th century, when wealthy visiting sportsmen enjoyed a dance hall, pool room, movie houses, and an elegant hotel (which burned in 1978).

Recreation

Ask at the Wachapreague Marina (757/787-4110) or **Captain Zed's Tackle Shop & Marina** (757/789-3222) about fishing charters starting at $500 for flounder and $1,100 for marlin. Four-person 16-foot skiffs are available for rent for $125 per day.

Accommodations and Food

On the waterfront, the **Wachapreague Motel** (1 Main St., 757/787-2105, www.wachapreague.com) has 21 newly renovated rooms, efficiencies, and two-bedroom apartments starting at $90 in season ($65 off-season), as well as a large, refurbished rental house that sleeps 11 ($380). It also books trips with several local charter boats. Across the street is the **Island House Restaurant** (757/787-4242, www.islandhouseentertainment.com, lunch and dinner daily, weekends only in winter), overlooking the marsh across the street and enclosing the self-declared finest raw bar on the Eastern Shore. Platters are $10–19, including great crab cakes and Black Angus steaks.

Events and Information

The **Wachapreague Volunteer Fireman's Carnival** (757/787-2105) comes to town mid-June to mid-July. Several fishing tournaments swing through town as well during the summer; call the Wachapreague Motel for more information.

ONANCOCK

One of the Eastern Shore's prettiest towns sits on Onancock Creek near one of the two deepwater harbors on the peninsula. Chock full of 19th-century houses with gingerbread trim and wraparound porches, Onancock (o-NAN-cock) has enough cultural offerings and quiet allure to justify a stay of a weekend or more.

The name, meaning "foggy place" in an Indian language, comes from a native tribe whose King Ekeeks introduced Englishman John Pory to oysters and "batata" (potatoes) in 1621. (After burning his mouth on a steaming tuber, Pory groaned, "I would not give a farthing for a truckload.") the settlement, founded in 1680 as Port Scarburgh, weathered frequent raids by British privateers during the Revolutionary War. Growth arrived with steamships plying the Chesapeake Bay, leaving Onancock one of the largest communities on the Eastern Shore.

For more information, visit the websites www.onancock.com and www.onancock.org.

Sights

On Market Street (Rte. 179) before the center of town stands **Kerr Place** (757/787-8012, www.kerrplace.org, 11 A.M.–4 P.M. Tues.–Sat. Mar.–Dec., $5 pp), one of the Eastern Shore's finest antique manor homes. Built in 1799 by a Scottish merchant, the elegant Federal mansion once presided over an estate of 1,500 acres. It's been restored by the Eastern Shore of Virginia Historical Society, which has set up offices, a museum, and a museum store inside. Intricate woodwork and plaster carvings decorate the walls and ceiling around period artwork and furniture. Notice the false window in the brick facade, included for symmetry.

Shopping

The **Willie Crockett Gallery** (39 Market St., 757/787-2288, www.williecrockett.com) offers nautical-themed works by the Tangier-born artist. Look to **gardenART** (44 King St., 757/787-8818) for plants, flowers, and whimsical garden decor. The funky shop has a friendly Portuguese water dog on hand as a greeter and is situated in a former power plant.

Off U.S. 13 south of Onancock, **Turner Sculpture** (757/787-2818, www.turnersculpture.com, 9 A.M.–5 P.M. daily) is the largest personal foundry and gallery in the country. Renowned sculptors William and David Turner count the National Audubon Society, the American Museum of Natural History, and the White House among dozens of public commissions for their realistic wildlife bronzes. Here in the gallery, more than 300 different animals are frozen in vivid poses that work especially well for the aquatic creatures—otters, dolphins, humpback whales, and the like. Prices range from $50 for palm-size works into the thousands for larger pieces.

Accommodations and Food

The **Colonial Manor Inn** (84 Market St., 757/787-3521, www.colonialmanorinn.com, $100–140) got its start as a boardinghouse in the 1930s, making it the oldest continually operating inn on the Eastern Shore. Full use of two acres of grounds and full breakfasts served at the huge dining table are included in the price.

Charlotte Heath and Gary Cochran purchased the building that began as the White Hotel in 1907, and turned it into the charming **Charlotte Hotel & Restaurant** (7 North St., 757/787-7400, www.thecharlottehotel.com). Gary made all the beds by hand, and Charlotte's artwork hangs in the dining room. They offer eight guest rooms ($115–160), a dining room (breakfast and dinner Wed.–Sun.), and a full-service bar. All the food is made in-house, with a seasonally changing "creative American" menu of entrées ranging $15–35 for dinner.

Originally built around 1880 as a private residence, the **Inn & Garden Café** (145 Market St., 757/787-8850, www.theinnandgardencafe.com) was entirely renovated in 2004. Four guest suites are $96–130 in season, and the 50-seat fine-dining restaurant (dinner Tues.–Wed. and Fri.–Sat., brunch Sun., $20–32, weekday specials for less) has seating inside or in an enclosed outdoor gazebo overlooking the gardens. Seafood entrées with a Southern flair run $20–28.

Bizotto's Gallery-Caffe (41 Market St., 757/787-3103, lunch Mon.–Sat., dinner daily, closed Sun. off-season) is a gallery for hand-tooled leather handbags and briefcases made by the owner as well as a popular restaurant that's packed at lunchtime. Dishes like veal picatta and filet mignon start at $7 for lunch and $18 for dinner. Another good dining choice is **Mallard's on the Wharf** (2 Market St., 757/787-8558, lunch and dinner daily). It's inside the venerable Hopkins Bros. Store, which began in 1842 as a feed and farm store and the village post office, making it one of the oldest general stores on the East Coast. Soups, salads, and sandwiches are $7–11, and entrées like broiled rockfish are $15–28. It's part of chef Johnny Mo's local restaurant portfolio, which also includes Mallard's Sidewalk Café in Accomac.

ONANCOCK TO CHINCOTEAGUE

Accomac

A wealth of Colonial architecture fills the tree-shaded streets in this historic burg, founded as Drummondtown in the 18th century. On Courthouse Green stands the early-1900s **Courthouse** next to the Victorian brick **Clerk's Office,** where the Accomac County Orders of 1714–1717 bear the vitriolic inscription "God Damn the King" instead of the more traditional "God Save the King."

Elaborate paintings inside the Greek Revival **St. James Episcopal Church** (built in 1838) simulate columns, doors, and arches. Call 757/789-3247 to arrange a visit to the 1782 **Debtors' Prison,** which housed the financially irresponsible and unlucky until it was rendered obsolete in 1849 by a state law that abolished imprisonment for debt. It's run by the Association for the Preservation of Virginia Antiquities.

Parksley

The **Eastern Shore Railway Museum** (18468 Dunne Ave., 757/665-7245, 10 A.M.–4 P.M. Mon.–Sat., 1–4 P.M. Sun., $2 adults, free children under 12) starts with a gift shop and collection of antique cars in the 1906 New York, Philadelphia, and Norfolk Railroad passenger station. An original freight station across the yard holds uniforms, maps, and lanterns from back when railroads were the lifeline of the Eastern Shore, while the yard is full of dining cars and cabooses from the Richmond, Fredericksburg & Potomac, Norfolk & Western, and Wabash lines. The museum is two miles west of U.S. 13 on VA 176 (Parksley Rd.).

CHINCOTEAGUE

From killdeer nesting in parking lots to gales that redefine the sandy shoreline, life on Chincoteague Island is shaped by the natural world. Known for its annual pony swim and auction, the largest community on the Eastern Shore combines a seasonal beach resort with a timeless offshore sanctuary, home to plenty of coastal life besides the famous fillies.

History

The story goes that on October 25, 1662, this island, sandwiched between the mainland and Assateague, was granted to Capt. William Whitington by Wachawampe, emperor of the Gingo Teagues. Over time the tribe's name would evolve into Chincoteague (SHINK-a-teeg), meaning "Beautiful Land Across the Water." A tiny settlement was destroyed by a tidal wave that swept over both islands in 1821, but the area gradually resettled over the next decades.

In 1861, a 132–2 vote to remain part of the Union set Chincoteague against the rest of its parent state. Several attempts by mainlanders to storm the island were repelled. The railroad arrived in 1876, ending an era of lawlessness, illiteracy, and bare feet with the introduction of schools, churches, a newspaper, and new homes.

Incorporated as a town in 1908, Chincoteague was connected to the mainland by an automobile causeway in 1922. Marguerite Henry's 1947 book, *Misty of Chincoteague,* propelled the town into the collective imagination of children worldwide as only a book about horses can. Many local residents appeared in the movie made from the children's story in the 1960s, and the town's name has been synonymous with ponies on the beach ever since.

Orientation

The town of Chincoteague occupies most of the island of the same name, connected to the mainland and U.S. 13 by Route 175. A long, straight causeway crosses marshland and a drawbridge to Main Street, running the length of the island's western shore. Head north (left) on Main Street for a few blocks and turn east (right) onto Maddox Boulevard, where signs lead to the visitors center and the Chincoteague National Wildlife Refuge.

Sights

The world's only oyster museum is right here in Chincoteague. The **Oyster and Maritime Museum** (7125 Maddox Blvd., 757/336-6117, 10 A.M.–5 P.M. daily in season, $4 adults, $2 children) holds the huge lens from the Assateague Island Lighthouse and exhibits on the history of the local oyster industry.

Fishing

Dozens of places in Chincoteague rent boats and fishing tackle for visitors interested in exploring the fringes of Chincoteague Bay. Expect to pay $50–75 per day for a midsized fishing boat for 3–4 people and upwards of $100 for a 12-person pontoon boat for four hours. Rods and reels, crab pots, and clam rakes are $5–10 per day. Try **Barnacle Bill's Bait & Tackle** (3691 Main St., 757/336-5920, www.chincoteague.com/barnaclebills), which runs scenic tours starting at $15 per person, or **Capt. Bob's Marina** (2477 Main St., 757/336-6654, www.captbobs-marina.com). **Snug Harbor Resort** (7536 East Side Rd., 757/336-6176) rents boats, canoes, kayaks, and personal watercraft starting at $29 per boat for a half day, $39 per boat for a full day.

Charters let you venture offshore for the big ones: tuna, marlin, swordfish, and shark. Two- to four-hour bay fishing trips run about $50 including all bait and tackle, with offshore trips varying in price depending on the size of the party and what you're after. Captain Fred Gilman of **Reel Time Charters** (757/336-2236, www.chincoteague.com/reeltime) offers offshore, big game, and wreck fishing from a 33-foot sportfishing boat. The ***Chincoteague View*** (757/336-6861, www.chincoteague.com/cview) is a pontoon boat out of Curtis Merrit Harbor that's available for morning or afternoon fishing charters after flounder, bluefish, sea bass, and other species.

Tours and Excursions

Captain Barry's Back Bay Cruises (6262 Marlin St., 757/336-6508, www.captainbarry.net) leave from the dock at the Chincoteague Inn Restaurant for early-morning bird-watching ($25 pp) and half-day Coastal Encounters for $45 per person, with historical tidbits and natural-history stops galore. Reservations are required. The ***Linda J*** (757/336-6214, http://mysite.verizon.net/lindajcharters) is a 24-foot pontoon boat that can be booked for sightseeing and nature trips for $30 per person.

No less than six tours a day are on the roster for the ***Assateague Explorer*** (757/336-5956 or 866/766-9794, www.assateagueisland.com/explorer.htm), including pony-spotting, bird-watching, fishing, and sunset cruises ($40 adults, $30 children under 12), leaving from Curtis Merritt Harbor.

Other Recreation

If you can't visit during the Pony Roundup, you can still get a close-up view at the **Chincoteague Pony Centre** (6417 Carriage Dr., 757/336-2776, www.chincoteague.com/ponycentre), offering afternoon pony rides daily. Despite the name, **Jus' Bikes** (6527 Maddox Blvd., 757/336-6700) rents bikes (single and tandem) but also scooters, mopeds, kiddie carts, and helmets.

Shopping

Another unmistakable sign of beach resorts is dozens of stores selling everything from crafts, dolls, and candles to framed seascapes and Christmas goodies in July, and Chincoteague is no exception. Ronald Justis's **Decoys Decoys Decoys** (4039 Main St., 757/336-1402) offers one of the largest selections on the East Coast. The **Main Street Shop Coffeehouse** (4288 Main St., 757/336-6782) has an eclectic selection of artwork and great coffee. Local artist Nancy West has oil paintings, woven clothing, and unique jewelry at **Island Arts** (6196 Maddox Blvd., 757/336-3113), while Welsh native Hal Lott sells silk-screens through **Lott's Arts & Things** (4281 Main St., 757/336-5773).

Events

Many of Chincoteague's annual events require advance tickets; call the Chincoteague Chamber of Commerce for information.

Bring a bib to the **Seafood Festival** at Tom's Cove Campground the first Wednesday in May. All you can eat of bushels of raw oysters, shoals of fish, and tens of thousands of clams are yours for the price of a ticket, but the event is popular, so you have to buy that ticket in advance from the Eastern Shore Chamber of Commerce (757/787-2460). If you can, return for the **Blessing of the Fleet** at the end of the month, where local ministers ask for local watermen to come home safe with plenty of fish.

The **Pony Roundup and Swim** is Chincoteague's biggest happening and one of the largest on the Virginia coast. Held since 1925, this event is preceded by the Fireman's Carnival on multiple weekends (Friday and Saturday evenings) throughout July. At the end of the month, members of the Chincoteague Volunteer Fire Company dress up as cowboys and round up the herd of wild ponies that lives in the Chincoteague National Wildlife Refuge. After swimming across the channel, the horses step ashore at Memorial Park at the southern end of the island. Here they're penned until the famous auction, attended by 50,000 or more people. The pony auction began in 1925 as a fundraiser for the Chincoteague Volunteer Fire Department, and continues in this capacity today. It also helps control the size of the herd. Each pony has already been cleared for travel by veterinarians, so if you succumb and buy one, you can take it right home. This event fills the town to capacity, so book accommodations well in advance. The **Chincoteague Blueberry Festival** happens at the beginning of Pony Penning Week.

October brings more food festivals. First the **Chincoteague Island Oyster Festival** rolls into town. It's been held since 1972 and brings all the oysters you can eat ($35 pp), in every variety imaginable, to the Maddox Family Campground, along with tons of other food and musical entertainment (buy tickets early; 757/336-6161). Then the **Chili & Chowder Cookoff** arrives midmonth to the town's waterfront park.

Accommodations

As befits a seasonal resort town, many hotels in Chincoteague close or drop their prices by as much as half in the off-season.

The T-shaped **1848 Island Manor House** (4160 Main St., 757/336-5436 or 800/852-1505, www.islandmanor.com, $125–215) was built by a local Union surgeon and a postmaster who married a pair of sisters. Apparently the wives didn't get along under the same roof, prompting their husbands to split the house in two. It's since been rejoined and decorated in Federal style. All lodgings come with a full Southern-style breakfast and trail mix, and special romantic getaway packages are offered.

Miss Molly's Inn (4141 Main St., 757/336-6686 or 800/221-5620, www.missmollys-inn.com, $110–180) occupies a Victorian home built in 1886 by J. T. Rowley for his daughter Molly, who lived there until age 84. Marguerite Henry stayed here while writing *Misty of Chincoteague,* and the room has since been named after her. Prices include full breakfasts in the gazebo and scones at teatime. The same owners also operate the **Channel Bass Inn** (6228 Church St., 757/336-6148 or 800/249-0818, www.channelbass-inn.com, $125–225), dating to 1892. Some of the five rooms and one suite have a view of the Chesapeake Bay, and the public is welcome to stop by for Barbara's famous scones at afternoon tea in the Tea Room—just call ahead for reservations.

A wraparound veranda and scallop shingles adorn **The Watson House** (4240 Main St., 757/336-1564 or 800/336-6787, www.watsonhouse.com, $130–175), built in 1898 by David Robert Watson. Guests have access to complimentary bicycles and beach chairs.

A hot tub, crabbing dock, and solarium are only some of the amenities at the **Waterside Inn** (3761 S. Main St., 877/870-3434, www.watersidemotorinn.com, $135–160). The **Refuge Inn** (7058 Maddox Blvd., 757/336-5511 or 888/257-0038, www.refugeinn.com) has rooms for $90–190 and suites for $180–320, depending on the season, as well as a three-bedroom Cape Cod–style cottage on the north end of the island, where ponies sometimes graze just beyond the fence ($585 for three nights or $1,400 per week).

Camping

The **Maddox Family Campground** (6742 Maddox Blvd., 757/336-3111, www.chincoteague.com/maddox) has 550 sites open March–November for $37–42, depending on whether you want hookups. It also offers a pool, showers, and crabbing equipment and takes reservations. **Tom's Cove Campground** (8128 Beebe Rd., 757/336-6498, www.tomscovepark.com) has waterfront sites within sight of the pony swim for $31–50, open March–November, along with three fishing piers and an Olympic-sized pool. A site at the **Pine Grove Campground** (5283 Deep Hole Rd., 757/336-5200, www.pinegrovecampground.com) is $30–40 during the April–November camping season. It has all the amenities, as well as a small motel (open May–Oct., $50–85), two waterfront cottages nearby ($1,600–1,800/week), and six ponds that are popular with birds.

Food

Dining in Chincoteague is a lesson in convergent evolution: Most of the 23 restaurants are named after someone and offer family-style food, usually seafood, for all meals daily. Many are only open Memorial Day to Labor Day, and most of the rest limit their hours in the off-season. Steak, seafood, and chicken entrées tend to run $12–17.

Popular spots include **Etta's Channel Side Restaurant** (7452 East Side Dr., 757/336-5644, dinner daily, from noon Sun.) and **Mr. Baldy's Family Restaurant** (3441 Ridge Rd., 757/336-1198). **AJ's on the Creek** (6585 Maddox Blvd., 757/336-5888, lunch and dinner Mon.–Sat.) is an intimate, romantic place with some of the better seafood in town. It also serves steaks and pasta and has a screened-in porch.

Don's Seafood Restaurant (4113 Main St., 757/336-5715, lunch and dinner daily) also has a lounge with a raw bar and dancing past midnight. Not to be outdone, **Bill's Seafood Restaurant** (4040 Main St., 757/336-5831, all meals daily) has all the surf and turf you could hope to eat, and gets the locals' vote (dinner entrées $13–30).

Steamers (6251 Maddox Blvd., 757/336-5300, dinner daily) is an informal seafood joint popular with tourists and locals and is almost always packed in season. All-you-can-eat feasts start in the low $20s and include soup, salads, biscuits, hush puppies, corn on the cob, sweet potatoes, and the seafood of your choice. Butcher paper and a garbage can for every table keeps the mess to a minimum.

Information

The Chincoteague Chamber of Commerce operates a **visitors center** (6733 Maddox Blvd., 757/336-6161, www.chincoteaguechamber.com, 8:30 A.M.–4:30 P.M. Mon.–Sat.) in a traffic circle about one mile west of the bridge to Assateague Island. For more information, visit the website www.chincoteague.com.

Near Chincoteague

The National Advisory Committee on Aeronautics (NACA) opened an aeronautical research center at Wallops Island in 1945. NACA became a full federal agency, the National Aeronautics and Space Administration (NASA), in 1958, and over the years, the **Wallops Flight Facility** has tested and launched thousands of orbital and suborbital rockets and balloons. An agreement also allows launches of commercial satellites. The agency runs a **visitors center** (757/824-2298 or 757/824-1344, 10 A.M.–4 P.M. daily July–Aug., Thurs.–Mon. off-season, free), tracing the history of flight, rockets, and space travel through video displays, photos, and real relics of the space program. Space-suit demonstrations and launchings of model rockets take place during the summer. Call ahead for a launch schedule, although many rockets launched from here aren't all that big or impressive.

CHINCOTEAGUE NATIONAL WILDLIFE REFUGE AND ASSATEAGUE ISLAND

Assateague Island, a thin ribbon of sand 37 miles long, extends from Ocean City, Maryland, to just past Chincoteague Island. In numerous places along the way its solitude is in striking juxtaposition to both resorts. The entire spit has been designated a National Seashore, and Virginia's end of the island was set aside in 1943 as the Chincoteague National Wildlife Refuge to protect dwindling habitat for migrating snow geese.

There's much more to the fishhook tip of sand than the graceful white birds with black wingtips, though. Virginia's portion of the wild pony herd draws plenty of visitors, while enough birds pass through during migrating season to guarantee additions to most bird-watchers' life lists. Even though they're not open to camping on this end of the island, 10 miles of wild oceanside beaches offer wave-soothed solitude for hikers who venture off the more popular beaches.

Habitats

Tidal salt marshes and mudflats line the ragged landward side of the island, facing Chincoteague Island and Chincoteague Bay. Pine and hardwood forests fill the interior, dotted with pools and the large bight of Toms Cove at the southernmost end. The smooth Atlantic edge is almost pure sand, which is slowly being pushed southward by the endless caress of the ocean.

Assateague Island, where the Chincoteague National Wildlife Refuge is located, faces the open Atlantic, with sea breezes and ocean waves.

Species

More than 300 species of **birds** depend on the rich harvest of plants, mollusks, insects, and crustaceans provided by Assateague Island's freshwater impoundments, marshes, mudflats, tidal pools, and maritime forests. Herons, egrets, gulls, terns, and sandpipers arrive in the summer, followed in the fall by migrating shorebirds and peregrine falcons, which are easier to spot on Assateague than almost anywhere else on the East Coast. Migrating waterfowl, including mallards, pintails, black ducks, Canada geese, and greater snow geese, take advantage of the island's mild winter climate during their thousand-mile journeys. Keep an ear out for the distinctive call of the willet, and be aware of area closures (usually most of Toms Cove Hook) to protect the nesting sites of the threatened piping plover.

Most famous of Assateague's 44 mammal species are undoubtedly the **wild ponies,** separated into two herds by a fence at the Maryland state line. The Virginia herd is owned by the Chincoteague Volunteer Fire Company and allowed to graze on federal land by special permit. It's fun to hear the legend that they swam ashore from a shipwrecked Spanish galleon, but it's more probable (and prosaic) that they're the descendants of herds hidden on the island in the 17th century by mainland colonists trying to avoid livestock taxes. This means they're actually stunted horses, not true ponies.

With their shaggy manes and stubby legs, they look cute enough to pet, which many people do—bad idea. These are not tame horses, and visitors get bitten and kicked every year and promptly blame the refuge staff for their own foolishness. The horses' short stature and their bloated bellies, which can't handle human handouts, are most likely the result of generations of salty marsh grass and brackish water.

Your best chance of spotting them is from the Woodland Trail in Black Duck Marsh, but you might bump into a few just about anywhere. While the Maryland herd grazes at large, the Virginia herd grazes in two fenced compartments, to keep them out of sensitive habitats and away from people.

© KATIE GITHENS

With stubby legs and shaggy manes, the famous Chincoteague wild ponies are cute – but remember to give them a wide berth.

© KATIE GITHENS

Great white egrets can be found fishing in the ditches around Assateague island.

© KATIE GITHENS

A quarter-mile hike up a sandy rise brings you to the Assateague Island Lighthouse.

A small herd of Asian **sika deer**—actually an elk species—was released by a Boy Scout troop in 1923 at the northern end of the island, and the deer now outnumber the native **white-tailed deer.** If you come across a large, relatively unfazed rodent with a big bushy tail, it's probably an endangered **Delmarva Peninsula fox squirrel.**

Visiting the Refuge

The refuge encompasses the Virginia portion of the **Assateague Island National Seashore** (757/336-6577 or 410/641-1441, www.nps.gov/asis). (To further complicate things, part of the Maryland section of the seashore is also a state park.) The refuge entrance, at the end of Maddox Boulevard, is open 5 A.M.–10 P.M. daily in season for $5 per car. The U.S. Fish and Wildlife Service operates the **Herbert H. Bateman Center** (757/336-6122, http://chinco.fws.gov, 9 A.M.–5 P.M. daily in summer, until 4 P.M. rest of year), with wildlife information, trail brochures, and schedules of interpretive activities. Be sure to pay homage to the **Assateague Island Lighthouse,** painted in jaunty red and white stripes and standing 142 feet tall. Completed in 1867, the lighthouse is still in use today, warning ships of shoals that once sank President Harrison's yacht. The beams are visible up to 22 nautical miles offshore.

Parts of the beach are open to surfing, fishing, swimming, clamming, and crabbing. Fifteen miles of trails include the 1.6-mile Woodland Trail to an overlook over pony-favored Black Duck Marsh; the 3.2-mile Wildlife Loop, open to vehicles 3 P.M.–dusk; and the Toms Cove Nature Trail, out along the southern tail. Miles of untracked beach stretch north from the National Park Service's **Toms Cove Visitor Center** (757/336-6577, 9 A.M.–5 P.M. daily in summer, until 4 P.M. rest of year), at the entrance to Toms Cove Hook. Inside the visitors center, kids will want to explore the aquarium and touch tank. Back outside, cyclists are welcome on paved trails. Boaters should check ahead of time for permitted landing sites.

Camping isn't allowed in the Virginia end of the refuge, but it is north of the Maryland border. You can pick up backcountry permits ($5) at Toms Cove, but the closest campsite is a 12-mile paddle or hike over sand while carrying drinking water and provisions for the trip. From the Maryland side, the distance is less daunting, only two miles away, and car camping is also available (410/641-3030, www.nps.gov/asis, $16–20). Dog owners take note: Pets are *only* permitted in the Maryland campground in the national wildlife refuge. No dogs are allowed anywhere on the Virginia side—not even inside cars.

Across the state line, **Assateague State Park** (410/641-2120 or 888/432-2267, www.dnr.state.md.us/publiclands/eastern/assateague.html, $4 pp) also has campsites for $30–40 from May to October.

Both the Park Service and the U.S. Fish and Wildlife Service offer naturalist programs in the refuge daily during summer and on spring and fall weekends. Annual events start with the **International Migratory Bird Celebration** in May, with guided walks, speakers, and workshops, and continue through **National Wildlife Refuge Week** in October. **Waterfowl Week,** in late November during the southward migration of Canada and snow geese, is the only time visitors can drive to the northern end of the refuge via the Northern Service Road.

The **Assateague Coastal Trust** (410/629-1538, www.actforbays.org) is a grassroots nonprofit organization dedicated to preserving Assateague Island and its surrounding ecosystem through outreach programs and advocacy efforts. It organizes occasional conferences, lectures, and workshops.

THE TOWN THAT TURNED PAUL NEWMAN DOWN

The Great Movie Controversy of 1998 showed clearly that increasing tourism hasn't changed the stubbornly independent local attitude of Tangier all that much.

Actor Paul Newman had selected Tangier as the perfect place to film *Message in a Bottle,* a movie starring himself and Kevin Costner. Everything looked great until a core of conservative, born-again Christians on the town council forced a last-minute change of plans. Despite a petition bearing 200 names, the possibility of $23,000 worth of repairs to the town dock, and work for hundreds of hard-up island residents, a 6-0 vote said that the PG-13 script, with its profanity, premarital sex, and alcohol, was inconsistent with community values and therefore unwelcome.

Many indignant islanders pointed out that swearing, procreating, and even illicit drinking all occurred on Tangier – and that legions of locals had taken the boat to Salisbury, Maryland, to see the disaster epic *Titanic.* But the arguments fell on deaf ears, and Newman, who had scoped out the island incognito, had to look elsewhere for a film site.

TANGIER ISLAND

Only 10 or so miles of Chesapeake chop from the mainland, Tangier is decades away from even the atavistic air of the Eastern Shore. The insularity of this tight little fishing community is something you don't come across every day. The pace of life is a little different and the accent hard to place, making a visit as much a cultural experience as a sightseeing jaunt. Even in a state that has as many curious nooks as Virginia does, Tangier stands out.

History

Indians fished and hunted on the island for centuries, but Tangier wasn't "discovered" by Europeans—Captain John Smith, to be precise—and named until 1608. The first settlement came in 1686, after native tribes, according to a (probably bogus) legend, sold the island for two overcoats. Cornishman John Crockett, along with his eight sons and their families, was the first to arrive. By the 19th century, the island was home to 100 residents, half of them Crocketts, who made a living fishing and grazing livestock.

The outside world intruded during the Revolutionary War, when British troops used the island as a base for raiding American ships. During the War of 1812, 12,000 more redcoats stood under the pines in preparation for an attack on Fort McHenry. Local reverend Joshua Thomas harangued the invaders, claiming that the word from above was that they could not take Baltimore. (He was right.) In 1814, Francis Scott Key boarded a British boat on Tangier to negotiate the release of an American prisoner. During his voyage, Key witnessed the American flag "gallantly streaming" through the Battle of Baltimore, inspiring him to write what would become "the Star-Spangled Banner."

A cholera outbreak in 1866 forced an almost total evacuation of the island, and a huge storm in 1933 inundated everything on the low-lying island but the top floors of houses. Three years later, the Army Air Corps had to drop supplies onto the school playground when the "Big Freeze" clogged the entire northern bay with a foot of ice. Electricity arrived in 1946, and satellite dishes have begun sprouting in the last decade or two.

Tangier Today

A little more than five square miles in area, the island consists of three inhabited "ridges," none more than five feet above the Chesapeake waterline, which are split by canals and connected by bridges. Most is marsh and wetlands, hunting grounds for Virginia rails, muskrats, herons, and egrets. About 530 people currently live on Tangier—fewer than half as many as did at the turn of the 20th century—and most are related. One-third are Crocketts, with the names of other settlers including Pruitt, Dise, Parks, and Wheatley covering most of the remainder. Crabbing and clamming sustain the community, which is still considered the "soft-shell capital of the world." Men leave before dawn to check the farms alongshore where the famous local crabs are raised.

Tangier has always been a tightly knit community. In the early 1900s, a book by resident Thomas Crockett rattled so many local skeletons that his descendants later gathered up and destroyed as many copies as they could find. During a World War I visit, president Woodrow Wilson found Tangier's doors locked when islanders suspected his aides of being a German raiding party off a submarine. When Accomack County officials sent over a metal jail in the 1930s, island residents threw it into the water, saying they had no need for one.

A peculiar accent, the product of generations of isolation, evokes England's West Country, turning "time" into "toime" and "mind" into "moind." Front yards (the highest ground on the island) are often crowded with graves and headstones, some centuries old, and highly religious roots continue to sprout—a 1995 revival left one-third of the population born-again Christians. All children attend one school, rebuilt in the mid-1990s, which consistently has the highest percentage of graduates (sometimes six out of six) going on to college in the state. Health care comes in the form of mainland physicians who come twice a week, and dentists and optometrists visit monthly.

Everyone knows each other, of course, and welcomes visitors with a wave from golf carts, bright cruiser bicycles, and a handful of cars and trucks. Stacked crab pots fill backyards lined with chain-link fences, and motorboats zoom around the wharf area, a maze of pilings, crab shanties, and trays called "peeler boxes" where crabs are held until they shed their shells.

Recreation

The Sunset Inn rents **golf carts** ($25 half-day, $50 overnight), and the Waterfront Restaurant rents **bicycles** ($5 per day), which can be left sitting around anywhere (where's a thief going to go?). Head to the south end of the island for a nice beach.

The Tangier Island Museum has about a dozen **kayaks** available for visitors to borrow for free, as well as maps of five suggested routes to explore the island by sea. For information on **watermen's tours** around the island, contact Denny Crockett (757/891-2331) or James Eskridge (757/891-2900).

Accommodations and Food

Because lodging options are limited, reservations are essential on Tangier. Alcohol is technically forbidden on the island. Shirley and Wallace Pruitt run **Shirley's Bay View Inn** (16408 West Ridge Rd., 757/891-2396, www.tangierisland.net, $125–140). Wallace was born in the 1806 house, which has a wraparound porch and plantings in abundance. Two rooms in the house and nine cottages behind are open year-round, with air-conditioning, cable TV, and breakfast included. Grace and Jim Brown's **Sunset Inn** (757/891-2535), also on Ridge Road at the south end near the beach, has cottages for $115–130 including breakfast. They also rent golf carts for getting around the island.

Hilda Crockett's Chesapeake House (757/891-2331, www.chesapeakehousetangier.com) is in town a few blocks south of the church. This local legend, open since 1939, offers rooms in season for $135–145 including breakfast. The restaurant is also open to the public, serving all-you-can-eat meals for $9 (breakfast) and $22 (lunch and dinner) daily. (Children eat for $5–10.)

Lorraine's Seafood & Sandwich Shop (4417 Chambers Ln., 757/891-2225, all meals Mon.–Sat., lunch Sun.) is one of the few restaurants on the island open year-round, serving subs, pizza, and seafood ($5–11). Near the docks are the **Fisherman's Corner Restaurant** (757/891-2900, lunch daily, dinner Mon.–Sat., May–Sept.) and the **Waterfront Restaurant** (lunch daily May–Oct., 757/891-2248), both serving fresh seafood in season. Sandwiches are $6–12, and seafood plates are $10–26—nothing fancy, but as fresh as it comes. The Waterfront also rents bikes for $5 per day.

CRAB LINGO

Backfin: large fin containing choice meat
Buster: crab within hours of shedding
Doubler: male and female crab caught in mating embrace
Jimmy: legal-size male
Peeler: crab ready to molt
Pot: crab trap
Sook: mature female

Information

Tangier doesn't have a centralized tourism body, but the **Tangier Island History Museum and Interpretative Cultural Center** (16215 Main Rd., 302/234-1660, www.tangierhistorymuseum.org, 11 A.M.–4 P.M. daily) comes close. Swing by the museum for a quick orientation when you arrive.

Getting There

Several tourist ferries run May through October. **Tangier & Rappahannock Cruises** (804/453-2628, www.tangiercruise.com) sends the *Chesapeake Breeze* from the Buzzard's Point Marina near Reedville, Virginia, at 10 A.M. daily May–October, returning at 4 P.M. ($25 adults, $13 children for day trips, $30 adults, $15 children for overnight stays). Phone reservations are a must in the summer.

The modern 300-passenger ***Stephen Thomas*** (410/968-2338) departs Crisfield, Maryland, at 12:30 P.M. daily May–October, returning at 4 P.M. Tickets are $25 per person for same-day round-trip, $35 per person for overnight.

The 36-foot ***Joyce Marie II*** (757/891-2505) leaves from Onancock at 10 A.M. Tuesday–Sunday May–October, returning at 4:30 P.M. ($25 pp round-trip). The ***Courtney Thomas,*** aka "the mail boat," runs year-round ferry service in addition to being Tangier Island's postal service. It leaves Crisfield, Maryland, at 12:30 P.M. Monday–Saturday, and departs Tangier Island at 8 A.M. (no Sunday travel). Call for rates (757/891-2240).

CENTRAL VIRGINIA

The Piedmont, Virginia's heartland, is also known as "Mr. Jefferson's Country." Two and a half centuries later, the man who left his indelible stamp on the central part of the state is still spoken about with a curious mixture of awe and familiarity, like a distinguished uncle who's just in the next room. These rolling hills, achingly beautiful in the late afternoon sunlight, echo every aspect of a true renaissance life.

Thomas Jefferson was born on his father's farm at Shadwell in 1743, and plows still turn the rich soil of large parts of Albemarle and Orange Counties every spring. Along with the land for Monticello, Jefferson inherited a taste for things patrician, a value system carried on with gusto by the Piedmont's current upper crust. Grand 19th-century homes anchor wealthy neighborhoods in Richmond, while in rural areas shaded country lanes lead to historic estates, each with its own name and legion of caretakers. Packs of foxhounds in the care of riders on purebred horses are blessed outside Grace Episcopal Church on Route 231 in an annual ritual Jefferson would have undoubtedly appreciated.

Although the author of the Declaration of Independence failed in his first few attempts at coaxing a decent grape from the fertile soil, central Virginia now cradles some of the best wineries in the East. Jefferson's fascination with classical architecture lives on in the neoclassical lines of the state capitol in Richmond, the porticoes of Monticello, and the unmistakable Rotunda of the University of Virginia in Charlottesville.

Above all, the third American president

© KATIE GITHENS

HIGHLIGHTS

White House and Museum of the Confederacy: Richmond, the onetime headquarters of the Confederacy, guards this residence of would-be president Jefferson Davis (page 217).

Richmond National Battlefield Park Visitors Center: This impressive museum in the old Tredegar Ironworks along the James River sheds light on the Civil War battles around Richmond (page 226).

James River Park: With 550 acres of shoreline, islands, and trails – not to mention Class I to IV white water – it's no wonder Richmond's largest park system has some of the nation's best urban paddling and mountain biking (page 227).

Kings Dominion: Fifteen roller coasters await at one of Virginia's best amusement parks, along with the WaterWorks water park and the Peanuts-themed Planet Snoopy for younger visitors (page 239).

University of Virginia: Charlottesville, an astonishingly cozy college town, is centered on the Lawn, Rotunda, and pavilions of one of the country's premier public universities (page 254).

Montpelier: James Madison's 2,700-acre retirement home – along with Jefferson's Monticello and James Monroe's Ash Lawn-Highland – proves the founding fathers knew their real estate and offers a glimpse into centuries-ago life at the top. An ambitious four-year restoration of the mansion concluded in 2008 (page 269).

Monticello: Thomas Jefferson's pet project (and the home we all know from the back of the nickel) is one of the great American architectural achievements, with more than 1,000 acres of lush gardens to explore (page 274).

Appomattox Court House National Historical Park: The Civil War ended here – in a home owned by the man on whose property it all began in Manassas (page 286).

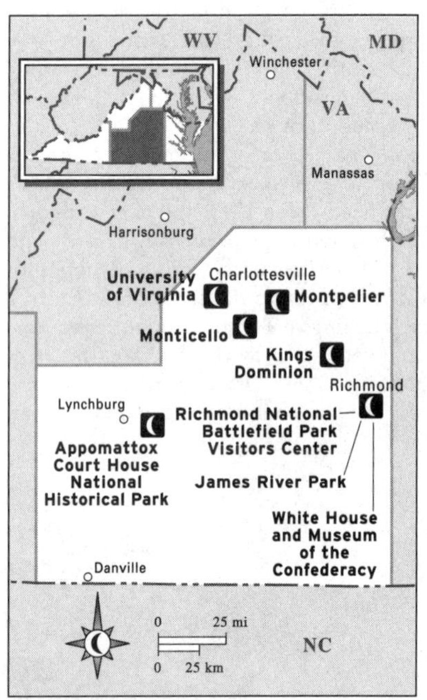

LOOK FOR TO FIND RECOMMENDED SIGHTS, ACTIVITIES, DINING, AND LODGING.

carried himself with an air of humility. He described how he found the greatest happiness when up to his elbows in his gardens or tinkering on one of the items on an endless list of projects and schemes both mechanical and political. Despite all the new money and celebrities that have poured into the Piedmont lately, central Virginia is still earthy and simple at heart. Whether it's the hand-poled Hatton Ferry across the James River at Scottsville, a well-worn tractor resting in a field of alfalfa, or the way everyone knows your name down at the general store after a couple of visits, this part of the state carries on Jefferson's greatest, quiet legacy: that of things of quality, appreciated slowly.

PLANNING YOUR TIME

You could easily spend weeks exploring central Virginia, one of the largest regions of the state, but it's possible to absorb the highlights—mostly in and around Richmond and Charlottesville, about an hour apart—in 3–4 days. Either city can serve as a home base; if you absolutely have to pick one, head to Richmond, where you'll find the outstanding **White House and Museum of the Confederacy** and the **Richmond National Battlefield Park Visitors Center**—and **James River Park,** for fresh air after all the museum-hopping. The city has been bursting with history ever since Patrick Henry gave his "liberty or death" speech here in 1775. Today Richmond remains Virginia's political and commercial capital, humming with life in restored historic neighborhoods full of museums, restaurants, shops, and nightclubs.

For more Civil War history, head to Fredericksburg (a good day trip from Richmond) or **Appomattox Court House National Historical Park** south of Charlottesville. This cozy college town is another city not to miss, home to fabulous restaurants and Thomas Jefferson's beloved **University of Virginia,** one of the country's premier public universities and a living museum of historic architecture. Speaking of founding fathers, Jefferson's enviable hilltop home at **Monticello** is nearby,

the Museum of the Confederacy in Richmond

as is his residence at **Poplar Forest,** James Madison's **Montpelier,** and James Monroe's **Ash Lawn-Highland.** It's easy to see a few of these places in a day or all of them in a weekend. **Kings Dominion** offers diversions of a different kind—think roller coasters and a water park—north of Richmond.

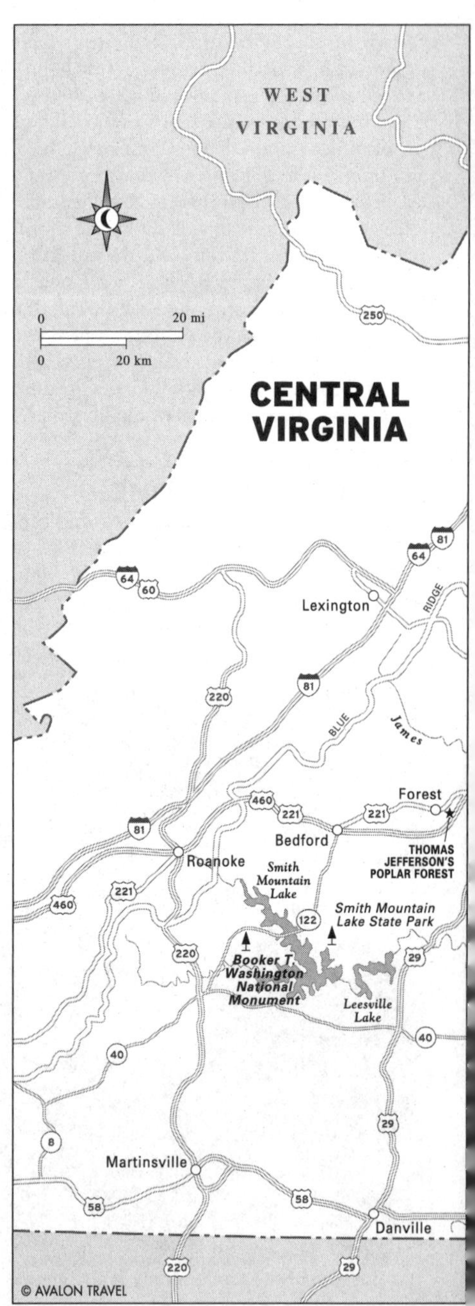

Access

All roads—or in this case, interstates—lead to Richmond. I-64 connects Virginia's capital with the Blue Ridge, Charlottesville, and the coast, while I-95 skewers Richmond on its way from Washington, D.C., to North Carolina. I-85 is an alternate route south, while I-295 encircles Richmond and reaches down to Petersburg. Beyond the interstates, federal highways such as U.S. 15, U.S. 60, and U.S. 522 offer more direct and scenic drives between major Piedmont cities. U.S. 29 is the quickest route between Charlottesville and Washington, D.C., via I-66, but watch for speed traps around Culpeper. Smaller state roads like Route 20, Route 231, and Route 40 take their sweet time meandering across the farmlands and up into the Blue Ridge foothills.

Events

In June, the **James River Batteau Festival** (www.batteau.org) brings a week of one of the East Coast's most unusual waterborne celebrations, centered on reproductions of 18th-century shallow-draft merchant boats. In their time, each 60-foot craft could carry up to 20 tons of goods to Richmond and back much faster than horses and wagons. A few were discovered near Richmond in the early 1980s, allowing carpenters to rebuild the time-tested design. The festival follows the river, with reenactors stopping at towns such as Scottsville and Lynchburg along the way.

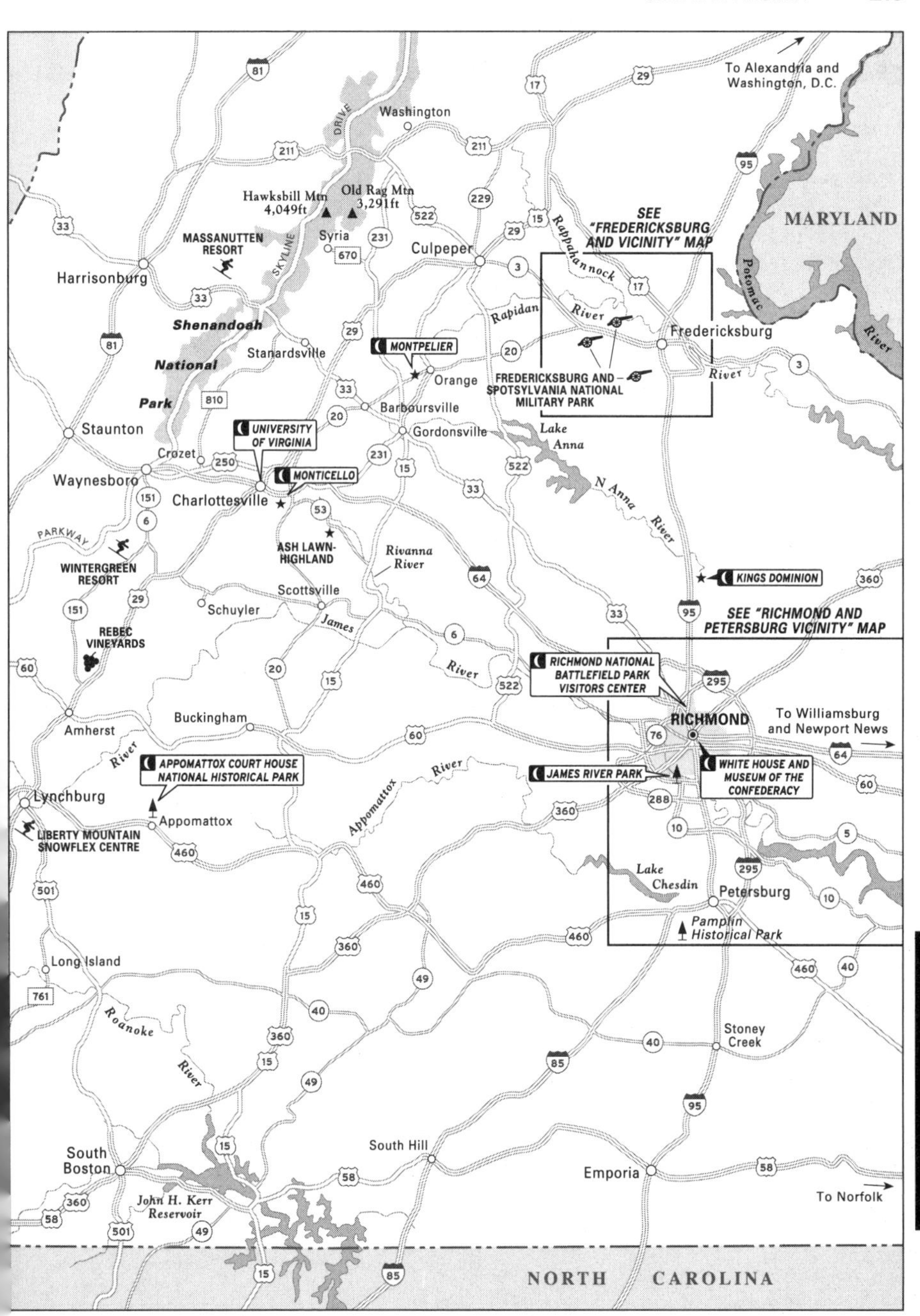
To Alexandria and Washington, D.C.
MARYLAND
Washington
Hawksbill Mtn 4,049ft
Old Rag Mtn 3,291ft
SKYLINE DRIVE
MASSANUTTEN RESORT
Syria
Culpeper
SEE "FREDERICKSBURG AND VICINITY" MAP
Rappahannock River
Potomac River
Harrisonburg
Shenandoah National Park
Rapidan
Fredericksburg
Stanardsville
MONTPELIER
Orange
FREDERICKSBURG AND SPOTSYLVANIA NATIONAL MILITARY PARK
Barboursville
Gordonsville
Lake Anna
Staunton
UNIVERSITY OF VIRGINIA
Crozet
Waynesboro
MONTICELLO
Charlottesville
N Anna River
PARKWAY
ASH LAWN-HIGHLAND
WINTERGREEN RESORT
Rivanna River
KINGS DOMINION
Scottsville
Schuyler
SEE "RICHMOND AND PETERSBURG VICINITY" MAP
James River
REBEC VINEYARDS
RICHMOND NATIONAL BATTLEFIELD PARK VISITORS CENTER
RICHMOND
To Williamsburg and Newport News
Buckingham
Amherst
APPOMATTOX COURT HOUSE NATIONAL HISTORICAL PARK
JAMES RIVER PARK
WHITE HOUSE AND MUSEUM OF THE CONFEDERACY
Lynchburg
Appomattox River
Appomattox
LIBERTY MOUNTAIN SNOWFLEX CENTRE
Lake Chesdin
Petersburg
Pamplin Historical Park
Long Island
Roanoke River
Stoney Creek
South Hill
South Boston
Emporia
To Norfolk
John H. Kerr Reservoir
NORTH CAROLINA

Richmond and Vicinity

Since its miraculous rebirth from the ashes of the Civil War, the capital of Virginia has learned to look forward as well as back. Without ignoring its role as one of America's consummate Southern cities—and all the respect for tradition that entails—Richmond has become a busy, affluent, eclectic metropolis that anchors its mother state in the past while propelling it toward the future.

Visitors, swayed by descriptions a decade or two out of date, might expect a crumbling, dreary place full of unrepentant ghosts and the stale smell of tobacco. Granted, some parts of downtown still aren't all that pleasant. Others, though, have undergone an amazing transformation. Luxury lofts and some of the liveliest nightlife in the state have bloomed by the James River, while streets to the west are packed at noon with browsers and the business lunchtime crowd. Outdoor athletes, too, have made themselves at home in Richmond's cityscape, taking advantage of the country's best urban white

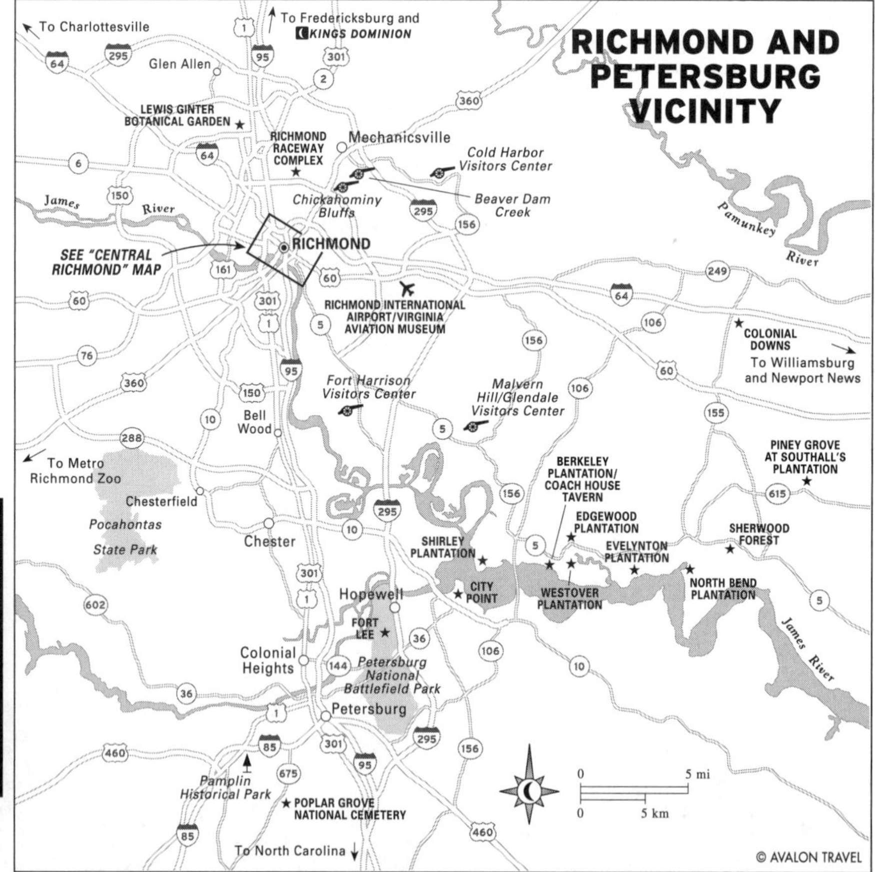

the Richmond skyline

water and an extensive trail system. In fact, the Xterra East Coast Championship, a high-profile off-road triathlon, is held each June on the banks of the James. And of course, other historic neighborhoods go about their business and tend their historic buildings as proud and conservative as ever.

The Richmond region, which includes the city and Chesterfield, Hanover, and Henrico Counties, is home to more than one million people. Thirty percent of the region's residents, and over half of the city's 200,000 inhabitants, are African American. Many younger residents are here attending schools such as the University of Richmond, Virginia Commonwealth University and its Medical College of Virginia branch, Virginia Union University, and the Union Theological Seminary.

Richmond has always been one of Virginia's commercial hubs, and even as trade along the James has faded, it has found new ventures to take over. A half-dozen Fortune 500 companies have their corporate headquarters here, and Richmond's title of "tobacco capital of the world" lives on in cigarette billboards, cigar shops, and the sprawling state-of-the-art headquarters of Philip Morris—the city's fourth-largest private employer—south of the James.

Revitalization is a never-ending process, and you'll see the fruits of the city's labor in the $1 billion Downtown Master Plan. The completed transformation of 32 acres of Tobacco Row along the river from 5th to 17th Streets, complete with walkways, plazas, and apartment buildings, was considered one of the country's most ambitious recent redevelopment projects.

History

Captains Christopher Newport and John Smith scouted this stretch of the James by Richmond in 1607, within weeks of the English settlers' landing. The name came from William Byrd II, who decided the falls at this spot on the James reminded him of Richmond-on-Thames in England. Several forts protected the bustling port, which was plotted out in 1737.

In April 1780 the Colonial capital was moved here from Williamsburg to protect it from the invading British, but to no avail;

infamous traitor Benedict Arnold put the town of 700 to the torch in January 1781. Richmond recovered, largely because of a canal system completed in 1840 that connected to the western Piedmont. The canal bypassed the falls and helped the city become a regional hub for transport, milling, banking, and trade. By the turn of the 19th century, Richmond's population had passed 5,000, and local culture blossomed. Planters brought their families into town in the winter to enjoy the stars of Europe and America performing on city stages. Edgar Allan Poe wrote scathing book reviews for the *Southern Literary Messenger* from August 1835 through January 1837, and at one party Charles Dickens acquired his nickname of the "artful dodger" as his host boasted how the famous author had bypassed Philadelphia and Baltimore in favor of Richmond.

FIGHTING FOR RICHMOND

The Confederate capital saw two major Civil War campaigns reach her doorstep. The first, in 1862, crushed the possibility of a short war, and the second two years later set the stage for the war's end.

THE SEVEN DAYS' BATTLES

Gen. George B. McClellan's Peninsular Campaign advanced to within sight of Richmond in June 1862. Robert E. Lee, recently named commander of the Confederate army, recalled Stonewall Jackson and his troops from the Shenandoah Valley and struck first on June 26 with 90,000 men. McClellan's army was flushed out of Mechanicsville and attacked by the Confederates (unsuccessfully) at Beaver Dam Creek.

The next day 55,000 Rebels attacked at Gaines' Mill, securing a last-ditch victory after being driven back repeatedly from the blue line along Boatswain's Creek. The heaviest fighting of the Seven Days' Battles resulted in 6,000-9,000 casualties, about one and a half times as many Confederates as Federals. McClellan began a fighting retreat, clashing with Lee at Savage's Station on June 29 and White Oak Swamp and Glendale (Frayser's Farm) on June 30. On July 1 the Union army managed to reach the safety of gunboats on the James River at Malvern Hill. Having reached the safety of the river, the Union army turned to defend Malvern Hill. Maj. Gen. Fitz-John Porter lined his troops up in battle formation and mowed down enemy ranks forced to cross open ground. Gunboat artillery helped slaughter more than 6,000 advancing troops, causing Confederate Gen. E. M. Law to remark, "It was not war – it was murder."

The Seven Days' Battles forced McClellan to abandon his advance on Richmond for the time being. Although (and in part because) McClellan kept demanding more men, Lincoln ended the campaign in August. A week of fierce combat had cost 35,000 casualties and untold suffering. One Georgian soldier wrote home, "I have seen, heard, and felt many things in the last week that I never want to see, hear, nor feel again."

THE BEGINNING OF THE END

By 1864 Richmond was heavily defended behind two rings of defensive earthworks and a series of forts on the outskirts of the city. Ulysses S. Grant had taken command of Union forces and put Richmond in the crosshairs once again. After much maneuvering by both sides, Confederate troops dug in at Cold Harbor just in time for Grant's assault on June 3.

A massive frontal attack in pre-dawn fog and misty rain threw 60,000 men against the impregnable Confederate lines in what quickly became the bloodiest charge of the war. Some 6,000 Federal soldiers were cut down with appalling speed by Rebel rifles and artillery. More than half fell in the first hour of fighting.

Ten more days of fighting proved the futility of infantry assaults against strongly held trenches, changing the course of the Civil War and all wars thereafter. Grant eventually withdrew and crossed the James toward Petersburg, where a 10-month siege would lead to the fall of Richmond and the end of the Civil War.

The most industrialized city in the south at the start of the Civil War became the Confederate capital on May 29, 1861. Jefferson Davis presided over a city flush with Southern pride and hosted lavish balls where hoop-skirted belles flirted with officers in crisp uniforms. After three years of fighting, however, high hopes had been replaced by rude reality. Richmond's population tripled as wounded and captured soldiers flooded the city. Belle Isle in the James became one of the war's largest prison camps, local factories cranked out thousands of weapons, and basic necessities like food and clothing grew scarce as the sound of gunfire grew ever nearer.

The Union army marched within hearing distance of the city's church bells in 1862 and again in 1864, but it wasn't until April 1865 that Robert E. Lee's Army of Northern Virginia found itself cornered. Davis and the Confederate government fled to Danville as the defensive lines at Petersburg collapsed on April 3. Retreating troops marched out by the light of fires raging among the warehouses of the riverside commercial district, set ablaze to keep their contents out of Yankee hands.

Once again Richmond rebuilt itself. Still an important shipping center, the city enjoyed an economic boom around the turn of the 20th century, when tobacco factories, flour mills, and iron foundries were built. Three major railways fed 1,245 manufacturing plants. Prohibition and the Great Depression came and went, shaking but sparing the city that by the late 1930s was the fastest-growing industrial center in the country. The historian Mary Newton Standard wrote how "business buzzes, traffic roars, skyscrapers soar to heaven, and numberless smokestacks proclaim that everything in the world, from matches to locomotives, is made in Richmond."

Dozens of antebellum homes in the downtown area fell to the wrecking ball of progress while wealthy citizens built Tudor estates to the west. A growing black population made the integration of city schools an inevitability and has shifted the political power structure away from its traditional Southern paradigm.

Orientation

Downtown Richmond, the heart of the Richmond Metropolitan Area, spreads along the northern side of a bend in the James River. Navigation is simple: The only kink in the simple grid street layout is in Carytown and the Fan, where everything has a 30-degree slant. Aside from this, and the fact that many streets are one-way, Richmond is an easy city to navigate. (Parking can still be tricky.) Broad Street (U.S. 60) is the main east–west thoroughfare, running the entire length of the city. As you'll soon find out, Richmonders love to carve their city up into neighborhoods, although they're not always so eager to delineate them clearly.

Safety

It's better to drive than walk through the downtown area at night, especially from one neighborhood to the next (say, Jackson Ward to Shockoe Slip). Wandering within popular, well-lit districts like Carytown and the Fan is considered safe. Some hotels offer shuttle service, but beyond that, you should drive or call a cab.

SIGHTS

Central Richmond

Richmond's historic heart beats in the neighborhood of **Court End** between Leigh Street and the state capitol. Centuries-old mansions and churches sit next to the dome of the Richmond Coliseum, modern office buildings, and the halls of the Medical College of Virginia (MCV), a branch of Virginia Commonwealth University.

WHITE HOUSE AND MUSEUM OF THE CONFEDERACY

The largest collection of Confederate relics in the world starts with pieces of the C.S.S. *Virginia* out front and continues inside. For its location in the heart of the Rebel capital, the presentation is surprisingly objective, with only a slight Southern slant peeking through from time to time. The moving collection ranges from the prosaic—more than 500 flags; dozens of swords, pistols, and rifles; and soldiers'

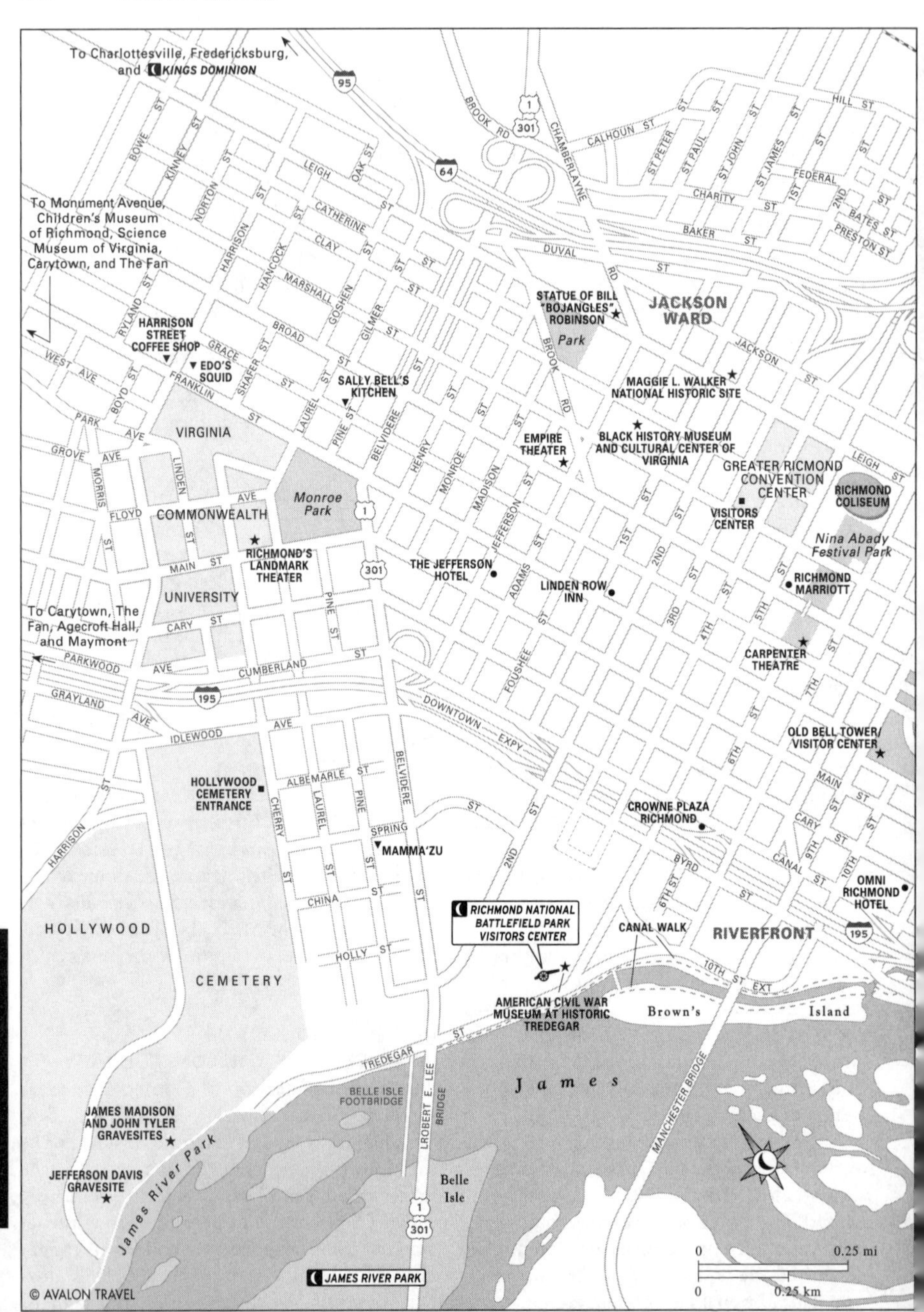
To Charlottesville, Fredericksburg, and KINGS DOMINION
To Monument Avenue, Children's Museum of Richmond, Science Museum of Virginia, Carytown, and The Fan
To Carytown, The Fan, Agecroft Hall, and Maymont
JACKSON WARD
STATUE OF BILL "BOJANGLES" ROBINSON
HARRISON STREET COFFEE SHOP
EDO'S SQUID
SALLY BELL'S KITCHEN
MAGGIE L. WALKER NATIONAL HISTORIC SITE
BLACK HISTORY MUSEUM AND CULTURAL CENTER OF VIRGINIA
EMPIRE THEATER
VIRGINIA
COMMONWEALTH
UNIVERSITY
Monroe Park
RICHMOND'S LANDMARK THEATER
THE JEFFERSON HOTEL
LINDEN ROW INN
GREATER RICMOND CONVENTION CENTER
VISITORS CENTER
RICHMOND COLISEUM
Nina Abady Festival Park
RICHMOND MARRIOTT
CARPENTER THEATRE
OLD BELL TOWER/ VISITOR CENTER
HOLLYWOOD CEMETERY ENTRANCE
MAMMA'ZU
CROWNE PLAZA RICHMOND
OMNI RICHMOND HOTEL
RICHMOND NATIONAL BATTLEFIELD PARK VISITORS CENTER
CANAL WALK
RIVERFRONT
AMERICAN CIVIL WAR MUSEUM AT HISTORIC TREDEGAR
Brown's Island
James
HOLLYWOOD CEMETERY
BELLE ISLE FOOTBRIDGE
Belle Isle
JAMES MADISON AND JOHN TYLER GRAVESITES
JEFFERSON DAVIS GRAVESITE
James River Park
JAMES RIVER PARK
0 0.25 mi
0 0.25 km
© AVALON TRAVEL

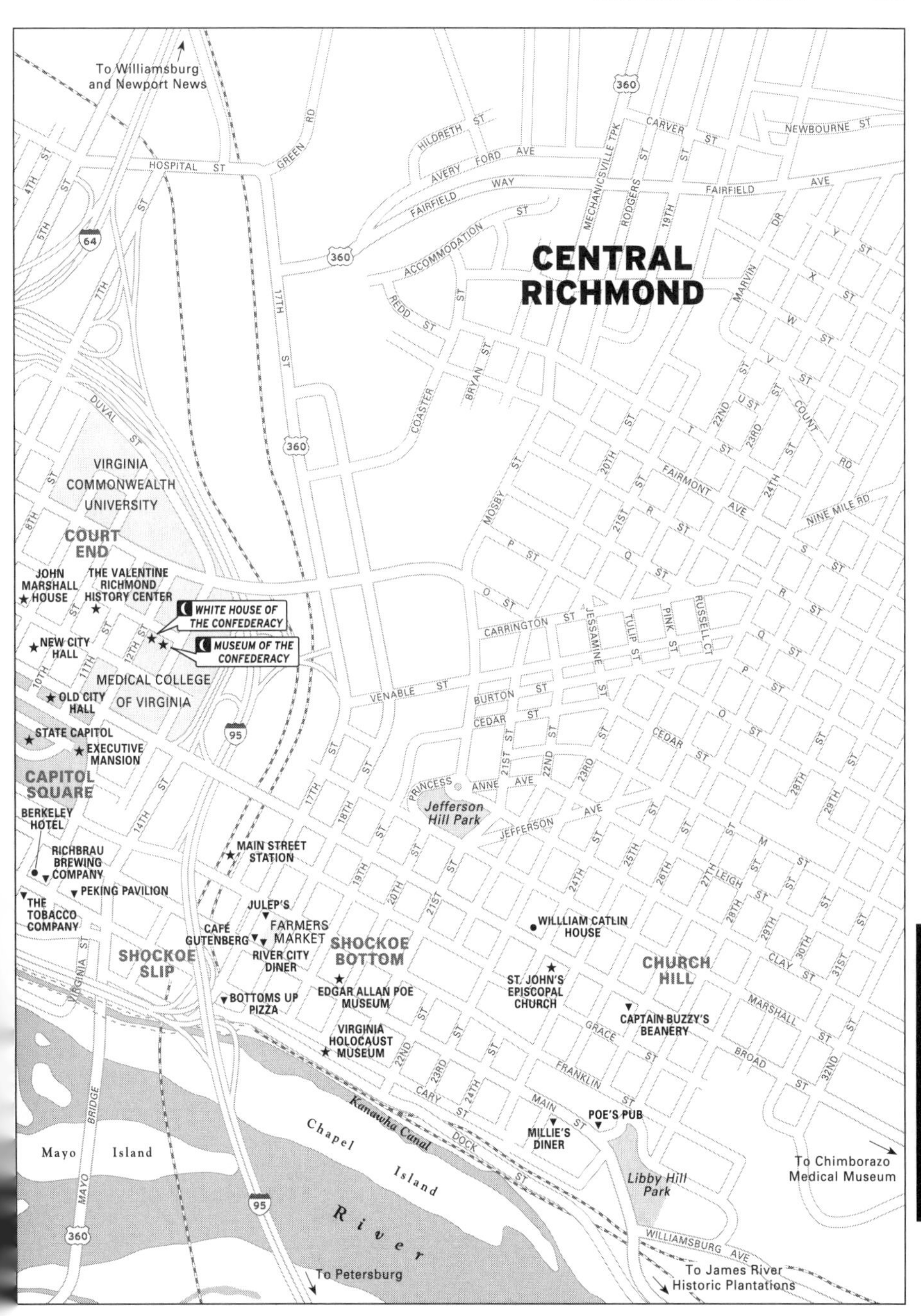

CENTRAL RICHMOND
To Williamsburg and Newport News
VIRGINIA COMMONWEALTH UNIVERSITY
COURT END
JOHN MARSHALL HOUSE
THE VALENTINE RICHMOND HISTORY CENTER
WHITE HOUSE OF THE CONFEDERACY
MUSEUM OF THE CONFEDERACY
NEW CITY HALL
MEDICAL COLLEGE OF VIRGINIA
OLD CITY HALL
STATE CAPITOL
EXECUTIVE MANSION
CAPITOL SQUARE
BERKELEY HOTEL
RICHBRAU BREWING COMPANY
PEKING PAVILION
THE TOBACCO COMPANY
MAIN STREET STATION
JULEP'S
FARMERS MARKET
CAFÉ GUTENBERG
RIVER CITY DINER
SHOCKOE SLIP
SHOCKOE BOTTOM
BOTTOMS UP PIZZA
EDGAR ALLAN POE MUSEUM
VIRGINIA HOLOCAUST MUSEUM
Jefferson Hill Park
WILLLIAM CATLIN HOUSE
ST. JOHN'S EPISCOPAL CHURCH
CHURCH HILL
CAPTAIN BUZZY'S BEANERY
POE'S PUB
MILLIE'S DINER
Libby Hill Park
Kanawha Canal
Mayo Island
Chapel Island
River
To Petersburg
To James River Historic Plantations
To Chimborazo Medical Museum
CENTRAL VIRGINIA

The Museum of the Confederacy contains the world's largest collection of Confederate relics.

The sword and uniform worn by Robert E. Lee at Appomattox are on display at the Museum of the Confederacy.

letters home—to the particular, in its prized assortment of personal effects from Confederate luminaries.

J. E. B. Stuart's plumed hat and Stonewall Jackson's revolver are highlights, along with the sword and coat Lee wore to Appomattox and the pen with which he signed the surrender documents. Upstairs you'll find changing exhibits addressing the experiences of different social groups during the war, while downstairs hangs *The Last Meeting of Lee and Jackson,* a monumental 1869 oil painting depicting the commanders' final parley at Chancellorsville.

Next door stands the building leased by the Confederate government as a home for Jefferson Davis, his family, and a dozen or so slaves from August 1861 to April 1865. Built in 1818, it became the Federal headquarters during Reconstruction. Lavish period decorations include many original Davis pieces, such as his favorite horsehair rocking chair (sat in by Lincoln less than 48 hours after the evacuation of Richmond) and a marble bust of the president of the Confederacy that was buried by a neighbor to keep it safe from Union troops. Notice the "gasaliers," hanging glass globes lit by coal gas, and the toy cannon in the nursery (the Davis kids were hellions, apparently).

Both buildings (1201 E. Clay St., 804/649-1861, www.moc.org, 10 A.M.–5 P.M. Mon.–Sat., noon–5 P.M. Sun., $12 adults, $7 children 7–13 to visit both buildings, $9 adults, $5 children to visit one) are so engulfed by the larger buildings of the Medical College of Virginia that it's hard not to be reminded of a losing army. There has been talk of moving the museum's collection elsewhere, although as of 2010 there were no takers.

CAPITOL SQUARE

A statue of George Washington on horseback surveys this grassy oasis dominated by the classical lines of the **Virginia State Capitol** (804/698-1788, www.virginiacapitol.gov, 8 A.M.–5 P.M. Mon.–Sat., 1–5 P.M. Sun., free tours every hour starting at 9 A.M. Mon.–Sat., 1 P.M. Sun.). The original central section, begun in 1785, was designed by—who else—Thomas

© KATIE GITHENS
the ornate columns of the Virginia State Capitol

Jefferson, based on the Maison Carrée, a 1st-century Roman temple in France. Even though it wasn't yet completed, the Virginia Assembly held its first meeting here in 1788. The Jean-Antoine Houdon statue of George Washington that stands under the cupola was unveiled the same year. It's considered one of the most valuable marble sculptures in the country because it's the only one Washington posed for in person. House and Senate chambers were added to the structure in 1904–1906, and since then the building has seen only two renovations, once in the 1960s and again in 2005–2007. Enter the Capitol via the new visitor entrance on Bank Street.

To one side is the **Executive Mansion** (804/371-8687), the oldest continually inhabited governor's residence in America. Call for hours and a current schedule of free tours. **Old City Hall** fills Broad Street with a block of Victorian Gothic pomp in gray stone. Built in 1886–1895, the structure was restored in the mid-1980s. The 1st floor is open to visitors—don't miss the ornate splendor of the painted pillars and two-story atrium. Across Broad Street stands the **New City Hall** (804/646-7000, 8 A.M.–5 P.M. Mon.–Fri.) with a 19th-floor observation deck, and the Old Bell Tower (1824) at the southwest corner of the square.

THE VALENTINE RICHMOND HISTORY CENTER

A collection of photos, old clothing, and antique tobacco tools captures the Life and History of Richmond from the 17th to 20th centuries. The museum (1015 E. Clay St., 804/649-0711, www.richmondhistorycenter.com, 10 A.M.–5 P.M. Tues.–Sat., noon–5 P.M. Sun., $8 adults, $7 children 7–18) abuts the Wickham House, built in 1812 by John Wickham, Richmond's wealthiest citizen and the lawyer who defended Aaron Burr against charges of treason in 1807. It's hard to decide which is more beautiful—the rare set of neoclassical decorative wall paintings or the Oval Parlor, designated one of the "100 most beautiful rooms in America." Behind the museum is a small garden, café, and the studio of

Richmond sculptor Edward Valentine, moved here in 1937 from its original spot at Leigh and 8th Streets.

JOHN MARSHALL HOUSE

The home of the third U.S. Supreme Court chief justice (1801–1835) reflects the astonishing career of one of the most brilliant men to ever hold the post. Revolutionary War veteran, lawyer, ambassador to France, secretary of state—Marshall did it all. He even had the temerity to oppose his cousin Thomas Jefferson in the political arena. The house (818 E. Marshall St., 804/648-7998, www.apva.org/marshall, noon–4 P.M. Wed.–Fri., 10 A.M.–5 P.M. Sat., noon–5 P.M. Sun., by appt. only Nov.–Feb., $8 adults, $4 children under 7) was built in 1788–1790 in the Federal style and contains many original architectural features and relics from Marshall's life and times.

Jackson Ward

This National Historic District is best known as a cradle of African American business and culture in the early and mid-20th century. Many black business and social leaders found a home along Quality Row, as Leigh Street west of 2nd Street was known. Banks, fraternal organizations, and other businesses benefited from a foundation of prominent figures such as Maggie Walker and Bill "Bojangles" Robinson. The Hippodrome Theater on 2nd Street (called The Deuce) swung through Prohibition to the tunes of Duke Ellington, Cab Calloway, and Billie Holiday, who handed down the crown to Ella Fitzgerald, Nat King Cole, and James Brown in turn. For a time, the neighborhood was known as the Harlem of the South.

The construction of I-95 in the 1950s destroyed hundreds of homes in Jackson Ward, although the Sixth Mount Zion Baptist Church, organized in 1867, stood strong and forced the interstate to reroute around it. Much of Jackson Ward fell into disrepair in the mid-20th century, but now gentrification is well underway, with new condos, art galleries, and restaurants popping up daily. Many of Jackson Ward's stately row houses have been restored as homes and offices, many with shallow covered front porches and fine ornamental ironwork; the only place you'll find more is New Orleans.

MAGGIE L. WALKER NATIONAL HISTORIC SITE

The daughter of a former slave, Maggie Walker overcame physical disability and racial prejudice to become the first female bank president in America at the turn of the 20th century, as well as owner of a newspaper, insurance company, and department store. Her St. Luke Penny Savings Bank is now called The Consolidated Bank and Trust Company and is the oldest black-operated bank in the United States. Walker lived at this two-story brick row house with her family 1904–1934, leaving many family pieces behind. The house (600 N. 2nd St., 804/771-2017, www.nps.gov/mawa, 9 A.M.–5 P.M. Mon.–Sat., free) is operated by the National Park Service, which has restored it to its 1930s appearance and offers free tours.

BLACK HISTORY MUSEUM AND CULTURAL CENTER OF VIRGINIA

Exhibits on Richmond's black history, with a focus on the immediate area, are displayed in this 1832 house (00 E. Clay St. at St. James St., 804/780-9093, www.blackhistorymuseum.org, 10 A.M.–5 P.M. Tues.–Sat., $5 adults, $3 children under 13), which served as a high school and black public library over the years. The collection includes work by artists such as Sam Gilliam, John Biggers, and P. H. Polk, and textiles and artifacts from Africa.

STATUE OF BILL "BOJANGLES" ROBINSON

The King of Tapology got his break in 1907 as a waiter at the Jefferson hotel, supposedly dancing his way out of a mixed-up order all the way back to the kitchen. He went on to perform his trademark stair dance on Broadway and in the movies, appearing in the first black "talkie" and starring alongside Shirley Temple in *The Little Colonel.* The 10-foot aluminum sculpture was erected in 1973 at the corner of Adams and Leigh Streets, where the dancer had donated a traffic light to help local children cross in safety.

The Fan

Full of thrift shops, worn-in apartments, and combination deli-launderettes that cater to students of Virginia Commonwealth University (VCU), the Fan is one of the largest intact Victorian neighborhoods in the country. The Fan takes it name from the way the streets spoke out from Monroe Park at the corner of Belvidere and Franklin. Million-dollar mansions and renovated early-1900s townhouses along Monument Avenue contrast with funky pastel buildings along Main Street west toward Carytown, with rooftop gardens and cobblestone alleys adding an extra touch of character. North of the I-95 downtown expressway, the Fan turns purely residential, with brightly painted houses along tree-lined streets.

MONUMENT AVENUE

The northern border of the Fan has been called one of the most beautiful boulevards in the world, and even if statue-happy Richmond has you worn down already, it is impressive. Huge likenesses of Confederate heroes—with one notable exception—pose on raised platforms, each surrounded by a traffic circle and linked to the next by grassy medians. **J. E. B. Stuart** sports his trademark plumed hat at Monument Avenue and Lombardy Street, followed by **Robert E. Lee** at Allen Avenue and **Jefferson Davis** at Davis Street. **Stonewall Jackson** faces boldly north at Boulevard, and **Matthew Fontaine Maury,** the father of modern oceanography, stands at Belmont Avenue. (Ironically, Maury's work helped the Union blockade seal up the Southern coast during the Civil War.)

Monument Avenue's latest addition almost didn't make it. Born in Richmond in 1943, **Arthur Ashe Jr.** began playing tennis at age seven and went on to win the U.S. Open and Wimbledon, becoming the first black man to receive a number-one international ranking. After retiring, Ashe used his fame to promote black athletics and education, even writing

Monument Avenue

a book about the history of black athletes. Controversy surrounded the decision to erect Ashe's likeness in such traditional company, but it was unveiled in 1996 nonetheless. The statue renders him offering a tennis racket and book to children reaching up at his feet.

Fittingly, Monument Avenue is home to the **Virginia Center for Architecture** (2501 Monument Ave., 804/644-3041, www.virginiaarchitecture.org, 10 A.M.–5 P.M. Tues.–Fri., 1–5 P.M. Sat.–Sun., $2), one of the few architecture museums in the United States. A learning center, gift shop, and exhibitions on topics like modern prefabs and livable communities fill a Tudor Revival mansion designed by John Russell Pope.

South of the Fan

BYRD PARK

Three lakes, picnic shelters, sports fields, trails, and tennis courts fill one of Richmond's most popular parks, along Boulevard south of I-195. During the summer you can rent pedalboats on Boat Lake and feed the ducks on the other two lakes. **The Carillon,** a 240-foot tower with 56 bells, was renovated in the 1990s and is a centerpiece of the city's Fourth of July fireworks. Outdoor concerts, children's performances, and the Festival of the Arts in July and August are held in the **Dogwood Dell** outdoor amphitheater.

MAYMONT

The former dairy farm of Maj. James Dooley, Confederate veteran and millionaire, and his wife, Sallie May, has become the city's most family-friendly sanctuary. Their Romanesque Revival mansion, completed in 1893, is full of European and Asian curios acquired over years of traveling, including oriental rugs, stained glass, frescoes, and porcelain. Maymont's grounds, though, are its real treasure: 100 acres of rolling open parkland, a riot of buds, birds, and blossoms in the spring and inviting at any time of year. Three decades of work went into the herb, formal Italian, and Japanese gardens that slope down toward the James River. Children love the aviary, farm barn, and the Nature & Visitors Center, with exhibits on the plants, animals, and ecology of the James River.

Maymont is run by the nonprofit Maymont Foundation (804/358-7166, www.maymont.org). A donation of $5 is suggested for admission to the house and the nature center, open noon–5 P.M. Tuesday–Sunday along with the children's farm barn ($2). The grounds, gardens, and visitors center are open 10 A.M.–5 P.M. daily. A wealth of children's activities include tram tours (noon–5 P.M. weekends, $3 adults, $2 children), carriage rides (call ext. 340 for dates and times, $5 adults, $3 children), and hayrides (1–4 P.M. weekends June–Aug., $3 adults, $2 children). Annual events start with a Flower and Garden Show in February and include a Family Easter and Christmas open house. Call about periodic Barn Days, garden tours, and history and nature programs.

To get to Maymont's main entrance at 2201 Shields Lake Drive, take Boulevard (VA 161) south two miles from I-64/I-95 exit 78. (You can also reach Boulevard by heading west on Cary Street.) Bear right at the Columbus statue and left at the Carillon (on Boulevard the whole way), then turn left onto Shirley Road. Bear left after one block into Byrd Park, and take a right after another block onto Shields Lake Drive.

HOLLYWOOD CEMETERY

It's hard to imagine a more tranquil resting place than this bluff over the James River. Acres of headstones, winged monuments, and mausoleums alternate between eerie and almost inviting, depending on the whims of weather and the time of day. Jefferson Davis, James Monroe, and John Tyler are the three most famous residents, along with J. E. B. Stuart and 21 other Confederate generals, six Virginia governors, and the first battle casualty of the Civil War. A 90-foot pyramid of rough stone marks the graves of 18,000 Confederate soldiers. To reach the cemetery (412 S. Cherry St., 804/648-8501, www.hollywoodcemetery.org, 8 A.M.–5 P.M. daily, until 6 P.M. Apr.–Oct., free, tour maps available for $1), enter

Hollywood Cemetery

off Albemarle Street. Contact the Valentine Richmond History Center (804/649-0711, ext. 334) for information on guided walking tours offered at 10 A.M. Monday–Saturday April–October.

Carytown

The 2800–3500 blocks of Cary Street, west of Boulevard, are filled with an eclectic mix of antiques stores and unusual restaurants.

VIRGINIA MUSEUM OF FINE ARTS

Richmond's most outstanding collection is on par with any along the eastern seaboard. Everything from Egyptian sculptures to Andy Warhol's *Triple Elvis* makes an appearance in the multifarious museum (200 N. Boulevard, 804/340-1400, www.vmfa .state.va.us, 10 A.M.–5 P.M. daily, until 9 P.M. Thurs.–Fri., free, except for special exhibitions). The 20,000-piece collection includes original works by Monet, Renoir, Picasso, and Degas, along with strong showings from the ancient Mediterranean, medieval Europe, and American art nouveau and art deco.

Locals rate the museum shop as outstanding, and the **Arts Cafe** is convenient for a bite on the outside patio in the sculpture garden. A complete $150 million transformation and expansion of the museum opened to the public in May 2010.

VIRGINIA HISTORICAL SOCIETY CENTER FOR VIRGINIA HISTORY

Next door to the art museum, this collection center (428 N. Boulevard, 804/358-4901, www.vahistorical.org, 10 A.M.–5 P.M. Tues.–Sat., galleries only 1–5 P.M. Sun, free) has a state's worth of portraits, weapons, tools, and books on display to catalog Virginia's cavernous past. Dugout canoes and Richmond streetcars are displayed near the library and murals of Virginia history.

Along the River

The riverside site of Richmond's Tredegar Iron Works, origin of most Confederate cannonballs and artillery pieces during the Civil War, is now threaded by the 1.5-mile **Canal Walk** along the old Haxall and Kanawha canals on the north side of the river. **Brown's Island** at the bottom of 7th Street, site of numerous summer festivals, marks one end of the trail. Richmond's canal was part of a network first envisioned by George Washington to reach all the way to Mississippi. It was extended through Lynchburg to Buchanan, where bateaux boats carried cargo in the early and mid-19th century, but the transport was eventually overtaken by railroads and the canal network mostly forgotten.

Today, historical markers tell the history of the riverfront from here to the other end near the Triple Crossing in Shockoe Slip—in the early 20th century, Richmond was the only city in the world with a triple main-line railroad crossing, which is still in use today. Access the path by heading south on 5th, 10th, 12th, Virginia, 14th, or 17th Streets.

RICHMOND NATIONAL BATTLEFIELD PARK VISITORS CENTER

The squat brick buildings of the Tredegar Ironworks, once so crucial to the doomed Confederate cause, are now the main visitors center (804/771-2145) for the Richmond National Battlefield Park (804/226-1981, www.nps.gov/rich, 9 A.M.–5 P.M. daily). Churning day and night during the Civil War, the ironworks produced 1,100 cannons, ammunition, and the armor plating that protected the CSS *Virginia.* Armed workers prevented its destruction at the hands of a mob during the burning of Richmond, and the factory went on to produce cast-iron artillery shells until 1957.

Three floors of displays contrast Civil War artifacts with high-tech exhibits that tell the story of the desperate fighting that encircled the city for most of the war. Park rangers can answer any questions left after your tour of the museum and a short film, and they sell a CD ($16) for a self-guided **auto tour,** which runs northeast of the city. The 70-mile loop takes you past sites from the Seven Days' Battles of 1862. There are smaller visitors centers at **Chimborazo Medical Museum** (804/226-1981) and **Cold Harbor** (804/730-5025), on Route 156 five miles southeast of Mechanicsville, as well as at **Fort Harrison** and **Glendale Cemetery,** both southeast of downtown and open seasonally. All visitors centers are open 9 A.M.–5 P.M. daily. Living-history

© KATIE GITHENS

The Tredegar Ironworks now houses the main visitors center for the Richmond National Battlefield Park.

demonstrations include Richmond Civil War Day at Tredegar (late Apr.) and the anniversaries of the battle of Cold Harbor (early June), Fort Harrison (late Sept.), and Seven Days' Battles at Malvern Hill (mid-July).

AMERICAN CIVIL WAR MUSEUM AT HISTORIC TREDEGAR

Richmond's newest Civil War experience (804/780-1865, www.tredegar.org, 9 A.M.–5 P.M. daily, $8 adults, $2 children) fills the ironworks' gun foundry. It endeavors to tell the story of the conflict from three sides—Union, Confederate, and African American—and does an impressive job of it, using both artifacts and high-tech media. Recordings and videos show how the war affected nearly everyone in the country, not just the unfortunate ones who had to fight it.

JAMES RIVER PARK

Several islands and a substantial chunk of riverbank, including most of the fall line of the James, have been set aside as a nature and recreational reserve right in the heart of Richmond. Five hundred fifty acres of urban wilderness stretch from the Robert E. Lee (U.S. 1/301) bridge upriver to the **Pony Pasture** and **Huguenot Woods** sections beyond the Powhite Parkway (Rte. 76) bridge—in short, it's a daily playground for Richmond's runners, bikers, climbers, boaters, dog walkers, and sunbathers. There are entrances to the south side from 22nd and 42nd Streets, and at Reedy Creek, where you'll find park headquarters.

A suspended pedestrian footbridge beneath Lee Bridge leads from the 22nd Street entrance to **Belle Isle,** with a great view of the Richmond skyline, 19th-century industrial ruins, and the remains of a notorious Civil War POW camp that held as many as 8,000 prisoners at one time. Migrating thrushes and warblers flock to Pony Pasture in the spring, accompanied by the blooms of Virginia bellflowers, morning glories, and Dutchman's breeches. The old Belle Isle quarry and pond has a handful of rock-climbing routes with top-rope anchors, as does the Manchester Wall, a 60-foot abandoned railroad pier on the south side of the James River near the new Manchester Bridge.

A **visitors center** (804/646-8911, www

Runners, bikers, climbers, dog walkers, paddlers, and loafers all find something to do in James River Park.

.jamesriverpark.org) sits along Riverside Drive on the south bank, one mile east of Huguenot Bridge. Pick up information on fishing and multiuse trails such as the Geology Interpretive Trail near Belle Isle, crossing a favorite 19th-century dueling ground. Naturally, floating draws the most visitors: The calm stretch of river from Huguenot Woods to the visitors center is fine for tubing, but beyond that you'll need a raft or kayak and an experienced guide. Call 804/646-8228 for the current river level.

Shockoe Slip

The Confederate capital's warehouse and commercial district, reduced to charred rubble in 1865, has been resurrected within the last few decades as a lively local hot spot. Fashionable shops and art galleries are open by day, and at night old-fashioned street lamps light the cobblestone avenues in front of renovated warehouses now holding restaurants and nightclubs. A portion of Thomas Jefferson's Virginia Statute for Religious Freedom has been emblazoned on the wall of a parking lot at the corner of Cary and 14th Streets.

Shockoe Bottom

Farther east under the I-95 overpass, Shockoe Bottom was once Richmond's oldest commercial district, replete with produce markets and warehouses. Tall sailing ships hailed from Africa with bodies for the district's slave auction houses, while canal barges and rail lines brought in raw materials for towering brick tobacco factories. Until recently, Shockoe Bottom was plagued by periodic flooding—a 1972 surge courtesy of Hurricane Agnes caused $350 million in damage, and in 2004 Tropical Storm Gaston caused another $25 million—but a multimillion-dollar flood wall now protects dozens of restaurants, pubs, and shops.

Tobacco Row between 20th and Pear Streets has been the target of Richmond's latest urban redevelopment project, aimed at transforming crumbling warehouses into apartment buildings. The unmistakable **Main Street Station,** whose ornate clock tower once welcomed countless rail travelers to the city, was restored to its former glory in 2003 and once again serves Amtrak customers. The **17th Street Farmers' Market** (17th and Main Sts., 804/646-0477, www.17thstreetfarmersmarket.com, 3–7 P.M. Wed., 10 A.M.–7 P.M. Thurs., until 4 P.M. Sat., Apr.–Nov.) has been active since 1779, making it one of the oldest in the country. Stop by for flowers, crafts, produce, and antiques.

EDGAR ALLAN POE MUSEUM

The genius of ghoul was raised and married in Richmond, spending more time here than in any other city. Poe gained his first national attention here on the staff of the local *Southern Literary Messenger.* Although he didn't actually live here, the Old Stone House (1914–16 E. Main St., 804/648-5523 or 888/213-2763, www.poemuseum.org, 10 A.M.–5 P.M. Tues.–Sat., 11 A.M.–5 P.M. Sun., $6 adults, $5 students, free children 7 and under) is the oldest residence in Richmond, built in the 1730s. It now houses Poe's personal effects and daguerreotypes of that famous haunted visage.

© KATIE GITHENS

A visit to the Edgar Allan Poe Museum provides an insightful look at the life and death of the master of macabre.

Sip a lemonade in the Enchanted Garden before embarking on a guided tour of the house, where you'll see his writing desk, childhood bed, and a model of Richmond in Poe's day.

VIRGINIA HOLOCAUST MUSEUM

Opened in 1997 by a group of volunteers, some of whom are concentration camp survivors, this museum (2000 E. Cary St., 804/257-5400, www.va-holocaust.com, 9 A.M.–5 P.M. Mon.–Fri., 11 A.M.–5 P.M. Sat.–Sun., free) offers a poignant look into the horrors of Europe during World War II. Self-guiding tours with CD players and headphones lead you through a re-created boxcar and family room frozen in mid-capture. Archives and a library are available to researchers.

Church Hill

A mosaic of 19th-century architectural styles adorns the city's oldest residential neighborhood, named for St. John's Church. Lovingly restored homes in Victorian, Greek Revival, and Federal style gaze out over the city and river. One of the best views of downtown Richmond is from atop Libby Hill Park at 29th and East Franklin Streets.

ST. JOHN'S EPISCOPAL CHURCH

Built in 1740–1741, Richmond's oldest house of worship is also one of the oldest wooden buildings in Virginia. It's best known as the site of Patrick Henry's "Give me liberty or give me death" speech to George Washington, Thomas Jefferson, and the rest of the Second Virginia Convention on March 23, 1775. The parish dates to 1611, and services are still held here. Edgar Allan Poe's mother is buried in the surrounding cemetery, which was the only public burial ground in Richmond until 1826.

Half-hour tours of the church (2401 E. Broad St., 804/648-5015, www.historicstjohnschurch.org) are given 10 A.M.–3:30 P.M. Monday–Saturday and 1–3:30 P.M. Sunday for $6 adults, $4 children 7–18. Reenactments of the Second Virginia Convention, complete with Henry's speech, are held at 2 P.M. every Sunday from Memorial Day to Labor Day, with a special reenactment on the Sunday closest to March 23.

© KATIE GITHENS

Patrick Henry gave his fiery "Give me liberty, or give me death" speech inside St. John's Episcopal Church.

CHIMBORAZO MEDICAL MUSEUM (RICHMOND NATIONAL BATTLEFIELD PARK)

The site of one of the Confederate's largest wartime hospitals is now a unit of the Richmond National Battlefield Park (3215 E. Broad St., 804/226-1981, www.nps.gov/rich, 9 A.M.–5 P.M. daily, free) and a medical museum. At its peak, Chimborazo Hospital was the largest of its kind in the world, eventually treating 76,000 patients in 150 buildings and 100 tents. Displays trace the practitioners and unenviable recipients of late-19th-century war medicine.

Other Sights

AGECROFT HALL

For a truly unique house tour, visit this 15th-century Tudor mansion (4305 Sulgrave Rd., 804/353-4241, www.agecrofthall.com,

10 A.M.–4 P.M. Tues.–Sat., 12:30–5 P.M. Sun., $8 adults, $5 children) that was dismantled in England in the 1920s and moved to the ritzy Windsor Farms neighborhood of Richmond to save it from destruction. From the Great Hall to the Great Parlour, the house features period furniture and decorations and original woodwork, and the magnificent gardens overlook the James River. The mansion offers a general 30-minute tour as well as specialty kids' tours and lectures on period dining habits.

Agecroft Hall is in Windsor Farms, a short drive west of downtown Richmond. To get there, head west on Cary Street past Carytown and I-195, take a left onto Malvern Avenue, and bear left onto Canterbury Road, which curves around to the right and becomes Sulgrave Road. Agecroft Hall is on the right.

SCIENCE MUSEUM OF VIRGINIA

It's hard to miss the green copper dome atop monumental Union Station, which now houses an excellent museum (2500 W. Broad St., 804/864-1400 or 800/659-1727, www.smv.org, 9:30 A.M.–5 P.M. Tues.–Sat., 11:30 A.M.–5 P.M. Sun., $10 adults, $9 children 4–12, $15/$14 including IMAX movie) full of hands-on displays on subjects such as aviation, computers, crystals, astronomy, and static electricity. Even harder to miss is the 29-ton Earth globe of black granite out front, suspended and rotating on jets of water. (The moon, about 300 feet away, is only 1,000 pounds, and you can rotate this one by hand if you try.) IMAX films and planetarium shows are shown in the 270-degree Ethyl Universe Theater. Other exhibits include the Bioscape, Crystal World, and the Reynolds Aluminaut, an aluminum submarine built by Reynolds Metals, which was headquartered in Richmond for decades and introduced the world to aluminum foil in 1947.

CHILDREN'S MUSEUM OF RICHMOND

The *m*-word can strike fear into the heart of the bravest 10-year-old, but this is more playhouse than museum. It was voted one of the best of its kind in the country, and will leave youngsters begging for more. After dressing up for the kid-sized TV studio, inventor's lab, and grocery store, children can learn about computers or crawl through a giant digestive tract in the Tour de Tummy. For the artistically inclined, there's a stage and materials for painting, drawing, and sculpting. Special family programs year-round bring storytellers, puppeteers, chefs, and musicians to explain their crafts or just entertain. The museum (2626 W. Broad St., 804/474-2667, www.c-mor.org, 9:30 A.M.–5 P.M. daily, closed Mon. Labor Day–Memorial Day, $8) is next to the Science Museum of Virginia.

VIRGINIA AVIATION MUSEUM

Fans of the early days of air travel will love this hangar full of restored vintage planes at the Richmond International Airport. The impressive collection (5701 Huntsman Rd., 804/236-3622, www.vam.smv.org, 9:30 A.M.–5 P.M. Tues.–Sat., noon–5 P.M. Sun., $6 adults, $5 children 4–12) includes the 1927 Fairchild FC-2W2 used by Admiral William Byrd (a Virginian) to make the first flight over Antarctica, a Cold War–era SR-71 spy plane, and a luxury monoplane that carried Clark Gable, Carole Lombard, and William Randolph Hearst.

LEWIS GINTER BOTANICAL GARDEN

Patrick Henry once owned these grounds north of Richmond where Lewis Ginter, founder of the American Tobacco Company, opened the Lakeside Wheel Club in the 1880s for Richmond's cycling gentry. Ginter's niece began converting the property into gardens, which she named Bloemendaal after Ginter's home in the Netherlands and left to the city at her death. The largest perennial gardens on the East Coast include plants native to Africa, Asia, and the Americas, including the Standard Reference Collection of the American Ivy Society. Streams gurgle past wildflower meadows, a formal Victorian garden, and a typical English "cottage" garden.

In 2003 the gardens (1800 Lakeside Ave., 804/262-9887, www.lewisginter.org,

9 A.M.–5 P.M. daily, $10 adults, $6 children 3–12) proudly opened a new $7 million domed conservatory, the only one of its kind in the mid-Atlantic. It houses exotic and unusual subtropical and tropical plants from around the world in a palm house and two wings, one filled with orchids.

The gardens are at the intersection of Hillard Road (Rte. 356) and Lakeside Avenue (Rte. 161), 1.5 miles north of I-95 exit 80. The Bloemendaal House has a horticultural gift shop, and the Garden Café and Robins Tea House serve light meals.

ENTERTAINMENT

Nightlife

With so many college-age residents, Richmond certainly has no deficit of bars, pubs, and music halls. The city's traditional attitude ensures plenty of more refined alternatives as well, some of which may require dressing up. Most of the action centers on Shockoe neighborhood restaurants, thanks to Virginia licensing laws, which require establishments that serve alcohol to serve food as well.

Look for up-to-the-minute information on after-hours fun in the entertainment section of the *Richmond Times-Dispatch,* the hipper *Style Weekly* (www.styleweekly.com), or the handbills plastering any utility pole.

DOWNTOWN

Over 200 different kinds of beers grace the menu at the **Capital Ale House** (623 E. Main St., 804/643-2537). **Godfrey's** (308 E. Grace St., 804/648-3957) has DJs in spades and a Sunday brunch drag show to boot.

CARYTOWN AND THE FAN

Coffee shops and alternative tunes, mostly along Main Street from VCU to Boulevard, cater to a hip college crowd. **The Sidewalk Cafe** (2101 W. Main St., 804/358-0645) may not look like much from the outside—it used to be a college dorm—but inside it's a well-worn, friendly place that's been around since 1991. It's a restaurant, too, with a simple menu, but stick around for the disco ball to be called into play and find out why it's near the top of many locals' lists for cheap eats and fun.

On weekends, jazz floats from the intimate confines of **Bogart's in the Fan** (1903 W. Cary St., 804/353-9280), the new location of one of the oldest clubs in the area, in the back of Bogart's restaurant. The **Cary Street Cafe** (2631 W. Cary St., 804/353-7445) welcomes an eclectic mix of acoustic and bluegrass nightly.

SHOCKOE BOTTOM AND SHOCKOE SLIP

Richmond's main nightlife districts throb with music on weekend evenings. There's a parking deck on 12th Street between Canal and Cary Streets, and a valet parking system (13th and Cary Sts., Mon.–Sat.) makes access even easier. Another large parking lot is underneath the I-95 overpass near Main Street Station.

If your tastes don't run to beer-fueled frat rock, there are still plenty of choices. Across the street from Bottom's Up Pizza is the **Canal Club** (1545 E. Cary St., 804/643-2582), whose entrance is on South 17th Street and Dock Street facing the canal. A relatively new entry into the Shockoe Bottom music scene, it's already becoming known as a dependable spot for good live tunes. Regional and national acts play here, and there are a ton of beers on tap. **Poe's Pub** (2706 E. Main St., 804/648-2120) is, fittingly, a dark and quirky place, with an anti-yuppie atmosphere of bikers, wood panels, and great live music—blues, bluegrass, acoustic, and jazz.

The Tobacco Company lounge brings quality blues, rock, acoustic, and jazz acts Friday and Saturday evenings. The **Tobacco Club** downstairs draws the professional crowd for pop and Top 40 music, with a moderate dress code befitting the classy setting. Just as stylish is the rooftop of **Havana '59** (16 N. 17th St., 804/780-2822), where patrons sip Cuba libres while DJs spin. Cigar smoke (allowed on the 2nd floor) and salsa dancers transport you far away from antebellum Virginia.

On Brown's Island, at the end of 7th Street on the river, a free summer concert series has been a TGIF tradition in Richmond for 25 years. **Friday Cheers,** as it's called, is organized by Venture Richmond (804/788-6466, www.venturerichmond.com) and has brought local and national acts such as Rusted Root to town. The shows kick off on Fridays at 6 P.M. May–June.

The Arts

MUSIC AND DANCE

The **Virginia Opera** (866/673-7282, www.vaopera.org) has gained national attention since its inception as the Official State Opera in 1975. Productions are held at the Carpenter Theatre in Richmond, as well as the Harrison Opera House in Norfolk and George Mason University's Center for the Arts in Fairfax. Even older, the **Richmond Symphony** (804/788-1212, www.richmondsymphony.com) began in 1957 and went on to receive the American Society of Composers, Authors and Publishers (ASCAP) Award for the fifth time in 1996. Two hundred annual performances range from classical masterworks to all-star pops with guest artists such as Itzhak Perlman and Bruce Hornsby.

A beloved holiday performance of *The Nutcracker* is only one great production of the **Richmond Ballet** (804/344-0906, www.richmondballet.com), one of the finest companies on the East Coast. They perform at their glass-walled space at 407 East Canal Street. **Concert Ballet of Richmond** (804/798-0945, www.concertballet.com) presents classical and contemporary performances at the Woman's Club auditorium (211 E. Franklin St.) year-round, as well as a number of other auditoriums and stages in the community. Check with the local colleges and universities for information on performances by their various music and dance departments.

THEATERS AND PERFORMANCE SPACES

Everyone who visits Richmond should see a movie at the **Byrd Theater** (2908 W. Cary St., 804/353-9911), in a setting as palatial as anything on Broadway. Opened on Christmas Eve 1928, the Byrd still has its original red velvet drapes, crystal chandelier, and a Wurlitzer organ that rises from the stage and is still played before Saturday evening shows. Tickets for second-run movies are only $2—just eight times as much as they were when the theater opened.

Another Roaring Twenties movie house has been transformed into the **Carpenter Theatre** (600 E. Grace St.), with even better acoustics and lighting. A ceiling painted to look like the open sky caps a lavish array of Moorish adornments, plush rugs, and a sweeping grand staircase. With 1,760 seats, the Carpenter Theatre is large enough to host the Richmond Ballet and opera performances as well as concerts and traveling Broadway productions. It's part of **Richmond CenterStage** (804/225-9000, www.richmondcenterstage.com), a downtown performing-arts complex completed in 2009.

Richmond's Landmark Theater (6 N. Laurel St., 804/646-4213, www.landmarktheater.net) began in 1927 as a Shriner meeting hall with 4,600 seats, six lobbies, 42 hotel rooms, and a bowling alley. With an Arabic tile design in the lobby, it was known as the Mosque until 1995, when a $6 million renovation brought back 3,500 seats. It has hosted the same range of performances as the Carpenter Theatre, including Garrison Keillor's *American Radio Hour*.

The **Empire Theater** (114 W. Broad St.) is Richmond's oldest (1911) and home to **Theater IV** (804/282-2620, www.theatreivrichmond.org), offering shows for young audiences. Outdoor concerts, children's performances, and the Festival of the Arts in July and August come to **Dogwood Dell** in Byrd Park (600 S. Blvd., 804/646-3355).

VISUAL ARTS

The strong arts program at Virginia Commonwealth University adds its creative juices to Richmond's burgeoning artistic scene. Galleries are concentrated in three main areas. On Main Street you'll find the **Visual Arts Center** (1812 W. Main St., 804/353-0094, www.visarts.org), hosting exhibits, classes, and other arty events, and galleries like the ultra-modern **Page Bond Gallery** (1625 W. Main

St., 804/359-3633, www.pagebondgallery.com). On up-and-coming West Broad Street are aptly named **Quirk** (311 W. Broad St., 804/644-5450, www.quirkgallery.com) and **1708 Gallery** (319 W. Broad St., 804/643-1708, www.1708gallery.org), a nonprofit space for new art. Manchester, a neighborhood south of the river, has even more galleries.

RECREATION

Tours

River District Canal Cruises (804/788-6466, www.venturerichmond.com, Fri.–Sun. Apr.–Nov., call for seasonal hours, $5 adults, $4 children 5–12) runs 40-minute historic narrated tours of the James River and Kanawha Canal aboard 38-passenger covered boats. The tours leave from 14th and Dock Streets.

If you'd rather stroll, contact the Valentine Richmond History Center (804/649-0711) for information on walking tours of various neighborhoods (Apr.–Oct., $10). Or for a zippy change of pace, contact **Segway of Richmond** (804/343-1850, www.segwayofrichmond.biz), based out of Shockoe Slip, for a two-wheeled tour of the city, starting at $50 per person.

Spectator Sports

The **Richmond Flying Squirrels** (804/359-3866, www.squirrelsbaseball.com) started their inaugural season in 2010, continuing a strong baseball tradition that has left Richmond without a baseball team for only two years since 1884—one of those was 2009, when the Richmond Braves relocated to an Atlanta suburb to many fans' dismay. The newly dubbed Flying Squirrels, a AA farm team for the San Francisco Giants, plays April–September at the Diamond ballpark (3001 N. Blvd.).

The **Richmond Kickers** (804/644-5425, www.richmondkickers.com) compete in the second division of the United Soccer Leagues (USL) and have won the championship not once, but twice since 2006. Home games during the April–August season take place at the University of Richmond Stadium at Maplewood Avenue and McCloy Street.

The **Richmond Coliseum** (601 E. Leigh St., 804/780-4965, www.richmondcoliseum.net) hosts a wide range of professional and college sports and other events, from pro wrestling and monster-truck extravaganzas to ice shows and the circus.

All of the universities and colleges in town have their own sports teams, from the U of R's Spiders on down, that compete on campus and in city venues such as the Coliseum. Contact the athletic departments of the University of Richmond (804/289-8388, www.richmondspiders.com) and Virginia Commonwealth University (804/828-7267, www.vcuathletics.com) for schedules and locations.

Horse-racing fans breathed a sigh of relief in 1997 with the opening of **Colonial Downs** (804/966-7223, www.colonialdowns.com), the first pari-mutuel betting racecourse in the state since the 1800s. With a five-level grandstand, restaurants, lounges, and monitors, the track is one of the largest and most luxurious of its kind in the country. The fall thoroughbred season culminates with the Breeder's Cup. Colonial Downs is in New Kent, near exit 214 off I-64 heading east to Williamsburg and Newport News.

On weekends in April, May, and September, crowds of close to 100,000 descend on the **Richmond International Raceway** (866/455-7223, www.rir.com) to watch that thunderous mix of gas fumes and adrenaline known as NASCAR racing. The track, Virginia's largest sports facility, hosts various events, from the Nationwide Series 250 to the Crown Royal Your Name Here 400. Tickets can get scarce, so call ahead. To get to the Richmond Raceway Complex, take I-95 exit 82 to Chamberlayne Avenue (Rte. 301), turn left at the third traffic light onto Azalea Avenue, and follow the signs for 2.5 miles.

Outdoor Recreation

The **Richmond Area Bicycling Association** (www.raba.org) has information on group rides for roadies, along with local cycling maps and tips. Mountain bikers will want to connect with the Richmond chapter of the **Mid-Atlantic Off Road Enthusiasts** (www.richmond-more.org)

for information on trails in the region. **Richmond Road Runners** (www.rrrc.org) organizes races and fun runs. The **Richmond Recreation & Parks Department** (804/646-5733, www.richmondgov.com/parks) is the best source of information on Richmond's parkland. It organizes various outdoor adventure classes, trips, and seminars throughout the year.

As one of the few cities in the world with serious white water churning through its center, Richmond knows its rapids. The James River can hit Class IV near Hollywood Cemetery and Belle Isle, making Richmond enough of a **white-water rafting** destination that many people live here just to paddle. Milder sections of the James welcome paddlers and tubers during the March–November season.

For the full experience, book a guided raft, kayak, or canoe trip with **Riverside Outfitters** (6836 Old Westham Rd., 804/560-0068, www.riversideoutfitters.net, $45–80 pp), which operates year-round. The best white water, though, is usually during November–May. Another outfitter running Richmond trips is **River City Rafting** (100 Stockton St., 804/232-7238, www.rivercityraft.com). Two- to four-hour trips go for $55–65 and four- to six-hour trips with a catered lunch cost $70–80. River City also rents tubes for $22 per person.

Providing a totally different perspective of the river—from above—Riverside Outfitters also offers tree-climbing expeditions along the James with a certified arborist. Trips can include harnessed walks along tree limbs, zip lines, and plunging tree swings. Prices vary, but for example a two-hour outing with five climbers starts at $150 per person.

SHOPPING

Funky gift, thrift, and clothing shops share space in Carytown with pricey boutiques and stores selling housewares and furniture (www.carytownrva.org). Drop in on places such as **World of Mirth** (3005 W. Cary St., 804/353-8991) for a taste of the kitschy and the unusual and plenty of cool stuff for kids. **Bygones Vintage Clothing** (2916 W. Cary St., 804/353-1919) sells vintage clothing, jewelry, and art next to the Byrd Theater. **Pink** (3158 W. Cary St., 804/358-0884) stocks funky-casual women's clothing.

For new, used, and rare books on all things American, Southern, and Virginian, stop by **Owens & Ramsey Booksellers** (2728 Tinsley Dr., 804/272-8888). They also have a selection of maps and fine-art prints. Find many more titles on the shelves at **The Fountain Bookstore** (1312 E. Cary St., 804/788-1594) in Shockoe Slip.

The HGTV set shouldn't miss **Caravati's** (104 E. 2nd St., 804/232-4175, www.caravatis.com), Richmond's oldest supplier of architectural salvage. Caravati's 40,000-square-foot warehouse in the Manchester neighborhood has every scrap of old houses imaginable, from brass doorknobs to stained-glass skylights.

EVENTS

April's **Easter on Parade** fills Monument Avenue with an old-fashioned parade, carnival rides, and jazz, blues, and Dixieland music. May brings Richmond's rite of spring: the **Strawberry Hill Races,** a steeplechase event and so much more. Citywide carriage parades and balls get everyone in the mood for the extravagant tailgate parties on the day of the races, some of which are so elaborate there's a competition for the best theme and costumes. All proceeds go to charity.

May's perfect softball weather also ushers in the **Round Robin Softball Tournament,** said to be the largest in the world. More than 400 teams from 20 states compete on Memorial Day weekend in parks around the city.

The second weekend in August, the **Carytown Watermelon Festival** fills nine blocks of Carytown with melons and music. The next weekend is the **Down Home Family Reunion,** with African dancing and music and "down-home" food in Abner Clay Park.

Everything that makes fairs great—rides, livestock exhibits, fattening food, the circus—can be enjoyed for 10 days in late September at the **State Fair of Virginia** at the Meadow Event Park next to Kings Dominion at exit

98 of I-95. Check www.statefairva.org for updates.

In early October the **Second Street Festival** celebrates Jackson Ward's African American heritage with theater, soul food, vendors, and ragtime and gospel music. More soulful music comes to the waterfront in October at the **Richmond Folk Festival** (www.richmondfolkfestival.com), a three-day event with six stages of ongoing music and dance performances, ethnic food, and folk art.

The December holidays bring open houses at historic homes like Maymont and the Lewis Ginter Botanical Gardens. Area boats are festooned with lights during the **James River Parade of Lights** in mid-December. A local favorite is the **Grand Illumination** of the tree and holiday displays at the James Center downtown, accompanied by choral concerts and wagon rides. Richmonders are also fond of the **Tackiest Christmas Decorations Tour,** which links places so gaudy they stop traffic. Look in the *Richmond Times-Dispatch* or online in late November or early December for a map.

ACCOMMODATIONS

A construction boom in the 1980s resulted in a city with 16,000 rooms in hotels and motels. The most distinctive—and expensive—lodgings congregate downtown, led by the magnificent Jefferson hotel. More generic options scatter into the Greater Richmond area, with a concentration near the Richmond International Airport.

Under $100

A little farther out of downtown there's an **Econo Lodge** (8350 Brook Rd., 804/262-7070, $55–65) next to the Hungary Brook Shopping Center. All the rooms at **Extended StayAmerica** (6811 Paragon Pl., 804/285-2065, $70) and **Homestead Studio Suites** (241 Arboretum Pl., 804/272-1800, $75) have kitchens for longer stays.

$100-150

This price range offers you more choices downtown. A row of 1840 Greek Revival townhouses has been converted into the lovely **Linden Row Inn** (100 E. Franklin St., 804/783-7000 or 800/348-7424, www.lindenrowinn.com). Period Victorian furnishings decorate the 63 rooms ($120–170) and seven parlor suites ($270), and guests have access to the first-class sport facilities of a YMCA a few blocks away. Garden rooms are in a restored carriage house dating to the late 1800s. According to local legend, the gardens that stood here in the 19th century were the "enchanted garden" that Poe mentions in his poem "to Helen."

Chain hotels downtown are represented by a **Holiday Inn Express** (201 E. Cary St., 804/788-1600, $100–150).

$150-200

In the Fan district, the **William Miller House** (1129 Floyd Ave., 804/254-2928, www.williammillerhouse.com, $190–210, two-night minimum on weekends) occupies a Greek Revival home built in 1869. The current owners, Patricia and Mike, have kept the marble mantels and period window glass but renovated just about everything else, and they serve a "killer" breakfast. Resident cockapoo Nuggett welcomes visitors to the two guest rooms.

The 361 rooms at the **Omni Richmond Hotel** (100 S. 12th St., 804/344-7000, $140–260) fill 19 stories overlooking the canal and river. It has a heated indoor-outdoor pool, a restaurant, and a deli.

$200-250

A step up in luxury and a step down in size is the **Berkeley Hotel** (1200 E. Cary St., 804/780-1300 or 888/780-4422, www.berkeleyhotel.com, $155–200). This small European-style place in the heart of Shockoe Slip earned the AAA four-diamond rating for its excellent service and terraces over the street. Its dining room (804/225-5105), open daily, is whispered to be as good as (and perhaps a better value than) the Jefferson's hallowed Lemaire.

The **Richmond Marriott** (500 E. Broad St. at 5th, 804/643-3400, $140–240) offers guests spa facilities, a sun deck, and exercise rooms near the Convention Center and Coliseum.

Over $250

Maj. Lewis Ginter spared no expense when he created the country's finest hotel in Richmond's most fashionable neighborhood near the turn of the 20th century. Millions from Ginter's cigarette fortune went into its design and construction, and in 1895 **The Jefferson** (101 W. Franklin St. at Adams St., 804/788-8000 or 800/424-8014, www.jeffersonhotel.com, $275–400) opened in time for the wedding of the year—the union of Charles Dana Gibson and Irene Langhorne, the original Gibson Girl.

An eye-popping smorgasbord of styles from rococo to Edwardian has wowed a who's who of famous guests over the years, including Charlie Chaplin and nine presidents. After a steady decline through the 20th century, this National Historic Landmark received a multimillion-dollar face-lift in the late 1980s and early 1990s that brought back much of its original splendor.

A tourist destination almost as much as it is a hotel, the Jefferson starts with the opulent Rotunda Lobby, with a 70-foot ceiling and huge faux-marble pillars dripping with carved nuts and fruits. A central staircase (often credited, though wrongly, with inspiring the set designers of *Gone with the Wind*) flows upward to the Palm Court, where sunlight pours through a Tiffany stained-glass dome onto a life-sized statue of Thomas Jefferson by Edward Valentine. The court once featured a grass lawn around a pool filled with live alligators; today classical music wafts over guests enjoying a traditional afternoon tea.

Along with a salon and health club, the Jefferson offers the **Lemaire** restaurant (804/649-4644, dinner daily), whose numerous dining rooms have earned it not only awards for best brunch and best overall restaurant in Richmond but also a AAA five-diamond rating. Lemaire was renovated in 2009 and its menu redone to offer more affordable small plates and a farm-to-table approach. **T.J.'s Grill and Bar** serves more casual and less expensive Southern fare such as Virginia peanut soup and bacon-wrapped meatloaf.

Rooms at the **Crowne Plaza Richmond Downtown** (555 E. Canal St., 804/788-0900, $160–260) overlook the river and are within easy walking distance of the Shockoe neighborhoods.

Camping

The closest campgrounds to Richmond are still some distance out of the city center. In Ashland, off I-95 exit 89 nine miles north of downtown, the **Americamps KOA** (11322 Air Park Rd., 804/798-5298 or 800/628-2802, www.americamps.com) has 198 full-hookup sites for $33–53. **Pocahontas State Park** (804/796-4255, www.dcr.virginia.gov/state_parks/poc.shtml), about 20 miles south of downtown Richmond, has sites with water and electric hookups for $25, along with a 500,000-gallon pool, one of the largest in the region. The **Kings Dominion** theme park about 30 miles north of Richmond welcomes campers as well; call 804/876-5355 for its latest rates.

FOOD

For a conservative city, Richmond has an astonishing variety of restaurants. From cheap retro diners to upmarket haute cuisine, almost every style and ethnicity imaginable is represented among hundreds of eateries. You might even detect a postmodern jab at the city's slowly eroding traditionalism in places that mix the traditional with the irreverent.

Snacks and Cafés

One of the few vegetarian *and* vegan menus in the city is found in the Fan at the **Harrison Street Coffee Shop** (402 N. Harrison St., 804/359-8060, breakfast and lunch Mon.–Fri.) along with bottomless cups of coffee and space for local artists, musicians, and poets to display their talents. Soups, salads, and sandwiches are all inexpensive here.

The **Strawberry Street Cafe** (421 N. Strawberry St., 804/353-6860, lunch and dinner daily) is a Fan tradition, with healthy, filling food and a popular "bathtub brunch," where a breakfast buffet is dished up in, you guessed it, a claw-foot tub. Homemade soups and pot pies, great gourmet sandwiches ($7), and entrées such as spinach lasagna and Mediterranean wraps ($9–14) pack them in.

With the best name and the freshest roast, **Captain Buzzy's Beanery** (2623 E. Broad St., 804/377-6655) is a friendly corner coffee shop in Church Hill. Try a slice of red velvet cake with a steaming mug of the rich and faintly cinnamony Church Hill blend, which owner Bob Buffington concocted to reflect the diversity of the neighborhood.

Near VCU, grab a box lunch ($7.70) from **Sally Bell's Kitchen** (708 W. Grace St., 804/644-2838, lunch Mon.–Fri.), a redbrick landmark that's been doling them out since 1924. Southern fare is the time-tested rule, including deviled eggs, chicken salad, and upside-down cupcakes.

In Shockoe Bottom, all of the things that make a classic diner—table jukeboxes, breakfast all day, and the Rochester Garbage Plate—come together in the endearing '50s throwback called the **River City Diner** (7 N. 17th St., 804/644-9418, all meals Tues.–Sat., breakfast and lunch Sun.–Mon.).

The **Café Gutenberg** (1700 E. Main St., 804/497-5000, lunch and brunch daily, dinner Wed.–Sun.) has evolved from Shockoe Bottom's beloved three-in-one coffee shop–wine bar–bookstore into a true restaurant, owned by the chefs who cook in it. While the bookshelves are gone, the café still serves Illy coffee, only now with a new slogan: "Brunch all day for carnivores and vegans." Try the pumpkin spice waffle, the braised pork lettuce wraps, or whatever else strikes your fancy (entrées $12–17).

Casual

Look for the big sun over the outdoor patio in Carytown to find **Nacho Mama's** (3449 W. Cary St., 804/358-6262, lunch and dinner daily), serving Richmond's best burrito along with combo dinners ($9–15) and a mouthwatering Mexican crab cake platter. Lunch specials are around $6–7, along with a few vegetarian options and the requisite range of margaritas.

In the Fan District, **The White Dog** (2329 W. Main St., 804/340-1975, dinner Tues.–Sun.) is known for its regional American cuisine and amiable waitstaff. Entrées run $14–28, with vegetarian and seafood specials offered daily and 10 beers on tap. Meat lovers will enjoy Max's Carnivore Special, named for owner Barry Pruitt's dog, a rescue from the Richmond SPCA. The bread pudding, a secret recipe that transforms ordinary baguettes into caramelly, whiskey-spiked goodness, draws particularly rave reviews.

Also in the Fan, **Edo's Squid** (411 N. Harrison St., 804/864-5488, lunch and dinner daily) is an Italian joint tucked away up a flight of rickety stairs. Known for sparse service and standout food, Edo's makes a mean eggplant parmesan and a to-die-for rockfish ($8–15). The chalkboard specials are consistently good too, though a bit pricier (up to $24). Make reservations if you can, or arrive early—the cozy tables get packed.

The **Richbrau Brewing Company** (1214 E. Cary St., 804/644-3018, lunch and dinner daily) owns the distinction of being the first brewpub to open in Richmond. It's classier than you might think, with everything from beer-battered fish-and-chips to filet mignon ($10–28) to go along with the homemade beers. Try a Big Nasty Porter (it's not so bad) or the Old Nick Pale Ale. They also make root beer and cream soda, and there's a bar and pool room upstairs.

Despite an unfortunate location right under the I-95 overpass, **Bottoms Up Pizza** (1700 Dock St., 804/644-4400, lunch and dinner daily) thrives thanks to outstanding pizza with thick sourdough crusts, served inside or on two open decks. Try one of the specialty pies like the Remocaldo Renegade, with crabmeat, spinach, and artichoke hearts, to learn why this place keeps getting voted the best pizzeria in the city (a large pie costs $22.50–25.50). Upstairs, with its pink-lit bar, is a popular place to meet for a late-night bite before hitting the Shockoe scene.

Millie's Diner (2603 E. Main St. at 26th St., 804/643-5512, lunch and dinner Tues.–Sun., brunch Sat.–Sun.) puts a gourmet spin on countertop meals, with great lunch sandwiches ($7–11) and dinner entrées ($18–28) like Thai spicy shrimp and pork osso bucco with corn pudding. Once a lunch spot for tobacco-plant workers on the edge of Shockoe Bottom, Millie's was reborn in 1989 as a place for "good food served right." It's still definitely a diner—there's a jukebox on the counter and the grill sizzles right next to the door—but the superb food guarantees you'll have to wait for a table if you don't show up early, especially for brunch. The 44-seat restaurant serves as many as 350 people on any given Sunday.

Upscale

Stone lions flank the entrance of **Peking Pavilion** (1302 E. Cary St., 804/649-8888, lunch and dinner daily), an elegant Chinese dining room in Shockoe Slip that's packed at lunch (specials are $6–9) and often at dinner as well. Dinner specials like Peking duck ($10–25) are worth every penny.

Even if only to peek inside, check out **The Tobacco Company** (1201 E. Cary St., 804/782-9555, lunch and dinner daily). Dim light, wicker chairs, iron scrollwork, a wooden cigar-shop Indian, and plenty of plants evoke Richmond's early-1900s heyday when this restaurant began as a tobacco warehouse. The Victorian lounge on the 1st floor is great for an afternoon drink and the "Contemporary American" menu is heavy on the seafood, beef, and veal, with a tasty four-seafood pasta ($16–36).

It's only a short walk to Shockoe Bottom to **Julep's** (1719–21 E. Franklin St., 804/377-3968, dinner Mon.–Sat.), specializing in "New Southern Cuisine." Housed in the oldest commercial building in Richmond (built in 1817 as a lumber house), Julep's has atmosphere to spare: brick walls, timber ceilings, and slushy mint juleps served in the traditional pewter cup, cold enough to frost on the outside. Two floors of fine dining are the perfect setting for plates such as veggie gumbo and venison ($17–27).

© KATIE GITHENS

Brunch at Millie's Diner draws a crowd – for good reason.

Two hotels in town have outstanding restaurants as well: the five-diamond **Lemaire** (804/649-4644, dinner daily, $19–30) of the Jefferson hotel and the **Berkeley Hotel's Dining Room** (804/225-5105, all meals daily, $20–32). The Jefferson also offers an extensive Sunday champagne brunch, served on the Mezzanine, for $42 adults, $20 children, as well as afternoon tea in the Palm Court lobby 3–4:15 P.M. Friday–Sunday.

And many would argue the best French food in Richmond isn't downtown, but at fireplace-lit **Chez Max** (10622 Patterson Ave., 804/754-3464, dinner Tues.–Sat.), about a 20-minute drive northwest on Route 6. Chef Alain Lecomte is a Master Chef of France, one of only five chefs in Virginia and D.C. to hold this distinction (Citronelle's Michel Richard is another). Expect classically prepared escargots and foie gras, with a few curve balls: You can also get beer-battered onion rings. Entrées, such as roasted duck breast with a green peppercorn sauce, come with a mixed green salad and chef's choice of vegetable and run $22–36. Reservations recommended.

INFORMATION

The **Richmond Metropolitan Convention & Visitors Bureau** (401 N. 3rd St., 800/370-9004, www.visitrichmondva.com) operates three **visitors centers.** The main visitors center is located at the convention center at 405 North 3rd Street (804/783-7450, 9 A.M.–5 P.M. daily), but you'll find another one at the Richmond International Airport (804/236-3620, 9:30 A.M.–4:30 P.M. Mon.–Fri.), and another at the Bass Pro Shops in Ashland (11550 Lakeridge Pkwy., 804/615-5412, 10 A.M.–6 P.M. Thurs.–Mon.).

For even more travel itineraries, swing by the **Old Bell Tower Visitors Center** (101 N. 9th St., 804/545-5585, 9 A.M.–5 P.M. Mon.–Fri.) by City Hall. It's operated by the state-run Virginia Tourism Corporation, so there's information about both Richmond and the rest of the Commonwealth.

For Richmond information online, check the websites of *Richmond* magazine (www.richmondmagazine.com), the *Richmond Times-Dispatch* (www.timesdispatch.com), and www.richmond.com.

GETTING THERE AND AROUND

Getting There

Amtrak trains began stopping once again at the restored **Main Street Station** in Shockoe Slip (1500 E. Main St., 804/646-6246) in 2003. Future upgrades to the ornate National Historic Landmark, originally opened in 1901, will include bus, trolley, airport shuttle, taxi, and limousine services. The **Greyhound** terminal (2910 N. Boulevard, 804/254-5910) is near I-95 exit 78.

Once known as Byrd Field, the **Richmond International Airport** (804/226-3000, www.flyrichmond.com) is off I-64 exit 197 east of downtown. Nine carriers connect Richmond with roughly 20 destinations in the East and Midwest. GRTC buses run to downtown, and **Groome Transportation** (804/222-7222 or 800/552-7911, www.groometransportation.com) leaves from the terminal for downtown around the clock. Most high-end hotels also run shuttles. Eight car rental agencies operate here, including National (804/222-7477), Avis (804/222-7416), and Hertz (804/222-7228).

Getting Around

Richmond is served by the **Greater Richmond Transit Company (GRTC)** (804/358-4782, www.ridegrtc.com). Call for bus schedules and routes.

Local taxi companies including **Veterans Cab Association** (804/275-5542) and **Metro Taxicab Service** (804/353-5000) can take you to the airport from downtown for about $28–32.

NEAR RICHMOND

◖ Kings Dominion

Fifteen roller coasters—one of the largest collections on the East Coast—are the main draw to one of the mid-Atlantic's favorite amusement parks. Start with a few of the classic wooden rattlers, like the 1975-vintage Rebel Yell and the Grizzly, consistently voted one of the best in America by enthusiast groups, before risking gastrointestinal distress on something more modern. Volcano: the Blast Coaster shoots passengers from the top of a "live" volcano at 70 mph, and Outer Limits: Flight of Fear uses an electromagnetic launching system to shoot cars horizontally onto a darkened indoor track. The Intimidator 305 plunges riders 305 feet at speeds faster than 90 mph, making it the tallest and fastest gravity-driven ride on the eastern seaboard when it opened in 2010.

Other rides include the Xtreme Skyflyer in Wayne's World, sort of a swinging bungee jump, and guaranteed soakers such as Whitewater Canyon, the Log Flume, and WaterWorks, a 20-acre water park with slides, rafts, and a 650,000-gallon wave pool that's included in the park admission. For children, there's Planet Snoopy and KidZville, and a one-third scale model of the Eiffel Tower for a bird's-eye view of the whole park.

Kings Dominion (804/876-5000, www.kingsdominion.com, $57, $34 for those under 48 inches tall, opens at 10:30 A.M. daily Memorial Day–Labor Day, weekends Apr.–May and Sept.–Oct.) is on Route 30 off I-95 exit 98. Closing hours vary 6–10 P.M.; call or check the website for a schedule. Parking is $10.

Metro Richmond Zoo

In Moseley, just south of Richmond, the Metro Richmond Zoo (8300 Beaver Bridge Rd., 804/739-5666, www.metrorichmondzoo.com, 9:30 A.M.–5 P.M. Mon.–Sat., $11.25 adults, $9.25 children 3–11) is a little-known gem that kids and parents alike will love. Even many longtime Richmonders don't know they have a zoo in the area, so you're likely to have some breathing room as you gaze at more than 600 animals, including penguins, giraffes, kangaroos, and a rare white Siberian tiger. The penguins are fed at 11 A.M. and 4 P.M., and you're allowed to pet and feed the giraffes—one of the strangest-looking animals you'll ever see up close.

Petersburg and Vicinity

Best known as the site of the last major battle of the Civil War, Petersburg (pop. 32,000) sits sleepily alongside the Appomattox River within day-trip distance of Richmond. The friendly residents of historic Olde Towne still recall with a shiver the tornado that passed through in August 1993, causing more damage in a few minutes than the Union army did during a 10-month siege. Luckily, most of the city's major sights escaped unharmed. Petersburg is only a short drive from the historic plantations along the upper James River.

History

Established in 1784, Petersburg weathered a destructive visit by Benedict Arnold and 2,500 British soldiers on their way to Yorktown during the Revolutionary War. For the next hundred years, the town served as a popular stopover for travelers drawn to its theater, racetrack, and taverns.

By June 1864, Ulysses S. Grant realized the key to taking Richmond was this vital road and rail junction a day's ride to the south. He managed to sneak 75,000 troops almost within striking distance before Robert E. Lee caught on and scrambled to reinforce Gen. P. G. T. Beauregard's force of 15,000.

Poor coordination kept Union forces from taking advantage of an early victory on June 15 over the northern Confederate bulwarks, and five days later the two armies settled down to 10 months of trench warfare and waiting. Opposing lines were so close that soldiers on both sides could tell time by the tolling of the courthouse clock. Supplies quickly ran low inside the city, but the unflappable Confederates held thrifty Starvation Balls rather than submit. The brutal Battle of the Crater did nothing to break the stalemate.

In time Grant was able to lengthen Union lines until they stretched from here to

AFRICAN AMERICAN HISTORY IN PETERSBURG

Petersburg's rich vein of African American history starts with the **First Baptist Church** (236 Harrison St., 804/732-2841, www.firstbaptistpetersburg.org), which opened in 1774 as the earliest organized black church in America (guided tours by appointment). By the mid-19th century, the city had the largest free black population in Virginia, though two-thirds of the black population remained slaves. Former slaves who had been manumitted (given their freedom) or bought it themselves organized small, self-contained communities in places like Pocahontas Island on the Appomattox River near Petersburg. Joseph Jenkins Roberts, the first president of Liberia (1848-1855, and again 1871-1876), left Petersburg, his hometown, in 1829, and 1888 saw the election of Virginia's first black congressman, Petersburg resident John Mercer Langston. The visitors center has more information.

Richmond. Scattered skirmishes peaked on March 25, 1865, when Lee tried to break out with a failed attack at Fort Stedman to the east. The Confederate commander realized his hopeless position, and on the night of April 2, Lee evacuated Petersburg and Richmond and led his army on its final march west.

SIGHTS

Petersburg's historic hub centers on the Appomattox River, where the **Appomattox Iron Works** hunkers on Old Street. The beautiful Exchange Building, built in the 1840s as a commodities market, is the home of Petersburg's **Siege Museum** (15 W. Bank St., 804/733-2404, 10 A.M.–5 P.M. daily, call for winter hours, $5 adults, $4 children under 10). Farmers once gathered to trade and auction produce under the Greek Revival dome in the two-story central hall, but now the focus is on civilian life during the terrible 10 months before the city fell. Hoop skirts, tourniquets, and cannonballs help to illuminate day-to-day life as Grant waited on the doorstep.

The prominent Bolling family built **Centre Hill Mansion** (1 Centre Hill Court, 804/733-2401, 10 A.M.–5 P.M. daily, call for winter hours, $5 adults, $4 children under 10) in 1823. Originally in the Federal style, Centre Hill was remodeled as a Greek Revival building in the 1840s. Don't miss the nine-foot 1886 grand piano.

The story of the U.S. Army Quartermaster Corps, the oldest corps in the army, is told in the **Quartermaster Museum** (1201 22nd St., 804/734-4203, www.qmmuseum.lee.army.mil, 10 A.M.–5 P.M. Tues.–Fri., 11 A.M.–5 P.M. Sat.–Sun., free) at Fort Lee four miles east of downtown along Washington Street (Rte. 36). Everything from Ulysses S. Grant's saddle to General Patton's Jeep (with custom Mercedes seats) is on display, including the first 50-star flag and the collection of the U.S. Army Women's Museum.

Petersburg National Battlefield

Comprising four major units, this park protects Petersburg's substantial Civil War legacy. Nine and a half months—almost a quarter of the entire war—was fought near Petersburg, mostly during what is still the longest siege in American history. Start at the Eastern Front Unit, 2.5 miles east of downtown on Washington Street (Rte. 36), where the **Eastern Front Visitors Center** (804/732-3531, www.nps.gov/pete, 9 A.M.–5 P.M. daily, $5 per car for all units for one week) is located. Take the trail past the grassy knolls, the remnants of Civil War fortifications, to the massive Dictator mortar that once hurled 250-pound shells toward Confederate troops. At night, citizens watched the lit fuses arc overhead before impact. From here a 33-mile auto tour leads past 13 sites along the battle line, including the Battle of Fort Stedman and the gaping hole left by the Battle of the Crater on July 30, 1864. During the summer, ranger-led walking tours give visitors the chance to see the grounds where soldiers lived, fought, and died.

The 16-mile Siege Line auto tour heads south and west of town past six more stops. **Poplar Grove National Cemetery** is filled with 6,000 Union casualties. There's a visitor contact station at the **Five Forks Battlefield** (804/469-4093, 9 A.M.–5 P.M. daily) farther west at the intersection of White Oak and Courthouse Roads in Dinwiddie County. This spot, considered by some the "Waterloo of the Confederacy," is where Union generals Joshua Chamberlain, Philip Sheridan, and George Custer battled Confederate general George Pickett's troops, who were desperately trying to protect the last of Petersburg's supply lines.

The town of Hopewell, where the Appomattox empties into the James, was the site of Grant's siege headquarters at **City Point** (Cedar Ln. and Pecan Ave., 804/458-9504, 9 A.M.–5 P.M. daily). A visitor contact station occupies Appomattox Plantation, an 18th-century home built by the Eppes family. City Point was the site of a massive supply base for Union forces surrounding Petersburg and Richmond.

Blandford Cemetery

Most of the siege's 30,000 Confederate casualties are buried here, off Crater Road (U.S. 301/480) south of Washington Street. A set of Tiffany stained-glass windows was donated to the **Blandford Church** (319 S. Crater Rd., 804/733-2396, 10 A.M.–5 P.M. Mon.–Sat., 1–5 P.M. Sun., closed Mon. and reduced hours Tues. in winter) by Southern states in memory of their Civil War dead. Weathered tombstones date to the 1700s. It's been said that the sight of girls putting flowers on Confederate graves at Blandford Cemetery later prompted Union general John A. Logan to push for Memorial Day to be established in 1866, although this is one of many stories surrounding the beginning of the holiday.

THE CRATER FIASCO

The idea was simple and daring: covertly dig a 500-foot tunnel under the Confederate trenches at Petersburg, fill it with explosives, and with one lit match avoid a torturous siege and perhaps even end the Civil War early. Union officials dismissed the idea as "claptrap and nonsense," but Lt. Col. Henry Pleasants managed to convince Maj. Gen. Ambrose E. Burnside that his corps of Pennsylvania coal miners could pull it off.

Burnside in turn persuaded a reluctant Ulysses S. Grant to give the go-ahead, and on June 25, 1864, digging began. How Union sappers managed to dig a tenth of a mile directly under hundreds of listless Confederate troops without being heard is anyone's guess, especially with two Confederate counter-tunnels in the vicinity, but on July 23, the cramped passage was completed. It took four days to pack the end with 8,000 pounds of gunpowder and seal the shaft for 38 feet, and at 3:30 A.M. on July 30, the fuse was lit.

Nothing happened. A nervous volunteer was sent below with another match, and at 4:45 A.M. the earth beneath the sleeping Confederates erupted. Nine entire companies were suddenly airborne above a hole 170 feet wide and 30 feet deep. Nearly 300 men were killed instantly or mortally wounded.

Members of Brig. Gen. James Ledlie's division spearheaded the assault into the smoking hole, although he stayed in his tent, drunk, and refused to come out. The troops were so shocked by the carnage they found that they milled about in leaderless confusion. The enraged Rebels regrouped and struck back, firing on the clump of blue uniforms without mercy. A black Union division (originally picked to lead the attack but switched at the last minute to avoid charges of racism) was ordered in to help but found itself trapped as well. Many were shot by Confederates after surrendering. By 1 P.M., the Union troops had been pushed back to their original line after suffering 3,798 casualties, more than twice as many as their opponents.

Grant later called the event "the saddest affair I have witnessed in the war," and Ledlie its "greatest coward."

ENTERTAINMENT

The **Cockade City Grill** (305 N. Sycamore, 804/862-2537) has a big bar, karaoke, and live entertainment until late on weekdays and weekends. **Longstreet's Delicatessen** (302 N. Sycamore, 804/722-4372) has a full bar and a wide variety of live acts—blues to folk to punky-tonk—on Friday and Saturday nights.

SHOPPING

The sign says Complete Home Furnishings at the **Trading Post** (314 N. Sycamore, 804/733-4772), but you'll find much more in this salvage shop supreme. Antiques addicts can get their fix within a few blocks of the visitors center at **Woody's Antiques and Used Furniture** (3 W. Old St., 804/861-9642) and **America Hurrah Antiques** (406 N. Market St., 804/861-9659).

EVENTS

In mid-April the Petersburg Art League sponsors a citywide **Artfest** at Poplar Lawn Park at Sycamore and Fillmore. The **1771 Battersea Revolutionary War Reenactment** takes place in April as well. You can take **Hallows Eve tours** of Blandford Cemetery in late October. Call the visitors center for more information.

ACCOMMODATIONS

$50–100

A treasury of French antiques fills **La Villa Romaine** (29 S. Market St., 804/861-2285 or 800/243-0860 ext. 1234, www.lavilla.tierranet.com, $95), from a carved armoire to matching twin Louis XVI beds. A full European breakfast in the country French dining room is included. A **Comfort Inn** (12001 S. Crater Rd., 804/732-2000, $70–110) and a **Days Inn** (12208 S. Crater Rd., 804/733-4400, $65–75) are both on U.S. 301 near I-95 exit 45.

$100–150

A turret tops the gorgeous Queen Anne Victorian mansion now known as the **High Street Victorian Inn** (405 High St., 804/733-0271, www.thehighstreetinn.com, $85–125). Rooms have antique four-poster beds and brass washbasins, and a full breakfast is included. On August 6, 1864, the Federal Court of Inquiry of the Battle of the Crater was held at the **Walker House** (3280 S. Crater Rd., 804/861-5822, www.walker-house.com, $100–120). Four rooms are each named after a season, and the spacious spread includes a walnut-paneled library and koi goldfish in the lily pond. The 1815 farmhouse is one mile off I-95 exit 48B.

Also in this price range is a **Hampton Inn** (11909 S. Crater Rd., 804/732-1400, $80), just east of I-95 exit 41. Some of the rooms have whirlpool tubs ($150).

Camping

The **Camptown Campground** (22802 Campground Dr., 804/469-4569) has 21 sites for $20–35. It's 11 miles southwest of town off Dabney Mill Road.

FOOD

In the Old Towne historic district is the long-standing **Alexanders** (101 W. Bank St., 804/733-7134, lunch Tues.–Sat, dinner Wed.–Sat.), serving respectable Greek fare for $7–10 for lunch and $10–19 for dinner. The **Dixie Diner** (250 N. Sycamore, 804/732-7425, breakfast and lunch Mon.–Fri., late night 8 P.M.–3 A.M. Fri.–Sat.) is a local institution with rock-bottom prices and famous hot dogs (ask about the Dixie Dog song).

Longstreet's Delicatessen (302 N. Sycamore, 804/722-4372, lunch Mon.–Sat., dinner Tues.–Sat.) is an inviting gourmet deli–cum–music venue that sells Reuben sandwiches with house-made potato chips ($8–12) and lots of wine and beer. Dinner options include heartier entrées such as steak too. Next to the visitors center, **The Brickhouse Run** (407–409 Cockade Alley, 804/862-1815, dinner Tues.–Sat.) is a classic British pub and probably the best dining option in town. Better-than-average pub fare such as fish-and-chips and shepherd's pie runs $12–23. For Italian, go to **Maria's** (16 W. Old St., 804/862-3100, lunch and dinner Mon.–Sat.). Many of the

Sicilian recipes immigrated to Petersburg right along with owners Enza and Giovanni, who were born and bred in Palermo. Entrées such as chicken marsala and penne *arrabiatta* cost $8–15, and finish nicely with a cappuccino and a bite of tiramisu.

INFORMATION

The Petersburg **visitors center** (425 Cockade Alley at Old St., 804/733-2400 or 800/368-3595, www.petersburg-va.org, 9 A.M.–5 P.M. Mon.–Sat., 1–5 P.M. Sun.) is just south of the U.S. 1/301 bridge. From April to October you can buy block tickets to certain Petersburg sights. There is another visitors center at the Carson Rest Area off I-95 exit 37.

GETTING THERE AND AROUND

Intercity service is provided by **Amtrak** (3516 South St., 804/526-4077), which is in Ettrick, across the river on U.S. 36 past Virginia State University, and **Greyhound** (108 E. Washington St. at Adams, 804/732-2905). Get around town on local buses ($1) run by **Petersburg Area Transit** (804/733-2413).

NEAR PETERSBURG

Pamplin Historical Park and the National Museum of the Civil War Soldier

This relatively new addition to Virginia's Civil War experience encompasses a high-tech history museum, four historic homes, and some of the best-preserved earth fortifications from the conflict. Start at the museum, which focuses on the life of an everyday soldier. Choose a real soldier from a list of 13, and then follow his career through a series of listening stations that play computerized recordings of actual diary entries. Videos, life-size models, and over 1,000 original artifacts round out the collection.

Reenactors, including gunners that fire cannons and soldiers training in the military encampment, populate the rest of the grounds. Sixty yards of field fortifications, complete with ditch, parapet, and obstacles, have been built near actual earthworks dug by Confederate soldiers. Tudor Hall Plantation (c. 1812), home to ancestors of the Pamplins, has been restored to its 1860s appearance, when it served as headquarters for a Confederate general. Tours of the plantation are offered daily. Nearby is a reconstructed slave house where a film addressing slavery's impact on the war plays continuously.

The park and museum (6125 Boydton Plank Rd., 804/861-2408 or 877/726-7546, www.pamplinpark.org, 9 A.M.–5 P.M. daily, to 6 P.M. in summer, weekends only Dec.–Feb., $10 adults, $5 children) are three miles south of Petersburg. Food is available at the Hardtack & Coffee Café, and they offer a variety of immersive history programs including one- and two-night camps for kids and Civil War weekends (www.civilwaradventurecamp.org), where participants live and train like soldiers.

Fredericksburg and Vicinity

The largest city between Washington, D.C., and Richmond, Fredericksburg eases up against a bend in the Rappahannock River just below its tumble over the fall line. The home of the University of Mary Washington and dozens of antiques and relic shops, Fredericksburg (pop. 22,000) counts estates, battlefields, and a historic riverfront area among its attractions. Herb and flower gardens bursting with tulip magnolias, crepe myrtles, and Bradford pear blossoms separate trim, neatly spaced houses in the downtown National Historic District. It's a popular escape from the U.S. capital and a good base for exploring the Northern and Middle Necks.

History

Fredericksburg was established in 1727, named for the Prince of Wales and father of King

George III. Wagons loaded with tobacco, flax, wheat, hemp, and flour rolled into the port city from surrounding farms for shipment downriver and on to Europe. George Washington spent part of his childhood at Ferry Farm across the Rappahannock. He attended school briefly in town and returned decades later to buy his mother, Mary, a house on Charles Street. Trade was brisk at the Rappahannock falls, and Fredericksburg thrived for a time. Three-masted schooners docked in her port, and wealthy plantation owners enjoyed horse races and lavish balls.

Revolutionary fervor reached a peak in Fredericksburg in the 1770s as the courthouse green rang with the shouts of officers drilling their troops. In 1777, Thomas Jefferson, George Mason, and other founding fathers met in Weedon's Tavern to draw up the Virginia Statute of Religious Freedom, which would eventually become the First Amendment to the U.S. Constitution.

A century later, its strategic riverside position midway between the Federal and Confederate capitals put Fredericksburg and its 4,000 inhabitants in the middle of some of the Civil War's hottest fighting. From 1861 to 1865 it changed hands seven times, but the city saw its worst

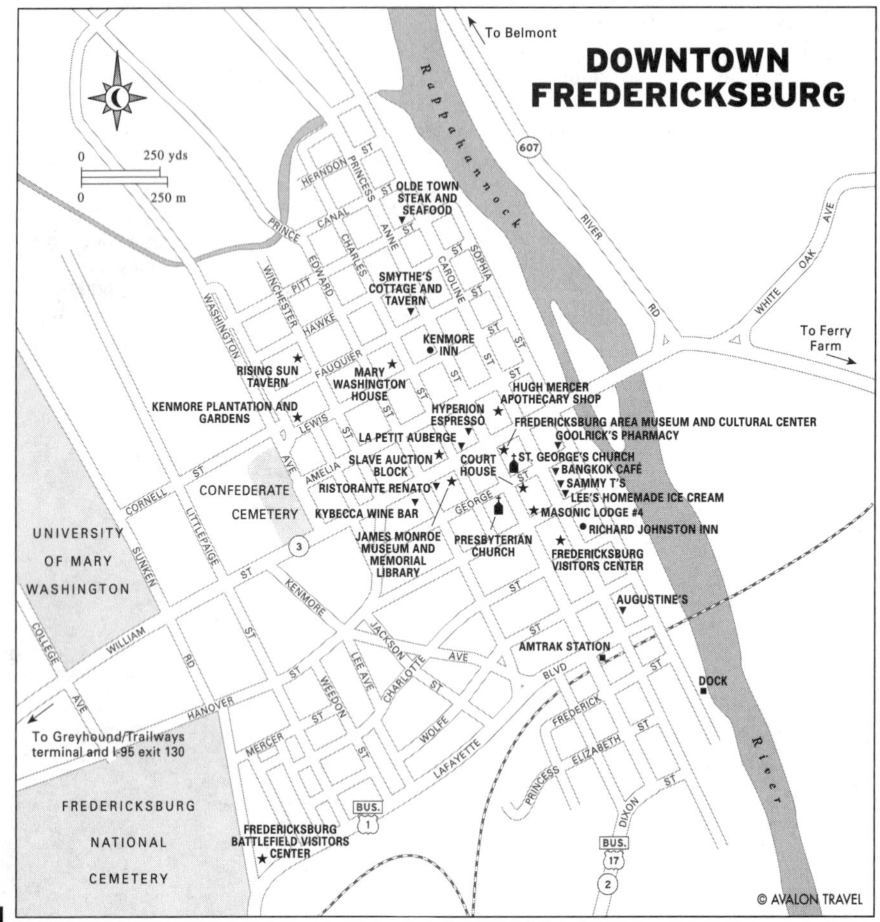

moments in 1862–1863. A Union bombardment two days before the Battle of Fredericksburg reduced parts of the city to rubble. Thirty thousand occupying soldiers found little left to loot before their officers imposed order. Lincoln visited on May 23 to meet with his generals, and Clara Barton tended wounded Federal soldiers inside the Presbyterian Church. In 1863 and 1864, Lee repeatedly trounced Grant in the fields to the west, resulting in 17,000 bodies to fill the Fredericksburg National Cemetery, part of the Fredericksburg and Spotsylvania National Military Park.

SIGHTS

Most of Fredericksburg's historic sites are preserved in a 40-acre National Historic District along the river, home to more than 350 buildings from the 18th and 19th centuries. Operating hours are shorter December–February.

George Washington's younger brother Charles built the **Rising Sun Tavern** (1304 Caroline St., 540/373-1776, 10 A.M.–5 P.M. Mon.–Sat., noon–4 P.M. Sun., $5 adults, $2 children) around 1760. It served as a stagecoach stop and post office during its heyday, when a beer cost three times as much as a bed (which you might have had to share with four other people), and the bathwater was changed after every third person. Self-described "wenches" in Colonial costume guide you through the separate rooms for women (resting and primping) and men (drinking and gambling), explaining along the way why tankards have glass bottoms and the genesis of expressions such as "mind your Ps and Qs" and "cold shoulder."

Some of the remedies at the **Hugh Mercer Apothecary Shop** (1020 Caroline St. at Amelia St., 540/373-1776, 9 A.M.–4 P.M. Mon.–Sat., noon–4 P.M. Sun., $5 adults, $2 children) are guaranteed to make you glad you weren't born 200 years ago. Mercer practiced here for 15 years, treating George Washington, among many other patients. He was killed in the Revolutionary War. Nowadays tour guides demonstrate tooth extractors, amputation tools, and the 18th-century inoculation technique for smallpox. Don't miss the tools for inducing bleeding, including a jarful of live leeches and a handheld razor device. (Back then it was thought that human bodies held 12 quarts of blood, a mistake that may have helped kill Washington.) Other medicines aren't so bad: cobwebs for open wounds, coltsfoot for asthma, and saffron to "quicken the brain."

Mary Ball Washington spent the last 17 years of her life in the **Mary Washington House** (1200 Charles St., 540/373-1569, 11 A.M.–5 P.M. Mon.–Sat., noon–4 P.M. Sun., $5 adults, $2 children), bought for her by her son George. The simple home still contains some original pieces, such as china bearing the Washington family wheat pattern. Behind the building is a separate kitchen and a small garden that's been restored to Mary's standards.

Furnishings, arts, weapons, and personal objects make up the collection of the **James Monroe Museum and Memorial Library** (908 Charles St., 540/654-1043, www.umw.edu/jmmu, 10 A.M.–5 P.M. Mon.–Sat., 1–5 P.M. Sun., $5 adults, $1 children). The fifth president was the only one besides Washington to fight in the Revolutionary War and the only one to have a foreign capital named after him (Monrovia, Liberia). The University of Mary Washington administers the museum, which holds many pieces from the Monroe White House.

The **Fredericksburg Area Museum and Cultural Center** (907 and 1001 Princess Anne St., 540/371-3037, www.famcc.org, noon–5 P.M. Mon. and Thurs.–Sat., 1–5 P.M. Sun., until 4 P.M. in Dec., closed Jan.–Feb., $7 adults, $4 students, free children under 6) holds two buildings of excellent exhibits from the prehistoric to the present. See the Bible on which George Washington took his Masonic pledge and a kid-friendly, hands-on exhibit about the history of Fredericksburg as a bustling port town, among numerous other displays.

Incredible plasterwork by the same itinerant artist who decorated Mount Vernon is just one highlight of the **Kenmore Plantation and Gardens** (1201 Washington Ave., 540/373-3381, www.kenmore.org, 10 A.M.–5 P.M. daily Mar.–Oct., until 4 P.M. Nov.–Dec., closed Jan.–Feb., $8 adults, free children under 6). One of the rooms in the elegant 18th-century mansion, built for George Washington's brother-in-law and his wife, is considered one of the 100 most beautiful in the country. A wide lawn balances the elaborate boxwood gardens behind. Stop by the kitchen for a nip of tea and a cookie.

A few other buildings in downtown Fredericksburg are worth a visit, starting with the Greek Revival **Presbyterian Church** at George and Princess Anne Streets. Built in 1833, it still has a cannonball from the Union barrage embedded in one wall. **St. George's Episcopal Church,** on Princess Anne Street between George and William Streets, has three Tiffany windows. Union troops set up temporary barracks in the basement of the Victorian Gothic **courthouse** across George Street and watched the nearby battles from its cupola.

Colonial ladies once mounted horses from the small **slave auction block** at the corner of Charles and William Streets, and the

horse-chestnut tree on Faquier Street between Charles and Edward is the only one left of 13 planted by George Washington to symbolize the original states.

RECREATION

Outdoor Recreation

The **Virginia Outdoor Center** (3219 Fall Hill Ave., 540/371-5085, www.playva.com) arranges instruction, rentals, and guiding in everything from canoeing and kayaking to backpacking and fly fishing. They'll rent you an inner tube for the Rappahannock for $17–20 and teach you rock climbing for $90. For more paddle sports, check with **Clore Brothers Outfitters** (5927 River Rd., 540/786-7749, www.clorebros.com), where canoe and kayak rentals are $35–60 for one day and $65–130 for two days, including all relevant gear and transportation to the put-in spot.

Tours

Jane Beale's **Living History Company** (904 Princess Anne St., Ste. C7, 540/899-1776, www.historyexperiences.com) leads a wide range of guided tours, from daylight history walks to lantern-lit "Phantoms of Fredericksburg" excursions. Town tours—sorry, "first-person custom driving experiences"—are $15 adults and $10 children, led by professional actors in character; battlefield rambles cost $60–120 for 2–4 hours. Buy tickets at the visitors center for **Trolley Tours of Fredericksburg** (706 Caroline St., 540/898-0737 or 800/979-3370, www.fredericksburgtrolley.com), which cover the major sights in town and on the battlefield in an hour and 15 minutes. These tours ($17 adults, $6 children 6–16) leave from the visitors center four times daily June–October, twice daily the rest of the year, and once in the evenings June–September.

Horse-drawn carriage tours with the **Old Time Carriage Company** (540/371-0094, www.oldetownecarriages.com) range from private evening jaunts to daily outings in the historic town center. Contact them for a schedule and their latest rates. Hop aboard the 100-foot paddle wheeler ***City of Fredericksburg*** (804/453-2628, www.tangiercruise.com) for lunch ($26 adults, $16.50 children), dinner ($38/$23.50), and brunch ($33.50/$21) cruises, leaving Tuesday–Sunday May–October from City Dock on Sophia Street. They also offer Sunday brunch ($33.50/$21) and Friday-night dinner/dancing ($45/$27) cruises. Reservations are recommended.

SHOPPING

You could outfit a mansion (or a brigade) with all the antiques and Civil War artifacts for sale along Caroline Street. The Downtown Retail Merchants of Fredericksburg keeps a listing of stores on its website (www.downtownfred.com) under the neat summary: "Eighteen blocks of shopping and the rest is history."

Try the **Picket Post** (602 Caroline St., 540/371-7703) or **Way Back When** (918 Caroline St., 540/371-7841) for starters. Every Saturday morning during the growing season you can procure seasonal produce from the **Fredericksburg Farmers Market** in Hurkamp Park at Williams and Prince Edward Streets. For crafts and antiques, try the **Manor Mart Flea Market** (540/898-4685), open on weekends only along U.S. 1 just south of town.

At the **Art First Gallery & Studios** (824 Caroline St., 540/371-7107), you can peruse the works of local artists and buy whatever catches your fancy. Works by potter Dan Finnegan and a few dozen other local artists are available at the **LibertyTown Arts Workshop** (916 Liberty St., 540/371-7255). LibertyTown also offers summer arts classes. **The Copper Shop** (1707-B Princess Anne St., 540/371-4455) specializes in the handcrafted Fredericksburg lamp, a glass and candle creation made by local coppersmiths Allen H. Green II and III.

EVENTS

Fredericksburg's **Heritage Festival** around the Fourth of July brings live music, crafts, food, and a raft race on the river. The story of October's **Dog Festival** begins in pre-Revolutionary days, when Indians were said to have traded furs for the settlers' exotic animals.

Revived in 1927, it's evolved into a small event with music, food, and a dog parade.

ACCOMMODATIONS

$50-100

There's a **Quality Inn** (543 Warrenton Rd., 540/373-0000, $60–85) near the intersection of U.S. 17 and I-95, and the **Best Western Central Plaza** (3000 Plank Rd., 540/786-7404, $60–100) sits next to the Spotsylvania Mall. Fountains, flags, and kites decorate the atrium of the **Ramada Inn South** (5324 Jefferson Davis Hwy., 540/898-1102, $50–100), which has a sauna, exercise room, and a heated indoor pool.

Over $100

The **Kenmore Inn** (1200 Princess Anne St., 540/371-7622, www.kenmoreinn.com, $130–175) dates back to the early 1800s. It has an excellent restaurant with outdoor dining and an English pub with jazz and blues on weekends. Guests can relax on the veranda facing Princess Anne Street or in front of the fireplace in the sitting room.

Facing the visitors center is the **Richard Johnston Inn** (711 Caroline St., 540/899-7606 or 877/557-0770, www.therichardjohnstoninn.com, $110–210), a multiaward-winning place that occupies a pair of joined townhouses built in the late 1700s by the mayor of Fredericksburg. Seven sumptuous bedrooms and two suites are dressed out with antiques such as a huge mahogany queen bed from the 1830s.

Rooms at the **Fredericksburg Hospitality House** (2801 Plank Rd., 540/786-8321), formerly a Holiday Inn Select, are $90–140.

Camping

Campers should head to the **Fredericksburg KOA Kampground** (7400 Brookside Ln., 540/898-7252, www.fredericksburgkoa.com). Located near I-95 exits 126 (southbound) and 118 (northbound), it has over 100 sites for $31–45, along with cabins ($52–58) equipped with charcoal grills, plus a fishing pond, hayrides, and a heated pool. A campground lodge has efficiencies with flat-screen TVs for $120–130.

FOOD

Snacks and Cafés

Goolrick's Modern Pharmacy (901 Caroline St., 540/373-9878, breakfast and lunch Mon.–Sat.) is a step back in time with its 1940s soda fountain and lunch counter. (By some accounts it's the oldest continually operating soda fountain in the country.) It serves an inexpensive breakfast, homemade soups, and sandwiches along with the obligatory egg creams and floats—everything on the menu costs less than $4. **Hyperion Espresso** (301 William St., 540/373-4882) serves the black diesel in an eye-catching setting daily from 7 A.M. (an hour later on Sundays), and **Lee's Homemade Ice Cream** (821 Caroline St., 540/370-4390) serves over 100 flavors of you-know-what.

Casual

It may seem like an oxymoron, but **Sammy T's** (801 Caroline St. at Hanover St., 540/371-2008, lunch and dinner daily) serves healthy pub fare, like bean and grain burgers and an apple-cheddar melt. Sandwiches are $5–10 and entrées, including many vegan and vegetarian options, cost $8–22. With more exotic offerings like Thai-style soft-shell crabs and pineapple-fried rice on the menu at **Bangkok Café** (825 Caroline St., 540/373-0745, lunch and dinner Wed.–Mon.), it's almost a shame to order the usual pad thai ($9–17).

On William Street, you can't miss the bright red awning of the wine bar **Kybecca** (400 William St., 540/373-3338, dinner Tues.–Sun.). Bison blue cheese sliders, platters of fresh figs, and other small bites go for $3–14 each, though it's the Sunday brunch that sent Washingtonians speeding down I-95 after a rave review from the *Washington Post.* The wine store next door has an eclectic mix, with 32 wines to sample on any day.

Established in 1954, **Allman's Bar-B-Que** (1299 Jefferson Davis Hwy., 540/373-9881, lunch and dinner Mon.–Sat.) is still run by Mary "Mom" Brown and serves up time-tested pork barbecue along with homemade shakes and coleslaw from her 100-year-old family recipe. Dishes run $5–13.

Upscale

A traditional take on French is found at **La Petit Auberge** (311 William St., 540/371-2727, lunch and dinner Mon.–Sat.), home to yet another D.C. chef who fled to the quieter reaches downstate. Local paintings hang on bare brick walls in the dining room adjoining a small pub. Excellent entrées such as rack of lamb crusted with Dijon herb crust and mint jelly are $10–25 for lunch and $12–30 for dinner, and the wine list includes a wide variety from Europe, Australia, and the United States.

Generous portions of authentic northern Italian dishes are standard at the excellent **Ristorante Renato** (422 William St., 540/371-8228, lunch Mon.–Fri., dinner daily). Lunch and dinner specials include side dishes, dessert, and even a glass of wine (for dinner). Most dinner entrées are $15–25, and all the breads, pastas, and pastries are cooked on the premises.

Prime rib is the house specialty at **Olde Town Steak and Seafood** (1612 Caroline St., 540/371-8020, dinner Tues.–Sun.), but carnivores and pescatarians will find lots of choices ($22–35). All entrées are served with a baked potato or fries and a garden salad.

The only AAA four-diamond restaurant in town, **Augustine's** (525 Caroline St., 540/310-0063, dinner Tues.–Sat.) occupies the lower level of an 1837 mansion in Fredericksburg Square. The setting is intimate and romantic, and the service is top-notch. Prix-fixe menus including such delicacies as Kobe beef carpaccio and roasted venison loin are $87 per person and change monthly. Reservations are recommended.

INFORMATION

Stop by the **Fredericksburg Visitor Center** (706 Caroline St., 540/373-1776 or 800/678-4748, www.visitfred.com, 9 A.M.–5 P.M. Mon.–Sat., 11 A.M.–5 P.M. Sun.) for walking-tour maps and a short movie on the area. They have free parking passes and sell a block ticket ($32 adults, $10 children) to nine attractions in the area, including Belmont, Ferry Farm, Kenmore, the battlefield, and most of the historic sights downtown.

GETTING THERE AND AROUND

Fredericksburg has a **Virginia Railway Express** and **Amtrak** station at 200 Lafayette Boulevard and Princess Anne Street, with commuter service via Alexandria to D.C.'s Union Station, as well as a **Greyhound** depot (1400 Jefferson Davis Hwy., 540/373-2103). The **local bus service,** called FRED, offers rides around the region for $0.50–1.25.

ACROSS THE RIVER

Belmont

The home of American figure painter Gari Melchers (1860–1932) has been turned into a museum and park overlooking the river and city. The house dates to the turn of the 18th century and was left untouched during the Federal occupation because its owner was a Union sympathizer. Many of Melchers's original furnishings, including a linen press and a series of plates designed to teach children the story of the Prodigal Son, reflect his fascination with Holland and the simple lives of the Dutch peasants that he painted. A granite studio holds these works and reproductions of famous portraits of Teddy Roosevelt and Mark Twain.

The house and studio (244 Washington St., 540/654-1015, www.umw.edu/gari_melchers, 10 A.M.–5 P.M.Thurs.–Tues., $10 adults, $5 children 6–18) are administered by the University of Mary Washington and open for tours. By dictate of Melchers's widow's will, the gates to the peaceful parklike grounds—perfect for a picnic—are never locked.

George Washington's Ferry Farm

In 1738 the Washington family moved to a small farm on the east bank of the Rappahannock, near a dock from which ferries ran to the newly founded city of

Fredericksburg. Here the future president, still only a child, grew up alongside three brothers and a sister and began his education. Ferry Farm (268 Kings Hwy., 540/370-0732, www.kenmore.org, 10 A.M.–5 P.M. daily Mar.–Oct., until 4 P.M. Nov.–Dec., closed Jan.–Feb., $5 adults, $3 students, free children under 6) is also the scene of two of the more enduring Washington myths: chopping down the cherry tree and throwing the silver dollar across the river. At his death in 1743, Augustine Washington left Ferry Farm to his son George, who turned to surveying for income. Nine years later he inherited Mount Vernon from his half-brother Lawrence, leaving his mother in residence at Ferry Farm until he sold it in 1774 and moved her into town.

There aren't any original buildings still standing, but excavations are in progress and the site of the Washington house was unearthed in 2008. Start at the visitors center, occupying a 1960s boys' school, which has exhibits on Washington's childhood and artifacts unearthed at the site. Self-guided tour brochures are available for a walk around the grounds.

FREDERICKSBURG AND SPOTSYLVANIA NATIONAL MILITARY PARK

From 1862 to 1864, some of the most brutal engagements ever fought on North American soil shook the landscape around Fredericksburg. It's estimated that 10,000 soldiers were killed out of 100,000 casualties on the four major battlefields near the city.

Park headquarters are across the Rappahannock from Fredericksburg in **Chatham Manor** (120 Chatham Ln., 540/371-0802, www.nps.gov/frsp, 9 A.M.–4:30 P.M. daily, free). This Georgian mansion was built in 1771 with a commanding view from the riverside heights. A series of Union officers established command posts here, and Walt Whitman, Clara Barton, and Abraham Lincoln all passed through during the fighting (making it one of the few buildings both Lincoln and George Washington visited).

Battle of Fredericksburg

During the cold winter of 1862, Union Gen. Ambrose Burnside, who had replaced McClellan after his defeat at Antietam, Maryland, pursued Robert E. Lee south toward Richmond. Despite Lincoln's urgings for speed, Burnside hesitated long enough to allow the Army of Northern Virginia to dig in on the high ground west of Fredericksburg by early December. Pontoon bridges across the icy Rappahannock were finally erected, in the face of Confederate sniper fire, and 120,000 Federal troops poured across the river on December 13 to attack Lee's force of 70,000.

Stonewall Jackson initially drove Gen. George Meade's forces back from Prospect Hill. Viewing the battle, Lee said to Gen. James Longstreet: "It is well that war is so terrible, or we should grow too fond of it." Burnside then sent 30,000 troops to take Marye's Heights from 5,000 Confederate soldiers, who were crouched behind a stone wall along the Sunken Road, and the real slaughter began. Wave after wave of Federal soldiers were mowed down by rifle fire from ahead and artillery shells from above. None came closer than 100 feet to the wall, but Burnside's orders held and the futile attacks continued until 8,000 men lay broken on the ground.

Never had anyone present seen such a massacre. "It can hardly be in human nature," wrote a Northern war correspondent, "for men to show more valor, or generals to manifest less judgment." Pacing in his tent the next day, Burnside was overheard muttering, "Those men. Those men."

A 19-year-old South Carolina infantryman named Richard Kirkland was so tormented by the cries of the wounded that he left the safety of the stone wall to offer men water from his canteen. Union gunners stopped firing at this act of mercy, and the Angel of Marye's Heights entered Civil War legend. Kirkland's deed is commemorated on the Sunken Road in a monument done by the same sculptor who created the Marine Corps Iwo Jima Memorial in Arlington.

The **Fredericksburg National Cemetery**

© MICHAEL MILLS / 123RF.COM

Fredericksburg National Cemetery

now occupies Marye's Heights in the center of the city. More than 15,000 soldiers are buried here, of whom only 15 percent have ever been identified. As you stand on the crest of the hill, imagine thousands of Federal troops swarming from the fields to the east "like some huge blue serpent," in the words of one Confederate witness, "about to encompass and crush us in its folds." At the foot of the slope, a **visitors center** (540/373-6122, 9 A.M.–5 P.M. daily) offers a 22-minute film overview of the battle (the only thing that requires a ticket, $2 adults, free children under 10), and you can also rent or purchase a CD to guide you along approximately 45 miles of a self-guided auto tour ($5 to rent, $13 to buy).

Battle of Chancellorsville

Union spirits ran low after the debacle at Marye's Heights. In late April 1863, Gen. Joseph "Fighting Joe" Hooker replaced Burnside and set about reorganizing the Union forces and restoring morale. So as not to repeat Burnside's mistake, Hooker divided his 134,000 troops into two groups and moved them across the Rapidan and Rappahannock Rivers to attack Lee from the west in a pincher movement.

True to form, Lee took the initiative and rushed west to attack first at Chancellorsville, after making the risky decision to leave 10,000 men under Maj. Gen. Jubal Early to defend the Fredericksburg position. Although outnumbered more than two to one, Lee threw his forces against the Union defensive lines. Jackson was sent with 25,000 troops on a 12-mile march to attack the Federal army from the west, which the savvy commander managed to pull off undetected. Had he failed and Hooker attacked Lee's remaining 15,000, the Confederates would have been crushed.

As it happened, Jackson's brigades charged from the woods behind a terrified horde of deer and rabbits, destroying the Union right flank. Fierce gunfire shredded nearby trees so badly they were useless as lumber afterward. The victory was short-lived, though, because on May 2 Jackson was mistakenly shot by Confederate soldiers while out scouting the battlefield at dusk. He died eight days later.

Meanwhile, Gen. John Sedgewick had finally wrested Marye's Heights from Jubal Early. J. E. B. Stuart took over Jackson's position and drove Hooker back to the Rappahannock. The Union general withdrew his forces across the river and stepped down from his command a few months later. The Confederates had won a huge victory but lost one of their finest commanders.

The **Chancellorsville Visitor Center** on Route 3 (540/786-2880, 9 A.M.–5 P.M. daily) is near a four-mile loop trail that covers major sites and can be shortened to a 20-minute walk. Historians lead guided walking tours daily in summer and on weekends in the spring and fall. Considered one of the most endangered Civil War sites by the Civil War Preservation Trust, Chancellorsville is the site of an ongoing dispute that pits preservationists against developers. Imagine the fields replaced by lanes of traffic and super-sized retail stores, and then decide with which side you agree.

Battle of the Wilderness

In March 1864 Ulysses S. Grant became commander-in-chief of all Union forces and was determined to track down and annihilate Lee at all costs. By May 5 Grant had marched almost within sight of the Confederate position around Fredericksburg. Once again Lee struck first in the tortured undergrowth west of Chancellorsville known as the Wilderness.

Federal coordination and their advantage of numbers dissolved in the confusion. Heavy gunfire ignited the dense brush, burning wounded soldiers to death in a hellish confusion of smoke and bullets. One Union survivor remembered it as "a blind and bloody hunt to the death, in bewildering thickets, rather than a battle." After two days of fighting, both armies had lost close to 15 percent of their ranks: the Federals 17,500 and the Confederates nearly 12,000.

The **Wilderness Exhibit Shelter** is on Route 20, 1.3 miles west of Route 3.

Battle of Spotsylvania Court House

Refusing to accept defeat at the Wilderness, Grant resolved to lead his army south, a decision greeted with cheers by his soldiers. Lee, however, won the race to Spotsylvania Court House, which controlled the shortest route to Richmond. Federal troops found themselves facing an entrenched Confederate army of 50,000, dug in behind hastily constructed earthworks.

"I propose to fight it out on this line if it takes all summer," Grant wrote Lincoln, but the battle was decided in two weeks of the war's most savage combat. On May 12, the Battle of Bloody Angle raged around a bulge in the Rebel line called the Mule Shoe. Twenty hours of desperate hand-to-hand combat in the pouring rain saw men trampled into knee-deep mud and others shot and bayoneted through gaps in the wooden breastworks. Point-blank rifle fire cut two-foot oaks in half, prompting one solider to remark later, "We had not only shot down an army, but also a forest."

Days later, the square-mile patch of ground that had resulted in an estimated 20,000 casualties was abandoned by both sides. Both armies, each one-third smaller, eventually moved southeast together for 11 more months of fighting. The Confederacy could not replace its fallen soldiers as easily as the Union could, and Lee's goal changed to delay instead of victory.

The **Spotsylvania Exhibit Shelter** is on Route 613. Loop hiking trails up to seven miles long pass the Bloody Angle and Lee's final line.

Stonewall Jackson Shrine

After his accidental wounding, Jackson was moved to a plantation office in Guinea Station, where he died on May 10. The building (804/633-6076) is open 9 A.M.–5 P.M. daily in summer, on weekends in the off-season.

LAKE ANNA STATE PARK

Created in 1971 to cool a nuclear plant, this lake with its 8.5-mile shoreline makes for a welcome stop during the swelter of a Virginia summer. Most people come for the swimming, boating, and fishing (largemouth bass, crappie, and bream are popular), but not many know that this area used to be known as Gold Hill and was one of the reasons Virginia was the country's third-leading producer of gold in the mid-19th century. You can tour the ruins of Goodwin's Mine with an interpreter on summer weekends, or try your hand at panning along the shore (and keep any ore you find!). More than a dozen miles of easy hiking trails wind through the trees.

The park (540/854-5503, www.dcr.virginia.gov/state_parks/lak.shtml, $4 per vehicle, $5 weekends) is on Lawyers Road between Charlottesville and Fredericksburg, west of Route 208. There's a small beach for swimming, with a concession stand and bathhouse (swimming is another $2–4 pp from Memorial Day to Labor Day). If you'd like to stay overnight, choose from a two-bedroom cabin ($79–130) or a spot in the campground ($24–30).

Charlottesville

Home to an eclectic mix of old values and liberal intellectualism, "C-Ville" combines fraternity parties and yoga groups, Colonial architecture and Wal-Marts, all in a setting that's close to perfect—the Blue Ridge Mountains half an hour west, the ocean two hours east, and farmland and winding rivers in almost every direction. It's no wonder, then, that many publications have listed Charlottesville (pop. 41,000) as one of the most pleasant cities of its size in the country. In 2010, *Men's Journal* named it one of the top five healthiest places to live in the United States.

It's a wealthy town—just head out into the countryside in any direction to find estates galore—but still surprisingly down-to-earth. Coffee shops and bookstores abound near the University of Virginia, and the pedestrian Downtown Mall teems with locals and tourists alike on warm evenings. A diverse local music scene boasts some impressive talent, and new plays and gallery shows open like dogwoods in the springtime.

History

Named in 1762 for Queen Charlotte, wife of George III, Charlottesville depended on Rivanna River trade until well into the 1800s. In 1781, Col. Banastre Tarleton raided the town intent on capturing Thomas Jefferson and other revolutionary leaders. British troops destroyed stores of tobacco and seized the county courthouse, but a heroic 40-mile ride by Capt. Jack Jouett through pitch-dark forests—on a par with Paul Revere's historic gallop—enabled Jefferson to escape.

Along with Jefferson, Charlottesville has hosted over the years James Monroe, James Madison, and the exploring duo of William Clark (born in Buena Vista) and Meriwether Lewis (born near Ivy). Although it was positioned along one of the main roads from the coast to the mountains, it remained a small town until the early 19th century. In 1822 Jefferson wrote:

> *In our village...there is a good degree of religion, with a small spice of fanaticism... Episcopalian and Presbyterian, Methodist and Baptist meet together...listen with attention and devotion to each others' preachers, and all mix in society in perfect harmony.*

When Jefferson opened the University of Virginia in 1825, the town consisted of 600 people, a courthouse, a church-in-progress, and a handful of taverns. River traffic faded after the Virginia Central Railroad reached Charlottesville in 1848, and many university buildings became hospitals during the Civil War. Sheridan's troops did little damage when they occupied the town in 1865. When chartered as a city in 1888, Charlottesville's population was 4,200.

Orientation

Charlottesville really has two downtown areas: the elbow of University Avenue/Main Street known as the Corner and the historic district around the Downtown Mall. West Main Street connects the two. The first few miles of U.S. 29 north toward Culpeper is crammed with shopping centers, office buildings, fast-food restaurants, and service stations. Often the easiest way to get from one end of town to the other is to hop on the U.S. 250 bypass, which loops around the northern side, or on I-64 to the south as it cruises between Staunton and Richmond.

SIGHTS

University of Virginia

In his epitaph, Thomas Jefferson wished to be remembered not only as the author of the Declaration of Independence but also as the father of the University of Virginia

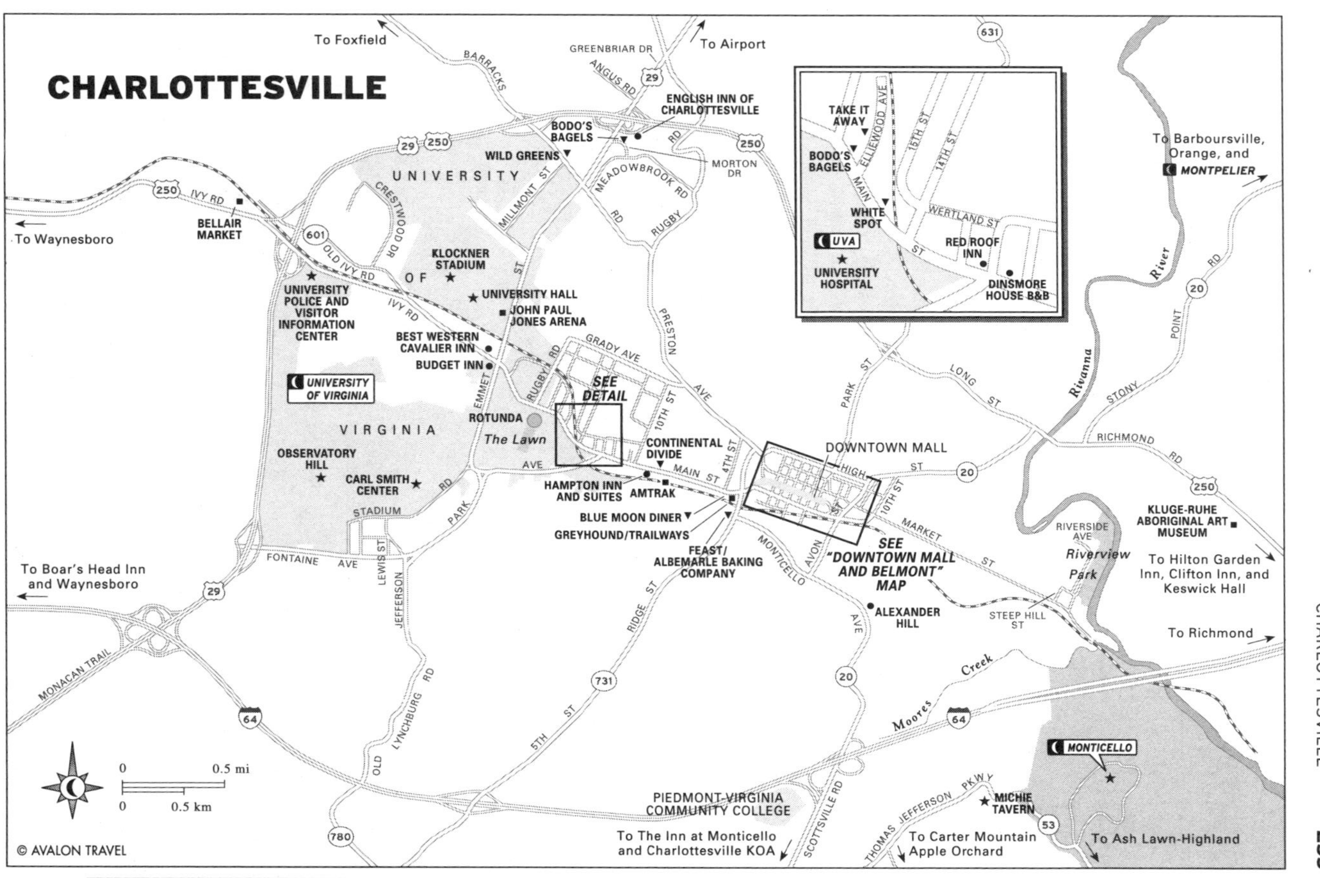
CHARLOTTESVILLE
To Foxfield
To Airport
To Barboursville, Orange, and MONTPELIER
To Waynesboro
BELLAIR MARKET
ENGLISH INN OF CHARLOTTESVILLE
BODO'S BAGELS
WILD GREENS
UNIVERSITY OF VIRGINIA
KLOCKNER STADIUM
UNIVERSITY HALL
JOHN PAUL JONES ARENA
UNIVERSITY POLICE AND VISITOR INFORMATION CENTER
BEST WESTERN CAVALIER INN
BUDGET INN
ROTUNDA
The Lawn
SEE DETAIL
OBSERVATORY HILL
CARL SMITH CENTER
CONTINENTAL DIVIDE
HAMPTON INN AND SUITES
AMTRAK
BLUE MOON DINER
GREYHOUND/TRAILWAYS
FEAST/ ALBEMARLE BAKING COMPANY
DOWNTOWN MALL
SEE "DOWNTOWN MALL AND BELMONT" MAP
ALEXANDER HILL
KLUGE-RUHE ABORIGINAL ART MUSEUM
Rivanna River
Riverview Park
To Hilton Garden Inn, Clifton Inn, and Keswick Hall
To Richmond
To Boar's Head Inn and Waynesboro
Moores Creek
MONTICELLO
MICHIE TAVERN
PIEDMONT VIRGINIA COMMUNITY COLLEGE
To The Inn at Monticello and Charlottesville KOA
To Carter Mountain Apple Orchard
To Ash Lawn-Highland
TAKE IT AWAY
BODO'S BAGELS
WHITE SPOT
UVA
UNIVERSITY HOSPITAL
RED ROOF INN
DINSMORE HOUSE B&B
ELLIEWOOD AVE
MAIN ST
WERTLAND ST
14TH ST
15TH ST
0 0.5 mi
0 0.5 km
© AVALON TRAVEL

(434/924-0311, www.virginia.edu). Jefferson planned to bring the values and intellectual excitement of the Enlightenment to America in his envelope-pushing "academical village," the first secular college in the country. Ground was broken in 1819 within sight of Monticello, where in his later years the ex-president could gaze down on his pet project. The school opened in 1825 with 68 students and 10 teachers, centered on the present-day Lawn and its surrounding buildings.

Today, UVA is one of the highest-rated state universities in the country, excelling in English and its graduate schools of business, law, and medicine. Many of the approximately 21,000 Cavaliers (the nickname comes from the school's nationally ranked football team) hail from Virginia, and competition for admission among out-of-staters is fierce. It's an interesting place that combines history and high-powered academics with a healthy dose of tradition and old-school spirit.

In school lingo, a freshman is called a "first-year" and so on up the ladder—and don't let anyone hear you call the *grounds* a "campus." The **Lawn,** the school's centerpiece, has been declared a UNESCO World Heritage Site as well as an "outstanding achievement of American architecture" by the American Institute of Architects. At the head of the grassy sloping expanse stands the striking white dome of the **Rotunda,** modeled after the Pantheon in Rome. Jefferson envisioned the grounds as a living architectural museum where students couldn't help but be inspired to learn, so each of the five **pavilions** on either side reflects a different classical style. Notice how they're set farther apart heading downslope, to account for perspective when seen from the Rotunda. The pavilions are still divided between professors' residences and classrooms, although now only a select few seniors—sorry, *fourth-years*—get to live in the Lawn's tiny brick rooms, which is still considered an honor even if the bathrooms are outside and around the corner. Many rooms have their own story—one occupied by Edgar Allan Poe has been sealed off with glass. Behind each is a unique Pavilion

© KATIE GITHENS

Thomas Jefferson modeled the Rotunda at the University of Virginia after the Pantheon in Rome.

garden lined by distinctive serpentine brick walls, designed (of course) by Jefferson for stability as well as beauty.

Free, lively tours are offered five times a day year-round by the **University Guides** (434/924-3239, www.student.virginia.edu/~uguides), whose elite ranks are filled in an annual competition.

The outstanding **Bayly Art Museum** (434/924-3592, www.virginia.edu/artmuseum, noon–5 P.M. Tues.–Sun., free) is a block down Rugby Road from the Rotunda. Opened in 1935, it boasts a permanent collection of art from the 15th to 19th centuries with an emphasis on American works, especially those from Jefferson's era (1775–1825). A dozen or so temporary exhibits get floor space every year.

Downtown Mall

Charlottesville's pedestrian mall on West Main Street between 2nd Street East and 6th Street East has become a shining example for similar setups around the country. Trees, fountains, benches, and whimsical statues mingle with outdoor cafés, unique shops, and vendors selling everything from Mennonite bread to Rastafarian incense. The controversial addition, in the mid-1990s, of a six-screen movie theater and ice rink to the west end has turned out to be a crowd-drawing blessing in disguise, even though it opened one cross-street to traffic.

At the eastern end is the big white tent of the **Charlottesville Pavilion** (434/245-4910, www.charlottesvillepavilion.com) where Fridays After Five and headliner music concerts are held. Down here you'll also find the **Virginia Discovery Museum** (434/977-1025, www.vadm.org, 10 A.M.–5 P.M. Tues.–Sat., 1–5 P.M. Sun., $4) with hands-on science and history exhibits, including a Colonial log house, a treehouse, a working beehive, and a walk-in kaleidoscope.

Other Downtown Sights

A few blocks off the mall sits the **Albemarle County Courthouse** (501 E. Jefferson St., 434/972-4083, 8:30 A.M.–4:30 P.M. Mon.–Fri.), the historical hub of downtown activity since its completion in 1860. Jefferson's will and some of his correspondence are stored inside. The **McGuffey Art Center** (201 2nd St. E., 434/295-7973, www.mcguffeyartcenter.com, 10 A.M.–6 P.M. Tues.–Sat., 1–5 P.M. Sun., free) occupies an old school named for Dr. William McGuffey, author of the McGuffey Eclectic Reader series for children at the turn of the 20th century. Close to 50 artists have workshops and studios here, which are opened free to the public twice a year through the Artisans Center of Virginia's Annual Artisans Studio Tour (540/946-3294, www.artisanscenterofvirginia.org).

A statue of **Robert E. Lee** astride his faithful steed Traveler graces a small park at the corner of Jefferson and 1st Street East, and a dynamic **Stonewall Jackson** urges Little Sorrel forward from Jefferson and 4th Street East. The statue of **Lewis and Clark** at Main and Ridge Streets is the subject of occasional grumbles for its depiction of Sacajawea, who basically kept them alive most of the trip, in a kneeling, subservient position. **William Clark,** explorer of the Northwest territory, stands at West Main Street and Jefferson Park Avenue.

Belmont

Good things are blooming on the wrong side of the train tracks from downtown Charlottesville. The burgeoning neighborhood of Belmont was first a sleepy farm and then a working-class neighborhood; in its current renaissance the hilly southeast corner of the city has come to own some of C-ville's best restaurants as well as its most progressive arts space.

Belmont is an easy 10-minute walk from downtown. Walk to the east end of the pedestrian mall—you'll know it when you see the white Pavilion tent ("shaped like a big potato chip," says one local). Loop around the block to cross the Belmont Bridge (9th St./Avon St.). At the opposite end of the bridge use the crosswalk to turn left onto Graves Street. The **Spudnut Coffee Shop,** which serves potato-donuts and is something of a

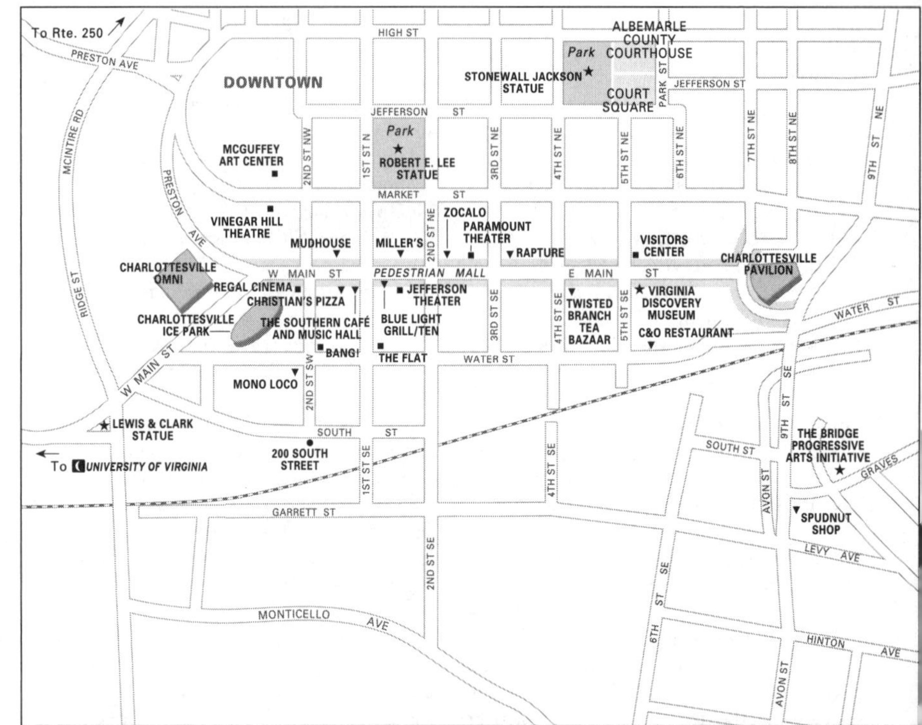

local landmark, will be on your right, and The Bridge Progressive Arts Initiative gallery will be in front of you. From here turn right onto Monticello Road, minding traffic along this one-way street, to reach most of Belmont's restaurants. If traveling by car, follow the same directions as above but turn left on Hinton Avenue (two blocks after Graves Street) instead.

THE BRIDGE PROGRESSIVE ARTS INITIATIVE

Fresh, edgy, unconventional. That's how the *C-ville Weekly* describes the artistic bent of the Bridge (209 Monticello Rd., 434/984-5669, www.thebridgepai.com), and the description fits. Silvery ribbons of smoke are painted across the facade of the Bridge's brown brick building that, by turns, serves as a gallery, live music venue, community hub, and small stage for avant-garde productions, films, and readings. The building's distinctive mural is the work of Brooklyn artist David Ellis.

The gallery is open noon–3 P.M. Wednesday–Saturday during active exhibitions, with later hours for the art space's varied special events. See the website for current happenings. Admission to its concerts, screenings, and gallery openings usually hovers around a budget-friendly $5.

Kluge-Ruhe Aboriginal Art Museum

One of the world's premiere private collections of Australian Aboriginal art—considered the oldest living art tradition on Earth—is housed in this museum (400 Worrell Dr., Peter Jefferson Pl., 434/244-0234, www.virginia

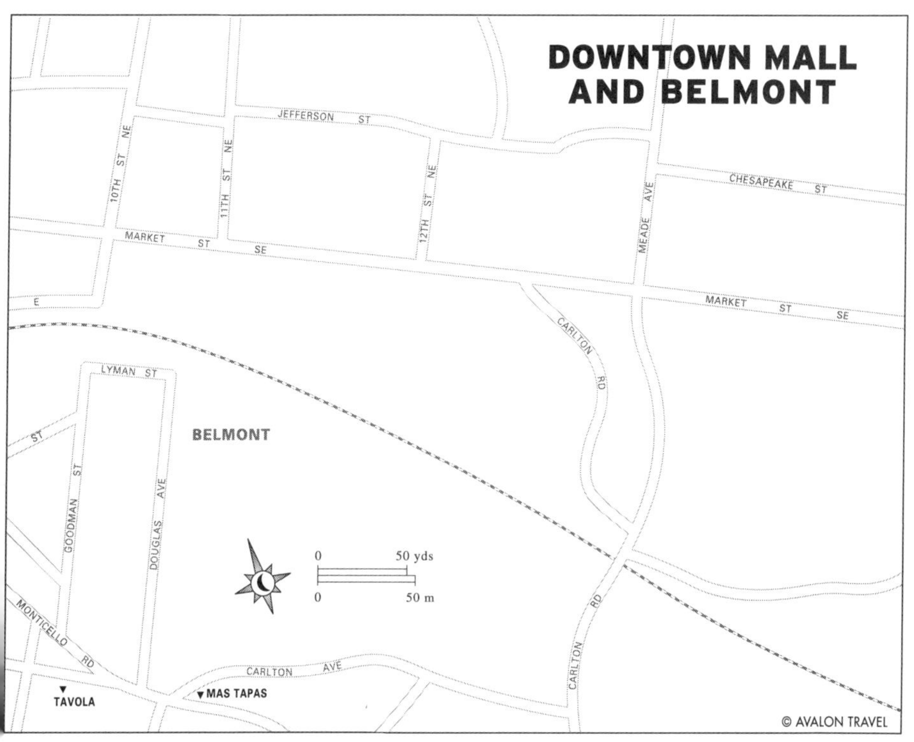

.edu/kluge-ruhe, 10 A.M.–4 P.M. Tues.–Sat., 1–5 P.M. Sun., free) on the east side of town. Bark paintings and other kaleidoscopic works are rotated on a regular basis.

ENTERTAINMENT

The local paper *C-Ville Weekly* (www.c-ville.com) and its spinoff publication *Bites and Sights* are the best sources for entertainment news and schedules. The Piedmont Council of the Arts (www.charlottesvillearts.org, 434/971-2787) offers cultural calendars on their website.

Performing Arts

Charlottesville's premier performance company is **Live Arts** (434/977-4177, www.livearts.org), with a full schedule of theater, poetry, dance, performance art, and music held in its new digs—the "enormous metal and concrete cube" at 123 East Water Street. Buy tickets on the company's website or by calling 800/594-8499.

At the university, the **Charlottesville and University Symphony Orchestra** (www.cvillesymphony.org) gives a dozen concerts per year at Cabell Hall Auditorium (box office, 434/924-3984), at the lower end of the Lawn. Shows are on Saturday evenings and Sunday afternoons (at the Monticello High School Auditorium), and individual tickets are $10–35. Also in Cabell Hall Auditorium, the Tuesday Evening Concert Series (www.tecs.org) brings high-caliber chamber music performances from around the world.

Contact the **McIntire Department of Music** (www.virginia.edu/music, 434/924-3052) for more information on performances by school groups such as the Jazz Ensemble

CENTRAL VIRGINIA WINERIES

Afton Mountain Vineyards
234 Vineyard Ln., Afton
540/456-8667
www.aftonmountainvineyards.com

Autumn Hill Vineyards
301 River Dr., Stanardsville
434/985-6100
www.autumnhillwine.com

Barboursville Vineyards and Historic Ruins
17655 Winery Rd., Barboursville
540/832-3824
www.barboursvillewine.com

Blenheim Vineyards
31 Blenhem Farm, Charlottesville
434/293-5366
www.blenheimvineyards.com

Burnley Vineyards
4500 Winery Ln., Barboursville
540/832-2828
www.burnleywines.com

Cardinal Point Vineyard & Winery
9423 Batesville Rd., Afton
540/456-8400
www.cardinalpointwinery.com

Cooper Vineyards
13372 Shannon Hill Rd., Louisa
540/894-5253
www.coopervineyards.com

DelFosse Vineyards & Winery
500 DelFosse Winery Ln., Faber
434/263-6100
www.delfossewine.com

First Colony Winery
1650 Harris Creek Rd., Charlottesville
434/979-7105
www.firstcolonywinery.com

Gadino Cellars
92 Schoolhouse Rd., Washington
540/987-9292
www.gadinocellars.com

Grayhaven Winery
4675 E. Gray Fox Circle, Gum Spring
804/556-3917
www.grayhavenwinery.com

Hartwood Winery
345 Hartwood Rd., Fredericksburg
540/752-4893
www.hartwoodwinery.com

Hill Top Berry Farm & Winery
2800 Berry Hill Rd., Nellysford
434/361-1266
www.hilltopberrywine.com

Horton Vineyards
6399 Spotswood Trail, Gordonsville
800/829-4633
www.hvwine.com

Jefferson Vineyards
1353 Thomas Jefferson Parkway, Charlottesville
434/977-3042
www.jeffersonvineyards.com

Keswick Vineyards
1575 Keswick Winery Dr., Keswick
434/244-3341
www.keswickvineyards.com

King Family Vineyards
6550 Roseland Farm, Crozet
434/823-7800
www.kingfamilyvineyards.com

Kluge Estate Winery and Vineyard
100 Grand Cru Dr., Charlottesville
434/977-3895
www.klugeestate.com

Mountain Cove Vineyards
1362 Fortunes Cove Ln., Lovingston
434/263-5392
www.mountaincovevineyards.com

Old House Vineyards
18351 Corkys Ln., Culpeper
540/423-1032
www.oldhousevineyards.com

Peaks of Otter Winery
2122 Sheep Creek Rd., Bedford
540/586-3707
www.peaksofotterwinery.com

Pollak Vineyards
330 Newtown Rd., Greenwood
540/456-8844
www.pollakvineyards.com

Prince Michel & Rapidan River Vineyards
154 Winery Ln., Leon
800/800-WINE (800/800-9463)
www.princemichel.com

Rebec Vineyards
2229 North Amherst Hwy., Amherst
434/946-5168
www.rebecwinery.com

Rockbridge Vineyard
35 Hill View Ln., Raphine
888/511-9463
www.rockbridgevineyard.com

Rose River Vineyards & Trout Farm
Rte. 648, Syria
540/923-4050
www.roseriverwine.com

Stone Mountain Vineyards
1376 Wyatt Mountain Rd., Dyke
434/990-9463
www.stonemountainvineyards.com

Sugarleaf Vineyards
3613 Walnut Branch Ln., North Garden
434/984-4272
www.sugarleafvineyards.com

Veritas Vineyards & Winery
151 Veritas Ln., Afton
540/456-8000
www.veritaswines.com

White Hall Vineyards
5282 Sugar Ridge Rd., White Hall
434/823-8615
www.whitehallvineyards.com

Wintergreen Winery
462 Winery Ln., Nellysford
434/361-2519
www.wintergreen-winery.com

or the University Singers. Likewise, call the UVA **Drama Department** (www.virginia.edu/drama, 434/924-3376) for information on seasonal plays held in Culbreth Theatre.

Closed for 30 years, the gorgeous **Paramount Theater** (215 E. Main St., 434/979-1333, www.theparamount.net), opened in 1931 on what would become Downtown Mall, was fully restored and reopened in 2004. Now it hosts acts like Norah Jones, Iron and Wine, and Herbie Hancock.

At the western end of the Downtown Mall, students and townspeople alike pack the grassy amphitheater and large white Charlottesville Pavilion tent (www.charlottesvillepavillion.com) for live music. Buy tickets for the big acts, or just bring a blanket and a snack for the free **Fridays After Five** concerts May–October and get down to everything from funk and rock to blues and country.

Theaters

Independent cinema is the hallmark of the **Vinegar Hill Theatre** (220 W. Market St., 434/977-4911, www.vinegarhilltheatre.com). **Cinematheque** (434/924-3556, www.uvaupc.com) at the university shows an equally diverse roster of films.

Opened on the Downtown Mall in 1912, the **Jefferson Theater** (110 E. Main St., 434/245-4980 or 800/594-8499, www.jeffersontheater.com) hosted the Three Stooges and Harry Houdini over the years, before taking a turn as a second-run movie house. Finally, after a three-year renovation, the Jefferson reopened in 2009 as one of the best live music venues in town—which is saying something in Charlottesville.

Nightlife

For its size, Charlottesville has an astonishing amount of local musical talent. Any coffee shop or bar worth its salt has a band booked for the weekend, if not the weekdays too. It's best known as the home of the Dave Matthews Band (Dave used to tend bar at Miller's), and local jazz guru John D'Earth has toured with Bonnie Raitt and Bruce Hornsby. Red neon and jazz fills **Miller's** (109 W. Main St., 434/971-8511) on the Downtown Mall, which used to be a hardware store.

In the former home of the popular and now closed Gravity Lounge, **The Southern Café and Music Hall** (103 S. 1st St., 434/977-5590, www.thesoutherncville.com) has risen up from the ashes as another smaller venue plugged into the circuit of up-and-coming bands and artists (tickets usually cost $7–15). **The Twisted Branch Tea Bazaar** (4141 E. Main St., 434/293-9947, www.teabazaar.com) also regularly books live music.

With its improved acoustics and sound and lighting systems, the renovated **Jefferson Theater** tends to attract bigger names like Amos Lee and Donna and the Buffalos. Advance tickets can be purchased through www.jeffersontheater.com or by phone at 800/594-TIXX (8499).

The **X Lounge** (313 2nd St. SE, 434/244-4389, 5:30 P.M.–2 A.M. Tues.–Sat.) occupies half of the distinctive glass building near the Downtown Mall. There's a big bar and hip, global food from dim sum shrimp dumplings with apricot sauce to stuffed poblano peppers (appetizers $5–9, main dishes $13–20). It's a popular watering hole for C-Ville's chic and restless.

Rapture (301 E. Main St., 434/293-9526, lunch and dinner Mon.–Sat., open until 2 A.M. Fri.–Sat.) is another stylish international eatery on the Downtown Mall, offering eclectic Asian-inspired dishes such as Thai, peanut, and dragon noodle bowls and grilled salmon ($9–20). Out front is a patio, while in back the atmosphere borders on bordello, with purple pool tables and velvet around a modish bar and dance club that goes by the name R2.

RECREATION

Spectator Sports

Cavalier football games at UVA's **Scott Stadium** are as much a display of tradition as school spirit. Semiformal attire is the norm, especially among the fraternities and sororities. Listen for the Wahoo song after each home-team touchdown, sung (or at least hummed) to the tune of "Auld Lang Syne." A strong **soccer** program has turned out powerhouse teams and sent members to the Olympics.

Soccer and lacrosse games are held in **Klöckner Stadium** next to **John Paul Jones Arena** (295 Massie Rd., 434/243-4960), where you'll catch basketball in season and major events and concerts. Contact the **Virginia Athletics ticket office** (434/924-8821 or 800/542-8821, www.virginiasports.com) for more information.

Two major steeplechase events are held every year at **Foxfield** (434/295-9501, www.foxfield races.com), about five miles out Barracks Road into the countryside after it turns into Garth Road. One event occurs the last Saturday in April, and the other on the final Sunday in September; both are full-day occasions complete with tailgate picnics, socializing, and hip-flask nipping (among Cavaliers, at least). Tickets are available via the Foxfield website or by calling 800/594-TIXX (8499).

Hiking

At the **Ivy Creek Natural Area,** seven miles of easy walking trails explore 215 acres of maples, walnut trees, poplars, and hemlocks. The red trail is the main 1.6-mile loop; all the others loop off of it. To get there, head 2.3 miles west on Hydraulic Road from U.S. 29 north, then turn left at the fourth light; there will be a sign after another half mile. Contact the Ivy Creek Foundation (434/973-7772, www.ivycreek foundation.org) for information on this and the **Ragged Mountain Natural Area,** 980 forested acres with two lakes and another seven miles of trail near town. **Riverview Park** borders a bend of the Rivanna River east of downtown. The paved Rivanna Greenbelt trail is part of the 20-mile Rivanna Trail, a pedestrian path that circles the city. Trail maps are usually available in the **Ragged Mountain Running Shop** near the Corner (3 Elliewood Ave., 434/293-3367).

Other Activities

You can carve the rink at the **Charlottesville Ice Park** (434/817-2400, www.icepark.com), even in the middle of the Piedmont's summer swelter. Anchoring one end of the Downtown Mall, it has a skating school, hockey leagues, and public skating time along with a pro shop, rentals, and lessons. Public skating is $8 adults, $3.75 children under five, with skates to rent for $1.50. Book hot-air balloon flights through the **Bear Balloon Corporation** (434/971-1757 or 800/932-0152, www.2comefly.com), which sends balloons aloft March–November for $150–250 per person.

The **Albemarle Charlottesville Historical Society** (434/296-1492, www.albemarlehistory.org) offers guided walking tours of historic downtown Charlottesville on Thursdays at 5:30 P.M. and Saturdays at 10 A.M. April–October for $5 per person. They leave from the McIntire Building (200 2nd St. NE) near Lee Park and take about an hour.

SHOPPING

The Downtown Mall has Charlottesville's best browsing-per-block quotient. Here you'll find places like **Blue Whale Books** (115 W. Main St., 434/296-4646) and **Daedelus** (123 4th St. NE just off the Mall, 434/293-7595), with used and rare books stacked up to the roof. Or **Cha Cha's** (201B E. Main St., 434/293-8553), a self-described funky, campy, kitschy boutique. Try to keep a straight face among the inflatable moose heads, adult Mad Libs, and leg lamps—yes, like in the cult classic *A Christmas Story.*

At **C'Ville Arts Cooperative Gallery** (118 E. Main St., 434/972-9500) you'll see the priced-to-sell handiwork of more than 60 artists, most of whom live locally. Knitters won't want to miss **The Needle Lady** (114 E. Main St., 434/296-4625) with its walls of high-quality yarns and needlework supplies. For a great selection of Virginia wines and cheeses, stop by the **Market Street Wineshop** (311 E. Market St., 434/979-9463).

For farm-fresh produce, visit the **Charlottesville City Market,** open 7 A.M.–noon on Saturdays in April–October in the parking lot at Water and First Streets.

There are stacks of new and used books to peruse at Blue Whale Books, in downtown Charlottesville.

EVENTS

Mid-April's **Dogwood Festival** (www.charlottesvilledogwoodfestival.org) is Charlottesville's largest. For two weeks the ephemeral blooms are the occasion for fireworks, a carnival, barbecue, and citywide parade. Mid-March heralds the five-day **Virginia Festival of the Book** (www.vabook.org), described by one attendee as "Spring Break for book lovers." In the same vein, the **Look3 Festival of the Photograph** (www.look3.org) attracts flocks of photographers for three days of exhibits, outdoor screenings, and workshops in June.

In early November, University of Virginia's Media Studies Program holds the **Virginia Film Festival** (434/982-5277 or 800/882-3378, www.vafilm.com), focusing on American films with a different theme every year, such as film noir or animals. Showings range from classics and Hollywood premieres to documentaries and experimental films, drawing big-name stars and critics such as Roger Ebert and Anthony Hopkins.

ACCOMMODATIONS

$50-100

Alexander House (1205 Monticello Rd., 434/327-6447, www.alexanderhouse.us, $40–75) is a pleasant hostel with single and double dorm beds as well as private rooms with shared bathroom facilities. A continental breakfast is included, and guests have access to a kitchen, living room, and sunroom. The **Red Roof Inn** (1309 W. Main St., 434/295-4333, $80–100) is right on the Corner. At the intersection of Emmet Street (U.S. 29) and Ivy Road/University Avenue is the **Budget Inn** (140 Emmet St., 434/293-5141, www.budgetinncha.com, $50–90).

$100-150

The Tudor-style **English Inn of Charlottesville** (2000 Morton Dr., 434/971-9900 or 800/786-5400, www.englishinncharlottesville.com, $110–150) sits in the elbow of U.S. 29 and the Route 250 bypass and offers an exercise room, heated indoor pool, and complimentary breakfast buffet.

Further down U.S. 29 (Emmet St.), the **Best Western Cavalier Inn** (105 Emmet St., 434/296-8111, www.cavalierinn.com, $90–150) is at the intersection with Ivy Road/University Avenue. The **Hilton Garden Inn** (1793 Richmond Rd., 434/979-4442, $120–160) is another good choice in this price range. It sits on the east end of town and has 124 guest rooms, an indoor pool, and free wireless Internet and business center. Kids under 18 stay free.

$150-200

A **Hampton Inn and Suites** (900 W. Main St., 434/923-8600, $140–240) recently renovated its guestrooms and is conveniently located on West Main Street between the university area and the Downtown Mall.

Since it was built in 1856, **200 South Street** (434/979-0200 or 800/964-7008, www.southstreetinn.com) has passed through various phases as a boardinghouse, brothel, and girls' finishing school. A columned neoclassical veranda wraps all the way around the cream-colored building, perfect for an evening cup of tea. English and Belgian antiques and a private collection of local historical photos decorate the interior. Rooms include whirlpool baths, canopied beds, and a continental breakfast. Rates range from $160 to $295, with most in the $160–225 range. Most weekends require a two-night stay.

Over $200

Along with Monticello and several buildings at the University of Virginia, Thomas Jefferson's master builder James Dinsmore designed and built the home that is now the **Dinsmore House Bed and Breakfast** (1211 W. Main St., 434/974-4663 or 877/882-7829, www.dinsmorehouse.com). It's the closest inn to the university. Rooms are $110–260, with a suite for $150–260 and a cozy enclosed sleeping porch for $110–160. Also on Main Street, the **Omni Charlottesville** (235 W. Main St., 434/971-5500, $200–270) anchors the east end of the Downtown Mall. It has two heated pools, a fitness center, and the Pointe Restaurant & Bar, featuring local vintages.

Take Monticello Avenue (Rte. 20) south past I-64 to reach **The Inn at Monticello** (1188 Scottsville Rd., 434/979-3593 or 877/735-2982, www.innatmonticello.com, $200–250). Built around 1850 at the foot of Monticello Mountain, this country inn roared in the 1920s with a horse racing track and swimming pool in the front yard. Twin fireplaces face each other across the main entrance room, where famous gourmet breakfasts are served. Upstairs are five bedrooms, some of which have fireplaces, private porches, and period antiques. To fill the afternoons there's croquet, a hammock, and checkers on the front porch.

The **Boar's Head Inn** (200 Ednam Dr., 434/296-2181 or 800/476-1988, www.boarsheadinn.com) is on Route 250 two miles west of town. The 573-acre country resort has 170 rooms and suites furnished with Colonial art and reproductions overlooking green hills and a lake. Dining choices include the four-star Old Mill Room, the Bistro 1834, and the more casual Birdwood Grill. Guests have access to its famous Sport Club with its Birdwood championship golf course, a top-rated tennis facility with 20 courts, a pool, and a gym. If this isn't enough, try an afternoon at the spa or a flight in a hot-air balloon. In-season rates start at $215 for a room and range as high as $315.

It's a little farther to **Keswick Hall** (701 Club Dr., Keswick, 434/979-3440 or 888/778-2565, www.keswick.com), but guests who can afford it won't be disappointed. The late Sir Bernard Ashley, husband of designer Laura, turned this 1912 Italianate villa into an exclusive award-winning country resort that's meant to feel like someone's home rather than a hotel. Hence there's no concierge desk, but there is a lounge with a fireplace opening onto a patio overlooking part of the 600-acre estate. Guests are spoiled with French and Italian cuisine, and accommodations include temporary membership to the Keswick Club, boasting one of Arnold Palmer's favorite golf courses on the East Coast, tennis courts, spa, and pools. Rooms start at $325. To get there, take Route 250 east to Shadwell, take Route 22 east for 1.5 miles, and follow the signs.

In the same direction off Route 729 is the **Clifton Inn** (1296 Clifton Inn Dr., 434/971-1800 or 888/971-1800, www.cliftoninn.net), a winner of the coveted Relais & Châteaux designation for luxury hotels. The manor house was built around 1800 as an office for Thomas Mann Randolph, Thomas Jefferson's son-in-law, who liked it so much he moved in. Each of the 18 rooms is unique, and private guest cottages like the Carriage House are all within a stone's throw of the Rivanna River. A lap pool flows into a waterfall near the hot tub and clay tennis court. Rooms start at $295.

Services

Guesthouses (434/979-7264, www.va-guesthouses.com) has been arranging stays in bed-and-breakfasts and private cottages throughout Albemarle County since 1976.

Camping

The **Charlottesville KOA** (3825 Red Hill Rd., 434/296-9881, www.charlottesvillekoa.com) is on Route 708 south of the city. You can get there via I-64 east exit 118A and U.S. 29 south, or I-64 west exit 121 and Route 20 south. It's open March–November, with sites for $26–41 and cabins for $50–72.

FOOD

Snacks and Cafés

Just off the Corner, **Take It Away** (115 Elliewood Ave., 434/295-1899, lunch daily) serves up great deli sandwiches on fresh bread that you can eat there or elsewhere. Grab a microbrew beer or bottle of wine if you're planning a picnic. The **White Spot** (1407 University Ave., 434/295-9899, all meals daily) is a quintessential greasy spoon famous for its Gusburger, topped with a fried egg and usually devoured at 2 A.M. during the stumble home.

Down West Main Street in "Midtown" is the classic **Blue Moon Diner** (512 W. Main St., 434/980-6666, all meals Mon.–Sat., brunch Sun.), a local tradition with excellent hash browns, organic eggs, sandwiches, and entrées such as chicken pot pie ($6–14). Breakfast is served all day. Down the street in the Main

Street Market, a hip collection of sustainably minded shops and eateries in a former car dealership, is **Feast** (416 W. Main St., 434/244-7800, lunch Mon.–Sat.). This café and market features local and seasonal ingredients from central Virginia farms as well as artisanal cheese and charcuterie from around the globe. It's a bit pricey—$8.50 for a cup of soup and half-sandwich—but the chorizo, bacon, and vegetable soup bursts with flavor. Perhaps the best part is you can nosh on samples of candied nuts, savory dips, and chocolate bits while you wait for your order. While in the Main Street Market, also be sure to swing by the award-winning **Albemarle Baking Company** (418 W. Main St., 434/293-6456, breakfast and lunch Mon.–Sat.).

On the Downtown Mall, the **Mudhouse** (213 W. Main St., 434/984-6833, all meals daily) is an über-coffeehouse with comfy sofas, Internet access, and live music some nights. Fresh-squeezed juices and local art complete the picture. At **The Flat** (111A E. Water St., 434/978-3528, lunch Tues.–Sun., dinner Thurs.–Sat.), you'll find fresh crepes served out of a tiny brick building near the Downtown Mall. The wait can be long but it's worth it. Cash only.

For a selection of more than 45 loose-leaf teas and a very bohemian vibe, try the **Twisted Branch Tea Bazaar** (4141 E. Main St., 434/293-9947, lunch and dinner Mon.–Sat.). Besides serving Middle Eastern and vegetarian fare, it's Charlottesville's only hookah bar and a live music venue in the evenings.

Finally, you can't come to Charlottesville without having a bagel at **Bodo's Bagel Bakery,** serving thousands of authentic New York–style "water" (i.e., boiled) bagels every day. A long line at mealtimes is a given at all three locations—1418 North Emmet Street (434/977-9598), 505 Preston Avenue (434/293-5224), and on the Corner (1609 University Ave., 434/293-6021)—but whether you're on a budget or not, you just can't beat the bagel sandwiches for $2–5, famous Caesar salads, and homemade soups. All locations are open for breakfast and lunch daily and dinner Monday–Saturday.

True to a college town, Charlottesville has no shortage of great coffee shops, such as Mudhouse on the Downtown Mall.

Casual

In Midtown across from the Amtrak station is **Continental Divide** (811 W. Main St., 434/984-0143, dinner daily), the quintessential Tex-Mex hole-in-the-wall—heck, the restaurant is in an unmarked storefront! You'll know it by the fluorescent green sign in the window that reads "Get in Here" and the throng of diners chowing on tuna tostadas. Everything on the menu is under $12 and there's often a wait.

For a quick slice of avocado and feta pizza and good people-watching on the pedestrian mall, try **Christian's Pizza** (118 W. Main St., 434/977-9688, lunch and dinner daily). An extra-large 18-inch pie costs $14–20, and the overflowing patchwork of fliers in the entryway gives the scoop on upcoming concerts and campus events.

On the west end of the Downtown Mall on the Water Street side is **Mono Loco** (200 W. Water St., 434/979-0688, dinner daily), a colorful slice of Cuba. Masa-crusted oysters and other appetizers run $4–10, with roasted pork and mushroom burritos for dinner ($12–18). Don't miss the margaritas or the Crazy Monkey cookies for dessert.

True to its name, which translates roughly as "center of town," **ZoCaLo** (201 E. Main St., 434/977-4944, dinner Tues.–Sun.) sits squarely in the middle of the Downtown Mall. In warm weather the 70-person patio has ample seating for dining outdoors. Entrées such as chili-dusted sea scallops, key lime free-range chicken, and other Spanish- and Latin American–inspired fare run $18–26.

Also on the Water Street side is **Bang!** (213 2nd St. SW, 434/984-2264, dinner daily). Choose from dozens of tapas-sized dishes ($6–12) with Asian leanings, made with local meats and produce. The martini menu alone is worth a stop. Murals grace the walls at **Wild Greens** (2162 Barracks Rd., 434/296-9453, lunch and dinner daily), where the excellent menu enjoys fresh ingredients and a stylish presentation. The wine list is extensive, and every entrée ($8–14 for lunch, $13–20 for dinner) comes with the signature "wild greens" salad.

Grab a quick slice at Christian's Pizza on the pedestrian mall.

The Belmont neighborhood, just south of the CSX Railroad tracks from downtown, boasts a handful of delicious, cozy restaurants. Tops is **Mas Tapas** (501 Monticello Rd., 434/979-0990, dinner Mon.–Sat.), reputed to have the best small bites in town—and that's no small feat in Charlottesville. Begun by UVA grad and now chef-owner Tomas Rahal, the long menu of Spanish-style tapas at Mas changes often. While the wines and cheeses hail from Spain, most of the other ingredients are sourced locally. You can order tapas (for two, ranging $4–15) or *raciones* (for four, $8–30). Mas does not take reservations, so arrive early for a spot under a yellow umbrella on the patio.

Newer to the neighborhood, but also mouthwateringly good, is **Tavola** (826 Hinton Ave., 434/972-9463, dinner Tues.–Sat.), a rustic Italian place. Start the meal with *cozze ai ferri* (skillet-roasted mussels, garlic butter, and parsley), choose from pancetta-peppered pastas and milaneses for the main course ($15–22), and finish with a scoop of gelato—the flavors change weekly.

Upscale

Two of C-Ville's favorite high-end eateries have the same address on the Downtown Mall. The **Blue Light Grill** (120 E. Main St., 434/295-1223, dinner daily) is a swank red-walled joint that serves outstanding seafood. The wine list and microbrew selection are both excellent, and there's a raw bar for fans of fresh-from-the-ocean fare. Seared trout, grilled tuna with truffle vinaigrette, and other entrées run $17–25. Upstairs is **Ten** (120B E. Main St., 434/295-6691, dinner Mon.–Sat.), a sushi spot that seems straight out of SoHo. Charcoal-grilled Kobe beef, sushi, sashimi, and tempura are all on the menu, along with an extensive sake list.

The Pepsi sign out front doesn't seem to promise much, but the **C&O Restaurant** (515 E. Water St., 434/971-7044, dinner daily) is often called the best in town. Brick walls, worn wood floors, and candlelight give this former railroad flophouse the feel of an old country home, the perfect setting for innovative French cooking. Six dining areas, from the bistro and mezzanine to the covered patio and open terrace, are available. Try an appetizer like smoked Medjoul dates stuffed with mascarpone ($5–14) before digging into a Cuban steak or braised veal short ribs ($19–30).

INFORMATION

The **Charlottesville-Albemarle Convention and Visitors Bureau** (610 E. Main St., 434/293-6789 or 877/386-1103, www.pursuecharlottesville.com, 9 A.M.–5:30 P.M. daily) is located on the Downtown Mall next to the white-tented Pavilion. Besides maps, brochures, and friendly advice, the visitors center provides two hours of free parking validation.

GETTING THERE AND AROUND

Getting There

There's a **Greyhound** bus terminal at 310 West Main Street (800/229-9424) and trains leave the **Amtrak** station a few blocks away (810 W. Main St., 434/296-4559). The **Charlottesville-Albemarle Airport** (434/973-8342, www.gocho.com) is eight miles north of town on the west side of U.S. 29. It's served by US Airways Express, Delta Connection, United Express, and Northwest Airlines. It also has three car rental agencies: Avis (434/973-6000), Hertz (434/297-4288), and National (434/974-4664).

Getting Around

Charlottesville is best appreciated on foot, especially since convenient parking is at a premium. Things are a bit spread out, though, so it's a good thing the **Charlottesville Transit Service** (CTS, 434/970-3649) sends buses around the city Monday–Saturday. Regular fare is $0.75.

Free trolleys run from the Downtown Mall to the Corner and UVA every 15 minutes 6:40 A.M.–midnight (shorter hours Sun.). Hop aboard the free blue and orange **University Transit Service** buses to get around the UVA grounds. For taxi service, try **Yellow Cab** (434/295-4131).

Vicinity of Charlottesville

NORTH OF CHARLOTTESVILLE

Barboursville Vineyards and Historic Ruins

Virginia governor James Barbour lived here 1810–1815 in a mansion designed by Thomas Jefferson (which accounts for the octagonal central room). It burned on Christmas Day 1884, leaving a roofless brick hulk with columns pointing skyward. The ruins are a great place for a picnic accompanied by a bottle of wine from the winery. If you can, come by in August when the Four County Players (540/832-5355, www.fourcp.org) perform their annual **Shakespeare in the Ruins** under the stars.

The winery (17655 Winery Rd., 540/832-3824, www.barboursvillewine.com, 10 A.M.–5 P.M. Mon.–Sat., 11 A.M.–5 P.M. Sun.) is near the intersection of Routes 20 and 33. Tours are offered noon–4 P.M. on weekends, and the **Palladio Restaurant** (540/832-7848, www.palladiorestaurant.com) is open for lunch Wednesday–Sunday and dinner Friday–Saturday, offering two-, three-, and four-course menus with wine pairings, starting at $46 for lunch and $100 for dinner. Reservations and a jacket are required for dinner.

Lodgings are available at **The 1804 Inn** (540/832-5384, www.the1804inn.com, $400 and up), filled with antiques beneath 11-foot ceilings, and the restored 18th-century **Vineyard Cottages** with three full suites for $240–260 each.

Montpelier

James Madison, known as the chief proponent of the Federal Bill of Rights, was actually the third generation to make his home here on 2,700 acres of Piedmont farmland. His father built the original redbrick Georgian house, which Madison enlarged twice under

Montpelier, the residence of James Madison

the advisement of Thomas Jefferson. In 1817 he retired to Montpelier with his wife, Dolley, after serving four congressional terms and the fourth presidency. He died in 1836 and was buried on the property; his wife, who inspired the title "First Lady," died in 1849.

In 1900 the property was purchased by William and Anna Rogers DuPont, who further enlarged the house, creating a total of 55 rooms plus added outbuildings. Their daughter Marion, one of Virginia's foremost horsewomen, took over the property in 1928 and began the well-known Montpelier Hunt Races.

Today the restored house and grounds, formally opened in 1987 by the National Trust for Historic Preservation, are a memorial to Madison's life and work. The view of the Blue Ridge Mountains is impressive, as is the acreage of replanted formal gardens, pasturelands, and forests. An ambitious five-year restoration of the mansion to its original form and furnishings was concluded in 2008. This reversed changes made after Madison's death,

THE INN AT LITTLE WASHINGTON

Virginia's flagship country inn sits at the main (and only) crossroads of a small village at the eastern foothills of the Blue Ridge. Washington itself, long ago prefixed by "Little" to distinguish it from the capital, was surveyed by its 17-year-old namesake in 1749; it is the only place named for him before he became the first president. Almost abandoned by the 20th century, Washington now brims with bed-and-breakfasts and antiques stores. Much of this is thanks to the Inn, which Patrick O'Connell and Reinhardt Lynch bought in 1977.

After 100 years as a general store, gas station, and dance hall, the building needed some serious renovations. But the work was worth it: the Inn was the first place ever to get five stars from both the Mobil Travel Guide and AAA for its accommodations and food. One reviewer gave it five stars out of a possible four.

Flags and flowers drape the white clapboard facade of the modest two-story building. Inside, rich fabrics and wall coverings set off the owners' collection of art and antiques. Eight rooms and two suites were decorated by a London stage designer whose drawings hang on the walls. Personal touches like framed tarot cards, crystal balls, and bouquets of flowers create a small world of exotic luxury. The rooms don't have TVs or radios, but they do have king-size canopy beds and chilled champagne waiting at check-in. Suites have whirlpool tubs and loft bedrooms; two more rooms fill detached guesthouses.

It's hard to believe, then, that what the Inn is really known for is its cuisine. Chef Patrick O'Connell derives inspiration from the 18th-century portrait of French gastronome Anthelme Brillat-Savarin ("Tell me what you eat and I'll tell you what you are") in turning out meals one critic described as "so good it makes you cry." Craig Claiborne of the *New York Times* called his dinner "the most fantastic meal of my life," and most consider it to be one of the 10 best restaurants in the country. Something perfect from the 14,000-bottle wine cellar is only one highlight of the five-course masterpieces, whose entrées add a French zest to regional Virginia favorites like Chesapeake Bay crabmeat and wild duck. Breakfast can be served in your room or in the Terrace Room overlooking the garden, and picnic lunches are available.

The Inn (Middle and Main Sts., 540/675-3800, www.theinnatlittlewashington.com) offers rooms and suites starting at $410; prices are higher on weekends and in the summer and October. Prix-fixe dinners are $148-178, served daily. Rooms and tables fill up months ahead – on some Saturday nights they've received 3,000 requests for only 65 seats – so book your stay as far in advance as possible. The Inn is popular for getaways, both romantic and illicit: Ten engagements happened on a single Valentine's Day, and the maître d' has described his job as like directing a French movie.

including returning the mansion to its original 22 rooms.

Montpelier (540/672-2728, www.montpelier.org, 9 A.M.–4 P.M. daily, to 5 P.M. Apr.–Oct., $16 adults, $8 children) is just south of the town of Orange on Route 20. Admission includes a short movie on the Madisons and the mansion restoration, and guided walking tours are offered daily, including special hands-on activities such as an archaeological dig for kids in April–October. The birthdays of James and Dolley Madison are celebrated on March 16 and May 20, respectively, with graveside ceremonies and receptions at the home. Early May brings the **Montpelier Wine Festival** (540/672-5216 or 800/594-8499, www.montpelierwinefestival.com), and the **Montpelier Hunt Races** (540/661-0196, www.montpelierraces.org), held on the first weekend in November, feature Jack Russell Terrier Races and the Liberty Cup.

VIRGINIA'S BEST PIZZA: THAT'S AMORE

The best pizza in the state is within half an hour of Charlottesville. In fact, the only reason most people have heard about the tiny burg of Crozet, 13 miles west of Charlottesville, is because it's the home of **Crozet Pizza** (5794 Three Notch'd Rd., 434/823-2132, www.crozetpizza.net, lunch Sat.-Sun., dinner daily). Before passing ownership to his daughter and son-in-law, founder-chef Bob Crum had been making pizzas for almost 30 years, with toppings ranging from the usual (peppers, pepperoni) to the unusual (asparagus, eggplant, jalapeños). While the menu now includes a few salads, the pizza dough is made from the same recipe that Karen Crum created in the early 1970s. Photos of fans from around the world wearing Crozet Pizza shirts decorate the walls. Prices start at $13.50 for a large pie, and reservations are definitely recommended for dinner.

Graves Mountain Lodge

The Graves family has offered food and lodging in Syria for almost 150 years, starting with stagecoaches crossing the Blue Ridge and now five generations later with this rustic retreat within sight of Hawksbill and Old Rag Mountains. *National Geographic Traveler* magazine included the lodge on its 2009 "Must Stay" list of 129 iconic accommodations across the country.

Thirty-eight motel rooms are $93–126 per person, rooms in an old farmhouse are $84–100 per person, and a plethora of cottages and cabins start at $95 per person. Rates include three meals a day of honest farm fare, served family-style at long wooden tables. Locally caught catfish and baked ham, sugar-cured on the premises, are augmented by fruits and vegetables grown on the 5,000-acre farm. For nonguests, meals are still available (breakfast $10, lunch $11–17, dinner from $23), but reservations are required.

Here at the foot of the Blue Ridge, the opportunities for hiking and fishing are almost endless. The lodge stables organize horseback rides by the hour or day and will teach you to round up cattle. If that's not enough, you can fish for trout, swim in the pool, or play tennis or horseshoes. Yearly events pack the place to the gills. May brings the **Graves Mountain Festival of Music**—bluegrass, that is—the weekend after Memorial Day. The second and third weekends in October are claimed by the **Apple Harvest Festival** with hayrides, apple-picking, cider-making, and country music.

Graves Mountain Lodge (540/923-4231, www.gravesmountain.com) is near Syria, reached from Route 231 via Route 670. It's open mid-March–November.

SOUTH OF CHARLOTTESVILLE

Michie Tavern

On Route 53 to Monticello, you'll pass this restored tavern, which was originally in Earlysville, 17 miles northwest of

THOMAS JEFFERSON

President, author of the Declaration of Independence, and potent political philosopher, Thomas Jefferson began his life on April 13, 1743, in what is now Albemarle County. When his father, surveyor and cartographer Peter Jefferson, died in 1757, Jefferson followed his father's wishes and pursued a classical education at the College of William & Mary. In school he made friends among the faculty and local government, who introduced him to the pleasures of urbane society, as well as the law, the natural sciences, and the pursuit of knowledge for its own sake.

After a five-year study of law and admittance to the bar, Jefferson entered politics in 1769 as a member of the Virginia House of Burgesses. Relations with Britain were already sliding downhill, and Jefferson soon found himself leading Patrick Henry and others who favored strong resistance to the mother country. In 1776, as a member of the Second Continental Congress, Jefferson found an outlet for his growing intellectual radicalism and profound, passionate writing skills by drafting the Declaration of Independence.

As his country struggled to fight itself free, Jefferson tried to put the ideas of the declaration into action as governor of Virginia 1779-1781. This proved easier said than done; his Statute of Religious Freedom encountered vigorous opposition that delayed its enactment until 1786, and his lackluster performance during the British invasion of 1780-1781 inspired the editor of a local paper to label him "a coward, a calumniator, a plagiarist, [and] a tame, spiritless animal." On September 6, 1782, the worst blow fell. Martha Wayles Skelton Jefferson, with whom Jefferson had enjoyed "ten years of unchequered happiness," died soon after the birth of their sixth child. "A single event," he wrote, "wiped away all my plans and left me a blank which I had not the spirits to fill up." He never remarried.

Jefferson was able to escape somewhat on a five-year diplomatic trip to France 1784-1789 in the company of Benjamin Franklin and John Adams, who had helped him draft the declaration. Here he wrote his only full-length book, *Notes on the State of Virginia* (1787). This volume, which answers a series of questions posed by a French diplomat on North America and its rapidly changing society, is considered by many to be one of the most insightful works of the 18th century.

After stints as secretary of state and vice president, Jefferson became the third U.S. president in 1801, narrowly defeating Aaron Burr in a close race that characterized the early polarization of American politics. In

© KATIE GITHENS

A 6-foot-3-inch life-size bronze statue of Mr. Jefferson greets you at the Monticello visitors center.

contrast to Burr's Federalists, Jefferson's Republicans supported policies claimed both by today's Democrats, in their championship of human rights and opposition to plutocracy and oligarchy, and modern Republicans, in the idea that the best federal government is small, noninterfering, and decentralized.

During his first term (1801-1805), Jefferson nearly doubled the size of the United States through the Louisiana Purchase. He originally intended to buy only a small part of the Mississippi River valley, but when a cash-poor Napoleon offered to sell everything from the Great Lakes to the Rockies and beyond for only $15 million, Jefferson jumped at the chance (even though, as he admitted, he had no constitutional authority to do so). Under his orders, Meriwether Lewis and William Clark's Corps of Discovery left to explore the territory, resulting in one of the greatest adventures the country has ever seen.

Jefferson's second term didn't go as well, thanks in part to growing controversy over the role of the federal government. His efforts to avoid involvement in the Napoleonic Wars led to more charges of timidity and vacillation. In 1809, deeply in debt, he handed over the reins of office to James Madison.

Jefferson's later life at Monticello gave him ample time to pursue the endless interests pushed aside by a career in politics. Over his lifetime Jefferson wrote volumes of letters that give a remarkably detailed picture of the man himself. He considered himself part of an educated gentry that owed its existence to the same public that held it responsible to govern justly. At six feet, two inches tall, Jefferson was lanky and angular and carried himself with a relaxed dignity.

Jefferson observed the construction of the University of Virginia by telescope until its opening in 1819, when he was finally able to indulge what he called his "canine appetite" for learning. He was one of the most educated men of his time, able to understand Latin, Greek, French, Spanish, Italian, and Anglo-Saxon. At age 71, he read Plato's *Republic* in the original Greek and pronounced it overrated.

His interest in architecture left its neoclassical stamp on dozens of buildings in Virginia and Washington, D.C., and as an amateur naturalist Jefferson collected and tried to classify fossils from all over the country. Mathematics and meteorology both fascinated him, and he always had some experiment in planting going in the fields of Monticello in the hopes of improving the prosperity of American farmers.

Yet, even as almost every event of his daily life went down on paper, certain aspects of the private man have remained a mystery. In 19,000 surviving letters, for example, not one exists between him and his wife. Then there's the question of how the country's foremost champion of natural rights and the equality of man could own hundreds of slaves. His *Notes on the State of Virginia* addresses the issue most directly, calling it a "great political and moral evil." But from there Jefferson falls back on limp justifications that reflect the prevailing prejudices of his era. Arguing that blacks were inferior to whites in physical beauty, foresight, and imagination, Jefferson couldn't bring himself to imagine both races living peacefully side by side. Slavery, in his view, was a necessary evil, crucial to the economy of the state and preferable to the "dynamite of class struggle" between rich and poor white planters.

Jefferson died on July 4, 1826, the 50th anniversary of the signing of the Declaration of Independence and only hours before his friend John Adams. He lies at Monticello under the inscription: "Here was buried Thomas Jefferson, author of the Declaration of American Independence, of the Virginia Statute of Religious Freedom, and father of the University of Virginia."

Charlottesville. Built by William Michie (MICK-ee) in 1784, it served stagecoach travelers for decades before falling into disrepair. In 1927, a wealthy businessman paid to have it moved here and restored.

Behind the tavern proper are reproductions of "dependencies," including a smokehouse, ice house, and root cellar. The Meadow Run gristmill is said to have seen no rest since 1797. After perusing the general store and crafts shops, try an Old Dominion vintage. Admission is $7 adults, $4 children 6–11. Entrance is free to President's Pass holders, a block ticket that covers Monticello, the Michie Tavern, and Ash-Lawn Highland for $31–36 for adults, $17.50 for children 6–11 (www.monticello.org/visit/ppass_guides.html).

If you didn't pack a lunch for your visit to Monticello, a stop at the "Ordinary" will leave you bursting at the seams. This log cabin sports original wood-beam walls and ceilings, creating the perfect atmosphere for a Colonial-style Southern buffet served on pewter plates. The Tavern (434/977-1234, www.michietavern.com) serves buffet lunches year-round for $16 adults, $9–11.50 children.

Monticello

Even if you're not a history fanatic, you know this landmark—it's on the back of a U.S. nickel, with a portrait of its creator on the flip side. If you're into history, or architecture, or can at least appreciate a stunning spread, don't miss Monticello, one of the country's outstanding architectural achievements.

Monticello (Mon-ti-CHELL-o) was Thomas Jefferson's pet project, which he designed, expanded, and refined over four decades. The first version of the house was radically redesigned after a five-year trip to France, where the future president acquired a loathing for the British-style Georgian brickwork so common to contemporary Colonial architecture. (Williamsburg's design, he wrote, was "the most wretched I ever saw.")

What took its place was a blend of the Italian style of architect Andrea Palladio and the French design of the court of Louis XVI. Eight rooms became 21, and Monticello Mark II was essentially finished in 1809. Jefferson died here on July 4, 1826, on the 50th anniversary of the signing of the Declaration of Independence. He's buried in a family plot on the grounds, though when he died his debt was so great that his family had to sell the estate.

The manor house tops a columned, classical portico with a large dome, the first on a residence in North America. Touches of Jeffersonian whimsy fill the interior, where the 1st floor is open to the public. A private museum in the entrance hall holds mastodon bones, a model of the Great Pyramid of Egypt, and objects from Lewis and Clark's expedition to the Pacific Ocean. In the corner a seven-day clock has weights that slowly fall from the ceiling to the basement through a special hole in the floor.

Almost every room is a different size and shape. In the study an ingenious handwriting copier allowed Jefferson to pen two letters at once, and don't miss the view from the parlor. The president's private suite features a bed alcove open to both the dressing room and the study, allowing him to rise in either room depending on his mood and the time of day.

The estate's true kingly feel, though, comes from the grounds. More than 1,000 acres of lush gardens have been restored to their original glory, doing proud Jefferson's sentiment that "no occupation is as delightful to me as the culture of the earth, and no culture comparable to that of the garden." Service quarters in Mulberry Row were placed so as not to obscure the stunning view (Monticello means "little mountain" in Italian). Even though he called slavery an "abominable crime," Jefferson did own about 200 slaves, whose homes and lives are currently being excavated and examined.

Monticello (434/984-9822, www.monticello.org, 9 A.M.–5 P.M. daily Mar.–Nov., 10 A.M.–4 P.M. daily Dec.–Feb., $17–22 adults, $8 children 6–11) commands a hilltop three miles southeast of Charlottesville on Route 53 (Thomas Jefferson Pkwy.). From I-64, take exit 121 (westbound) or 121A (eastbound) to Route

© KATIE GITHENS

just like on a nickel: Thomas Jefferson's Monticello estate

20 south (if traveling westbound, turn south, or left, on Rte. 20); make a left on Route 53, at the second stoplight. The entrance to Monticello is located on the right, approximately 1.5 miles from Route 20. You'll have to park at the visitors center, and from there you can walk or take a shuttle bus half a mile up to the house. Arrive early for tickets, as this place is understandably popular. A half-hour guided tour of the house is included in admission, and special gardens and grounds tours are also offered April–October. The **Cafe at Monticello** in the visitors center serves lunch and snacks year-round, featuring produce grown in Jefferson's restored vegetable garden.

Carter Mountain Apple Orchard

Pick your own peaches in the summer and apples in the fall at this orchard (1435 Carters Mountain Trail, 434/977-1833, www.cartermountainorchard.com, 10 A.M.–5 P.M. daily mid-Apr.–Nov., longer hours June–Oct.) that's three-quarters of a mile up the James Monroe Highway/Route 58 on the way to Monticello. Picnics, apple cider, warm donuts, and hayrides in the fall all benefit from the views 1,150 feet above town.

Ash Lawn-Highland

It seems that Jefferson's sense of style was contagious. In 1793 James Monroe, whom some historians call Jefferson's protégé, bought 1,000 acres just south of Monticello. When George Washington sent Monroe to France for three years, Jefferson hired gardeners to give his friend's orchards a jump-start. From 1799 to 1823 Monroe lived at Highland with his family. He found comfort in the view of Monticello to the north and borrowed from his mentor's style in designing his own house (which remained a much more modest affair).

Sadly, one year after his second term as president ended in 1825, Monroe was forced to sell Highland, where he had hoped to retire, to pay off a $75,000 debt. Subsequent owners added the name Ash Lawn in 1838 and in 1884 built a Victorian-style house next to the original building.

The College of William & Mary, Monroe's alma mater, maintains Ash Lawn–Highland as a working farm. A collection of period furnishings fills the main house, including some from the Monroe White House and others that were presented as gifts from South American republics in thanks for the Monroe Doctrine of noninterference in political matters.

Keep an eye out for the chair that's been seen to rock on its own on repeated occasions. Legend says it was Monroe's favorite, so some think the spirit is his. Another story says that a nanny died in the chair when a stray spark from the fireplace caught her long hair on fire.

Ash Lawn–Highland (434/293-8000, www.ashlawnhighland.org, 9 A.M.–6 P.M. daily Apr.–Oct., 11 A.M.–5 P.M. daily Nov.–Mar., $10 adults, $5 children 6–11) is near Monticello and the Michie Tavern on Route 795, 0.5 mile south of the intersection with Route 53. A gift shop and picnic tables await after a 40-minute house tour, which is included in the admission. **James Monroe's birthday** on April 28 is a special day here, and the annual **Ash Lawn Opera Festival** (434/293-4500, www.ashlawnopera.org) spans July and early August. The house is lit with candles during the holidays.

Waltons' Mountain Museum

Author Earl Hamner Jr. based his autobiographical stories on vivid memories of growing up in the rural village of Schuyler during the Depression. The 1970s-era TV series they inspired won six Emmys and two Golden Globes its first year and went on to run for 211 episodes over eight more years. This museum occupies the Schuyler Community Center, once Hamner's own elementary school, and includes replicas of some of the sets from the show. Fans will recognize locations such as the Waltons' kitchen and living room and John Boy's bedroom. Ike Godsey's country store now houses a gift shop that sells local crafts. The museum (434/831-2000, www.waltonmuseum.org, 10 A.M.–4 P.M. daily Mar.–Nov., $7 adults and children over 6) is on Route 6 east of U.S. 29. Call or see website for directions.

Scottsville

The first seat of Albemarle County (1745) occupies a horseshoe bend in the James River. This choice location made it the chief port above Richmond for freights and passengers during a golden era in the mid-1800s, but also has made it prone to floods. The barges are long gone, but you can still drift gently downstream on a canoe or inner tube from **James River Reeling and Rafting** (434/286-4386, www.reelingandrafting.com). Rentals with shuttle service start at $20 per person (May–Oct.). A floating cooler—key in summer—is another $8, and the company also offers canoeing, kayaking, and overnight camping and fishing trips for $52–62 per person. Children must be at least six years old to participate in floats. **James River Runners** (434/286-2338, www.jamesriver.com) also plies the James aboard tubes, canoes, kayaks, and rafts. It's based five miles outside of Scottsville.

Wintergreen Resort

Twenty-six ski slopes ranging from novice to expert have earned Wintergreen Resort

THE VIRGINIA WINE & GARLIC FESTIVAL

The humble, pungent bulb of *Allium sativum* is the subject of a weekend's worth of fun in mid-October at **Rebec Vineyards** (434/946-5168, www.rebecwinery.com), five miles north of the town of Amherst. Virginia's most fragrant fair has 100 vendors selling the "stinking rose" in just about every form imaginable, along with pony rides for children and music on four stages. Some 12,000 people turn out to see the selection of the Garlic King and Queen and the Best Garlic Costume and taste the entries in the Garlic Cook-Off. (Winning recipes are posted on the winery's website.)

the *Washington Post Express*'s "best snow skiing spot" in the 2009 readers choice awards. Five lifts, including two high-speed six-person chairs, serve the 1,000-foot vertical drop of the Highlands, and there's a 900-foot snow-tubing facility called the Plunge nearby. Many runs are lit for night skiing, or you can opt for a cappuccino in front of the fireplaces in the cozy stone lodge. Adult lift tickets are $47–69 or $34 at night, and ski rentals are $36 for adults, $31 for children 6–12, and $25 for children under 5 (snowboards are $36–41). Beginners' group ski or snowboard lessons are half off with rentals.

Two outstanding golf courses (one designed by Rees Jones) draw guests during the summer, along with tennis courts, pools, and 20-acre Lake Monocan. You can rent bikes, horses, and ponies, or simply hike from the nature center along miles of trails operated by the Wintergreen Nature Foundation. The Wintergarden Spa has hot tubs, a whirlpool tub, saunas, and workout rooms. Dining options include the **Copper Mine Bistro** and the **Devils Grill.** The Out of Bounds Adventure Center boasts facilities for paintball, rock climbing, basketball, in-line skating, volleyball, and skateboarding. Rental choices include hundreds of mountaintop villas and dozens of slopeside homes, most of which have kitchens and fireplaces.

Wintergreen (434/325-2200 or 800/266-2444, www.wintergreenresort.com) is on Route 644, off Route 151 south of Nellysford. You can also get there from the Blue Ridge Parkway via the Reeds Gap exit at milepost 13.

Lynchburg and Vicinity

Virginia's classic tobacco town goes by a few different monikers. As the City of Seven Hills, Lynchburg (pop. 72,000) bulges with lofty historic districts and stately inns. As the center of Virginia's conservative religious heartland, it's also called the Buckle in the Bible Belt, with more than 130 houses of worship, Jerry Falwell's Liberty University, Dial-the-Bible listings in the White Pages, and radio preachers who end every sentence in "-uh." And its tourist slogan, the Real Virginia, rings true thanks to Lynchburg's combination of the new (ideas debated in several medium-sized colleges) and the old (Thomas Jefferson's Poplar Forest and Appomattox Court House, both nearby).

History

After earning his freedom from a wealthy Quaker planter, indentured Irish servant Charles Lynch went on to marry the boss's daughter and build the town's first warehouses and commercial buildings on land he had acquired along the upper James River. In 1757, his son John set up a ferry terminal at the bottom of today's 9th Street, and Lynchburg was off and running as a regional commercial center.

Trade poured in along the James River and Kanawha Canal from Richmond, and railroads from Petersburg and Alexandria. A dark, coarse-leafed local variety of tobacco soon became the area's main cash crop. Farmers hummed popular songs like "Goin' Down to Lynchburg Town to Carry my Tobacco Down" as they brought huge hogsheads to dozens of warehouses along the riverbanks. Small boats called *bateaux,* usually manned by a trio of skilled, brawny slaves, waited on the water to take the containers to Richmond.

By the mid-19th century, Lynchburg was second only to New Bedford, Massachusetts, in per capita income (whale oil still brought in more money than tobacco). Soon more than 30 million pounds of tobacco were passing through the city's warehouses every year. Lynchburg served as a major Confederate storage depot during the Civil War and as one of four quartermaster (horse) depots in the

THE BEALE TREASURE

Virginia's best-known lost fortune is said to consist of thousands of pounds of gold and silver and a fortune in jewels. Some say it's a hoax, but hundreds of hopeful treasure hunters believe otherwise.

In 1817, a party of 30 Virginians led by Thomas Jefferson Beale left to try their luck mining in Colorado. They struck a rich vein of gold and silver in the south-central part of the state, which they worked for a year and a half before the accumulating wealth started to make some uncomfortable. Beale and eight others went back to Virginia to bury two truckloads of nuggets while the others stayed and mined.

The party arrived at Goose Creek in Bedford County in November 1818, following a faint trail through a gap in the Blue Ridge foothills near the Peaks of Otter. Snow covered their tracks as they dug a square pit six feet deep, lined it with flat stones, and filled it with iron cooking pots filled with treasure. The last concealing spadeful fell in December, and within two months they had rejoined their comrades.

After two more years of mining, Beale led another trip back to the same spot and a second load joined the first. This time he decided to leave a message for his partners in Colorado in case something happened to his group on the return. Three numerical ciphers detailing the location of the hoard, the contents of the vault, and the name of the party were put in a strongbox and given to Lynchburg innkeeper Robert Morris, with instructions to open it if no one returned in 10 years.

Beale and his crew left once more for Colorado, and Morris never saw any of them again. Two months later he received a letter saying the keys to the code were in the mail, and then nothing. As the years passed, Morris gradually forgot about the strongbox, until he happened upon it decades later while searching for a harness in a shed. After trying for years to decipher the codes, Morris showed them to a friend, who managed to break the one describing the vault using a key based on the Declaration of Independence. The other two were made public (see, for example, http://unmuseum.org/bealepap.htm) but remain a mystery despite the efforts of decoding experts and computer codebreakers.

Here is the beginning of page 1, describing the location of the vault: 71, 194, 38, 1701, 89, 76, 11, 83, 1629, 48, 94, 63, 132, 16, 111, 95, 84, 341, 975, 14, 40, 64, 27, 81, 139, 213, 63, 90, 1120, 8, 15, 3, 126, 2018, 40, 74, 758, 485, 604, 230, 436, 664, 582, 150, 251, 284, 308 . . .

Confederacy. On June 18, 1864, Gen. Jubal Early narrowly managed to save the city from destruction by running empty trains back and forth with much noise and commotion, convincing Union generals that reinforcements had arrived.

The tobacco trade carried Lynchburg into the early 20th century, but as demand slackened, the city turned to its wealth of antiquity to lure visitors. Many antebellum houses marred by midcentury neglect have been restored as homes and offices.

SIGHTS

Museums and Historic Districts

Five of Lynchburg's seven hills are now historic districts with lofty views of the James River. Two Baptist church spires bookend **Court House Hill,** where the 139 steps of **Monument Terrace** lead past a row of war memorials to the steps of the **Lynchburg Museum at the Old Court House** (901 Court St., 434/455-6226, www.lynchburgmuseum.org, 10 A.M.–4 P.M. Mon.–Sat., noon–4 P.M. Sun., $6 adults, $3 children 6–17). The dome-capped Greek Revival temple houses exhibits ranging from native Monacan tribes to life in Lynchburg during the tobacco boom.

Many of the grand houses on **Diamond Hill** were built during Lynchburg's golden age near the turn of the 20th century. Once one of the city's most exclusive neighborhoods, Diamond Hill embraces a wealth of architectural styles, including Queen Anne and Greek, Gothic, and Georgian Revival. **Federal Hill** to the west was Lynchburg's first residential suburb, filled with Federal-style homes along steep, dead-end streets. Once known as Quality Row as it passed through the **Garland Hill** district, Madison Avenue is still partially paved in century-old brick.

On the far side of Blackwater Creek rises **Daniel's Hill,** dominated by the octagonal bay facade of **Point of Honor** (112 Cabell St., 434/847-1867, www.pointofhonor.org, 10 A.M.–4 P.M. Mon.–Sat., noon–4 P.M. Sun., $6 adults, $3 children 6–17). Built in 1815 by Dr. George Cabell Sr., who treated Patrick Henry and other revolutionary figures, the Federal mansion is named for duels once fought over matters of principle on this bluff above the James. Among the activities offered are cooking demonstrations given in a reconstructed plantation kitchen and an exhibit on medicine in early Virginia that displays tools, methods, and illnesses that Dr. Cabell would

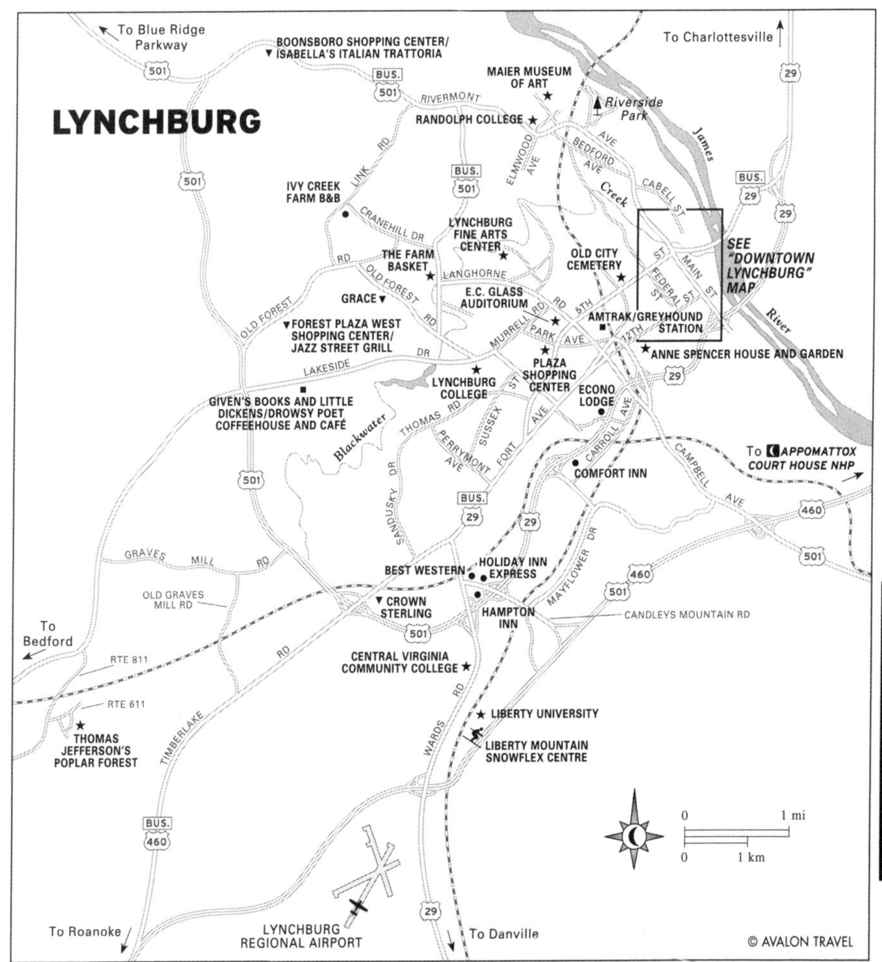

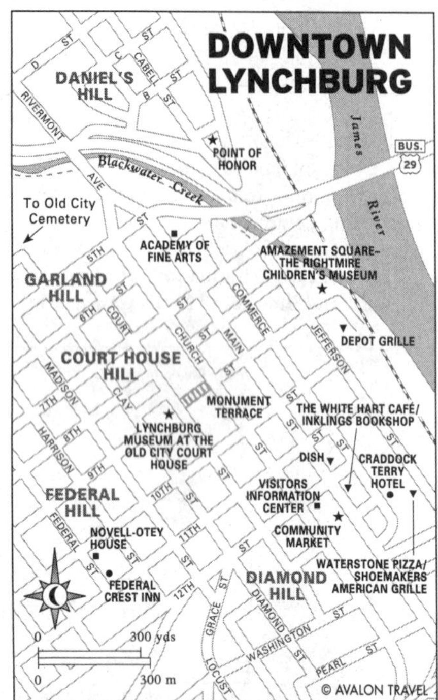

have seen as a physician. Admission includes a guided tour.

A few blocks farther up the James you'll find Randolph College's **Maier Museum of Art** (1 Quinlan St., 434/947-8136, www.maiermuseum.org, 1–5 P.M. Tues.–Sun., 1–4 P.M. Wed.–Sun. in summer, free), which houses an impressive collection of 19th- and 20th-century American works, including paintings by Edward Hopper, Winslow Homer, and Georgia O'Keeffe.

Other Sights

The 26-acre **Old City Cemetery** (401 Taylor St., 434/847-1465, www.gravegarden.org, dawn to dusk daily, free) came into use in 1806. A loop trail starting at Taylor and 4th Streets passes ancient family plots, Revolutionary War graves, and the final resting place of Blind Billy, a local street musician and former slave whose freedom was paid for by Lynchburg residents. Beyond the Confederate section, containing 2,200 soldiers from 14 states, you'll find butterfly and medicinal herb gardens, a lotus-studded goldfish pond, and a row of 60 varieties of antique roses from the 16th to 19th centuries. A dozen self-guided tour brochures are available, or you can set up a guided tour ($5 pp) by prior appointment.

The Cemetery Center (11 A.M.–3 P.M. daily Mar.–Oct., 11 A.M.–3 P.M. Mon.–Sat. Nov.–Feb.) includes four small museums, including the **Museum of 19th Century Mourning Customs** and the **Pest House Medical Museum** (434/847-1811), once the medical office of local physician John J. Terrell. During the Civil War, Dr. Terrell turned it into a "House of Pestilence" for his experiments in isolating victims of smallpox and measles. The 1840s building, viewed through glass doors, contains medical tools from the era, including an amputation kit, "asthma chair," and "poison chest" (presumably for medicines). These buildings are open for guided tours only ($5 adults, $2 children) by prior appointment.

At the **Anne Spencer House and Garden** (1313 Pierce St., 434/845-1313, www.annespencermuseum.com), the Lynchburg poetess who wrote of love and reverence of beauty in humankind and nature is memorialized in her home and the gardens that inspired many of her stanzas. Spencer (1882–1975) is considered part of the Harlem Renaissance and is the only Virginian included in the *Norton Anthology of Modern American and British Poetry.* While living here she entertained visitors such as George Washington Carver, Martin Luther King Jr., Thurgood Marshall, and W. E. B. DuBois, when she wasn't composing in the small garden cottage she called Edenkraal. Guided tours of the house are by appointment only ($5 adults, $2 children under 12); unguided tours of the gardens are possible year-round.

Amazement Square – the Rightmire Children's Museum (27 9th St., 434/845-1888, www.amazementsquare.org, 10 A.M.–5 P.M. Tues.–Sat., 1–5 P.M. Sun., $7, free children under 2) is a hands-on learning center oriented toward kids, but exhibits with names like

Raceways and Voltageville and Once Upon a Building just might end up intriguing grown-ups as well. At the center of the building is a four-story agglomeration of tunnels, stairs, and paths called the Amazement Town.

Parks and Natural Areas

Daniel's Hill continues upriver into **Riverside Park**—look for a sign along Rivermont at the Virginia School of the Arts building. Trails along the hillside lead to the keel of the packet boat the *John Marshall,* typical of the 19th-century craft that were pulled by mules as far as Richmond. This particular one carried Stonewall Jackson's body to Lexington for burial.

Snaking through downtown Lynchburg, the **James River Heritage Trail** (515 Monticello Ave., 434/847-1640) comprises eight miles of bicycle and foot trails along old railroad beds that link together two of Lynchburg's favorite trail networks: the RiverWalk in the downtown waterfront and the 300-acre Blackwater Creek Bikeway further inland. The trail is breeziest in the jaunt to reach its eastern terminus; you cross the James River on a former railroad bridge before traversing the one-mile length of Percival Island and then a second former rail bridge into Amherst County. Maps and additional information are available at the Lynchburg Visitor Information Center and you can also download a trail map from the City of Lynchburg website (www.lynchburgva.gov).

Liberty Mountain

Year-round skiing has come to Lynchburg with the **Liberty Mountain Snowflex Centre** (1971 University Blvd., 434/582-3539 or 866/504-7541, www.liberty.edu/snowflex, \$5/hr Mon.–Wed., \$7/hr Thurs.–Sun., \$12 skis/board rental, \$8 tube rental). Opened in 2009 on Liberty University's campus, the ski slopes are blanketed in a European-made synthetic material that simulates snow, which made its debut on U.S. soil here.

The complex includes a bunny slope, a main slope with intermediate and advanced sections, and a freestyle park with an 11-foot quarter pipe, triple kickers, and other features. A tubing chute and a two-story ski lodge decked out in taxidermy of every huntable game in North America complete the picture. It's open noon–midnight Monday–Thursday, until 1 A.M. Friday, 8 A.M.–1 A.M. Saturday, and 2 P.M.–midnight Sunday. From Richmond Highway (U.S. 29/U.S. 460), take the University Boulevard ramp and turn left onto Liberty University Drive.

Liberty Mountain is also interwoven with more than 65 miles of **mountain biking** on single- and double-track trails and logging roads that are open to the public during daylight hours. Download a trail map from Liberty University's website (www.ultimatelu.com).

ENTERTAINMENT

Nightlife

Cattle Annie's (4009 Murray Pl., 434/846-3206, www.cattleannies.com) features both kinds of music—country *and* western—as well as a bar, restaurant, and 4,500-square-foot dance floor. The music ranges from live bands to DJs. The **Jazz Street Grill** (3225 Old Forest Rd., 434/835-0100), in the same shopping center, sounds like Dixieland on weekends.

Fine Arts

The **Academy of Fine Arts** (600 Main St., 434/528-3256, www.academyfinearts.com) is Lynchburg's clearinghouse for art and dance classes and theater performances. In 2010, their plan to restore the 1905 Academy of Music Theatre downtown and join it with art galleries, an education center, and a multipurpose studio space was well underway.

The **Lynchburg Symphony Orchestra** (621 Court St., 434/845-6604, www.lynchburgsymphony.com) performs at the Lynchburg City Stadium or the E. C. Glass High School Auditorium.

SHOPPING

Two dozen antiques shops sell bits and pieces of Lynchburg's rich history, from Victorian hatpins to antique linens. Many are along Main Street, like **Scarlet's Main Street Antique**

Mall (1026 Main St., 434/528-0488) and **Sweeney's Curious Goods** (1220 Main St., 434/846-7839). But the best treasure hunting can be found inside all three locations of **Estate Specialists** (1300 Main St., 1225 and 1228 Commerce St., 434/845-1972, www.estatespecialistsinc.com), one of the largest single-owner companies selling antiques and estate items on the East Coast.

The Farm Basket (2008 Langhorne Rd., 434/528-1107) is a fun collection of shops offering art, flowers, jewelry, and crafts. Wander around inside to unearth a gem or two, then take a break on the deck overlooking Blackwater Creek with a box lunch from the food shop (and don't miss the homemade apple butter and hot pepper jelly).

EVENTS

In mid-September, the city **Art Festival** (434/384-2723) brings local and regional artists to the E. C. Glass High School grounds on Memorial Avenue. The Diamond Hill Historical Society sponsors a guided **Victorian Home Tour** in early December. Seven to ten restored homes are usually open to the public, decorated for the holiday season.

ACCOMMODATIONS

$50-100

Two choices in this price range are the **Econo Lodge** (2400 Stadium Rd., 434/847-1045) and the **Holiday Inn Express** (5600 Seminole Ave., 434/237-7771), both with rooms for $80–100.

$100-150

It's chain hotels in this price range as well, including the **Hampton Inn** (5604 Seminole Ave., 434/237-2704, $95–115) and a **Best Western** (2815 Candlers Mountain Rd., 434/237-2986, $85–110).

$150-200

You'll recognize the **Craddock Terry Hotel** (1312 Commerce St., 434/455-1500, www.craddockterryhotel.com, $160–200) by the enormous red high heel adorning its brick exterior, a tip of the hat to the circa-1901 building's history. This posh boutique hotel is the latest incarnation of the Craddock Terry Shoe Company, which at its height churned out 5,000 pairs of shoes daily, making it the fifth-largest shoe company in the world. It continues to be a family-run affair; the great-grandson of the original shoe company's owner was the architect for the project to convert the rundown factory and adjoining tobacco warehouse into the 44-room hotel and conference center that opened in 2007. The hotel rooms, which feel more like classy studio apartments, have high ceilings, exposed beams, and large windows facing downtown, the Blue Ridge, or the river. Amenities include two highly praised restaurants (more on that later), a fitness center, and, of course, a complimentary overnight shoe shine.

© KATIE GITHENS

The posh Craddock Terry Hotel was once the fifth-largest shoe factory in the world.

The biggest and finest mansion in the Federal Hill Historic District is now the **Norvell-Otey House** (1020 Federal St., 434/528-1020 or 877/320-1020, www.norvelloteyhouse.com, $125–165). Built in 1817, it offers canopied beds, afternoon tea, and a full Southern breakfast to start the day right.

English boxwoods frame the **Ivy Creek Farm B&B** (2812 Link Rd., 434/384-3802 or 800/689-7404, www.ivycreekfarm.com, $150–200), with three guest rooms on eight private acres, along with an old barn left from a previous life as a dairy farm. Oriental carpets, period furnishings, and antique pewter embellish the inside, and there's a brick-floored pool room inside.

Phil and Ann Ripley's **Federal Crest Inn** (1101 Federal St., 434/845-6155 or 800/818-6155, www.federalcrest.com) commands a stately view from the top of Federal Hill, especially from the Eagle's Nest Theater on the 3rd floor, built as a stage for the original owner's children (and now home to a large-screen TV). Seven fireplaces, each with a unique mantel, are spread throughout the 1909 house, which has two guest rooms ($145–195) and two suites ($185–235) with down comforters.

FOOD

Snacks and Cafés

Aside from an eight-year time-out, the **Lynchburg Community Market** (1219 Main St., 7 A.M.–2 P.M. Mon.–Sat.) has been open since 1783, making it the third-oldest farmers market in the country. It's the place in town for picnic fixings, baked goods, and seasonal produce.

The Farm Basket (2008 Langhorne Rd., 434/528-1107, lunch Mon.–Sat.) also offers fresh produce in season, box lunches, and healthy fare along the lines of cucumber sandwiches on fresh-baked bread ($5–7).

Inside Givens Books and Little Dickens, Lynchburg's oldest and largest independent bookstore, the **Drowsy Poet Coffeehouse & Cafe** (2336 Lakeside Dr., 434/385-4505, all meals Mon.–Sat.) serves up various caffeinated beverages along with sandwiches and salads for around $6. They even have wireless Internet.

Downtown, try **The White Hart Café and Inklings Bookshop** (1206–1208 Main St., 434/845-2665, all meals Mon.–Sat.), another merger of fair-trade coffee, finger food, and books—with a particular fondness for C. S. Lewis. Especially delicious is the Mugwumper sandwich, a concoction of roast beef with sautéed spinach, scallions, roasted red peppers, and sun-dried-tomato mayo. Breakfast plates, sandwiches, and entrées cost $5–10. The White Hart also hosts live music.

College students gab at The White Hart Café and Inklings Bookshop.

Casual

Families with small children visiting the Amazement Square will be pleased that casual dining and a kids' menu are right across the street. The riverfront **Depot Grille** (10 9th St., 434/846-4464, lunch and dinner daily) serves steaks, seafood, and pastas in the old N&W Depot building for $14–23.

Further down the riverfront, **Waterstone Pizza** (1309 Jefferson St., 434/455-1515, lunch and dinner daily) occupies the ground level of the Craddock Terry Hotel. Besides delivering on chewy thin-crust fire-roasted pizzas, Waterstone will appease hopheads with its locally brewed draughts from **Jefferson Street Brewery.** A 10-inch individual pizza costs $8–10.

Isabella's Italian Trattoria (4925 Boonsboro Rd., 434/385-1660, lunch and dinner Mon.–Sat., brunch Sun.) is a chic but casual bistro serving northern Italian fare. The menu includes brick oven–baked pizzas ($12), pastas ($12–18), and dishes such as parmesan-crusted grouper for $14–26.

Upscale

Cheese and wine lovers unite at the turquoise-walled **Dish** (1120 Main St., 434/528-0070, lunch and dinner Tues.–Sat.), another bastion for small plates and oenophiles. In addition to daily chalkboard specials, the coconut green curry shrimp and the duck confit spring rolls are two to try (small plates cost $7–9; plan to order several). Don't miss the extensive cheese plates, from a mozzarella made right in Lynchburg to an epoisses from Burgundy, France. You can order samples of 3, 4, 5, or all 14 cheeses ($10.50–49).

Shoemakers American Grille (1312 Commerce St., 434/455-1510, lunch Mon.–Fri., dinner Mon.–Sat.) serves more traditional American fare such as Virginia trout with roasted pecans and crab cakes with a spicy remoulade ($13–21). Salads, like the iceberg wedge with blue cheese and bacon, and assorted sandwiches ($6–13) are on the menu too. Shoemakers is, unsurprisingly, part of the Craddock Terry Hotel, with several clever nods in the decor alluding to the property's history in the shoe-making business, though the restaurant is actually located in a converted tobacco warehouse. An open-air courtyard overlooking the river offers alfresco dining.

Cooking seasonally with herbs cut from his own garden, chef Kent Trebilcox dishes up the best of "slow food" at **Grace** (2627 Old Forest Rd., 434/386-9666, www.savorgrace.com, dinner Thurs.–Sat., $17–29). Grace serves contemporary American dishes in Locust Thicket, one of Lynchburg's oldest historic homes, built in 1790. A friend called a Grace dinner one of the best meals she's ever had. The trick is being in town when the restaurant is open. Mid-May through September, Trebilcox, who hails from San Francisco and trained at the Cordon Bleu Cooking School in Paris, is chef and cellarmaster for the "A Bar A" guest ranch in Wyoming. During this summer hiatus, Grace is only open for special events and occasional prix-fixe dinners (see website for details).

Crown Sterling (6120 Fort Ave. at U.S. 501, 434/239-7744, dinner Mon.–Sat.) bills itself as "Central Virginia's oldest fine dining restaurant," because it's been locally owned and operated for more than 40 years. It serves aged beef charcoal-grilled to perfection, as well as chicken and seafood entrées ($17–34) such as teriyakis, grilled swordfish, and filets.

INFORMATION

For walking-tour brochures and advice on anything in the region, stop by the **Lynchburg Visitors Information Center** (216 12th St., 434/847-1811 or 800/732-5821, www.discoverlynchburg.org, 9 A.M.–5 P.M. daily).

GETTING THERE AND AROUND

Getting There

The **Lynchburg Regional Airport** (434/455-6090) is eight miles south of downtown on U.S. 29. It's served by US Airways Express and Delta Connection. You can rent a car from Avis (434/239-3622), Budget (434/237-6101), or Hertz (434/237-6284). The Crescent line between New York and New Orleans stops at the local **Amtrak** station (825 Kemper St. at Park Ave., 800/872-7245) daily. **Greyhound** (434/846-6614) is in the same building.

Getting Around

The **Greater Lynchburg Transit Company** (434/856-2489, www.gltconline.com) serves the city and surrounding area from its main terminal at the Plaza Shopping Center. Local fares are $1.50 per person.

THOMAS JEFFERSON'S POPLAR FOREST

In 1773 Thomas Jefferson inherited a 4,812-acre working tobacco farm from his father-in-law, providing the future president with a welcome source of cash income. In 1806 he laid the foundation there for a house he would come to cherish almost as much as Monticello, saying "when finished, it will be the best dwelling house in the state, except that of Monticello; perhaps preferable to that, as more proportioned to the faculties of a private citizen." Poplar Forest served as a year-round retreat from that other "curiosity of the neighborhood," which had already become a magnet for visitors. Eventually Jefferson was making the three-day ride from his official residence three or four times a year and staying here anywhere from two weeks to two months at a time.

Poplar Forest left the Jefferson family when it was sold in 1828, two years after Jefferson's death. A nonprofit organization bought it in 1984 and began restoration in the early 1990s. Restoration is an ongoing process; the exterior has been completely restored, but work continues inside. The interior is sparsely furnished, emphasizing the simple, classical lines of the structure. Guided tours are included with admission.

A winding gravel drive leads to the north portico. The entire house forms a perfect octagon, reflected in the shape of two brick privies on the opposite side. Similarities to Monticello appear in the three-piece windows that fill the parlor with light from floor to ceiling, and alcove beds, one of which has been reproduced here. Twin earth mounds on either side of the house were formed from soil excavated from the wine cellar and sunken lawn and were once planted with aspens and weeping willows.

To reach Poplar Forest (434/525-1806, www.poplarforest.org, 10 A.M.–4 P.M. Wed.–Mon. Apr.–Nov., $14 adults, $6 children 12–18, $2 children 6–11), take VA 811 from U.S. 221 or 460, then turn onto VA 661 (Bateman Bridge Rd.) and follow the signs.

BEDFORD

The self-proclaimed "World's Best Little Town" lost a larger proportion of its population to the horrors of World War II than any other community in the country; 21 of 35 local boys, out of a town of about 3,200 people, died storming the beaches of Normandy. This explains why the otherwise unremarkable town was chosen as the location for the **National D-Day Memorial** (540/587-3619 or 866/219-6900, www.dday.org, 10 A.M.–5 P.M. Tues.–Sun., $5 adults, $3 children, guided tours $2 walking, $3 riding), dedicated in 2001. Set on a hilltop, the memorial re-creates the beach landing down to sculptures of fallen soldiers and jet fountains that simulate bullets pinging off metal and cratering the reflecting pool. A large arch is striped like Allied planes, and walls record the names of the dead. It's worth paying for a guided tour because your guide may have some hair-raising first-person experiences to relate. The memorial is near the intersection of the U.S. 460 bypass and VA 122.

Angus cattle graze on a farm near Bedford.

Bedford is also home to the inimitable **Holy Land USA** (1060 Jericho Rd., 540/586-2823, www.holylandusaonline.com, 9 A.M.–5 P.M. Tues.–Sat., $10, reservations required), a curious mix of faith and farming on the property of retired supermarket owner Bob Johnson. Sheep graze and geese waddle among life-size dioramas depicting scenes from the Bible using unmistakable imagery: The wise man's house stands firm on a rock, while the foolish man's house (built on sand) is a pile of scrap. A three-mile trail into placid fields passes old farm machinery and enough quotations for a month of Sundays. Holy Land USA is three miles west on Dickerson Mill Road (Rte. 746) from Route 122 just south of town.

For another dose of the offbeat, take a pilgrimage to **Peaks of Otter Winery and Johnson's Orchard,** in the Blue Ridge foothills near Bedford. You can't miss the 15-foot-tall **Johnny Appleseed statue** that watches over the vineyard and apple trees with a permanently befuddled look. The **winery's tasting room** (2122 Sheep Creek Rd., 540/586-3707, www.peaksofotterwinery.com, noon–5 P.M. daily Apr.–Dec., noon–5 P.M. weekends only Jan.–Mar.) is really the reason to visit, as is the **Horse & Hound Wine Festival** hosted here in July. From Bedford, take U.S. 460 west for one mile, then turn right on 680 and continue for 5.5 miles, turning left at the entrance sign.

For more information on Bedford, contact the town's tourist office (540/587-5681, www.visitbedford.com).

APPOMATTOX COURT HOUSE NATIONAL HISTORICAL PARK

Following the fall of Petersburg and Richmond in early April 1865, Robert E. Lee led his exhausted Army of Northern Virginia on a fighting retreat west. The goal was to link up with Gen. Joseph Johnston and his Army of Tennessee near Danville, but Ulysses S. Grant's forces harried the Rebels at every step. On April 6, the Battle of Sailor's Creek cost Lee 7,000 men, one-fifth of the remaining Confederate ranks, including Lee's son Custis and seven other generals who were captured. The next day, Lee refused Grant's request for a discussion of surrender, saying he would rather "die a thousand deaths." But after Lee's supplies were captured at Appomattox Station on

ROLFMUELLER / WIKIMEDIA COMMONS

the McLean House in Appomattox Court House National Historical Park

CENTRAL VIRGINIA

the evening of April 8, Lee was compelled to meet with the Union leader.

On Sunday morning, April 9, the two generals met in the parlor of Wilmer McLean's home in Appomattox Court House. They drafted the terms of surrender—the Confederates would be allowed to return home unmolested, they could keep their horses and officers their side arms—and Lee signed the paper, surrendering his army and signaling the end of four years of bloodshed and chaos. At a ceremony on April 12, the ragtag Rebel army laid down its flags and weapons and each man received a printed parole. "The war is over," said Grant, prohibiting any celebration among his troops out of respect. "The rebels are our countrymen again." During the ceremonial stacking of arms, the Federal soldiers rendered a salute to the surrendering Confederates, which was returned in kind.

The McLean House was dismantled in 1893 amid plans to ship it to the capital and rebuild it as part of a war museum, but this never happened, and the pieces lay decaying for decades. Luckily the largely abandoned village was designated a National Historical Park in 1954 and eventually restored to its 1865 appearance.

Visiting Appomattox Court House

Appomattox Court House National Historical Park (434/352-8987, ext. 26, www.nps.gov/apco, 8:30 A.M.–5 P.M. daily, $4 pp or $10 per vehicle in summer, $3 pp or $5 per vehicle off-season) is on Route 24, three miles north of U.S. 460 and the town of Appomattox. Start at the **visitors center** and get your bearings with two 15-minute slide presentations and a map display of Lee's retreat. Take a look at the museum, which holds relics such as little Lula McLean's doll, the "silent witness" to the signing.

In the village, a reconstructed version of the McLean House is decorated as accurately as possible from paintings and firsthand accounts. The nearby Clover Hill Tavern dates to 1819. The park includes a section of the Richmond–Lynchburg Stage Road where the Confederates stacked their arms during the surrender ceremony. Park interpreters can answer questions and point you down the trails to both Lee's and Grant's final headquarters. Living-history programs are held daily from Memorial Day to Labor Day.

Town of Appomattox

Numerous restaurants are available for a quick bite in the present-day town of Appomattox, including the inexpensive, home-style **Granny Bee's** (179 Main St., 434/352-2259, all meals daily except Sunday dinner, entrées $6–14). You can find **campsites** near the 150-acre lake in **Holliday Lake State Park** (434/248-6308, www.dcr.virginia.gov/state_parks/hol.shtml, $2–3 per vehicle) in the Appomattox Buckingham State Forest 12 miles east on Route 24, for $22 with electric and water hookups.

For more information on the area, including details on the **Railroad Festival** in mid-October, contact the **Appomattox Visitor Information Center** (214 Main St., 434/352-8999, www.tourappomattox.com, 9 A.M.–5 P.M. daily).

YOGAVILLE

Integral Yoga guru Sri Swami Satchidananda (1914–2002) was born in India and established the **Satchidananda Ashram – Yogaville** (434/969-2048 or 800/858-9642, www.yogaville.org) to further his goals of peace, universal understanding, and enlightenment. The 750-acre rural retreat centers on the Light of Truth Universal Shrine (L.O.T.U.S.), shaped like a 100-foot blooming lotus. Inside are a neon-lit meditation chamber and 12 altars symbolizing the 10 major religions, "Other Known," and "Those Still Unknown."

The ashram hosts workshops and retreats year-round, and guests are welcome to stop by for an afternoon, day, week, or longer. Lodging options include camping ($85–90 d), dorms ($70–80 pp with shared bath or $155–195 d for private room with shared bath), and the Lotus Guest House ($170–215 d), all of which include three buffet vegetarian meals, hatha yoga classes, and meditation sessions every day. Pickup or drop-off service from Charlottesville is $45–55 per person each way.

SMITH MOUNTAIN LAKE

Central Virginia's favorite aquatic escape was formed in 1966 by the damming of the Roanoke River in Smith Mountain Gap. The resulting 40-mile lake has more than 500 miles of gorgeous shoreline (featured in the movie *What About Bob?* with Richard Dreyfuss and Bill Murray). Oak and pine forests shelter wild turkeys, deer, and woodchucks, and year-round bird species such as pine warblers, tanagers, ospreys, and the rare bald eagle are joined by migratory ducks, geese, loons, and occasionally great tundra swans.

Information and Activities

At Bridgewater Plaza, on the south side of Hales Ford Bridge (Rte. 122 south from Bedford), you'll find a **visitors center** operated by the Smith Mountain Lake Chamber of Commerce (800/676-8203, www.visitsmithmountainlake.com), along with one of two dozen marinas scattered along the shoreline. At just about any of these marinas you can rent personal watercraft, canoes, sailboats, pedalboats, and fishing boats by the hour or day, as well as buy bait and equipment; try **Bridgewater Plaza Marina & Boat Rentals** (540/721-1639 or 800/729-1639, www.bridgewaterplaza.com) or the **Parkway Marina** (540/297-4412, www.parkwaymarina.com) at the end of Route 626 on the north side. Learn to sail with the **Smith Mountain Lake Sailing School** (540/719-0009, www.smlsailing.com), which offers classes for all levels.

Fishing in Smith Mountain Lake is outstanding, especially for black bass, muskie, and walleye. Striped bass are in season year-round. (Remember, Virginia fishing licenses are required.) Saddle up at **Smith Mountain Farm & Stables** (7661 Grassland Dr., Sandy Level, 434/927-5199, www.smithmountainstables.com), where two-hour horseback rides (by appointment only) are $70.

The ***Virginia Dare*** paddle wheel tour boat (540/297-7100 or 800/721-3273, www.vadarecruises.com) takes passengers on lunch and dinner cruises April–December. Tours are $38–42 per person for lunch (daily) and $41–45 for dinner (Mon.–Sat.). Sightseeing-only tours (without a meal) cost $20 for adults and $10 for children 12 and under.

There are plenty of shopping possibilities in the gourmet markets and antiques stores along Route 122 on both sides of the bridge. Three lakefront golf courses—**Mariner's Landing** (540/297-7888, www.marinerslandinggolf.com), **Sycamore Ridge** (540/297-6490), and the **Westlake Golf & Country Club** (540/721-4214, www.golfthewestlake.com)—are open to the public. You can tour the Appalachian Power Company's **Smith Mountain Dam** (540/985-2587, 10 A.M.–6 P.M. daily), built in 1967, at the east end of the lake.

Smith Mountain Lake State Park

Sixteen miles of shoreline and the only public swimming beach on the lake fall within this small park (540/297-6066, www.dcr.virginia.gov/state_parks/smi.shtml, $3 per vehicle weekdays, $4 weekends) on the north shore of the lake off Route 626. Not all of the fun is in the water (it's $3 pp to swim): Four short hiking trails wind through pine and hardwood forests to secluded coves. Facilities include pedalboats for rent, hiking trails, and campsites for tents and vehicles ($20–25), open March–November. Two- and three-bedroom cabins with docks and wood-burning stoves can fit 4–6 people each for $75–129 per night. A small visitors center explains the local human and natural history.

Events

Mariners Landing hosts an **Antique and Classic Boat Show and Rally** (800/676-8203, www.woodenboats.net, free) in mid-September, with mahogany and cedar cruisers, runabouts, and sailboats on display. Over two dozen Virginia wineries come for the **Smith Mountain Lake Wine Festival** (800/676-8203, $15–22 admission) in late September.

Accommodations and Food

In Hardy, the **Lake Inn Motel** (45 Enterprise Ln., 888/466-5253, www.lakeinnmotel.com) has rooms for a reasonable $65–96. A plethora of real-estate agencies can help with lakeside lodging rentals. Try **Lake Retreat Properties** (540/297-6002 or 800/421-6980, www.lakeretreat.com) or **Lakeshore Rentals** (540/297-5610 or 800/572-6098, www.lakeshorerentals.com).

Bridgewater Plaza offers several casual dining options: **Mango's Bar & Grill** (540/721-1632, lunch and dinner daily) features an outdoor grill and a "tropical state of mind"; **Moosie's** (540/721-5255, from 11 A.M. daily) cooks up barbecue and Mexican dishes; and the **Pizza Pub** (540/721-1234, lunch and dinner daily) explains itself.

The Landing restaurant (540/721-3028, lunch Fri.–Sat., dinner Tues.–Sun.) is nearby at 773 Ashmeade Road in Moneta. It's a more upscale place, with dinner appetizers for $7–16 and entrées such as pan-seared ahi for $12–35.

BOOKER T. WASHINGTON NATIONAL MONUMENT

The most influential and powerful black activist in early-1900s America was born a slave on a small Virginia tobacco farm in 1856. Freed by the Emancipation Proclamation, the Washington family moved to West Virginia, where young Booker struggled to take advantage of a startling new opportunity: education. First he rose every day before dawn to work in a salt mine so his afternoons would be free for school. Then, at age 16, Booker walked most of the 500 miles back to Virginia to attend the Hampton Institute, one of the country's leading schools for blacks, where he would eventually become a teacher.

In 1881 Washington opened his own school, the Tuskegee Institute in Alabama. A low point in race relations, personified by the rising Ku Klux Klan, intensified the fine balance between educating fellow blacks in useful skills and antagonizing whites. His nonconfrontational stance, calling for interracial cooperation without abolishing social segregation too abruptly, drew protests from within his own race.

Nonetheless, Washington endured critical attacks and racial slurs to become the leading black figure of his day. His famous Atlanta Compromise Address of 1895 crystallized his conservative viewpoint, which gradually became more liberal in his later years. In 1901 he published an autobiography, *Up from Slavery,* and he died at Tuskegee in 1915.

The farm where Washington was born into servitude is on Route 122 west of Smith Mountain Lake. Start your visit to the monument (540/721-2094, www.nps.gov/bowa, 9 A.M.–5 P.M. daily, free) at the visitors center, which has a short video and a touch-screen information program on Washington's life. From there, a short walking trail leads past reconstructed buildings and stone outlines of the original structures, including the owners' home and the building where Washington was born. The 1.5-mile Jack-o-Lantern Trail heads off into the woods, and rangers offer guided tours in the summer; contact the park for times.

Danville

The manufacturing center of southern Virginia, just a hair north of the North Carolina border, Danville (pop. 45,000) was until recently one of the most important tobacco auction centers in the country, though even here they've all but petered out. Along with one million square feet of now-empty auction space, the legacy of its Victorian-era economic heyday lives on in the stunning architecture along Millionaires' Row.

History

William Byrd, trying to determine the true boundary between North Carolina and Virginia in 1728, was so captivated by the surrounding scenery that he said he felt as if he had wandered "from Dan to Beersheba." The Biblical praise stuck in the name of the Dan River and, in 1793, the town, which was named the same year its first tobacco warehouse was

THE WRECK OF THE OLD 97

September 27, 1903, began as just another quiet Sunday morning in Danville. At the helm of locomotive No. 1002, Engineer Joseph Broady, a 20-year veteran of the Southern Railroad, was running late from Lynchburg. Luckily the "Old 97" was the fastest engine on the Southern Line, and Broady opened the throttle wide. At the top of White Oak Mountain, he realized he was going too fast for the three-mile downhill grade that loomed ahead. At the bottom was the 500-foot curved trestle above the Dan River.

In vain Broady reversed the engine, locking the wheels in a scream of metal. As the five-car train hit the trestle, it leapt from the rails and vaulted 75 feet into the rocky creek bed below. Nine passengers were killed and seven were injured in the disaster. Images of the twisted wreckage leapt from front pages nationwide.

The famous ballad inspired by the crash inspired controversy of its own. Initially recorded by Virginia musicians Henry Whitter and G. B. Grayson, it was released by singer Vernon Dalhart and went on to become the country's first platinum record, before the term was even invented. It eventually sold five million copies. The song's true author, however, was still in dispute. In 1933, the first major copyright lawsuit was resolved when the courts ruled against the RCA Victor Company, stating that David George, a telegraph operator at the scene of the accident, was the original author. Even though George himself probably added new lyrics to an older folk tune, he was awarded $65,000. RCA Victor, in turn, tied up the case through appeals for so long that George never collected a penny for "The Wreck of the Old 97."

A plaque marks the crash site on U.S. 58 between Locust Lane and North Main Street.

established. "Twelve fit and able men" elected the first mayor in 1833, and during the Civil War Danville's population of 5,000 expanded when Federal soldiers were imprisoned there.

After the destruction of Richmond in April 1865, Jefferson Davis and the rest of the Confederate cabinet moved into the home of prominent Danville citizen Maj. William T. Sutherlin. Less than two weeks later, the Rebels would lay down their arms—they were there long enough, however, to earn Danville the title of Last Capital of the Confederacy.

In the meantime, Danville's manufacturing industry kept growing. Riverside Cotton Mills, founded in 1882, came to be known as Dan River Inc., which, until the employer of 3,500 folded in 2008, was the largest single-unit textile facility in the world. You've likely slept between Dan River sheets at some point in your life—so perhaps take a moment of silence for the 126-year-old mill as you drive by.

Orientation

Danville is spread on both sides of the Dan River, which runs roughly east to west. Downtown is mostly on the southern side of the river, sandwiched between it and the North Carolina line.

SIGHTS

The section of Main Street near the 1000 block, listed in the National Register of Historic Places, is the architectural equivalent of a wedding cake catalog. Dripping scrollwork and sweeping porches decorate mansion after mansion, each one gaudier than the one before. Cupolas and minarets thrust skyward as stately columns keep everything grounded. Every architectural style of the Victorian era, plus a few more to boot, is represented: Queen Anne (#926), High Victorian Gothic (#878), Early Federal (#770), Georgian Revival (#776), and Italianate (#753). The gorgeous monster at #1020 is simply known as the "Wedding Cake House." Pick up a walking-tour brochure at the visitors center.

Danville Museum of Fine Arts and History

This 1857 Italianate mansion on Millionaires' Row was home to Maj. William T. Sutherlin, tobacco merchant and wartime quartermaster, before Jefferson Davis and company arrived on April 3, 1865. Davis issued his final proclamation as Confederate president a day later, and left for North Carolina on April 10 after the arrival of the news that Lee had surrendered at Appomattox Court House. Today the museum (975 Main St., 434/793-5644, www.danvillemuseum.org, 10 A.M.–5 P.M. Tues.–Fri., 2–5 P.M. Sat.–Sun., $5 adults, $4 students, free children 6 and under) houses exhibits of local history and art, with a small auditorium where local groups perform.

The Crossing at the Dan

The former Southern Railroad Yard at 677 Craighead Street in the tobacco warehouse district has been renovated and filled with shops, restaurants, and entertainment facilities. The 1899 passenger station is now the **Danville Science Center** (434/791-5160, www.dsc.smv.org, 9:30 A.M.–5 P.M. Tues.–Sat., 1–5 P.M. Sun., $6 adults, $5 children 4–12). A satellite of Richmond's Science Museum of Virginia, the center is full of hands-on family-oriented displays of science and natural history. An outdoor butterfly garden is open in summer.

Danville's **Community Market** (434/797-8961, 8 A.M.–noon Sat. May.–Oct.) occupies the 1904 Southern Railroad Freight Warehouse. Farm-fresh produce, baked goods, and crafts are among the offerings in season. Nearby **Carrington Pavilion** (629 Craighead St., 434/793-4636), also known as Auctioneers Park, has an outdoor amphitheater with room for thousands. This is where you'll find one end of a 3.5-mile bike and foot trail along the riverfront to Dan Daniel Park, passing over an early-1900s railroad bridge along the way.

Birthplace of Lady Astor

Born here on May 19, 1879, Nancy Witcher Langhorne would grow up to become the Viscountess Astor, the first woman to sit in the British Parliament. She was the source of such immortal quotes as "I married beneath me—all women do" and "the only thing I like about rich people is their money." Her sister Irene would make a name for herself in turn by marrying artist Charles Dana Gibson and providing the inspiration for the famous Gibson Girls. The house (117 Broad St. at Main St.) is open by appointment only; call the visitors center for information (434/793-4636).

American Armoured Foundation Tank Museum

The world's largest collection of international tanks and cavalry artifacts consists of almost 100 pieces spanning 200 years of history, including a 62-ton tank and a missile transport. The museum (3401 U.S. 29 N., 434/836-5323, www.aaftankmuseum.com, 10 A.M.–4 P.M. Mon.–Sat., $10 adults, $9.50 children) is impressive in its breadth, from 500 pieces of military headgear to 140 weapons, such as bazookas, flamethrowers, and machine guns. The collection includes Panzer and Patton tanks, eight artillery pieces, and more than 100,000 pieces of military memorabilia.

Virginia International Raceway

Originally built in 1957, this racetrack situated 12 miles east of Danville got a face-lift in the 1990s. A year-round schedule of motor events includes motorcycle races and historic sportscar rallies. An 1830s plantation home serves as a clubhouse, complete with restaurant and lounge. Most events are held April–October, led by the Virginia Festival of Speed in late June and early July.

The raceway (1245 Pine Tree Rd., 434/822-7700, www.virclub.com) is in Alton, Virginia. To get there, take U.S. 58 east to Route 62 south. In Milton, North Carolina, take Route 57 onto Racetrack Road back over the state line. Tickets are $10–60 per person; contact the raceway for events listings and information.

EVENTS

Mid-May's **Festival in the Park** brings arts and crafts, entertainment, and food to Ballou Park, and concerts are held at the Crossing of the Dan the first Friday evening of every month in summer during **Fridays at the Crossing.** In November, hopheads head to the **Bright Leaf Brew Fest** ($21 pp, $5 designated driver) held in the Crossing. Contact the Danville welcome center to buy tickets.

ACCOMMODATIONS

$50-100

The **Innkeeper Danville West** (3020 Riverside Dr., 434/799-1202) is on U.S. 58 west of the U.S. 29 junction, and its sister motel, the **Innkeeper Danville North** (1030 Piney Forest Rd., 434/836-1700), is on U.S. 29 2.5 miles north of U.S. 58. Both offer accommodations for $50–150. The **Hampton Inn Riverside** (2130 Riverside Dr., 434/793-1111, $80–110) is on Route 58, half a mile from the junction of Routes 86 and 29.

Cabins made of logs from century-old tobacco barns provide the accommodations at **Fall Creek Farm** (2556 Green Farm Rd., 434/791-3297, www.fall-creek-farm.com, $75–95). Inside are stone fireplaces, antiques, and whirlpool tubs, and outside are porch rockers. Breakfast is delivered each morning, and there's even a heated pool for guests to use. To get there, take U.S. 29 north (Main St.) to Route 726 East (Malmaison Rd.), and go 3.5 miles to Route 360 South (Old Richmond Rd.). From there it's another mile to Route 719 (Green Farm Rd.). Rates including full breakfast are $100–120.

$150-250

Lodgings at the **Courtyard by Marriott** (2136 Riverside Dr., 434/791-2661) run $100–120, with suites from $160. It has high-speed Internet and an exercise room.

FOOD

It's mostly chain food in Danville, but a few locally owned places serve simple and straightforward cuisine. **Mary's Diner** (1203 Piney Forest Rd., 434/836-5034, lunch and dinner daily, specials for $5) has been family owned and operated since 1951. Mary's boasts the best fried chicken and soup in town.

In the Riverside Shopping Center, **Joe & Mimma's Italian Restaurant and Pizza** (3336 Riverside Dr., 434/799-5763, lunch and dinner Tues.–Sat.) has pastas for $8–13 and entrées for $15–21, along with healthier and vegetarian entrées, gourmet pizzas, and seafood. Come for the ribs, stay for the pulled pork sandwiches at **Short Sugar's Bar-B-Q** (2215 Riverside Dr., 434/793-4800, all meals Mon.–Sat.). Prices are mostly in the $6–10 range.

INFORMATION

Danville's **welcome center** is across from Dan Daniel Memorial Park at 645 River Park Drive (434/793-4636, www.visitdanville.com, 8 A.M.–5:30 P.M. daily).

MARTINSVILLE

About 30 miles west of Danville is Martinsville, home to the exceptional **Virginia Museum of Natural History** (21 Starling Ave., 276/634-4141, www.vmnh.net, 9 A.M.–5 P.M. Mon.–Sat., $7 adults, $3 children), an affiliate of the Smithsonian Institution. Exhibits highlight the state's geology, biology, and paleontology, including ongoing research projects. From the deer-hunting tiger to the allosaurus skeleton cast, this place is a real find in south-central Virginia.

Martinsville is also home to the **Martinsville Speedway** (877/722-3849, www.martinsvillespeedway.com), the shortest track (just over half a mile) in the Sprint Cup circuit. The NASCAR-sanctioned track hosts the Goody's Fast Pain Relief 500, the Kroger 250, and other races from March through October.

THE SHENANDOAH

"To everyone, especially to those who live in narrow streets where automobiles are thicker than ants in an ant hill and where trolleys clang, sirens screech, and people rush about, we say, come to this beautiful Blue Ridge area for recreation . . ." So began one letter, written in the 1920s, encouraging the creation of Shenandoah National Park. Today, Shenandoah entices visitors for much the same reasons.

But what *is* the Shenandoah, exactly? The word comes from a Native American term meaning "beautiful daughter of the stars," which should give you a clue as to this corner of Virginia's deep and glittering legacy.

In name, it's a lazy-rolling river—two, actually, born in the valleys on the west side of the Blue Ridge. The North and South Forks of the Shenandoah River flow northeast before joining near Front Royal and entering West Virginia. By the time it reaches the Potomac near Harpers Ferry, the Shenandoah has become the larger river's main tributary. It's the perfect waterway for fishing, tubing, or canoeing: slow, winding, and lined with green most of the way.

In legend, the Shenandoah refers to the wide, fertile valley dividing the Blue Ridge Mountains from the Alleghenies—which was elevated to near-mythic status by some of the most dramatic fighting of the Civil War. The fruitful soil drew settlers centuries ago, as first- or second-generation German farmers moved down from Pennsylvania to the valley where, it was said, the summer grass grew high enough to tie across a horse's saddle.

HIGHLIGHTS

Luray Caverns: The Shenandoah has most of the state's commercial caverns, including this, the largest and most spectacular on the East Coast (page 310).

Hiking in Shenandoah National Park: Waterfalls, windswept ridgetops, and the Appalachian Trail, steps away from Skyline Drive, are just some of the attractions you'll see hoofing it through Virginia's premier outdoor destination (page 318).

Grand Caverns Regional Park: Cathedral Hall is the highlight of this, another astounding network of caves. Be sure to check out the Civil War-era "graffiti" (page 327).

Frontier Culture Museum: Learn what rural life was like in the 18th and 19th centuries at Staunton's first-rate Frontier Culture Museum. The buildings, farming techniques, and even the livestock are all rigorously authentic (page 330).

Polyface Farms: Hop on a hay bale for a tour of one of the most sustainable farms in the nation (page 335).

The Homestead: Depending on the season, you can golf, ski, or just relax with a soothing soak at the most venerable and lavish resort hotel in the state (page 340).

Natural Bridge: Despite all the commercial hoopla surrounding it, it's still an impressive – and beautiful – stretch of stone. Bonus points for spotting George Washington's initials carved into the base (page 350).

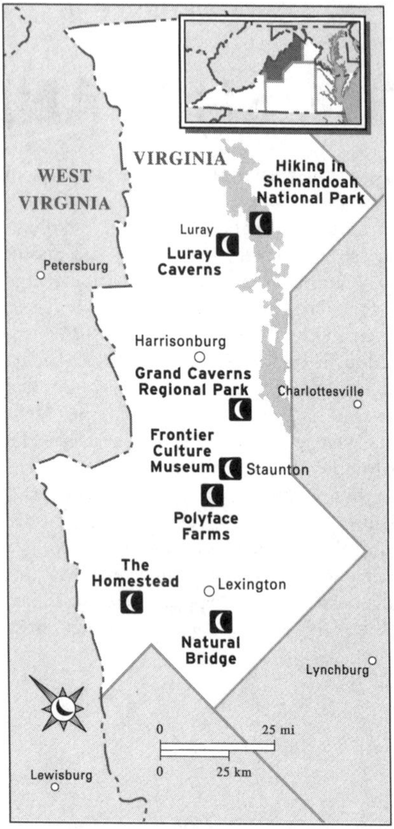

LOOK FOR ☾ TO FIND RECOMMENDED SIGHTS, ACTIVITIES, DINING, AND LODGING.

During the war the valley's productivity and strategic importance almost proved to be her undoing. Over three years, the area endured more battles than any other region in the country, and in so doing, buried tragedy and lore beneath the rich farmland.

In essence, the Shenandoah is equal parts legend and locale, embodied in the rich odors of farmland in morning mist, snow on ragged granite peaks, and the simple pleasures of small-town hospitality evident even in the larger cities.

PLANNING YOUR TIME

Aside from its intangible enticements of atmosphere, the Shenandoah is replete with things to do and see. Set aside at least 4–5 days to hit the highlights. The approach is obviously linear, but Winchester and Staunton both make good staging points from the north and south ends of the valley, respectively. Several good half- and full-day excursions are possible from Winchester, including the towns of White Post and Middletown. Moving south down the valley, **Luray Caverns** and **Grand Caverns** are two of the state's best subterranean attractions. Head up, not down, to reach **Shenandoah National Park,** which you can access from the north, south, or middle entrances.

History fans should be sure not to miss the living exhibits at the **Frontier Culture Museum** near Staunton. While near this city, take a farm tour at **Polyface Farms** and find out what on earth an "Eggerator" is. The Allegheny Highlands make a good two- or three-day excursion from Staunton; head up to Monterey and swing by the **Homestead** on your way back for some golf, spa treatments, or skiing in the winter. Lexington and the famous **Natural Bridge** can be combined into another good day trip from Staunton. You could easily take a week driving from Front Royal to the North Carolina border along the crest of the Blue Ridge, following the Skyline Drive through Shenandoah National Park and the Blue Ridge Parkway thereafter.

Access

I-81 runs the length of the valley along the well-worn route of the Old Valley Pike, once worn deep into the soil by native tribes, European settlers, and Civil War troops. As one of the main north–south routes in the mid-Atlantic, this interstate is clogged with 18-wheelers, which use the route as a toll-free alternative to I-95. (The situation is getting so bad there is talk of building a second four-lane "truckway" parallel to the interstate.) The older, more scenic route of the Old Valley Pike lives on as U.S. 11, worlds away from the interstate, although the two are often within sight and sound of each other. Up north, I-66 leads to Front Royal and the mountains for the weekend hordes from Washington, D.C.

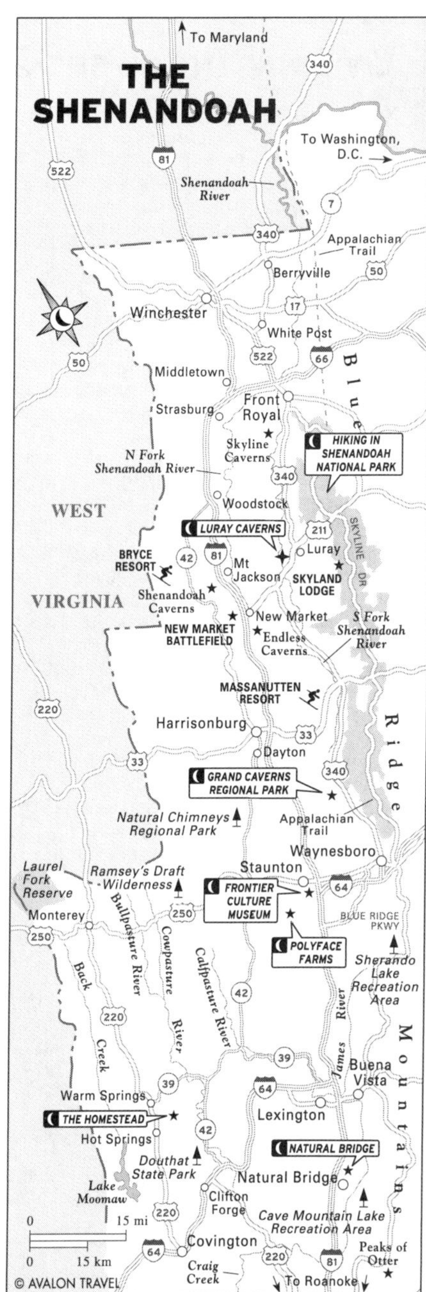

CIVIL WAR IN THE SHENANDOAH

As the Civil War slowly tore through Virginia, the strategic value of the Shenandoah made it crucial to the strategies of both sides. The valley was not only the fertile breadbasket of the Confederacy, but it could also allow troops to march unseen practically to the steps of Washington, D.C. – or, in the other direction, to flank Richmond. "If the valley is lost," declared Stonewall Jackson, "Virginia is lost." The Rebel commander would add his own legend to the two short but bloody years that transformed a pastoral landscape into a smoking wasteland.

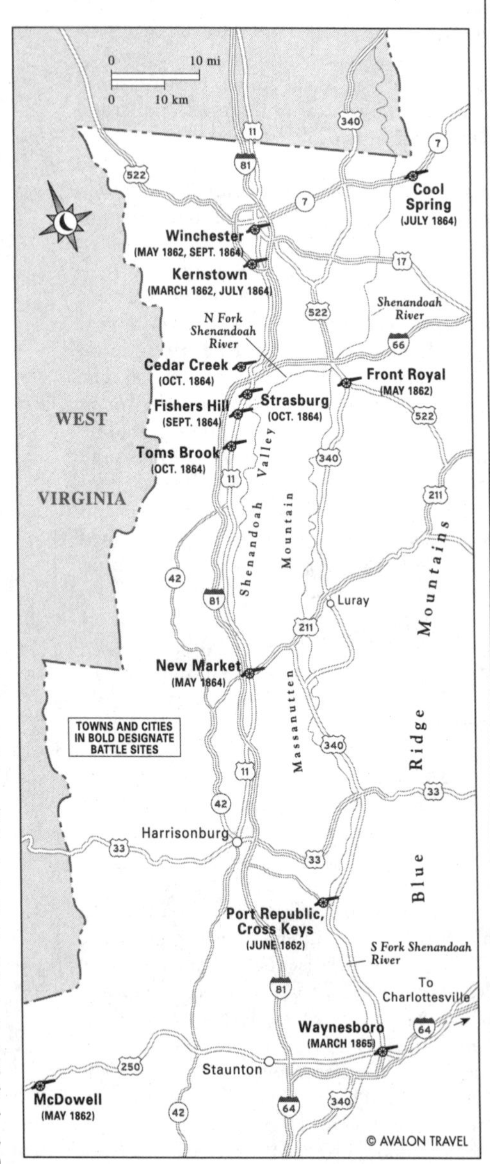

SPRING 1862: JACKSON'S VALLEY CAMPAIGN

Robert E. Lee's orders to Jackson were simple: defend the valley, and prevent Federal reinforcements from joining the attack on Richmond. With that in mind, Jackson pitted his 17,000 troops against heavy odds in an incredible display of cunning, endurance, and luck. In seven weeks, Jackson's famous "foot cavalry" – consisting of the 2nd, 4th, 5th, 27th, and 33rd Virginia infantry regiments and the elite Rockbridge Artillery – fought four battles and six skirmishes, marched more than 600 miles, and eventually immobilized and inflicted casualties (twice as many as they suffered) on some 60,000 Federals.

"There are two things never to be lost sight of by a military commander," said Jackson. "Always mystify, mislead, and surprise the enemy if possible...[and] never fight against heavy odds, if by possible maneuvering you can hurl your own force on only a part, and the weakest part, of your enemy and crush it." Not surprisingly, he employed a strategy of surprise and deception that suited the uneven terrain perfectly and had his dogged troops showing up whenever and wherever they were least expected. Jackson realized that speed was of the essence, and once led his troops 350 miles in

30 days. His tactics worked: As of 1864, the Stonewall Brigade had yet to be driven from a field that it defended.

At the First Battle of Kernstown, on March 23, 1862, Jackson attacked a force he thought to be only a few regiments strong, but which turned out to be Gen. James Shields' entire division. Both sides raced for the cover of a wall in the middle of an open field. The Confederates won, though they eventually had to retreat in the face of overwhelming numbers. The Rebels did, however, manage to keep Shields from joining McClellan's peninsular campaign.

On May 3, Jackson mystified even his own subordinates when he ordered half his army to march eastward out of the valley. Almost to Charlottesville, the troops suddenly found themselves herded onto railroad cars and shipped back to Staunton. There they disembarked and marched off for a surprise attack at McDowell on May 8, forcing Union troops under Gen. Robert Milroy to flee into West Virginia.

With help from the spirited spy Belle Boyd, the Confederates captured Front Royal on May 23 after joining with Jubal Early's command in a surprising move and passing through a gap in Massanutten Mountain. During this battle, members of the 1st Maryland Division from each side found themselves facing, greeting, and then fighting their own neighbors and relatives.

The First Battle of Winchester, on May 25, followed a race toward the important supply city that was lost by Union Maj. Gen. Nathaniel Banks. At sunset, Banks, believing the fighting ended, went upstairs to take a bath. Under Jackson, though, the Confederate attacks continued, sending the Union troops scurrying in retreat toward Washington, D.C. (When Banks asked one retreating soldier if he loved his country, the man replied, "Yes sir, and I'm trying to get back to it as fast as I can.") Pursuit was eventually called off because Jackson's men were too worn out from marching the previous nights.

Two more victories in June near Port Republic secured the Confederate hold on the valley. On June 8, Gen. Richard S. Ewell sent a larger army under Gen. John C. Fremont packing, and the next day Jackson defeated Brig. Gen. Erasmus Tyler.

In a tragic turn of events, Jackson was accidentally killed by his own men following the Confederate triumph at Chancellorsville one year later.

SUMMER 1864: THE TIDE TURNS

As the war dragged on, Lincoln and his Union commanders realized they would have to bring the South to its knees by any means possible to keep the war from continuing indefinitely. Soon after the Battle of New Market on May 15, in which 10 VMI cadets were killed, Union Lt. Gen. Ulysses S. Grant began a massive statewide offensive intended to end the war once and for all. Lee sent Lt. Gen. Jubal Early to defend the valley. Early's Maryland Campaign, as it became known, began with successes at Cool Spring on July 19 and the Second Battle of Kernstown on July 24. By August, Early had his sights set on Washington, D.C., itself.

Embarrassed by the continued defeats and alarmed by the threat to the capital, Grant realized that the Union had to win the valley at all costs. He sent Maj. Gen. Philip Sheridan south with orders to raze the Shenandoah so completely "that a crow flying over it will have to carry his provender [provisions] with him." Sheridan's Valley Campaign spelled doom for the area as surely as Jackson's had meant its temporary salvation. Early's 12,000 remaining troops found themselves facing 40,000 Union soldiers who advanced down the valley slaughtering livestock, ruining fields, and putting buildings to the torch. Scattered stone foundations still recall the frenzy of destruction remembered for generations as "The Burning."

The Battle of Opequon (Third Winchester), on September 19, was the largest in the valley, leaving 5,000 Federal and 3,500 Confederate casualties in its wake. Despite the numbers, it was considered a Union victory. Three more wins – Fishers Hill on September 22, Toms Brook on October 9, and Cedar Creek (near Strasburg) on October 18 – marked the beginning of the end for the Confederate hold on the valley. At the Battle of Waynesboro, on March 2, 1865, Sheridan crushed Early's remaining forces and condemned the South to defeat.

The Blue Ridge is pierced by another interstate (I-64), roughly paralleled by the Amtrak line from Charlottesville to West Virginia via Staunton, and several smaller roads (U.S. 211 from Luray, U.S. 33 from Harrisonburg, and U.S. 60 from Lexington).

Resources

The **Shenandoah Valley Travel Association** (540/740-3132 or 800/847-4878, www.visitshenandoah.org) can provide more information on touring the area. ShenandoahValley.com is another useful website.

Winchester and Vicinity

A map of Virginia is like a salute to our Second Amendment rights, what with city names like Remington and, of course, Winchester. Known for its apple blossoms and Civil War battles, Winchester (pop. 25,000) has alternately enjoyed and endured its position as the gateway to the northern Shenandoah Valley. The largest and fastest-growing city in Virginia's apple heartland of Frederick and Clarke Counties, Winchester is surrounded by acres and acres of orchards, filled with delicate buds in the spring and teams of migrant harvest workers in the fall. From padded shoulder buckets to wooden crates in the backs of rumbling trucks, the fruit eventually makes its way to dozens of processing plants near town that infuse the air with the sweet smell of cider, vinegar, apple butter, and applesauce in the making. More than half of each yearly crop of 200–300 million pounds is sold fresh across the country.

Several natives of this region have gone on to nationwide fame, including progressive 1920s governor Harry Byrd. Country singer Patsy Cline hailed from the nearby town of Gore and worked in Gaunt's Drug Store at the corner of South Loudoun Street and Valley Avenue. She is buried in the Shenandoah Memorial Park cemetery, and a boulevard was named in her honor east of the interstate.

The quaint Old Town Pedestrian Mall (www.oldtownwinchesterva.com), on Loudoun Street between Piccadilly and Cork, is crowded with restaurants.

History

Virginia's oldest city west of the Blue Ridge, Winchester began as a Shawnee campground that was settled by Pennsylvania Quakers in 1732. Settlers soon arrived from all over Europe, including Scotch-Irish, Welsh, English, and French. Germans left their mark in trim houses set flush against sidewalks with tidy gardens in back.

In 1748, an eager red-haired 16-year-old

PATSY CLINE CHRONOLOGY

1932	Born Virginia Patterson Hensley in Winchester
1957	Records "Walkin' After Midnight," which hit #2 on country charts and #12 on pop charts
1958	Moves to Nashville, joins Grand Ole Opry
1961-1962	#1 Female Recording Artist; records Willie Nelson's "Crazy"
1962	#1 country song "I Fall to Pieces"
1963	Dies at age 30 in a plane crash in Tennessee
1973	Inducted into Country Music Hall of Fame
1992	Commemorative stamp issued
1994	Inducted into Cowgirl Hall of Fame
1995	*Greatest Hits* album sells six million copies
	Honored with Grammy Lifetime Achievement Award

arrived to survey thousands of rolling acres belonging to Lord Fairfax. Within a decade, George Washington had set about building Fort Loudoun to protect the frontier town from Indian attacks and French encroachment. Soon he was elected to his first political office in the House of Burgesses.

During the Civil War, Winchester saw as much action as any city in Virginia. On the cusp of the Shenandoah Valley, with Maryland less than 50 miles to the north, Winchester changed hands 72 times during the course of the war—13 times in one day. Some of these capitulations were questionable—a single soldier left in town after the opposition retreated, for instance—but no fewer than five major battles were fought within the city limits. The Third Battle of Winchester (aka Opequon), on September 19, 1864, was the largest fought in the valley. Confederate forces under Lt. Gen. Jubal Early killed more than 5,000 of Sheridan's Federal troops, but the battle was still considered a Union victory. Thousands of wounded were brought here from Gettysburg and Antietam, helping fill close to 8,000 graves in two major cemeteries along Woodstock Lane—Stonewall for the Confederates, National for the Federals.

SIGHTS

The **Museum of the Shenandoah Valley** (901 Amherst St., 540/662-1473 or 888/556-5799, www.shenandoahmuseum.org, 10 A.M.–4 P.M. Tues.–Sun., house and gardens Mar.–Nov. only) combines the 18th-century homestead of Winchester founder James Wood, six acres of

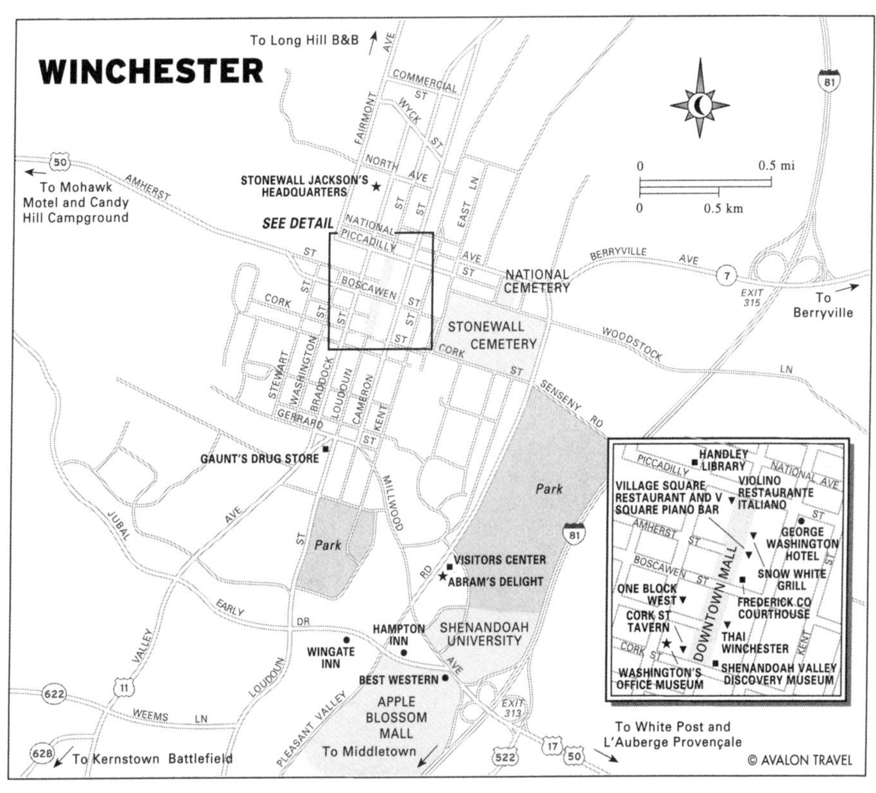

spectacular gardens, including an arched tunnel of flowering crab apple trees, and a modern museum for an in-depth overview of the valley's history, art, and culture. Opened in 2005, the museum displays fine art, antiques, and a beguiling gallery of miniature rooms and houses. Admission to all is $12 adults, $10 children 7–18, with less expensive options to visit the house, gardens, or museum only.

Block tickets to Winchester's three main historical sights can be purchased ($10 adults, $4 children 7–18) at any of the three locations. Separate admission is also available ($5/$2.50). Abram's Delight, Stonewall Jackson's Headquarters, and George Washington's Office Museum are all open 10 A.M.–4 P.M. Monday–Saturday, noon–4 P.M. Sunday April–October.

Abram's Delight (1340 S. Pleasant Valley Rd., 540/662-6519, www.winchesterhistory.org), the oldest home in Winchester, sits across from the visitors center and next to pleasant Wilkins Lake Park. This stone building was built by Isaac Hollingsworth in 1754 to replace a log cabin built by his father, Abraham, who had called his 582 acres "a delight to behold." The limestone main house served as the city's first Quaker meetinghouse. Five generations of Hollingsworths furnished the home with what are now beautiful antiques, and rope beds upstairs had to be tightened every night with a special crank (hence the phrase "sleep tight"). Abraham's ghost is said to move things around when nobody's looking.

The 1854 Gothic Revival building that served as **Stonewall Jackson's Headquarters** (415 N. Braddock St., 540/667-3242, www.winchesterhistory.org) originally belonged to Lt. Col. Lewis Moore, great-grandfather of Mary Tyler Moore (who donated the reproduction gilt wallpaper). The building was taken over by the Confederate general from late 1861 to the start of his Valley Campaign in 1862. Civil War–era furniture and relics include original Confederate flags, uniforms, and Jackson's prayer book and camp table. Heft an 1861 Springfield rifle and try to figure out whether *you* could have handled the percussion caps, minnie ball bullets, and ramrod quickly enough to load and fire it three times in one minute.

Between September 1755 and December 1756, future founding father George Washington, still a 23-year-old colonel in the Virginia militia, organized the frontier town's Revolutionary War defenses from a three-room structure preserved today as **George Washington's Office Museum** (32 W. Cork St., 540/662-4412, www.winchesterhistory.org). The museum is filled with Revolutionary War memorabilia, antique surveying tools, and an interactive map of early Winchester. Bloodstains under one window bear witness to one of the city's many battles, and there is a lock of Washington's hair on display.

The **Old Court House Civil War Museum** in the Frederick County Courthouse (20 N. Loudoun St., 540/542-1145, www.civilwarmuseum.org, 10 A.M.–5 P.M. Wed.–Sat., 1–5 P.M. Sun., $5 adults, $3 children 5–17) contains excavated relics from the war that illustrate the lives of common soldiers. The building served as a hospital and prison for both sides. Graffiti left by prisoners on the upstairs walls, including a curse to Confederate president Jefferson Davis by a Union soldier, have been framed behind glass.

At the corner of Braddock and Piccadilly sits the **World's Largest Apple,** built to top a 5,200-pound monument in rival apple town Cornelia, Georgia (which was actually a 1927 gift from Winchester). A few blocks over on the downtown mall, children can try their hand at a mock apple-packing center, one of the many interactive exhibits at the **Shenandoah Valley Discovery Museum** (54 S. Loudoun St., 540/722-2020, www.discoverymuseum.net, 9 A.M.–5 P.M. Mon.–Sat., 1–5 P.M. Sun., $6). You can browse the museum shop for free.

With its extensively carved exterior and three-story rotunda topped by a copper dome, the 1913 **Handley Library** (100 W. Piccadilly St. at Boscawen, 540/662-9041, www.hrl.lib.state.va.us) is considered the best example of beaux arts architecture in the state.

U-PICK ORCHARDS

You can't come to Winchester and not pick a few apples for the ride home. There are at least a half-dozen u-pick orchards within a short drive of town. **Marker-Miller Orchards** (3035 Cedar Creek Grade, 540/662-1980, www.markermillerorchards.com) has 325 acres of familiar varieties like Gala and Granny Smith as well as lesser-known Nittanys and Staymans. The apple-cider donuts at the bakery are the real reason you want to come. **Richards Fruit Market** (6410 Middle Rd., 540/869-1455, www.richardsfruitmarket.com) holds an Apple Festival in October with pony rides, live music, and ice cream to go with slices of apple pie. Apple-picking season usually begins in late August and continues through late November. The Virginia State Apple Board (434/984-0573, www.virginiaapples.org) and the Winchester–Frederick County Visitors Center will have more suggestions.

ENTERTAINMENT

From mid-June to early August, you can enjoy a Broadway performance by the **Shenandoah Summer Music Theatre** (877/580-8025, www.shenandoahsummermusictheatre.com). Tickets for productions such as *Annie, Fiddler on the Roof,* and *Oklahoma!* are around $28. It's based out of Shenandoah University near Abram's Delight.

Look for live music at **Brewbaker's Restaurant** (168 N. Loudoun St., 540/535-0111) and **Sweet Caroline's** (29 W. Cork St., 540/723-8805, www.sweetcarolines.net).

SHOPPING

At the north end of the mall, the **HandWorks Gallery** (150 N. Loudoun St., 540/662-3927) sells unusual and beautiful handicrafts from all over the world, including handcrafted wooden boxes from Poland, batik masks from Indonesia, and Peruvian carved gourds. The **Winchester Book Gallery** (185 N. Loudoun St., 540/667-3444) stocks a large selection of gardening and Civil War titles, as well as cookbooks and children's picture books.

The wood floor and handhewn beams of an old apple-packing warehouse lend the perfect setting for antiques shopping at **Millwood Crossing** (381 Millwood Ave., 540/662-5157), with about 10,000 square feet of antiques and specialty shops.

EVENTS

To usher in spring and its acres of blooming orchards, normally conservative Winchester erupts with pink and green clothing, parades, music, and parties. The first **Shenandoah Apple Blossom Festival** (540/662-3863, www.thebloom.com) was organized in 1924, and except for a break during World War II, it's been going strong ever since. Six days of entertainment, food, and fun, including a circus, a 10K race, and the coronation of the Apple Blossom Queen, take place every May the weekend before Mother's Day.

The **Winchester City Market** is held at the south end of the mall 9 A.M.–1 P.M. on Saturdays during growing season (roughly May–Oct.). Finally, Winchester's **Hot Air Balloon Festival** takes place in mid-October at Historic Long Branch, an 1811 Greek Revival mansion in Millwood. Rides, launches, music, artisans, and wine tasting are all part of the fun. To get there, take Route 624 (Red Gate Rd.) 10 miles east of White Post.

ACCOMMODATIONS

Here is what you'll find in town, but some of the most interesting lodgings in the area are outside the city, in Berryville, White Post, and Middletown.

$50–100

Exit 313 onto U.S. 50 off I-81 has most of Winchester's midpriced hotels, including the **Hampton Inn** (1655 Apple Blossom Dr., 540/667-8011, $80–100) and the **Best Western Lee-Jackson** (711 Millwood Ave., 540/662-4154, $70–80). The **Mohawk Motel** (2754 Northwestern Pike, 540/667-1410, $56) has offered budget quarters for close to 50 years. It's worth the drive out of town (three miles south on Rte. 37 from I-81 exit 317, then two miles west on U.S. 50) for the views.

Four miles from Old Town, the **Long Hill Bed & Breakfast** (547 Apple Pie Ridge Rd., 540/450-0341 or 866/450-0341, www.longhillbb.com) has three rooms for $95. The house is an interesting custom design with stained glass and artwork. Owners George and Rhoda Kriz offer sunny hospitality and award-winning breakfasts. There's a pool table and a vintage pinball machine in the game room downstairs. The gardens outside are certified wildlife habitat, with bird feeders galore. To get there, take Fairmont Avenue north from downtown. It turns into Frederick Pike (Rte. 522) and crosses the Route 37 bypass. Take an immediate right onto Apple Pie Ridge Road, and the turn-off will be on your left.

$100-150

Winchester's **Wingate Inn** (150 Wingate Dr., 540/678-4283, $89) is among the most modern in town, with a business center, conference center, and heated pool. In addition to 145 rooms, the **Travelodge of Winchester** (160 Front Royal Pike, 540/665-0685, $65) has a heated pool and wireless Internet.

$150-250

The **George Washington Hotel** (103 E. Piccadilly St., 540/678-4700, www.wyndham.com/hotels/DCAGW, $120–130) features a Roman bath–style indoor swimming pool and the Dancing Goat restaurant, and is the most opulent place to stay in town. Built in 1924, Winchester's landmark historic hotel features luxurious guest rooms, fireplaces, whirlpool tubs, restaurants, lobby bar, and high-speed Internet.

Camping

Sites at the **Candy Hill Campground** (165 Ward Ave., 540/662-8010 or 800/462-0545, www.candyhill.com) are $35–50. It's open year-round, just beyond the Route 37 bypass, and has a pool, bathhouse, game room, and grocery store.

FOOD

Casual

The snugly casual **Cork Street Tavern** (8 W. Cork St., 540/667-3777, lunch and dinner daily) serves burgers ($7–8), award-winning ribs, and other hearty entrées ($12–23) in front of a big stone fireplace and bar. The building has quite a history; some parts date to the 1830s, it was shelled during the Civil War (it's said ghosts still haunt the place), and as the Rustic Tavern it survived the Depression and World War II.

On the downtown mall, the **Snow White Grill** (159 N. Loudoun St., 540/662-5955, lunch Mon.–Sat., open late Fri.–Sat.) is a diner that's usually crammed with locals who come in for ice cream and cheap eats ($2–6), especially the mini-burgers with grilled onions and pickles on a steamed roll. The grill has been serving inexpensive lunch-counter fare since 1949. If you're craving spice, look no further than **Thai Winchester** (24 S. Loudoun St., 540/678-0055, lunch and dinner daily, $8–14).

Upscale

Starting at the north end of the mall, the **Violino Restaurante Italiano** (181 N. Loudoun St., 540/667-8006, lunch and dinner Mon.–Sat.) serves creative Italian fare that earned four stars in one local review. Franco and Marcella Stocco from Turin offer classic Northern cuisine, graced by excellent sauces, in the $15–35 range, including many vegetarian plates. Reservations recommended.

A bit farther down is the **Village Square Restaurant** (103 N. Loudoun St., 540/667-8961, lunch and dinner Mon.–Sat., brunch Sun.), serving American fare with staid European influences—starting with hand-prepared stock for sauces. There's outdoor seating under a canopy of trees along the mall. Lunch ($8–12) and dinner entrées ($17–29), such as pan-seared rockfish, are excellent. The Sunday champagne brunch ($28) features live music, and the stylish V Square Piano Bar is open until 1 A.M.

Just one block off the mall is, fittingly, **One Block West** (25 S. Indian Alley, 540/662-1455, lunch and dinner Tues.–Sat.), offering a changing menu of fresh local products, many from Virginia. Lunch plates are mostly $8–14, and dinner entrées ($19–33) such as grilled Virginia lamb loin chop with pesto always have a helpful suggested wine pairing on the menu. As a prelude to dinner, or to find recipes after a delicious meal, check out chef Ed Matthews's blog (http://oneblock-west.blogspot.com).

INFORMATION

The **Winchester-Frederick County Convention and Visitors Bureau** (1400 S. Pleasant Valley Rd., 540/542-1326 or 888/316-6189, www.visitwinchesterva.com, 9 A.M.–5 P.M. daily) has videos of the area, the Civil War, and Patsy Cline, a small shrine to the singer, and brochures of walking and driving tours.

NEAR WINCHESTER

Berryville

For a change of pace from the usual hotels, motels, and bed-and-breakfasts, consider a spiritual stay at the **Holy Cross Abbey** (901 Cool Spring Ln., 540/955-4383, www.hcava.org), one of 17 working Trappist monasteries in the country. Members of the Cistercian Order of the Strict Observance, begun in France in 1098, live a quiet life on 1,200 acres in the rolling Blue Ridge foothills alongside the Shenandoah River. The monastery's main means of support is a bakery, where the monks find time, between their six daily services, to turn out 24,000 famous fruitcakes a year.

An elegant guesthouse located a short distance from the monastery can be rented by anyone interested in joining the monks in quietness and prayer. Retreats run Monday–Friday for a suggested donation of $300–500 per person ($75 deposit) for the duration of the stay, including meals, or Friday–Sunday ($150–300 pp, $75 deposit). Guests are welcome to join in the services, sung liturgy, and family-style meals. Reservations should be made as far in advance as possible. A gift shop and information center (1:15–5 P.M. Sun.–Fri., 10 A.M.–noon and 1:15–5 P.M. Sat., longer hours mid-Oct.–Dec.) sells Cistercian publications and monastery products, including Trappist preserves, creamed honey, fudge, and bread, but not, alas, any abbey ales.

To get there, follow Route 7 east from Berryville, turning left immediately before crossing the Shenandoah River onto Route 603, and watch for a sign on the right after one mile.

White Post

Eight miles south of Winchester at the intersection of U.S. 522, U.S. 340, and Route 277 looms **Dinosaur Land** (3848 Stonewall Jackson Hwy., 540/869-2222, www.dinosaurland.com, 9:30 A.M.–5:30 or 6:30 P.M. daily Mar.–Dec., $5 adults, $4 children 2–10), a Jurassic-themed landmark that's been around for decades. More than 50 dinosaur replicas, including all those tongue-tying names your kids know by heart—brontosaurus, stegosaurus, yaleosaurus, and saltoposuchus—stand next to a 60-foot shark, a 70-foot octopus, and a 20-foot cobra (and don't miss the fake caveman).

In the same town but at the other end of the cultural spectrum is **L'Auberge Provençale** (13630 Lord Fairfax Hwy., 540/837-1375 or 800/638-1702, www.laubergeprovencale.com). Innkeepers Alain and Celeste Borel have created a small, charming French country inn in the middle of the fields and pastures of the Shenandoah. Three buildings huddle near an expansive flower garden, full of tulips in the spring and sunflowers every fall. Over the years the American Historic Inns, the *Washington Post,* AOL, and *Washingtonian* magazine have all called it one of the most romantic inns in the country. Alain, the French-born chef, draws regular visitors from the nation's capital for a taste of his native Avignon in the dining rooms of the 18th-century stone manor house. Fresh ingredients from the gardens and local farmers add the final touch to gourmet candlelit dinners featuring foie gras, smoked rabbit, and fresh Shenandoah trout—and that's just for appetizers. Breakfast is almost as much of a production: Scones, salmon, poached eggs, and croissants may all grace your plate. The four-diamond restaurant is open to visitors as well as guests for dinner Wednesday–Monday, with a three-course ($58 pp) or five-course ($88 pp) meal, or a seven-course chef's tasting menu ($115) including dessert. It also offers a Sunday bistro lunch.

Provençal fabrics, canopy beds, and fireplaces fill seven guest rooms and four suites available for $165–325. Two more suites and another room ($245–295) are available in the Villa La Campagnette, set on 18 wooded acres three miles from L'Auberge. This equally impressive spread, decorated like a Mediterranean villa, has a brick terrace next to a pool and outdoor whirlpool tub.

Middletown

Antiques stores and a curious mix of old and new houses line U.S. 11, called Main Street as it passes through the center of Middletown. There you'll find the **Wayside Inn** (7783 Main St., 540/869-1797 or 877/869-1797, www.alongthewayside.com), one of the oldest inns in the United States. It received its first guests in 1797 as Wilkerson's Tavern, and it later served as a stagecoach rest stop and way station for soldiers from both sides of the Civil War. With the arrival of the automobile, it became America's first motor inn, regaining much of its antique charm during a restoration in the 1960s.

An antique parlor off a lobby welcomes guests with chiming clocks and brick-and-stone fireplaces. Antiques and books are everywhere, including a combination chess and cribbage board. The stately Colonial dining room of Larrick's Tavern dates to the 1720s, with lunch entrées for $8–11. Traditional dinner plates such as peanut soup at the Wayside Restaurant run $15–25. Each of the 22 rooms has a distinct personality, and the hotel offers popular romantic escapes for honeymoons and anniversaries that include champagne, breakfast in bed, and a special late checkout. Rooms are $100–170.

Just south of the inn, the small, intimate **Wayside Theater** (7853 Main St., 540/869-1776, www.waysidetheater.org) began as a movie house in the 1940s before being converted with a stage in 1962. The second-oldest professional theater in Virginia, it's now under the management of a nonprofit community foundation, which has welcomed actors such as Susan Sarandon and Kathy Bates. Tickets are $23–30 adults, $10 children under 17.

Cedar Creek Battlefield and Belle Grove Plantation

In the predawn mist of October 19, 1864, 17,000 famished Confederates under Lt. Gen. Jubal Early made a surprise attack on 30,000 Union troops. The Rebels soon had the larger force on the run to the north of Middletown ("they jumped up running," recalled one attacker), but Maj. Gen. Philip Sheridan managed to gallop from Winchester in time to rally his forces, a ride later celebrated in song and legend. More than three times as many Confederate soldiers were killed or wounded as Union soldiers as the Federals pushed their opponents back to the south and eventually out of the valley altogether, signaling the end of Confederate military power in the Shenandoah.

In 2002, Congress approved the creation of the **Cedar Creek and Bell Grove National Historical Park** (www.nps.gov/cebe), encompassing the battlefield and the historic Belle Grove mansion nearby. It's intended to be a different sort of Park Service unit; private landowners and organizations will still be able to live, work, and operate within the park's 3,000 acres. As of 2010, though, the National Park Service hadn't yet put any visitor facilities in place.

In the meantime, head to the Cedar Creek Battlefield **visitors center** (540/869-2064 or 888/628-1864, www.cedarcreekbattlefield.org, 10 A.M.–4 P.M. Mon.–Sat., 1–4 P.M. Sun., Apr.–Oct.), run by a nonprofit foundation on Route 11 one mile south of Middletown. The fields have changed little in the years since the battle, which is reenacted with gusto every year on the weekend closest to October 19. More than 5,000 participants take part under the gaze of 20,000 spectators, usually just as the fall leaves are reaching their colorful peak.

Belle Grove Plantation (540/869-2028, www.bellegrove.org, 10 A.M.–4 P.M. Mon.–Sat., 1–5 P.M. Sun., Apr.–Oct., $8 adults, $4 children 6–12) sits in the middle of the battlefield opposite the visitors center. Once one of the valley's most prestigious homes, it was built in 1794–1797 by Major Isaac Hite Jr. with design help from Thomas Jefferson. Sheridan used the mansion as his headquarters for his devastating march down the valley, and James and Dolley Madison later honeymooned here. A quilt and fabric shop fills the basement, and Colonial craft demonstrations are held in the smokehouse, icehouse, and blacksmith shops.

The Northern Valley

FRONT ROYAL

Known as Hell Town during its frontier days, this riverside city is thought to have been unintentionally renamed by an exasperated Colonial drill sergeant. His repeated orders for his troops to "Front the royal oak!" in the center of town (oaks were considered the royal tree of England) struck someone's fancy, and the name stuck. In the Civil War, Stonewall Jackson captured Front Royal in May 1862 with the help of spy Belle Boyd.

Today, a long bridge over the Shenandoah River leads to tree-lined Royal Avenue (U.S. 340). Turn left onto East Main Street at the Warren County Courthouse to reach the Village Commons with its gazebo, big red caboose, and the town visitors center. Front Royal serves as the northern gateway to Shenandoah National Park and the Blue Ridge, which rises to the south of town.

Sights

Learn more about life during the days of Belle Boyd, along with details about her spy life, at the **Belle Boyd Cottage** (101 Chester St., 540/636-1446, www.warrenheritagesociety.org, 10 A.M.–4 P.M. Mon.–Fri., 11 A.M.–4 P.M. Sat.–Sun. June–Oct., $3).

MATA HARI OF THE CONFEDERACY

Belle Boyd, the Confederacy's most colorful secret agent, was born in Martinsburg, Virginia, in 1843 and reveled in attention from an early age. With the arrival of the Civil War, the vivacious young woman used her quick mind and feminine charms to coax military secrets from Union troops and pass them on to Confederate officers. By age 21, she had achieved a measure of infamy within Union forces: She had been reported 30 times, arrested six or seven, and thrown in jail twice. During one stay in Washington, D.C.'s Old Capital Prison, Boyd put intelligence messages in India rubber balls and threw them to an accomplice waiting outside her window.

Fellow Southern belles were shocked at Boyd's life of risk. She often traveled alone, meeting with officers from both sides in their private tents with little concern for decorum. Refusing to disguise her handwriting or encode her messages, the socialite spy found herself an international celebrity called "La Belle Rebelle" in France and "That Secesh Cleopatra" in New York.

Front Royal served as her main base of operations. When a Federal regiment under Gen. Nathaniel P. Banks occupied the city in May 1862, Boyd invited the officers to a ball and plied them for information. After her guests had fallen asleep, she reportedly rode 30 miles in the dead of night to pass the intelligence to Stonewall Jackson, who attacked the next morning and captured three-quarters of the Union forces.

After the war ended, Boyd tried her hand at acting and gave public lectures on her secretive adventures. In 1865, she published *Belle Boyd in Camp and Prison,* a dramatic tell-all of life as a female secret agent. She died in 1900 in Wisconsin.

A local chapter of the United Daughters of the Confederacy owns and operates the **Warren Rifles Confederate Museum** (95 Chester St., 540/636-6982, 9 A.M.–4 P.M. Mon.–Sat., noon–4 P.M. Sun., Apr. 15–Oct., $4), containing a large collection of arms, uniforms, flags, pictures, and personal items that evoke the Civil War exploits of Stonewall Jackson, Mosby's Rangers, J. E. B. Stuart, and Robert E. Lee.

There's an interesting **elephant mural** by nationally known artist Patricia Windrow entitled *The Not-So-National Zoo* on the side of a barn at High and Jackson Streets.

Recreation

Several local outfitters take advantage of the fact that one of Virginia's favorite rafting rivers flows practically through their backyard. Most operate campsites down the South Fork of the Shenandoah for overnight visitors during the floating season of March–November. Prices should include equipment, brief instruction, maps, and shuttle service.

The **Front Royal Canoe Company** (8567 Stonewall Jackson Hwy., 540/635-5440 or 800/270-8808, www.frontroyalcanoe.com) runs canoe, raft, and kayak trips starting at $40, with longer excursions of 2–3 days also available. Tubing ($16 pp) is popular, and it also rents canoes, kayaks, and rafts.

Take a guided horseback ride with **Highlander Horses** (5197 Reliance Rd., 540/636-4523, www.highlanderhorses.com) for $30–90 per person for 1–2 hours. They have year-round access to 200 acres of riding terrain. If you'd like to polish your equine technique, group instruction is $30 per person per hour, and semi-private and private instruction runs $40–50 per person per hour. (Reliance Rd./Rte. 627 is off Rte. 532 north of town.) A flight with **Blue Ridge Hot Air Balloons** (540/622-6325 or 877/743-3247, www.rideair.com) will set you back $200 per person, but the views are wonderful—and the champagne toast afterward doesn't hurt either.

Shopping

On summer weekends and holidays, the **Front Royal Antique and Flea Market** (S. Commerce Ave. btwn. Stonewall Dr. and South St., 540/535-7330) is *the* place for assorted treasures, junk, and crafts spread among 100 booths. The **Royal Oak Bookshop** (207 S. Royal Ave., 540/635-7070) stocks thousands of rare, used, out-of-print, and new books.

Events

Front Royal is home to the **Virginia Wine and Craft Festival** (540/635-3185, www.wineandcraftfestival.com), held the third Saturday of May. In early August, the **Warren County Fair** (540/635-5827, www.warrencountyfair.com) brings a 4-H livestock auction, tractor pull, car show, music, rides, and pageants.

Accommodations and Camping

You can find rooms for $50–65 at the **Budget Inn** (1122 N. Royal Ave., 540/635-2196), for $70–90 at the **Quality Inn Skyline Drive** (10 Commerce Ave., 540/635-3161), and for $55 at the **Twi-Lite Motel** (53 W. 14th St., 540/635-4148), which offers an outdoor pool.

Innkeepers Tom and Kathy Conkey run the impressive Edwardian mansion known as **Killahevlin** (1401 N. Royal Ave., 540/636-7335 or 800/847-6132, www.vairish.com), built by a local limestone baron on one of the highest hilltops in town. A strong Irish influence pervades, from the reproduction wallpaper to the private pub with its oak bar and Irish beer on tap. The four "color" rooms (Green, White, Blue, and Raspberry) are $155–225, while two suites in the early-1900s Tower House out back, near the koi pool and gazebos, cost $255–285.

Lackawanna (236 Riverside Dr., 540/636-7945, www.lackawannabb.com) is a bed-and-breakfast in an 1869 Italianate-style home and a big porch overlooking the junction of the North and South Forks of the Shenandoah River. An outdoor pool is open seasonally, nice for a dip and sunbathing after a long hike in nearby Shenandoah National Park. Accommodations including a filling breakfast are $140–170.

Besides Shenandoah National Park itself, campers should head to Gooney Creek

Campground (7122 Stonewall Jackson Hwy., 540/635-4066, www.gooneycreek.com). Full hookups are $27 and tent sites go for $19. The campground is open April through October.

Food

Cajun-fried catfish and slow-cooked jerk chicken will nourish the body and taste buds at **Soul Mountain Restaurant** (300 E. Main St., 540/636-0070, lunch and dinner Tues.–Sun.) for $13–22. At lunchtime, salads, wraps, and sandwiches come served with pasta salad and fries for $7–11. **Wynn's** (219 E. Main St., 540/635-5956, breakfast and lunch Tues.–Sat.) is a popular breakfast and lunch spot open from 5 A.M. On Saturdays Wynn's serves breakfast all day. **L Dee's Pancake House** (522 E. Main St., 540/635-3791, breakfast and lunch Wed.–Mon.) also offers breakfast all day starting at $3, along with daily lunch specials.

The **Royal Oak Tavern** (101 W. 14th St., 540/551-9953, lunch and dinner daily) serves American standards in a casual setting, including the "best ribs in the Valley." Sandwiches and burgers go for $7–8 (lunch) and entrées run $11–22 (dinner).

Set in the old Proctor Biggs feed mill building next to the town park, the **Main Street Mill** (500 E. Main St., 540/636-3123, lunch and dinner daily) serves sandwiches and burgers for around $5–10 and heartier entrées such as ribs, pork chops, and pastas for $10–16. Dine inside by the animal paintings or out on the patio. There's a tavern upstairs as well.

Above **Element** (206 S. Royal Ave., 540/636-9293, lunch Tues.–Sun., dinner Wed.–Sun.), a casual bistro specializing in gourmet soups, salads, and sandwiches perfect for a picnic, is **Apartment 2G** (540/636-7306, dinner Fri.–Sat.), a snug restaurant with a full bar. Apartment 2G serves five-course dinners on Friday and Saturday ($50) with starters like shrimp with saffron risotto and finishers like roast rack of lamb. The experience is like having dinner in the apartment of a gourmet friend, and everything is prepared on the premises daily. The evening's party trick is that you get to watch the chefs prepare your meal on a closed-circuit camera projected onto TVs in the dining room. As the chefs say, it's an alternative to "the ennui of the countless chain restaurants." Reservations are required.

To satisfy a sweet tooth, go to **Spelunker's Custard** (116 South St., 540/631-0300, lunch and dinner daily) for frozen custard or a chocolate malt. Inexpensive cheeseburgers and Philly cheesesteaks are also on the menu.

Information

The **Front Royal-Warren County Visitor Center** (414 E. Main St., 540/635-5788 or 800/338-2576, www.discoverfrontroyal.com) sits in the restored train station in the town park. Open 9 A.M.–5 P.M. daily.

Near Front Royal

Opened to the public in 1939, **Skyline Caverns** (800/296-4545, www.skylinecaverns.com, 9 A.M.–6 P.M. daily, to 4 P.M. off-season, $16 adults, $8 children 7–13) were discovered a few years earlier by means of a giant sinkhole where the parking lot now sits. The highlights of these caves, otherwise overshadowed by their southern neighbors, are glittering calcite formations called anthodites. These delicate spikes are found in only one other cave in the United States (and there in much smaller quantities). They grow one inch every 7,000 years, and are either pure white or stained brown by iron oxide. Skyline Caverns' crop sprouted in a vacuum left by a receding underground pool.

Throughout the rest of the cave, high, smooth passages evoke the slot canyons of the American southwest. Kids love the Skyline Arrow, an outdoor miniature train that crawls near the entrance. The caverns are on Route 340, about one mile south of Route 55.

One of the newest additions to Virginia's state park system, the **Raymond R. "Andy" Guest Jr. Shenandoah River State Park** (540/622-6840, www.dcr.virginia.gov/state_parks/and.shtml, 8 A.M.–dusk daily, $2–3 per car) encompasses 1,600 rolling acres along the South Fork of the river eight miles south of Front Royal, including 5.6 miles of river frontage. Most people come to fish or boat, but there are also 13 miles of trails and campsites ($20–30).

STRASBURG

One of the earliest settlements in the valley, Strasburg has been a crafts center since being chartered in 1761. A tradition of earthen and stoneware pottery was once manifested in six shops going at once in a section called Pot Town. Antiques are now the main draw of the self-proclaimed "antiques capital of Virginia," with local ceramics running a close second.

Try any of the dozen or so shops in town for furniture, clothing, folk art, and rugs, such as **Vilnis and Company Antiques** (329 N. Massanutten St., 540/465-4405). For a larger-scale approach, stop by the 65,000-square-foot **Strasburg Antique Emporium** (160 N. Massanutten St., 540/465-3711), one of the largest antiques centers in the state. More than 100 dealers and artisans sell vintage clothing, paintings, furniture, jewelry, and more in a former silk mill.

WEST OF THE INTERSTATE

Bryce Resort

Only a few miles from the West Virginia border, this small resort features two chairlifts and eight ski slopes ranging from beginner to expert. Voted the mid-Atlantic's most family-friendly resort in 2008, Bryce Resort is sure to tucker out kids and grown-ups looking for a winter escape. Lift tickets sell for $40 adults and $33 children on weekdays ($57/$50 on weekends), with half-days for $28/$23 ($44/$39). The ski instruction program, developed by German National certified instructor Horst Locher, starts with children as young as four. Night skiing, snowboarding, snow tubing, and ski rentals are all options.

Dine at the Restaurant @ Bryce Resort (540/856-8187, dinner Fri.–Sat., brunch Sun.) or the more informal Copper Kettle Bar & Lounge (lunch and dinner daily, drinks until late). In the summer, an 18-hole, par 71 golf course enjoys mountain views and all the amenities. Guests can also choose from grass skiing (just what the name implies), mountain boarding (ditto), tennis, and boating on Lake Laura.

To get there, take I-81 exit 273 onto Route 263 and head 11 miles to the entrance on the right. For more information on the resort and lodging options, including rental properties, contact the resort directly (540/856-2121 or 800/821-1444, www.bryceresort.com).

Orkney Springs

Five weekends between late May and the end of August are filled with symphony, big band, jazz, and folk music during the **Shenandoah Valley Music Festival** (540/459-3396 or 800/459-3396, www.musicfest.org) in this tiny town in the hills. A benefit ball kicks things off, and ice cream socials and children's concerts are part of the program. Tickets for individual events are $25–40 in the open-air pavilion and $20–27 on the lawn.

The concerts have been held since the early 1960s at the Shrine Mont Retreat and Conference Center, a venerable mineral springs resort dating to the turn of the 20th century. The town is 15 miles west of I-81 exit 273 via Route 263.

Mount Jackson

Originally housed in an old feed store in Middletown when the company began in the 1990s, the **Route 11 Potato Chip Factory** (11 Edwards Way, 540/477-9664 or 800/294-7783, www.rt11.com) was said to be the smallest of its kind in the country. In 2008, the chipmakers expanded into a factory space in Mount Jackson, but everything is still hand-cooked. Watch the spudmasters at work and sample the chips 9 A.M.–5 P.M. Monday–Saturday.

NEW MARKET AND VICINITY

Two major Indian pathways gave this spot on the upper North Fork of the Shenandoah its first official name of Cross Roads. The first inhabitants, the Senedo tribe, were wiped out by the Catawbas from the south when their paths crossed around 1700. In 1796, the town of New Market was established, named after the city in England with a famous racetrack (there was also a racetrack here, to the west of the settlement). A famous Civil War clash nearby left the town with memories of children lost in battle and a three-inch shell hole in a post at the intersection of Breckinridge Lane and Congress Street (U.S. 11 through town).

New Market Battlefield State Historical Park

On May 15, 1864, one of the last Confederate victories in the valley campaign featured a famous charge by Virginia Military Institute (VMI) cadets against a line of Union artillery. On his way to destroy the railroad and canal complex at Lynchburg with 10,000 men, Maj. Gen. Franz Sigel was attacked by a makeshift force of 4,100 Confederates led by Maj. Gen. John C. Breckinridge. Among the Rebel forces were 257 VMI cadets, who were meant to be kept in reserve. In the heat of battle, however, the boys—whose average age was 15—were put on the front line. Five were killed and dozens wounded. (Five more later died from their wounds.) The students were able to hold the line for half an hour and capture a cannon, helping defeat the superior Union forces and earning themselves a place in Civil War legend.

Whether or not you think children in combat is something worth celebrating, the well-preserved battlefield (866/515-1864, www2.vmi.edu/museum/nm/index.html, 9 A.M.–5 P.M. daily, $10 adults, $6 children 6–12) is easily understood and absorbing. Inside the **Hall of Valor** run by VMI is a visitors center and a museum covering the entire Civil War. An Emmy-winning docudrama, shown on the hour, re-creates the battle using actors and historic images.

Pick up a walking-tour brochure and step outside to begin the mile-long loop trail. Imagine yourself as one of the students, your high spirits drenched by four days' marching in the rain. A headlong charge takes you through the buildings of the Bushong farm, where the terrified family hides in the basement, and across the mud-clogged "field of lost shoes" toward the deafening thunder of the Union guns.

A 200-foot vista over the peaceful Shenandoah River marks where the trail turns back. The cadets' role in the battle is honored in a formal ceremony every May 15 at VMI. The costumed reenactment of the battle and the cadets' charge is one of the oldest in the country, held around the same date.

Commercial Caves

North of New Market at I-81 exit 269, **Shenadoah Caverns** (540/477-3115 or 888/422-8376, www.shenandoahcaverns.com, tours 9 A.M.–6:15 P.M. daily, to 5:15 or 4:15 off-season, $22 adults, $10 children 6–14) were unearthed in 1884 during the construction of the valley railroad. Opened to the public in 1922, they're the only ones in the state with an elevator and feature flowstone slabs called the Bacon Formations as well as other formations. Your ticket includes admission to **Main Streets of Yesteryear,** a set of window displays filled with miniatures, and **American Celebrations on Parade,** a 40,000-square-foot exhibit of 50 years of parade floats from around the country.

The largest billboard in the eastern United States points off I-81 toward **Endless Caverns** (800/544-2283, www.endlesscavern.com, tours 9 A.M.–6 P.M. daily, to 4 P.M. off-season, $16 adults, $8 children 4–12), a serpentine network of passages and tunnels discovered in 1879 by two boys hunting a rabbit. Five miles have been mapped so far, with no end in sight, giving Endless Caverns the most untamed feel of any of Virginia's caves. New passageways are still being discovered, and they've even unearthed a mammoth tooth in here. Refreshments (including bottled cave water) are available in the 1920s limestone lodge, and 145 campsites ($40 and up) are available, some with full hookups.

Other Activities

New Market Walking Tours (www.new-market-virginia-walking-tours.com, $10 adults, $5 children) depart from the Apple Blossom Inn at 10:30 A.M. Monday–Saturday May–October, with some afternoon tours as well (call for details). Costumed guides leads visitors through the town's historic district and tell tales of Colonial times and the Civil War, as well as local folklore. Evening lantern tours are offered in October.

Shopping

A handful of antiques stores lines Congress Street within a few blocks of the center of town at Old Cross Road. Places such as **Shop Civil War** (9398 S. Congress St., 540/740-2729) stock everything from art and flags to real Civil War relics. Find functional and fine art pottery at **Art Studio Pottery** (346 Endless Caverns Rd., 540/896-4400, www.artstudiopottery.com).

Accommodations

One mile north of I-81 exit 264, you'll find **Quality Inn Shenandoah Valley** (162 W. Old Cross Rd., 540/740-3141, $80–100), offering a pool and the Johnny Appleseed Restaurant.

Dating to the end of the 18th century, the **Rosendale Inn** (17917 Farmhouse Ln., 540/740-4281, www.rosendaleinn.com) sits on 20 acres off Route 793 on the way to Endless Caverns. Four rooms and a separate guest cottage are $105–160, and there's a veranda with rocking chairs for enjoying the evening. The **Jacob Swartz House** (574 Jiggady Rd., 540/740-9208 or 877/740-9208, www.jacobswartz.com) can put up guests in a two-bedroom cottage with a living room, full kitchen, wood-burning stove, and screened porch set along a river bluff. Rates start at $125 single occupancy per night ($25 each extra adult/teen, $15 each child), including full breakfast. Enjoy an on-site therapeutic or aromatherapy massage as an add-on to your stay. Call for directions.

The **Cross Roads Inn Bed & Breakfast** (9222 John Sevier Rd., 540/740-4157 or 888/740-4157, www.crossroadsinnva.com, $75–135) was built in 1925 for Claude Hoover, one of the driving forces behind the creation of Shenandoah National Park. The late Victorian home has six rooms, several with whirlpool tubs and fireplaces, and beautifully landscaped grounds. It's at the intersection of Route 211 to Luray and John Sevier Road, just east of Route 11 north.

Rent the 1806 **Apple Blossom Inn** (9317 N. Congress St., 540/740-3747, www.appleblossominn.net, $135 d, $25 each extra person) in the Historic District and have it entirely to yourself: two bedrooms, a full kitchen, parlor, gardens, secret courtyard, and all. It holds up to four guests and comes with a country breakfast.

Campsites at the **Shenandoah Valley KOA** (12480 Mountain Valley Rd., 540/896-8929) in nearby Broadway, Virginia, are $35–55. It's 3.3 miles east of I-81 exit 257 on Route 608.

Food

With a real 1950s-diner feel, the **Southern Kitchen** (9576 S. Congress St., 540/740-3514, all meals daily) has sandwiches for $5–8 and dinners for $10–18. A big statue of the man himself marks the **Johnny Appleseed Restaurant** at the Quality Inn Shenandoah Valley (162 W. Old Cross Rd., 540/740-3141), serving home-style food daily for all meals. Homemade apple fritters and buttermilk biscuits from scratch are on the menu.

Information

Just off I-81 exit 264 is the **Shenandoah Valley Visitor Center** (277 W. Old Cross Rd., 540/740-3132, 9 A.M.–5 P.M. daily).

LURAY

The seat of Page County is best known for what it's near: the central entrance for Shenandoah National Park and the most impressive caverns in the East. The U.S. 211 bypass serves as Main Street, divided into east and west at Broad Street (U.S. 340).

Luray Caverns

The most impressive of Virginia's commercial caves, this U.S. Registered Natural Landmark (540/743-6551, www.luraycaverns.com, 9 A.M.–7 P.M. daily, to 4 P.M. off-season, $21 adults, $10 children 6–12) encloses the most-visited caverns in the East. From the start, the ceilings bristle, the floors bulge, and the walls

© KATIE GITHENS

Stalactites and stalagmites come in all shapes and sizes at Luray Caverns.

flow in a scale that makes you wish the tour lasted longer than an hour. Fifty-foot drapery (a type of rock formation that looks like curtains) is pulled so thin that some parts are translucent; nearly pure white calcite columns and a 170-ton fallen stalactite the size of a school bus are other highlights. Dream Lake, 2,500 feet square, is only 1–6 inches deep, with a reflection that's otherworldly.

The most famous feature of Luray Caverns, though, is only half natural: a "stalacpipe organ," which produces tones with electronically controlled rubber mallets striking stalactites to produce music that brings to mind a subterranean marimba—and somehow Tim Burton. Covering 312 acres, the organ is listed in Guinness World Records as the largest natural instrument in the world.

Back out in the fresh air is the Car and Carriage Caravan Museum (included in admission), with 140 models as old as 1625. No cavern resort complex would be complete without a garden maze ($6 adults, $5 children), gas station, airport, restaurant, golf course, and gift shop, selling everything from pottery to handcuffs.

© KATIE GITHENS

A visit to the Car and Carriage Caravan Museum, replete with classic Model Ts, is included in admission for the Luray Caverns.

Other Diversions and Recreation

The **Luray Zoo** (540/743-4113, www.lurayzoo.com, 10 A.M.–5 P.M. daily, shorter hours in spring, fall, and winter, $10 adults, $5 children 3–12) is home to one of Virginia's largest scaly collections, both extinct and living. Cobras, alligators, and 20-foot pythons coexist with exotic birds and mammals along Route 211 one-half mile west of town, with live educational shows and a petting zoo for the children and batrachophobes. The zoo is a rescue zoo, meaning it specializes in serving as a home for unwanted, abused, or confiscated exotic animals. The owners are both licensed falconers and eager to talk about their high-flying pastime.

A carillon of 47 bells fills the **Luray Singing Tower** on West Main Street opposite the caverns. Free live concerts are given weekends in the spring and fall and during the week in summer.

The South Fork of the Shenandoah from Luray to Front Royal is known for great bass fishing, packing the placid waters with canoes, tubes, and private boats on busy weekend afternoons from spring to fall. **Shenandoah River Outfitters** (6502 S. Page Valley Rd./Rte. 684, 540/743-4159 or 800/622-6632, www.shenandoahriver.com) offers rentals and trips along the river 10 miles northwest of town. Beginning white-water rentals start at $55 for a two-person canoe and $36 for a kayak, or you can opt for an eight-mile flatwater float for the same price. Tube rentals and cookouts are only two of the other options. They also operate fully furnished log cabins ($100–150 d), a mountain cottage ($100–180; sleeps up to three), and campground ($8 pp).

Events

Luray's **Festival of Spring** in mid-May fills the streets with pony and llama rides, antiques dealers, and food vendors. A traditional maypole dance and historic home tours are also part of the festivities. This coincides with the New Market battle reenactment weekend. Taking place around Columbus Day in October, the **Page County Heritage Festival** has been known for arts and crafts since 1969. More than 10,000 people show up for the antique tractor and engine show, chili cook-off, and pony rides.

Accommodations

Rooms at the nearly identical **Luray Caverns Motel East** (831 W. Main St., 540/743-6551 or 888/941-4531) and **Luray Caverns Motel West** (U.S. 211 W., 540/743-6551 or 888/941-4531) range $72–94. **The Mimslyn** (401 W. Main St., 540/244-9445 or 800/296-5105,

SHENANDOAH AREA WINERIES

Barren Ridge Vineyards
984 Barren Ridge Rd., Fishersville
540/248-3300
www.barrenridgevineyards.com

Cave Ridge Vineyard
1476 Conicville Rd., Mt. Jackson
540/477-2585
www.caveridge.com

Crooked Run Cellars
1685 Crooked Run Rd., Mt. Jackson
540/477-9030
www.crookedruncellars.com

CrossKeys Vineyards
6011 E. Timber Ridge Rd., Mt. Crawford
540/234-0505
www.crosskeysvineyards.com

Lexington Valley Vineyard
80 Norton Way, Rockbridge Baths
540/462-2974
www.lexingtonvalleyvineyard.com

North Mountain Vineyard & Winery
4374 Swartz Rd., Maurertown
540/436-9463
www.northmountainvineyard.com

Rockbridge Vineyard
35 Hill View Ln., Raphine
888/511-9463
www.rockbridgevineyard.com

Shenandoah Vineyards
3659 S. Ox Rd., Edinburg
540/984-8699
www.shentel.net/shenvine

Veramar Vineyard
905 Quarry Rd., Berryville
540/955-5510
www.veramar.com

www.mimslyninn.com) opened in 1931 on top of a commanding hill just outside the center of town. Renovated in 2007, the "grand old inn of Virginia" still sits amid 14 acres of lawns and gardens overlooked by a terrace and solarium. from the front doors, a red carpet flows up the central staircase.

Rooms in **The Cardinal Inn** (1005 E. Main St., 540/743-5010 or 888/648-4633, www.luraybestvalueinn.com) are $50–80, and the hotel has a porch with a view of the mountains. Rates include continental breakfast.

The **Woodruff Inns** (330 Mechanic St., 540/743-1494, www.woodruffinns.com) are headquartered in **The Woodruff House,** an 1882 Fairytale Victorian, but there is also the **Victorian Rose,** an 1890 French Country Victorian, and a **cabin** and **cottage** along the riverfront. Room rates range $110–250 (the cottage and cabins are $160–250), with an additional charge for gourmet meals if you want them. Amenities include outdoor garden hot tubs, flower gardens, whirlpool tubs, and private balconies.

Under new management, **The Victorian Inn** (138 E. Main St., 540/860-4229, www.victorianinnluray.com) is an 1885 Fantasy Victorian building with three rooms priced $160–250.

Camping

Yogi Bear's Jellystone Park (540/743-4002 or 800/420-6679, www.campluray.com) is off Route 211 three miles east of town. Campsites are $35–57, and cabins range $90–160. On hand are a stocked fishing pond, two pools, camp store, and laundromat. **The Country Waye RV Resort** (3402 Kimball Rd., 888/765-7222, www.countrywaye.com, mid-Mar.–mid-Nov.) offers great views and 100 campsites for $20–30. All the amenities are included: pool, hot tub, game room, laundry, and even an Internet café. Maintained by the National Forest, **Camp Roosevelt** (540/984-4101) has 10 basic sites for $10 each, 8.5 miles northwest of Luray on Route 675.

Food

On Luray's Main Street, the **Artisans Grill** (2 E. Main St., 540/743-7030, lunch and dinner Wed.–Mon.) serves art-themed sandwiches ($6–7), soups, and salads made with fresh organic produce. Dinner specials ($18–28) include stuffed portobello mushrooms and barbecue baby-back ribs. Sticking with the artisanal motif, an on-site gallery shows work by local and national artists and 7–9 P.M. Wednesdays local musicians strum Eagles and James Taylor tunes.

Just up the street, **A Moment to Remember** (55 E. Main St., 540/743-1121, breakfast and lunch Mon.–Sat., dinner Thurs.–Sat., brunch Sun.) is both a casual restaurant serving German and American cuisine and an espresso bar. Owners and husband and wife John and Elke Thomas know their schnitzel—Elke hails from Germany, and John spent eight years there. The two met in Elke's previous German restaurant, 25 miles north in Front Royal. Deli sandwiches and paninis go for $5–8 at lunch, and dinner dishes, such as a bratwurst sampler, run $13–17.

Swing by **Main Street Bakery** (127 E. Main St., 540/743-6909) for cinnamon-raisin bread warm from the oven, served with a generous pat of butter. The bakery is open for breakfast and lunch Tuesday–Saturday, and serves vegan baked goods, too.

The Farmhouse Restaurant (326 Hawksbill Park Rd., 540/778-2285 or 888/418-7000, www.jordanhollow.com, all meals daily) at the Jordan Hollow Inn in nearby Stanley is the area's most acclaimed eatery. Featured on the Food Network and in *Bon Appetit,* the restaurant offers gourmet breakfasts, a full bar, and excellent entrées like chicken marsala and Virginia ham steak with wild mushrooms for $18–32 at dinner. Two of the four dining rooms are in a 200-year-old log farmhouse.

Information

For information on festivals and other activities in town, contact the **Luray-Page County Chamber of Commerce** (18 Campbell St., 540/743-3915 or 888/743-3915, www.luraypage.com), which also operates a visitors center 9 A.M.–5 P.M. daily.

Sperryville

The mid-Atlantic's most famous hike goes by a funny name, Old Rag—as in "Old Ragged

Mountain." The popularity of this rocky scramble is hard to exaggerate. You can even buy a Christmas ornament to commemorate your hike. While Old Rag falls within the jurisdiction of Shenandoah National Park, it sits a short distance from the Blue Ridge near the tiny hamlet of Sperryville. To get to the trailhead, you (and a myriad of other hikers) must pass through town, where a number of cafés and shops line the petite Main Street.

If you can freshen up after hiking, go to **Thornton River Grille** (3710 Sperryville Pike, 540/987-8790, www.thorntonrivergrille.com, lunch and dinner Tues.–Sat., brunch Sun.), a place that Luray residents will cross the mountains to visit for special occasions. Items such as grilled rib eye with sautéed mushrooms and a house-ground cheeseburger on a challah roll go for $13–29 (lunch is $9–14).

Shenandoah National Park

One of the country's most popular national parks protects nearly 300 square miles of the Blue Ridge Mountains, from some 60 rough-edged peaks to the stream-filled nooks and wildflower-dotted crannies in between. Zipping it all together is the Skyline Drive, stretching for 105 miles along ridgetops from Front Royal to Waynesboro. Arguably the most beautiful drive in the eastern United States, this meandering byway continues as the Blue Ridge Parkway south toward North Carolina and Great Smoky Mountains National Park.

Few visitors venture far off the road, either because they're content with the countless overlooks or because they're in a hurry to move on. Those who do leave their cars discover gushing spring waterfalls, quiet wooded glades, and mountaintop views that often beat anything available from the road. It takes little effort to put space between you and the asphalt, and you won't be disappointed.

All mileposts (mp) are measured from 0 at Front Royal.

The 105 miles of Skyline Drive stretch from Front Royal to Waynesboro.

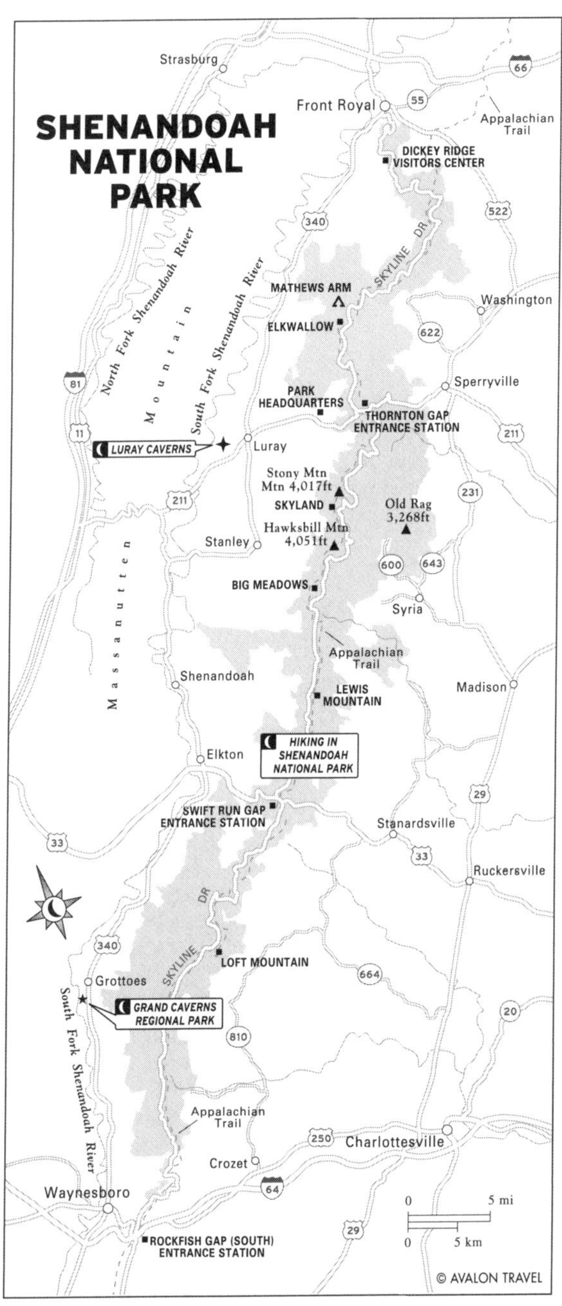

HISTORY

The idea of protecting a large swath of Virginia's mountains had been around since the turn of the 20th century, but it took governor Harry Byrd's creation of a state conservation and development commission in 1926 to get the ball rolling. Without federal money to buy land, the Virginia state legislature passed an act that required landowners to sell their plots within 10 years. The project received the enthusiastic support of President Hoover, who spent every moment he could spare at a fishing camp on the upper Rapidan River within the borders of the proposed park.

Ground was broken for the Skyline Drive in 1931, supposedly after Hoover got the idea during a horseback ride along the crest of the mountains. In 1933, president Franklin Roosevelt's Civilian Conservation Corps pitched in with the construction of sturdy scenic overlooks, picnic areas, and landscaping. More than a thousand mountain residents were compelled to find somewhere else to live by the time the park was dedicated in 1936. The road was finished three years later, and the land was returned to its natural state. In 1976, Congress declared two-fifths of the park (more than 79,000 acres) wilderness.

HABITATS

Shenandoah National Park straddles the mid-Atlantic transition between the Northern and Southern Appalachian ecosystems, giving it an incredible variety of plant and animal life.

Flora

With elevations ranging from 600 feet at the northern entrance to more than 4,000 feet on mountain peaks, Shenandoah National Park encloses a constantly changing deciduous forest. More than 95 percent of the park is forested now with close to 100 tree species and 47 species of mosses and ferns. The chestnut blight near the turn of the 20th century wiped out most of that native species. Oaks and hickories are among the most common trees in the park today. Mixed hardwood forests in the middle elevation include birch and maples. Pines and scrub oak grow on drier slopes, while ash, basswood, and yellow poplar line many streams. The forests explode into brilliant color in autumn, peaking around mid-October. The National Park Service posts weekly foliage reports and live images from a "leaf cam" in autumn so you can time your visit accordingly (www.nps.gov/shen/parknews/fall_colors.htm).

Azaleas and mountain laurel fill the understory; the latter blooms pink in June. Huckleberries, blueberries, and blackberries ripen in mid- to late summer, attracting animals on two and four legs. At the right time of year the park sparkles with over 1,000 species of wildflowers, especially along Skyline Drive and in Big Meadows. Higher elevations help the spring blossoms of violets, chickweeds, and bloodroots persist after summer heat has claimed the Piedmont. (Look along low-elevation streams for more spring blooms.) Periwinkles, pink ladyslippers, trillium, and geraniums flower close behind, followed by gaudy yellow cowslips in May, touch-me-nots in June, and black-eyed Susans and Queen

THE APPALACHIAN TRAIL STORY

Classic though it is, the Appalachian Trail has a relatively short history. The "impossible" idea began as a 1921 proposal by Massachusetts regional planner Benton MacKaye, who envisioned it as an escape for residents of the increasingly populated East. (Today close to two-thirds of the population of the United States lives within 500 miles of the trail.) The Appalachian Trail Conference (now the Appalachian Trail Conservancy), a loose organization of local hiking clubs, was formed in 1925. Thanks to its unpaid efforts, the first continuous trail opened in 1937, but various highways, extreme weather, and the privations of World War II almost buried the project. In the early 1950s, the entire pathway was again cleared and re-marked, and in 1968 it was declared the nation's first National Scenic Trail, akin to a linear National Park but without the funding.

At its northern end, the trail starts at the peak of Maine's Mt. Katahdin (5,267 ft.), winding its most isolated miles through the Maine backwoods. From there it passes through the White Mountains of New Hampshire and the Green Mountains of Vermont before clipping off the western ends of Massachusetts and Connecticut. Southern New York state, where the trail crosses the Hudson River, marks the beginning of the trail's least rural section. Northern New Jersey is next, followed by the Cumberland Valley in eastern Pennsylvania. Eventually the ATC headquarters in Harpers Ferry, West Virginia, comes into sight, where thru-hikers sign a logbook and have their pictures taken.

Virginia contains a quarter of the AT and some of its most breathtaking scenery. Winding down around the Skyline Drive through Shenandoah National Park, the trail then steers west to touch the West Virginia line. It crosses the Blue Ridge Parkway nine times on its way through some of the state's most beautiful wilderness, including the Mount Rogers National Recreation Area. South of Virginia, the AT follows the state line between Tennessee and North Carolina on its way through the rugged undulations of the Great Smoky Mountains National Park. The finish line (or starting point, if you're heading north) comes at the peak of Springer Mountain (3,782 ft.) in Georgia's Chattahoochee National Forest.

Anne's lace in August, when sunflowers also reach their peak.

Fauna

More than 50 species of mammals call the park home. You may spot squirrels, raccoons, and a trundling opossum or groundhog. A few lucky hikers may see a bobcat or gray fox among the trees. At dawn and dusk, white-tailed deer congregate in open areas, particularly Big Meadows, browsing on tender plants until spooked by a car or breeze. A few colonies of beavers have reestablished themselves along the Thornton and Rapidan Rivers. Shenandoah National Park has one of the highest densities of black bears of any park in the country—about one per square mile. In a terrifying moment, our dog once chased one from a tree! (Do follow the leash laws in the park—trust us, it's worth it.) Bear boxes and proper food storage are a must if camping or backpacking.

Two hundred species of birds include permanent residents such as the barred owl, ruffed grouse, and wild turkey. Migratory woodcocks arrive in the early spring, while warblers, thrushes, tanagers, and flycatchers move in during the summer. A hawk or six-foot turkey vulture circling the updrafts is a common sight along the Skyline Drive. Virginia's first breeding pair of peregrine falcons in 40 years was found nesting in the park in 1994.

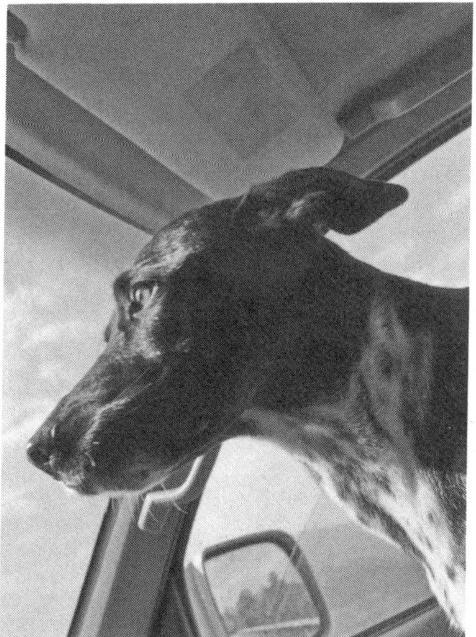

© KATIE GITHENS

Dogs eagerly anticipate a trip to Shenandoah National Park, but they must be leashed at all times.

ACCESS

Shenandoah National Park is divided into three sections by roads bisecting the Skyline Drive. The Northern District stretches from the entrance station at Front Royal (U.S. 340, mp 0) to Thornton Gap (mp 31.5), where U.S. 211 connects Luray to the Piedmont. The Central District continues south to Swift Run Gap (mp 65.5), where U.S. 33 crosses the park as it runs to Harrisonburg. Rockfish Gap (mp 104.6) marks the boundary of the Southern District and the Skyline Drive, with access to I-64 and U.S. 250.

Each entrance has an information booth where you can pay your admission fee and receive a map of the park and, in summer and fall, a copy of the *Shenandoah Overlook* visitor guide. Various hiking trails enter the park from the base of the mountains on either side, often continuing as far as the crest and the Skyline Drive.

Fees

Shenandoah National Park's early years—when it cost a quarter to enter and a buck for an annual pass—are long gone. In the mid-1990s, national park fees were raised throughout the country in an effort to make up for chronic underfunding and to direct more dollars back into the parks. Today, entrance to the park costs $15 per car ($10 Dec.–Feb.) and $8 per pedestrian or bicyclist ($5 Dec.–Feb.); the pass is good for seven consecutive days.

A year-long pass good for any federal recreation site that charges admission is $80. U.S. citizens over age 62 can buy a senior pass ($10), and visitors with disabilities can receive a free access pass with similar privileges. Fees in all national parks are suspended the last Saturday in September for National Public Lands Day.

When to Go

For the height of the fall foliage display in October, you'll probably have to make accommodation reservations—sometimes as much as a year in advance. The best time to avoid the million or so people who visit per year, then, while still getting the view, vegetation, and wildlife you came for, is in the spring and on weekdays during the summer and fall. In the winter, all facilities shut down and parts of the Skyline Drive are often closed due to inclement weather. Then you'll have most of the park to yourself, which can be a magical experience if you're prepared. Bring a full tank of gas, tire chains or snow tires, water, and warm clothing, and call ahead for conditions.

HIKING

Over 500 miles of trails crisscross the park. City softies beware: They're most often uphill or downhill, and occasionally precipitous. More than a dozen waterfalls accessible only on foot are a highlight of any sweaty ramble, as are the pools below and in between. Remnants of former homesites are visible in crumbling walls and chimneys and mossy cemeteries hidden in the underbrush.

© KATIE GITHENS

A hike up Old Rag is an all-hands-and-feet endeavor with narrow passageways and the occasional rock scramble along the way.

Each visitors center has trail maps, along with topographical maps and detailed maps of the entire park. Various trail guides are available at the bookstore in the park visitors centers. **Pets** are allowed on most trails, but only on leashes; ask at the visitors centers about which trails are off-limits. **Bicycles** are only allowed on Skyline Drive and other paved areas—but wow, what a scenic cycling route even so.

A 101-mile segment of the **Appalachian Trail** threads its way along Skyline Drive, making it ideal for short hikes as it crosses and recrosses the road. Many loop trails include part of the AT.

Listed here, by difficulty from north to south, is just a sample of the park's plethora of trails.

Easy Hikes

A self-guided walk on the **Fox Hollow Trail** starts at mile 4.5, passing an old homesite and cemetery in a 1.2-mile circuit. Another short self-guided trail, the **Stony Man Trail,** climbs the second-highest peak in the park from Skyland Resort (mp 42). Also near Skyland, the 1.2-mile **Limberlost Trail** heads past laurel bushes and evergreens. A crushed greenstone walkway makes it the first and only fully ADA-accessible trail in the park.

Near milepost 51 spreads **Big Meadows,** the largest treeless area in the park. These 135 acres of fields and wetlands make up one of the most popular destinations along the Skyline Drive, offering various visitor facilities and a good chance of spotting herds of deer that are unimpressed by cars or people. Trails lead to different waterfalls, including the popular **Dark Hollow Falls,** a 70-foot flow over green volcanic stone (1.4 miles round-trip). Or, head down the 1.8-mile **Story of the Forest Trail.**

Toward the southern end of the park, the **North Fork of Moormans River** bears the scars of a catastrophic flood in June 1995 following six straight days of rain in the park. It's still a beautiful walk along the river, although

EXODUS OF THE MOUNTAIN PEOPLE

Hiking in the "wilderness" of Shenandoah National Park, you might be startled to stumble across an old cemetery overgrown with underbrush or the foundation of a derelict cabin. What is a cemetery doing in a national park? It was there first, as it turns out.

For all the National Park Service literature about how the New Deal and the Civil Conservation Corps shaped Shenandoah National Park as we see it today, far less has been published about the 500 or more families forced to relocate for its creation. Congress approved creating the park in 1926, prompting alarm and a letter-writing campaign among the literate living in the mountain hollows.

Skyline Drive was already under construction when Arno Cammerer, director of the parks service, officially announced in 1934 that the federal government would require residents to vacate the Blue Ridge. His policy decision drew few questions from outside Appalachia, given a widely held perception that the mountain people were barefoot hillbillies, backwards and "disreputable" to begin with (the cottage industry of moonshining had something to do with this reputation).

While some Blue Ridge families left willingly, even happily, others went down swinging, particularly tenant farmers who received no payment for leaving the land since they were not the landowners, and landowners who felt the government had undervalued their land. "Time and again we were threatened with sudden death by infuriated landowners," said William Carson, chairman of the state agency charged with handling the legalities of acquiring parkland. All told, the national park comprises more than 3,000 individual tracts of land bought or condemned under eminent domain in the 1930s.

Vacated homes were then demolished in an effort to return the land to its natural, pre-human state as quickly as possible, with few exceptions. Even so, the observant hiker can still run across lasting artifacts of these Appalachian communities. For a vintage photo gallery of mountain residents before their exodus into the valley, see the National Park Service website (www.nps.gov/shen/historyculture/mtnresidents.htm).

the footing can get tricky at times. It's a little over 1.5 miles upstream to Big Branch, which spills in from the left (west). Park officials estimate that, for a time, there was as much water rushing in here as spills over Great Falls on the Potomac at low flow. The river has begun to recover well, and there are many spots to take a dip or fish along the way. The trail starts at the park boundary and leads outside the park. Reach the trailhead by taking Route 614 upriver from Route 810, north of Crozet. Up and back, the hike should take about three hours.

Moderate Hikes

If solitude is what you're after, head to **Jeremy's Run,** a beautiful stream valley full of luxuriant forests, waterfalls, and pools. It's a six-mile round-trip hike down and back up, and it's steep in spots. Combined with an ascent of **Knob Mountain,** this makes a modestly challenging 12-mile loop from Elkwallow Picnic Area (mp 24). From the lower section of the picnic area, follow the brown Jeremy's Run trail marker. Be ready to cross the stream numerous times.

Just south of Skyland Resort, you'll find the parking lot and trailhead for **White Oak Canyon** (mp 42.6), a spectacular (and popular) hike down a steep gorge past pools, huge boulders, and six waterfalls ranging 35–85 feet high. The 1,000-foot climb to the first waterfall is steep. It connects with the **Limberlost Trail,** where you'll find old-growth hemlocks.

At mile 52.5, the **Mill Prong Trail** leads downhill to Rapidan Camp, President Hoover's weekend White House, which was donated to the proposed park in 1933. From the South River Picnic Area (mp 62.8), a trail leads to **South River Falls,** the third highest in the park at the head of a steep gorge. You'll climb 850 feet in 2.6 miles round-trip.

Near mile 90, the 6.8-mile **Riprap Hollow Trail** offers great views and access to one of the park's largest swimming holes. Include Calvary Rock, Chimney Rock, the Wildcat Ridge Trail, and the AT to make it a 9.8-mile circuit hike, bedecked with mountain laurel blossoms in the spring.

Strenuous Hikes

The trail to **Old Rag Mountain** begins at a parking lot on Route 600, which leaves Route 231 between Sperryville and Madison to the east of the park. The 7.2-mile circuit winds up, over, and around a huge jumble of granite boulders to the peak (3,291 ft.), dotted with water-filled depressions called "buzzard baths." As you enjoy the view, think about the fact that the rock you're standing on is thought to be some of the oldest exposed rock on the East Coast—around 1.1 billion years old. Return via the Weakley Hollow Fire Road.

Because it's one of the more spectacular hikes within day-trip distance of Washington, D.C., Old Rag is popular, and it can get staggeringly crowded on sunny weekends.

A great alternative to Old Rag, especially when the crowds are plentiful, is the 6.1-mile loop to the top of **Robertson Mountain.** It's also a strenuous climb, but after passing through peaceful Corbin Hollow and following a wonderful trout stream, you're rewarded with views that are easily comparable—you can even see Old Rag from the top. Park in the same place as Old Rag, but take the Weakley Hollow Fire Road up to the trailhead. (Combine with Old Rag to make a 12-mile trek that climbs 4,000 feet.)

A steep path leaves from Hawksbill Gap (mp 45.6) to the top of **Hawksbill Mountain** (4,049 ft.), the highest point in the park. Climbing 1,557 feet in less than one mile, the trail reaches an observation point at the peak, a great place to spot hawks.

ACCOMMODATIONS, CAMPING, AND SERVICES

Information and reservations for Big Meadows Lodge, Skyland Resort, and the Lewis Mountain Cabins can be obtained from **Aramark** (888/896-3833, www.visitshenandoah.com). Prices are highest in October, and a few different lodging and dining packages

Unlike most of Virginia's peaks in the Blue Ridge Mountains, Old Rag has a bald summit.

are available. Gasoline, oil, air, water, groceries, and camping supplies are available at all three waysides (Elkwallow, Big Meadow, and Loft Mountain).

The park's four main campgrounds are open spring through fall and feature roomy tent, trailer, and RV sites (no water or electric hookups) with picnic tables and grills for $14–19. The Potomac Appalachian Trail Club (703/242-0693, www.patc.net) maintains six primitive cabins with mattresses and pit toilets ($25–40). Backcountry camping is free, but you'll need a permit from one of the visitors centers, entrance stations, or park headquarters (also available by mail). Facilities start opening in March or April and start closing from October to late November, so call ahead if you plan to visit at either end of the season.

Starting from Front Royal, the **Mathews Arm Campground** at mile 22.1 has 179 sites and is near the trailhead for Overall Run Falls, the tallest waterfall in the park. **Elkwallow Wayside** (mp 24.1) has a snack bar, camp store, gas station, and gift shop. **Skyland Resort** (mp 41.8) began as Stony Man Camp in 1894. At 3,680 feet, it's the highest point on Skyline Drive, which means great views from most of the 179 rooms. "Rustic" cabin rooms are $106–250, motel-style rooms in the main lodge range $125–160, and suites are $160–220. Family cabins with room to sleep six to eight people are $250. (Prices are slightly higher in October.) None have phones, but some have TVs. The glass-walled restaurant lets you enjoy steaks, trout, and other basic fare while looking out over the forest, and the Tap Room has live entertainment on summer nights. Guided horseback and pony rides are available from the stables.

Built in 1939, the **Big Meadows Lodge** has a cozier feel, thanks to stone walls paneled with native chestnut wood. The sitting room features a fireplace and outdoor deck with the requisite gorgeous vista; otherwise, the facilities are similar to those at Skyland. Rooms in the main lodge are $106–160, cabins are about $100, and suites $160. At the same turn-off (mp 51.2) is the park's largest and most popular campground with 217 sites. You can reserve sites in advance (reservations are required between mid-May and November) by calling 877/444-6777. Next to the Byrd Visitors Center is the Big Meadows Wayside with a restaurant, gift shop, camp store, and gas station.

Lewis Mountain (mp 57.5) has cabins with one or two rooms for $106. All cabins are heated and linens are provided, but they don't have phones or TVs. Cooking is done outdoors on a grill. Tent cabins are also available for $30. Thirty-one campsites ($15) are offered first-come, first-served, right next to the information center, gift and food shop, showers, and laundry. At **Loft Mountain** (mp 80), you'll find the Loft Mountain Wayside gift shop and snack bar. More than 200 campsites are available mostly on a first-come, first-served basis, with a camp store, shower, and laundry.

Guided outdoor adventure programs, including hiking and rock climbing, are offered April–November for about $75. See www.visitshenandoah.com for more details.

INFORMATION

Maps and Information

The Potomac Appalachian Trail Club sells three topographical maps (numbers 9, 10, and 11) covering the entire park. The 1:75,000-scale map by National Geographic's **Trails Illustrated** (www.trailsillustrated.com) is printed on tearproof plastic for $12; get map number 228. More detailed quadrangle maps are available from the U.S. Geological Survey (USGS) information line (888/275-8747, http://topomaps.usgs.gov). Park visitors centers and most local outfitters sell these maps.

The nonprofit **Shenandoah Natural Park Association** (540/999-3582, www.snpbooks.org) offers a large selection of books and other items, whose sales help support the park's interpretation and education efforts.

The website **Hiking Upward** (www.hikingupward.org) has great local hiking suggestions and resources.

Visitors Centers and Entrance Stations

The park has two visitors centers: The **Dickey Ridge Visitors Center** is at mile 4.6, and the **Harry F. Byrd Sr. Visitors Center** is in Big Meadows at milepost 51. They are both open 8:30 A.M.–5 P.M. daily April–late November, with reduced hours in April and November, and are stocked with information, films, exhibits, maps, and books. The **Loft Mountain Information Center** at mile 79.5 is also open on weekends. There are **entrance stations** at Front Royal and Rockfish Gap at either end of the park and at Thornton Gap (mp 31.5) and Swift Run Gap (mp 65.5).

Park Headquarters (540/999-3500, www.nps.gov/shen, 8 A.M.–4:30 P.M. Mon.–Fri.) is four miles east of Luray on U.S. 211.

Harrisonburg and Vicinity

The urban center of the northern Blue Ridge is home to 40,000 people and some 20 major industries. Thousands of local farmers come together in huge farmers markets, where you might find yourself parked next to a black horse-drawn buggy; about 1,000 Old Order Mennonites live in the area in a simple lifestyle similar to Pennsylvania's Amish, with whom they share a common Anabaptist religious heritage.

A strong arts presence complements three of the Shenandoah's largest schools—James Madison University (JMU), Bridgewater College, and Eastern Mennonite University—which have campuses in or near the city. Harrisonburg also excels in outdoor options, sandwiched as it is between Shenandoah National Park and the mountains of West Virginia, with lots of nearby rivers, lakes, and caverns to explore.

History

Harrisonburg was founded in the 1740s by Thomas Harrison near the intersection of the Spotswood Trail and the main Indian road down the valley. Strict Methodists started the city's first school in 1794, outlawing gaming and "instruments of music" and decreeing that no student be "permitted on any account whatever to wear Ruffles or powder his hair." The Battle of Harrisonburg, on June 6, 1862, saw the death of Gen. Turner Ashby, one of Stonewall Jackson's most trusted and respected officers.

Today, surrounding Rockingham County leads the state in production of beef, dairy

GHOSTS OF HARRISONBURG

On December 1, 1900, an aunt was checking on a baby in an upstairs bedroom when she bent to blow out an oil lamp. Low on oil, the lamp suddenly exploded, igniting the woman's dress and burning her so badly that she died the next day. Local legend holds that glowing handprints from the unlucky aunt appear on the wall of the old house, now part of the Willow Hill subdivision. Previous owners have witnessed the door to the master bedroom slamming shut on its own.

Residents of the Funk House on Mason Street – usually college students – tell of blasts of cold air gusting through rooms and doors closing without visible assistance. One person reported in the early 1970s that she woke up in the middle of the night feeling as if she were suffocating and couldn't get out of bed. Folklore scholars point out the old English custom of "mattressing," in which poor families piled mattresses on sick or elderly people they couldn't afford to take care of and sat on them until they suffocated.

Harrisonburg's most famous specter is said to be Colonel Warren, of the Warren-Sipe House, killed during the Battle of the Wilderness by a bullet in the head. Several witnesses have spotted his ghost at the first landing of the stairway, standing in full uniform with its head wrapped in wide bandages.

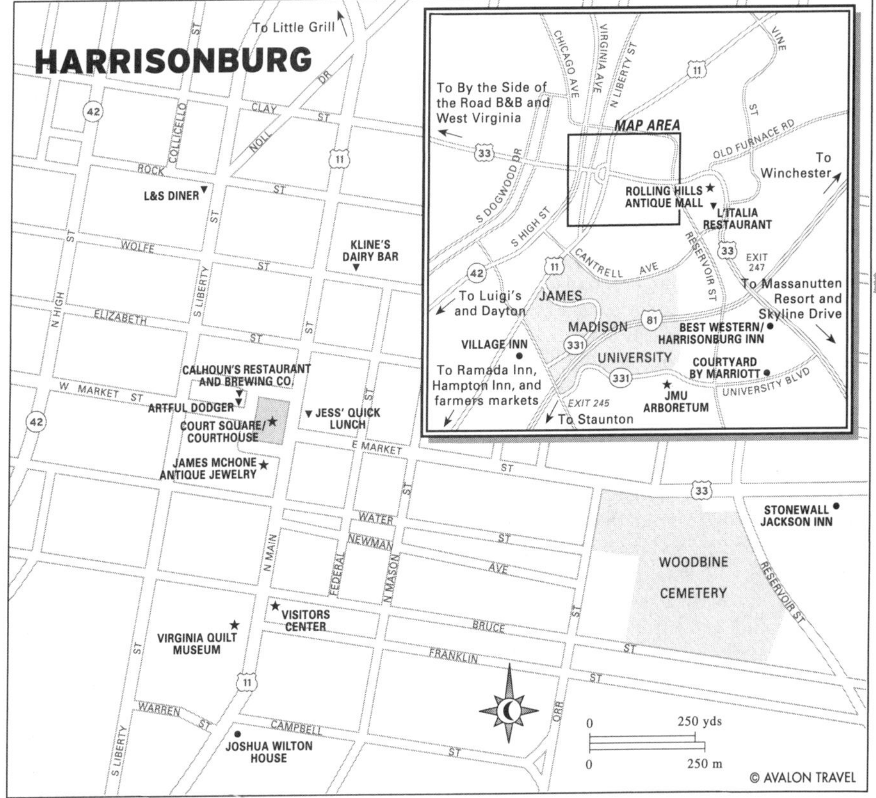

products, and poultry. Along with Staunton, Harrisonburg is a performing-arts hot spot of the Shenandoah, home to the Blue Ridge Theater Festival, the Court Square Theater, and the Valley Playhouse.

SIGHTS

Court Square

The heart of downtown rings the limestone-faced Rockingham County Courthouse. Dating to the turn of the 20th century, the imposing building is the fifth to sit on the original 1.5-acre plot of land donated by Thomas Harrison in 1779. Look for the round copper dome of the **springhouse** at the southwest corner, an exact replica, erected in 1995, of the original watering hole and meeting place.

Virginia Quilt Museum

Both traditional and modern masters of the art of quilting have works on display in the 1855 Warren-Sipe House (301 S. Main St., 540/433-3818, www.vaquiltmuseum.org, 10 A.M.–4 P.M. Tues.–Sat., $5 adults, $3 students 12–18, $2 children 6–12). People originally began making blanket covers from scraps out of necessity, because new bedclothes were expensive, but quilting has since evolved into its own art form. Rotating exhibits feature some wild, colorful examples edging toward fabric impressionism—notice the one made from old Bull Durham tobacco pouches.

James Madison University

This beautiful 696-acre campus is home to

17,000 students working towards a bachelor's or master's degree in the sciences, arts, business, health, or education. The well-rounded public university (540/568-6211, www.jmu.edu) is consistently cited by national publications as one of the top regional public institutions of higher learning. JMU also supports several successful sports teams that make regular appearances in the NCAA playoffs.

The gently sloping, grassy quadrangle is the perfect place for reading in the shade, Frisbee-throwing, or just taking a quiet stroll around this focal point of campus. The gracious red-roofed bluestone dormitory, classroom, and administration buildings, including the always-reliable Wilson Hall clock tower, constitute the original campus of the State Normal School for Women, a teachers' college founded in 1908.

At the other end of the spectrum, the **College of Integrated Science and Technology (CISAT)**—the first and most challenging curriculum of its kind—on the other side of I-81 is a modern marvel that is now the highest point in town (students call it the Emerald City). Sunset-watching is terrific from the parking lot outside the main building.

JMU administers the **Edith J. Carrier Arboretum** (540/568-3194, www.jmu.edu/arboretum) on University Boulevard. One hundred twenty-five acres of mature natural forest surround ponds and landscaped plots of shrubs and flowers. Nature trails weave through the leaves and across little Monet bridges over a stream. It's open dawn to dusk for free, with lectures, workshops, and tours offered 8 A.M.–4 P.M. Monday–Friday by prior appointment.

ENTERTAINMENT

Located in the same indoor plaza as Cally's restaurant, the **Court Square Theater** (61 Graham St., 540/433-9189, www.courtsquaretheater.com) operates under the auspices of the Arts Council of the Valley to bring theater, dance, movies, and live music to town. Call or check its website for a performance schedule.

JMU's **Masterpiece Theater** series (540/568-7000 or 877/201-7543, www.jmu.edu/cvpa/masterpiece) encompasses music, theater, and dance.

Tickets to **JMU Dukes** football and basketball games can be ordered from the JMU Athletic Ticket Office (540/568-3853, www.jmusports.com).

A wide variety of music acts perform at **The Pub** (1950 Deyerle Ave., 540/432-0610, www.dothepub.com), open until 2 A.M. daily.

SHOPPING

A Touch of the Earth (66 E. Market St., 540/432-1894) stocks a little bit of everything from far-off corners of the planet. Afghan carpets, Southwestern Indian pottery, Balinese carvings, and a roomful of drums are only the beginning. If you can't find something there, swing by **Gift & Thrift** (731 Mt. Clinton Pike, 540/433-8844, www.giftandthrift.org), covering the rest of the globe with Salvadoran painted boxes, Vietnamese ceramics, and Philippine shell ornaments. Half thrift shop and half international crafts store, this fascinating place is run by the Mennonites as a non-profit organization.

James McHone Jewelry (75 S. Court Square, 540/433-1833) specializes in estate jewelry both new and antique. Harrisonburg artists' cooperative **Oasis** (103 S. Main St., 540/442-8188) stocks paintings, jewelry, furniture, photography, and pottery. Sixty dealers fill the **Rolling Hills Antique Mall** (779 E. Market St., 540/433-8988), stuffed to the rafters with everything from kitchen collectibles to automobilia.

On Saturday mornings year-round, as well as Tuesday mornings April–November, the **Harrisonburg Farmers Market** (540/476-3377, www.harrisonburgfarmersmarket.com) features fresh produce, baked goods, flowers, and greenery in the Turner Pavilion in the municipal parking lot at South Liberty and West Water Streets.

EVENTS

The Rockingham County Fairgrounds hosts the **Annual Memorial Day Horse Fair and Auction** in late May. In June, Eastern

Mennonite University rings with the sounds of classical music during the **Shenandoah Valley Bach Festival** (540/432-4367, www.emu.edu/bach).

Biggest of all is the **Rockingham County Fair** (www.rockinghamcountyfair.com) in August, an agricultural expo rated as one of the top 10 in the country by the *Los Angeles Times*. Competitions in flowers, crops, livestock, and art compete with country music, tractor pulls, and demolition derbies for a week near the middle of the month.

ACCOMMODATIONS

$50-100

The Village Inn (4979 S. Valley Pike/U.S. 11, 800/736-7355, $75–100) has been family owned and operated since 1936. It has an outdoor pool, and many rooms have outdoor decks. The **Ramada Inn** (1 Pleasant Valley Rd., 540/434-9981, $70–90) is off I-81 exit 243, with an outdoor pool and restaurant. Also try the **Best Western Harrisonburg Inn** (45 Burgess Rd., 540/433-6089, $80).

$100-150

The Joshua Wilton House (412 S. Main St., 540/434-4464 or 888/294-5866, www.joshuawilton.com, $145–160, $85 corporate rates available midweek) vies for the titles of most elegant hotel and most elegant restaurant in the city. The Victorian mansion was built in 1888 by the owner of a hardware store on Court Square, who went on to start the local electric company. Wilton's residence, naturally, was the first in town with electricity—even before it had plumbing.

Much of the original materials and craftsmanship remain, including the leaded glass in the front door and the parquet floor and banister in the main hall, which even survived the house being used as a fraternity house for several years in the mid-1900s. Five bedrooms feature period antiques, four-poster beds, and faux-marble fireplaces. Enjoy the inn's award-winning cuisine, whipped up from locally sourced ingredients, in the two front rooms. More casual fare is served in three back rooms and on an outdoor patio café, with appetizers like Prince Edward Island mussels and entrées such as horseradish-crusted filet mignon. Rates include a gourmet breakfast in the sunroom.

Other good options in this price range include the **Hampton Inn** (43 Covenant Dr., 540/437-0090, $110–150) and a **Courtyard by Marriott** (1890 Evelyn Byrd Ave., 540/432-3031, $130–150).

$150-200

By the Side of the Road B&B (491 Garber's Church Rd., 540/801-0430 or 866/274-4887, www.bythesideoftheroad.com, $150–200) fills a Revolutionary-era Flemish bond building two miles to the east of downtown. It served as a hospital during the Civil War, during which Union soldiers tried to set fire to the foundation three times, unsuccessfully. Four suites in the main house and three separate cottages ($220–280) each have whirlpool tubs and breakfast delivered every morning.

The **Stonewall Jackson Inn** (547 E. Market St., 540/433-8233 or 800/445-5330, www.stonewalljacksoninn.com) near Old Town offers ten guest rooms ($130–180) named after Civil War figures. The restored circa-1885 mansion blends Queen Anne and New England cottage architecture. Enjoy a breakfast of crab soufflé or eggs Nova Scotia on the back porch.

FOOD

Snacks and Cafés

Retro couches, knickknacks, Wi-Fi, and local art on the walls make **The Artful Dodger** (47 W. Court Square, 540/432-1179, 8 A.M.–2 A.M. daily) a classic coffeehouse hip enough to make up for the lack of funk elsewhere in town. It also serves desserts and sandwiches ($5–7), and doubles as a cocktail lounge at night.

Look for the 20-foot ice cream cone in front of **Kline's Dairy Bar** (58 E. Wolfe St., 540/434-6980), where soft-serve ice cream, sundaes, and shakes have been served from the same Electro Freeze machine since 1943. Packed on weekend evenings in the summer, Kline's is so popular it has opened a second branch at 2425 South Main Street (540/434-4014), plus a third in Staunton and a fourth in Waynesboro.

The food at the quirky worker-owned **Little Grill Collective** (621 N. Main St., 540/434-3594, all meals Tues.–Sat., brunch Sun.) is healthy, inexpensive, and plentiful for the student-budget prices: mostly vegetarian and Mexican fare for $4–9. It's been operated as a restaurant since the 1940s and hosts live music at night. Cash only.

Casual

Jess' Quick Lunch (22 S. Main St., 540/434-8282) is an old city standby serving shakes, hamburgers, and the best hot dogs in town (three college students once ate 53 at a sitting). Low-priced breakfast, lunch, and dinner (hardly anything is more than $5) are served in diner booths and at the counter 9 A.M.–10 P.M. every day of the year.

"Home cooking from scratch" is the calling card of the bright-red **L&S Diner** (255 N. Liberty St., 540/801-0110), started in 1947 and with counter seating only for three inexpensive ($6 and under) meals Monday–Saturday.

Cally's Restaurant and Brewing Co. (41 Court Square, 540/434-8777, lunch and dinner daily) is a microbrewery popular with college students. It offers fresh beers brewed on-site, sandwiches ($7–10), and entrées ($14–19) ranging from pasta to seafood in a lively setting. A filling Sunday brunch runs $6–9, and there's rooftop dining overlooking Courthouse Square.

Upscale

Aside from the Joshua-Wilton House, Harrisonburg's other establishment of note is the Amato family's **L'Italia Restaurant** (815 E. Market St., 540/433-0961, lunch and dinner daily), serving Italian fare amid candles and romantic music. Entrées such as lobster ravioli and the broiled catch of the day start at $10.

INFORMATION

Harrisonburg Tourism operates the local **visitors center** in the Hardesty Higgins House (212 S. Main St., 540/432-8935, www.harrisonburgtourism.com, 9 A.M.–5 P.M. daily).

NEAR HARRISONBURG

Farmers Markets

The flowing valley farmland surrounding Harrisonburg sets the stage for two examples of the original rural version of the shopping mall. Follow South Main Street out of town as it turns into U.S. 11 to reach the **Shenandoah Heritage Market** (540/433-3929, www.shenandoahmarket.com, 10 A.M.–6 P.M. Mon.–Fri., 9 A.M.–6 P.M. Sat.) on Route 11 south of I-81 exit 243, where you can browse Civil War memorabilia, antique tractors, model trains, crafts, and furniture as well as produce. A few miles further south on Route 42 between Bridgewater and Dayton is the **Dayton Farmers Market** (540/879-3801, www.daytonfarmersmarket.com, 9 A.M.–6 P.M. Thurs.–Sat.). Homemade breads, cheeses, and jellies fill dozens of booths next to country hams, jams, and toys.

Dayton

The centerpiece of the **Heritage Center** (Bowman and High Sts., 540/879-2681, www.heritagecenter.com, 10 A.M.–4 P.M. Mon.–Sat., $5) is a huge electric map that traces the comings, goings, and clashings of Stonewall Jackson's Shenandoah Valley Campaign. A 20-minute narrated tape explains things in dramatic tones. Regional ceramics, textiles, paintings, and sculptures fill the folk art section, close to a genealogy research library and bookstore.

Green Valley Book Fair

Some 40 years ago, Kathryn and Leighton Evans got the idea of selling surplus new and used books out of an old family barn. Today the idea has evolved into a huge affair filling three floors with half a million volumes on all subjects. New titles from most major publishers are 60–90 percent off retail—enough to entice buyers from nearby states. The Book Fair (2192 Green Valley Ln., 800/385-0099, www.gvbookfair.com) is held six times a year, for about two weeks at a time, March–December. It's in Mount Crawford off I-81 exit 240. Head east onto Route 682 for 1.5 miles, then take a left on Route 681 at the Green Valley sign. Contact them for a schedule.

Massanutten Resort

Some of the state's best skiing waits east of Harrisonburg in a natural depression behind Massanutten Peak. With the longest vertical drop in Virginia, Pennsylvania, or Maryland (1,100 ft.), Massanutten (540/289-9441, www.massresort.com) boasts 14 runs ranging from beginner to expert and six lifts, including Virginia's first quad. Other attractions include night skiing, a popular snowboard park, kids' programs, and NASTAR races. Lift tickets cost $45–64 adults, $40–54 children; tickets good for two hours at the state's first snow-tubing park are $18–22. (The latter often sell out the day before; call 800/207-6277 for availability.) Equipment rentals start at $24–34 per day for adults and $18–28 for children 12 and under. Look for late-season discounts on lift tickets in March.

During the rest of the year, Massanutten keeps busy with an 18-hole golf course, a water park, tennis courts, canoeing, kayaking, and a skate park. The chairlifts are open for scenic rides, and the mountain's trails are open for mountain bikes, but only to guests of the resort. Held on the opposite side of the mountain, the **Massanutten Hoo-Ha!** (540/289-4954) is an annual cross-country mountain bike race in June that's one of the largest in the state.

The resort is 10 miles from Route 33 on Route 644.

Natural Chimneys Regional Park

Seven limestone towers 65–120 feet tall form the nucleus of this small park near Mt. Solon (I-81 exit 240). The columns used to be part of the same block of limestone left from when Virginia was covered by an inland sea, but a layer of harder rock on top protected them from erosion. Natural Chimneys' other claim to fame is the **jousting tournaments** held the third Saturday of August to much medieval fanfare. Begun in 1821 to decide who should marry a local woman, they are among the oldest continually held sporting events in the country, older than the Kentucky Derby. No one crashes to the ground in full armor here, though—the tournaments are based on accuracy, with contestants aiming their lances through small rings at full gallop. The jousting tournament is now part of the Stone Tower Glenn Renaissance Faire (540/337-6324, www.medievalfantasiesco.com).

The park (540/245-5727, www.co.augusta.va.us, dawn–dusk daily, $2 pp or $5 per car) also has a campground (open May–Oct.) with 145 sites for $19–33 each, a pool, store, hot showers, and playground.

Grand Caverns Regional Park

Up there with Virginia's best, this network of caves includes huge Cathedral Hall, one of the largest underground rooms in the East, and the 5,000-square-foot Grand Ballroom, where dances were actually held in the early 1800s. This one was discovered in 1804 by a 17-year-old looking for a raccoon trap, making it the oldest show cave in the country, and was once visited by Thomas Jefferson on horseback from Monticello. Signatures on the walls record the quartering of Stonewall Jackson's troops near here during the Valley Campaign. More than 200 formations called "shields" are a mystery to geologists.

The caverns (540/249-5705, www.ci.grottoes.va.us, 9 A.M.–5 P.M. daily Apr.–Oct., weekends in Mar.–Nov. by appt., $18 adults, $11 children 6–12) are east of I-81 exit 235. Winter hours might be extended, beginning in November 2010; call to confirm. The park also encloses picnic shelters, hiking and biking trails, a pool, tennis courts, and a miniature golf course, and is host of a bluegrass festival the weekend after Labor Day.

Staunton and Vicinity

One of the oldest cities in the Shenandoah Valley, Staunton (pop. 24,000) is a pretty, if hilly, town to amble through for an afternoon or three. The Augusta County seat is home to yet another president and to country music luminaries the Statler Brothers, who opened for Johnny Cash for years.

Since it was spared from Civil War destruction, Staunton still claims historic architecture to rival that of any city in the state. Faded advertisements for feed, fertilizer, and hardware on brick buildings give the downtown a railroad-era look, while grand private homes fronted by sloping lawns line West Frederick Street. Intense restoration efforts have resurrected the train station and are now being focused on the warehouses of the adjacent Wharf area.

History

For a railroad town, Staunton (STAN-ton) is a surprisingly white-collar community, and has been for more than a century. Originally homesteaded by Scottish-Irish immigrant John Lewis in 1732, the town first served as a way station at the intersection of the old Valley Pike and the westbound Midland Trail, where travelers could rest themselves and their horses and stock up on supplies.

A little more than 50 years after the town was chartered, in 1801, the Central & Ohio Railroad arrived, beginning Staunton's transformation from a rural outpost to a thriving commercial city and transportation hub of western Virginia. Early on Staunton was on the map for doctors, lawyers, and educators looking for work, starting with the establishment of the Augusta County Courthouse (1745), the Western Lunatic Asylum (1825), and the Virginia School for the Deaf, Dumb, and Blind (1839). Those last two, thankfully, go by abridged names these days.

Woodrow Wilson was born here in 1856 to

Spared by Civil War shelling and modern-day demolition, Staunton has some of the best-preserved 19th-century architecture in the state.

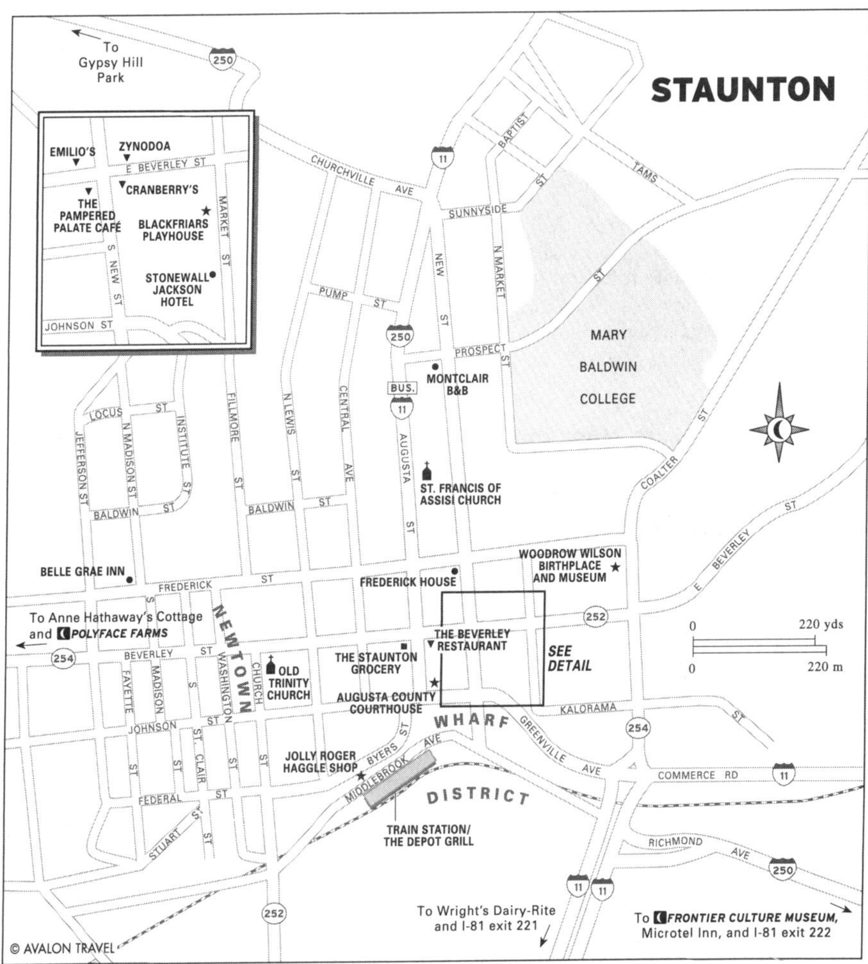

a local Presbyterian minister and his wife, and is immortalized in "Woody World" (the locals' nickname for the presidential library and museum). Staunton served as a supply base during the Civil War but was spared much of the destruction visited on other Virginia cities. That is why today Staunton boasts one of the best assemblages of 19th-century architecture in the state.

SIGHTS

No less than five lovingly preserved National Historic Districts earned Staunton a spot on the National Trust for Historic Preservation's 2001 list of a Dozen Distinctive Destinations nationwide. Historical-tour guide Marney Gibbs can give you the rundown aboard the Staunton Trolley (540/885-2403, www.stauntonguidedtours.com, $10 adults, $5 children) or one of her many walking or driving tours.

The cobble-lined **Wharf District** includes the early-1900s train depot (now an Amtrak station), with old cabooses at the end of a long platform that hummed with activity during the city's railroad heyday. Many of the nearby warehouses and mill buildings have been turned into galleries and antiques shops.

Beautiful Victorian buildings from the boom years of 1860–1920 fill the **Beverley** district, along the street of the same name between Lewis and Market Streets. West of Lewis Street is **Newtown,** actually the city's oldest residential area, home to prominent citizens and their less wealthy neighbors who labored in local factories. **Stuart Addition** adjoins the campus of Mary Baldwin College, and **Gospel Hill,** filled with elegant residences, gets it name from religious meetings originally held in the late 18th century.

Frontier Culture Museum

In the 1700s, four ethnic groups—English, German, Scottish-Irish, and slaves from West Africa—dominated the small-scale farming settlements of the Shenandoah Valley frontier. Over the next two centuries, their distinctive traditions would blend into a uniquely American heritage brought back to life in this fascinating living-history center (540/332-7850, www.frontiermuseum.org, 9 A.M.–5 P.M. daily, 10 A.M.–4 P.M. daily Dec.–Mar., $10 adults, $6 children). With a focus on the common man rather than the patrician, the costumed interpreters and working farms set out to show how American immigrants lived, both in their home countries and here in the Virginia countryside. Ignore the traffic hum from I-81, and it's easy to be carried back in time by the smells of fresh-cut hay and open-hearth cooking and the sounds of cows lowing, pigs rooting, and the clank of hammer on anvil.

Start off at the visitors center, which offers films and a small museum explaining the Colonial cultures you're about to experience. Then step outside to begin a self-guided walking loop through six distinct farms. Rural life from the 18th and 19th centuries has been rigorously re-created and—with one notable exception—all the buildings are original: disassembled where they stood, shipped here, and reassembled on-site. Everything was done as authentically as possible, down to bringing in thatchers from Ulster to roof the Irish cottage.

The 18th-century **German farm** from the Rhineland-Palatinate region is first. A framework of thick posts and beams is covered with wattle and daub (woven sticks covered with a mixture of soil, water, sand, lime, and manure). This style became common in Colonial America, though wooden planks would eventually replace the twigs and fertilizer. Twin walls of whitewashed stone separated by a layer of rubble make up the early 19th-century **Scottish-Irish cottage** and outbuildings, one of which encloses a working forge. A small field is planted every spring with flax to make linen, a common crop in northern Ireland at the time. The 18th-century **English farmhouse** from West Sussex is the most substantial so far, a two-story wooden building with an elaborate brick chimney. Next comes along life in the New World, with a 1770s **clapboard-covered log house** from Rockingham County and an 1850s **homestead and tobacco barn** from Botetourt County near Roanoke.

Until recently, one culture was noticeably missing from the re-creations: the African. Recognizing this absence, the Frontier Museum's newest site, slated to open in fall 2010, is a **West African farmers compound** modeled after an Igbo village. Why the Igbo? Extensive research showed that nearly 40 percent of all African captives brought to Virginia during the Colonial era were Igbo, located in present-day Nigeria. With the help of Igbo building experts and scores of volunteers (among them local football players) the village is being hewn together mud brick by mud brick using traditional methods adapted to the Virginia soil. When complete, the village will include four houses, a perimeter wall, and a traditional garden including yams and livestock such as pygmy goats.

As the first of its kind in the United States, the village fills a unique cultural gap, allowing African Americans of Igbo descent to see their heritage up-close without having to fly to Nigeria, and encouraging all visitors to learn about West African contributions to common American life—even the small stuff, like quilt designs and fried okra. But most importantly, it shares what was until now a missing chapter in the story of the Virginia frontier.

The museum is on U.S. 250, west of I-81 exit 222. Most of the grounds and buildings are wheelchair-accessible, and motorized scooters are available free of charge to mobility-impaired visitors. A long list of daily demonstrations varies throughout the year, including fabric weaving, sheep shearing, woodworking, and cooking. Some of the more popular activities and events such as Oktoberfest and holiday lantern tours have special admission fees and require preregistration; call or check the website for details.

Woodrow Wilson Presidential Library & Museum

Only a few original presidential birthplaces are still open to the public (that cabin in Kentucky probably isn't the one where Lincoln was born), and this quaint city boasts one of them. The birthplace of the 28th president (18–24 N. Coalter St., 540/885-0897, www.woodrowwilson.org, 9 A.M.–5 P.M. Mon.–Sat., noon–5 P.M. Sun., reduced hours Nov.–Feb., $12 adults, $3 children 6–12) features period furniture; personal belongings; a collection of books, memoirs, and World War I volumes; and Wilson's favorite 1919 Pierce-Arrow limousine. Boxwood gardens outside were restored in 1993 by the Garden Club of Virginia. Guided tours and exhibits trace his life from here to Princeton and the White House. (Wilson only lived here for the first year of his life before moving to Georgia, but what the heck, it's a nice place.) Admission is free on his birthday, December 28.

Other Landmarks

The cream-brick **Augusta County Courthouse,** on the corner of Johnson and Augusta Streets, is the fifth such structure on this particular site. Its classic design includes large stone columns supporting a dome topped by a weather-greened statue of Justice. Dating to 1855, the Gothic Revival **Trinity Episcopal Church** on Beverley Street replaced one that hosted the Virginia General Assembly in 1787 (look for the 12 Tiffany stained-glass windows). The lime-green **St. Francis of Assisi Catholic Church** sits on the highest hill in town.

Mary Baldwin College (540/887-7019, www.mbc.edu) was founded by the Rev. Rufous Bailey in 1842 as the Augusta Female Seminary, making it one of the oldest women's colleges in the South. Today it has an enrollment of about 2,200 students. The Greek Revival campus buildings sit on 54 acres on Sycamore Street overlooking downtown. Tennis courts, playgrounds, a golf course, a skate park, and a swimming pool fill **Gypsy Hill Park,** northwest of downtown along Churchville Avenue.

ENTERTAINMENT AND RECREATION

Local artists are thankful for the **Staunton-Augusta Art Center** (20 S. New St., 540/885-2028, www.saartcenter.org), which holds opening receptions from time to time. Crafts such as paintings, pottery, jewelry, and scarves are sold near the holidays.

From late May to late October, free **guided walking tours** leave from the Woodrow Wilson Presidential Library & Museum at 10 A.M. every Saturday. Brochures are also available for self-guided rambles from the Staunton Visitors Center (35 S. New St., 540/332-3971, www.visitstaunton.com), or contact the Historic Staunton Foundation (540/885-7676, www.historicstaunton.org) for more information.

Gypsy Hill Park, at the intersection of Churchill and Thornrose Avenues, is a 214-acre expanse that includes a lake, a pool, a public golf course, a gymnasium, sports stadiums and fields, playgrounds, and a bandstand. The Gypsy Express miniature train still runs through the park as it has for 50 years (noon–6 P.M. Sat., 1–5 P.M. Sun., May–Oct., $1).

Pay a visit to Elizabethan England at the **Blackfriars Playhouse** (10 S. Market St., 540/851-1733 or 877/682-4236, www.americanshakespearecenter.com), home to the internationally acclaimed American Shakespeare Center. This 300-seat indoor

© KATIE GITHENS

Staunton is best known for the Blackfriars Playhouse, but the Dixie is great for a movie.

playhouse—the only re-creation of the Bard's original indoor theater in the world—allows the productions to be staged as they originally were: on a simple stage sharing the same light as the audience section, giving a communal feel to the performances. The world-class venue is open year-round for Shakespeare productions and other special musical and theatrical events. Tours of the theater are also offered, often led by actors appearing in current productions (11 A.M. Mon.–Sat., plus 2 P.M. Mon.–Fri., $5).

Staunton also has two cool old-school cinemas. The **Dixie Theater** (125 E. Beverley St., 540/885-8445, www.thedixietheater.com, $6) has four screens and makes for a cheap date, and **Visulite Cinemas** (12 N. Augusta St., 540/885-9959, www.visulitecinemas.com, $8) has stadium seating with plush rocker-back chairs.

SHOPPING

Staunton's most interesting spot to browse is unquestionably the **Jolly Roger Haggle Shop** (27 Middlebrook Ave., 540/886-9527). Leave yourself an hour or more to do justice to roomfuls of old lunch boxes, turquoise jewelry, antique tools, militaria, books, and records piled to the ceiling. It boasts "more than one million items," and it's easy to believe. Other craft-antiques stores are clustered near Beverley and New Streets, including **Warehouse Antiques & Collectibles** (26 W. Beverley St., 540/885-0891), the city's largest antiques store, and **17 E. Beverley Antiques** (17 E. Beverley St., 540/885-1117, www.bevant.com), stocking vintage clothes, antique jewelry, quilts, and African art.

Sunspots (202 S. Lewis St., 540/885-0678) sells beautiful works in copper and handblown glass. You can watch the process during glass-blowing demos 10 A.M.–4 P.M. most days. The **Staunton/Augusta Farmers Market** (540/332-3802, www.safarmersmarket.com) features locally grown fruits, veggies, and other edibles on Saturday mornings April–November at Johnson and Byers Streets downtown.

EVENTS

The Stonewall Brigade Bandstand in Gypsy Hill Park is Staunton's music epicenter during the summer. The **Stonewall Brigade Band,** one of the nation's oldest continuous community bands, performs on Monday evenings June–August, and the **Jazz in the Park** series brings more music on Thursday evenings, rain or shine. In fact, you can basically pick a genre: There's also **gospel music** on Tuesday evenings and **bluegrass concerts** on Wednesdays. (All are free.) The **Staunton Music Festival** (540/569-0267, www.stauntonmusicfestival.com) offers classical and family music concerts at various locations around the city in August. Tickets are $20 per person.

ACCOMMODATIONS

$50-100

Near I-81 exit 222, the **Microtel Inn** (200 Frontier Dr., 540/887-0200) offers a heated outdoor pool, breakfast, and cookies at night.

$100-150

Fox-hunt decor distinguishes the **Montclair B&B** (320 N. New St., 540/885-8832 or 877 885-8832, www.montclairbnb.com). Sheri and Mark Bang have done an award-winning job of restoring the circa-1880 Italianate home, which features a library, private sitting rooms, and four guest rooms for $95–200.

The **Comfort Inn** (1032 Richmond Ave., 540/886-5000, $85–105) is between exit 222 off I-81 and downtown and offers free continental breakfast and an outdoor pool. There's also an **Econo Lodge** (1031 Richmond Ave., 540/885-5158, $60–130) in this price range near exit 222.

$150-200

The best way to top off a performance at Blackfriars Playhouse is a stay at **Anne Hathaway's Cottage** (950 W. Beverley St., 540/885-8885, www.anne-hathaways-cottage.com), a thatched-roof replica of Shakespeare's wife's cottage near Stratford in England. Rates for the three guestrooms are $160–210, including breakfast daily and afternoon tea on Friday and Saturday.

The most obvious place to stay in town is the restored **Stonewall Jackson Hotel** (24 S. Market St., 540/885-4848, www.stonewall

the historic Stonewall Jackson Hotel

© KATIE GITHENS

jackson.com); you can't miss the rooftop neon sign. Built in 1924, the historic hotel has 124 rooms and suites ($100–200) that were renovated in 2005, an indoor pool, fitness center, and 24 Market, serving all meals daily. Theater packages are also available (Blackfriars is literally next door).

Over $200

Frederick House (28 N. New St., 540/885-4220 or 800/334-5575, www.frederickhouse.com) is a European-style inn with an attached tearoom across from Mary Baldwin College. (Enter from the parking lot on New Street.) The building, some parts of which date to 1810, features a Federal-style curving stairway. Twenty-three distinctive rooms and suites are spread between the main house and nearby cottages and townhouses. Prices range $103–273.

Up on the high western end of Frederick Street perches the **Belle Grae Inn** (515 W. Frederick St., 540/886-5151 or 888/541-5151, www.bellegrae.com). Originally part of a 200-acre farm on the edge of town, the building known as the Old Inn was opened to the public in 1983. A front veranda and 12-foot ceilings grace the first of three Federal-style stories, and azaleas bloom in the garden in back. The circa-1873 Main Inn has three formal dining rooms and five rooms upstairs ($160–200). The Townhouse has two rooms and two suites ($160–220), and each of the four suites in the Jefferson House ($190) has a deck or porch overlooking the Victorian garden. The inn also serves up Thai specialties at the Ubon Thai Victorian Restaurant (540/886-4141, all meals daily).

Camping

In nearby Mint Springs off I-81 exit 217, the **Staunton Walnut Hills KOA** (484 Walnut Hills Rd., 540/337-3920 or 800/699-2568, www.walnuthillscampground.com) has a stocked fishing lake, pools, and laundry. The sites ($28–35) are open year-round, and cabins ($35–58) and cottages ($73–115) are available for rent as well.

FOOD

Snacks and Cafés

The **Pampered Palate Cafe** (28 E. Beverley St., 540/886-9463, lunch Mon.–Sat., dinner Fri.) offers quiches, pita sandwiches, and New York–style bagel sandwiches for $6–8. Many vegetarian and low-fat options are balanced by a gourmet goodie, coffee, and wine shop. Come by in the afternoon for "cappy hour" (i.e., cappuccino).

Staunton's oldest commercial building houses **Cranberry's** (7 S. New St., 540/885-4755), a natural grocery and eatery that serves excellent Lester's Best coffee and espresso, roasted daily by a local blues singer. Grab eggs and waffles for breakfast, or a smoothie and a BLT sandwich for lunch. Cranberry's also offers gluten-free items and has been certified by the Gluten-Free Restaurant Awareness Program. Open for breakfast and lunch Monday–Saturday, as well as dinner Thursday–Saturday, with shorter hours in winter.

Casual

Wright's Dairy-Rite (346 Greenville Ave., 540/886-0435, all meals daily) has been a local institution since 1952. Come inside or stay in your car for curbside service—either way, enjoy burgers, hot dogs, and sandwiches from $2 and up. The Statler Brothers, who hail from Staunton, used to fill up here.

Look for the stained-glass windows fronting the restored 1888 storefront of **The Beverley Restaurant** (12 E. Beverley St., 540/886-4317, all meals Mon.–Fri., breakfast and lunch only Sat.), serving home-style Southern food including chicken and dumplings, ham hocks and cabbage, and chipped-beef gravy breakfasts (all under $7). Both the chocolate milkshakes and the homemade pecan pies here are said to be "the best you'll ever eat" (let me know your verdict). They serve afternoon tea 3–5 P.M. Tuesday and Thursday.

Upscale

Today, more people head to the old C&O depot to try one of the two restaurants there than to board a train. **The Depot Grill** (42 Middlebrook Ave., 540/885-7332, lunch and dinner daily) boasts a marvelous 40-foot bar rescued from a luxury hotel that was demolished in Albany, New York. Seafood is also a favorite here, starting with shrimp, crab legs, and crawdads at the steamer bar. Sandwiches, burgers, and salads are $7–12, and entrées are $14–25.

Regional dishes like *pollo alla cacciatora* and gnocchi *alla bolognese* are a specialty of the cozy **Emilio's Italian Restaurant** (23 E. Beverley St., 540/885-0102, lunch and dinner daily). Casual lunches ($8–12) and dinners ($14–28) are enlivened by live music most nights in the upstairs Pompeii Lounge, boasting four fireplaces and a rooftop terrace that operate seasonally.

You won't mistake **The Staunton Grocery** (105 W. Beverley St., 540/886-6880, lunch Wed.–Sat., dinner Tues.–Sun.) for a supermarket; it's actually a fine-dining establishment renowned for chef Ian Boden's farm-to-table creations using fresh, local ingredients. Modern takes on Southern fare run $20–28 (appetizers are $7–11) in a stylishly casual setting with exposed brick walls and white tablecloths. Dishes follow the lines of roasted salmon with gnocchi, chestnuts, and brussels sprouts. Sundays are a three-course prix-fixe dinner for $35, and tasting menus paired with wine start at $55.

You know your culinary stars have aligned when the White House comes calling. Chef Michael Lund of **Zynodoa** (115 E. Beverley St., 540/885-7775, dinner daily, brunch at noon Sun.) cooks for the occasional presidential state dinner, but usually he's cooking up contemporary, locally sourced spins on fried green tomatoes and shrimp and grits here in Staunton. Start with cornmeal-dusted Chesapeake oysters (appetizers $9–12) before moving on to honey-brined pork tenderloin with apple sage bread pudding (entrées $18–27). One more vote of confidence: Lund trained at the Inn at Little Washington, widely considered the best in fine dining in Virginia.

INFORMATION

Look for the **Staunton/Augusta Travel Information Center** (1290 Richmond Rd., 540/332-3972 or 800/332-5219, 9 A.M.–5 P.M. daily) in the Museum of Frontier Culture, and the **Staunton Visitors Center** (35 S. New St., 540/332-3971, www.visitstaunton.com, 9 A.M.–6 P.M. daily, 9:30 A.M.–5:30 P.M. daily Nov.–Mar.) at the New Street Parking Garage. For information online, visit the city's website at www.staunton.va.us.

GETTING THERE AND AROUND

The free **Staunton Trolley** runs three different routes connecting downtown, the Wharf, and Gypsy Hill Park, among other destinations. There are designated stops, but you can also just flag them down. See the city website for hours and route details.

Trains leave the unstaffed **Amtrak** station for Charlottesville and Clifton Forge three times a week.

NEAR STAUNTON

Polyface Farms

Until recently, few living outside the Shenandoah Valley had heard of "beyond organic" farmer Joel Salatin and his 550-acre family-owned farm—no doubt because shipping farm-fresh meats runs counter to his commitment to buying and selling food locally. Then along came Michael Pollan's *New York Times* bestseller *The Omnivore's Dilemma* and the documentary *Food, Inc.*, and Salatin found himself standing front and center on the hay-bale soapbox of the sustainable agriculture movement.

Not that he had kept quiet before. The self-described Christian-Libertarian-Environmentalist-Capitalist-Lunatic has authored six books on raising pastured livestock and poultry using farming methods that focus on rotating animals' pastures daily to provide them with access to plentiful fresh air and grass (or, as he quips, "salad bars"). His goal is nothing short of changing the way we grow, buy, and sell food in America.

But don't just read about it here—see it for yourself. Polyface Farms (540/885-3590, www.polyfacefarms.com), so named for the "many faces," snouts, and beaks raised there, is deeply committed to the transparency of its operations and the treatment of its livestock. "Shake the hand that feeds you," the saying goes. Guided two-hour tours are available for $10.50 per person twice monthly (book early, they fill up).

Tour participants are invited to climb aboard a tractor-pulled flatbed of hay to visit the different pens and learn about farm operations and techniques. With Farmer Joel at the helm, it's kick-in-the-pants fun—really—and you'll see visitors there from all walks of life, from a retired couple from Ohio thinking about giving farming a go, to the usual suspects driving down from D.C. in an eco-friendly Prius. Kids especially will love the chick house, with all the downy yellow chicks milling about.

If you can't make it to one of the designated tours, visitors are still welcome to take a self-guided tour Monday–Saturday. Before you leave be sure to stock up on eggs, steaks, sausage, and chicken from the on-farm shop (9 A.M.–4 P.M. Sat. or by appointment). Polyface Farms is located in Swoope, about eight miles southwest of Staunton. Call or see website for directions.

Even if you never visit the farm, chances are good you'll eat a Polyface egg at some point during your time in Virginia. Once you start looking, you'll see "Polyface Farms" tattooed on restaurant menus from Washington, D.C., to Virginia Beach.

WAYNESBORO

Take exit 94 off I-81 to reach this industrial town just west of a major pass through the Blue Ridge. Accommodations await two blocks off Main Street at the **Belle Hearth B&B** (320 S. Wayne Ave., 540/943-1910 or 866/710-2256, www.bellehearth.com). Adorned with a gabled roof and wraparound porch, the early-1900s building is filled with Victorian furnishings and seven fireplaces—hence the name. Three rooms and one suite range $100–145.

The **P. Buckley Moss Museum** (150 P. Buckley Moss Dr., 800/343-8643, www.pbuckleymoss.com, 10 A.M.–5 P.M. Mon.–Sat., 12:30–5 P.M. Sun., free) houses dozens of works by the well-known local artist. Her distinctive "valley style," inspired by the scenery and people of the Shenandoah, is marked by bare, wiry trees, sensuous horses, chunky Canada geese, and elongated portraits of Amish and Old Order Mennonite farmers. There's a gift shop downstairs, where prices for even small prints can start in the hundreds.

Allegheny Highlands

Encompassing Highland, Bath, and parts of Augusta and Allegheny Counties, this wrinkled western spur is surprisingly accessible for such a wild area. Long, narrow peaks of the Allegheny Mountains ripple off into West Virginia, split by river valleys running arrow-straight southwest to northeast. With fewer than 3,000 people spread over 416 square miles, Highland County (aka Virginia's Switzerland) doesn't lack for open space. Most of it is above 4,000 feet elevation, making it one of the highest counties, in average elevation, east of the Mississippi. Many residents live off the land as their ancestors did, still referring to places as "three mountains over."

Bath County, in contrast, is one of the richest in Virginia, thanks to the fully realized resort possibilities of a series of thermal springs to which native tribes once ascribed healing powers. In 1750 a visiting doctor wrote, "the spring is very clear and warmer than new milk," although "the settlers would be better able to support travelers was it not for the great number of Indian warriors that frequently take what they want from them." Over the next few centuries, the wealthy residents of the Piedmont learned that the mountains and waters were the perfect escape from the summer mugginess. Thus began a tradition of lavish seasonal retreats, which is carried on today at the Homestead—possibly the grandest resort hotel in the state.

OUTDOOR RECREATION

Fishing is one of the top draws in this part of the state, attracting anglers from hundreds of miles away in search of bass (largemouth, smallmouth, and rock), trout, catfish, crappie, and muskies. Several of Virginia's major rivers have their headwaters in these choppy hills. Almost any of the streams and rivers flowing southwest, including the Maury, Bullpasture, and Cowpasture, offer great casting. The Jackson River flows into Lake Moomaw, a 12-mile flood-control reservoir with some of the best fishing in the state (bass in the three-to-four-pound range love the clear waters). The 60-acre Douthat Lake in Douthat State Park offers fee fishing for stocked trout.

Many wildlife management, recreation, and wilderness areas present boundless opportunities for hiking and camping amid the spruce and northern hardwood forests. Pocahontas County, just over the border in West Virginia, is a nationally known destination for mountain biking, and this side of the border is almost identical, although relatively less explored by knobby-tire enthusiasts. Finding your own track should be a cinch.

ACCESS

Possibly the prettiest road to the highlands—or anywhere in the state, for that matter—is Route 39, the "Avenue of Trees" from Lexington to Warm Springs via Goshen Pass. A 150-foot suspension bridge over the Maury River leads into tens of thousands of acres administered by the state. Frequent pull-offs and swimming spots galore can easily turn this 42-mile drive into a half-day trip. U.S. 250 from Staunton to Monterey comes in a close second, passing through the quaint burg of Churchville before becoming a rising corridor through the George Washington National Forest. A great view at the crest welcomes you to Highland County before the road inches its tortuous way down the other side of the ridge, only to rise and fall, again and again. Finally, no-nonsense I-64 heads from Lexington straight into West Virginia.

There's an unstaffed **Amtrak** station (307 E. Ridgeway St., 800/872-7245) in Clifton Forge, with trains to Staunton and White Sulphur Springs, West Virginia, and through bus service to Roanoke.

MONTEREY

Coming over the mountain on U.S. 250 when the leaves are lush and green can make the Highland County seat seem like a vision, nestled as it is in a narrow, gently sloping valley. It's a small town, with about 200 people at last count and only one traffic light (a flashing one, at that). U.S. 250 turns into Main Street as it runs through the center of town, lined with dozens of old buildings from the turn of the 20th century or before. The Landmark House, across from the courthouse, was built from logs in 1790 and renovated in 1977.

Recreation

For guiding and instruction in rock climbing, contact Rick Lambert at **Highland Adventures** (540/468-2722). Cyclists will be keen to explore the country roads; download maps and cue sheets of suggested routes from the Highland County Chamber of Commerce website (www.highlandcounty.org). In August, the **Mountain Mama Road Bike Challenge** (540/468-2946, www.bikemountainmama.homestead.com) stages a century ride with nearly 14,000 feet of climbing that quickly introduces you to the terrain and the vistas (there are shorter rides too).

Shopping

Opposite the courthouse sits the **H&H Cash Store** (540/468-2570, www.handh.homestead.com), an old-fashioned mercantile stocking maple sugar candy, buckwheat flour, tools, and clothing. As they say, "If we don't have it, you don't need it." Knitters and crocheters can pick up specialty yarns, many of them locally made, at **Wool Becomes Ewe** (50 Fleisher Ave., 540/468-2007, www.woolbecomesewe.com), a block north of Main Street. Highland County is typically one of Virginia's largest wool-producing counties, so you can thank the sheep you'll see grazing on the hillsides later. The **Highlands Farmers Market** runs Friday afternoons June through September at the Highland Center (540/468-1922), located south on Spruce Street just off U.S. 250.

Events

Fans of Virginia fairs know Monterey's **Highland Maple Festival** is one of the first major ones of the year. Held the second and third weekends in March, the festival centers on the fact that Highland is the only county in Virginia that produces maple syrup and all its tasty by-products. Some 50,000 people eager to see the sun after a long winter make the trek to enjoy crafts and an all-you-can-eat pancake breakfast—topped with fresh maple syrup, of course.

Accommodations

The pink stone **Montvallee Motel** (54 E. Main St., 540/468-2500, www.montvalleemotel.com) offers 1950s-style charm at the intersection of U.S. 250 and U.S. 220, with double rooms for $84–120. Farther on into town sits the Victorian **Highland Inn** (68 W. Main St., 540/468-2143 or 888/466-4682, www.highland-inn.com, $100–150), built in 1904 as a vacation getaway. Gingerbread trim decorates the stacked front porches, where rocking chairs sway in the breeze. Inside are the Black Sheep Tavern and a dining room, both heated by wood-burning stoves for cooler evenings.

The **Cherry Hill Bed & Breakfast** (224 W. Mill Alley, 540/468-1900 or 540/468-2020, www.cherryhillbandb.com, $85–110) perches on Mill Alley one block off Main Street. Bay windows look out over a wraparound porch to a great view of the town and valley, and a hammock sways in the quiet flower garden out back.

Contact the Highland County Chamber of Commerce (540/468-2550, www.highlandcounty.org) for information on the many other cabins, farms, and other rural getaways in the area.

Food

The **Monterey Dining Room** of the Highland Inn serves dinner Wednesday–Saturday and a brunch buffet on Sunday. Caesar salads and burgers are $8–9 and entrées such as locally caught rainbow trout and pecan-crusted chicken are $14–18, with nightly specials for a bit more.

Across the street, **High's Restaurant** (73 W. Main St., 540/468-1700, all meals daily) is the oldest in town and still going strong. You'll usually find it bustling with local folks. Burgers and sandwiches cost $4–6 while T-bones and trout can cost up to $20. The homemade pies and fresh bread are worth a stop. Cash only.

Information

The **Highland County Chamber of Commerce** (540/468-2550, www.highlandcounty.org) has an office in the Highland Center on Spruce Street.

Near Monterey

A wealth of hiking options await in **Laurel Fork,** a 10,000-acre special management area that covers the tip of the point sticking into West Virginia. This pristine region shelters "relic communities" left over from cooler times, including rare species such as the endangered Virginia northern flying squirrels, which soar through the red spruce forests.

Dozens of miles of trails roam through the craggy hills, many following old railroad grades. Popular ones include the Buck Run and Locust Springs Run Trails, following turn-of-the-20th-century railroad grades once used to log virgin timber. You can make an 11-mile loop (actually a figure eight) out of the Buck Run, Spring Run, Cold Spring, and Christian Run Trails, starting at the Locust Spring Picnic Area. (Be ready for a number of stream crossings.)

See the Highland County Chamber of Commerce website (www.highlandcounty.org) for directions to the trailhead, which involves a number of twists and turns on gravel roads. Contact the Warm Springs Ranger District of the George Washington & Jefferson National Forest (540/839-2521, www.fs.fed.us/r8/gwj/warmsprings) for more information.

If Monterey isn't far enough away for you, consider staying at the **Bear Mountain Farm and Wilderness Retreat** (540/468-2700, www.mountain-retreat.com, open Apr.–Oct.), a lodge so far into the hinterlands that you could throw a rock and hit West Virginia. The center welcomes everyone from individuals to groups of up to 20, who can stay in three simple, snug pine cabins with shared bathhouse ($90–125) or the larger Allegheny Mountain log cabin ($125), which sleeps five and feels straight out of the Wyoming foothills. The latter has a large common room with a piano, cooking facilities, a hot tub, and spectacular views from the wide windows and wraparound porch. The owners offer naturalist weekend workshops and guided hikes. Relax in the evening in front of the wood-burning stove in the main room or in the sand-floored sauna. Camping is $35, or $45 with use of the kitchen and bathhouse. The stargazing, as you can imagine, is divine, but be sure to arrive at Bear Mountain before dark to avoid getting lost.

Some of the most isolated and craggy territory in the George Washington National Forest fills the 6,500-acre **Ramsey's Draft Wilderness,** which you enter off U.S. 250 about 21 miles east of Monterey. Thousands of acres of virgin forest—spared the axe thanks to their inaccessibility—include yellow poplar, white oaks, and hemlocks, making up one of the largest expanses of old-growth forest in the East. ("Draft" means creek, and you'll cross plenty while hiking here.) The 6.8-mile Ramsey's Draft Trail winds alongside a stream of the same name, and a National Forest campground sits nine miles north of U.S. 250 on Route 715 (continue one mile northeast on Forest Road 95, then one mile southwest on Forest Road 95B). Call the North River Ranger District of the George Washington & Jefferson National Forests in Staunton (540/885-8028, www.fs.fed.us/r8/gwj/northriver) for more information.

WARM SPRINGS

The Bath County seat nestles in a valley near a small set of natural thermal springs. Eighteenth-century buildings, many white with green trim, constitute the original town center known as Old Germantown off Route 39 just west of U.S. 220.

Recreation

A pair of oddly shaped buildings at the Route 39/U.S. 220 intersection house the **Jefferson Pools,** owned by the luxury resort The Homestead. These large stone pools of naturally warm water were built in the late 18th century, when the Virginia elite would make the rounds of different pools in the area. Thomas Jefferson may have lent his design flair to the structures: the men's pool house has 8 sides and the women's has 22. Jefferson spent three weeks here in 1818, soaking three times a day and deeming the spring waters "of first merit."

As you relax in the 98°F water, be thankful fashions have changed since the 1830s, when according to one account stylish bathers had to don "a large cotton gown of a cashmere shawl pattern lined with crimson, a fancy Greek cap, Turkish slippers, and a pair of loose pantaloons." For a change of pace, try hydrotherapy, where part of the 1,200-gallon-per-minute flow is released onto your back as you sit in a special chamber outside and below the pool. The clothing-optional pools are open noon–5 P.M. seasonally for $17 per hour. Call the Homestead concierge to confirm hours (540/839-7741).

Accommodations and Food

Take Old Germantown Road (Rte. 692) off Route 39 toward the center of Warm Springs to reach the **Anderson Cottage Bed & Breakfast** (540/839-2975, www.bbonline.com/va/anderson) on your left. The two buildings are among Bath County's oldest, having served over the years as a tavern, a girls' school, and a summer inn. They've been in the present owner's family since the 1870s. Rates range $100–150; the separate guest cottage, formerly an early-19th-century brick kitchen, is $150 for the first night and $125 per night thereafter.

To find **The Inn at Gristmill Square** (540/839-2231, www.gristmillsquare.com), look for the waterwheel on Old Mill Road (Rte. 645) in the heart of Warm Springs. A mill has stood here since 1771, but the present buildings date to the 19th century. Janice and Jack McWilliams, who bought the place in 1981, have added tennis courts, a pool, and a sauna in the process of restoring four buildings: the Blacksmith Shop, the Miller House, the Steel House, and the Hardware Store. All 17 guest rooms have wood-burning fireplaces and are tastefully furnished with antiques and exotic curios. Rates ($110–175) include a continental breakfast. Fine food is served with a country flair in the adjacent **Waterwheel Restaurant.** Dinner, served daily, features savory dishes such as roast duck with apricots ($24–30). Sunday brunch is also available.

Three **National Forest campgrounds** can be found within 20 miles of Warm Springs, all starting west on Route 39. From nearest to farthest, they are Hidden Valley ($10), Blowing Springs ($10), and Bolar Mountain

($16–20) on Lake Moomaw. Blowing Springs is open year-round; the other two just April–November. Contact the George Washington & Jefferson National Forest (540/839-2521, www.fs.fed.us/r8/gwj/warmsprings) for exact directions and more information.

ON THE ROAD TO HOT SPRINGS

Virginia novelist Mary Johnson *(to Have and to Hold)* built the central part of **Three Hills Inn & Cottages** (540/839-5381 or 888/234-4557) in 1913. Today the hotel, which is reached by a winding driveway from U.S. 220, commands an impressive view from 38 acres of hillside just south of the Route 39/U.S. 220 intersection. Rooms in the main house are $130–150, suites are $180–270, and several cottages with kitchenettes can hold four people for $300. Some rates include a full breakfast.

This neck of the woods also happens to be home to one of Virginia's most celebrated musical venues, the not-for-profit **Garth Newel Music Center** (540/839-5018 or 877/558-1689, www.garthnewel.org). Top-flight classical performances are held in the concert hall on Saturday and Sunday afternoons. You can enjoy a four- or five-course set meal (reservations required) or picnic before or after the shows. In mid-June, the music center hosts the **Virginia Blues & Jazz Festival,** which has featured renowned musicians like Taj Mahal. Contact the center for prices and a current schedule.

HOT SPRINGS

The Homestead

Virginia's premier resort (540/839-1766 or 866/354-4653, www.thehomestead.com) is more like a richly endowed university than a hotel. So big that U.S. 220 curves around it and little arrows are posted to help navigate the hallways, this world-class spread covers 15,000 acres of Bath County with spotless grounds, stately brick buildings, and one of the finest mountain golf courses in the country.

The first lodge here was built in 1766 by Lt. Thomas Bullitt, a frontier militiaman. The facilities were improved to the status of "modern hotel" in the mid-19th century, just in time to serve as a field hospital during the Civil War. The first spa, golf course, and tennis courts were opened in 1892, but most of the buildings vanished in a fire in 1901 and were rebuilt.

Inside the main structure, the cavernous Great Hall is lined with fireplaces surrounded by cozy chairs. The opulent President's Lounge has a view of the inner courtyard, and the Jefferson Parlor features wall paintings of Thomas Jefferson and the Homestead. For meals, guests can choose between the formal main dining room, 1766 Grille, and several more casual options, such as the Casino Club or Sam Snead's Tavern. Cottage Row off the Great Hall contains a small mall's worth of shops selling fine gifts, children's items, and gourmet foods. Golf, ski, and tennis shops elsewhere in the complex rent and sell sporting goods.

The Homestead offers more than enough activities to keep guests busy year-round, both indoors and out. Three golf courses—including the regular top-100 contender Cascades Course, restored to its original 1923 William Flynn design—draw the most visitors. One boasts the oldest first tee in the country, in use since 1890. Instruction and full equipment services are available for golfers and patrons of the hotel's six tennis courts. Canoeing, mountain biking, and 100 miles of hiking trails lure hikers into the hills, and there's a four-mile private trout stream and a shooting club for the sporting types. Guests can take lessons in both fly fishing and falconry.

One of the first European-style spas in the country offers aromatherapy, hydrotherapy, massage therapy, facials, and an indoor spring-fed pool opened in 1903. Bowling alleys and a movie theater keep night owls busy, and the Homestead Kids' Club keeps children occupied. In the winter, a small **ski area**—the South's first—has nine slopes, a snowboard park, snow-making equipment, and a full-service ski shop. If you're not a downhill speed demon, snowshoe and snowmobile tours and cross-country ski lessons are also available.

The hotel has 480 rooms and suites. Standard room rates range $175–315 per night on summer weekends. Suites can cost as much as triple that rate. Various golf, spa, and romance packages are also available.

DOUTHAT STATE PARK

Virginia's oldest state park (540/862-8100, www.dcr.virginia.gov/state_parks/dou.shtml, $2 per car, $3 weekends) is also one of its best. It boasts 40 miles of hiking and mountain biking trails winding through 4,493 rugged acres, blustery ridges, and deep forest surrounding 50-acre Douthat Lake, stocked twice a week with rainbow trout (as is Wilson Creek below the dam). Three miles of the creek have been designated children-only, giving budding anglers easy access and clearings to perfect their casts into well-stocked pools. Douthat is the only Virginia state park split by a road—Route 629, which leaves I-64 north from exit 27.

Campsites (open Mar.–Nov.) are $24–25 each, and reservations are essential on busy weekends from Memorial Day to Labor Day. One-room, one-bedroom, and two-bedroom cabins are priced $88–112 (less on weekdays and off-season). Two five-bedroom lodges can be rented by the week or for a minimum of two nights: The **Creasey Lodge** is $270–301 per night for up to 18 people, and the **Main Lodge** is $318–354 per night for up to 15 (both are also cheaper on weekdays and off-season). Three new cabins were under construction in 2010. Swimming from the beach area is $2–3 per person. A restaurant overlooking the lake serves lunch and dinner Wednesday–Friday and all meals on weekends from Memorial Day to Labor Day, and weekends in April and October. There's also a camp store and gift shop.

Lexington

Take a smallish mannerly town, steep it in Civil War history, overlay with a nationally recognized college or two, and you'll end up with something approaching this quiet community (pop. 7,000), close to both Natural Bridge and the Blue Ridge Parkway. Crew-cut cadets stroll in gray full dress uniform down tree-shaded streets, while other students jog in red and yellow school colors past grand colonnaded houses. Within the town limits lie two of the most honored heroes of the Confederacy: Robert E. Lee and Stonewall Jackson.

Founded in 1777, Lexington was leveled by fire in 1796 and rebuilt with lottery proceeds. Less than 30 years after its founding, the Virginia Military Institute (VMI) had a chance to prove its mettle, when dozens of cadets were thrown into the Battle of New Market in May 1864. VMI was the target of Union Gen. David Hunter's guns a month later. The barracks and much of town were left in ruins.

Since then, things have improved. In 2000 the city was included in the National Trust for Historic Preservation's list of a Dozen Distinctive Destinations, representing some of the best-preserved and unique communities in America.

SIGHTS

Washington and Lee University

Known as "W and L," this small private college (540/458-8400, www.wlu.edu) enjoys a national reputation, with an overwhelming percentage of students arriving from the top of their high school classes. It was founded in 1749 and saved from bankruptcy in 1796 by a substantial gift from George Washington. Soon after conceding the Civil War at Appomattox, Robert E. Lee served as its president from 1865 to 1870. Today, 2,000 students enjoy a beautiful central campus that was declared a National Historic Landmark in 1972. A row of dark redbrick buildings are fronted by bright white colonnades.

In the center of the campus stands the **Lee Chapel and Museum** (540/458-8768, http://chapelapps.wlu.edu, 9 A.M.–5 P.M. Mon.–Sat., 1–5 P.M. Sun. Apr.–Oct., to 4 P.M. Nov.–Mar.,

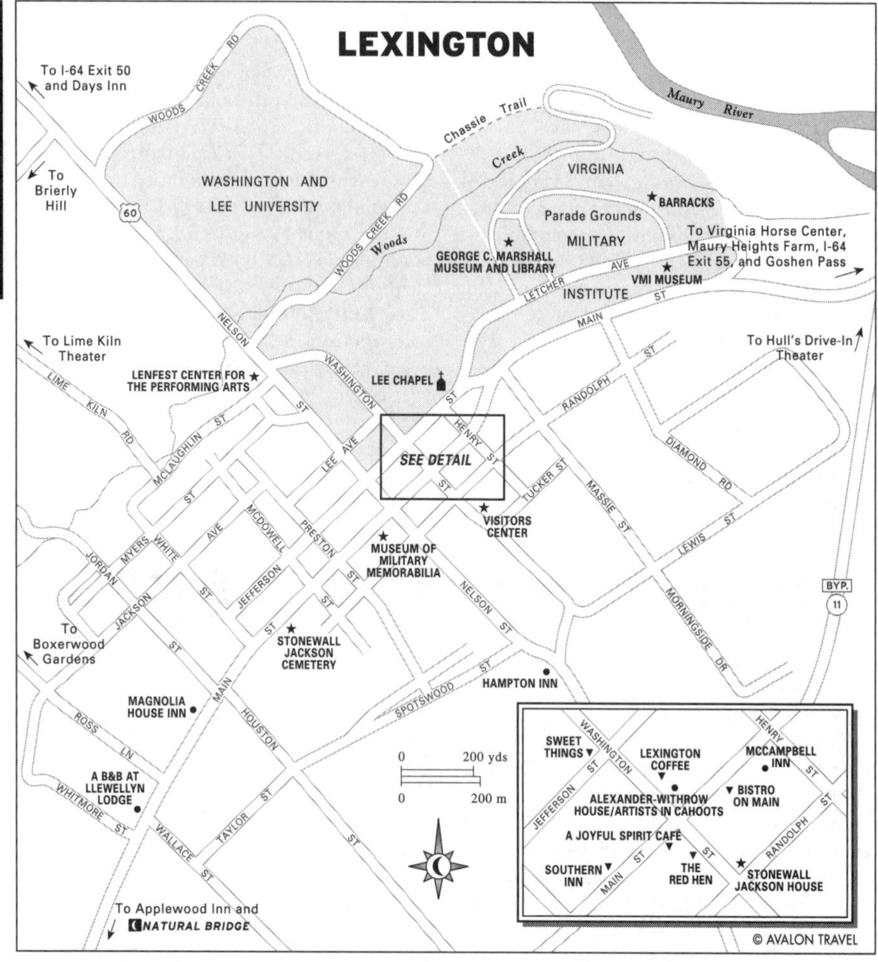

free). The former Confederate commander supervised its construction in 1867–1868 and set up his offices in the lower level. The simple, pretty Romanesque chapel (not to be confused with the Robert E. Lee Episcopal Church, at Washington St. and Lee Ave.) was actually never consecrated, serving instead as a hall for meetings and weddings. Inside is Charles Wilson Peale's portrait of George Washington—the first Washington ever sat for—in the incongruous uniform of a British colonel. A famous Edward Valentine statue of Lee in repose is surrounded by Confederate flags. Notice that Lee is represented not as dead, but resting: His feet are crossed and his hand rests on the hilt of his sword. Downstairs are the Lee family crypt and a small museum, which includes Lee's office just as he left it on September 28, 1870. Lee's horse Traveler is buried outside.

Virginia Military Institute

The country's first state military college

(540/464-7211, www.vmi.edu), VMI was founded in 1839 on the site of the Lexington Arsenal and had an initial class of 23. Twenty-five years later, 1864 was a big year for VMI: in May, her cadets fought in the Battle of New Market, and in June the barracks were shelled to the ground by Federal forces. The next big news came more than a century later. In 1996, the U.S. Supreme Court ruled that the school's males-only policy was unconstitutional, and a year later 30 female cadets were allowed to endure the infamous freshman Rat Line, a harsh rite of passage that claims 25 percent of each incoming class. The "cadettes" lived on the same floors as the men, wearing the same crew cuts, under the rule that any fooling around will result in the dismissal of both parties. New outdoor security lighting, emergency phones, and modified communal bathrooms made the adjustment slightly easier. In 2001, the institute's first coed class graduated without any major incidents to mar the transition.

Crenellations (battlements) top somber gray buildings around the huge central parade ground where cadets practice sports and military drills. (The Corps of Cadets gives a review parade most Friday afternoons.) At the southwest corner, the **George C. Marshall Museum and Library** (540/463-7103, www.marshallfoundation.org, 9 A.M.–5 P.M. Tues.–Sat., 1–5 P.M. Sun., $5 adults, $2 students) commemorates the 1901 graduate who went on to serve as general of the army, the highest military rank possible. While he was secretary of state, his Marshall Peace Plan for the rebuilding of Europe after World War II won him the Nobel Peace Prize. The museum contains army memorabilia, personal papers, and a narrated map of World War II.

The **Virginia Military Institute Museum** (540/464-7334, www.vmi.edu/museum, 9 A.M.–5 P.M. daily, free) is located in Jackson Memorial Hall at the opposite corner of the parade ground. Stonewall Jackson's field desk and a statue of his favorite horse, Little Sorrel, are both on display along with period clothes, weapons, and historical VMI artifacts. The museum reopened in 2006 following a two-year $3.3 million expansion.

Stonewall Jackson House

The only home the Confederate commander ever owned stands in the heart of Lexington (8 E. Washington St., 540/463-2552, www.stonewalljackson.org, 9 A.M.–5 P.M. Mon.–Sat., 1–5 P.M. Sun., Mar.–Dec., $6 adults, $3 children 6–17). Jackson occupied the modest brick townhouse for two years with his second wife, Anna Morrison, before riding off to war in April 1861, never to return. Restored in 1979, the brick building contains many of his possessions and other Civil War–era pieces, along with a gift shop. The kitchen garden has been replanted behind the house. Tours are given every half-hour until 4:30 P.M.

Stonewall Jackson Cemetery

After being accidentally shot by his own men at Chancellorsville, "Old Jack" was finally laid to rest in this burial ground at the south end of Main Street. An Edward Valentine statue

© KATIE GITHENS

Stonewall Jackson Cemetery

STONEWALL JACKSON

Born Thomas Jonathan Jackson on January 21, 1824, in Clarksburg, Virginia, the Civil War's most famous field commander found himself an orphan by age seven. He grew up in the house of an uncle, before squeaking into the U.S. Military Academy at West Point. (The first choice from the local congressional district, it seemed, had quit after his first day.) There he survived, in his own words, "by the skin of my teeth," graduating in 1846, 17th in a class of 59.

During the Mexican-American War, Jackson saw action in Cerro Gordo, Veracruz, and Chapultepec, and his outstanding conduct in the artillery earned him early promotions. In 1851, though, he left the rank of major to become a professor of military tactics and physics at the Virginia Military Institute (VMI). Students derided his dull teaching style and classroom quirks, starting with a shrill voice that belied his six-foot, 170-pound frame. Jackson lived in Lexington for the next decade, joining the Presbyterian Church and local Bible society. Two of those years were spent in the house on Washington Street, which is now a museum.

Within weeks of the outbreak of the Civil War, Jackson was back in the ranks, assuming a post as infantry colonel on April 21, 1861. Quickly promoted to brigadier general, the former teacher marched a group of VMI cadets to Richmond to help train the budding Confederate Army. His famous nickname came at the First Battle of Bull Run, in July 1861, soon after Confederate forces had begun to flee the fight. Seeing Jackson's troops holding their ground, Brig. Gen. Barnard E. Bee cried, "There stands Jackson like a stone wall! Rally behind the Virginians!" Bee was killed minutes later, but the tide of battle turned, and the name stuck.

Shortly after being promoted to major general, Stonewall cemented his place in history with his famous Valley Campaign in the spring of 1862, often called one of the most brilliant in military history. He continued to shine through the battles of Antietam and Second Bull Run, where his unorthodox tactics and uncanny rapport with General Lee won him fight after fight. Stonewall worked best when he was free to march and attack at will, pushing his men to the limit and always appearing when and where his opponents least expected.

Through it all, "Old Jack" remained a strange bird, obsessed with secrecy and concealing his plans even from direct subordinates. (Maj. Gen. Richard Ewell eventually concluded that his superior was a few pecks short of a bushel.)

At Chancellorsville in early May 1863, Jackson detached from General Lee's forces to flank the Federal XI Corps under Maj. Gen. Joseph Hooker. The risky but inspired maneuver routed the enemy troops in one of the most dramatic and decisive Confederate victories of the war. But Stonewall's finest hour was too soon followed by his final one: Out riding the evening of May 2, he was fired on by mistake by Confederate soldiers. Two of his aides were killed, and Jackson was shot in the right hand and left arm. In a nearby home that served as a field hospital, doctors decided to amputate the shattered limb. "He has lost his left arm," Lee said as Jackson lay dying, "but I have lost my right."

Jackson gave a good fight, but pneumonia set in and his condition deteriorated. On May 10, his doctors decided that he wouldn't last until sundown. The Confederacy's star commander died that afternoon after a final request: "Let us cross over the river and rest in the shade of the trees." His valiant Stonewall Brigade, hardened by dozens of battles, was never the same after losing its leader, though eight of its men went on to become generals.

WIKIMEDIA COMMONS

© KATIE GITHENS

The fabled general and 144 Confederate veterans are buried in Lexington's Stonewall Jackson Cemetery.

marks his tomb in the center, surrounded by the graves of other Civil War notables and prominent local citizens. Open dawn–dusk.

Boxerwood Gardens

Local doctor Robert Munger began planting rare trees and shrubs around his house in 1952. After his death in 1988, his gardener bought the place and opened it to the public in 1997. More an arboretum than a flower garden, Boxerwood (963 Ross Rd., 540/463-2697, www.boxerwood.org, dawn–dusk daily, free) encloses 15 bucolic acres of exotic species such as Japanese maples and dwarf conifers alongside local dogwoods, rhododendrons, and azaleas, all with a panoramic view of the Blue Ridge Mountains. Everything is labeled, but the atmosphere is more raggedly natural than neatly pruned. Maps are available for self-guided tours, but half the fun is simply wandering around and seeing what you find.

Museum of Military Memorabilia

Uniforms, weapons, flags, and accoutrements from France, Great Britain, Germany, and the United States fill this small gallery (122 S. Main St., 540/464-3041, noon–5 P.M. Wed.–Fri., 9 A.M.–5 P.M. Sat., Apr.–Oct., $3 adults). The collection spans wars from 1740 to the Gulf War, and guided tours are available. Cadets in uniform are admitted free.

Virginia Horse Center

On Route 39 just north of I-64 lies one of the most outstanding equine complexes in the country. The 600-acre state-of-the-art center (540/464-2950, www.horsecenter.org) hosts shows, clinics, and sales year-round, including the Spring Arabian Classic, the Virginia Horse Trials, and the Southern States Showdown. The **American Work Horse Museum** includes just about everything horse-powered you can think of, from farm equipment to rural postal wagons. It's open most weekends or whenever an equine event takes place.

ENTERTAINMENT AND RECREATION

Theaters

On the outskirts of Lexington, the ruins

of a 19th-century kiln have been converted into one of the more unusual and enjoyable places to see a play in the entire mid-Atlantic region. Founded in 1983, the **Lime Kiln Theater** (540/463-7088, www.theateratlimekiln.com) seems to rise up out of the ground, amid the vine-covered stones where workers once smelted lime and cut stones. Actors and musicians now perform on summer evenings on one of three stages—two open to the stars and one in a tent in case of rain. The outdoor theater season runs April–October. Tickets for plays and concerts are $8–55 and are available for purchase by calling 540/463-7088 or at the Lexington Visitors Center. Reach the theater from Lime Kiln Road off White and McLaughlin from Main Street, or via Border Road south off U.S. 60 West.

Washington and Lee's **Lenfest Center for the Performing Arts** (U.S. 60 West and Glasgow St., 540/458-8000, http://lenfest.wlu.edu) also hosts plays and concerts by students and professionals. The W&L Film Society also screens movies at the **University Commons** at the corner of Main and Henry Streets, often free. Head north on Route 11 about five miles to reach the classic dinosaur called **Hull's Drive-in Theater** (540/463-2621, www.hullsdrivein.com, $6 pp over age 12), one of only a handful of drive-in theaters left in the state. It's the real thing, Sno-Cones and all. Open since 1950, it's been operated by a nonprofit group called Hull's Angels since 2001, making it the country's only nonprofit, community-owned drive-in theater.

Nightlife

Students name **The Palms** (101 W. Nelson St., 540/463-7911) as the biggest and most popular bar in town. It's open from lunch (sandwiches and burgers) through dinner (light fare to chicken and pasta) until 1 or 2 A.M.

Tours

Lexington is one of the most pleasant towns in Virginia to wander around on foot. Pick up a self-guided **walking-tour brochure** from the visitors center, detailing four different routes.

From late May to October, **Haunting Tales of Historic Lexington** (540/464-2250) guarantees a scare—or at least a shiver—on candlelit rounds of ghostly sites around town. The 90-minute walking tour leaves at 8:30 P.M. from the visitors center, where tickets ($12 adults, $6 children 4–12) are available. Reservations are required; cash only.

A daytime option is a tour of Lexington's major historical sights by horse-drawn carriage with the **Lexington Carriage Company** (540/463-5647, www.lexcarriage.com). Its 45-minute tours leave from Washington Street across from the visitors center, 11 A.M.–5 P.M. daily April–October, 10 A.M.–6 P.M. daily June–August, $16 adults, $7 children 7–13.

The folks at the Applewood Inn (242 Tarn Beck Ln., 540/463-1962 or 800/463-1902, www.applewoodbb.com) organize two-hour **llama treks** into the surrounding countryside for $24 per person ($18 for guests of the inn).

Outdoor Recreation

Narrow but pretty **Woods Creek Park** follows the creek of the same name for two miles along the length of Lexington. At the northern end, where it reaches the Maury River, you can pick up the **Chessie Nature Trail,** a seven-mile stretch of the old Chesapeake and Ohio rail line through rural countryside to Buena Vista. Damage from Hurricane Camille in 1969 caused the line to be abandoned, allowing the Nature Conservancy to acquire it in 1978. Along the way you'll pass old canal locks and cross a 235-foot bridge over the South River near its confluence with the Maury River. To reach the starting point, cross U.S. 11 near VMI Island using the foot bridge; the pedestrian trail begins near the north end of the U.S. 11 bridge.

Fly-fishing guide extraordinaire **John Roberts** (540/463-3235 or 800/882-1145, www.vatrout.com) will take you casting in trout-rich local streams for $350–490 per day and offers casting instruction for $30 per hour. Prices include all equipment except waders, which he rents.

Afternoon canoeing, kayaking, and tubing trips on the Maury and James Rivers can

THE DEVIL'S MARBLEYARD

A short but challenging hike up the west side of the Blue Ridge leads to a singular hillside strewn with white quartzite boulders. Split by frost wedges during the last Ice Age, these rocks cover eight acres, leading to a great view of Arnold's Valley from the top. (Watch for spiders and biting insects in the summer, though.) To get there, take Route 130 south from Natural Bridge to Natural Bridge Station, then take a right on Route 759 (Arnold's Valley Rd.). Cross the James River and the Shenandoah Valley, pass a correctional center on the left, then head left on Petite's Gap Road at a three-way intersection. Parking is on the left, marked Belfast Trail. The trail is only a mile long but strewn with stones, and a few creek crossings are necessary. You can access the Appalachian Trail from the top, and it's easiest to descend on the trail to the right of the rockslide.

be arranged through **Twin Rivers Outfitters** (653 Lowe St., Buchanan, 540/261-7334, www.canoevirginia.com) for $15–40 per person. Longer trips are also possible. Based in Natural Bridge Station, the **Wilderness Canoe Company** (631 James River Rd., 540/291-2295, www.wildernesscanoecampground.com) will send you down the James River in a canoe, kayak, or tube ($15–60); prices include shuttle service, maps, and equipment.

SHOPPING

Local artists have formed a cooperative gallery in the Alexander-Withrow House called **Artists in Cahoots** (1 W. Washington St., 540/464-1147), showcasing beautiful crafts from photography and stained glass to hand-painted silks and delicate carved birds. Some artists also work here. **Virginia Born and Bred** (16 W. Washington St., 800/437-2452) stocks Americana like hand-carved nutcrackers and folk art alongside jellies, hams, and wines.

You'll find a little bit of everything—and then some—at **Goodharts Second Hand Shop** (7 S. Jefferson St., 540/463-7559), from crates of records and old guitars to photographs, clothes, and antiques. For books, head to Nelson Street: Try **The Bookery** (107 W. Nelson St., 540/464-3377) or **Books & Co.** (29 W. Nelson St., 540/463-4647), which also sells CDs and maps.

Lexington has too many antiques stores to mention—practically one on every block—but for sheer volume you can't beat the **Lexington Antique Center** (1495 N. Lee Hwy., 540/463-9511), with 250 dealers spread over 20,000 square feet. It's in the College Square Shopping Center, north off Lee-Jackson Highway, near both I-81 exit 191 and I-64 exit 55.

EVENTS

Lee-Jackson Day commemorates the birthdays of Robert E. Lee (January 19) and Stonewall Jackson (January 21) with celebrations throughout the South, but particularly in Stonewall's hometown. Free tours of Jackson's home and other festivities honor the local hero.

In March of election years, Lexington comes alive with Washington and Lee's famous **Mock Convention** (http://mockcon.wlu.edu), an outrageous parade and party that also happens to be one of the most accurate predictors of presidential politics in the country. Since William Jennings Bryan defeated John A. Johnson in 1908, the counterfeit caucus has correctly predicted presidential nominees 18 of 24 times, an accuracy rate of 75 percent. Despite the festive atmosphere, a year's worth of serious research goes into keeping up such a good track record (recently broken in 2008, when Barack Obama was chosen for the Democratic nomination over Hillary Clinton—but that was only the second misfire in choosing the party's nominee in W&L's history). The convention happens early in the actual races, making it the subject of national interest.

Every July, Lexington hosts the **Fourth of July Balloon Rally** at the VMI parade grounds. Activities include piloted balloon flights, tethered balloon rides, live music, fireworks, and children's activities.

ACCOMMODATIONS

Befitting its role as one of the state's most popular getaway towns, the Lexington region is positively rife with guesthouses.

$50-100

Maury Heights Farm (1080 Maury River Rd., 540/463-7458, www.mhfarm.com) offers two guest rooms ($60–90) in a pastoral valley three miles from the visitors center. The building also has a den/office room with Wi-Fi, and rates include a continental breakfast.

Off I-64 exit 55 is a **Super 8 Motel** (1139 N. Lee Hwy., 540/463-7858) with rooms for $70–90.

$100-150

John Roberts, the owner of **A Bed & Breakfast at Llewellyn Lodge** (603 S. Main St., 540/463-3235 or 800/882-1145, www.llodge.com, $95–190) was born in the Stonewall Jackson house and knows the Lexington area like the back of his hand. He's even written a local hiking guide he's happy to share with guests. His place, a brick Colonial-style building, is the longest-running bed-and-breakfast in town, and rooms include a celebrated full gourmet breakfast cooked by his wife, Ellen. They're happy to help organize fishing and canoeing trips too.

The **Applewood Inn** (242 Tarn Beck Ln., 540/463-1962 or 800/463-1902, www.applewoodbb.com, $130–155) is an environmentally friendly bed-and-breakfast offering 37 acres of rustic comfort south of town. A California redwood hot tub sits on an enclosed porch that's part of the house's solar envelope construction, where a layer of heated air surrounding the entire building provides warmth well into the night. Guests are welcome to use the pool and kitchen, and the owners offer two-hour llama treks into the hills for guests and day visitors for $18–24 per person. To get there, take Route 11 for 4.5 miles south of town and make a right onto Buffalo Bend Road, following signs for the next 1.2 miles to Tarn Beck Lane.

On U.S. 60, 4.5 miles west of Lexington, is the **Days Inn Lexington** (325 W. Midland Trail, 540/463-2143), with rooms for $82–200.

The **Best Western Inn at Hunt Ridge** (25 Willow Springs Rd., 540/464-1500, $100–120) is a modern place with a Colonial flair. Rates include a continental breakfast. Head north of town on Lee Highway (Rte. 11), cross under I-64, take a quick left on Maury River Road (Rte. 39), and Willow Springs Road will be on your right.

$150-200

The **Magnolia House Inn** (501 S. Main St., 540/463-2567, www.magnoliahouseinn.com) dates to 1868 and boasts high ceilings, spacious rooms, and a cottage garden. Guests are greeted with a cool drink and a warm cookie and can choose from three rooms and two suites ($140–190).

Historic Country Inns of Lexington (11 N. Main St., 877/283-9680, www.lexingtonhistoricinns.com) offers 32 rooms and 12 suites in two beautifully restored historic townhouses downtown—the 1809 **McCampbell Inn** and the 1789 **Alexander-Withrow House**—as well as in the 1850 **Maple Hall Country Inn** seven miles north of town, which comes complete with guest house, pond house, pool, and tennis court. Rooms and suites range in price $110–180, including expanded continental breakfast.

An 1827 manor home has been converted into the **Hampton Inn Lexington** (401 E. Nelson St., 540/463-2223, $144–265), graced by a Palladian porch and many antiques.

Camping

The **Virginia Horse Center** (540/464-2966, www.horsecenter.org) has two campgrounds with water and electric hookups; call for details.

FOOD

Snacks and Cafés

The **Lexington Coffee Shop** (9 W. Washington St., 540/464-6586, breakfast and lunch daily) serves stiff brews and baked goods in a relaxed wood floor–and-burlap atmosphere. The beans are fair trade and freshly roasted each week, and accompanied by free Wi-Fi and occasional live music.

A Joyful Spirit Café (26 S. Main St., 540/463-4191, breakfast Mon.–Sat., lunch daily) is a vegetarian-friendly place serving breakfast, bagels, salads, and grilled sandwiches and wraps for $6–8.

Sweet Things (106 W. Washington St., 540/463-6055, lunch and dinner daily) offers homemade ice cream and frozen yogurt in just about every conceivable permutation, with hand-rolled waffle cones to boot.

Casual

A big green neon sign lights the way to the **Southern Inn** (37 S. Main St., 540/463-3612, lunch and dinner daily), a long high-ceilinged place open since 1932. The Southern-style food is well prepared from scratch, whether it's the roasted portobello mushroom sandwich for lunch ($8–14) or the arugula salad and the sautéed calf's liver and onions for dinner ($12–25).

© KATIE GITHENS

Southern cooking is on the menu at the Southern Inn, as are fresh salads.

There is a wide selection of wines as well. Try to sit at the bar for a casual, cozy evening buzzing with locals and visitors alike.

The Southern influence continues in a contemporary vein at the **Bistro on Main** (8 N. Main St., 540/464-4888, lunch and dinner Tues.–Sat., brunch Sun.), serving jambalaya, shrimp and grits, and the tasty Bistro burger. Lunch runs $4–9 and dinner $12–24, with fresh seafood specials and vegetarian dishes too.

Upscale

Half a mile from downtown, **Café Michel** (640 N. Lee Hwy., 540/464-4119) offers fine French-inspired fare such as lobster in puff pastry and steak au poivre ($13–23) for dinner Monday–Saturday. In the summer you can sit on the outdoor patio, and the bar room is available for a drink at any time.

Back in town, the jaunty red café on the corner of Washington and Main Streets is the **Red Hen** (11 E. Washington St., 540/464-4401, dinner Tues.–Sat.), a farm-to-table Lexington favorite. In fine weather, grab a seat on the patio. You can catch a glimpse of herbs cultivated for dinner. Plates like seared trout with lentils and bacon run $16–32. Reservations strongly recommended.

Enjoy the tastes of northern Italy at **Tuscany** (24 N. Main St., 540/463-9888), with homemade sauces and desserts complemented by Continental wines. Tuscany is open for lunch and dinner daily (entrées $14–25) and features a piano lounge every evening. The dining room at the **Maple Hall Country Inn** (11 N. Main St., 540/463-2044 or 877/283-9680, www.lexingtonhistoricinns.com) is another excellent option for a fine dinner, with a glass-walled patio and home-baked bread.

INFORMATION

Lexington's well-organized **visitors center** (106 E. Washington St., 540/463-3777 or 877/453-9822, www.lexingtonvirginia.com, 9 A.M.–5 P.M. daily Sept.–May, 8:30 A.M.–6 P.M. daily June–Aug.) features a miniature museum, a short video presentation, and helpful employees.

South of Lexington

NATURAL BRIDGE

Rockbridge County derives its name from this 215-foot-tall limestone span—all that remains of a huge cavern carved out over thousands of years by tiny Cedar Creek. Thomas Jefferson, who once owned Natural Bridge, called it "so beautiful in archeology, so elevated, so light, and springing as it were up to Heaven, [that] the rapture of the spectator is really indescribable."

Natural Bridge is spectacular, to be sure—it's one of Virginia's most impressive natural sights. Almost as fascinating, though, is what has evolved around it. Interstate billboards are stacked like dominoes for hundreds of miles in every direction, and even ticket sellers can't keep a straight face describing the nightly *Drama of Creation* colored-light show, complete with music and solemn narration on the origins of the universe. If you run out of money, there's an ATM; if you find religion, there's a Baptist church. In the end, the whole package, which has little to do with the bridge, gives a new shade of meaning to the slogan "the Wonder of It All."

COURTESY NATURAL BRIDGE OF VIRGINIA

Natural Bridge

History

According to native legend, the "Bridge of God" materialized to help a band of Monocan Indians fleeing from raiding Shawnee and Powhatans. In 1749, British Lord Fairfax hired Col. Peter Jefferson—who, six years earlier, had fathered a son destined to become president—to survey the land around today's Route 11. One young assistant carved his initials on the stone wall; the faint "GW" is still visible, making George Washington the only president to have officially defaced a Virginia landmark. In 1773, Thomas Jefferson gained title to the bridge and 157 surrounding acres from King George III for 20 shillings. Near the base he built a log cabin and installed a "sentiment" book in which prominent visitors could record their impressions. During the Revolutionary War, soldiers made bullets by pouring molten lead from the bridge into the creek below and mined saltpeter from nearby caves for gunpowder.

The Bridge

All visits to the bridge (800/533-1410, www.naturalbridgeva.com, 8 A.M.–dusk daily) start at the main ticket building, which encloses a gargantuan gift shop, an indoor pool, a miniature golf course, an ATM, and a post office. Brochures in French, German, Spanish, Russian, Chinese, and Japanese describe what you're going to see, as soon as you've decided which ticket package to buy. Options include the bridge and the wax and toy museums only ($18 adults, $10 children 5–12), or the bridge, museums, and caverns ($26/$14). (The bridge and toy museum are open year-round, but the other attractions are closed in the off-season.) You can drive over the bridge for free—Route 11 heading east toward the Blue Ridge Parkway crosses right over it—but you can't see anything from above.

Walk downhill or take a shuttle bus to the beginning of the trail, where the **Summer House Cafe** offers light fare in an open patio alongside the creek. Children's voices echo up the deep, wooded gorge, where you'll get your first glimpse of the sheer size of the thing. At 50–150 feet wide and 90 feet long, it's massive, but surprisingly graceful for 36,000 tons of stone. The trail continues along the creek, a pleasant walk when it's not too crowded. Past an open space where Easter sunrise services have been held since 1947 are an old saltpeter mine, picnic areas, and the Lace Waterfalls.

Other Sights

George Washington, Daniel Boone, and Robert E. Lee share quarters with some 175 others in the **Natural Bridge Wax Museum** (10 A.M.–5 P.M. daily). Narrated historic scenes include the Garden of Eden and a theatrical presentation of Leonardo da Vinci's *Last Supper.* An explanation of the making of wax figures is part of the tour.

It's said that the ghost of a woman haunts the **Natural Bridge Caverns** (10 A.M.–5 P.M. daily Mar.–Nov.), the deepest cave on the East Coast. Guided tours to spots including the Wishing Well Room, Colossal Dome Room, and Mirror Lake leave every half hour.

The **Toy Museum** (10 A.M.–5 P.M. daily) is billed as the largest collection of childhood memorabilia on display in the world. More than 45,000 toys, games, and dolls range from Revolutionary War–era dolls to Star Wars figures.

Natural Bridge Zoo (540/291-2420, www.naturalbridgezoo.com, 10 A.M.–5 P.M. daily Mar.–Nov., longer hours in early summer and on weekends, $12 adults, $8 children), on Route 11 south, harbors the usual—giraffes, camels, bears, and monkeys—along with rare and endangered species such as a white tiger born in 1997. It also boasts the largest petting zoo in the state. If you haven't had your critter fix by now, stop by the **Virginia Safari Park** (540/291-3205, www.virginiasafaripark.com, 9 A.M.–5 P.M. daily Mar.–May and Sept.–Nov., until 6 P.M. Apr.–Oct., $14 adults, $10 children 3–12), a 180-acre drive-through zoo. A three-mile road takes you past bison, zebra, antelope, and ostriches roaming free (more or less), and there's also a petting zoo, an aviary, and a primate house. Kids love the giraffe feeding station. Wagon rides ($4 pp) run at 1 and 3 P.M. on weekends.

A tour of **Professor Cline's Haunted Monster Museum and Dark Maze** (4942 S. Lee Hwy., 540/464-2253, 11 A.M.–7 P.M. daily June–Aug., noon–5 P.M. weekends in spring and fall, closed in winter, $8 adults, $5 children) begins with your greeter, in top hat and tails, leading you into the former Stonewall Inn and locking the only door behind you. You have no choice but to proceed onward, past moving bookcases, the professor's secret lab, lunging monsters, and rattling séance tables. (The scare factor can be toned down for small children.)

Accommodations and Food

Next to the ticket building, the **Natural Bridge Hotel** (800/533-1410) has rooms in the hotel year-round for $70–140 and four- to six-room cottages across the road starting at $82 (mid-Mar.–Oct.). There's also an Olympic-sized pool and a restaurant serving all meals daily, with outdoor dining on the veranda and popular weekend buffets. Various packages include lodging, meals, and admission to the attractions.

Yogi Bear's Jellystone Park Camp-Resort at Natural Bridge (540/291-2727 or 800/258-9532, www.campnbr.com) has full-hookup sites for $44–54, tent spots for $40, and cabins for $90–160 per night. It rents boats, canoes, and tubes to enjoy the nearby James River and charges a small fee for fishing in its stocked pond. To get there, take Route 130 east from I-81 exit 175 for 4.5 miles, take a right onto Route 759, then your first left onto Route 782. Sites at the **Natural Bridge KOA** (540/291-2770, www.naturalbridgekoa.com) are $25–50. It's just off I-81 exit 180 on Route 11.

HUMPBACK COVERED BRIDGE

Virginia's oldest covered bridge spans Dunlap Creek, three miles west of Covington on U.S. 60. Built in 1835, Humpback Covered Bridge was restored for foot traffic in 1953, and the surrounding land was set aside as a park and picnic area. Ropes dangle underneath for (illicit) swings into the water, and the inside of the bridge, sadly, is defaced by graffiti. It's one of only eight covered bridges in Virginia, three of which are on private property.

Near Natural Bridge

Since no natural wonder is complete without a replica megalithic observatory, don't miss **Foamhenge,** a full-sized model sculpted in foam blocks, one mile north of the bridge (free). Six miles east of Natural Bridge on Route 130 is the tiny town of **Glasgow,** "the Town That Time Forgot," where a dozen full-size dinosaur replicas have invaded buildings and backyards.

A short drive up into the Jefferson National Forest brings you to the **Cave Mountain Lake Recreation Area** (540/291-2188, www.fs.fed.us/r8/gwj/gp), centered on a cold, clear seven-acre lake formed in the 1930s by a dam built by the Civilian Conservation Corps. It's popular for swimming and fishing, with showers and a sandy beach area, and there's a log picnic shelter available. Campsites are $15–30 each (open May–Oct.). Hikers can choose from the half-mile Panther Knob Natural Trail or the four-mile Wildcat Mountain Trail loop. Head further afield into the nearby James River Face Wilderness, the state's first designated wilderness. It's bisected by the Appalachian Trail and miles of other hiking paths, including the route up the Devil's Marbleyard.

To get to Cave Mountain Lake, take Route 130 east from I-81 exit 175 or 180 for 3.2 miles, turn south onto Route 795 for another 3.2 miles, and turn right onto Route 781 for 1.6 miles to the recreation area's paved entrance road.

BLUE RIDGE PARKWAY

Like a vine connecting two ripe grapes, this scenic highway unites the Shenandoah and Great Smoky Mountains National Parks in one long, lovely stretch of Appalachia. It was begun during

Foamhenge, a full-sized replica of Stonehenge, near Natural Bridge

the Great Depression as a federal public-works project. Designers took liberties with the philosophy of the shortest distance between two points, choosing instead to follow the wandering ridgeline wherever it chose to go. Of the parkway's 469 miles, 217 are in Virginia, and the first 114, between Waynesboro and Roanoke along the crest of the Blue Ridge Mountains, are widely thought to be the most impressive. Miles of tranquil farm scenes are punctuated by crumbling graveyards and "gaps," which open to grand panoramas in either direction. The Appalachian Trail follows the parkway from the northern end at Rockfish Gap south to Roanoke, where it veers off to the west. In 2010, the Blue Ridge Parkway celebrated its 75th anniversary.

Access

The parkway is open year-round, although few facilities outside Peaks of Otter are open beyond May–October, and parts of the road may be closed due to inclement weather. In foggy conditions, blinking lights lining the road are sometimes your only guiderail, so be careful. Entry is free. Between I-64 at Waynesboro and U.S. 460 at Roanoke, drivers can reach the road via U.S. 60 near Buena Vista, Routes 30 and 501 east of Natural Bridge, and Route 43 between Bedford and Buchanan.

Flora and Fauna

Vegetation along the parkway is more southern (drier) than in Shenandoah National Park. Forests of white pine, hemlock, and hawthorn burst into color during an extended fall season, thanks to the wide range of altitudes along the entire road (649–6,047 ft.). In the autumn spectrum, reds are probably maples or dogwoods, yellows hickory, and orange sassafras. Spruce, fir, and pine provide a green backdrop. Spectacular flame azalea bloom throughout the park in May and June, followed by purple Catawba rhododendron near Peaks of Otter in June. Many of the larger animals come out at dusk and are gone by dawn, leaving daytime to the groundhogs, squirrels, and chipmunks. White-tailed deer, bobcats, raccoons, and black bears all make occasional appearances.

Camping

Of the four campgrounds along the Virginia section of the Blue Ridge Parkway, two are north of Roanoke: **Otter Creek** (434/299-5941, Apr.–Oct., $16), on the James River at the parkway's lowest elevation, and **Peaks of Otter** (540/586-4357, mid-May–Oct., $16), at milepost 86 near the Peaks of Otter Lodge. Campsites in Virginia are first-come, first-served, and limited to a 21-day maximum stay. Some are accessible to visitors with disabilities. Trailers up to 30 feet are permitted, and all campgrounds have dump stations (but no water or electrical hookups). Pets must be kept on leashes. Off the parkway, backcountry camping is permitted in the George Washington National Forest.

Rockfish Gap to Sherando Lake

All locations along the parkway are measured in mileposts (mp), from milepost 0 at the southern end of Shenandoah National Park at Rockfish Gap to milepost 218 at the North Carolina border. The speed limit along the entire parkway is 45 mph, but traffic can crawl during high season.

At the **Humpback Rocks Visitor Center** (mp 5.8), a self-guided trail leads through a reconstructed 19th-century farmstead, with exhibits on life in the rural Blue Ridge. Across the road, a steep 0.75-mile trail climbs to the jagged top of Humpback Rocks (3,080 ft.) for a 360-degree view of the mountains. Watching the sun rise from the top of Humpback with a steaming Thermos of coffee is one of the best vistas in the whole state. Past **Devil's Knob** (3,851 ft.) is a turn-off to Route 664 east toward Wintergreen Ski Resort.

Head west on Route 664 to reach the **Sherando Lake Recreation Area,** centered on a pair of lakes created in the early 1900s by the Civilian Conservation Corps for recreation and flood control. The 25-acre lower lake is open to swimming and boating, with a sandy swimming beach, while the seven-acre lake above it is known for trout, bass, and bluegill fishing. There are 65 campsites arranged around three loops near the water.

Mountain biking enthusiasts know Sherando as the home of one of the burliest trails in this part of the state. Head up the steep, rocky Blue Loop trail past the lake toward the park entrance—you'll end up carrying your bike, trust me—to the yellow-blazed Torrey Ridge Trail 1,000 feet above. Go down the ridgeline, carrying your bike yet again through a nasty rock garden, then head down the blue-blazed Slacks Trail to the orange-blazed White Rock Trail back to the lake. The whole thing is an 11-mile loop, and all the carrying makes the ride down that much sweeter.

Sherando Lake to Otter Creek

Below the **Twenty Minute Cliff Overlook,** the Tye River spills east to eventually join the James. At **Tye River Gap** (2,969 ft.), take narrow, winding Route 56 east to the trailhead for **Crabtree Falls Trail,** leading to the highest waterfall east of the Mississippi. Five large waterfalls and many smaller ones tumble over 1,200 feet all told. It's best in the spring, when the water levels are high. An easy trail with steps and railings leads along the water, which can be filled with splashing families in the summer. There's a good rock for picnicking at the top. You can also access the three-mile trail from above, at a parking lot on Route 826 (4WD only) at Crabtree Meadows, where it's possible to make a primitive camp.

This is also a good spot to access two of the state's newest and choicest wilderness areas. The 5,742-acre **Priest Wilderness** encloses eight peaks higher than 4,000 feet, including the Priest (4,063 ft.), the Friar, and the Cardinal. The 4,748-acre **Three Ridges Wilderness** is probably one of the most rugged and wild sections of Virginia's Blue Ridge. Both were set aside in 2000 and are connected to the parkway by the Appalachian Trail.

Yankee Horse (mp 34.4) is named for an unfortunate Union mount that had to be shot after it fell from exhaustion. Here an overlook trail leads along a remnant of an old logging railway from the 1920s to 30-foot Wigwam Falls in a shady grove.

Otter Creek to Roanoke

The **Otter Creek Campground** (mp 60.8) has 69 sites ($16), a coffee shop, and a service station. The creek rolls down the hillside toward the James River, lined by blooming mountain laurel in May and June.

The parkway hits its lowest point (649 ft.) where it crosses the James River. Here you'll find a visitors center at the **James River Overlook** (mp 63.6). A self-guiding trail leads over a footbridge and along the river bluff to restored locks along the Kanawha canal.

After climbing to its highest point in Virginia (3,950 ft.), the parkway winds into the **Peaks of Otter** (mp 86), with a visitors center, 151 campsites, and the **Peaks of Otter Lodge** (540/586-1081 or 800/542-5927, www.peaksofotter.com), the only place on the parkway guaranteed to be open year-round. Sixty rooms overlooking Abbott Lake each have two double beds but no TVs or phones, with prices around $115–130 (as low as $85 in off-season). The view from the dining room is justly famous, and the hotel has two restaurants, a lounge, and a gift shop. Trails near the campground lead to the restored 1930s Johnson Farm. Thought to be the highest point in the state by Thomas Jefferson, Sharp Top (3,875 ft.) can be reached by foot and sweat via a steep 1.5-mile trail, or on a tour bus from the hotel that drops you off near the peak.

From here it's another 34 miles to the campground at Roanoke Mountain.

Information

The Blue Ridge Parkway is administered by the National Park Service in Asheville, North Carolina (828/298-0398 or 828/271-4779, www.nps.gov/blri). Each visitors center sells excellent books detailing hikes, history, and wildlife along the road. **Friends of the Blue Ridge Parkway** (800/228-7275, www.blueridgefriends.org) is a nonprofit volunteer organization dedicated to preserving and protecting the parkway. For more information, check out the Blue Ridge Parkway Association's online travel guide (www.blueridgeparkway.org).

SOUTHWEST VIRGINIA

Virginia's rugged western tail—by far the least-tamed, and often most-forgotten, part of the state—dangles in the hilly country bordered by North Carolina, Tennessee, Kentucky, and West Virginia. The area has few Civil War battlefields or founding fathers to anchor it in memory, but that doesn't seem to bother its residents or its visitors. It can take a full day to drive here from Washington, D.C., so the area sees much less traffic and operates at an even slower pace than the rest of the state.

History here has a rougher edge to it, too, beginning with the frontier families who pushed their way into the rippling hills, cleared virgin land, set up shop, and began a legacy that still lives on. Pockets of Brethren and Friends (Quakers) keep alive the faith handed down from their 18th-century German forebears. Later the hillsides were gouged open to make way for coal mining and railroads, creating new towns and greatly expanding others while covering everything with a layer of fine grit.

Today, countless narrow roads wind past forested hillsides, some still laid bare by strip mines, and cities struggle to find a way to fill the economic vacuum left by the departure of extractive industries. Still, this part of the state is home to some great nuggets of history, art, music, and nature, if you know where to look. Old-time mountain music was born in these ancient Appalachians, and in its legacy the genres of bluegrass and country. From the peak of Mt. Rogers to impromptu fiddling competitions in isolated coves and back rooms, southwest Virginia can leave you feeling like you discovered something special.

HIGHLIGHTS

Taubman Museum of Art: The architecture on the outside and the art on the inside are worth the trip to Roanoke's premier art museum (page 361).

O. Winston Link Museum: Roanoke, the "Star City" of Southwest Virginia, is a former railroad town whose steam-powered legacy is preserved in the photographs on display at this fascinating museum (page 362).

Mount Rogers National Recreation Area: This natural area encloses 117,000 acres of wildness and the highest peak in the state (page 378).

Grayson Highlands State Park: Pick wild blueberries in season and hike to some of the most beautiful vistas in Virginia – with wild ponies for company (page 380).

Barter Theatre: In Abingdon, make sure to catch a show at the historic theater where patrons could once trade food or supplies for a taste of the arts (page 383).

Pocahontas Exhibition Coal Mine & Museum: Here you can go underground with a former miner, hard hats and all (page 388).

Carter Family Fold: American country music can trace its lineage all the way back to the famous Carter Family's music hall. Listen to foot-tappin' bluegrass and mountain music where Johnny Cash played his last concert (page 392).

Cumberland Gap National Historical Park: Colonial gateway to the American West, the Cumberland Gap is preserved in much the same condition it was in when Daniel Boone blazed the trail (page 395).

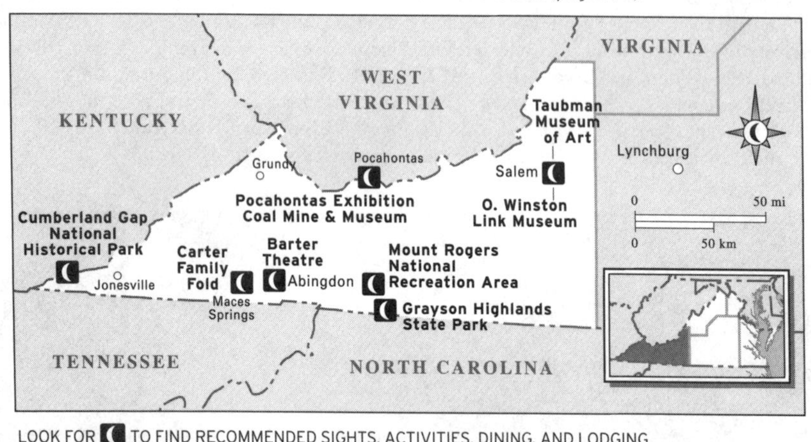

LOOK FOR ☾ TO FIND RECOMMENDED SIGHTS, ACTIVITIES, DINING, AND LODGING.

PLANNING YOUR TIME

Allow yourself plenty of time to drive between destinations down here. Don't be deceived by the short hops across the map; these winding roads are longer than they look.

Most visits to southwest Virginia start and end at the "Star City" of Roanoke, a railroad town reborn as a lively, forward-thinking metropolis. You can't miss the silver silhouette of the **Taubman Museum of Art,** the city's latest arty addition. Be sure to swing by the historic Market Square to grab some fresh produce in season. From there, 3–5 days are enough to see the highlights of this part of the state. Abingdon makes a good base for visiting the farthest reaches; if you can, stay at the

© KATIE GITHENS

The modern architecture of Roanoke's Taubman Museum of Art contrasts with the historic brick buildings of the downtown center.

Martha Washington Inn and visit the **Barter Theatre** while you're here.

If Abingdon is the region's cultural hub, Damascus is the center of all things outdoors. Thousands of acres of beech, maple, hickory, and ash stand within the Jefferson National Forest, including the **Mount Rogers National Recreation Area,** which contains the highest peak in the state and some of the best single-track around.

The hills here are alive with the sounds of fiddles, banjos, and stomping feet at famous hoedowns such as the Galax Old Fiddler's Convention, the Carter Family Memorial Music Center (better known as the **Carter Family Fold**), and the Floyd Flatfoot Jamboree. Take a peek beneath the surface at the **Pocahontas Exhibition Coal Mine,** and explore the famous gateway to the American West encompassed by the **Cumberland Gap National Historical Park.**

Access

I-81 runs most of the length of southwestern Virginia, paralleled by the slower, more scenic U.S. 11. I-77 slices across briefly from North Carolina to West Virginia. West and north of Abingdon, most rural roads are two-lane, meandering, and gorgeous. The only major airport is in Roanoke, and the nearest Amtrak service 45 miles north, in Clifton Forge.

Resources

Contact the **Blue Ridge Travel Association** (www.virginiablueridge.org) for more information on the region. If you plan to be among the thousands who flock here during autumn, call the Shenandoah Valley Travel Association's Fall Foliage Hotline (800/434-LEAF) to find out when and where colors are peaking. For details on Virginia's heritage music trail—from regular jams to fiddling festivals—contact **The Crooked Road** (276/492-2085, www.thecrookedroad.org).

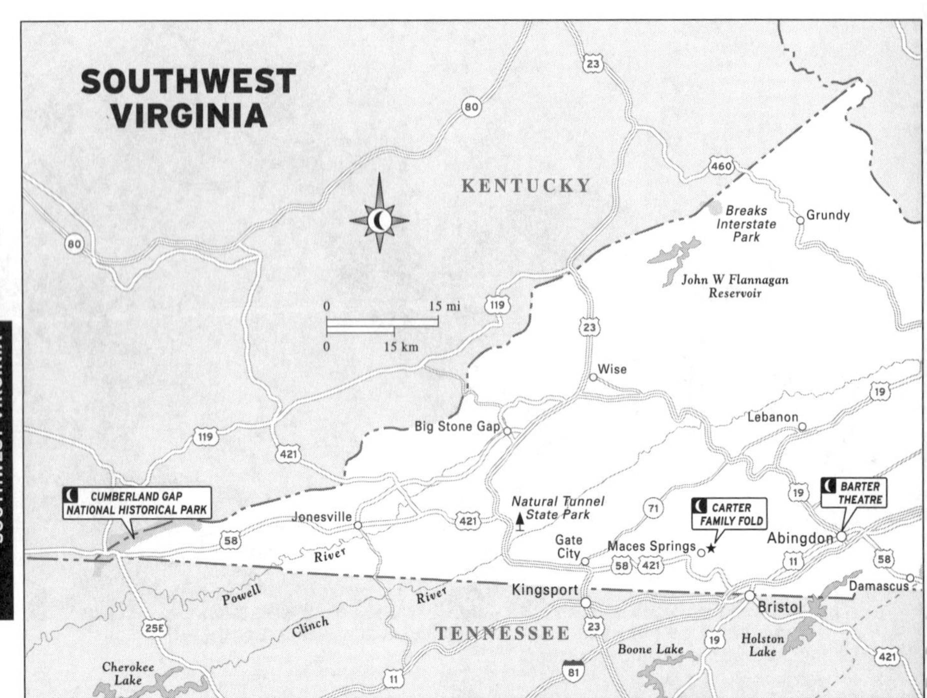

Roanoke and Vicinity

Settled in a valley and split by the Roanoke River, Roanoke, the largest city in southwest Virginia (pop. 300,000 in the metro area), offers metropolitan convenience with a surprising amount of flair. The "capital of the Blue Ridge" serves as the transportation and medical center for the entire region, and it was the first community in North America to offer citywide recycling. Various polls have put it in the top 10 or 20 cities nationwide for quality of life, lack of stress, and tourism potential. Much of this potential is linked to the city's vibrant downtown area, anchored by Market Square, the Center in the Square arts complex, and more recently, the striking Taubman Museum. Having the Blue Ridge Parkway only a short drive away doesn't hurt, either.

History

The city's unenviable original name, Big Lick, refers to the area's salt deposits, sought out by animals, which were in turn hunted by Native Americans. The first European settlers arrived near the end of the 1700s, stopping along the Great Road down the Shenandoah Valley. By the early 1800s, the town's central streets had been laid out and, with the completion of a road over the Blue Ridge from Lynchburg, Big Lick was on its way to becoming a crossroads for western Virginia.

Explosive growth arrived with the steam and clatter of the railroads shortly after the Civil War. In 1882, the Shenandoah Valley and Norfolk & Western railroads chose the town of 700 as a junction point, changing its name in

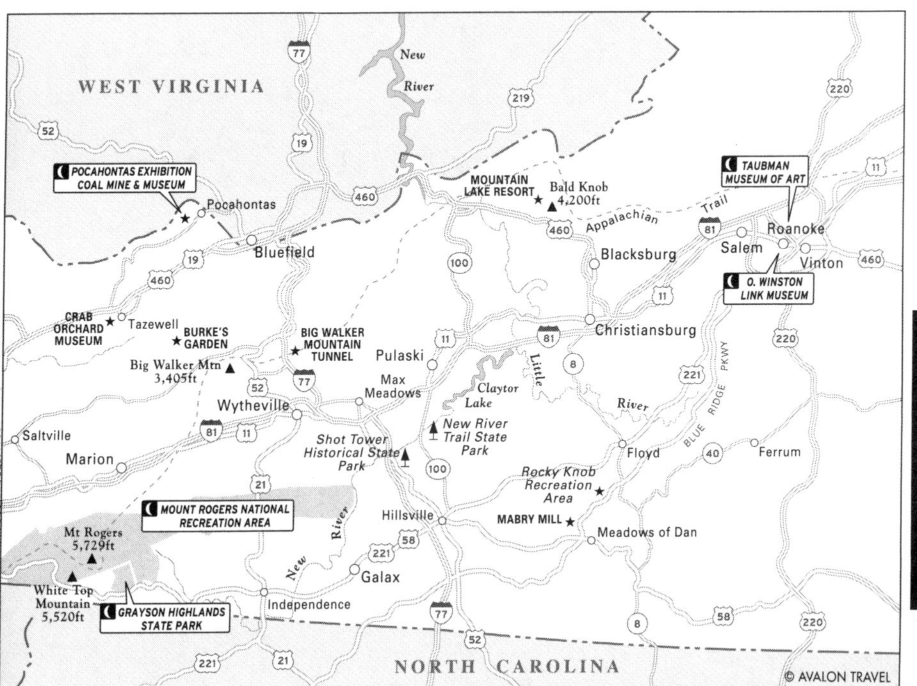

the process to the more presentable Roanoke, from the native word *rawrenock* for "shell money." By 1892, some 25,000 people called the valley home. The Virginia Railway arrived in 1906, bringing coal traffic and passengers, including Mark Twain, who rode on the first coach into the city. The largest rayon plant in the world opened here in the early 1900s.

During the award-winning downtown revitalization planning in 1979, wise city planners drew heavily on public opinion through questionnaires, interviews, and live television "design-a-thons." The result is a lively example of how an urban center can be brought back to life without losing touch with its roots.

Orientation

The easiest way to navigate is by landmarks and highway exits. Heading south on I-581 from I-81, exit 4 sits between the Roanoke Civic Center on the east and the tan spire of St. Andrew's Catholic Church, one of the highest points in the city. Next, look for the unmistakable Tudor bulk of the Hotel Roanoke and Conference Center, followed by the spaceship tower of the Wachovia Bank.

Exit 5, onto Williamson Road, carries you past the visitors center, the Taubman, and the H&C coffeepot neon sign and the Dr. Pepper bottle-cap clock on Salem Avenue. Head toward Market Square along Campbell or Salem Avenues. To reach Mill Mountain and the Blue Ridge Parkway, hop on Walnut Avenue from Jefferson Street south and follow the signs.

SIGHTS

Market Square

Begun in the 1880s with only a handful of vendors, this is one of Virginia's oldest markets in continuous use. After following the city's

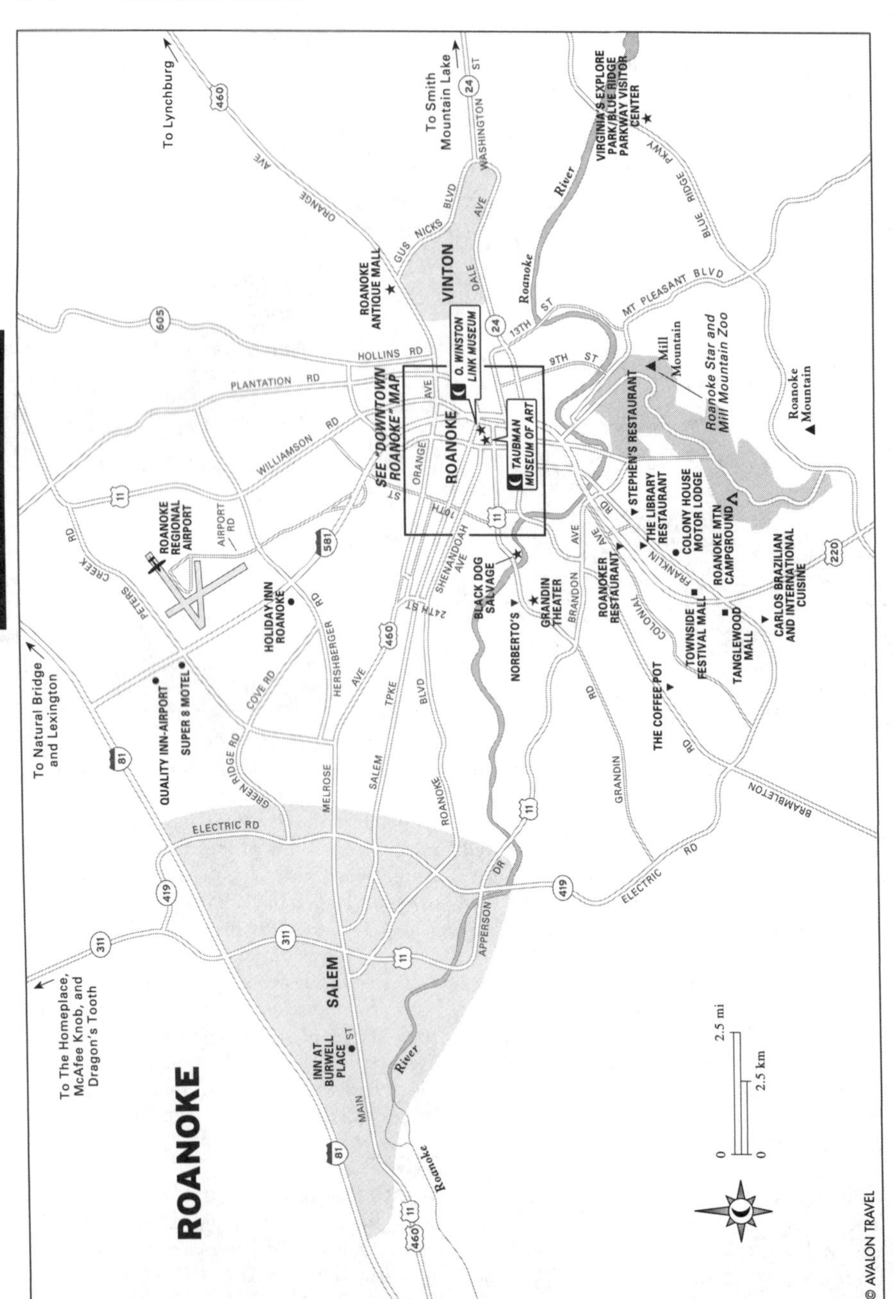
ROANOKE
To Lynchburg
To Smith Mountain Lake
To Natural Bridge and Lexington
To The Homeplace, McAfee Knob, and Dragon's Tooth
VIRGINIA'S EXPLORE PARK/BLUE RIDGE PARKWAY VISITOR CENTER
ROANOKE ANTIQUE MALL
VINTON
O. WINSTON LINK MUSEUM
TAUBMAN MUSEUM OF ART
SEE "DOWNTOWN ROANOKE" MAP
ROANOKE
ROANOKE REGIONAL AIRPORT
HOLIDAY INN ROANOKE
QUALITY INN-AIRPORT
SUPER 8 MOTEL
BLACK DOG SALVAGE
NORBERTO'S
GRANDIN THEATER
ROANOKER RESTAURANT
STEPHEN'S RESTAURANT
THE LIBRARY RESTAURANT
COLONY HOUSE MOTOR LODGE
ROANOKE MTN CAMPGROUND
TOWNSIDE FESTIVAL MALL
TANGLEWOOD MALL
CARLOS BRAZILIAN AND INTERNATIONAL CUISINE
THE COFFEE POT
Mill Mountain
Roanoke Star and Mill Mountain Zoo
Roanoke Mountain
Roanoke River
SALEM
INN AT BURWELL PLACE
MAIN ST
ORANGE AVE
GUS NICKS BLVD
WASHINGTON AVE
DALE AVE
HOLLINS RD
PLANTATION RD
WILLIAMSON RD
PETERS CREEK RD
AIRPORT RD
HERSHBERGER RD
COVE RD
GREEN RIDGE RD
ELECTRIC RD
MELROSE AVE
SALEM TPKE
ROANOKE BLVD
SHENANDOAH AVE
24TH ST
10TH ST
13TH ST
9TH ST
MT PLEASANT BLVD
BLUE RIDGE PKWY
BRANDON AVE
GRANDIN RD
FRANKLIN RD
COLONIAL AVE
BRAMBLETON AVE
APPERSON DR
460
24
605
11
581
81
419
311
220
0
2.5 mi
2.5 km
© AVALON TRAVEL

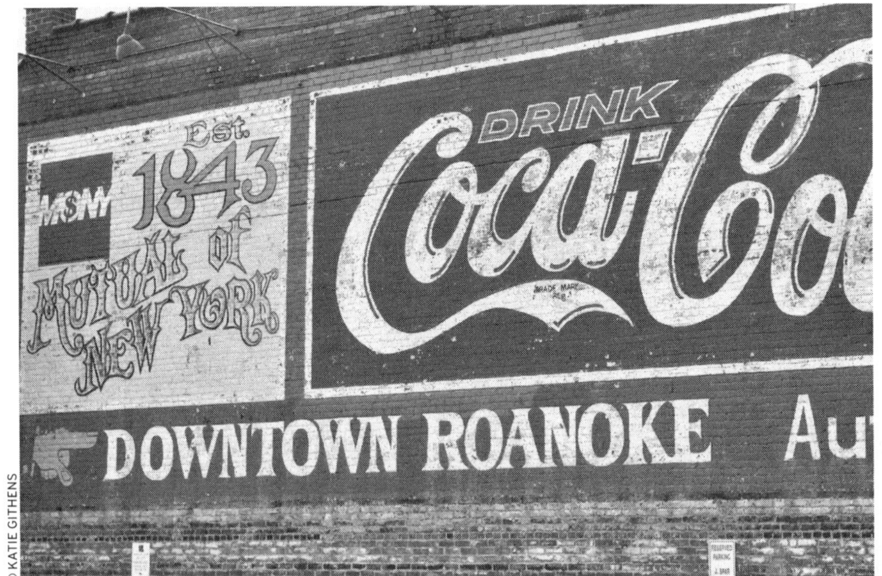

© KATIE GITHENS

an antique advertisement near the Market Square in downtown Roanoke

boom-and-bust cycles through most of the 20th century, the market has become one anchor of Roanoke's downtown renaissance. Today, permanent awnings shade sidewalk stands brimming with country-market staples: fresh seasonal produce, baskets of flowers, eggs, dairy products, and seeds (vendors usually open 8 A.M.–5 P.M. Mon.–Sat., 10 A.M.–4 P.M. Sun.). Old Victorian shops, now nouveau country stores, have shelves that groan under gourmet wines, cheeses, and preserves, while restaurants, gift shops, and art galleries take up any extra space for blocks around. Local legend has it that anyone who drinks from the small **dog mouth fountain** at Salem Avenue and Market Street will someday return to Roanoke.

The historic **City Market Building,** erected in 1922, is home to a neon-lit international food court featuring everything from sushi to Cuban sandwiches. In 2010, there was much debate and discussion about plans to close the City Market Building for renovations that would last the better part of a year. Contact the market clerk for an update (540/342-2028, ext. 15).

Taubman Museum of Art

In a $66 million gamble to put Roanoke on the nation's cultural map, the Art Museum of Western Virginia reopened in 2008 under a new name in a striking new glass-and-steel building on Salem Avenue. The Taubman Museum of Art (110 Salem Ave. SE, 540/342-5760, www.taubmanmuseum.org, 10 A.M.–5 P.M. Tues.–Sat., until 7 P.M. Thurs., noon–5 P.M. Sun., $10.50 adults, $5.50 children), renamed for a major donor, still features 19th- and 20th-century American art, decorative crafts, and works by regional artists, only now it resides in a modern 81,000-square-foot space designed by Los Angeles architect Randall Stout, a protégé of Frank Gehry. The modern space engenders gutsy, thought-provoking special exhibits—for example, a tent city of woodblock prints on themes of social justice and the recession juxtaposed with tiny etchings Rembrandt made of beggars in the 17th century. Even a peek at the light-filled lobby is worth a stop.

© KATIE GITHENS

the glass-and-steel Taubman Museum of Art

Under the undulating metallic roof, the permanent collection includes works from Winslow Homer, John Singer Sargent, and Norman Rockwell, as well as the Art Venture, a family-oriented interactive art center. Hungry patrons can grab lunch or afternoon tea at **Norah's Café** (540/204-4154, $7–12) in the museum complex.

Center in the Square

At the southwest corner of Market Square, this converted warehouse (540/342-5700, www.centerinthesquare.org) houses five floors of some of southwest Virginia's finest cultural attractions.

Ten thousand years of local goings-on, from Native Americans to the present day, are covered in the **History Museum of Western Virginia** (540/342-5770, www.history-museum.org, 10 A.M.–4 P.M. Tues.–Fri., 10 A.M.–5 P.M. Sat., 1–5 P.M. Sun., $3 adults, $2 children over 6). It's free 1–4 P.M. the second Friday of each month (except Dec.).

Hop the elevator to the **Science Museum of Western Virginia** (540/342-5710, www.smwv.org, 10 A.M.–5 P.M. Tues.–Sat., 1–5 P.M. Sun., $8 adults, $6 children 3–12), a place full of noises, voices, and flashing lights that proves that museums can be anything but boring. Hands-on exhibits geared toward kids—but fun for anyone—include holograms, fiber optics, and a giant xylophone. The Hopkins Planetarium helps the museum maintain its consistent status as one of the best in the region. Shows in the planetarium and the large-format MegaDome Theater are extra, with various options for combined admission. The 4th floor of the museum is free 3:30–6 P.M. the second Friday of each month, with reduced admission to the shows.

O. Winston Link Museum

The Norfolk & Western was the last steam railroad in the United States, and the last passenger train to Roanoke was in 1971, but here you'll all but hear the whistles blowing and see the steam clouds rising. The museum (101 Shenandoah Ave., 540/982-5465, www.linkmuseum.org, 10 A.M.–5 P.M. daily Mar.–Dec., 10 A.M.–5 P.M. Mon.–Sat., noon–5 P.M. Sun. Jan.–Feb., $5 adults, $4 children under 11) fills the old railway passenger station across the train tracks from downtown with Link's evocative black-and-white photographs of the waning days of steam railroads in the United States. Next to the photos, displays show how Link shot his carefully planned images: Most were shot at night so he could control the lighting, and the railroad obliged by backing up trains for reshoots.

Other Museums

From the O. Winston Link Museum, a pedestrian bridge leads across the tracks to the Market Square and the Center in the Square areas. On the opposite side, a path leads to the **Virginia Museum of Transportation** (303 Norfolk Ave. SW, 540/342-5670, www.vmt.org, 10 A.M.–5 P.M. Mon.–Sat., 1–5 P.M. Sun., $8 adults, $6 children 3–11) serves as a monument to the many methods of simply getting from one place to another. Inside the restored freight station three blocks west of Market Square are an O-scale model railroad, a gift shop, and a gorgeous collection of antique autos, including a 1934 Ford V-8 Model A Sedan and a 1950 Studebaker Landcruiser, more spaceship than car. Dozens of train engines and cars—a few of which are open to visitors—fill the lot out back. Steam engines, diesel locomotives, post office cars, and a classic caboose cover virtually the entire history of rail travel. A discounted joint ticket with the O. Winston Link museum is available.

The Harrison School, opened in 1916 as the city's first public high school for African American students, is home to the **Harrison**

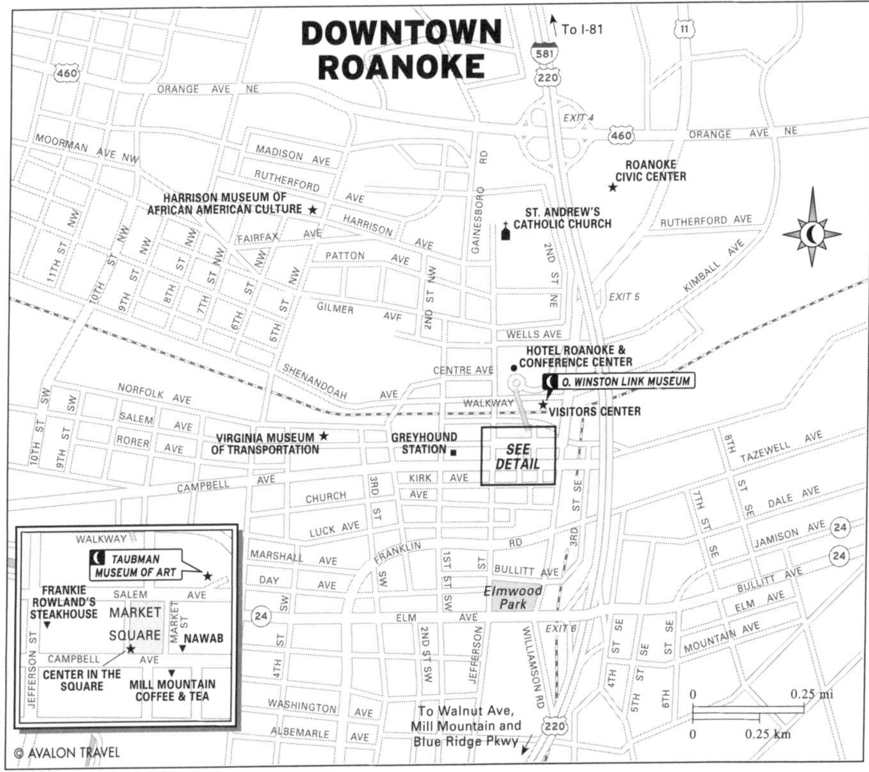

Museum of African American Culture (523 Harrison Ave. NW, 540/345-4818, www.harrisonmuseum.com, 1–5 P.M. Mon.–Fri., free). Changing exhibits relating to African American culture focus on the Roanoke area, and African crafts fill the gift shop.

Mill Mountain

Sandwiched between the city and the Blue Ridge Parkway sits this lone peak, disconnected from the rest of the Appalachian chain. A trolley to the summit was built in 1910 but was soon abandoned because people preferred to drive up winding Walnut Avenue instead. At the peak stands the **Roanoke Star,** the city's most famous landmark. The World's Largest Manmade Illuminated Star is 100 feet tall, with 2,000 feet of neon tubing visible for 60 miles. Airplane pilots navigate by it occasionally, and even Elvis Presley once snuck up here after a concert to take a closer look. The view of the city and valley from the base and the picnic area nearby are excellent on a clear day.

A short walk away, the **Mill Mountain Zoo** (540/343-3241, www.mmzoo.org, 10 A.M.–4:30 P.M. daily, $7.50 adults, $5 children under 12) is a five-acre zoo with 50 species of mammals, birds, and reptiles, including many exotic, endangered examples such as Japanese macaques, Nepalese red pandas, and snow leopards. Children will love the prairie dog village and the miniature ZooChoo train that circles the park ($2 pp), and their parents with enjoy the wildflower garden and the views.

ENTERTAINMENT

Two of Roanoke's major cultural institutions host performances in the Jefferson Center at 541 Luck Avenue SW: the **Roanoke Symphony Orchestra and Chorus** (540/343-9127, www.rso.com) and **Opera Roanoke** (540/982-2742, www.operaroanoke.org). Contact each for its latest performance listings. On a more visceral level, the **Roanoke Civic Center** (710 Williamson Rd., 540/853-2241, box office 540/853-5483, www.roanokeciviccenter.com) hosts rock concerts.

For the drama-inclined, **Showtimers** (2067 McVitty Rd. SW, 540/774-2660 or 877/336-9294, www.showtimers.org) is the oldest continuously performing community theater in Virginia. The players put on drama, comedy, music, and dance performances; call for a schedule and tickets.

Two of the city's shopping malls—Valley View and Tanglewood—have multiplex theaters nearby. For a more personal experience, though, head out to the **Grandin Theatre** (1310 Grandin Rd., 540/345-6177, www.grandintheatre.com), ornate in a style that's all but disappeared. Built in 1931, it closed in 1976, 1985, and 2001. A benefit by Bill Murray in 1986 helped keep it alive, and it was restored and reopened in 2002 by a nonprofit foundation. The theater runs current and older films and occasionally offers ticket specials.

A Cigar & Billiards sign outside the **Corned Beef & Co. Bar and Grill** (107 S. Jefferson St., 540/342-3354) advertises the restaurant's major draw after hours, when live and DJ music drifts through the haze in the scotch and cigar lounge toward the pool tables. Established in 1936, **The Coffee Pot** (2902 Brambleton Ave. SW, 540/774-8256) is a Virginia historic landmark and the oldest roadhouse in the state, hosting acoustic, R&B, and rock on occasion. Look for the big coffee pot on top of the building.

RECREATION

For trail maps, outfitter listings (such as mountain bike rentals), and all things outdoors in the Roanoke Valley by land or by lake, check out RoanokeOutside.com, hosted by the Roanoke Regional Partnership.

Virginia's Explore Park

Only 10 minutes from downtown Roanoke, Explore Park fits snugly between the Roanoke River Gorge and milepost 115 of the Blue Ridge Parkway. Mountain bikers love its 8.5 miles of IMBA-certified trails that range from beginner to expert.

The National Park Service maintains a **Blue Ridge Parkway Visitor Center** (9 A.M.–5 P.M. daily May–Oct., 9 A.M.–5 P.M. weekends in Apr.) here as well.

SOUTHWEST VIRGINIA

SOUTHWESTERN VIRGINIA WINERIES

Abingdon Vineyard & Winery
20530 Alvarado Rd., Abingdon
276/623-1255
www.abingdonwinery.com

AmRhein Wine Cellar
9243 Patterson Dr., Bent Mountain
540/929-4632
www.roanokewine.com

Château Morrisette
Blue Ridge Parkway Milepost 171.5, Floyd
540/593-2865
www.thedogs.com

Davis Valley Winery & Vineyard
1167 Davis Valley Rd., Rural Retreat
276/686-8855
www.dvwinery.com

Fincastle Vineyard & Winery
203 Maple Ridge Ln., Fincastle
540/591-9000
www.fincastlewine.com

Hickory Hill Vineyard
1722 Hickory Cove Ln., Moneta
540/296-1393
www.hickoryhillvineyards.com

MountainRose Vineyards
10439 N. Reservoir Rd., Wise
276/328-2013
www.mountainrosevineyard.com

Tomahawk Mill Winery
9221 Anderson Mill Rd./Rte. 649, Chatham
434/432-1063
www.tomahawkmill.com

Valhalla Vineyard
6500 Mt. Chestnut Rd., Roanoke
540/725-9463
www.valhallawines.com

Villa Appalaccia
752 Rock Castle Gorge, Floyd
540/358-0357
www.villaappalaccia.com

West Wind Farm Vineyard & Winery
180 West Wind Dr., Max Meadows
276/699-2020
www.westwindwine.com

White Rock Vineyards & Winery
2117 Bruno Dr., Goodview
540/890-3359
www.whiterockwines.com

McAfee Knob Hike

This lofty rock outcropping is one of the most photographed spots along the more than 2,000-mile length of the Appalachian Trail (AT), and it's easy to see why. McAfee Knob rewards you with nearly 270-degree views of the Catawba Valley, North Mountain, Tinker Ridge, and, weather permitting, the Roanoke Valley—all from the dizzying vantage point of the Knob itself, which bears resemblance to a stone gangplank. Besides scenic views, the seven-mile-round-trip hike passes by some good bouldering. To reach the AT parking area from Roanoke, take I-81 south to exit 141, then head north up Route 311 about six miles.

Dragon's Tooth Hike

A jagged prow of rock juts from the peaks of the Jefferson National Forest, offering great views from a moderately strenuous climb, this time just off the Appalachian Trail. The hike is 4.6 miles round-trip and climbs 1,250 feet, but it's worth it. Start by passing through a pleasant creek valley, then angle up a ridgeline to join the AT. Turn right and put your head down—it's a steep slog up switchbacks from here. Metal steps have been placed in some of the more dangerous spots, but it's still not something you want to do in bad weather. At the top of Cove Mountain, take a left to reach the Tooth.

Take Route 311 north eight miles from I-81

exit 141, and look for the parking area on the left just past the Catawba Grocery. For more information on this and other hikes in the area, contact the Eastern Divide Ranger District of the Jefferson National Forest (540/552-4641).

SHOPPING

In addition to the farmers market in Market Square, a wide range of shops provides enough spending opportunities for days. Gourmet country foods are the specialty of **Sumdat Farm Market** (209A Market St. SE, 540/982-2164).

The largest selection of antiques awaits at the **Roanoke Antique Mall** (2302 Orange Ave. NE/Rte. 460, 540/344-0264), with more than 120 dealers open daily. The real gem, though, is **Black Dog Salvage,** an architectural antiques and salvage warehouse with design-minded staff and a darling black Labrador to help (902 13th St. SW, 540/343-6200, www.blackdogsalvage.com).

EVENTS

Roanoke isn't called the Festival City of Virginia for nothing. Call the city's visitors center for details of the following events. Come in late April for the **Blue Ridge Kite Festival,** which attracts about 10,000 spectators. On Memorial Day weekend, the **Festival in the Park** ushers in summer with concerts, arts and crafts, and many other goings-on in Elmwood Park. Also in May, the **Virginia State Championship Chili Cook-Off** has participants begging for water the first Saturday of the month. This often coincides with the **Strawberry Festival.**

In late September, Elmwood Park, at the corner of Jefferson Street and Elm Avenue, hosts the **Henry Street African American Heritage Festival,** and again in early October it hosts the **Big Lick Blues Festival and Rib Cook-Off** (www.biglickblues.org).

ACCOMMODATIONS

$50-100

On a hilltop just north of the airport, you'll find the **Quality Inn Airport** (6626 Thirlane Rd. NW, 540/366-8861, $70–160) and a **Super 8** motel (6616 Thirlane Rd. NW, 540/563-8888, $60–70). Also in this category is the **Colony House Motor Lodge** (3560 Franklin Rd. SW, 540/345-0411, $55–80), off I-581/U.S. 220 near the Franklin Road/Salem exit.

$100-150

The **Holiday Inn Roanoke** (3315 Ordway Dr., 540/362-4500) has rooms just south of the airport for $80–160.

You'll have to head to nearby Salem (a 20-minute drive) to reach the **Inn at Burwell Place** (601 W. Main St., 540/387-0250, www.burwellplace.com), the area's most comfortable nonhotel lodging. The first thing you'll notice is the wraparound front porch, great for an afternoon lounge. Upstairs are two rooms ($115–125) and two suites ($175), luxuriously appointed with antique tubs and guest robes. The back garden is beautiful enough to host weddings, which it does quite often.

$150-200

With a history almost as long as the city, the **Hotel Roanoke and Conference Center** (110 Shenandoah Ave., 540/985-5900, www.hotelroanoke.com, $140–190) has anchored Roanoke's downtown for more than a century. It was built in a wheat field in 1882, and, thanks to its popularity with vacationers, outlasted the railroads that financed it. Anyone who's anyone passing through the area has stayed here, from presidents to celebrities, Amelia Earhart to Elvis.

Even if you're staying elsewhere, a peek inside the classic Tudor facade is worth the walk through the glass-enclosed walkway over the train tracks from Market Square. In the lobby, Florentine marble floors set off vaulted ceilings, while Southern idyll paintings on the walls and ceilings make the Palm Court off the lobby perfect for afternoon tea. Guests enjoy a fitness center, pool, the Regency Room's famous peanut soup, and the hotel's trademark fresh-baked cookies on arrival.

Camping

The National Park Service maintains a

campground at Roanoke Mountain (540/767-2492, mid-May–Oct., $16) off Mill Mountain Road between the Roanoke Star and the Blue Ridge Parkway at mile 120.4, as well as at a 107-site campground (540/745-9660, mid-May–Oct., $16) at mile 167.1. You can also camp at Dixie Caverns (540/380-2085, www.dixiecaverns.com, $28 for RV, $8 pp for tents).

FOOD

Snacks and Cafés

One of the city's best nightspots has nothing to do with dancing or alcohol, although intoxicating drinks are still a cornerstone. **Mill Mountain Coffee & Tea** (112 Campbell Ave. SE, 540/342-9404, all meals daily) is one of five in Virginia. Beans roasted here are served in a good, strong brew, alongside dozens of flavors of teas, Italian sodas, and desserts to die for. They're open late (to 11 P.M. or midnight).

A virtual United Nations of eateries fills the Market Square food court, packed at lunch with the downtown crowd. Most are open Monday–Friday and have entrées for $5–9.

Casual

The best Indian food in Roanoke is conveniently close to the downtown historic center. **Nawab Indian Cuisine** (118-A Campbell Ave. SE, 540/345-5150, lunch and dinner daily) has a large menu ranging from vegetable samosas to *chana masala* to goat curry ($11–20 dinner). The best deal is the weekday lunch buffet ($8).

For a bite before a movie at the Grandin Theatre, try **Norberto's** (1908 Memorial Ave. SW, 540/342-1611, dinner daily), an unpretentious but solid Italian eatery serving pasta, veal, chicken, and seafood entrées ($12 and up).

Montano's International Gourmet (3733 Franklin Rd. SW, 540/344-8960, lunch and dinner Mon.–Sat.) is a popular lunch spot. It's in the Townside Festival Mall and has received numerous local awards: best bar, best beer selection, best wine selection, and best healthy business lunch. Specialties include paella and pasta, with entrées around $7–12 for lunch and $9–24 for dinner.

Stephen's (2926 Franklin Rd. SW, 540/344-7203, dinner Tues.–Sat.) serves authentic Creole cuisine under high ceilings and wrought iron. Fresh seafood is flown in for the gumbo and étouffée, and soft-shell crabs and crawfish are available in season. Dinner entrées run $19–36.

Ask around for Roanokers' favorite place for dinner, and chances are good that **Carlos Brazilian & International Cuisine** (4167 Electric Rd., 540/776-1117, dinner Mon.–Sat.) will come up. Casually classy styling, good prices, and outstanding food make this one so popular you'll need reservations on weekends. Try the authentic Brazilian *feijoada*—a full meal of black beans seasoned with salted pork that's the national dish. Entrées start at $15 and run up to $44 for dinner.

Don't forget **The Roanoker** (2522 Colonial Ave. SW, 540/344-7746, all meals Tues.–Sun.), a local favorite since 1941. City residents pack several dining rooms for down-home staples like the biscuits-and-gravy breakfast, homemade breads, and fresh vegetables. Dinner entrées usually run less than $13.

Eating at **The Homeplace** (4968 Catawba Valley Dr., 540/384-7252) is like nothing so much as dinner at Grandma's. This old country home features a set menu of classic country items—fried chicken, roast beef, or country ham, mashed potatoes, beans, fresh flaky biscuits, coleslaw, gravy, and cobbler for dessert—and they'll keep bringing it out until you beg them to stop. Meals ($13 for two meats, $14 for three) are served 4–8 P.M. Thursday–Friday, 3–8 P.M. Saturday, 11 A.M.–6 P.M. Sunday. To get there, take I-81 exit 140 or 141 to Route 311 north, and it's seven miles farther on your left, in Catawba.

Upscale

With an entryway lined with awards, **The Library** (3117 Franklin Rd. SW, 540/985-0811, dinner Tues.–Sat.) is easily one of the state's better restaurants. Top-notch service,

SOUTHWEST VIRGINIA

an extensive wine list, and the candlelit atmosphere of book-lined walls set off exceptional French cuisine. Try the oysters Rockefeller for starters, followed by the dover sole à la meuniere. Reservations are recommended for dinner ($21–39).

Enjoy a prime cut of chop in an atmosphere of mahogany, leather, and candlelight at **Frankie Rowland's Steakhouse** (104 Jefferson St., 540/527-2333, dinner Mon.–Sat.), where entrées are $24–39.

INFORMATION

The Roanoke Valley **Visitor Information Center** (101 Shenandoah Ave., 540/345-8622 or 800/635-5535, www.visitroanokeva.com, 9 A.M.–5 P.M. daily) shares the old Norfolk & Western Railway passenger station with the O. Winston Link Museum. For more information on the city, visit the *Roanoke Times* website (www.roanoke.com).

GETTING THERE AND AROUND

Getting There

The **Roanoke Regional Airport** (5202 Aviation Dr. NW, 540/362-1999, www.roanokeairport.com) is the only large airport in southwest Virginia. It's served by U.S. Airways, United Express, Allegiant Air, and Delta. Several car rental agencies have offices there, including Avis (540/366-2436) and Hertz (540/366-3421). **Roanoke Airport Transportation Services** (540/345-7710) offers town car, van, and limousine service between the airport and the rest of the city.

There's a **Greyhound** station (26 Salem Ave. SW, 540/343-5436), but **Amtrak**'s nearest station is in Clifton Forge, 45 miles northwest. For information on a Thruway bus connection, call 800/872-7245.

Getting Around

The **Valley Metro** bus network (540/982-2222, www.valleymetro.com) serves the entire city from its main transfer point at Campbell Court (17 W. Campbell Ave.). Buses run 5:45 A.M.–8:45 P.M. Monday–Saturday, and route maps are available at the visitors center or online. For cab service, try **Yellow Cab** (540/345-7711) or **Quality Cab** (540/265-0467).

NEAR ROANOKE

Dixie Caverns

This hole in the earth was discovered by a pair of Civil War soldiers whose dog—named Dixie—disappeared while chasing an animal across the hillside. They found the hole the dog had gone into and managed to rescue their canine companion with lanterns and rope. The caverns the dog unwittingly discovered creep upward into the mountain instead of down, so for most of the tour you're actually above the parking lot where you started.

Fifty-minute tours leave whenever a large enough group materializes. Hundreds of couples have been married beneath the 57-ton Wedding Bell formation (a statement on the beauty of the union or the weight of the commitment—you be the judge). Notice where early tourists broke off small stalactites for souvenirs, a practice that would get you thrown in jail today.

The caverns (540/380-2085, www.dixiecaverns.com, tours 9:30 A.M.–6 P.M. daily, to 5 P.M. Oct.–May, $12 adults, $6 children 5–12) are off I-81 exit 132 just west of Salem.

Ferrum

This tiny town erupts every fall with the **Blue Ridge Folklife Festival** at Ferrum College, the largest showcase of rural tradition in the state. Animals are the stars, from the State Championship Coon Mule Jumping Contest to sheep-herding demonstrations. Visitors enjoy all the deep-fried, golden-brown down-home cooking they can stuff down—barbecue, apple pie, pork rinds, spare ribs, and fried chitterling sandwiches, for starters—while listening to gospel, country, and blues music. Storytellers and a petting zoo will keep the kids busy as parents peruse the quilt and crafts displays.

The festival is held the fourth Saturday in October. For more information and directions, contact the Blue Ridge Institute and Museum (540/365-4416, www.blueridgeinstitute.org).

Floyd

One of the more interesting counties in the state, Floyd shelters a small pocket of the 1960s that's apparent in subtle but distinct signs. Earthships (houses made of recycled materials and earth), gasohol, and tie-dyed T-shirts in crafts stores all reflect a countercultural legacy that combines intriguingly with the surrounding rural lifestyle. One restaurant's logo depicts a farmer, a businessman, and a hippie standing happily side by side.

There's only one stoplight in the town of Floyd, which makes it easy to find the **Floyd Country Store** (206 S. Locust St., 540/745-4563, www.floydcountrystore.com), famous for its weekly Flatfoot Jamboree. Every Friday at 6:30 P.M., the floor is given over to *real* country music and shuffling feet. The store is the fourth building on the right to the west of the stoplight, and the show is $4 per person. Granny Rules are good-naturedly enforced: "no smokin', no cussin', and no drinkin'." Nationally famous country and bluegrass acts play most Saturdays for about $15. Show up early to get a seat.

Oddfellas Cantina (110 N. Locust St., 540/745-3463, lunch and dinner Wed.–Sun., brunch Sun.) offers "whole food for whole people" and more live music. Lunch goes for $6–10, dinner $8–22. Two miles north of town, **The Historic Pine Tavern Restaurant** (611 Rte. 221 N., 540/745-4482, dinner Thurs.–Sun., brunch Sun.) offers family-style meals on shared platters for $11 per person (kids $4–6).

The **Jacksonville Center for the Arts** (220 Parkway Ln. S., 540/745-2784, www.jacksonvillecenter.org, 10 A.M.–2 P.M. Mon.–Tues., 11 A.M.–4 P.M. Wed.–Sat.) is an old farm complex that has been transformed into a center for art, mountain music, theater, dance, crafts, and rural heritage. It's half a mile south of town on Route 8, with a gallery and gift shop on the premises.

In late July, a different kind of arts collective comes to town: **Floydfest,** a 13,000-attendee folk music festival in the school of Bonnaroo, but with a more family-friendly vibe. The four-day festival's venue is near milepost 171 of the Blue Ridge Parkway; it also hosts the **Floyd Fandango Beer & Wine Festival** in early July. Across the Way Productions organizes both festivals; see its website for details (www.atwproductions.com).

The **Floyd County Chamber of Commerce** (202 S. Locust St., 540/745-4407, www.visitfloyd.org, 10 A.M.–4 P.M. Mon.–Wed., 10 A.M.–2 P.M. Thurs.–Fri., 11 A.M.–4 P.M. Sat.) is happy to supply more information on the area, or you can log on to www.floydvirginia.com.

Southern Blue Ridge Parkway

The **Roanoke Mountain Campground** (540/767-2492, mid-May–Oct., $16) is off Mill Mountain Road between the Roanoke Star and the Blue Ridge Parkway at mile 120.4. At mile 167.1 is a 107-site campground (540/745-9660, mid-May–Oct., $16), followed by a visitors center at **Rocky Knob Recreation Area** at mile 169. The rustic stone **Rocky Knob Cabins** (540/593-3503, May–Oct., $65) at mile 174 have fully furnished kitchens and linens and share a bathhouse.

A National Recreational Trail winds 11 strenuous miles down into **Rock Castle Gorge,** 1,500 feet deep and studded with outcroppings of quartz. Apple orchards and stone chimneys are all that remain of numerous homesteads once inhabited by several families. The Black Ridge Trail offers a more moderate hike of 3.1 miles from the visitors center to Black Ridge and Grassy Knoll. A one-mile loop trail also leaves from the visitors center parking lot.

Seven miles farther south at mile 176.1 is one of the most popular stops on the Parkway: **Mabry Mill** (276/952-2947), a restaurant and gift shop complex centered on a gristmill operated commercially 1910–1935. Fresh-ground cornmeal is sold near a restored sawmill and blacksmith shop.

Cool nights and loamy soil give the **Meadows of Dan,** at the intersection of the Parkway and U.S. 58, the distinction of raising the sweetest cabbage in the world. The **Meadows of Dan Campground** (2182 Jeb

Stuart Hwy., 276/952-2292, www.meadowsofdancampground.com) has sites for $20–25. On the fourth Saturday of August, thousands of people show up for the **Cabbage Festival** at Poor Farmers Farm in nearby Vesta (276/952-2560, www.poorfarmersfarm.net), with bluegrass music, games for the kids, and plenty of cabbage.

Blacksburg and Vicinity

A quiet residential town on the surface, Blacksburg harbors the secret heart of one of the fastest-growing, most progressive communities in Virginia. Its scenic setting, on a plateau right at the edge of farm country, seduces all ages—Blacksburg is rated one of the best places in the country to retire, while the 25,000 students of Virginia Tech University make up a majority of the town's population.

This influx of brainpower makes Blacksburg a bit difficult to classify. The town celebrated its bicentennial in 1998, a year after several tattoo parlors downtown hosted the two-day Piercefest VIII. The municipal bus system has won national awards, even as the town lends itself so well to strolling. Its nearness to the mountains means there are trails galore practically on the town's doorstep.

Over everything spreads the wings of Virginia Tech, southwest Virginia's major learning center and one of the largest universities in the state. The entire town was one of the first to be wired to the Internet, and Hokie basketball and football are NCAA Division One mainstays.

Whatever category you file it under, Blacksburg is an inviting and intriguing city. It's tragic that the event that brought it to the world's attention was the shooting of 32 Tech students on April 16, 2007, by one of their own, who then killed himself. The disaster has drawn the student body and the town even closer together in a determined, united effort at recovery.

History

This gorgeous slice of Appalachia was originally the farming settlement of Draper's Meadow, a mixed community of European settlers and the first permanent English-speaking colony west of the Alleghenies. Much of the land was granted in 1748 to Col. James Patton's Woods River Company.

A Shawnee attack in July 1775 left all but four settlers dead, wounded, or captured; Patton was shot after cutting down two attackers with his sword. One female captive managed to escape later and made an incredible 800-mile trek back to the settlements. Another, Mrs. John Draper, was adopted by the chief's family and remained a prisoner until she was ransomed in 1781.

Col. William Preston arrived in 1772 and built Smithfield Plantation, which still stands on the edge of the Virginia Tech campus. Blacksburg was founded in 1798 on 38 acres donated by William Black and set up as a 16-block grid bounded by today's Draper Road and Wharton, Jackson, and Clay Streets.

Dr. Henry Black petitioned the Virginia General Assembly in 1872 to establish a land-grant university in the area. It opened with a single building and 43 students; 125 years later, it thrives as southwest Virginia's largest university and employer.

VIRGINIA TECH

The original Virginia Agriculture and Mechanical College became the Virginia Polytechnic Institute and State University in the late 1800s, now known simply as Virginia Tech (540/231-6000, www.vt.edu), or around here just "Tech." It's one of the state's powerhouse universities, ranking among the nation's best in research and scholarship. A yearly research budget runs in the hundreds of millions. More than 25,000 undergraduate and graduate students study within eight colleges, including agriculture, veterinary medicine, and forestry.

Stately limestone neo-Gothic architecture dots the 3,000-acre campus in the heart of Blacksburg. Burruss Hall presides over the huge grassy drill field, and the tree-lined duck pond, west of the central campus, provides a peaceful spot to escape the pressures of academics. (And by the way, "Hokie" is a nonsense word coined by a member of the class of 1896 for a school cheer.)

The April 2007 shooting shook the institution to its core, but the worldwide expression of sympathy that followed helped kick-start the healing process. As professor Nikki Giovanni said at a memorial convocation the day after the event, "We are the Hokies. We will prevail."

Tech's **Museum of Geological Sciences** (2062 Derring Hall, 540/231-6894, 8 A.M.–5 P.M. Mon.–Fri., free) contains the largest collection of Virginia minerals in the state, alongside full-scale dinosaurs, gemstones, and other fossils.

Smithfield Plantation

Follow signs down Duck Pond Drive to reach this classic plantation home built by Scottish-Irish immigrants William and Susanna Smith Preston in the 1770s. Over the years, two Virginia governors, James Patton Preston (1816–1819) and John Buchanan Floyd (1849–1852), were born here. Today, the Tidewater-style mansion (540/231-3947, www.smithfieldplantation.org, 10 A.M.–5 P.M. Mon.–Tues. and Thurs.–Sat., 1–5 Sun., Apr.–early Dec., $7 adults, $3 children) is a living museum, with costumed interpreters leading one-hour tours of the house and the demonstration kitchen garden, planted with culinary and medicinal herbs.

ENTERTAINMENT AND RECREATION

Nightlife

For live music, **Top of the Stairs** (217 W. College Ave., 540/953-2837) is the local hot spot with the campus's Greek life, booking mostly alternative bands. Thursday is karaoke night. The **Lyric Theater** (135 College Ave., 540/951-0604, www.thelyric.com, $5) is yet another old-school movie house (1930) that was rescued and restored by concerned citizens. The films show a university-town inclination toward the unusual and innovative, and the Lyric also hosts live music. Or watch a movie under the stars during the summer at the **Starlite Drive-In Theater** (305 Roanoke Rd., 540/382-2202, www.starlitedrivein.biz, $4 adults, $2 children) in Christiansburg, one of the few remaining original drive-ins in the country.

At the College

Virginia Tech football is almost a way of life for die-hard fans. Games against the archrival Cavaliers of the University of Virginia fill parking lots at either school with tailgate parties and boisterous alumni. For information and tickets, contact the school's athletic department (540/231-6731 or 800/828-3244, www.hokiesports.com or www.hokietickets.com).

Art happenings on campus range from nationally known musicians and speakers to Virginia Tech's Theater Arts Programs and Audubon Quartet. Call the main campus number (540/231-6000) for a current schedule.

Outdoor Recreation

The right-of-way of the old Huckleberry Train, which began running in 1904, is now the six-mile **Huckleberry Trail,** a foot and bike path that runs from the Blacksburg library (200 Miller St.) to the New River Valley Mall in Christiansburg.

The surrounding acres of the Jefferson National Forest provide Blacksburg residents and visitors with plenty of opportunities to hike, bike, ride horses, and camp. Head west from town on Route 460 to reach a few of the more popular trails.

Four miles from town up Route 460, turn right onto the dirt Forest Service Road 188.2 for the great intermediate mountain-bike loop around **Brush Mountain.** It's just over eight miles around and can get tough in spots. Head up Forest Service Road 188.2 past the old lookout tower, then turn right and head down the steep red-blazed trail 2.5 miles from Route 460. Cross Poverty Creek and turn right onto the orange-blazed trail, which eventually takes you right (southeast) back across the creek toward Forest Service Road 188.2. (If you reach Pandapas Pond, you've gone too far.)

Shortly past the turn-off for Forest Service Road 188.2 on the left is the parking area for **Pandapas Pond,** an eight-acre pond surrounded by pines and hardwoods with a loop trail around it. Fishing and canoeing are allowed, but bikes and horses are prohibited within 300 feet.

Keep going up Route 460 to Pembroke, 17.5 miles from Blacksburg, then turn right onto Route 623 and go four more miles to the parking lot for the **Cascades Recreation Area,** where a National Recreation Trail climbs two miles up a gorge to a 66-foot waterfall.

Both **Blue Ridge Outdoors** (1560 S. Main St., 540/953-7060) and **Back Country Ski & Sports** (3710 S. Main St., 540/552-6400) sell outdoor gear and can provide you with information on outfitters in the area.

ACCOMMODATIONS

$50–100

The most economical options are in nearby Christiansburg, eight miles south by I-81. Here the **EconoLodge** (2430 Roanoke St., 540/382-6161) and the **Super 8** (55 Laurel St., 540/382-5813) have rooms in the $50–65 range (though they can be double that in spring).

Over $100

Blacksburg proper has surprisingly few guesthouses, considering how many students and parents come and go over the course of the year. The **Maison Beliveau** (5415 Gallion Ridge Rd., 540/961-0505, www.maisonbeliveau.com) is a French Country–style home with wraparound porches and great views on 165 acres. Five bed-and-breakfast rooms are $225–300, although rates go up and a two-night stay is required during Tech football games.

In Christiansburg, **The Oaks Victorian Inn** (311 E. Main St., 540/381-1500 or 800/336-6257, www.theoaksvictorianinn.com) is an 1889 Queen Anne Victorian with six large rooms ($160–230) with hot tubs and fireplaces. The garden cottage ($190–210) features a sauna and a 400-gallon hot tub outside.

In terms of chain hotels, pick from **Amerisuites** (1020 Plantation Rd., 540/552-5636, $90–110) or the **Comfort Inn** (3705 S. Main St., 540/951-1500, $100–120). Both establishments charge nearly double on football weekends.

FOOD

Snacks and Cafés

Pies, breads, and French pastries are the manna of **Our Daily Bread** (1329 S. Main St., 540/953-2815, 7 A.M.–6:30 P.M. Mon.–Fri., 7 A.M.–5:30 P.M. Sat.). They also offer daily sandwiches and salads ($4–8) and gourmet coffees.

Casual

Top of the Stairs (217 W. College Ave., 540/953-2837, lunch and dinner daily) boasts the best barbecue in the New River Valley and has live music on many nights. Burgers are around $5, and a rack of slow-cooked St. Louis ribs run $11.

Grab a house-made margarita and a grilled tuna taco ($8.50) at **Cabo Fish Taco** (117 S. Main St., 540/552-0950, lunch and dinner daily, open late), which combines the tastes of coastal Mexico with healthy California flavors.

Upscale

Options for when the parents come to town include **Zeppoli's Restaurant and Wine Shop** (810 University City Blvd., 540/953-2000, lunch and dinner Sun.–Fri., lunch Sat.), serving excellent fresh pastas in the University Mall for $9–16. They occasionally host wine tastings from local vineyards.

Boudreaux's Cajun Restaurant (205 N. Main St., 540/961-2330, lunch and dinner daily) offers lots of seafood, Cajun spice, and a Sunday brunch. Lunch plates start at $7, and dinner entrées run $15–25.

INFORMATION

For more details on Blacksburg attractions, contact the **Montgomery County Chamber of Commerce & Visitors Center** (103 Professional Park Dr., 540/522-2636, www.montgomerycc.org, 9 A.M.–5 P.M. daily). Another good source is the **Blacksburg Electronic Village** (www.bev.net), a virtual online community and one of the first of its kind in the nation.

GETTING THERE

Home Ride of Virginia (540/953-2266 or 800/553-6644, www.homeride.com) offers weekend bus service between Blacksburg and Vienna, stopping at Harrisonburg and Charlottesville, and between Blacksburg and Hampton, stopping at Richmond. Buses run September–April; contact Home Ride for the latest schedule and prices.

MOUNTAIN LAKE AND VICINITY

In the shadow of 4,200-foot Bald Knob, Mountain Lake is Virginia's highest, and one of only two natural lakes in the state. (The other is in the Great Dismal Swamp.) No one is quite sure how it formed up here at 4,000 feet, making it the highest lake east of the Mississippi, but the altitude is enough to earn it the record for the lowest temperatures in the state (it hit -30°F in 1985). One theory about its formation holds that a small rockslide blocked a natural outlet sometime during the late 19th century, back when the spot was called Salt Pond by farmers looking for salt for their cattle.

Mountain Lake Resort

The first hotel was built on the shore of the chilly lake in the late 19th century, providing lodging for people making the east–west trip through the mountains. In the hands of the Porterfield family near the turn of the 20th century, the hotel became known as a luxury stop. Guests were allowed to build their own cottages until the main stone lodge was constructed in 1936. The movie *Dirty Dancing* was filmed here in 1986, two years after major renovations were completed, and made the hotel's classic mountain ambience world famous.

Guests have no excuse to cry boredom. The daily roster overflows with things to do, starting with hikes and rides on a network of trails of different difficulty levels around the lake and into the surrounding hills. You can wander to the Mountain Lake Biological Station, run by the University of Virginia, or as far as Minnie Ball Hill, named for small-caliber Civil War cannonballs still found there more than 150 years after a Union general abandoned his supply wagons because his horses couldn't pull them up the steep grade. Some trails are open to mountain bikes, which are available for rent, as is equipment for volleyball, horseshoes, and croquet.

During warmer months, the small sandy beach is packed with swimmers, while the farther reaches of the lake are open to boats and canoes. Relaxation comes in the form of massages at the health spa, a day camp for children, or simply enjoying the view from a deck chair while families compete at lawn chess nearby.

While you're browsing the row of shops and galleries, notice Bob Evans's whittled wooden Nobbits ("cousins to Hobbits"). He bases them on the German legend of Wurtzelgrabbers (root diggers), said to run around carving their own likenesses out of roots and leaving them on the doorsteps of friends to bring good luck. At the height of fall comes Oktoberfest, with Teutonic food, beer, and live polka music.

The hotel and restaurant are open from the first Friday in May through the last Sunday in October, as well as weekends and Thanksgiving in November. Rooms are around $200, suites are in the $250 range, and cottages with 1–4 bedrooms are $250–800. A two-night minimum stay is required. For more information, contact the hotel (540/626-7121 or 800/346-3334, www.mountainlakehotel.com).

To get there, take U.S. 460 west (which actually runs north) from Blacksburg, turning right onto Route 700, a precipitous back road that winds through seven gorgeous miles of rural Virginia. As you chug the last seven miles uphill, keep in mind that this stretch was included in a Tour duPont bicycle race as a Category One climb—as hard as it gets.

Near Mountain Lake

This corner of the state conceals one of the wilder chunks of the Jefferson National Forest, marked by high, windswept ridges blanketed with hemlock and spruce. Steep ravines within the 10,000-acre **Mountain Lake Wilderness** conceal stands of centuries-old white oak, with mushrooms, bogs, and berry bushes in more moderate valleys. The three-mile **War Spur hike** leads to a rocky overlook on the north side of Salt Pond Mountain, a prime spot for a picnic. To reach the trailhead, continue past the resort and lake on Route 613 for 1.5 miles, then take the left fork for another 1.5 miles to a parking area on your right.

The **Peters Mountain Wilderness** spreads farther north to intersect with the Appalachian Trail, skirting the West Virginia border near the **White Rocks Recreation Area** off Route 613. All three wild areas are open only to primitive camping. For more information, contact the **Eastern Divide Ranger District** (540/552-4641) of the Jefferson National Forest.

A few miles west of the Mountain Lake turn-off is the **Cascades Recreation Area,** known for a four-mile round-trip trail up Little Stony Creek Gorge. Wooden bridges span the creek as the trail climbs through hemlocks and birches to a 66-foot waterfall. Trout fishing is good in the creek. To get here, take a right turn (north) off U.S. 460 onto Route 623 in Pembroke, following signs four miles to the recreation area.

New River Valley

WYTHEVILLE

First of all, it's pronounced "WITH-vul," and has been ever since the town was incorporated in 1839 along the Wilderness Road (part of which still serves as the town's Main Street). During the Civil War, Wytheville saw plenty of action, as troops from both sides passed through on a regular basis. A Union attack in 1863 was beaten back by a local militia, but by the end of the war, most of the town lay in ruins.

Sights

Wytheville's two museums are both part of the **Wytheville Heritage Preservation Center** (Monroe and Tazewell Sts., 276/223-3330, 10 A.M.–4 P.M. Mon.–Fri.). Admission to both is $6 adults, $3 children, and guided tours leave on the hour. The Haller-Gibboney Rock House Museum served as a hospital during the Civil War—bloodstains are still visible on the floor of one of the second-story bedrooms. Out back, an herb garden showcases plants used for medicine in the 1800s. The historical collection in the Thomas J. Boyd Museum includes the town's first fire truck (1855), Civil War uniforms, and hands-on displays of local history for children.

On Main Street, the 30-foot **Big Pencil** was built in the late 1950s to advertise an office supply store.

Entertainment

At the **Wohlfahrt Haus Dinner Theatre** (170 Malin Dr., 276/223-0891 or 888/950-3382, www.wohlfahrthaus.com, dinner Tues.–Sat.), a German-themed dinner theater, you can enjoy a four-course meal and then a Broadway-style musical without changing your set. Choose from a Rhineland wurst ($15) next to the fireplace in the Matterhorn Restaurant and Lounge or a pilsner in the outdoor Bier Garten. Dinner and a show is $42 adults, $25 children, and the schedule includes workhorses like *The Sound of Music* and *Grease.*

Shopping

Both **Snooper's Antique & Craft Mall** (276/637-6441) and the **Old Fort Antique Mall** (276/228-4438) are located on the service

SODA SOURCE

Southwest Virginia claims parenthood of not one but two famous soft drinks within miles of each other. Mountain Dew was created in Marion, about midway between Wytheville and Abingdon (I-81 exit 45), where its original spokesperson was a hillbilly shouting, "Ya-hoo, Mountain Dew!" Every Fourth of July, a chili cook-off and Mountain Dew Day celebrate the highly caffeinated chartreuse beverage.

Just up the interstate is Christiansburg, where a doctor lived in the late 19th century. As the story goes, a certain Wade Morrison was in love with the doctor's daughter. Morrison moved to Texas in the 1870s, alone, where he ended up running a drug store in Waco. In 1885, the store's pharmacist invented a uniquely flavored drink that became famous nationwide. Perhaps in honor of his long-lost love, Morrison named it after her father: Dr. Pepper.

road between exits 77 and 80 off I-81. They're both open daily year-round and stock industrial quantities of antiques, collectibles, and snacks.

Accommodations

Your only options here are chain hotels, and all are in the $50–100 range. Choose from a **Best Western** (355 Nye Rd., 276/228-7300), a **Comfort Inn** (2594 E. Lee Hwy., 276/637-4281), or a **Days Inn** (150 Malin Dr., 276/228-5000).

Just east of town is the **Wytheville KOA Kampground** (276/228-2601 or 800/562-3380, www.koa.com/where/va/46112, $30–45), boasting a heated pool with water slide, an activity center, nature trails, and live music in the summer. To get there, take exit 77 off I-81/I-77, then head south 0.5 mile on Route 758. The U.S. Forest Service maintains the **Stony Fork Campground** at the foot of Big Walker Mountain, eight miles north on U.S. 52 and 0.3 mile east on Route 717. Sites here are $12–22.

Food

Most of Wytheville's eating options are of the generic interstate-exit variety, but there are a few exceptions. **Skeeters** (165 E. Main St., 276/228-2611, breakfast and lunch Mon.–Sat.) on Main Street supposedly serves the best chili dogs in the world—it says so right there on the front—and they've been doing it for more than 90 years.

The **Peking Restaurant** (105 Malin Dr., 276/228-5515, lunch and dinner daily) sits on top of a hill near exit 73 off I-81. This ornate place has tasty Chinese plates for lunch ($4–8) and dinner ($8–16), plus the Flaming Volcano Drink consisting of "rums fired with sacred nectars, served aflame for two people."

Information

Contact the **Wytheville Convention and Visitors Bureau** (975 Tazewell St., 276/223-3355 or 877/347-8307, www.visitwytheville.com) for more information on the area.

Near Wytheville

North of town, the Appalachians crest with surprising speed, forcing I-77 to dive into a tunnel through Big Walker Mountain within a few miles. A small loop beginning at exit 47 has been deemed a Scenic Byway: Take Route 717 west to the junction with U.S. 52, which you'll climb to the **Big Walker Lookout** (276/663-4016, 10 A.M.–5 P.M. daily, depending on weather, $5 adults, $3.50 children). The 100-foot tower sits at 3,405 feet, commanding an Olympian view of the surrounding hills. Afterward, dispel your vertigo by following U.S. 52 north and east back to I-77, crossing Walker Creek.

Nearly 800 years ago, a small, hospitable mountain valley a short drive from Wytheville was settled by a small group of Native Americans. About 100 people lived here, but where they came from and where they went is still unknown. Today, the **Wolf Creek Indian Village and Museum** (276/688-3438, www.indianvillage.org, 10 A.M.–5 P.M. Tues.–Sat., $10 adults, $6 children 5–16) shares the site with an archaeological excavation, as well as nature trails and picnic facilities. To get there, take I-77 exit 58 and follow the signs to the town of Bastian.

GALAX

Early Scottish-Irish settlers would have been proud to know that their fiddles and bagpipes still echo in Galax (GAY-laks), the current World Capital of Old Time Mountain Music. Turn off the U.S. 58/221 strip (E. Stuart Dr.) onto Main Street to the center of town to reach the massive brick **Grayson County Courthouse,** built near the turn of the 20th century when the town first sprang to life as Bonaparte.

From Main Street, head west on Oldtown Street, then south on Old Stuart Drive to reach the **Jeff Matthews Museum** (606 W. Stuart Dr., 276/236-7874, www.jeffmatthewsmuseum.org, 11 A.M.–4 P.M. Wed.–Sat., free). Barely across the threshold, you're accosted by the biggest stuffed bear you've ever seen, an 8.5-foot Kodiak grizzly from Alaska, presiding over enough animal carcasses to stock a taxidermy shop. Check out everything an early-1900s family (or three) would need to survive, including a fully stocked country store, a 1902 Sears & Roebuck catalog, an 1899 map of Virginia, more than 1,000 knives, and an 800-pound whetstone. Don't miss the antique hair curler, straight out of a Frankenstein movie. Two reconstructed cabins out back date to the mid-19th century.

The **Galax Farmer's Market** fills North Main Street with produce, baked goods, crafts, and flowers every Friday and Saturday morning June–October.

Music and Events

The quiet village is brought to raucous life during the annual **Old Fiddler's Convention** (276/236-8541, www.oldfiddlersconvention.com), the oldest and largest mountain-music convention in the country. It was begun in 1935 with the stated purpose of "Keeping alive the memories and sentiments of days gone by and mak[ing] it possible for people of today to hear and enjoy the tunes of yesterday," and that still holds true. More than $10,000 in prizes is awarded each year. The clack of clogs and the slap of flatfoot combine with arts, crafts, and food booths the second week of August. Tickets are $6–12 per day, and camping is $70 per night; both are sold on a first-come, first-served basis.

Every Friday evening 8–10 P.M., WBRF (98.1 FM) and the Galax Downtown Association sponsor **Blue Ridge Backroads,**

© KATIE GITHENS

Arrive early for a seat at Galax's Rex Theater on Friday evenings to hear live music.

one of the few remaining live bluegrass radio shows in the country. It's held at the historic **Rex Theater** (111 E. Grayson St., www.rextheatergalax.org), which also hosts live bluegrass and country bands. Admission costs $5.

If all of these great tunes inspire you to pick up an instrument, stop by **Barr's Fiddle Shop** (105 S. Main St., 276/236-2411), where Tom Barr makes and sells fiddles. In mid-July, Galax hosts over 10,000 people during the two-day **Virginia State Barbecue Championship** (www.smokeonthemountainva.com).

Accommodations and Food

You'll see **Galax Hampton Inn** (205 Cranberry Rd., 276/238-4605, $100) on Route 58 coming into town. Touted the nicest place to stay in Galax proper, it's clean, quiet, and comes with a continental breakfast. Free wireless Internet and an indoor pool and fitness room round out the amenities.

In nearby Independence 15 miles west, the **Davis-Bourne Inn** (119 Journey's End Dr., Independence, 276/773-9384, www.davisbourneinn.com) is a genteel bed-and-breakfast in a restored Victorian mansion, circa 1865, with a wide wraparound porch. Each of the four bedrooms has a private bath, and **The Journey's End Restaurant** serves brunch and dinner (entrées $12–24). Rates are $100–145 double occupancy and include breakfast and afternoon tea. No pets or children under 12. Reservations recommended.

Kitty-corner to the Rex Theater is **The Galax Smokehouse** (101 N. Main St., 276/236-1000, lunch and dinner Mon.–Sat., lunch Sun.), a barbecue joint with all the "secret sauces" you could hope for. Sandwiches go for about $5, dinner platters $8 or $9.

Also within easy walking distance of the Rex Theater, **Flossies on Grayson** (117 W. Grayson St., 276/238-3300, all meals Mon.–Fri., breakfast and lunch Sat., very inexpensive) is a hole-in-the-wall home-style place that keeps a brisk business with the locals. Be sure to sample the real Southern cast-iron-skillet cornbread—it's not the sweet, cakey stuff you make from a boxed mix.

Information

The **Twin County Regional Chamber of Commerce** (405 N. Main St., 276/236-2184, www.gcgchamber.com) has more information on the town. Also try the **City of Galax** (276/238-8130, www.visitgalax.com).

NEW RIVER TRAIL STATE PARK

This "greenway" park protects a 39-mile stretch of the misnamed waterway and her banks. For 57 miles from Pulaski to Galax, you'll find people hiking, biking, riding horseback, and skiing down the old railroad bed, with occasional stops to fish or admire the cliffs and forest along the river.

Park headquarters (276/699-6778, www.dcr.virginia.gov/state_parks/new.shtml, 8 A.M.–4:30 P.M. Mon.–Fri., parking $2–3) are in Foster Falls, near **Shot Tower Historical State Park,** 17 miles south of Wytheville by either I-77 (exit 24) or U.S. 52. Here, a 70-foot tower was used in the 19th century for making lead rifle shot. From the top, molten metal was poured down through the tower and a 75-foot shaft beneath into a kettle of water at the bottom. The perfectly round balls were then recovered through a horizontal tunnel from the river's edge. Parking and restrooms are available at the base of the tower, and a loop trail accesses the New River Trail.

Four campgrounds ($15) are available en route, including one on an island in the river. Contact **Foster Falls River Company** (276/699-1034, daily Memorial Day–Labor Day, weekends in Apr.–May and Sept.–Oct.) for canoe, kayak, tube, and bicycle rentals and shuttle service. Try **Foster Falls Livery** (276/699-2460) for horse rentals. Seven other access points stretch along the river from Galax to Draper on I-81 near Pulaski.

Guided fishing trips for smallmouth bass start at $285 for a half-day with **Tangent Outfitters** (540/626-4567, www.newrivertrail.com) in Pembroke. Canoe trips start at $35 per person per day, and guided overnight trips are $65 per person. Bike rentals with shuttle service on the New River Trail run $40–75 per person (bike rentals only are $25).

Damascus

This small community is known as Trail Town USA for good reason. Damascus sits at the intersection of the Virginia Creeper Trail, the Trans-America "76" Bicycle Route from Virginia to Oregon, the prime single-track of the Iron Mountain Trail, and of course the fabled AT.

Every year the town's population swells from 1,000 to 25,000 the weekend after Mother's Day when Damascus hosts **Trail Days,** timed for the arrival of the first AT thru-hikers of the season. Future hikers come to ask questions, past hikers reminisce walking the length of the eastern seaboard, and the whole celebration culminates in a rowdy parade down Laurel Avenue, the town's main street.

PRACTICALITIES

At the hub of so many trail networks, Damascus is a useful stop for information and grub. Refuel at the **Whistlepig Bistro** (425 Douglas Dr., 276/475-3194, lunch daily, dinner Wed.–Sun., closed Mon.–Tues. in winter) for a Muenster-topped burger or, for vegetarians, a house-made black-bean burger. All entrées cost less than $7. For pizza and beer, try **Quincey's Pizza** (132 W. Laurel Ave., 276/475-5753, lunch and dinner daily), a long-time destination on the AT. A 16-inch pizza costs $11–17.50 and the menu also includes pastas, burgers, steaks, and salads.

While numerous bed-and-breakfasts operate nearby, the best-known lodging in Damascus is **The Place,** a hostel run by the United Methodist Church (200 E. Laurel Ave.) that is open *only* to AT thru-hikers and cross-country touring cyclists, should you meet that description. Expect to sleep on wooden bunk beds without mattresses and pay a $4 donation for your stay.

For maps, directions, and gear, pay a visit to the friendly staff at **SunDog Outfitter** (331 Douglas Dr., 276/475-6252 or 866/515-3441, www.sundogoutfitter.com) or **Mt. Rogers Outfitters** (110 Laurel Ave., 276/475-5416, www.mtrogersoutfitters.com). For more information on Damascus, see the town website (www.damascus.org).

MOUNT ROGERS NATIONAL RECREATION AREA

Places like Mt. Rogers prove that there are still spots east of the Mississippi as wild and gorgeous as any in the country. Throughout the 140,000 acres of the area, massive stone protrusions called "balds" jut skyward from high, wild alpine meadows ringed by fir and spruce forests.

Within the recreation area tower Virginia's two tallest mountains, two of only seven in the entire Blue Ridge that exceed 5,000 feet. Mt. Rogers (5,729 ft.), near the center of the Lewis Fork Wilderness, is covered with enough trees to block any sweeping vistas from the top. Whitetop Mountain (5,520 ft.) is more representative of the gently rounded southern balds found in Georgia and North Carolina. Some of the best views in the region come from the top of Wilburn Ridge, one mile from Mt. Rogers. Named for an 18th-century hermit and bear hunter, the ridge offers views of up to 100 miles.

The west end sees the most traffic through the trail hub of Damascus, with access to the Virginia Creeper and Appalachian Trails. Equestrians prefer the eastern end, as do hikers seeking solitude. In between is more than 25,000 acres of the highest country in the state. About 10,000 acres of this falls within the Lewis Fork and Little Wilson Creek Wilderness Areas, and 5,000 acres are in Grayson Highland State Park. Two herds of free-roaming ponies call the high country home.

Hiking Mt. Rogers

Bring your boots: Some 400 miles of trails creep through the area, offering wandering options ranging from easy to difficult. Most famous of these paths is the **Virginia Creeper National Recreation Trail** (www.vacreepertrail.com), which winds 35 miles along Whitetop Laurel Creek from Abingdon to Whitetop Station at the North Carolina line. What began centuries

© KATIE GITHENS

The Blue Ridge Mountains are an outdoor recreation haven for nearby towns such as Damascus.

ago as an Indian footpath had been claimed as a railroad bed by the turn of the 20th century. Timber and passengers were ferried from Abingdon to West Jefferson, North Carolina, up grades so steep the engines would slow to a crawl—hence the name.

The last train whistle split the forest silence in 1977, and since then the Virginia Creeper has become a shining example of the nationwide rails-to-trails initiative. It's relatively flat from Abingdon to Damascus, and therefore packed with hikers and horseback riders on weekends. Mountain bikers love to drive to the top of White's Mountain and glide back toward Abingdon.

Along with the Creeper, the **Appalachian Trail** snakes through the entire Recreation Area, 64 miles from end to end. The **Mt. Rogers Scenic Trail** leaves the Grindstone Campground and climbs to join the AT. It's 6.5 miles to the peak, as you climb from wooded forest through rock outcroppings to the top of the mountain.

The orange-blazed **Crawfish and Channel Rock Trails** form a moderate 10-mile loop starting in Crawfish Valley. From here the Crawfish Trail climbs Brushy Mountain and descends Channel Rock hollow. Keep an eye open for wildlife on this out-of-the-way route. Another good moderate hike is the **Seven Sisters Trail,** a five-mile route from Stony Fork Campground that passes rhododendrons and old-growth white pines to the top of a ridge on Little Walker Mountain.

A relatively easy eight-mile loop hike will take you up on top of Iron Mountain, a seemingly endless ridge that forms Mt. Rogers' backbone. Start at a pull-off on Route 58 at Laurel Creek, and make a loop via the Feathercamp Branch Trail, the Iron Mountain Trail, and the AT. Keep an eye peeled for ripe blackberries in season. Feathercamp Branch is a pretty stream lined by rhododendrons.

To reach the summit of Virginia's highest peak takes a seven-mile hike from the Grindstone Campground on the Mt. Rogers Trail. It's a moderately difficult hike with a 2,900-foot elevation gain, but the views, of course, are worth it. Make a 13.3-mile loop of it by coming back via the Pine Mountain, Cliffside, and Lewis Fork Trails.

Other Activities

Mountain bikers rave about the eight-mile loop up and around **Iron Mountain.** Start six miles east of Damascus on U.S. 58, then head left on

Forest Service Road 90. The route includes part of the Iron Mountain Trail and Forest Service Road 615; see the guidebook *Mountain Bike America: Virginia* for a detailed description.

Roadies will be pleased to pedal on Route 76, part of the **TransAmerica Trail** (www.adventurecycling.org) that passes through the region.

Although some of the best horseback riding around is found in Grayson Highlands State Park, Mt. Rogers offers the orange-blazed **Virginia Highlands Horse Trail,** running from Elk Garden to VA 94. Horses are also permitted on the Virginia Creeper and Iron Mountain Trails within the boundaries of the recreation area. (The Virginia Highlands Horse Trail lies just outside.) Mountain bikes are welcome on many of the same trails.

Even if you don't get out of your car, you can still enjoy the prettiest drive in this part of the state. The **Mt. Rogers Scenic Byway,** consisting of 34 miles of U.S. 58 from Damascus to Volney, earns the title of highest road in Virginia as it climbs the flank of Whitetop. A 23-mile side branch of Route 603 to Volney passes closer to Mt. Rogers.

Anglers can find trout in Hale Lake and 14-acre Beartree Lake, which also has a small sandy beach for swimming. Whitetop Laurel Creek is popular with fly-casters.

Outfitters

In Damascus, the **Blue Blaze Bike and Shuttle Service** (226 W. Laurel Ave., 276/475-5095 or 800/475-5095, www.blueblazebikeandshuttle.com) rents mountain bikes ($20 per day) and runs a bike shuttle service for $8–18 per person. **Adventure Damascus** (128 W. Laurel Ave., 276/475-6262 or 888/595-2453, www.adventuredamascus.com) rents ($17–25), sells, and repairs bikes, and offers trail maps, private showers, and lockers. Bike tours are also an option, and their trail shuttle costs $13 per person. Both offer rental-plus-shuttle deals.

The **Virginia Creeper Fly Shop** (276/628-3826, www.vcflyshop.com) in Abingdon is a full-service fly-fishing shop that offers instruction and catch-and-release drift trips starting at $230 per person, $280 for two people.

Camping

The recreation area has seven developed camping areas, ranging $5–40 per night. Most have water, but only a few have hot showers. Camping is also permitted off-trail.

Information

The **W. Pat Jennings Visitor Center** (3714 Hwy. 16, 276/783-5196 or 800/628-7202, www.fs.fed.us/r8/gwj/mr, 8 A.M.–4:30 P.M. Mon.–Fri., 9 A.M.–4 P.M. Sat.–Sun., weekdays only mid-Oct.–mid-May) sits off Route 16 six miles south of Marion (I-81 exit 45).

GRAYSON HIGHLANDS STATE PARK

On the southern side of the Mount Rogers National Recreation Area is this hidden gem, off U.S. 58 just west of Volney. Stunning views of the Blue Ridge make this the most beautiful approach up the Old Dominion's tallest mountain.

Hikers and backpackers can access the AT and Mt. Rogers from the Massey Gap parking area and the eight-mile out-and-back **Rhododendron Trail,** where rhododendrons flourish in early summer as do wild blueberries in fall. Or else head up the 1.6-mile **Twin Pinnacles Trail,** an interpretive nature loop, or the **Cabin Creek Trail,** a two-mile streamside loop that's great in the fall.

Virginia's highest state park is also its only one with horse camping facilities, including stalls for horses. Special orange-blazed equestrian trails climb Haw Orchard Mountain—named for the prickly hawthorn trees found there in abundance—for 360-degree views from Big Pinnacle and Little Pinnacle. Mountain bikers find that the eight-mile Virginia Highlands Horse Trail makes a great moderate loop ride (remember to give horseback riders the right of way).

The wing beats of wild turkeys thunder in the underbrush, while wild ponies—part of a herd of 30 released years ago—may sidle up looking for handouts. The 120-strong herd is rounded up twice a year and checked for disease, and some are auctioned off during the **Grayson**

Highlands Fall Harvest Festival at the end of September, which also includes Appalachian crafts and music. The **Wayne Henderson Music Festival & Guitar Competition,** the third Saturday in June, features music, instrument-making demonstrations, and food.

A total of 96 developed campsites ($20–25) are available, and primitive camping is $15. Information is available from park headquarters in Mouth of Wilson (276/579-7092, www.dcr.virginia.gov/state_parks/gra.shtml, parking $2–3). Be extra cautious of icy conditions here; the park is a mile above sea level, and its weather doesn't necessarily match the valley's—and there are no guardrails to keep you from skidding off the road.

Abingdon

As the oldest English-speaking settlement west of the Blue Ridge Mountains, Abingdon is the genteel nexus of southwest Virginia, a town that is aware and proud of its heritage. Abingdon centers on the historic streets of Main—split into East and West at Court Street—and Valley, more residential but just as charming. In places it seems as though every building along the rolling brick sidewalks is an antique, either original or restored to its former grandeur through the careful ministrations of its owners. Along with two of southwest Virginia's biggest cultural draws—the Barter Theatre and the Martha Washington Inn—Abingdon is the nearest town of substance to the Mount Rogers National Recreation Area, making this quiet burg of nearly 8,000 one of the area's most popular destinations.

History

Abingdon's first name, Wolf Hills, came during a visit by Daniel Boone in 1760, when a group of wolves attacked the dogs in his hunting party near where the town is today. The name stuck until 1774, when Joseph Black erected Black's Fort on this site to protect hundreds of local settlers from Cherokee raids. Abingdon proper, named for Martha Washington's home parish in Oxfordshire, England, was established two years later as the seat of Washington County.

The early 19th century saw Abingdon bloom into a focal point of southwest Virginia, handling most of the mail and traffic to the western frontier along the Wilderness Road. It escaped the damage of the Civil War until December 1864, when 10,000 Federal troops

THE SALTVILLE MASSACRE

Though not as obvious as men or munitions, salt played a major strategic role in the Civil War. It was used in medicine and gunpowder, and to preserve meat for army rations. Only two spots in the entire South produced significant amounts – one mine near Atlanta and one in Saltville, Virginia, the "Salt Capital of the Confederacy."

Saltville also saw one of the war's worst massacres. On October 4, 1864, about 3,600 Union troops, including 400 members of the U.S. Colored Cavalry, had been beaten back repeatedly as they tried to take the town from 2,800 ragtag Confederates under Capt. Champ Ferguson and Brig. Gen. Felix Robertson. By nightfall, hundreds of Federal wounded covered the ground after the rest had retreated.

The next morning, Confederate soldiers advanced across the field, shooting black soldiers as they lay helpless. It's uncertain exactly how many were killed this way, but accounts from both sides put the total at well over 100.

Union troops managed to occupy and level much of the town within a few months, but justice took time. Ferguson was eventually captured, tried, and hanged for murder in October 1865. Robertson not only escaped punishment but lived well into the 20th century. He died, the last surviving Confederate general, in 1928.

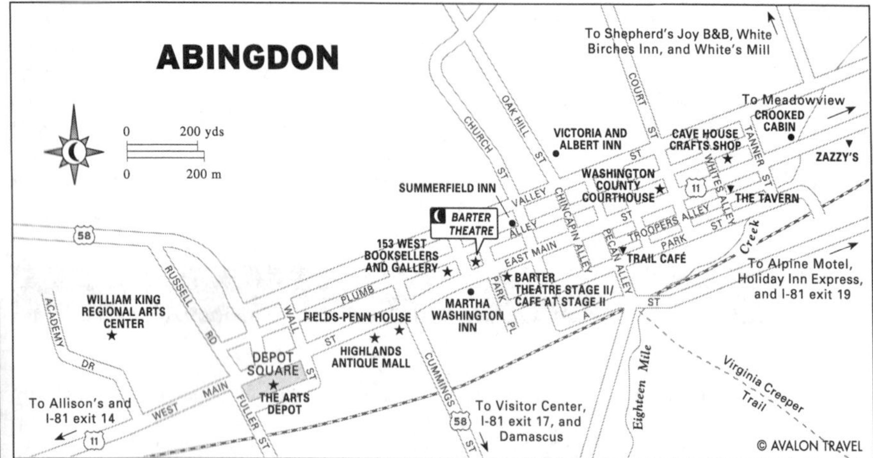

under Gen. George Stoneman burned several buildings, including the depot and the town jail, that were being used to store Confederate supplies. Over the years, other fires have claimed other historic structures, but many more remain standing.

SIGHTS

A good place to start your stroll down Main Street is **The Arts Depot** (276/628-9091, www.abingdonartsdepot.org, 11 A.M.–3 P.M. Thurs.–Sat., free) in Depot Square at West Main Street and Russell Road. The old Virginia & Tennessee Railroad freight station was abandoned for years before being rescued and claimed by Abingdon's visual, performing, and literary artists. You can watch artists at work, browse the sales galleries, or attend various workshops and lectures held throughout the year.

More exhibits and classes are held in the **William King Regional Art Center** (415 Academy Dr., 276/628-5005, www.williamkingmuseum.org, 10 A.M.–9 P.M. Tues., 10 A.M.–5 P.M. Wed.–Sat., 1–5 P.M. Sun., $5). A partner of the Virginia Museum of Fine Arts in Richmond, the center concentrates on the artistic heritage of Appalachia and hosts the works of national artists along the lines of Ansel Adams, Andrew Wyeth, and Winslow Homer.

One block away stands Abingdon's **Martha Washington Inn,** one of the town's outstanding landmarks (and a functioning inn). Across the street is Abingdon's other landmark, the **Barter Theatre.**

East Main Street starts to dip and rise as it reaches the old commercial and administrative center of town. Soon you'll pass the **Washington County Courthouse,** the fifth such building to stand at Main and Court Streets. This one was built in 1869 and boasts a World War I memorial stained-glass window designed by the Tiffany studio. In the "jockey lot" behind the courthouse, horse merchants used to gather on the first Saturday of each month while court was in session for a boisterous day of trading and gambling. (Women and children were encouraged to keep their distance.)

A short walk further brings you past **The Tavern,** Abingdon's oldest building and finest restaurant. It'll take a bit longer to get to **White's Mill** (12291 White's Mill Rd., 276/628-2960, www.whitesmill.org, 10 A.M.–5 P.M. Wed.–Sun., closed Jan.–Feb., free), southwest Virginia's only remaining water-powered gristmill, which sits a short drive or moderate bicycle ride into the countryside north of town. Built around 1840, it's painfully photogenic and redolent of history, with a great musty smell, creaking floorboards, and antique machinery filling four floors. It's still used to grind cornmeal, which is offered for sale across the street in White's Mill Mercantile.

ENTERTAINMENT AND RECREATION

Barter Theatre

In 1933, aspiring but frustrated Virginia actor Robert Porterfield opened a theater in this structure, built in 1832 as a church on West Main and College Streets, with the novel idea of bringing theater to the masses. Not only would hungry, out-of-work actors and playwrights be given a place to perform their works, but theatergoers short of the cash for a ticket could exchange produce for seats. Playwrights would be given a Virginia ham for the use of their works. The barter system caught on, and farmers and townspeople began exchanging "hams for Hamlet" along with, perhaps, cabbages for Coward and spinach for Shaw (a vegetarian). The first season's profits amounted to $4.35 in cash, two barrels of jelly, and a collective weight gain among the actors of more than 300 pounds.

Since declared the State Theater of Virginia, over the decades the Barter Theatre (127 W. Main St., 276/628-3991, www.bartertheatre.com) has hosted stars including Ernest Borgnine, Gregory Peck, and Kevin Spacey, making it one of the longest-running professional repertory theaters in the country. Major renovations in the mid-1990s resulted in a vastly improved—yet still intimate—theater. Productions, including many world premieres, range from musicals to farce and Shakespeare. Between productions, storytellers take the stage to entertain children. Visitors hail from around the world; the guests coming the longest distance receive a door prize every evening. Tickets usually run $25–40.

Outdoor Recreation

The western end of the **Virginia Creeper Trail** starts off Pecan Street just across the train tracks, near the huge Norfolk and Virginia locomotive, the last one to run these rails. **Highlands Ski & Outdoor Center** (302 Green Spring Rd., 276/628-1329, www.highlandsoutdoor.com) rents mountain bikes and stocks camping, hiking, and climbing gear for anyone eager to tackle Mt. Rogers; additional outfitters in Damascus are available to help too. Call for rates.

COURTESY OF BARTER THEATRE

Barter Theatre: the State Theater of Virginia

SHOPPING

Craftaholics shouldn't miss the **Cave House Crafts Shop** (276/628-7721, www.cavehousecraftshop.org), named for the cave beneath the store, from which, according to legend, the wolves that attacked Daniel Boone's dogs emerged. The historic home, built in 1858, formerly housed Barter Theatre actors, until in 1971 the Holston Mountain Arts and Crafts Cooperative moved in and began selling crafts of every description: quilts, musical instruments, clothing, baskets, pottery, and toys, to name a few. By 2010, the house closed for badly needed repairs and in the interim, the co-op has relocated to "The Jailhouse" (the former sheriff's office) at 214 Park Street.

Across from the Martha, **153 West Booksellers & Gallery** (153 W. Main St., 276/628-1232) exhibits fine handicrafts, especially pottery, alongside a peaceful bookstore.

EVENTS

As if it didn't already have enough going for it, Abingdon also hosts one of the top 100 tourist events in North America, known as the **Virginia Highlands Festival** (www.vahighlandsfestival.org). Officially a showcase for Appalachian musicians, artists, craftspeople, and writers, the festival—held for two weeks near the beginning of August—features one of the largest antiques markets in the southeast, wine tasting, garden workshops, and a hot-air balloon rally. For kids, there's storytelling, writing workshops, puppetry, and interactive theater.

Get down to music from rock to swing, funk to Celtic, in between sampling food from around the world and choosing your favorites from the exhibits of local and national artists. About 200,000 people pack the town during the festival, so make reservations as early as possible. Most events are free.

During the second week in September, the **Washington County Fair** (276/628-6222, www.washcofair.com) brings country music and the sounds of livestock to the fairground on U.S. 11 west of town. Carnival rides, tractor pulls, and the Miss Washington County pageant round out the fun.

And should you be in Abingdon in mid-January, check out a quirky event for a canine cause. For an annual fundraiser, a Bristol husky rescue league stages a **local Iditarod** along the Virginia Creeper Trail from Abingdon to Damascus, reenacting the 1925 dogsled run that brought badly needed diphtheria antitoxin serum 674 miles from Nenana to Nome, Alaska. In the years without enough snow to run a sled—which, thus far, has been every year—mushers hitch their dog teams to wheeled carts. The cheering bystanders and grinning huskies don't seem to mind.

ACCOMMODATIONS

$50-100

The classic 1960s-era **Alpine Motel** (822 E. Main St., 276/628-3178, $70–80) offers well-kept rooms with mountain views and cable TV. Rooms at the **Holiday Inn Express** (940 E Main St., 276/676-2829) are in the $80–110 range. Note that NASCAR races in nearby Bristol, Tennessee, tend to drive up room prices in Abingdon.

$100-150

Joyce Ferratt was born in the same Queen Anne country–style house in which she and her husband, Jack, now operate the **Shepherd's Joy Bed & Breakfast** (254 White's Mill Rd., 276/628-3273, www.shepherdsjoy.com, $135–185). The friendly couple runs a small sheep farm out back, complete with well-trained sheep dogs. The house is decorated with family heirlooms and a sheep motif.

$150-200

Next door to the Shepherd's Joy, the **White Birches Inn** (268 White's Mill Rd., 276/676-2140 or 800/247-2437, www.whitebirchesinn.com) features four rooms and a suite ($150–180) named after famous playwrights who traded words for food at the Barter Theatre. Just off the back porch, a small pond is stocked with koi and goldfish.

The **Victoria and Albert Inn** (224 Oak Hill St., 276/676-2797 or 800/475-5494, www.abingdon-virginia.com, $130–175) sits across from the town library. It was built in 1892 and features four rooms named for the colors of their walls. They also operate the nearby **Love House B&B,** an 1850 Colonial-style home with two rooms and two suites ($135–160) that feature gas-log fireplaces and jetted tubs.

A large front deck graces the **Summerfield Inn B&B** (101 Valley St. NW, 276/628-5905 or 800/668-5905, www.summerfieldinn.com, $160–190). The entire house is sunny and spacious, with four large rooms in the main Parsonage and three more modern ones in the newer Carriage House, featuring whirlpools. The bed-and-breakfast organizes special packages including tickets to the Barter Theatre or bike rentals and shuttle service on the Virginia Creeper Trail.

$200-250

Known locally as "the Martha," **Martha Washington Inn** (150 W. Main St., 276/628-3161 or 888/999-8078, www.marthawashingtoninn.com, $185–245) is a gargantuan structure that fills an entire block of West Main Street with true Colonial class. It began in 1832 as the home of Gen. Francis Preston, who built the original central brick structure for his family. In 1858, the building became the Martha Washington College, a high-class school for young women. During the Civil War, students served as nurses for soldiers wounded in skirmishes near Abingdon, and the Martha became a makeshift hospital while the Washington Mounted Rifles trained on the grounds outside.

By 1934, the place had become a true hotel, housing actors in town for productions at the Barter Theatre and such presidential luminaries as Harry Truman, Eleanor Roosevelt, Lady Bird Johnson, and Jimmy Carter. An $8 million renovation in 1984 transformed the Martha into a fully modern luxury inn while preserving much of the original architecture and antebellum appeal.

Antique treasures await around almost every corner. Notice the marble fireplaces, crystal chandeliers, and the beautiful paintings in the Grand Ballroom, formerly the school chapel. Other paintings on the walls of the entranceway are copies of ones in the White House, depicting Niagara Falls, Natural Bridge, Boston Harbor, West Point, and New York City as they looked in the 1830s. The full-service spa and saltwater pool are more modern additions.

Rooms and suites (up to $700) are filled with rich fabrics and antiques. Rates include daily continental breakfast, afternoon tea on weekends, and a nightcap of port in the library. Some suites have fireplaces and whirlpool tubs.

The original **Crooked Cabin** (303 E. Main St., 276/628-9583, www.crookedcabinprop.com) was built in 1780, making it one of Abingdon's oldest buildings. Today it's a cozy self-contained cottage appointed with antiques and quilts, featuring three bedrooms, a dining room, and a patio and garden out back. The same owners also rent out the Meadow Cottage on a two-acre meadow nearby, which can also sleep six people. A two-night stay (minimum) is $195–245.

Camping

The **Riverside Campground** (18496 North Fork River Rd., 276/628-5333) lies seven miles north of town on Route 19, then two miles east on Route 611. More than 200 tent and RV sites ($25–35) are open April–November, with facilities that include a convenience store, game room, swimming pool, and a sports field. (Tent river sites and bath house closed December–March.)

FOOD

Snacks and Cafés

Next to the Barter Theatre's Stage II is **The Barter Cafe** (110 W. Main St., 276/619-5462, lunch daily, dinner Wed.–Sun.). This arty little place is decorated with memorabilia from past productions and features dishes named after actors and producers for $6 or $7.

Wild Flour Bakery (24443 Lee Hwy., 276/676-4221, lunch and dinner Mon.–Sat.) serves excellent soups, salads, and breads made from scratch. For a dose of literature (and unorthodox spelling) with your morning coffee, try bookstore-beanery **Zazzy'z** (380 E. Main

St., 276/698-3333, breakfast and lunch daily). Breakfast sandwiches are on the morning menu and wraps, salads, and paninis round out the lunch menu for under $6.

Casual

Fuel up before tackling the Virginia Creeper Trail at the **Trail Café** (128 Pecan St. SE, 276/698-3159), conveniently located close to the trailhead. Along with caffeine and homemade trail mix, it serves full breakfasts and deli-style offerings for lunch Tuesday–Sunday. Friendly home-style cooking is the hallmark of **Alison's** (1220 W. Main St., 276/628-8002). Come for the baked-potato soup or fresh fish and steaks; linger on the enclosed patio, which is opened in the spring. Open for lunch ($6–12) and dinner ($10–20) Monday–Saturday.

Upscale

Abingdon's oldest building (and that's saying something) houses **The Tavern** (222 E. Main St., 276/628-1118, dinner Mon.–Sat.), serving excellent continental food with a German flair. It was built in 1779 as a tavern and overnight stop for stagecoach traffic on the Wilderness Road. President Andrew Jackson and Louis Phillippe, king of France, were among the many guests. The first post office west of the Blue Ridge operated out of the east wing, where the mail slot is still visible in the door.

Over the years the building passed through various incarnations as a private residence, general store, bank, barber shop, bakery, and, oh yes, tavern. During the Civil War, wounded soldiers from both armies were tended to on the 3rd floor—the charcoal numbers for each bed are still visible on the plaster walls. In 1984, it was restored using original materials and techniques, including hand-forged hinges, hand-planed lumber, and handmade bricks in the two-foot walls. It was reopened in 1994 by German native Max Harmann. Tilted tables, rustic fixtures, low ceilings, and dark worn wood evoke the informal air of an old tavern, but the food is excellent. German standbys like Wiener schnitzel and *kasseler rippchen* occupy the menu along with salmon and jambalaya, and the beer list is extensive. Entrées are around $18–36.

The **Martha Washington Inn** has two restaurants. Sisters (276/628-9151, dinner daily, brunch Sun.) is a classy affair serving Southern dishes; reservations are suggested for dinner and especially Sunday brunch. Martha's Market (276/619-5272, breakfast and lunch Mon.–Sat.) is a more casual lunch café where you can grab a sandwich or salad.

INFORMATION

The Abingdon Convention and Visitors Bureau runs the town **visitors center** (335 Cummings St., 276/676-2282 or 800/435-3440, www.abingdon.com, 9 A.M.–5 P.M. daily).

MEADOWVIEW

In Meadowview, 15 minutes east of Abingdon on I-81, readers of Barbara Kingsolver's book on local eating, *Animal, Vegetable, Miracle,* will find the same philosophy dished up in delicious style at the **Harvest Table Restaurant** (13180 Meadowview Square, 276/944-5142,

slices of heaven: down-home desserts at the Harvest Table Restaurant

www.meadowviewfarmersguild.com, all meals Wed.–Sat., lunch only Tues.). Kingsolver's husband, Dr. Steven Hopp, opened the restaurant in 2007, intent on supporting local farmers through comfort food from their freshest ingredients. If it's possible for a pot roast sandwich to be an epiphany, it is here, served with au jus on dill bread. Lunch entrées cost $7–9 and dinner $9–23, and—no surprise—the menu rotates seasonally. The desserts are plate-scraping good and there's live music every second Thursday at 8 P.M. You might recognize a poster of "The Vegetannual" on the wall behind the bar; it shows a fictitious plant that bears all the crops grown over the harvest season. It's the handiwork of artist Richard Houser, who moonlights in the kitchen—in fact, he's spent 30 years in the restaurant business—where he joins chef Philip Newton.

Next door, the **Meadowview Farmers' Guild General Store** is part of the same operation. You'll find signed copies of Kingsolver's novels tucked in the shelves between natural soaps, homemade preserves, hand-dyed yarns, and other handicrafts by more than 100 people, another effort to create a local economy.

Far Southwest

TAZEWELL AND VICINITY

From Marion, drive north on Route 16—a gorgeous corkscrew of a road—to the hub of Tazewell (TAZ-wul) County, incorporated in 1866 after a fistfight settled a dispute over where to establish the local government seat. If you stop by in mid-July, you might catch the **Main Street Moments Festival,** with carriage rides, street dancing, and an antiques show. Also in mid-July, the **Tazewell County Fiddlers' Convention** comes to the county fairgrounds in town.

Crab Orchard Museum and Pioneer Park

Nearly every phase of the state's history finds a voice on this 110-acre archaeological site (276/988-6755, www.craborchardmuseum.com, 9 A.M.–5 P.M. Tues.–Sat. Apr.–Oct., plus 1–5 P.M. Sun. Memorial Day–Labor Day, $4 adults, $2 children), three miles west of Tazewell on U.S. 19/460. Mastodon fossils and frontier furniture and weapons fill the central gallery building, while the nearby Pioneer Park consists of log homes dating to the 1800s. Park staff discuss crops typical of the pioneer era and explain the uses of various buildings, including a blacksmith shop, lardhouse, and dairy. Near a recently discovered Cherokee burial ground, descendants of

BURKE'S GARDEN

Discovered in 1748 by surveyor James Burke, this small bowl-shaped valley east of Tazewell is almost entirely circled by Garden Mountain. Even though it's only 10 miles long (hence its nickname of "God's thumbprint"), it's considered one of the prettiest corners of the state. At 3,100 feet, it does gets chilly up here, but that doesn't stop local farmers from taking advantage of some of Virginia's richest limestone soils.

To get there, take VA 61 east from Tazewell, then turn right onto Route 623 after about eight miles, which takes you up and over the edge of the mountain bowl. From here you can explore the valley at will. The town of Burke's Garden is little more than a store, a post office, and a church, where some headstones in the graveyard date to the 16th century. Leave the same way you came in, or else take Route 623 as it continues up over Garden Mountain to the south – a twisting dirt road that can get sketchy quickly – and passes through the Jefferson National Forest before connecting with VA 42.

local Cherokee groups have built indigenous houses typical of the 16th century. Farther on, a barn contains horse-drawn farm equipment and antique cars.

In late April, the park hosts the **Skirmish at Jeffersonville** Civil War reenactment.

Pocahontas Exhibition Coal Mine & Museum

Some time during the 19th century, a blacksmith discovered a small outcropping of coal poking out of a nearby hillside. Finding himself with more than enough to power his forge, he amiably allowed neighbors to take home wagonloads for their own homes, despite his wife's warning that there soon wouldn't be enough even for them. In 1882, the Pocahontas Coalfield opened with the arrival of the Norfolk & Western Railroad, giving birth to the town. Over the next 73 years, it would produce more than 44 million tons of coal, including the "famous" Pocahontas Number Three,

KING COAL

The legendary coal deposits of Appalachia began taking shape hundreds of millions of years before Loretta Lynn's daddy tried to eke a living out of the side of a mountain. Over the centuries, organic matter was compressed, dried, and hardened into the black substance known as bituminous or "soft" coal, the most common type still found in the Norton formation that underlies Kentucky, West Virginia, Tennessee, and Virginia.

Coal mining took off with the country's economic expansion after the Civil War, especially at the turn of the 20th century, when fresh-cut passages through the hills allowed railroads to transport the fuel to ships and factories for the first time. Demand for coal peaked in the 1920s, both to power vehicles and to make coke, a precursor to the steel used in gleaming new structures that rose from rapidly expanding cities. The industry declined after World War II as oil and natural gas began to take over the market, but in the 1970s – about the time women began to work in the mines – the worldwide oil crisis drove demand and coal prices back up. The most recent trend has been back down, because worldwide competition, the decline of the steel industry, and a decreasing demand for electric power have all cut demand for coal.

THE INDUSTRY IN ITS INFANCY

Conditions during the early heyday of mining in southwest Virginia (roughly 1910-1930) were brutal and dangerous. Labor was cheap, and mining was often the only work around. Miners had to supply their own tools, which included a soft hat, carbide lamp, and low-vein shovel, so-called because its shallow bend allowed a miner to work under a ceiling only a few feet high. A strong worker could swing a short, double-pointed miner's pick at 40 strokes per minute.

Mines were laid out in grids, with long "main streets," or "headings," crisscrossed by "cross streets," or "rooms," up to 20 feet wide and 60 feet high. The 50-foot square pillars of coal in between were mined (or "robbed") last, to hold the ceiling up as long as possible. In the meantime, hand-cut timbers supported the ceiling, at least most of the time.

To blast out the coal, a miner would drill holes by hand using a six-foot breast auger braced against his sternum. A tamping bar was used to place the explosive charge, filled with the miner's own black powder, and ignited with a small firecracker-type charge called a squid. The final steps were to light the fuse and run for cover.

The resulting broken pieces of coal were then loaded into carts pulled to the surface by ponies or mules, a method that persisted into the 1950s. Miners noted bitterly that the animals seemed more valuable than they did, and the beasts of burden were certainly harder to replace. The horses and mules were brought out of the mines on weekends to keep them from going blind in the darkness, though many still did.

Flammable methane, which seeps naturally from exposed coal, was the most immediate danger underground. The slightest spark could

chosen by the U.S. Navy for its ships for its clean burning.

Today, a short section of the mine is open to the public, providing a fascinating glimpse into the industry that underpinned the economy of this section of Appalachia for most of the past century. In the museum (276/945-2134, http://wvweb.com/www/pocahontas_mine, 10 A.M.–5 P.M. Mon.–Sat., noon–6 P.M. Sun., Apr.–Sept., $7 adults, $4.50 children 6–12), formerly the power house for the mine, visitors learn just how dangerous the industry was. Peruse accounts of the coal-dust explosion in March 1884 that killed everyone in the mine, filling the cemetery on the other side of town. Look for the mine-accident diagrams in the old shower room.

Tours into the mine begin with a video on modern mining. Then you enter the shaft, lined with rusted equipment and the famous 13-foot coal seam. The shaft remains a cool 52°F year-round, so bring a jacket or sweater.

ignite the invisible gas and set fire to coal dust or the coal itself, causing explosions of awesome power. One blast in the Pocahontas mine in March 1884 killed at least 114 people and hurled coal cars out the mouth of the tunnel with enough force to dash them to pieces against the far bank of a ravine. Such explosions were frighteningly common.

It was the unenviable job of the fire boss to track down methane pockets with the help of caged canaries, who succumbed to the odorless fumes more quickly than humans. The gas was then ignited before it gathered into dangerous concentrations.

Other dangers included falling rocks and "widowmakers" – petrified tree stumps that slid from the ceiling. The most insidious threat by far, though, was black lung or miner's lung (pneumoconiosis), a chronic pulmonary condition caused by breathing coal dust.

For all this, miners received an average of $2.15 per hour in 1952, which works out to less than $1 for a hand-blasted load of 2.5 tons of coal. Sometimes they were paid in company scrip good only in the overpriced company store, with the excuse that real U.S. currency was hard to come by in such rural areas.

MODERN MINING

Plastic hard hats and electric lamps have replaced leather and carbide, and self-rescue kits with 30-minute breathing filters are now carried by every miner. Six-foot roof bolts are epoxied into holes drilled in the ceiling, and blasting has become a less hazardous activity thanks to safety fuses, detonating cords, and electric blasting caps. Dust controls imposed by the government in 1969 have cut cases of miner's lung dramatically, and digital methane and oxygen monitors make sure the underground workspace is safe.

The days of digging by hand are also long gone. Massive machines called shearers, armed with twin cutting drums, can gouge out 50 tons of coal – enough to supply the electricity needs of one household for 15 years – every minute. Hydraulic roof supports called shields, each of which can support 500 to 1,000 tons, are electronically controlled to follow the shearer and set themselves in place. A typical shearer can work strips up to 1,000 feet wide and two miles long, eating through 30-40 inches at a time over a period of 9-12 months.

Such blazing efficiency has its consequences, though. With all the automated machinery in use, jobs in Appalachia are running out, and so is the coal. Virginia's coal production has been on the decline since 1990, according to the U.S. Geological Survey. By some estimates, recoverable coal resources across the country could be exhausted within less than 150 years. While mining has been the economic lifeblood in southwest Virginia for well over a century, its latest chapter of extraction – mountaintop removal and aggressive strip-mining – is altering the Old Dominion's topography and waterways. Though hailed as safer for miners, these methods risk leaving nothing of the mountains behind but the memories of a coal miner's daughter.

To get here, take Route 102 nine miles northwest from Bluefield on the West Virginia border. A walking tour of the historic town of Pocahontas will take you past the 1883 Old Company Store, the 1884 Silver Dollar Saloon and the 1895 Opera House. The mine is on the other side of the town of Pocahontas, over the bridge and railroad track.

BREAKS INTERSTATE PARK

What could break a mountain? In this case, it took the Russell Fork River and a few hundred eons to carve through Pine Mountain on the border between Virginia and Kentucky. The result, nicknamed the Grand Canyon of the South, is said to be the deepest gorge in the country east of the Mississippi. Numerous overlooks line the five-mile canyon along a broad curve in the river, so deep that you can't even hear the Class V white water 1,600 feet below the famous pyramidal Towers.

The Cherokee once hunted here, although by 1769 (only a few decades after English silversmith John Swift supposedly buried a fortune in silver near the Towers) they had relinquished rights to the area. Daniel Boone passed through twice on a reconnaissance mission through the canyon, carving his name in trees in both 1767 (coming) and 1771 (going). Shawnee raids during the late 18th and early 19th centuries only slowed the inevitable influx of settlers.

Overnight guests can choose from **campsites** ($12–20) or more permanent accommodations. The **Breaks Motor Lodge** has 83 rooms overlooking the canyon ($75), open year-round. Two-bedroom **cottages** and **log cabins** are available by the night or by the week and can hold up to four people. The glass-walled **Rhododendron Restaurant** (all meals daily Apr.–Dec.) boasts an impressive view from its deck.

It may be hard to spot from the top, but the Russell Fork River rages within the confines of the park. Class III to V+ rapids make the run one of the most challenging on the eastern seaboard; names like Triple Drop and El Horendo emphasize that this river is for experienced rafters and kayakers only. **Wahoo's Adventures** (828/262-5774 or 800/444-7238, www.wahoosadventures.com) in Boone, North Carolina, sends rafts and kayaks downstream—no first-timers on the Russell Fork, though!

Over 15 miles of **hiking trails** lead down to the river or out to overlooks. (Clinchfield Overlook has the best view of the gorge here, but is outshone by the Towers Overlook.) Twelve-acre Laurel Lake is stocked with bluegill and bass, and boats can be rented Memorial Day to Labor Day. Likewise, horse rentals and a pool are limited to the summer season.

A **visitors center** (276/865-4413 or 800/982-5122, www.breakspark.com, 9 A.M.–5 P.M. daily May–Oct., 8 A.M.–4 P.M. daily in Apr., parking $2 Memorial Day–Labor Day) includes a small museum on the history of the area, with a focus on coal mining.

BIG STONE GAP

Southwest Virginia's "other" gap has played second fiddle to Cumberland since the early days of the republic, when passages through the mountains were few and precious. The various names over the years of its central town reflect its strategic location. Initially called Three Forks—for tributaries of the Powell River that meet in or near the town center—the settlement became Mineral City from 1882 to 1888, thanks to major coalfields nearby. By the end of the late 19th century, three separate railroads served the gateway settlement, hauling out the black gold and leaving a rather drab mining town behind.

The town and its colorful characters have been lovingly immortalized and fictionalized in former local resident Adriana Trigiani's best-selling trilogy: *Big Stone Gap, Big Cherry Holler,* and *Milk Glass Moon.* The first of these books is in production to become a major motion picture.

Sights and Entertainment

Big Stone Gap's favorite son, John Fox Jr., made this corner of Appalachia famous in the 19th century with his short stories and novels, most notably in *The Trail of the Lonesome Pine.* The bare-knuckled romance between the Virginia mountain girl and the eastern mining engineer has metamorphosed into the Official State Outdoor Drama of Virginia, presented at the **June Tolliver Playhouse** (518 Clinton Ave. near E. 4th St., 276/523-1235 or 800/362-0149, www.trailofthelonesomepine.org), named for its real-life heroine. A rollicking mix of humor and heartbreak, folk music and fantasy, the melodrama unfolds Thursday–Saturday at 8 P.M. late June–late August for $15 adults, $8 children.

The heroic mountain girl is also memorialized where she once lived at the 1896 **June Tolliver House** (Jerome St. at Clinton St., 276/523-4707, 10 A.M.–5 P.M. Tues.–Sat., 2–5 P.M. Sun., Mar.–mid-Dec.), with free tours throughout the day.

The author is immortalized in the **John Fox, Jr. Museum** (Shawnee Ave. btwn. E. 2nd St. and E. 3rd St., 276/523-2747, 2–5 P.M. Thurs.–Sat. Memorial Day–Labor Day, $3 adults, $1 children 6–12), built in 1888. Ask the employees about Fox's wife, the opera star Fritzi Scheff (aka Mademoiselle Modiste), who, according to one account, "dazzled the world with jewels, gowns, pompadour, wasp waist, and sprightly charm." She married Fox less than 24 hours after divorcing her previous husband, a baron, but didn't last long in this decidedly non-cosmopolitan neck of the woods.

One of southwest Virginia's best historical collections is found, fittingly, at the **Southwest Virginia Museum Historical State Park** (10 W. 1st St., 276/523-1322, www.swvamuseum.org, 10 A.M.–4 P.M. Tues.–Thurs., 9 A.M.–4 P.M. Fri., 10 A.M.–5 P.M. Sat., 1–5 P.M. Sun., extended hours in summer, $3 adults, $2 children). This former mansion of a state attorney general houses well-presented exhibits tracing the boom-and-bust cycles of the area's coal and iron industries, along with the household utensils, clothes, and furniture of everyday citizens.

Finally, the **Harry W. Meador Jr. Coal Museum** (Shawnee Ave. and E. 3rd St., 276/523-9209, 10 A.M.–5 P.M. Wed.–Sat., 1–5 P.M. Sun., free) concentrates on Big Stone Gap's bituminous legacy. You'll know the place by the hulking mine equipment rusting out front, courtesy of the Westmoreland Coal Company, which also runs the museum.

Accommodations and Food

Both in-town lodging options sit along U.S. 23 on the way into the center of town. The **Country Inn Motel & RV Park** (627 Gilley Ave., 276/523-0374) offers 42 rooms for around $50. The **Comfort Inn** (1928B Wildcat Rd., 276/523-5911) has rooms for $90, as well as the **Huddle House** restaurant, open 24 hours daily and specializing in breakfast.

Fast food has taken over Big Stone Gap, with the usual plastic-roofed representatives scattered about. **Little Mexico** (117 Powell Valley Square, 276/523-3992) and the **Red Flower Chinese Restaurant** (323 Wood Ave. E., 276/523-2498) offer adequate Mexican and Chinese food, respectively, for lunch and dinner daily.

Information

Contact the Big Stone Gap town offices (505 E. 5th St. S., 276/523-0115, www.bigstonegap.org) for more information.

NATURAL TUNNEL STATE PARK

Another monument to geological persistence has been carved by modest little Stock Creek, whose carbonic acid gradually dissolved an 850-foot-long tunnel through limestone bedrock. The southern entrance opens off the amphitheater, a semicircular gallery with sheer walls that drop 150 feet to creek level. The gaping hole is large enough for the creek and a pair of train tracks, installed in the 19th century to take advantage of the natural passageway to and from the coalfields.

Several short trails, open until dusk, lead to the bottom and around the rim. Be careful near the edge at Lover's Leap, where an ancient myth holds that a Native American man and his love, prohibited from marrying by their warring tribes, leapt to their deaths. A chairlift runs into the gorge for $3 per person (daily in summer and weekends in spring and fall). About 10 coal trains per day still chug through the tunnel, so a guided tour is the only way to explore beyond the entrance. Cave tours and canoe trips on the Clinch River are offered on weekends and other dates by special request; both must be prescheduled. Contact the park's **Cove Ridge Interpretive Center** (276/940-1643) for more information.

The park is off Route 871, off U.S. 23 between Clinchport and Duffield. The **visitors center** (276/940-2674, www.dcr.virginia.gov/state_parks/nat.shtml, 10 A.M.–5 P.M. Mon.–Fri., 10 A.M.–6 P.M. Sat.–Sun. Memorial Day–Labor Day; 10 A.M.–4 P.M. Sat.–Sun. Apr.–May and Sept.–Oct., parking $2–3) houses a snack bar, gift shop, and a small museum on the geology and history of the immediate area. Campgrounds on the hilltop by the entrance cost $16–22 (reservations via 800/933-7275 or www.reserveamerica.com are required) and include use of the pool, which is open Memorial Day–Labor Day. The campground is open March–November.

CARTER FAMILY FOLD

One of the taproots of American music reaches all the way back to Maces Spring in southwest Virginia. It's well worth a side trip to visit the music center, especially if you're already in the vicinity of Natural Tunnel State Park.

Country Music's Legendary Carter Family

It all began with carpenter Alvin Pleasant "A. P." Carter, who grew up here and operated a grocery store on Route 614. His true passion, though, was collecting and playing the pure, haunting mountain music that recorded the loves, losses, and everyday events of life in rural Appalachia.

In 1927, Ralph Peer, a talent scout from RCA Victor Records, discovered A. P. playing in a trio with his wife, Sara, and sister-in-law Maybelle.

© KATIE GITHENS

As the sign says, the Carter Family Fold hosts old-time country music every Saturday at 7:30 P.M.

© KATIE GITHENS

© KATIE GITHENS

A collection of Carter Family memorabilia is on display in a renovated building that used to be A. P. Carter's grocery store.

They soon recorded what were known as the Bristol Sessions, today considered a watershed in commercial country music. Between 1927 and 1942, the Carter Family recorded more than 300 songs, including classics such as "Bury Me Under the Weeping Willow," "I'm Thinking Tonight of Blue Eyes," and "Keep on the Sunny Side," which is inscribed on A. P.'s tombstone in the cemetery just down the road from his old store.

In addition to the songs the family wrote, A. P. also collected songs on countless forays into the hills, where he'd obsessively scribble down lyrics and memorize tunes with the help of Sara and their daughter, Janette. This priceless form of musical anthropology introduced dozens of timeless tunes, including "Will the Circle Be Unbroken?", to the country and the world.

The original Carter Family broke up in 1943 after A. P. and Sara's marriage failed (various other combinations of Carters played together until the 1960s), but their effect on American music still echoes across the country, bluegrass, and folk categories. In 1993, their faces appeared on U.S. postage stamps along with Patsy Cline, Hank Williams, and other country music luminaries. That same year, Rounder Records began to re-release the complete Carter Family Victor recordings, a nine-CD set that includes almost 150 songs recorded 1927–1934.

A. P.'s grocery store fell into disrepair, serving briefly as a tobacco warehouse, before Janette cleaned it up and began to hold regular concerts there in an effort to preserve the family legacy. Soon the crowds drawn to the Saturday-night shows were packing the place to the roof. So with the help of friends and relatives (including Johnny Cash, who married Maybelle's daughter, June; he gave his last performance here), the Carter Family Fold was erected in 1976 and has been going strong ever since.

THE CROOKED ROAD

The Carter Family Fold, the Floyd Country Store, and the Rex Theater in Galax are all stops on The Crooked Road (www.thecrookedroad.org), a much welcomed tourism initiative to get word out about southwest Virginia's old-time musical legacy. As factories continue to close throughout the region, the value of this unique inheritance is becoming increasingly apparent and important.

"Virginia's Music Heritage Trail" winds for more than 250 miles, steering you to music jams and shows that are sometimes in unexpected places – say, a Dairy Queen or a grocery store on the Virginia-North Carolina border. That's because the Crooked Road strings together music that's been playing for years; now it's just inviting visitors to come listen.

The trail has five more major venues, including the **Blue Ridge Institute & Museum** (540/365-4416, www.blueridgeinstitute.org) at Ferrum College, the **Blue Ridge Music Center** (276/236-5309, www.blueridgemusiccenter.net) at mile 213 on the Blue Ridge Parkway, and the **Ralph Stanley Museum and Traditional Mountain Music Center** (276/926-5591, www.ralphstanleymuseum.com) in Clintwood. You'll recognize the distinctive voice of Ralph Stanley from the acclaimed soundtrack of the 2000 film *O Brother, Where Art Thou?*, which kicked off a popular renaissance for bluegrass.

Look for the banjo-emblazoned signs on the side of the road and wayside exhibits with FM radio stations you can check out to learn more while behind the wheel.

Visiting the Carter Family Fold

Shows begin every Saturday at 7:30 P.M. ($7 adults, $1 children 6–12) and present a wide range of traditional acoustic mountain music, including gospel and bluegrass. Janette passed on in 2006, but her daughter Rita Forrester now oversees the music center. Up to 900 people can squeeze into the arena (dirt-floored until 2004), although 200–400 is more typical. On summer evenings, the sides and back are opened to the night air, cooling down the cloggers and buck dancers who gyrate on the small concrete dance floor. A concession stand sells CDs, T-shirts, drinks, and snacks, but no alcohol—it's strictly prohibited, as are swearing and misbehaving.

A. P.'s old store is now the newly refurbished **Carter Family Museum,** open 6 P.M. to showtime every Saturday for a $5 donation. Alongside A. P.'s work clothes and tools you'll find Janette's first autoharp, bought at age 13 with her earnings from performing with the family ($0.25 per show); original 78 rpm records; photographs; and show clothes, including those worn by Johnny Cash and June Carter when they performed for President Nixon in 1970. The original cabin that is A. P.'s birthplace is also on-site, carefully moved from its inaccessible location nearby and restored board by board.

Every August, even more music lovers congregate in Maces Spring for the **Carter Family Memorial Festival,** held to commemorate the family's first recording session. Banjos, fiddles, guitars, and bass fill the Fold 6–11:30 P.M. Friday and 3–11:30 P.M. Saturday, while local artisans set up booths outside. National acts bring slightly higher prices ($10–20 pp per day).

Contact the Carter Family Fold (276/386-6054 or 276/645-0035, www.carterfamilyfold.org) for show lineups and other questions. To find the Fold, head toward the town of Hiltons on Route 58/421 from Weber City (east) or Bristol (west). In Hiltons, turn onto Route 709 and then immediately left onto Route 615, also known as the A. P. Carter Highway. Maces Spring is three miles farther, and you can't miss the Fold—on Saturdays, just look for the hundreds of cars lining the road.

CUMBERLAND GAP NATIONAL HISTORICAL PARK

One of frontier America's most famous landmarks is more accurately an absence of land: a break in the long Appalachian chain that allowed migrating deer and buffalo, Native Americans, and pioneers to pass through into the Ohio River Basin. It was discovered by European settlers in the mid-18th century to be the easiest way to "Kentuckee," easing crowding east of the mountains. Named after the Duke of Cumberland, son of King George II, the pass was called the Warrior's Path by the Cherokee raiding parties that came from as far as North Carolina to attack western tribes.

Daniel Boone made the pass famous, and vice versa. In 1796, the budding frontiersman set his legend on track when he and 30 "axemen" hacked out the Wilderness Road through the gap. Also known as Boone's Trace, the historic highway was barely a rutted track in spots as it wound from Kingsport, Tennessee, to Boonesborough, Kentucky. Still, between 1775 and 1810, more than 200,000 settlers crossed through "the first doorway to the West" as the new nation spread its wings.

Today this rugged corner of the Cumberland Mountains is preserved in the one of the nation's largest historical parks (20,271 acres). It's also one of the least visited parks, so any trip to the corner of Kentucky, Tennessee, and Virginia is automatically a step away from crowds as well as into the past.

Visiting the Gap

The visitors center is actually over the border, on U.S. 25E just south of Middlesboro, Kentucky (606/248-2817, www.nps.gov/cuga, 8 A.M.–5 P.M. daily, free), and contains exhibits and films on the history and geology of the park. Craftspeople demonstrate their skills, particularly on weekends. Almost 70 miles of trails wind through hemlock, pine, and oak forests (lusher here than farther north because scouring glaciers didn't make it this far south). Views from the 21-mile Ridge Trail and the Pinnacle Overlook (2,440 feet) can be spectacular if the weather cooperates; it's possible to see into Virginia, Kentucky, and Tennessee on a clear day, and even as far as the Great Smoky Mountains in North Carolina. The overlook is also accessible via a curvy four-mile road.

Other spots on the itinerary include **Hensley Settlement** on top of Brush Mountain, a self-sufficient homestead dating to the turn of the 20th century. Seasonal half-day tours (reservations recommended) are $10 adults, $5 children. Countless caves creep underground; two-hour tours of **Gap Cave** cost $8 adults, $4 children. On the Virginia side, 160 **campsites** with restrooms and hot showers are $12 (41 have hookups for $17). There's no cost for backcountry camping permits, available from the visitors center.

A $265 million pair of tunnels completed in 1996 rerouted U.S. 25 to the south of the original mountain pass, which has been restored to its unpaved "Boone-era" condition.

BACKGROUND

The Land

Heaven and Earth never agreed to frame a better place for man's habitation. Here are mountains, hills, plaines, valleyes, rivers, and brookes, all running into a faire Bay, compassed but for the mouth, with fruitful and delightsome land.

– Captain John Smith, 1607

GEOLOGY

During the Paleozoic Era (620–230 million years ago), all of Virginia west of the Blue Ridge and part of the Piedmont lay under a great inland sea. Geologic upheavals thrust beds of sediment to mountainous heights. Today we can see evidence of those upheavals in marine fossils embedded in limestone hillsides. The Appalachian Mountains began to rise in the Mesozoic Era (230–70 million years ago), only to be worn down by wind and water into their present rounded contours. Debris washed down from the eastern slopes created the deltas and floodplains of ocean-bound rivers, leaving rich farmland all the way to the coast.

© KATIE GITHENS

CLIMATE

It's hard to decide whether summer's gentle prelude or its fiery swan song is more beautiful, but weather-wise, spring and fall are definitely Virginia's more enjoyable seasons. On average the state manages to escape both the frigid northern winters and the incapacitating summer swelter of the Deep South, although high humidity levels can make temperatures in both seasons feel more extreme.

The warm weather of **spring** brings forth buds and blossoms throughout the mountains and Piedmont, although temperatures can still dip into the 30s at night (or even 20s in the mountains). Rivers swollen with melting snow surge past electric groves of blooming bluebells, marigolds, violets, and daffodils. According to local lore, spring climbs the Blue Ridge 100 feet a day, pushing skyward the green line of new leaves dotted with the flowers of dogwoods, pink azaleas, and purple and white rhododendrons. Migrating birds leave their winter nesting grounds along the coast, while others arrive in breeding plumage ready to build a nest and start a family.

Summer brings high temperatures and humidity. Averages of 80°F seem more like 100°F when there's enough water in the air to drink through a straw. Suddenly the coast is a lot more attractive than the muggy countryside, even with the sudden thunderstorms that condense in the afternoons. The mountains are also cooler than the lowlands in summer; nights can be downright nippy, making jackets and sleeping bags necessary for overnighters. Wildflowers bloom in succession the entire season, as newborn fawns and chicks take their first wobbly steps.

Virginia's famous **fall** colors peak near the middle of October with a vivid palette of yellow, gold, orange, and red, courtesy of maples, oaks, and hickories. Bird migrations also peak during this season, sending hawks, shorebirds, and songbirds for the warmer climates of the southern United States, the Caribbean, and Latin America. Harvest time brings roadside produce stands and huge rolls of hay scattered throughout farmland in the Shenandoah Valley and central Virginia. Balmy Indian summer weather gradually gives way to nighttime temperatures in the 40s by October.

© KATIE GITHENS

In June, Route 58 is blazing with rhododendrons; in December, it's dripping with icicles.

In **winter,** the shore is bleak but still beautiful, as boardwalks stand empty and the wind shoves whitecaps across the gray water. Snowfall in the Piedmont quickly turns into slush, but it can still block unplowed back roads for days. Temperatures in both regions average near 30°F, rarely dipping into the teens for long. You can experience clear, cold air and bare-branch views from the mountains, as long as the Skyline Drive and Blue Ridge Parkway aren't closed by snow. Waterfalls and seeps (small springs) turn into garlands of ice, and the occasional ice storm or freezing fog can coat everything in a glittering film of frost.

LANDSCAPE

Virginia stretches from the Appalachian Mountains to the Atlantic Ocean, encompassing the three distinct physical regions of the mid-Atlantic. The state's 40,767 square miles start in rugged **mountains** in the west, then spread across a flat, fertile **central region** known as the Piedmont. A defined drop-off, about even with Richmond, marks the beginning of the **coastal plain** or Tidewater, drained by rivers flowing into Chesapeake Bay. Across the bay the southernmost splinter of the peninsula that protects the Chesapeake Bay—Virginia's Eastern Shore—faces the open Atlantic.

More than anything, Virginia's landscape is defined by water. Natural waterways attracted the first colonizers to sheltered harbors and lured explorers upriver into the heart of the country. Four major rivers—the Potomac, York, Rappahannock, and James—reach as far as the West Virginia border. Rich soil provided the early colonists with productive farmland. Serpentine rivers carried flatboats laden with cotton and tobacco downriver on their first step to the warehouses of Europe, sometimes bypassing falls and rapids by means of ingenious canals. And always the dramatic backdrop of the mountains stood to the west.

Virginia's hills are part of the **Appalachian chain** that separates the watersheds of the Atlantic Ocean and the Gulf of Mexico. Once as tall and jagged as the Rockies, the much older Appalachians have mellowed with age into a soothing skyline. Although the mountains appear gentle, looks can be deceiving: Frozen snowdrifts can still trap your four-wheel-drive vehicle if you're not careful, and ice storms bring down large trees almost every year. The entire chain runs from Alabama to Canada, but "Appalachia" per se, as much a cultural term as a geologic one, only reaches as far north as south-central New York. In Virginia, narrow crests and steep slopes ease into smoother mountaintops in the south part of the range. Weathered granite outcroppings and mostly bare "parks" top many peaks, while slightly acidic groundwater has eroded an underlying stratum of limestone into a myriad of caves, sinkholes, pillars, and natural bridges.

The **Blue Ridge Mountains,** named for the natural haze that tints them, soar from nearly flat farmland to form the easternmost fringe of Virginia's slice of the Appalachians. West of the Blue Ridge, the **Allegheny Mountains** undulate into West Virginia like waves of stone, separated by rivers flowing through long, narrow valleys. Almost all of Virginia's southwestern tip is above 1,600 feet in elevation, ranging as high as 3,000 feet on the Cumberland and Kanawha plateaus that extend into Kentucky.

Between the Blue Ridge and the Alleghenies stretches the **Shenandoah River,** sharing its name with a bucolic valley and a way of life. Stretching from Staunton, Virginia, to Harpers Ferry, West Virginia, the fruitful river basin produces apples, chickens, corn, and cattle in such profusion that it was fought over nearly to death during the Civil War. Down the middle runs thin Massanutten Mountain, splitting the North and South Forks of the Shenandoah River for 50 miles before they join at Front Royal and flow north to the Potomac. Shallow and placid for most of its length, the Shenandoah River draws mineral nutrients from limestone springs to provide sustenance for minnows, crayfish, and their larger aquatic predators.

Most of Virginia's other major **rivers** also have their headwaters in or beyond the Blue Ridge, including the York, James, and Rappahannock. The New River to the southwest is actually the oldest in North America, and the second most ancient in the world—only the Nile is older. It began flowing before the Appalachians were formed, explaining why it's one of the few major rivers in North America that flows from south to north, across the grain of the mountains.

Virginia's midsection runs from the base of the Blue Ridge east across low, rolling hills

BEST VIRGINIA TOWN NAMES

Bumpass (BUM-puss)
Busthead
Bustleboro
Hurt
Lively
Modest Town
Mollusk
Nuttsville
Possum Trot
Scuffleburg
Short Pump
Simplicity
Village

The Potomac River is lazy in some spots and torrential in others.

rising no higher than 1,000 feet. It's also called the Piedmont, which translates roughly as "foot of the mountain." It is separated from the coastal plain by the **fall line,** a topographic stripe where the central plain's harder metamorphic rock crumbles into the sandier soils of the coast. Many of the state's rivers, winding slowly across the flat countryside, turn into white water over the edge of the fall line, which roughly parallels I-95 as it runs from Alexandria to Petersburg.

Ranging from 50 miles wide in the north to almost 200 miles wide at the North Carolina border, Virginia's central plain has endured more human impact over the years than other parts of the state. Centuries of tree-clearing, farming, city-building, and suburb-spreading have turned much of the gently forested slopes into pastures, ponds, and pavement. Although transformed, the Piedmont still retains a patrician grace most evident in the horse country near Charlottesville and Lexington, where miles of whitewashed fences border green meadows.

FLORA AND FAUNA

Reaching into two geographic provinces, Virginia hosts both northern and southern species of flora and fauna at the extremes of their natural ranges. Visitors can see two seasons in a day simply by driving from the base of the Blue Ridge, where spring buds are blooming, to the top, where bare trees of winter remain. It's also possible to see northern tree species such as fir and spruce in the mountains, then head east and find alligators in cypress swamps and shells on sandy beaches, all in a weekend.

The Mountains

Temperate forests include more than two dozen tree species from deep green eastern hemlocks to fragrant-budded tulip trees, whose trunks have measured more than 25 feet in diameter. Indians fashioned dugout canoes from these giants, and settlers boiled and ate the acorns of white oaks before cutting down the trees for their fine wood. Flowering dogwoods erupt in the spring along with azaleas and purple flame, or rose rhododendrons (called laurels locally).

Blossoming trees herald the arrival of spring.

The pink and white flowers of trilliums blanket the northeast foothills. Green and yellow violets, Dutchman's-breeches, lady's slippers, skunk cabbage, and 85 species of ferns all sprout in the undergrowth at various times.

Common animals in the mountains include rabbits, foxes, chipmunks, skunks, and raccoons. Many of Virginia's million or so white-tailed deer browse roadside grasses in Shenandoah National Park, while bobcats and coyotes are rarely seen. Black bears are also present, but shy. Classified as omnivores, they subsist mostly on nuts, berries, and the tender parts of trees.

Among the birdlife, the turkey vultures (buzzards) are the most impressive to see, riding updrafts on their six-foot wings. Their red heads are a good field mark. Black vultures are smaller and less common. The raven, another big black bird, alternates flapping with gliding, and croaks in one of a dozen particular ways. Wild turkeys, the largest birds in the hills, really do look like those Thanksgiving decorations, and if you do enough hiking you'll probably lose a few heartbeats to the sudden launch of ruffed grouse. Red-tailed hawks can spot rodents and small reptiles from hundreds of feet in the air before diving for a meal.

The southwestern tip of Virginia is as impressive, biologically speaking, as any part of the state. It's home to dozens of rare and endangered mussels and fish, one of the highest number of imperiled species in the country outside of Hawaii.

Central Virginia

Oaks prevail among the trees that are left, although mostly in second- and third-stage stands of chestnut, red, and white varieties. Maples, cypress, and black gum line the meandering rivers, while south of the James, coniferous forests of pine begin to replace deciduous species. Springtime brings the vibrant pink and magenta blooms of redbud and the creamy white petals of flowering dogwoods. Morning glories and bluebells display two of the more gaudy blossoms among the flowers.

Those animals that have learned to coexist with people are abundant, including deer,

Turkey vultures are a common sight winging along mountain ridges.

raccoons, opossums, and squirrels, along with the occasional quail and wild turkey in the underbrush. Once pushed into the mountains by settlers, the ever-adaptable coyote has gradually spread back into possibly every county in the state by now. Even though hundreds are killed by hunters and state animal-control officers ever year, some 30,000 coyotes are estimated to live in the Old Dominion today.

Edge communities (where two ecosystems meet, such as pastures and forests) are good places to spot wildlife, especially birds. Look for indigo buntings in hedgerows, and distinctive red-winged blackbirds in marshy land near water. Artificial lakes and riverbanks are prime habitat for muskrats, beavers, and kingfishers. By night your flashlight might catch the reflecting eyes of a Virginia opossum or bobcat. Reptiles include snapping and eastern box turtles and a nocturnal cacophony of bullfrogs, gray tree frogs, and spring peepers. The northern water snake is most common, bearing a superficial resemblance to the poisonous (but nonswimming) copperhead.

The big, fluffy-tailed Delmarva Peninsula fox squirrel is an endangered species. There are about 200 of them living in Chincoteague National Wildlife Refuge.

The Coast

Once past the fall line, the coastal plain begins its gentle descent to sea level. Virginia's 3,300 miles of shoreline display a vast network of marshes, creeks, and rivers that widen into estuaries drained and filled by the ocean tides. Dry hardwood groves likewise transform into **flooded forests** of bald cypress and black gum. Unlike their upland relatives, many of these wetter, less accessible forests have escaped the logger's ax, allowing their rich soils to support largely unaltered ecosystems.

As many as 35 species of warblers flit through the Spanish moss in the Great Dismal Swamp, which continues south across the state line into North Carolina. Unusual species like green anole—a lizard that looks like a salamander—and Creole pearly eye butterflies inhabit the otherworldly recesses of Virginia's coastal **swamps.** Tannin, a natural acid, stains the waters brown and keeps bacteria from growing, which led early sea captains to prefer these waters for drinking on long journeys.

Impenetrable, boggy tangles of shrubs and trees called *pocosins* are rare and little-studied.

Mixing mineral salts from the ocean and fertile soil washed downriver from central Virginia, **salt marshes** are some of the richest habitats in the state—indeed, in all of North America. Each acre can generate up to twice as much organic material as an acre of farmland, attracting migratory birds by the millions every spring and fall. Swans, geese, and ducks all float in the brackish waters at different times of year. Keep an eye out for the black-tipped blue bill of the redhead, a diving duck, and listen for the supernatural hoot of barred owls at night.

The coastal plain flows into the Chesapeake Bay, one of the largest estuaries in the world, fed by 100,000 streams and rivers in Maryland and Virginia. With an average depth of only 20 feet, the Chesapeake Bay meets the Atlantic at the superb natural harbor of Hampton Roads. Here, fresh and saltwater mix into a rich blend that supports a staggering diversity of life. The bay's name comes from the Algonquian word Chesepioc (Great Shellfish Bay), and bushels of oysters and crabs are still yanked up to the sunlight by the unique breed of surviving Chesapeake watermen (or waterpeople, nowadays) as they have been for generations.

Wading birds such as ibis, egrets, and great blue herons stalk the shoreline in search of smaller creatures. Birds of prey such as ospreys soar overhead in renewed numbers. Bald eagles have staged a heartening comeback along the coast from the dark days of DDT, from only 33 nests in the whole state in 1977 to more than 610 pairs in 2009. Now the huge, white-headed national bird competes with people for prime waterfront property along the James, Rappahannock, and Potomac Rivers, which it patrols for fish, waterfowl, and small mammals.

At the ocean's edge stretch long, shallow lagoons and salt flats just a shell's throw from open water. Change is the only constant along the beaches, especially in the case of the **barrier islands** that line the seaward side of the Eastern Shore. These narrow strips of sand are thought to shelter a greater variety of birds than any other ecosystem in the country. Here the whistle of the endangered piping plover echoes over beaches that are simultaneously eaten away and built up by the constant pounding waves.

Tall marsh grasses provide enough protection against erosion for stumpy trees to gain a foothold in the sand. Muskrats ply tidal pools for shellfish as the rare least tern lays its eggs in shallow pits in the dunes. Thanks to the warming effect of the Gulf Stream, you'll find many southerly plant and animal species at the northern extreme of their range along the Virginia coast, including live oak, sea oats, sawgrass from the Everglades, and the chicken turtle, with a neck longer than its shell.

Environmental Issues

The **Virginia Department of Conservation and Recreation** (www.dcr.state.va.us) began the comprehensive **Virginia Natural Heritage Program** (www.dcr.state.va.us/dnh) in 1989 with a goal of identifying, protecting, and managing Virginia's wide range of ecosystems. In less than a decade, scientists, resource managers, landscape architects, and computer jockeys worked together to identify more than 1,800 conservation sites containing rare species or communities—making the statewide program the most comprehensive of its kind in the United States. It was recognized by The Nature Conservancy in 1994 as one of the most outstanding natural heritage programs in the Western Hemisphere.

SAVE THE BAY

One of Virginia's main environmental challenges is keeping the Chesapeake healthy. Seventeen million people inhabit the bay and its watersheds, with a dramatic effect on this incredibly complex ecosystem—or rather, collection of ecosystems. The bay is doing better than it was 10 or

15 years ago, thanks to strict fishing limits and restrictions on the flow of industrial pollutants and nutrient-laden farmland runoff, but there's still plenty of work to be done.

Annual algal "blooms" thrive on the nitrogen, phosphorus, and other chemicals introduced into the bay by polluting industries, car exhaust, and agricultural and residential runoff. The tiny plants then cloud the water, inhibiting the growth of underwater grasses that shelter crabs and fish. Algae also decompose through a process that eats up the oxygen in the water, creating "dead zones" incapable of supporting life.

One proposed solution to restore the bay to its former glory is to bring **oyster** populations back to their ancient levels. A century ago, oyster shell banks were large enough to be a navigation hazard, and together the oyster population could filter the entire volume of water in the bay in 3–4 days. Only 1 percent of that population is left now, thanks to overfishing and disease, meaning it takes a year to filter the same water. Scientists predict that restoring even 10 percent of the original oyster populations would go a long way toward restoring the ecosystem.

Virginia and Maryland are developing disease-resistant oyster strains, and dumping millions of bushels of shells on old reef spots every year in the hope of reseeding faded breeding grounds. A plan to distribute one million Asian oysters—which grow larger and faster and are more resistant to disease than the native types—had been under way, but stopped short due to fears the foreign bivalves could become an invasive species. In the end it might take a nonfishing subsidy to equal the success achieved with the rockfish population, which was brought back from the edge of disaster through a cooperative effort among Maryland, Virginia, and Delaware agencies.

In the meantime, annual wade-ins are held each summer to measure the Chesapeake's progress, judging water clarity with the "Sneaker Index" (how far you can wade before your sneakers disappear) as a rough yardstick for water quality. The 25.5-inch wade-in of 2009 was better than the 8 inches of 1988, but a far cry from the 60 inches of the 1960s. In 2009, President Obama issued an executive order giving the EPA more teeth for enforcing Virginia and Maryland targets for reducing nitrogen and phosphorous levels, two key pollutants, but there's a long way to go before these waters again teem with grasses and blue crabs.

CONSERVATION ORGANIZATIONS

Alliance for the Chesapeake Bay
804/775-0951
www.acb-online.org

Chesapeake Bay Foundation
Virginia State Office: Capitol Place
1108 E. Main St., Ste. 1600
Richmond, VA 23219
804/780-1392
www.cbf.org

Civil War Preservation Trust
1156 15th St. NW, Ste. 900
Washington, D.C. 20005
202/367-1861
www.civilwar.org

Friends of the Shenandoah River
1460 University Dr./Gregory Hall
Winchester, VA 22601
540/665-1286
www.fosr.org

The Nature Conservancy – Virginia Chapter
490 Westfield Rd.
Charlottesville, VA 22901
434/295-6106
www.nature.org/virginia

Sierra Club – Virginia Chapter
422 E. Franklin St., Ste. 302
Richmond, VA 23219
804/225-9113
www.virginia.sierraclub.org

Virginia Conservation Network
422 E. Franklin St., Ste. 303
Richmond, VA 23219
804/644-0283
www.vcnva.org

THE BLUE RIDGE TURNS PURPLE

Visibility has never been perfect from the crest of the Blue Ridge; even early accounts of the views begin, "On a clear day . . ." Just like in the Smoky Mountains of North Carolina and Tennessee, water vapor combined with airborne dust and organic compounds given off by trees forms a natural hill-shrouding haze, especially in summer.

In recent years, though, industrial smog and auto exhaust have added a new tinge that began reaching the peaks around 1976. Increasing amounts of acid rain, originating in the emissions from old coal-fired power plants in the Ohio and Tennessee Valleys, hurt trees and fish in Shenandoah National Park. Visibility along Skyline Drive is roughly one-half what it was 50 years ago, and invasive and non-native plants and animals are encroaching, including the mile-a-minute weed, which reportedly can grow six inches in an hour, and a deadly Asian beetle that has infested all of the park's hemlock groves. Thanks to levels of ozone, acid rain, and smog that occasionally exceed those of nearby major cities, Shenandoah National Park is considered among the most polluted national parks in the country. An annual funding shortfall of millions of dollars makes problem solving even more difficult.

Pollution is having a terrible effect on Virginia's mountain streams, widely known as some of the finest brook trout habitat left in the United States. Acid rain is slowly making mountain streams and rivers in the mid-Atlantic region too acidic to support populations of native brook trout. Meanwhile, the conservation group American Rivers dubbed the Shenandoah River one of the country's 10 most threatened rivers in 2006, due to polluted runoff and other effects of overdevelopment.

History

Good Old Dominion, blessed mother of us all.

– Thomas Jefferson

PRECOLONIAL ERA

No one is sure when the first humans crossed the ice bridge over the Bering Strait to enter the Americas—current thinking is about 18,000 years ago—but anthropologists generally agree that they subsisted on seasonal hunting and gathering once they arrived. Musk ox and caribou fell to stone-tipped spears and wooden clubs, supplying the primitive nomads with food, clothing, and material for tools. Roots, nuts, and berries filled in when game was scarce, and early humans moved their temporary encampments to follow the herds or flee the harsher seasons.

Approximately 11,000 years ago, the glaciers of the most recent ice age retreated to 200 miles north of present-day Virginia. The future state's first inhabitants arrived from the west to find unfamiliar species of bison, deer, turkeys, bears, and elk moving up from the south. These family groups often camped alongside streams, leaving behind chipped stone tools and discarded rock flakes to record their passing. The chilly ice age weather claimed larger mammals like mastodons and mammoths, helped along by the spears of early natives.

Within a few thousand years, temperatures continued to climb, relegating cold-weather tree species such as hemlocks, birches, and firs (which had flourished at lower elevations) to the Appalachian peaks. Human populations increased slowly but surely, so that by the time of Christ, the **Woodland Period** was in full swing. Amid lowland forests of hickory, oak, and chestnut a more settled lifestyle emerged. Rudimentary agriculture produced crops of corn, squash, and beans, while the development of fragile pottery made continuous migration less practical. The discovery of the bow

WIKIMEDIA COMMONS

John White, an early English colonist, sketched native men cooking fish in Virginia.

and arrow made hunting and warfare more efficient. Relatively small numbers kept native Virginians' impact on their environment to a minimum, although they occasionally burned large swaths of forest to flush out game and drove herds of bison over cliff edges, killing more than they could use at one time.

Welcome to the "New" World

When they arrived in 1607, the first English settlers found the Tidewater area under the control of the **Powhatan Confederacy,** an Algonquian native group whose lands stretched from North Carolina to the Potomac River. Thirty tribes containing some 10,000 people lived in palisaded villages by rivers or on hillsides under the leadership of Wahunsonacock, called Chief Powhatan by the Europeans. The Powhatans fished, hunted, and grew corn, squash, pumpkins, and herbs in summer gardens. Dressed in animal hides and woven plant fibers, they decorated themselves with feathers, tattoos, and jewelry made of shells, clay beads, and pearls. High priests called Periku offered sacrifices to Okee or Mannith, worshipped as the "Creator of All Things."

Farther west and north lived the **Monacans** and **Manahoacs,** occupying the eastern edge of the Blue Ridge and the upper banks of the James, Potomac, and Rappahannock Rivers into the Allegheny Mountains. These traditional enemies of the Powhatans shared a common Siouxan cultural heritage and language. Other native groups included the **Nansemond**—who were such good farmers that they became known as the "granary" of the early English colony—the **Rappahannock** near present-day Richmond, and small groups of **Cherokee** up from the south.

THE COLONIAL PERIOD

Jamestown

At the turn of the 17th century, England was painfully aware that it needed to get a foothold in the New World. Spain, after all, had been busily colonizing, converting, and pillaging for the last century. Three decades of attempts finally bore fruit in 1607, when three ships—the *Sarah Constant,* the *Godspeed,* and the *Discovery*—brought 143 settlers to the mouth of the Chesapeake Bay. In contrast to the conquistadors financed by the Spanish Crown, the English expedition was a private venture organized by the London-based Virginia Company. Captain Christopher Newport led the ships 30 miles up the James River, which he named after the English king. On May 14, 1607, the colonists tied their ships to trees, disembarked, and set about building the first permanent English settlement in the Americas.

Soon James Fort stood guard over Virginia, the name given to all of North America not

KEY DATES IN VIRGINIA HISTORY

1607	Jamestown settled
1610	Jamestown almost fails due to winter famine, inept leadership, and poor planning
1612/13	John Rolfe plants first crop of West Indian tobacco
1619	First blacks brought to Virginia
1624	Virginia becomes a royal colony when Virginia Company's charter is revoked
1676	Bacon's Rebellion against Governor Berkeley's administration fails
1693	College of William and Mary founded in Williamsburg
1699	Colonial capital moved to Middle Plantation (now Williamsburg)
1774	British Gov. John Murray dissolves House of Burgesses
1775	Newly formed Virginia Convention calls for first Continental Congress
	Patrick Henry advocates rebellion in famous speech to House of Burgesses
	Revolutionary War begins at Lexington and Concord, Massachusetts
1776	Declaration of Independence signed in Philadelphia
	Virginia Convention adopts state constitution and bill of rights
1779	Richmond becomes state capital
1781	Lord Cornwallis surrenders to Gen. George Washington at Yorktown, ending American Revolution
1788	House of Burgesses, the first representative assembly in the New World, convenes at Jamestown
	Virginia ratifies U.S. Constitution
1789	George Washington becomes first president of United States
1831	Nat Turner's slave rebellion
1859	John Brown's raid on Harpers Ferry
1861	Civil War begins
	Virginia secedes from the Union, joins Confederate States
	Richmond becomes Confederate capital
1863	West Virginia splits from Virginia, admitted to Union
1865	Lee surrenders to Ulysses S. Grant at Appomattox, ending Civil War
1870	Virginia readmitted to Union
1889	Newport News opens Simpson Dry Dock, the largest in the world
1954	U.S. Supreme Court decision to end segregation in public schools meets massive resistance in Virginia
1957	Chesapeake Bay Bridge-Tunnel completed
1969	First Republican elected governor of Virginia since 1886
1971	State constitution rewritten
1990	L. Douglas Wilder, the country's first African American governor, is elected in Virginia

under the control of the Spanish or French, after the English Virgin Queen (Elizabeth I). The land was rich, game plentiful, and the natives friendly, at least at first, but the colony still almost failed within its first few years. Inept leaders, with the exception of adventurer John Smith, were ill suited to the hard decisions and harder labor. Despite warnings to avoid damp low-lying areas, they built their settlement in a salt marsh, which led to famine and disease. The winter of 1609–1610 became known as the "Starving Time." Things got so bad that colonists ate snakes, rats, their shoes—and worse. One colonist killed and ate his wife ("for which hee was executed, as hee well deserved," wrote a fellow sufferer; "now whether shee was better roasted, boyled or carbonado'd I know not"). The colony was abandoned in May 1610 by its 60 remaining colonists; however, their departing boat was met by two ships bearing Gov. Thomas Gates from England, and the survivors were convinced to turn around and stick it out.

Colonist John Rolfe began a legacy a few years later by planting the first crop of West Indian tobacco *(Nicotiana tabacum).* With some selective breeding, the large-leaf tobacco plant would prove a stable revenue crop in high demand back in England. Representative government, in a limited sense, began in June 1619, when the first legislative assembly in the New World convened for six days in a "generall Assemblie" in the Jamestown church. The first boatload of "20 and odd Negroes" from Africa arrived in Hampton Roads that same year as indentured servants.

© KATIE GITHENS

a reproduction of the 17th-century James Fort palisades, based on archaeological remains found in 1994

Things Get Worse Before They Get Better

Fewer than 1,200 out of 4,000 arrivals survived to 1624, the rest victims to Indian attacks and a major epidemic in 1622–1623 that killed 500 people. Although friendly at first with gifts of food and advice, the Powhatans turned hostile when they realized the Europeans were here to stay. Within two years all of the main native towns had been seized, Chief Powhatan had fled, and any colonist venturing beyond the walls of the settlement took his life in his hands. A temporary truce followed the marriage of Powhatan's 13-year-old daughter (and John Smith's alleged savior) Pocahontas to colonist John Rolfe (not for any "carnall affection; but for the good of this plantation, for the honour of our countrie"), but relations quickly deteriorated. A surprise attack in March 1622 by natives under Powhatan's successor Opechancanough killed 400 settlers. In 1624 the Virginia Company's charter was revoked and Jamestown came under British government rule, making it the first royal colony.

Nonetheless, by 1634 the colony counted 5,000 inhabitants concentrated along the James and York Rivers, the Eastern Shore, and the Hampton Roads area. Most settlers under Gov. Sir William Berkeley (1642–1652 and 1660–1677) were small-scale farmers, artisans, and tradesmen, many of whom had worked their way out of indentured servitude and found themselves owning land for the first time. Tobacco quickly became the major crop, creating a demand for slaves to work the labor-intensive crop. By 1660, the year before slavery was legalized, the colony counted one black for every 20 whites. Five hundred more colonists were killed in an Indian attack in 1644, which led to the capture and murder of the blind, elderly Chief Opechancanough. A treaty of submission signaled the beginning of the long, slow displacement of Virginia's native tribes.

Early Unrest and Bacon's Rebellion

Supporters of Charles I, who was deposed and killed in 1644, fled to the New World and set

CAPTAIN JOHN SMITH

The savior of Jamestown saw more action before setting foot in the New World than most of us see in a lifetime. Born in 1580 in Lincolnshire, England, Smith spent his childhood on his family's farm before being apprenticed as a teenager to a local merchant. At age 16 he ran away to fight in France for Dutch independence from Spain, worked on a merchant ship in the Mediterranean Sea, and went to Transylvania to battle the Turks.

Knocked out in battle and left for dead, Smith was captured and sold to a Turkish *pasha* who sent him as a present to his heartthrob in Constantinople. The lady, though reportedly smitten with her English prisoner, passed him on to her brother, who abused him so badly that Smith killed his master and fled. With an iron collar still around his neck, he escaped through Russia, ending up back in England in time to buy stock in the newly formed Virginia Company in 1606. He was 26 years old.

On December 20, 1606, Smith and 142 other hopeful setters sailed west. A stubborn, disputatious nature quickly got him in trouble with the trip leaders, who accused the adventurer of conspiracy and had him arrested. At their

© KATIE GITHENS

A statue of John Smith gazes across the James River. Standing nearby is a statue of Pocahontas, favorite daughter of chief Powhatan. Smith credited Pocahontas with saving his life twice.

down the roots of a gentry society with firm historical ties to England—hence Virginia's nickname of "the Old Dominion." Tobacco sales were funneled through a handful of London merchants, driving prices down and making it increasingly difficult for small Virginia farms to turn a profit. Charles II, placed in power in 1660 after the English Civil War, even tried to grant all of Virginia's northern neck—at the time, the entire colony—to English nobility.

Further impolitic decisions provoked a rebellion in 1676 led by 26-year-old firebrand Nathaniel Bacon. After the Colonial government had refused to help frontier settlers fight off repeated Indian attacks, the plantation owner spearheaded an unauthorized

arrival in Chesapeake Bay, though, the sealed expedition orders were opened and revealed that Smith had been named a member of the governing council. When other leaders kept him from assuming the position, he set out west to look for a passage to the Pacific. He got far enough to discover the falls on the James River near Richmond, and returned to find the settlement in dire straits. Local natives had become increasingly hostile, and the ill-prepared colonists were reduced to a daily ration of one pint of wormy grain boiled in water. In the words of one settler, "Our drinke was water, our lodgings, castles in the air."

Smith assumed leadership and began to whip the settlement and its inhabitants into shape. Sturdy houses and defenses were constructed, and relations with the Powhatan Indians were improved to allow colonists to trade for corn, fish, and other food. Around this time, Smith began a series of expeditions up the "Patawomeck" and "Topoahannock" Rivers, on which he based his famous 1606 map of Virginia. Accurate enough to serve local navigators for a century, Smith's map was used to survey the Mason-Dixon line between Pennsylvania and Maryland, which separated free states from slave states during the Civil War.

While searching for the source of the "Chickahamania" River in December 1607, Smith was captured by the Powhatans, who took him to a lodge on the banks of the York River. In a later account, he described Chief Powhatan as "a tall well proportioned man, with a sower looke...proudly lying uppon a Bedstead a foote high, upon tenne or twelve Mattes, richly hung with manie Chaynes of great Pearles about his necke...with such a grave Maiesticall countenance, as drave me into admiration to see such state in a naked Savage."

According to his own account, Smith was then condemned to death and laid out on the clubbing block. As the story goes, Powhatan's 13-year-old daughter Pocahontas rushed forward and pleaded with her father to spare Smith's life. Whatever really happened, he was eventually freed and returned to lead the colony, which had been hampered by laziness and inept leadership and was struggling through the winter of 1607. Appointed president of Jamestown in September 1608, Smith enforced a rigid discipline, strengthened fortifications, and started general military training. Idlers were spurred on with the edict, "He who does not work, will not eat." His efforts saw the group through the next hard winter until more settlers arrived with provisions in the summer of 1609. That September he was wounded severely enough in a gunpowder explosion to force him to return to England. He never went back to Virginia.

On later journeys, Smith explored and mapped the Maine and Massachusetts coastlines, dubbing the area New England with the approval of Prince Charles. On another voyage he was captured by pirates, escaped, and returned to England penniless. One final colonizing attempt in 1617 ended in failure. For the rest of his life, Smith praised the wonders of the Western continent in books such as *A Description of New England* (1625), *The Generall Historie of Virginia, New England, and the Summer Isles* (1624), and *The True Travels, Adventures and Observations of Captaine John Smith in Europe, Asia, Africa and America* (1630). He died in London in 1631.

campaign against the Susquehanna tribe, for which he was labeled a rebel and a traitor by aging Governor Berkeley. During the fighting that ensued, Bacon occupied the General Assembly, burned Jamestown to the ground, and spoke out against the increasingly corrupt and self-serving government. The rebellion collapsed soon after Bacon's untimely death from dysentery that October, but his point had been made.

Expansion and the Golden Age

Through the late 17th and most of the 18th centuries, the colony spread steadily west. In March 1669, German scholar John Lederer became one of the first white men to reach the crest of the Blue Ridge. Scotch-Irish and Germans moved down from Pennsylvania into the Shenandoah Valley near the middle of the 18th century, sparking friction with French settlers and their native allies that resulted in the **French and Indian War** (1754–1763), begun when a 22-year-old Lieutenant Colonel in the Virginia militia named George Washington attacked French troops near modern-day Pittsburgh.

At the conclusion of the "Seven Years' War" (as it was called outside the colonies), Britain was the world's dominant imperial power, on land and sea. It also started to wonder exactly how much money it could squeeze out of its American colonies, which after all had sparked an expensive war.

This era became known as the "Golden Age" of plantations, financed by huge tobacco profits and based largely on the aristocratic society of English estate owners. A core of First Families with names such as Carter, Randolph, and Byrd formed a "bourgeois aristocracy" that defended self-government jealously—as long as it served their own interests. Speculation in land and slave trading brought in even more money, while the basic concepts and advocates of American liberal thought were being born.

By 1715, the colony counted one black for every three whites. Settlers pressed westward, following Indian trails down the Shenandoah Valley to create the Great Wagon (or Valley) Road. Stretching some 700 miles west and south from near Philadelphia, the road led to what is now Roanoke, where paths split into southwest Virginia, east Tennessee, and the Carolina Road south. In 1730, German immigrants had settled near what is now Luray, followed by a medley of European ethnic groups including French Huguenots, Irish, and Welsh.

The Eve of Revolution

The more than 120,000 persons living in the British colony in 1715 lived modestly in a stable, if narrowly based, plantation economy tied closely to the Old World. The seeds of split had already been planted, however. Britain's determination to wring money from the colonies through taxes would provide the powder keg. France was no longer strong enough to serve as a bogeyman to scare the colonies into obedience. Colonists were prohibited many rights extended to English subjects across the Atlantic, and royal edicts kept overriding acts passed by the Virginia House of Burgesses.

In 1763 a ridiculous, unenforceable law prohibiting westward expansion angered frontier settlers and coastal land speculators alike. Taxation without representation reached its peak with the Stamp Act of 1765. A fiery speech in Williamsburg by the gifted orator Patrick Henry implied that the colonies might be better off without George III. (His words "Caesar had his Brutus, Charles the First his Cromwell, and George III . . ." were interrupted by cries of "Treason!") The Virginia General Assembly followed by passing the Stamp Act Resolves, which decreed that only Virginia had the right to tax Virginians. Repealed in 1766, the Stamp Act was replaced by heavy import duties the next year.

In 1773 the perpetrators of the Boston Tea Party received the support of the local government, even as the British Parliament closed the port to all commerce and sent in troops to maintain order. This harsh response only served to unify the colonies. When Virginia's Governor Dunmore dissolved the General Assembly in response, the burgesses met at

Raleigh Tavern in Williamsburg to propose a meeting in Philadelphia to discuss separation from England. George Washington, Patrick Henry, and Benjamin Harrison all made it to the first Continental Congress in September 1774, where a militia was organized to defend the colonies. "The die is now cast," said King George III that same month. "The Colonies must either submit or triumph."

At the March 1775 Virginia Convention at St. John's Church in Richmond, Patrick Henry made his most famous speech. Although nobody present actually wrote it down, witnesses recalled it ending along these lines: "I know not what course others may take; but as for me, give me liberty, or give me death."

THE REVOLUTIONARY WAR

Virginia managed to escape most of the fighting of the first three years of the American Revolution, beyond supplying leaders, troops, supplies, and the occasional landmark document. In May 1776, the same month Gov. John Dunmore fled to England, radicals and conservatives united in the decision for independence at the Virginia Convention in Williamsburg. By the time the ink had dried on the U.S. Constitution (penned mostly by Virginian Thomas Jefferson), two other papers had been completed: George Mason's Virginia Bill of Rights, asserting that "all power is vested in, and consequently derived from, the people" (this later served as the model for the Federal Bill of Rights); and Virginia's first constitution, ending 169 years as an English colony.

Patrick Henry was chosen as governor of Virginia. No one seemed to mind the irony that although Virginians had sounded the loudest demands for liberty, Virginia was still closest in sentiment to England of all the colonies. The Virginia gentry led the struggle for independence: "These gentlemen from Virginia appear to be the most spirited and consistent of any," wrote John Adams upon the arrival of the Virginia delegates to the first Continental Congress.

George Washington had been elected commander-in-chief of the Continental Army soon after the first shots were fired at Lexington and Concord. Many of his fellow Virginians made a name under him, including cavalry leader Col. Harry "Light-Horse" Lee, father of Civil War legend General Robert E. Lee, and George Rogers Clark, who managed to wrest the Northwest Territory from Britain in 1778–1779 during a hard-fought winter campaign. Crucial help came from French forces led by the Marquis de Lafayette, eager for some revenge for their recent defeat by Britain.

When Thomas Jefferson became governor of Virginia in 1779, he found the state treasury practically emptied by the expense of supplying the scrappy Continental Army. Life in Virginia remained more or less unaffected by the war until English ships invaded via Hampton Roads in 1779, forcing the capital to be moved to Richmond for safety. Jefferson resigned his position in June 1780, narrowly avoiding capture by the British, thanks to Capt. Jack Jouett, who rode all night to warn him at his Monticello home. Seven other legislators were captured.

Infamous traitor Benedict Arnold—one of Washington's most trusted commanders before becoming a brigadier general in the British Army—led troops to destroy Richmond in January 1781. Before the year was out, however, Britain's Gen. Lord Charles Cornwallis was surrounded on the Yorktown peninsula between 10,000 Continental troops under Washington and 8,000 under Lafayette, with the French fleet preventing escape by sea. On October 19, Cornwallis marched his troops (many, according to one witness, "much in liquor") across Surrender Field between the ragged Continental Army and the spotless French forces. A band played "The World Turned Upside Down," and a new country was born.

After the Revolution

The U.S. Constitution was adopted at the Philadelphia Constitutional Convention in 1787. Virginia's approval of it spurred a debate that pitted Virginians who had helped draft it, including George Washington and James

Madison, against fellow statesmen wary of an omnipotent national government, led by Patrick Henry and George Mason. The Bill of Rights proved a good compromise, and pro-ratification forces prevailed by a vote of 89–79. In 1788, Virginia became the new nation's 10th state, and a year later George Washington was elected its president, with Thomas Jefferson as secretary of state. The new nation was off and running.

Virginia played a dominant role in the early years of the republic. Many of the founding fathers hailed from the Old Dominion, including Jefferson, Madison, and George Mason. Virginia had one-fifth of the country's population and contributed one-third of its commerce. By 1790, thanks to a law that allowed owners to free their own slaves, there were more than 12,000 free blacks in the state.

BETWEEN THE WARS

Setting up a Country

Early American politics were marked by conflict over how much power the national government should have. Thomas Jefferson and James Madison championed states' rights, arguing that the federal apparatus should stick to what was specifically outlined in the Constitution and leave everything else to state and local governments. Federalists, on the other hand, followed the lead of New Yorker Alexander Hamilton in pushing for the widest possible role of the federal government. Regardless, Virginians dominated national politics for the first four decades, supplying four of the first five presidents, including an uninterrupted stretch 1801–1825. Virginian John Marshall served as chief justice of the U.S. Supreme Court 1801–1835.

The newly discovered Cumberland Gap, blazed in 1796 by Daniel Boone and 30 "axemen," let settlers move through the mountains to "Kentuckee" and beyond. Hundreds of thousands passed along Boone's Trace 1775–1810. By some estimates, one-quarter of all Americans have ancestors who used this route.

Antebellum Life

The first half of the 19th century is still remembered as one of the more idyllic times in Virginia's history, evoking the plantation nostalgia of hoop skirts, gentlemen on horses, and sun-drenched fields of cotton and tobacco. Of course, it was an ideal time—for a select few. All others worked themselves to the bone to make a living (or, in the case of slaves, simply to survive). Small-scale agriculture was still the norm—the average American farm in 1850 was only 340 acres—and most farmers were too poor to own slaves. Instead, they relied on family members for help in raising peanuts, potatoes, corn, hogs, chickens, and cattle. Rutted roads connected scattered towns, where courthouses served as social hubs and mercantiles sold everything from medicines to bolts of cloth. Any necessary tools or buildings were fashioned by the farmers or hired artisans.

Family connections were paramount, and served to emphasize—in a polite way—the gap between the gentry and the rabble. The gap existed even in worship: the upper class attended Presbyterian and Episcopal services while the populace mostly filled Methodist, Lutheran, and Baptist churches. Above all, the concepts of civility, humility, and honest hard work shaped Virginia society. "The Virginian," wrote historian Percival Renier, "liked to think of himself as a plain and homespun-appearing gentleman with a noble pedigree, which naturally put him above airs and snobbery and fine clothes. . . ." State politics were split between the demands for representation from burgeoning western counties, universal taxpayer suffrage, and freedom for slaves on one hand, and the interests of wealthy eastern landowners and merchants who granted certain grudging concessions on the other.

The Slavery Issue

The narrow-minded policies and political conservatism of the aspiring aristocrats of the East eventually began to mire Virginia's antebellum period in economic and political stagnation. Granted, the founding fathers were a hard act to follow, but still Virginia politicians faltered again and again, allowing the port of Hampton Roads to fall far behind those of New York, Baltimore,

MOTHER OF PRESIDENTS

The Old Dominion has supplied eight Chief Executives, more than any other state.

George Washington:
1789-1797 (1st)

William Henry Harrison:
1841 (9th;
died in office)

Thomas Jefferson:
1801-1809 (3rd)

John Tyler:
1841-1845 (10th)

James Madison:
1809-1817 (4th)

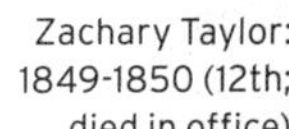

Zachary Taylor:
1849-1850 (12th;
died in office)

James Monroe:
1817-1825 (5th)

Woodrow Wilson:
1913-1921 (28th)

WIKIMEDIA COMMONS

Slaves were auctioned on stone blocks, such as this one on a plantation in central Virginia.

and Boston, and resisting the construction of a canal between the Potomac and Ohio Rivers. New England became the nation's textile center instead of Richmond, public education suffered (with the exception of the University of Virginia, founded by Jefferson in 1819), and a population exodus caused the state to lose 13 congressmen between 1810 and 1860.

Fostering the decline was the increasingly inefficient but entrenched plantation economy. Tobacco exhausted the soil and brought in less and less money, but even though the slave trade had been abolished in 1778, the practice of slavery continued and came to be seen as the rotten root of a slowly dying tree. By the turn of the 19th century, more than one-third of Virginia lived in bondage. Thomas Jefferson, the slave owner who extolled the equality of man, had foreseen the conflict: "Indeed I tremble for my country when I reflect that God is just: that His justice cannot sleep forever: that considering numbers, nature and natural means only, a revolution of the wheel of fortune, an exchange of situation, is among possible events . . ."

Northern states began to clamor for emancipation as scattered slave revolts gained momentum. In 1800 a huge slave named Gabriel was said to have led 1,000 others in a thwarted rebellion in Richmond. Thirty years later, black preacher Nat Turner led 60 slaves to kill 58 whites—mostly women and children—in Southampton County near the North Carolina line. Although the rebels were caught within 48 hours, the event threw gasoline on the fire. Pro-slavery forces blamed abolitionist propaganda and killed innocent blacks in retaliation.

Most arguments against slavery came from the rapidly industrializing North, where factories provided plenty of work for men of any color and smaller farms made a large labor force unnecessary. The disregard for slaves' human rights was an issue in the new western territories, while Southern abolitionists resented the political stranglehold held by the pro-slavery planter aristocracy. In the end, economics was probably the most important factor: A poor farmer in Georgia and the owner of a Massachusetts textile factory found it equally impossible to compete against slave labor.

Slave owners dreaded the thought of these regions unifying against them. They found too much of their declining income tied up in human beings—close to half of the taxable wealth of the Tidewater was in slaves—and argued that the system was better (for everyone but the slaves themselves) than the alternative of "wage slavery" for whites. It was also argued that there were too many slaves to simply set free. Southern whites found it impossible to imagine the transition to a stable, prosperous society in which two races worked side by side as equals. And who would pay to ship the freed slaves out west, or back to Africa?

An 1832 plan for gradual emancipation failed in the Virginia General Assembly, putting the issue to rest until the Mexican-American War (1846–1848). This conflict again raised a divisive issue last heard in the Missouri Controversy of 1819: whether new territories admitted into the Union would permit slavery or not. A slight midcentury economic recovery—including Virginian Cyrus McCormick's invention of the mechanical reaper in 1831, the construction of more railroads, and the flourishing of Richmond's slave-powered Tredegar Ironworks—did little to distract from the debate.

In the 50 years leading up to the Civil War, the population of the United States grew at six times the world average. It was still an overwhelmingly rural country, but this was changing, especially in the North. In the South, four million blacks still lived in bondage.

Prelude to War

In October 1859, the country was rocked by a raid on the federal arsenal at Harpers Ferry (now in West Virginia), led by militant abolitionist John Brown. Seventeen whites and five free blacks tried to steal enough weapons to arm slaves for a rebellion, and in the process killed the mayor and other townspeople. The group was eventually captured by U.S. Marines under the command of a young Lieutenant Colonel named Robert E. Lee, but their death sentences gained the abolitionist cause a white martyr and forced slave owners to face the reality that opponents of slavery were willing to fight, and die, for their cause. Brown's dying words echoed over the widening chasm: "The sins of this guilty land can only be purged with blood."

The final straw came in 1860 when Abraham Lincoln was elected president on a Republican platform, pledging to keep slavery out of the territories. On December 20, South Carolina seceded from the Union, followed soon after by Mississippi, Alabama, Florida, Georgia, Louisiana, and Texas. When Fort Sumter on the South Carolina coast was attacked by Southern artillery on April 10, Lincoln called for 75,000 volunteers to put down the "insurrection." Originally against secession, Virginia nonetheless withdrew from the Union on April 19, 1861. Fireworks exploded above Richmond as "ten thousand hurrahing men and boys" carried torches through the streets to celebrate the occasion. Six days later, Virginia became part of the Confederate States of America.

"They say Virginia has no grievance," reported one contemporary writer; "she comes out on a point of honor."

THE CIVIL WAR

In creating a new country, the American Revolution had left two major issues unresolved: the extent of the federal government's dominion over the states, and the contradiction between the assertions of the equality of all men in the Declaration of Independence and the fact that in America, more people owned other people than in any other country in the world. Before those questions would be answered, four years of fighting would make muddy wastelands of the same acres fought over in the Revolutionary War less than a century before, and close to 700,000 Americans—more than in both world wars put together—would perish.

As a border state located only a rifle shot from Washington, D.C., and home to the Confederate capital, Virginia suffered more major battles and witnessed more casualties

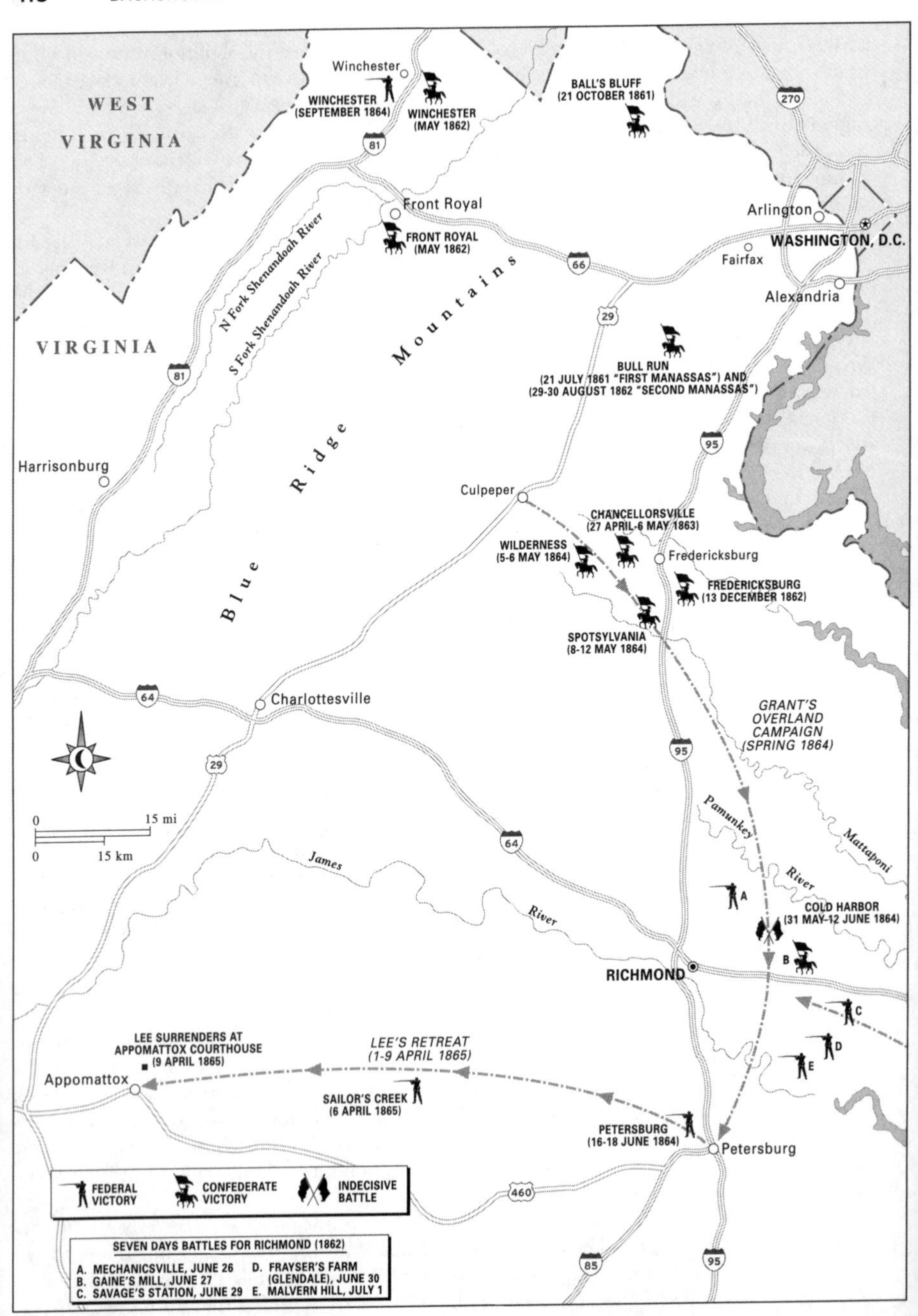
WEST VIRGINIA
VIRGINIA
Winchester
WINCHESTER (SEPTEMBER 1864)
WINCHESTER (MAY 1862)
BALL'S BLUFF (21 OCTOBER 1861)
Front Royal
FRONT ROYAL (MAY 1862)
Arlington
WASHINGTON, D.C.
Fairfax
Alexandria
N Fork Shenandoah River
S Fork Shenandoah River
Blue Ridge Mountains
BULL RUN (21 JULY 1861 "FIRST MANASSAS") AND (29-30 AUGUST 1862 "SECOND MANASSAS")
Harrisonburg
Culpeper
CHANCELLORSVILLE (27 APRIL-6 MAY 1863)
WILDERNESS (5-6 MAY 1864)
Fredericksburg
FREDERICKSBURG (13 DECEMBER 1862)
SPOTSYLVANIA (8-12 MAY 1864)
Charlottesville
GRANT'S OVERLAND CAMPAIGN (SPRING 1864)
0 15 mi
0 15 km
Pamunkey River
Mattaponi
James River
COLD HARBOR (31 MAY-12 JUNE 1864)
RICHMOND
LEE SURRENDERS AT APPOMATTOX COURTHOUSE (9 APRIL 1865)
LEE'S RETREAT (1-9 APRIL 1865)
Appomattox
SAILOR'S CREEK (6 APRIL 1865)
PETERSBURG (16-18 JUNE 1864)
Petersburg
81
270
66
29
95
64
460
85
FEDERAL VICTORY
CONFEDERATE VICTORY
INDECISIVE BATTLE
SEVEN DAYS BATTLES FOR RICHMOND (1862)
A. MECHANICSVILLE, JUNE 26
B. GAINE'S MILL, JUNE 27
C. SAVAGE'S STATION, JUNE 29
D. FRAYSER'S FARM (GLENDALE), JUNE 30
E. MALVERN HILL, JULY 1

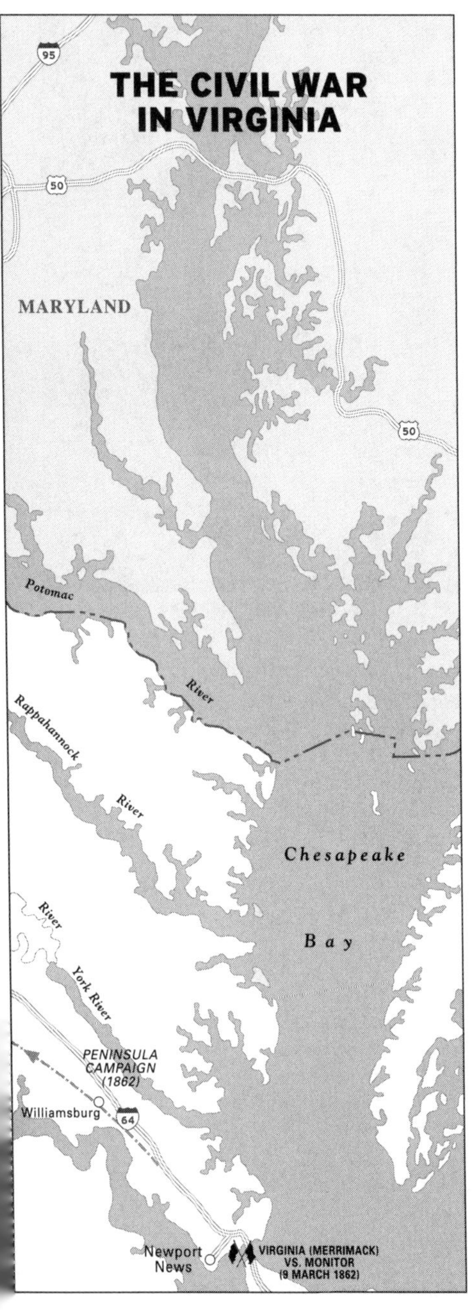

than any other state. Both the first major clash of the Civil War and the peace treaty that signaled its end happened in the Old Dominion, while the four intervening years would leave its graveyards full, its society in ruins, and literally tear the state in half.

Early Fighting

The Civil War began in earnest at the **First Battle of Bull Run** on July 21, 1861. Convinced the Rebels would turn and flee at the first hint of trouble, Washingtonians rode out from the city and spread out picnics on a hillside near Manassas to watch the battle. Fewer than half of the 57,000 troops present actually fought, and confusion reigned. Blue and gray uniforms appeared on both sides, along with highland kilts and baggy trousers straight from North Africa. The early Confederate flag resembled the Stars and Stripes so closely that gunners mistakenly fired on their own troops. The routed Federal soldiers fled in what became known as "the great skedaddle," and all hopes of a quick victory were extinguished.

Battle of the Ironclads

Union troops retreating from Portsmouth had burned, among other things, a steam frigate called the ***Merrimac.*** Desperate for any kind of naval weapon to help break the tightening noose of the Union blockade, Confederate shipbuilders restored the charred hulk, covered it with steeply sloping iron plates, and rechristened her the ***Virginia.*** In March 1862, the reborn ship steamed into Hampton Roads like a "floating barn belching smoke," according to one witness, rammed a carriage-sized hole through one Union warship, sank another with cannon fire, and drove off three more as shells and bullets bounced off her sides.

The next morning the Union unveiled its own metal ship called the ***Monitor,*** built with a round turret and a flat deck that was even with the waterline (a "Yankee Cheese Box on a raft"). Four hours of fighting and maneuvering accomplished little besides demonstrating both ships' resistance to gunfire. Hampton Roads remained under Union control, Gen. George

© KATIE GITHENS

Virginia has more Civil War battlefields than any other state, including Manassas National Battlefield Park, pictured above.

B. McClellan was able to move troops by water to occupy Norfolk, and the *Virginia* was blown up to escape capture. The *Monitor* sank in a storm off North Carolina in December, where it lay undiscovered until 1973.

The Rebels Forge Ahead

Virginia's Confederate Tidewater area was evacuated after the defeat of the *Virginia,* and the struggles for Richmond began. During what became known as the **Seven Days' Battles** in late June 1862, General McClellan propelled his newly trained Army of the Potomac to within sight of Richmond, but was pushed back by Robert E. Lee's inspired tactics. Gen. Thomas "Stonewall" Jackson helped Lee by tying up Union reinforcements in the Shenandoah Valley. Close to 35,000 soldiers died, but the threat to Richmond was lifted for the moment. At the **Second Battle of Manassas** in August and September, Union Gen. John Pope made the mistake of ordering pursuit when the Confederates weren't really retreating. Lee, Jackson, and Gen. James Longstreet took advantage, attacking with such ferocity that Pope barely managed a nighttime withdrawal back across the Bull Run River to safety.

With renewed confidence, Lee moved north, but the capture of a copy of Confederate marching orders led to a clash with McClellan at Antietam near Sharpsburg, Maryland, on September 17. This battle remains the single deadliest day in American history, leaving 12,410 Union soldiers and 10,700 Rebels sprawled in the dirt. Lincoln saw an opportunity he had been waiting for, and on January 1, 1863, he issued the Emancipation Proclamation, freeing all slaves in areas not held by Union forces.

This edict, which Lincoln called "the central act of my administration, and the greatest single event of the 19th century," made the fight against slavery, along with preserving the Union, the central goal of the Civil War. England and France couldn't afford to grant diplomatic recognition to the Confederacy without appearing to support the "peculiar institution" they themselves had outlawed long ago, and the Southern cause became forever linked with human bondage.

Lee still seemed invincible, beating back Federal attacks on Virginia time and again. At **Fredericksburg** on December 13, 1862, Gen. Ambrose Burnside, though warned by Lincoln, didn't move quickly enough in crossing the Rappahannock, allowing Lee to entrench his forces on higher ground and win the battle. The battle of **Chancellorsville** (April 27–May 6, 1863) resulted in triumph and tragedy for the Rebels. Lee sent Jackson on a daring flanking maneuver toward a weak point in Gen. Joseph Hooker's line of 160,000. The Federals were pushed back across the Rappahannock in defeat. On the evening of May 2, Jackson was mistakenly fired on by his own troops, and he died eight days later. "I know not how to replace him," mourned Lee, who had no choice but to press on without his star commander.

Union forces were carrying the war's western theater, threatening the South's control of the Mississippi River and occupying Tennessee. Nevertheless, General Lee and Jefferson Davis, president of the Confederacy, plotted an attempt to take the Federal capital. In June the Army of Northern Virginia crossed the Potomac.

The Tide Turns

Three days of fighting at **Gettysburg** in early July 1863 ended Confederate hopes of taking Washington, D.C., despite a final desperate charge by 11,000 Rebel soldiers under Gen. George Pickett into the face of point-blank gunfire. During the retreat, Lee told Pickett: "The men and officers of your command have written the name of Virginia as high today as it has ever been written before." One in three soldiers survived Pickett's Charge. When the smoke cleared, the Battle of Gettysburg—the bloodiest of any American war—had claimed more than 50,000 casualties. After a long siege, Vicksburg, Mississippi, fell on July 4, 1863. Although two more years of fighting would follow, the Confederate cause was all but lost.

Virginia's westernmost districts had voted against secession in 1861, and now that Union forces controlled the entire region from the Ohio River to the mountains, they took action. In 1863 all of Virginia's counties beyond the Alleghenies and two at the northern end of the Shenandoah Valley were accepted into the Union as West Virginia.

A Slow End

By 1864, the Confederate economy was in shambles. The Union naval blockade kept the shoreline sealed, causing barrels of flour to sell for $200 and spurring bread riots in Richmond. Morale plummeted and Confederate soldiers began to desert in droves as it became obvious that only a miracle would bring a Southern victory. Though few citizens publicly suggested surrender, many blamed Jefferson Davis and the Confederate government for the deteriorating situation. The last realistic hope was that the Southern armies could prolong the fighting long enough for public disgust in the North to unseat Lincoln in the 1864 elections, bringing about the possibility of a negotiated peace.

Instead, Ulysses S. Grant, newly appointed commander of all Union armies, moved south with Richmond and General Lee's battle-weary Army of Northern Virginia in his sights. "Wherever Lee goes," Grant ordered Gen. George Meade, "there you will go also." Lee repeatedly outguessed Grant's flanking maneuvers as the Confederate army, undersupplied and half the size, dogged the Federals

SOLDIERS AND POLITICIANS

Seven U.S. presidents served in the Union army during the Civil War. All were generals except McKinley, who was a major.

Chester A. Arthur
James A. Garfield
Ulysses S. Grant
Benjamin Harrison
Rutherford B. Hayes
Andrew Johnson
William McKinley

in a string of fierce battles that led slowly southward.

During the **Battle of the Wilderness** (May 5–6, 1864), the opposing forces clashed in dense undergrowth. More than 25,000 troops—two-thirds of them Federals—died in the confused fighting, many in wildfires set by cannon bombardment. At least 12,000 more fell struggling for one square mile of ground called the "Bloody Angle" in the **Battle of Spotsylvania Court House** (May 8–21) nearby. Union victories came at a heavy price. In two months during the spring of 1864, the Federals lost 77,452 men in Virginia—more soldiers than in Lee's entire army.

Realizing he stood little chance of defeating Lee in straightforward combat, Grant moved south to lay siege to Richmond and Petersburg, the Confederate capital's vital supply center. Through the summer and fall of 1864, the Confederates watched helplessly as Gen. Philip Sheridan razed the fertile Shenandoah Valley and Gen. William Sherman began his famous march to the sea from Atlanta to Savannah, cutting a swath of destruction through the Southern heartland.

Richmond was evacuated and burned on April 3, 1865, sending the Confederate government fleeing west to Danville. After fighting a final series of skirmishes in retreat across Virginia, Lee asked Grant for a meeting six days later on April 9. Grant later wrote: "I felt...sad and depressed at the downfall of a foe who had fought so long and valiantly, and had suffered so much for a cause, though that cause was, I believe, one of the worst for which a people ever fought."

The terms of surrender were drawn up and signed at Appomattox Court House, and on April 12, the ragged but unbowed Confederates turned over their arms and flags in a formal ceremony. The opposing armies saluted each other, and the war was over.

The Dust Settles

Virginia was readmitted to the Union in 1870, three years after Congress had placed the South under military rule. It's hard to overestimate

DOUG COLDWELL / WIKIMEDIA COMMONS

Today the reconstructed old Appomattox Court House is the visitors center in Appomattox Court House National Historical Park, the small village where the Civil War ended.

ELIZABETH VAN LEW: SOCIALITE SPY

Born into a wealthy and prominent Richmond family in 1818, Elizabeth Van Lew began life as a model Southern belle. Things changed when she went to school in Philadelphia, however, and she returned an ardent and outspoken abolitionist. "Slave power," she wrote in her diary, "is arrogant, is jealous and intrusive, is cruel, is despotic." She convinced her family to free their slaves, and when the Civil War erupted, she determined to help the Union cause from the heart of the Confederacy.

Van Lew wore tattered clothing and muttered to herself to elude pursuers and became known around town as "Crazy Bet." Nonetheless, she was able to smuggle notes to and from Union prisoners held in Libby Prison, and she helped some escape. She set up a complex messenger network to relay critical military information pried from unsuspecting Confederate soldiers out of Richmond and enlisted the services of Mary Bowser, a former slave, who worked as a servant in Jefferson Davis's White House of the Confederacy.

General Ulysses S. Grant came to rely on her information, which arrived so quickly it sometimes came with flowers still fresh from Van Lew's garden. "You have sent me the most valuable information received from Richmond during the war," he later told her. At the fall of Richmond in 1865, Van Lew raised the first Union flag in the city over her own house. When an angry mob gathered, Van Lew confronted them bravely: "I know you, and you... General Grant will be in town in an hour. You do one thing to my home, and all of yours will be burned before noon!"

After the war, Grant rewarded Van Lew with the job of postmistress of Richmond 1869-1877. She had exhausted her inheritance financing her spy network and was ostracized by her neighbors. She died penniless and an outcast in 1900. Friends later set a stone over her unmarked grave engraved with these words.

> *She risked everything that is dear to man – friends, fortune, comfort, life itself, all for one absorbing desire of her heart – that slavery might be abolished and the Union preserved.*

the effect of defeat on the consciousness of the South and on Virginia and her inhabitants in particular. Society as they knew it had been utterly transformed from orderly and stratified to chaotic. Richmond and most of Fredericksburg and Petersburg lay in ruins, along with large sections of dozens of other cities and towns. Local currency was worthless, 350,000 slaves no longer had to answer to anyone but themselves, and the rest of the workforce—two whole generations of men—was left demoralized, wounded, or dead. By 1877, Virginia's total war loss was estimated at $457 million, a staggering amount when divided among only 1.2 million inhabitants.

Paying the debt, including $45 million owed even before the war, became the central political issue of the late 19th century. Decades of dissension followed as "Readjusters" took the reins of government in an effort to reduce the debt and interest. Before a compromise was reached, hundreds of schoolhouses were shut down due to lack of funds. By the turn of the 20th century, the economy had begun to gain momentum again. Once it had been freed from the narrow-minded control of the planter aristocracy, Virginians were able to diversify into smaller-scale agriculture, mining, commerce, and manufacturing. Railroads again stretched across the state, and suburbs sprouted as the larger cities were rebuilt.

In contrast, the decades following the Emancipation Proclamation marked one of the lowest points in the history of American blacks. Slavery was gone, but freedom had yet to arrive. Even though a new state constitution drawn up in 1867 ratified universal male suffrage for both races, a series of rulings preserved slavery in everything but name for years. Restrictive "Black codes," poll taxes, and the 1896 Supreme Court decision in *Plessy v. Ferguson* kept minorities in a parallel existence that was definitely "separate" but far from "equal." Voting by blacks fell 90 percent (as did the turnout of poor whites, although not as much) when handwritten applications were required for voter registration. Although there was much less racial violence in Virginia than in states farther south, the mere appearance of the Ku Klux Klan in certain regions was enough to discourage any protest.

Meanwhile the myth of the Old South began to take root in books, songs, and popular culture. The past, real or imagined, provided comfort during the hard times following the Confederate defeat. The horrors of the war—still evident in missing limbs, ruined buildings, and mass graves—began to take on the sheen of chivalry, with gallant young soldiers fighting and dying in valiant defense of their homeland. Novelist James Branch Campbell noted that Southerners were creating "in the same instant that they lamented the Old South's extinction, an Old South which had died proudly at Appomattox without ever having been besmirched by the wear and tear of existence."

20TH CENTURY AND TODAY

As the digits clicked over from nines to zeros, Virginia found herself increasingly a contender on the national playing field. Chemical fertilizers made farmers less dependent on tobacco, and diversification into industry continued. World War I stimulated the economy even more by sparking an enormous expansion of the Newport News shipyard, bringing in money and workers. Tourism began to bring in significant income, and once again a Virginian sat in the White House, as Woodrow Wilson served two presidential terms 1913–1921. The Great Depression slowed mining and the wheat and tobacco markets, but the state suffered less than others thanks to the frugality of a new captain at the helm.

The Byrd Years

The governorship of 1926–1930 marked the beginning of half a century of political impact for Democrat Harry F. Byrd Sr. Tracing his lineage to 17th-century merchant and land speculator William Byrd, the Southern progressive brought Virginia's government into the modern age with a policy of honesty and efficiency. During his tenure as governor, various laws revised the tax system, expanded highways, set aside more money for social welfare programs including schools and mental hospitals, and promised severe penalties for lynching.

A solid core of Virginia conservatism remained, though; in 1928 the state voted for a Republican presidential candidate for the first time since 1872. Roosevelt's New Deal was viewed with skepticism even as it made the government the state's leading source of revenue from 1932 on. World War II brought thousands of soldiers to military camps throughout the state and caused Hampton Roads to grow even more to support the shipyards and the Norfolk Naval Base.

By mid-century, Virginia had shifted from a rural state to an urban one as its population, which had doubled since the turn of the 20th century, leapt by 25 percent 1940–1950. Thanks to the stability of the Byrd administration, employment rose, and rural blacks and big labor began to emerge as potent political forces.

Race Relations

Blacks in Virginia continued to struggle against a statewide system of segregation that kept nonwhite schools inferior and prohibited minorities from sitting on juries or holding public office. Even without the widespread violence that plagued the deeper South to spur them on, many black citizens emigrated from Virginia to Washington, D.C., and farther north in search of better lives. When the unanimous 1954 Supreme Court decision in ***Brown v. Board of Education*** declared segregation inherently unequal and therefore illegal, a massive statewide resistance blossomed. This would mark the last attempt to hold onto the old order in an embarrassing departure from the usual Virginian civility.

Spurred on by Sen. Harry Flood Byrd (son

of Harry Sr.), the General Assembly voted to withhold state funds from any school honoring integration. By 1958, integrated public schools in Charlottesville, Norfolk, and Front Royal had closed. One year later, Gov. Lindsay Almond bowed to popular protest, business pressure, and the federal courts by accepting limited integration—all the while railing against the "livid stench of sadism, sex immorality, and juvenile pregnancy" that he believed resulted from the integration of public schools in Washington, D.C.

Schools in Prince Edward County remained closed until 1964, focusing national attention on the fact that black children were receiving no education while white children attended private institutions. The 1965 Civil Rights Voting Act and the 24th Amendment to the Constitution ended the struggle, at least as far as the law was concerned, and assured minorities in Virginia and elsewhere of their right to representation.

THE SLAVERY APOLOGY

In early 2007, with the Jamestown 400th anniversary celebrations on the horizon, the Virginia House of Delegates voted unanimously to express "profound regret" for the Old Dominion's less-than-perfect track record when it comes to race relations. It was the first legislation of its kind in the country, and it was met with a mixed response from the black community, some of whom said it was time to look forward instead of making symbolic gestures about the past. The vote was joined by a resolution for the state to celebrate "Juneteenth," a holiday honoring the end of slavery in America.

Recent History

Virginia's economic and technological boom is best evidenced in the northern part of the state. Fairfax County, home to 41,000 residents in 1940, counted 533,000 in 1973—a 1,200 percent increase. The result has been, in the eyes of many, a lesson in development gone wrong as pastoral farmlands are transformed into faceless suburbs. On a brighter note, the country's first test-tube baby was delivered at Norfolk General Hospital on December 28, 1981.

Meanwhile, state politics have made the transition to a true multiparty democracy, controlled for the most part by Democrats. Harry F. Byrd Sr. died in 1966, and a series of liberal Democrats then came to power. After three successive gubernatorial elections were won by Republicans, a Democrat again carried the election in 1981. In 1990, L. Douglas Wilder became the first elected black governor of any U.S. state. Born in Richmond to children of former slaves, Wilder received a Bronze Star for heroism in the Korean War and a law degree from Howard University. He gained attention as the state's first black senator in 1969 for his efforts to change the state song and to establish a holiday for the birthday of Martin Luther King Jr. Wilder won the race for governor by fewer than 7,000 votes.

By the early 1990s, Virginia's population was more than six million, with two-thirds of Virginians living in cities; the state's per capita income ranked 12th in the country. The early years of the new millennium were marked by some unease, particularly in northern Virginia, which weathered the terrorist attacks on the Pentagon of 9/11 and the sniper shootings of October 2002 that left 10 people dead. In 2004, the state legislature created a scholarship fund for African Americans whose schools were closed between 1954 and 1964 during widespread resistance to racial integration.

The state has seen an extraordinary transformation from half a century ago, when two-thirds of the state's residents lived in rural areas. Satellite communities to Washington, D.C., have seen explosive growth—Loudoun and Stafford Counties are among the fastest growing in the nation—and the term "Fairfaxed" has been used to describe the negative effects of such rapid suburban development.

Crossing the Potomac from Washington,

D.C., used to be a step back in time to a proud but impoverished land living out its dreams of yesterday and insulated from the rest of the nation. Today it's a step forward into busy financial and manufacturing centers and a modern agricultural system tied into the global market, where the past still echoes but no longer impedes.

The state experienced both pride and heartbreak in April 2007. As the celebrations surrounding the 400th anniversary of the settling of Jamestown were gearing up, cementing Virginia's place as a true birthplace of America, a deranged student shot 32 people and himself on the Virginia Tech campus, the worst event of its kind in U.S. history.

Government and Economy

GOVERNMENT

The executive branch of Virginia's state government consists of three elected positions: governor, lieutenant governor, and attorney general. Each serves a four-year term, but governors cannot be reelected (Virginia is alone in this in the United States). Seven judges are appointed to the supreme court, the highest of four judiciary levels, for 12-year terms. The 10-member Virginia Court of Appeals was started in 1985.

Virginia's legislative body is the General Assembly, consisting of 40 senators serving four-year terms and 100 delegates elected every two years. The Assembly traces its roots to the House of Burgesses in Jamestown in 1619, leading to claims that it is the "oldest continuous law-making body in the New World." It meets every January in Richmond for sessions of 30 or 60 days. The state constitution, adopted in 1970, dictates a House of Delegates of 90–100 members, serving for two years each, and a Senate of 33–40 members, serving for four.

A moderately conservative electorate has voted for Republican presidents in a majority of elections since the middle of the 20th century. Democrats, though, have dominated state politics—only six governors since 1874 have been Republicans. In 2010, Virginia was represented by senators Mark Warner (D) and Jim Webb (D) and eleven representatives—five Republicans and six Democrats.

ECONOMY

Virginia bounced back from the ravages of the Civil War to join Georgia, Florida, and North Carolina as one of the South's wealthiest states. Its gross state product was $397 billion in 2008, and median household income stood at $61,210. Virginia typically has at least 10 counties in the country's 100 richest, mostly in the northern part of the state. In fact, in 2008, Loudoun County was #1 (median household income $111,582) and Fairfax County was #2 ($107,075). No wonder it costs an arm and a leg to live inside the Beltway.

With the nation's capital just across the Potomac, it's no surprise the federal government dominates Virginia's financial picture. Four hundred fifty square miles of military facilities, including the Pentagon in Arlington and the Marine Corps base in Quantico, provide a substantial chunk of the state's gross product. It's somewhat ironic that this traditionally conservative state has been buoyed so much by the midcentury expansion of military and federal agencies within her borders. Virginia is one of the top five recipients of federal funds in the country.

Concentrated in Hampton Roads, shipbuilding has a long legacy in the manufacturing sector, as does tobacco processing and light industry, producing chemicals, clothing, machinery, wood products, and food. High-tech firms have replaced dairy farms in northern Virginia, while mining consortiums supervise the extraction of coal, natural gas, granite, sand, clay, and other minerals from the hillsides. Tourism is the state's third-largest retail earner and employer.

© KATIE GITHENS

Apples are an important crop for the state of Virginia.

Agriculture is another big earner, centered on dairy products, livestock, fruit, and grains. As the productivity demands of the 20th century forced farms to become more mechanized, many smaller family operations closed, sending ex-employees to the cities in search of work. Surviving farms have tended to shrink. By 2007 there were about 47,000 farms throughout the state averaging 171 acres each, and farming—once the backbone of the state's economy—had fallen to about 1 percent of Virginia's annual economy. Corn, grains, soybeans, sweet potatoes, peanuts, apples, and cotton are all important crops. Virginia is the fifth-highest tobacco producer in the country. The coastal fishing industry is the state's smallest revenue producer, despite hundreds of millions of pounds of fish and shellfish pulled from the Chesapeake Bay each year.

The People

SETTLEMENT

For a group with such a strong historical identity, Virginians are a surprisingly diverse lot. Early European colonists almost all came from rural England, mostly the midland and southern counties near London. Arrivals from Wales and France in the 18th century had to make room for the large numbers of Irish, German, and Scotch-Irish farmers who flowed into the Shenandoah Valley from New Jersey, Pennsylvania, and Maryland. Native tribes were decimated by imported diseases they had no immunity against, until a mere fraction of tens of thousands of Native Americans remained.

The first blacks arrived in 1619 as indentured servants, but by the end of the century, thousands of African slaves were being hauled ashore and sold as labor on huge Tidewater plantations. Virginia quickly became the most crowded state in the New World, relatively speaking, with a population that doubled every 25 years after 1680. By the eve of the Revolutionary War, the colony counted 550,000 inhabitants, almost half of whom were black.

The state broke the one-million mark near the beginning of the 19th century, but lost many of its residents during the carnage of the Civil War and as a result of the secession of several western counties, which became West Virginia in 1863.

STATISTICS

In 2008, more than 85 percent of Virginia's 7.7 million inhabitants lived in metropolitan areas, primarily in the corridor stretching south from Washington, D.C., to Richmond and east to Hampton Roads. Virginia Beach led in population, followed by Norfolk, Chesapeake, Arlington (though it's technically a county, not a city), Richmond, and Newport News. Just under 75 percent of Virginians describe themselves as Caucasian. About 20 percent

VIRGINIA'S TRIBES TODAY

In 2008, the state's eight recognized native groups made up 0.4 percent of the population. One hundred members of the **Pamunkey** (pa-MUN-kee) tribe (www.baylink.org/pamunkey) live along the river of the same name in King William County, which contains the supposed burial site of Chief Powhatan. About 75 of the 450 members of the **Mattaponi** (ma-ta-poe-NYE) tribe occupy a reservation along the Mattaponi River dating to 1658. Another group called the **Upper Mattaponi** (www.uppermattaponi.com) live off the reservation.

Charles City County is home to about 875 **Chickahominy** tribal members mingled with the nonnative population. About 70 of the 130 **Eastern Chickahominy** live in New Kent County east of Richmond. On Bear Mountain in Amherst County, over 1,400 **Monacans** (www.monacannation.com) make up the westernmost group, and 200 **Nansemond** (www.nansemond.org) live in Norfolk, Chesapeake, Virginia Beach, and Portsmouth near their ancient hunting grounds around the Great Dismal Swamp. The **Rappahannock** tribe (www.rappahannocktribe.org) in King & Queen County elected the state's first female chief since the 1700s, G. Anne Richardson, in 1998.

EVENTS

Typical native powwows echo with heavy drums, dancing, and chanting by participants in buckskin clothes and eagle and turkey feathers. Native American veterans proudly display their U.S. Army uniforms beneath the flags of their county and tribe. Chiefs lead processions, followed by braves in war paint, women, and children. Native American food and crafts are also featured prominently.

In late May, the **Monacan Powwow** takes place on their reservation, and the **Nansemond Indian Powwow** comes to Lone Star Lake in Suffolk in August. The Rappahannock tribe hosts their own **Powwow** the second Saturday in October at their cultural center in Indian Neck.

INFORMATION

For more details on Virginia's tribes, contact the **Virginia Council on Indians** (804/225-2084, http://indians.vipnet.org).

are black, concentrated in the Piedmont and coast area; central Richmond and Charles City County on the Historic Peninsula are roughly half African American.

Other minorities, mostly Hispanic, Asian, and Middle Eastern, make up the remaining population. In the last decade, Hampton Roads had one of the country's fastest-growing Jewish communities, as well as growing numbers of immigrants from India.

ATTITUDES

It's almost impossible to summarize a state this varied, but if any quality holds true across the board, it's affability. A wave is the surest sign, whether it's from the driver of a pickup passing on a back road or a complete stranger helping you parallel park. Locals are more than happy to point you in the right direction or to give you their two cents on the most recent scandal across the Potomac; just be patient, because folks tend to choose their words carefully.

A mild but deeply rooted conservative streak, also called "a touch of old Southern values," runs beneath day-to-day affairs in more traditional parts of the state. This pride in the past can alternately—or simultaneously—glorify Virginia's rich heritage and sustain less-welcome parts of it. Race relations, while better than in most Southern states, have been irritated by recent controversies including the Virginia legislature's designation of the third Monday in January as Lee-Jackson-King Day (rather than just Martin Luther King Jr. Day), which was split into separate holidays honoring Confederate and Civil Rights heroes in 2000. Former senator (and governor) George Allen's "Macaca" faux pas (a patronizing and, many felt, racist characterization of a person of color in the audience during a campaign speech) during the 2006 congressional campaign helped cost him reelection.

In the early 1990s, former Gov. L. Douglas Wilder, the grandson of former slaves, led the fight to retire the state song "Carry Me Back To Old Virginia," written by black minstrel James Bland in the 1870s. The song, which depicts a slave fondly remembering the days when he "labored so hard for old Massa/Day after day in the fields of yellow corn," infuriated black legislators and mortified many white legislators as well. It hadn't been played at official functions since the 1970s but wasn't officially retired by the General Assembly until 1997. A 1998 competition was held to select a new state song and included entries by Donna and Jimmy Dean and A. P. Carter. As of 2010, however, the contest had been suspended indefinitely. (Check the website www.virginia.gov/song/song.html for updates.)

Virginia is a pious state, too, with a deep religious streak evidenced by broadcasts of the *700 Club* from Pat Robertson's Christian Broadcasting Network in Norfolk and by Jerry Falwell's Liberty University near Lynchburg. At the same time, a tradition of religious tolerance dates back to Thomas Jefferson's 1785 Statute for Religious Freedom. Today Protestants—mostly Methodists, Southern Baptists, and Presbyterians—outnumber other religious groups. You will come across pockets of Quakers and Mennonites in the Shenandoah and Hunt Country, and Richmond has one of the largest Jewish populations of any city its size in the country.

Arts and Culture

HISTORIC TRAVEL

The **Association for the Preservation of Virginia Antiquities** (804/648-1889, www.apva.org) owns, maintains, and operates 34 historic properties throughout the state, including the original Jamestown site, Smithfield Plantation near Blacksburg, and the Cape Henry Lighthouse at Virginia Beach. Membership ($40 single, $50 couple, $60 family) gives you free admission to its properties and a subscription to *Preservation Virginia Journal.*

CIVIL WAR-RELATED ACTIVITIES

With the most Civil War battlefields and sites of any state—one-third of the country's total—Virginia has the market cornered on Civil War sightseeing. From the first major battle at Bull Run to Robert E. Lee's surrender at Appomattox Court House, the Old Dominion boasts dozens of places where you can appreciate the war's effects on the lives of soldiers and everyday citizens.

Most of the National Battlefield Parks, administered by the National Park Service, are concentrated in the northern and eastern parts of the state. All charge entrance fees, but several special passes are available. A Golden Eagle Passport—good for one year at any Federal recreation site that charges an entrance fee—costs $80. U.S. citizens over age 62 can buy a Golden Age Passport ($10) for lifetime access, while disabled visitors can receive a free Golden Access Passport with similar privileges. Fees in all national parks are suspended on August 25 for Founders Day, celebrating the establishment of the National Park Service.

Presentations, exhibits, brochures, and park rangers are there to teach you about the history of each site before you take the tour, which can be self-guided or led by rangers. Picnic areas and gift shops are part of the package, but you'll have to look elsewhere for food and lodging.

Held on various dates at sites throughout the state, **Civil War reenactments** are history brought to vivid life. The attention to detail is amazing: For serious participants everything has to be authentic, down to the scratchy wool of their pants and the frames on their eyeglasses. Many carry expensive original weapons and accessories. In the field, the smoke of campfires and artillery firings mingles with the rattle of drums and the clop of horse's hooves. Back in camp you can watch a surgeon demonstrate his amputation technique or a local matron hand out hoecakes to hungry soldiers (many reenactors are women).

Tens of thousands of spectators gather for the larger events, usually paying a small fee to watch. Individual battlefields and sites can tell you about reenacting schedules or put you in touch with local reenactment organizations.

Inaugurated in 1997, **Virginia Civil War Trails** focus on different phases of the conflict in Virginia. Three special driving routes ("1862 Peninsula Campaign," "1864 Overland Campaign," and "Lee's Retreat") and two regions (the Shenandoah Valley and northern Virginia) link hundreds of sites of historic significance, often following the same roads the soldiers used. Some are in National Parks or Battlefields, and for the rest, special arrow signs point you down remote back roads far from the recent world, past private homes still bearing bullet scars, churches that once housed the wounded, and streams on whose banks soldiers rested more than a century ago. The website (www.civilwartraveler.com) has information on Civil War history in all parts of the state.

The range of publications dealing with Civil War travel alone shows how popular the subject is to many people. Publications such as ***Civil War Traveler*** and ***A Guide to Virginia's Civil War*** are updated yearly and available free at most visitors centers, historic sites, and National Parks in Virginia. Good magazines to check out include ***America's Civil War*** and ***Civil War Times Illustrated,*** both available through the website The History Net (www.historynet.com), as well as ***Blue & Gray Magazine*** (www.bluegraymagazine.com), which has driving tours, color maps, and plenty of photographs. The ***Camp Chase Gazette*** (800/624-0281, www.campchase.com) is primarily for reenactors.

Working to preserve historic battlefields from the encroachments of modern civilization are organizations such as the **Central Virginia Battlefields Trust** (www.cvbt.org) and the **Civil War Preservation Trust** (202/367-1861, www.civilwar.org). They also have lots of handy links on their websites for Civil War–related travel information.

The **Smithsonian Associates' Civil War Studies section** (202/633-3030, www.civilwarstudies.org) offers a wealth of articles, overnight study tours, online programs, tours, and events.

HOLIDAYS AND FESTIVALS

Every town has its own list of annual celebrations, from Monterey's Highland Maple Festival to Norfolk's Harborfest. At any given event, chances are you'll find live music, dancing, parades, displays of regional crafts, and tables groaning under platters of local food. Historical figures from a particular city are often remembered—or even brought to life by reenactors—on their birthdays, and local events are commemorated in services or parades. Some events charge admission, anywhere from $5 to $20 per adult, and the more popular ones start selling tickets months ahead of time.

Most national holidays, including Easter, the Fourth of July, and Labor Day, get their own celebrations, while Christmas and the week after bring religious services, buildings lit with strings of bulbs, and candlelight tours of historical sites. **First Night** heralds in the New Year in many cities; it's often an alcohol-free family-oriented cultural-performance event. During **Historic Garden Week** (804/644-7776, www.vagardenweek.org) in April, the grounds and gardens of more than 250 locations statewide (most otherwise closed to the public) are open to visitors. Tickets for individual events range $10–35 per person and are available from late January to the day before each event.

A good many of Virginia's best festivals have something to do with music, from **Floydfest** in Floyd in late July to the **Shenandoah Valley Music Festival** in Orkney Springs in August. Old-time country music has a strong showing; in southwest Virginia you can catch the **Floyd Flatfoot Jamboree** on Friday and get to the **Carter Family Fold** in Maces Spring in time for the Saturday show. In August, the **Old Fiddler's Convention** (www.oldfiddlersconvention.com) in Galax is one of the oldest and biggest in the nation. For more country and bluegrass music events, check out **Blue Ridge Music Trails** (www.blueridgemusic.org) and **The Crooked Road: Virginia's Heritage Music Trail** (www.thecrookedroad.org).

A good source on festivals in Virginia, besides the Virginia Tourism Corporation (VTC) and local chambers of commerce, is the Old Dominion edition of the bimonthly newspaper ***Southern Festivals*** (www.southfest.com/virginia.shtml). The Charlottesville-based **Blue Ridge Outdoors** (www.blueridgeoutdoors.com) usually publishes at least one issue on music jam festivals in the region.

Many businesses and all government offices are closed on national holidays. These include New Year's Day (January 1), Martin Luther King Jr. Day (third Monday in January), Presidents' Day (third Monday in February), Memorial Day (last Monday in May), Independence Day (July 4), Labor Day (first Monday in September), Columbus Day (second Monday in October), Veterans' Day (November 11), Thanksgiving Day (fourth Thursday in November, as well as the following day), and Christmas Day (December 25). Lee-Jackson Day (second Friday in January) is also widely observed.

SHOPPING

Virginia handicrafts come in an amazing range of styles and quality. Pottery is near the top of the list, produced in historic ceramics centers such as Strasburg or in the studios of hundreds of potters and ceramic artists across the state. On the coast you can watch decoy carvers at work, or take a class yourself. Keep an eye out for bronze wildlife sculptures and signs advertising Wood Carvings For Sale outside private homes. Craftspeople in Jamestown and Colonial Williamsburg keep historical skills alive as they produce silver pitchers, hand-blown glass, shoes, and musical instruments, many of which are for sale.

Heading west you'll come across hooked rugs, table linens, and quilts from the looms of local weavers, along with handforged iron and brass. Woodcrafters turn out tools, toys, musical instruments, and cane-seat chairs and other furniture. In southwest Virginia, look for the exquisite musical instruments produced in places like Galax. Throughout the state, artisans benefit from **art centers** like the Torpedo Factory, housed in an old munitions plant in Alexandria. Some, including Norfolk's d'Art Center and The Arts Depot in Abingdon, offer classes as well as display and sales areas.

Serious buyers and casual browsers agree that shopping for **antiques** can eat up a week as easily as an afternoon. Barns and attics throughout the state have been raided to stock tiny shops and huge antiques malls, with old stuff by the truckload for sale restored or "as is." Prices are often lower in Virginia than in Washington, D.C., drawing many shoppers down from the capital in search of that elusive but always possible Great Find. The list is practically endless but includes furniture, old toys, quilts, magazines, advertising posters, clothing, and lawn ornaments.

Furniture ranges from country standbys such as cupboards, dressers, wardrobes, rope beds, and blanket boxes to distinctive Hepplewhite, Sheraton, and empire desks, chairs, and chests. **Civil War relics** such as swords, guns, uniforms, and utensils can get pricey, but smaller items—for instance prints, maps, and minnie balls (bullets)—are often more affordable. Packaging and/or delivery can often be arranged on the spot.

Before you plunk down $600 on that creaking farm table, it helps to know a little about antiques pricing. Shop around to get an idea of price ranges, and look for various reference books that offer advice on how to get the most for your money. A wide range of publications cater to antiques buyers and sellers, including *Antique Week* (765/345-5133 or 800/876-5133, www.antiqueweek.com) and *Southeastern Antiquing and Collecting Magazine* (770/974-6495 or 888/388-7827, www.go-star.com/antiquing).

FOOD

Classic Country Cuisine

As soon as the Jamestown settlers were able to make it through a few winters in a row, they set about starting a tradition of rich dining that lives on in Virginia homes and restaurants today. All of the fruits of the fertile land went into the pot and onto the table, including fish from the rivers, bays, and ocean; corn from the Indians; produce brought from the Old World; and farm animals of every description. Every well-stocked dining room had a "groaning board" bent under the weight of overflowing platters.

Today historic-themed restaurants like Williamsburg's Shields Tavern and Charlottesville's Michie Tavern serve this culinary legacy in its truest form. Wherever you go in Virginia, though, you're liable to enjoy local specialties in some form or another. Odds of finding these local foods are better further into the countryside or at a restaurant that advertises "home cooking" as a specialty.

One quick disclaimer: This is not health food. Deep-fried, loaded with butter, and salted from here till Tuesday, home cooking Virginia-style can pack on the pounds quicker than a chocolate tour of Switzerland. But a couple meals won't clog your arteries overnight.

And anyway, it is *good.* The classic meal, served at a restaurant such as The Homeplace near Roanoke, goes something like this: Sides of coleslaw, beans (butter or baked), black-eyed peas, mashed potatoes (plenty of gravy), cornbread,

VIRGINIA WINE

Of all the eastern states, Virginia enjoys the best climate – and mindset – for growing and enjoying quality vintages. Vineyards planted 37-39° north latitude, the same as California's north coast, avoid both the harsh northern cold and the prolonged humid southern summers. Production is usually limited, with most bottles sold at wineries, festivals, wine shops, and supermarkets alongside beer. (Hard liquor by the bottle is found only in state-run Alcohol Beverage Control stores.) The quality of Virginia wine took a quantum leap in the 1990s, but since it is less known as a winemaking location than, say, Sonoma, it's still a good deal; you can get many excellent bottles for under $30.

HISTORY

Early Jamestown settlers grew grapes with the help of French *vignerons* sent by the Virginia Company, but even with the Assembly's "Acte 12" compelling each farmer to plant 12 grapevines or be punished, imported vines died and hardy local varieties turned sour. Cold weather, insects, disease, and the American Revolution undermined the 1769 Act for the Encouragement of the Making of Wine. Thomas Jefferson, the "father of American wine" (among a few other things), shipped in an Italian expert to help him plan Monticello's vineyards, but it wasn't until 1835 that Richmond viticulturist Dr. D. N. Norton bred the first "non-foxy" American wine grape, encouraging local vintners to give it another go.

By 1979 Virginia counted six wineries, and in 1988 Ronald Reagan presented former Soviet president Mikhail Gorbachev with a bottle of Virginia Seyval at the Moscow summit. Four years later, *Wine Spectator* magazine dubbed Virginia "the most accomplished of America's emerging wine regions." The awards had started rolling in, including the 1993 and 1995 *Wine Spectator* Critic's Choice awards bestowed on Williamsburg Winery, placing it among the world's 200 best. By 1997, Virginia was sixth in the country in fine wine production, and in 2009 counted over 140 wineries in production, spread over thousands of acres.

VARIETIES

White wines tend to grow best in the Old Dominion. Thanks to the state's comparably cooler climate, they tend to be light- to medium-bodied, closer to wines from Burgundy or the Pacific Northwest than California. Viogner is Virginia's best white, and it is approaching (some would say already equals – shh!) those

grits, and fresh, flaky, steaming biscuits sidle up to a centerpiece of crispy fried chicken, juicy roast beef, or salty country ham. Occasionally, soup—vegetable, chili, or hearty Brunswick Stew (with the original rabbits and squirrels replaced with chicken, ham, or beef)—is served on the side. Peanut soup is a local staple, just the right balance of sweet and spicy. "Salad" can mean anything from field-fresh tossed greens and dressing to canned fruit served on cottage cheese. Iced tea ("sweet" or "unsweet") is the drink of choice, followed closely by local apple cider. Dessert is often homemade peach or blackberry cobbler or pecan pie.

Main courses almost always include some kind of meat. "Country-fried" or "chicken-fried" steak is covered in breading before cooking, and "barbecue" usually means pork, with a more delicate flavor than the vinegar-fueled kick of Deep South barbecue. Pot roast, rib-eye steak, chicken and dumplings, and baked pork chops are all popular, but **ham** is by far the most distinctive Virginia centerpiece. The tradition began in Colonial days, when pork proved easier to preserve by smoking, drying, sugar-curing, or pickling than other meats. **Virginia ham,** also known as Williamsburg or country ham, is dry-cured with salt and then smoked. **Smithfield ham,** named after the small town on the James River west of Norfolk, is slowly smoked over a hickory fire and then aged, skin and all, for up to a year. This, along with a coating of pepper applied during curing, gives it strong, smoky

of France in quality. Chardonnay and Vidal Blanc do moderately well, with the latter usually made into a dessert wine. Whites to watch include Sauvignon Blanc and Petit Munsang.

Reds here are more temperamental. Cabernet Franc has been the state's premier red for a decade. Despite somewhat inauspicious beginnings, Merlot and Petit Verdot are both up-and-coming, with strong potential in the near future. Vintners have high hopes for Bordeaux-style blends, as well as Norton, the state's native grape. This non-vinifera variety is the only American grape that can age well, but it is still dismissed by many wine "experts." These last two are quite possibly the future of reds in Virginia.

VISITING WINERIES

Wine aficionados can find over 100 wineries from the coast to the mountains, with the highest concentration in the Piedmont. A visit to a winery combines a drive through beautiful countryside with the satisfaction of buying a quality vintage directly from the person who made it – and prices are always best at the source.

Tastings are usually offered free or for a small charge, allowing you to pick your favorite from a wide selection. Tours of the facilities can be guided or self-guided, leading you past crusher-stemmers, presses, fermentation tanks, oak aging barrels, and bottling setups. Many wineries allow you to enjoy your purchase immediately with a picnic on the grounds, and a few offer gourmet restaurants on the premises. October has been dubbed Virginia Wine Month, with dozens of different events held at wineries. During the rest of the year, wineries host everything from jazz concerts to food festivals.

Local wineries are listed in sidebars in the destination chapters of this guide. Visiting hours vary, so it's always a good idea to call before showing up. When driving, look for small grape-cluster road signs that point the way to wineries.

RESOURCES

For a free list of wineries and events, contact the **Virginia Wine Marketing Office** (804/344-8200, www.virginiawines.org) or see the **Virginia Tourism Corporation**'s website on vineyard tours (www.virginia.org/wine). For a regular taste of the Old Dominion, there's the **Virginia Wine of the Month Club** (800/826-0534, www.vawineclub.com), which charges only for wine and shipping – one bottle a month is $16, two are $27.

taste. Local stores often have Smithfield hams hanging in burlap sacks, which customers remove before soaking overnight and cooking. The secret is to slice it paper thin, ideal for the traditional ham biscuit.

Breakfast is often as serious an undertaking as dinner. Biscuits and gravy, chicken-fried steak, sausage, and ham slices may all make an appearance next to your eggs and coffee.

Seafood

The daily catch, served up in weather-beaten cafés on the Eastern Shore and Virginia Beach's great oceanfront restaurants, is the state's other gourmet specialty. Ask your server whether the selection is native or not—of course, fresher is better. Dozens of Virginia's 200 species of fish, including rockfish (striped bass), bluefish, shad, trout, pike, and crappie, are served broiled, fried, grilled, blackened, smoked, and baked.

The most famous Chesapeake shellfish is the famous **Chesapeake blue crab,** whose scientific name *(Callinectes sapidus)* translates as "savory, beautiful swimmer." An average of 44 million pounds of these little guys (and gals) are plucked from the bay every year, making up one-third of the nation's entire catch. Cracking open and eating crabs is an acquired art form, but well worth the effort; males are easier to pick apart, while the millions of eggs inside females can make the experience even messier. Crab cakes, made with cornmeal or cracker crumbs and eggs, are a more manageable alternative.

Soft-shell crabs are brought up within an hour after molting, while they sit on the bottom waiting for their new shells to harden. Those caught just before shedding are stored in floating boxes and watched around the clock until they get around to it. They're fried in batter and eaten whole, often on a bun—a true saltwater delicacy. Crab imperial (mixed with bread, egg, mayonnaise, and Worcestershire sauce), deviled crabs with horseradish and chili powder, and cream-based soups like bisque and sherry-laced "she-crab" are all recipes worth trying. If you're interested in catching your own, try renting a small crab pot from a sporting goods store or netting crabs in the shallows with fish or chicken leftovers as bait.

It was a brave soul who ate the first raw **oyster,** but somehow the slimy mouthful caught on. Chincoteague oysters on the half shell are the best around here. Oyster season runs September–April, with a peak around the holidays. **Clams** are served raw or steamed and are usually cherrystones (aka littlenecks, hardshells) or manoes (steamers, longnecks, or softshells). True Virginia-coast chowder isn't the creamy New England style nor red Manhattan style; here it's made with a clear base filled with potatoes, celery, onions, and herbs. Everything comes with a handful of small balls of fried cornmeal dough called hush puppies.

ESSENTIALS

Getting There and Around

GETTING THERE

By Car

Like most of the United States, Virginia is best explored in your own vehicle. Luckily, a network of interstate highways provides easy access to every corner. I-81, running the length of the western border, and I-95, connecting Washington, D.C., with Richmond and North Carolina, are the main north–south arteries. I-66 links the nation's capital with I-81, a popular north–south alternative to I-95. I-64 runs from the Norfolk area through Richmond to Staunton, continuing west from Lexington into West Virginia.

The speed limit on rural interstates is 65 mph; otherwise it's 55 mph or as marked. Radar detectors are illegal in Virginia. State-maintained routes may have a name (i.e., Old Mill Road) as well as a number (Route 645), so keep this in mind as you look for that out-of-the-way bed-and-breakfast. Give the state tourism office a call for a free map of the state's thousands of miles of official and proposed **scenic byways.**

In winter, state-maintained roads are generally plowed quickly, though a fast, heavy snowfall can take a day or two to clear. Nearly

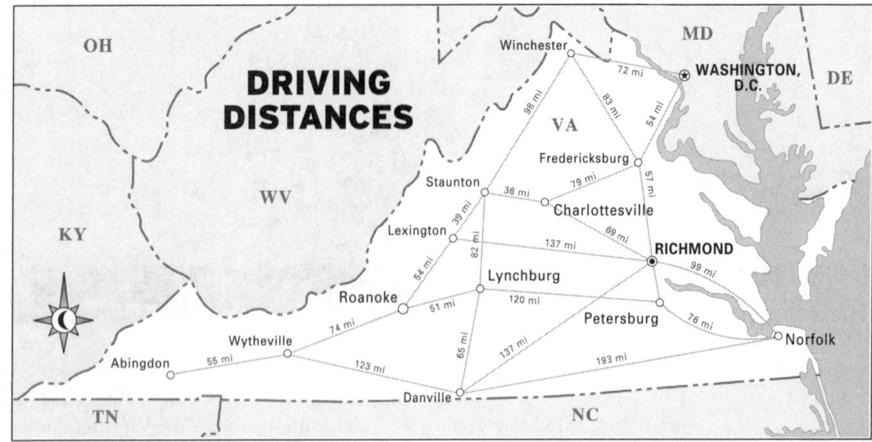

invisible **black ice** is the biggest winter driving hazard, especially at night and in the early morning before the sun melts it. **Fog** on the mountains is another concern; you'll most often encounter it along the Skyline Drive and Blue Ridge Parkway. Visibility can plunge to 50 feet or less, so go slow and turn on your headlights. (Some passes, like I-64 near Waynesboro, have lights in the roadway to make driving in fog safer.)

The **Virginia Department of Highways and Transportation** (www.virginiadot.org) offers many resources for drivers, including a Highway Help and Information line (511 or 800/367-7623), traffic webcams, road condition and construction maps, and details on carpooling and high-occupancy vehicle (HOV) lanes.

If you plan on doing a lot of driving, then joining the **American Automobile Association (AAA)** (www.aaa.com) can come in handy. Emergency roadside assistance, free maps, tourbooks, and campbooks are all included in the yearlong membership fee (about $65–130). Contact your local AAA office for details.

By Bus

Greyhound (800/231-2222, www.greyhound.com) connects most Virginia cities and tourist destinations. Tickets are cheaper if you buy them in advance. Its Discovery Pass program (www.discoverypass.com) offers discounted unlimited travel for certain periods (weeks or months). Ask about other discounts for students, seniors, and military personnel. Children under 12 travel for 25 percent off, and companions assisting a traveler with disabilities receive half-off tickets with 48 hours' notice. Call the toll-free number for route and fare information; local terminal numbers will handle all other inquiries.

By Train

Traveling on **Amtrak** (800/872-7245, www.amtrak.com) to Virginia is closer in price to flying, but more comfortable and convenient. Amtrak's high-speed Acela Express connects New York City to Washington, D.C.'s **Union Station.** From there, Metrorail lines run to destinations in northern Virginia.

In the rest of the state, service varies between one or more round-trips daily to 3–6 per week, with Amtrak Thruway buses connecting some cities. Student, senior, veterans', and children's discounts are available. Special seating, boarding assistance, and discounts for travelers with disabilities are possible with 24 hours' notice, and service dogs ride free. Once again, use the toll-free number for

AMTRAK VIRGINIA LINES

TRAIN	ROUTE	VIRGINIA AREA STOPS
Cardinal/Hoosier State	New York City to Chicago, IL	Washington, D.C., Alexandria, Manassas, Culpeper, Charlottesville, Staunton, Clifton Forge
Carolinian and Piedmont	Washington, D.C., to Charlotte, NC	Alexandria, Quantico, Fredericksburg, Petersburg, Richmond
Crescent	New York City to New Orleans	Washington, D.C., Alexandria, Manassas, Culpeper, Charlottesville, Lynchburg, Danville
Regional	Boston to Newport News, VA	Washington, D.C., Alexandria, Woodbridge, Quantico, Fredericksburg, Ashland, Richmond, Williamsburg
Silver Service/Palmetto	New York City to Miami	Washington, D.C., Alexandria, Richmond, Petersburg

route and fare questions; otherwise, local terminal numbers for baggage and other questions are given under individual city listings in this guide.

By Air

Most major airlines fly into one of two major airports in northern Virginia: **Washington Dulles International Airport** near Herndon or **Ronald Reagan Washington National Airport** on the Potomac between Arlington and Alexandria. National handles domestic flights from east of the Mississippi and is easily accessible from D.C. by Metro. There are also major airports near Richmond, Norfolk, Newport News–Williamsburg, Charlottesville, and Roanoke.

The cheapest flights are almost always round-trip and date-restricted (usually requiring a Saturday-night stay). You'll have to book in advance and purchase within a day or two of making a reservation to secure the fare. Try different airports and smaller or regional carriers, and it never hurts to search one of the many fare search engines such as Travelocity.com or Kayak.com for up-to-the-minute deals.

GETTING AROUND

Bus Tours

Cosmos (www.cosmos.com) offers a Historic Trails and Blue Ridge Mountains tour, covering Washington, D.C., Williamsburg, and Lexington, as well as parts of Maryland, Pennsylvania, West Virginia, Kentucky, and Tennessee (14 days, $1,729 pp). These tours are primarily booked through travel agents.

Gray Line (202/289-1995, www.graylinedc.com) sends daily bus tours from Washington, D.C., to Mount Vernon and Old Town Alexandria ($55 adults, $30 children), Arlington National Cemetery and Mount Vernon ($70/$45), and Monticello and Charlottesville ($92/$60). Most run March–October and end at Union Station in Washington, D.C., after a morning hotel pickup in the capital.

Outdoor Tours

Sierra Club Outings (415/977-5522, www.sierraclub.org/outings) can arrange extended hiking trips on the Appalachian Trail in the Shenandoah and week-long bicycle trips along the C&O Canal for about $1,000 per person. **New England Hiking Holidays** (800/869-0949, www.nehikingholidays.com) rambles through the Blue Ridge, exploring Civil War history and country inns along the way (six days, $1,725–1,825 pp). The Potomac Appalachian Trail Club organizes day and overnight hikes as well.

Bird-watchers could do much worse than **Field Guides Incorporated** (512/263-7295 or 800/728-4953, www.fieldguides.com). Its Virginia's Warblers tour explores Monticello, the James River, the Blue Ridge, and West Virginia's Monongahela National Forest (five days, $1,250). **Smithsonian Journeys** (877/338-8687, www.smithsonianjourneys.org) offers a wide range of educational seminars and study tours in Virginia covering topics as diverse as architecture, the Civil War, and opera. One example is a week-long scenic cruise of the Chesapeake Bay aboard the *American Spirit* ($3,715–4,555 double occupancy).

Recreation

With so many activities readily available, it's a surprise Virginians ever get anything done. Simply put, if you can do it on the East Coast, you can probably do it here, from skiing to surfing and most everything in between.

In general, hours and admission prices vary depending on the attraction and the season. Children's prices generally apply to kids under 12, with tots admitted free. Senior admission falls somewhere in between the adult and child prices. Taking pictures is against the rules in many museums and historical houses, so ask first.

GENERAL RESOURCES

Information on the state's incredible range of open-air activities can be ordered from the **Virginia Department of Conservation and Recreation** (203 Governor St., Richmond, 804/786-1712, www.dcr.state.va.us). This is also the place to go for information on Virginia's 35 **state parks** (800/933-7275, www.dcr.state.va.us/parks). The best are covered in this guide; see the individual listings for more details.

The Virginia section of the **Great Outdoor Resource Page** (http://gorp.away.com/gorp/location/va/va.htm) lists activities, tour operators, and links for the entire state. Another good source for articles and outdoor-activity listings in the mid-Atlantic states is ***Blue Ridge Outdoors*** (434/817-2755, www.blueridgeoutdoors.com), a free monthly magazine distributed throughout Virginia.

HIKING AND CAMPING

The simplest way to enjoy Virginia often reveals her humblest, but most profound, pleasures. Whether it's an evening amble down a

Log steps ease the climb on this trail in Shenandoah National Park.

VIRGINIA'S OFFBEAT BEST

Association for Research and Enlightenment, Virginia Beach: The catalogued prophecies of American psychic Edgar Cayce, plus massages and yoga.

Dinosaur Land, White Post: Fiberglass Tyrannosaurs and a 60-foot shark are just the beginning.

Holy Land USA, Bedford: Full-size replicas of Bible scenes on a central Virginia farm.

Jeff Matthews Museum, Galax: A Kodiak grizzly and over 1,000 knives.

Johnny Appleseed, Bedford: A 15-foot statue of Mr. Appleseed himself keeps a cockeyed watch over Peaks of Otter Winery and Johnson's Orchard.

Jolly Roger Haggle Shop, Staunton: More than a million items piled to the ceiling.

Professor Cline's Haunted Monster Museum and Dark Maze, Natural Bridge: What does this have to do with a 215-foot limestone span? Got me, but it's still fun.

Tangier Island: A unique, long-isolated fishing community in the bosom of the Chesapeake Bay.

Virginia Wine & Garlic Festival, Rebec Vineyards, Amherst (October): The "stinking rose" in just about every form imaginable.

Yogaville, Buckingham, and **Holy Cross Abbey,** Berryville: Two different takes on spiritual lodgings.

Look for the giant Johnny Appleseed at Peaks of Otter Winery and Johnson's Orchard near Bedford.

country lane or a predawn slog up some rocky peak, walking only requires a pair of boots and a little time and effort. For this small investment you can find yourself miles from anyone else, resting by an icy waterfall or enjoying a 50-mile view—or maybe just down the road, discussing bait fish with the folks at the local market.

Shenandoah National Park draws D.C. residents by the SUV-full, and for good reason—it encloses some of the choicest acres in all of Appalachia. Most visitors never go more than an hour from the asphalt, though, leaving the backcountry to the more determined travelers. Through the park coils part of the famous **Appalachian Trail,** tramped by hundreds of thru-hikers and thousands of day-ramblers every year. Farther south lie the **Mount Rogers National Recreation Area** and **Breaks Interstate Park,** both rugged and less trafficked.

Other established trails such as the Washington and Old Dominion, Virginia Creeper, and New River started out as railroad beds before being reborn as foot-power freeways. For details on these routes (which are also open to bikes and horses), call the **Rails-to-Trails Conservancy** in Washington, D.C. (202/331-9696, www.railtrails.org).

The **George Washington & Jefferson National Forests** cover more than one-eighth of the entire state. More information on the national forests can be found at local district offices listed in the destination chapters of this guide, or contact the Forest Supervisor's office in Roanoke (540/265-5100 or 888/265-0019, www.fs.fed.us/r8/gwj).

The **Potomac Appalachian Trail Club** in Vienna (118 Park St. SE, 703/242-0693, www.potomacappalachian.org) is a great resource for information on hikes, excursions, and work trips on the AT and elsewhere. Check the calendar tab of the club website for upcoming excursions, all of which are open to newcomers.

Swimming holes statewide (and along the entire East Coast, for that matter) are listed online at www.swimmingholes.org, and you can create, download, and order custom topographic maps from **TopoZone** (www.topozone.com) or **MyTopo** (www.mytopo.com). An excellent resource for hikers in Virginia and West Virginia is **HikingUpward.com.** The volunteer-run website organizes hikes by region on an interactive map, with hike listings that include photos, trail maps, driving directions, and ratings on a scale of 1–5 for difficulty, views, solitude, and the like.

BICYCLING

Virginia has an incredible diversity of cycling opportunities, from careening down rocky single-track in the mountains to spinning along the Virginia Beach boardwalk. It's not that big a state, and you can cover a lot of ground on two wheels, so long-distance rides are a great option, camping in state parks or national forest campgrounds along the way. The mid-Atlantic also has a very competitive cycling racing scene, to rival even California's.

Wherever you go, don't overestimate your abilities or underestimate the terrain. Take foul-weather gear, tire patches, a pump, and enough food and water to keep you going in case the next rest stop is farther along than you thought. In the countryside, angry dogs can be a nuisance and occasionally a danger. Outrunning them is an option (most will give

Cyclists will find that both competitive races and recreational group rides are popular throughout the state.

up the chase once you leave their territory), as is shouting and dismounting to put your bike between Cujo and yourself. Save kicking, pepper-spraying, or whacking with a pump for a last resort.

Mountain Biking

Fat-tire fanatics will quickly find that Virginia's high country offers some of the best steep dirt on the East Coast. *Mountain Bike* magazine voted Charlottesville the number eight "Dream Town" in the country for mountain bikers, while *Dirt Rag* has sung the praises of Harrisonburg. Many excellent foot trails are also open to knobby tires—just make sure to yield to walkers and horses, and don't do anything to give off-road riders a bad name. Trail difficulty ranges from countless miles of low-grade dirt roads to single-track descents to turn your hair white. Races occur year-round throughout the state; check out www.usacycling.org/mtb and www.active.com for mountain bike events. I-81 provides handy access to trails and approach roads following the length of the Blue Ridge. Bring your bike to Damascus if you're ever headed to Virginia's southwest tip.

Various guidebooks can tell you where to go, and a handful of tour companies can take you there. National forest district offices are good sources of information on trail conditions and maps, as are local bike shops, many of which also rent bikes and offer guide services. If you're looking for a more sedate ride, every former railroad trail has a host of agencies that offer rentals and shuttle service to cyclists.

For more details, contact the **International Mountain Biking Association** (303/545-9011 or 888/442-4622, www.imba.com), which offers a list of local cycling clubs on its website (www.imba.com/contacts/near_you/virginia .html).

Cycling Events and Information

The competitive cycling scene is very active in the mid-Atlantic. Dozens of teams train in Virginia, D.C., and Maryland and road races occur almost every weekend from April through September, with mountain bike and cyclocross races even later in the year. The **Mid-Atlantic Bicycle Racing Association** (www .mabra.org) oversees most races in the region and is a good resource. **GamJams** (www.gam jams.net) is another popular website for a race calendar and biker gossip.

Bike touring and more recreational trips also abound. **Bike Virginia** (804/261-0507, www .bikevirginia.org) is a five-day ride down back roads, past historical monuments and natural wonders. It's held every June and covers about 50 miles per day. Some 2,000 cyclists per year sign up to explore a different part of the state. For a fee of $360 per person, there are vehicles to carry your luggage, and the trip organizers can help arrange meals and accommodations every evening. Shorter group cycling events include the **Tour de Chesapeake** (www.bikechesapeake.org), covering 15–80 miles in three days in mid-May near the mouth of the Chesapeake Bay, and **River Ride** (www.riverride.org) on the Northern Neck in late September. In October the **Shenandoah Fall Foliage Bike Festival** (540/416-0267, www.shenandoahbike.org) takes advantage of Virginia's spectacular autumn colors with road rides of varying lengths that start and end in Staunton. Registration is $85 adults, $15 ages 6–17.

Riders from both camps can benefit from the **Adventure Cycling Association (ACA)** (800/755-2453, www.adventurecycling.org), a nonprofit organization that helps support the development and maintenance of more than 25,000 miles of roads and off-road trails nationwide. The ACA stocks long-distance gear, books, and excellent route maps.

For more information on events, see the website of the **Virginia Cycling Association** (www.vacycling.org), an organization of a dozen or so local cycling clubs. The **Virginia State Bicycle Coordinator** (804/371-4869 or 800/835-1203, vabiking@vdot.virginia.gov) is another good cycling resource.

ADVENTURE RACING

This relatively new sport typically combines several activities—running, mountain biking, and paddling—as well as route-finding and the occasional "challenge," like solving a puzzle or balancing across suspended ropes. You can compete alone or as part of a team, and races last from a few hours to multiple days. It's catching on quickly, particularly near urban areas, since it allows people trapped in offices all week to get out on weekends and challenge themselves. Plus, it's a good excuse to get in great shape, and it's a heck of a lot of fun.

Many adventure races are already becoming regular annual events in Virginia. **Odyssey Adventure Racing** (www.oarevents.com), with the motto "Your pain is our pleasure" (these races aren't cakewalks), sponsors running and mountain bike races and adventure race clinics near Roanoke. **EX2 Adventures** (www .ex2adventures.com) also holds trail running, mountain bike, and adventure races, including the Greenhorn in Prince William Forest Park in northern Virginia for first-timers. The headliner each June is the **XTERRA East**

Championship (www.xterra.com), when adventure-racing elite from 35 states and around the world descend on the James River Park System in Richmond to jockey over qualifying slots for the World Championship in Maui. There's a 10K and a half-marathon for the weekend warrior too.

For more information, and for a list of adventure races across the country, contact the **U.S. Adventure Racing Association** (979/703-5018, www.usara.com).

HORSEBACK RIDING

Settled as it was on horseback, Virginia still has hundreds of miles of trails open to riders. Lodges, farms, and outfitters throughout the Shenandoah and southwest Virginia can set you up for a day ride, including guided rides from Skyland Lodge in Shenandoah National Park. The Virginia Horse Center near Lexington hosts national equine events. Contact the **Virginia Horse Council** (888/467-7382, www.virginiahorsecouncil.org) for a statewide list of stables and public horse trails.

Riding takes on a more patrician air in the Piedmont area and the Hunt Country of northern Virginia, where horses have been a cornerstone of life for generations. **Fox hunts** in spring and fall evoke Old England (and horrify animal-rights activists), with groups of riders in traditional uniforms galloping after packs of baying hounds. In American hunts, the chase is more important than the actual fox, which is rarely caught. You'll have to be invited by a member of a hunt (local club) to participate; most observers follow by car and enjoy tailgate picnics along the way. During the November–March season, you might be able to catch the blessing of the hounds, a ritual in which a priest or minister invokes divine guidance on the pack.

Long before Virginia-born Secretariat won the Triple Crown in 1973, **horse races** have raised the blood pressure of both species involved. Dozens of steeplechases and assorted flat-track events take advantage of the state's prime horse stock, which goes back to thoroughbred stallions imported from England in the 18th century. Races are held from spring to fall at places such as Foxfield near Charlottesville, where dressy tailgate parties distract college students and race fans alike. The Plains, near Middleburg, hosts the Virginia Gold Cup in May and the International Gold Cup in October. **Polo** matches usually include the traditional divot-stomping at halftime. Recent referendums have begun to reverse religious-inspired prohibitions on pari-mutuel **betting,** making new tracks like the Colonial Downs in Richmond the place to lay your money down.

The Middleburg visitors center or the **Virginia Steeplechase Association** (www.vasteeplechase.com) can provide a listing of seasonal horse events. For information on some two dozen local hunts, steeplechase, and "point-to-point" races, contact the ***Chronicle of the Horse*** (540/687-6341, www.chronofhorse.com) for details on getting in touch with local clubs. You can get a free copy of *A Guide to Virginia's Horse Country* from the Virginia Horse Industry Board (804/786-5842, www.vhib.org) of the state Department of Agriculture.

ROCK CLIMBING

At least 30 climbing areas scattered along the Blue Ridge provide a respectable alternative to West Virginia's Seneca Rocks and New River Gorge, often with a fraction of the crowds. Most cliffs are 40–60 feet high and can be top-roped, with both traditional and sport routes. Access is easy and legal to routes in national forests and state and national parks. Great Falls on the Potomac is one of the most popular sites near D.C., with more than 100 routes of all levels. (Carderock just over on the Maryland side also gets lots of traffic.) Other popular spots include Old Rag Mountain and scattered areas near Harrisonburg and off Skyline Drive.

Don't trespass on private land, and clean up any mess you make to help ensure that future climbers will be welcome. Jeff Watson's *Virginia Climber's Guide* and Eric Hörst's *Rock Climbing Virginia, West Virginia, and Maryland* are both good sources. The Mountaineering

Section of the Potomac Appalachian Trail Club (118 Park St. SE, Vienna, 703/242-0693, www.potomacappalachian.org) organizes rock or ice climbs most weekends. Indoor climbing gyms such as **Sport Rock** (5308 Eisenhower Ave., 703/212-7625, www.sportrock.com) in Alexandria and **Peak Experiences** (11421 Polo Circle, Midlothian, 804/897-6800, www.peakexperiences.com) near Richmond will also have suggestions for outdoor climbing.

RAFTING, KAYAKING, AND CANOEING

Few things embody the Virginia landscape as much as flowing water, etching the Piedmont before widening into the watery highways of the Tidewater and the Chesapeake Bay. Some 380 miles of Virginia's waterways have been declared State Scenic Rivers for their beauty, historic significance, or recreational value. All told, nearly 200 rivers, creeks, and channels are open to boaters of every kind, many with excellent public access. Calmer waters fill tidal estuaries and more than 30 lakes ranging 500–50,000 acres. Dozens of outfitters and tour companies can put you on the water.

© KATIE GITHENS

A kayaker paddles down the James River near Richmond.

The foothills of the Blue Ridge are only the beginning of the journey for Virginia's biggest rivers, whose upper reaches often churn with white water, like the Russell Fork as it roars through the canyons of Breaks Interstate Park. Rafters and kayakers in search of a challenge should also look east to the fall line, where wide, slow rivers suddenly gush over a natural ledge that runs the length of the state. The Potomac River seethes near Great Falls Park into one of the finest white-water stretches in the East. The James River can reach Class IV, depending on the season, within sight of Richmond.

Between the chutes and holes lie placid stretches ideal for canoes and inner tubes: The Clinch, Maury, Mattaponi, upper James, and the South Fork of the Shenandoah are just a few of the most popular watercourses. A canoe is also the best way to explore the spooky depths of the Great Dismal Swamp or the boggy reaches of the Nottaway and Blackwater Rivers near Suffolk. Always bring food, drinking water, sunscreen, and a change of clothes in a waterproof container (trash bags work). River shoes and insect repellent can also come in handy.

The **Virginia Professional Paddlesports Association** (www.vappa.com) is a good place to direct questions on water sports. Member businesses are listed on its website. **Blue Ridge River Runners** in Lynchburg (www.brrr.ws) is a group that advocates river safety and the protection of Virginia's waterways, and it can help arrange paddling instruction. Further north, **Liquid Adventures** (301/229-0428, www.liquidadventures.org) teaches classes in the Potomac's tamer white water near Great Falls (they're good—even I learned how to roll). **American Whitewater** (866/262-8429, www.americanwhitewater.org) lists conservation information and river-level readings and protects public access to rivers. For ocean paddlers, the website www.seakayak.ws is a great resource for info on kayaking in the Chesapeake Bay.

BOATING

It may take more effort and money to hit the water of the Chesapeake Bay and the Atlantic, but it's almost guaranteed to be well worth it. **Excursion** or **cruise** boats, from restored wooden schooners to modest motorboats, take passengers on sightseeing junkets. The trips, which can last anywhere from an hour to all day, usually feature narration on points of interest and drinks, snacks, or even a full sit-down meal (on the luxury dinner yachts up the Potomac). You'll find more locals than tourists aboard **water taxis** and **ferries,** which simply shuttle between one shore and another.

Charter boats, under both sail and mechanized power, can be rented for a day or longer to go after trophy fish or to explore the farthest reaches of the seaward islands. Expect to have your references and credentials thoroughly checked if you plan to rent one "barebones," meaning without a captain. A hired skipper will tack on at least $100 to the price, which tends to be around $400–800 for one day (there's often a two-day minimum rental, and luxury boats go for significantly more). Charters often leave from **marinas,** shoreside establishments that are combination truck stops, mini-marts, and RV campgrounds. Mooring slips, electrical hookups, holding-tank pumps, freshwater fill-up, bait, tackle, and crusty advice are standard, with the occasional laundry, grocery, and shower facilities thrown in for good measure.

Various local schools offer **classes** in the operation and navigation of sailing and power boats. Your next step will probably be a **rental,** either of a full-sized craft or a smaller day sailer, windsurfer, or rowboat. Most major lakes and countless locations along the bay and coast have public launching ramps for boat trailers. Contact the Department of Conservation and Recreation (203 Governor St., Richmond, 804/786-1712, www.dcr.state.va.us) for a map of public access to the Chesapeake Bay and its tributaries, and look at the *Virginia State Road Atlas* for other river and lake access points.

SURFING

Virginia Beach is without a doubt the most popular surfing area on the coast. Be careful of local regulations: Surfing is prohibited in some spots and within 300 feet of piers, and you have to wear a leash to avoid a fine. Summer surfing hours typically run sunrise–10 A.M. and 5 P.M.–sunset. A good break curls near the jetty

© KATIE GITHENS

Sixteen-foot skiffs are available for rent at Capt. Bob's Marina on Chincoteague Island.

off 1st Street near the Lighthouse Restaurant. Conditions are just as promising along the Eastern Shore, but difficult access keeps many surfers away. You'll need a flat-bottomed boat to explore the outer islands of the Virginia Coast Reserve.

Swells are usually small (1–5 feet) but can grow to 9–10 feet during the winter and spring nor'easters or late-summer hurricanes. Early fall is most dependable. You'll probably need at least a partial wetsuit in the spring and fall, and an early start is essential to enjoy the summer warmth without the crowds. Bottoms are sandy. Virginia Beach is full of surf shops, some of which rent boards.

For more details, order *Mid-Atlantic Surf Report* (Vol. 8, #12, $8) from Surfer Publications (www.surfermag.com/travel/usa), or contact the Virginia District of the **Eastern Surfing Association** (http://va.surfesa.org).

FISHING

Tens of thousands of registered anglers have statewide conservation efforts to thank for the quality of fishing in Virginia. Both fly and bait casters can go after native Eastern brook trout in the hillside streams of Shenandoah National Park, part of 2,800 miles of trout waters within the Blue Ridge. Bass are ubiquitous throughout the state: The upper James River can't be beat for smallmouth, with more trophy fish per mile than any other Virginia river. Sunfish and catfish are also plentiful, joined by crappie and white perch downstream near Richmond.

Head to the South Fork of the Shenandoah River for redbreast sunfish, then try the New River for yellow perch, muskellunge, and walleye, and the Chickahominy near Walker's Dam in late spring for bluegill, chain pickerel, and herring. Almost all of the state's lakes and reservoirs also offer excellent fishing. Smith Mountain Lake near Roanoke is Virginia's top spot for striped bass, and largemouth bass fishing in the John H. Kerr Reservoir along the North Carolina border can't be beat. Charter boats ply the Chesapeake Bay for trout, bluefish, flounder, drum, and sharks, while deep-sea boats leave Virginia Beach in search of marlin, sailfish, and sea bass. Peak saltwater season is May–September.

The **Virginia Department of Game and Inland Fisheries** (804/367-1000, www.dgif.virginia.gov/fishing) can provide details on fishing spots and regulations, along with an annual guide to freshwater angling throughout the state. Freshwater licenses are available to nonresidents over 16 for $36 from sporting-goods stores, bait shops, and marinas (stocked-trout permits are another $36; tack on $3 to fish in national forest). No permits are required for saltwater fishing from Cape Henry to North Carolina. Call the permit information number (866/721-6911) for more details.

HUNTING

Hunting ranks near the top of the list of Virginia's most popular activities, although more among locals than visitors. So many permits are sold every year that, when combined with the sale of fishing licenses, it's almost enough to completely support the Virginia Department of Game and Inland Fisheries. Licenses are available for guns, bows, trapping, and falconry. In the western part of the state, most hunting occurs in the national forests, while back east hunters use private land or hunting clubs. With close to a million deer roaming the state, it's no surprise that white-tails are one of the most popular targets during the November–January season (dates vary for black-powder and bow hunters). Even if you're not hunting, be sure to wear blaze orange on public lands this time of year! Other fall seasons encompass duck, small game (rabbit and squirrel), quail, and bear. Waterfowl season includes Canada geese along the Eastern Shore, and turkey season spans five weeks in the spring.

Licenses and regulations vary locally, and a hunter education certificate is necessary for first-timers and younger hunters. ... contact the **Virginia Department o**
Inland Fisheries (804/367-10
.virginia.gov/hunting). Local h
know about public and private s
for clay, trap, and skeet.

Virginia has plenty of bird-watching opportunities.

BIRD-WATCHING

The uninitiated may dismiss it as an odd, pointless waste of time and energy, but once you've caught the bird-watching bug, you'll always wince at how much you were missing before peering through binoculars and poring over checklists taught you to see all of nature in a vivid new way.

The **American Bird Conservancy** (540/253-5780, www.abcbirds.org) has named 12 locations in Virginia among the top 500 "globally important bird areas" in the country, selected for their habitat value. The list includes a good chunk of the Shenandoah, as well as Assateague Island National Seashore, the Eastern Shore of Virginia National Wildlife Refuge, the Virgina Coastal Reserve, and the Great Dismal Swamp National Wildlife Refuge. See its website for bird-watching guides to each area.

The spring and fall migration periods are the best times for bird-watching in almost any art of the state, from hawk-spotting along the Ridge to waterbirds following the Atlantic p and down the coast. Bald eagles are making a comeback to the state's coastal waterways, even along the Potomac River and Tidal Basin of the nation's capital. Several guidebooks are indispensable for bird-watchers, and most Virginia parks and reserves can supply—or at least point you toward—a list of local species.

The first of its kind in the country, the **Virginia Birding and Wildlife Trail** is a network that links the state's best places to see birds and animals. It includes 18 driving loops on the coast, 34 in the mountains, and 13 in the Piedmont. Order a detailed guide courtesy of the state Department of Game and Inland Fisheries online at www.dgif.virginia.gov/vbwt for $8.50.

CAVES AND CAVERNS

Although not technically *outdoors,* Virginia's underground acres can provide a glimpse of a fascinating side of the state—its underside. Virginia is among the top spelunking states in the country, with more than 4,000 known caves. Most of them were formed when carbonic

© KATIE GITHENS

Luray Caverns are among a number of commercial caves worth exploring.

acid, a weak natural acid carried in groundwater, ate away at underground limestone (calcium carbonate) deposited as sediments on the floors of shallow seas eons before.

Over millions of years, the steady drip of mineral-laden water has worn away rooms and passages and filled them with a moonscape of fantastic formations like cave drapery, flowstone, and soda straws. Stalactites hang tight to the ceiling, often bearing a drop of water at the tip ready to slide off and leave another hairsbreadth of ore behind. Stalagmites grow up underneath, occasionally meeting their suspended twins and joining into columns. Everything down here happens excruciatingly slowly: It can take more than 100 years for a feature to grow one inch.

Expect cool temperatures year-round (55–65°F), confusing passages, and one of the only opportunities on earth to experience total darkness. On true spelunking expeditions, tight squeezes might mean you have to push your backpack through first, or assume the "Groucho walk"—bent over at the waist, with your head up to watch for stalactites. Guides show the way and provide assurance and helmets with carbide lamps. Emergency kits, instruction in their use, and three sources of light per person should be standard. Wear sturdy boots and reasonably warm clothes that you won't mind getting muddy, and bring food and water in a small backpack. Never go underground without an experienced guide.

No matter how sturdy they seem, don't touch any formations, because the oils from your fingertips can stop the accumulation of minerals (notice how slick and dead-looking the places you're allowed to touch in commercial caves are). Keep an eye out for bats hanging asleep along the walls and ceiling. (Just for the record, they're not dangerous or icky—just think of them as mice with wings—though if you're rodent-phobic, that might not help.)

Virginia's most impressive and accessible caves—almost all in the Shenandoah—have been tamed and opened to the public. These commercial caverns feature paved paths, handrails, colored lights, and towering monuments with ridiculous names like "Dairy Queen

FLY THE FRIENDLY SKIES

Should you become interested, for some strange reason, in experiencing the Virginia airspace up close, you have a few options. One option is drifting through it attached to a **parachute.** You can learn enough for a tandem jump in as little as half an hour, then take the plunge strapped to an instructor's chest for around $240. Static-line courses, in which your ripcord is pulled automatically – remember those World War II movies where the poor saps line up, clip in, and leap – cost about the same. An all-day Accelerated Free Fall (AFF) level-one course (it's the learning that's accelerated, not the fall) will have you yanking your own ripcord and set you back $300-380 per person.

Take the plunge on the Middle Neck at the **West Point Skydiving Center** (804/785-9707, www.skydivewestpoint.com), or with **Skydive Virginia** (540/967-3997 or 540/941-8085, www.skydive-virginia.com) at the airport in Louisa, between Charlottesville and Richmond. **Skydive Orange** (877/348-3759, www.skydiveorange.com) operates a small but respectable school out of the Orange County Airport, and is the closest drop zone to Washington, D.C.

If you'd rather stay in the plane, **Front Royal Fighter Command** (540/635-2203 or 800/809-5482, www.giftflight.com) offers flights in a WWII North American AT-6 "Texan" fighter trainer based out of Front Royal. Prices range from $445 for a 30-minute test flight to $695 for an hour-long session, with an optional tail-mounted videotape of the flight. Passengers on rides of a half hour or longer will be given a chance to fly the thing (under supervision, of course) and can opt to have the pilot demonstrate a series of aerobatic maneuvers.

Cone." Wide reflective lakes (always called "Fairy"-something) are often only inches deep and peppered with dozens of tiny growths. Guided tours are mandatory.

For more information on caving in Virginia, contact a local "grotto," the **Virginia Region of the National Speleological Society** (www.varegion.org), or the **Virginia Cave Board** (804/786-7951, www.dcr.virginia.gov/dnh/cavehome1.htm).

Be aware that in 2009 the U.S. Fish and Wildlife Service issued a voluntary moratorium on caving in Virginia in response to a mysterious illness decimating bat populations in the northeast United States and as far south as the Blue Ridge. White-Nose Syndrome, as it's called, has a 90 to 100 percent mortality rate for affected bat populations. While there's no known risk to humans, cavers may inadvertently spread the malady from cave to cave via clothes and gear. For more information, see www.fws.gov/northeast/wnscavers.html.

SKIING

In 1959, The Homestead, in the Shenandoah area, added the first ski slopes in the South to its long list of activities. Since then three other resorts have opened on Virginia's western mountains: Bryce, Massanutten, and Wintergreen. Conditions can be great for this far south—especially during fluke blizzard years. All four Virginia resorts welcome snowboarders (The Homestead boasts a 250-foot halfpipe), and most offer snowmaking and slopeside lodging. During the ski season of mid-December–mid-March, temperatures seldom drop below the teens even at night.

For year-round skiing, look no further than the Liberty Mountain Snowplex Centre in Lynchburg, where you can ski sleeveless in August. Opened in 2009, the center is the first synthetic ski hill in North America to use Snowflex, an artificial snow surface that cushions and grips well enough for softening landings in the terrain park.

GOLF

With its mild climate and endless undulating acres, Virginia has sprouted hundreds of public, resort, and semi-private golf courses. A few rival any in the country, including Wintergreen Resort and The Homestead. One course in Williamsburg clings so tightly to its Highland roots that sheep roam the grounds and a Scottish bagpiper plays at dusk each day. The **Virginia State Golf Association** (804/378-2300, www.vsga.org) lists courses, shops, tournaments, and instruction available statewide. Call 800/932-2259 for a free copy of the annual *Virginia Golf Guide.*

OTHER RECREATION

A host of **water sports,** including sailing, scuba diving, and riding personal watercraft, is offered by various businesses along the coast, concentrating in and around Virginia Beach. **Hot-air balloons** and **skydiving** planes lift enthusiasts above the fields of the Piedmont and northern Virginia (bringing them back to earth at slightly different speeds). Seasonal **college sports** such as football, basketball, soccer, and baseball demonstrate local spirit like nothing else.

Contact the Virginia Department of Agriculture and Consumer Services (804/786-2373, www.vdacs.virginia.gov/vagrown) for a copy of *Virginia Grown,* a booklet describing places around the state where you can **pick your own berries and farm produce,** as well as month-to-month produce availability charts and farmers market listings. Most of this information is available on its website as well. The crisp days of fall bring **apple picking** at orchards and wineries; contact the Virginia Apple Growers Association (434/984-0573, www.virginiaapples.org) for a list and schedule.

Accommodations

HOTELS AND MOTELS

Virginia law dictates that maximum prices must be posted in rooms. Beyond that, accommodation rates can vary drastically depending on the timing, your persistence, and the manager's desire to fill an otherwise empty room. **High season** (May–September and the October fall foliage displays) can double prices, as can holidays and local events such as college athletic games and graduations.

Always ask about discounts: Business/corporate, government, senior (AARP), auto club (AAA), and military rates are almost always lower. Weekend rates, except in resort areas like Virginia Beach, can save you a bundle if you stay Friday and/or Saturday night. Longer stays of a week or more are also discounted. Simply checking around in the evening can often score you a good deal because hotels are eager to fill empty rooms. Websites such as Orbitz (www.orbitz.com) and Travelocity (www.travelocity.com) let you find your own deals and often offer discounts for booking your flight, hotel, and/or rental car together.

Hotel chains' main reservation numbers can tell you the location of their nearest representative, list facilities, and even keep a room waiting; however, calling a hotel directly for a reservation (especially on a Sunday night) is often better than calling the chain's toll-free number or booking over the Internet. Ask to speak to the manager on duty or someone in the sales office, and ask them to put a note in your record requesting a room upgrade, just on the off chance that one is available and offered.

CAMPING AND HOSTELS

Whether you want to get completely away from it all or just relocate and bring most of it with you, camping is the most flexible and affordable way to travel for an extended period.

Campgrounds vary widely, but most are open from March or April through November or December. Reservations and/or deposits may be necessary at private campgrounds in resort areas or during peak seasons.

Public campgrounds include those at state parks, state fishing lakes, and wildlife management areas. A number of state parks also have **cabins** for rent March–December. Reserve these and state park campgrounds online at www.reserveamerica.com. Free primitive camping is permitted in the backcountry of the Jefferson and George Washington National Forests except where specifically prohibited. Backcountry and campsite camping are possible in the Shenandoah National Park.

Private campgrounds usually include grills, drinking water, flush toilets, hot showers, coin laundry, and a camp store. More elaborate sites, typified by **KOA Kampgrounds** (406/248-7444, www.koakampgrounds.com), come complete with pools, game rooms, hot tubs, saunas, and volleyball courts. Occasionally they'll have small **cabins** with air-conditioning and heat for about the price of a budget motel room. Features such as bicycle rental, miniature golf, and summer children's programs cost extra. You can reserve campsites online.

Hookups for water, electricity, and sewer are charged as a whole or occasionally available separately. RV drivers can contact the **Recreation Vehicle Industry Association** (703/620-6003, www.rvia.org) for information on choosing and operating an RV.

Virginia has Hostelling International (HI) outposts in Virginia Beach and on the Blue Ridge Parkway near Galax. Even without the member's discount, these modest lodgings can be cheaper than a hotel room at $20–35 per person per night (less for members). Hostels are sometimes closed during the day and lock their doors at 10 P.M., but increasing numbers of hostel lodgings allow 24-hour access. Contact the Potomac Area Council of Hostelling International USA (202/783-4943, www.potomachostels.org) for details.

HI membership is $28 per year for adults and can be acquired at any hostel or from **Hostelling International USA** (301/495-1240, www.hiusa.org). The online directory **Hostels.com** lists hotels worldwide.

BED-AND-BREAKFASTS AND INNS

Bed-and-breakfasts, although more expensive, can often be a reason for visiting in themselves. Staying at one is like being a guest in someone's house, which is often exactly what you are, except there's someone to cater to your every whim and the building is often an outstanding antique. Nobody opens a bed-and-breakfast to retire early (although many owners already are retired), so you know your hosts are in it for the joy of meeting people and sharing their love of the area. Owners have often grown up nearby or even in the same house, making them an ideal source of local guidance and trivia.

Multicourse silver-service breakfasts are the norm instead of the exception—no muffin-and–instant coffee "continental" fare here. Smoking is usually permitted outside only, if at all (one brochure reads, "The house is 200 years old and the fire department five miles away"). Private bathrooms are standard, or at least there's a separate bath just down the hall—these always seem to have large claw-foot tubs. Guests can often use a kitchen or kitchenette to prepare food.

Country inns straddle the line between hotels and bed-and-breakfasts, with the formalized quality of service of the former and much of the charm of the latter. Led by the world-class Inn at Little Washington, Virginia's inns offer privacy and luxury in a romantic, indulgent setting.

Advance reservations are desirable for both inns and bed-and-breakfasts, especially during weekends, high season, and special events. Popular ones fill up months or even years in advance. A deposit in the form of one night's fee is often required, and a minimum length of stay may be imposed during the high season. Cancellation requires prior notice—at least 24 hours, or as much as one week—to avoid paying a service charge. Deals on multi-night stays are possible. Rates given are per room, double occupancy.

The **Bed and Breakfast Association of Virginia** (888/660-2228, www.innvirginia.com) lists its members online. Anther helpful source is **Bed & Breakfast Inns Online** (www.bbonline.com/va).

OTHER WAYS TO TRAVEL

U.S. Servas (707/825-1714, www.usservas.org) oversees a worldwide network of hosts and travelers designed to promote peace and foster intercultural understanding through person-to-person contact. After an initial interview, travelers 18 and older pay a yearly fee ($85 international, $50 domestic, $25 student) to rent a list of hosts who offer free room and board for two nights. Becoming a Servas traveler is an excellent way to meet interesting local people and can easily recoup your initial investment. **Couchsurfing** (www.couchsurfing.com) is another similar budget travel option with a bit less paperwork involved.

If you're interested in a longer-term stay, consider a home exchange. **HomeExchange.com** (www.homeexchange.com) currently has the most listings in Virginia. The use of cars is often included, and you can also trade boats or RVs for homes, at least temporarily. Its list is free to search, but costs $10/month for a year membership ($16/month for a three-month membership), which you'll need to make the exchange.

Tips for Travelers

HEALTH AND SAFETY

For emergencies anywhere in the state, dial 911 from any phone (no charge) or the local sheriff or police department. On your cell phone, dial #77 to reach the State Police. Hospitals in larger cities are excellent, although emergency-room treatment is always much more expensive than scheduled appointments.

Outdoors

Whenever you go into the wild, always tell someone where you're going and when you expect to be back, and then contact them when you return. It's a good idea to carry a first-aid kit, available prepackaged at most camp, drug, or large discount stores, and bring extra clothing layers (including a waterproof layer) and a safety kit that includes a Swiss army knife, waterproof matches, compass, topographical map, flashlight, emergency blanket, signal whistle, and emergency food.

Even the clearest, highest mountain streams stand a good chance of containing **giardia,** a bacteria transmitted in human and animal waste that causes severe diarrhea. Filter or treat all water with iodine pills or drops. **Mosquitoes** are an annoyance everywhere in the summer and fall, along with **bees, wasps, yellowjackets,** and **hornets.** Female **black widow spiders,** identifiable by a tiny red hourglass on their black abdomens, live in dark, woody places like rotting logs and under benches and tables. Their bite causes severe abdominal pain. If you are bitten, consult a physician. **Lyme disease** is transmitted through deer-tick bites. The mid-Atlantic is prime tick territory, so use insect repellent and check yourself after passing through high grass or underbrush. If you notice a large red circular rash like a bull's eye around a bite, seek medical treatment—it's life-threatening if untreated.

Virginia is home to three species of poisonous snakes: **Rattlesnakes** live in the mountains, **cottonmouth moccasins** inhabit swamps, and **copperheads** are everywhere. Don't stick your feet or hands anywhere you can't see, and if you encounter a snake, back off slowly. They're more afraid of you than you are of them and strike out of fear at sudden movements. Swimming in the ocean could expose you to a brush with a **jellyfish.** The best thing to minimize the sting (besides staying out of the water) is—believe it or not—meat tenderizer.

Plants to avoid include **poison ivy, poison oak,** and **poison sumac.** Stay clear of waxy-looking leaves in groups of three. (Remember the saying, "Leaves of three, let it be.") The irritating oil transmitted by contact with these plants can be washed off with soap and water, and over-the-counter cortisone creams can relieve the itching. Several local types of **mushrooms** and **berries** are also dangerous if ingested: Don't eat any if you don't know what you're doing.

Weather

Being wet and tired in the cold mountains can lead to **hypothermia,** a dangerous plunge in the body's core temperature. Symptoms include shivering, slurred speech, and loss of coordination and mental clarity. Warm the affected person up by skin-to-skin contact and with liquids (no alcohol), and evacuate as a last resort. **Lightning** is a danger on exposed ridges, so stay away from lone trees and conductive materials such as power lines and metal fences. The summer sun along the coast can cause a nasty **sunburn,** so cover up with clothes and sunscreen, at least for the first week or so.

Crime

Although things have improved in the last few decades, the downtown areas of larger cities such as Richmond and Norfolk still pose a threat of **robbery,** especially at night. Check with hotel staff regarding safe and dangerous areas. To discourage **break-ins** and **car theft,** don't leave valuables in plain view in your vehicle, and always lock the doors. Consider using an antitheft device like The Club in questionable neighborhoods.

MAPS

The **AAA map** of Virginia is the handiest for general navigation. For every last back road and some city maps, pick up a copy of the large-format ***Virginia Topographic Atlas and Gazetteer*** published by DeLorme ($20). Hikers can get **topographical maps** ($8–10) put out by the U.S. Geological Survey (http://topomaps.usgs.gov) from the USGS, outdoor stores, or **Omni Resources** (800/742-2677, www.omnimap.com), which also carries city and recreational maps. USGS also allows you to download topo maps as PDF files directly from its website for free, the best deal of all.

If you're into maps as art, order a catalog from **Raven Maps & Images** (800/237-0798, www.ravenmaps.com). At 35 by 65 inches, its *Virginia, Maryland, Delaware, & D.C.* map is too large to carry in the car with you, but with tinted elevation and shaded relief, it's nice enough to frame and hang on the wall ($30 non-laminated, $50 laminated).

INFORMATION

The **Virginia Tourism Corporation** (800/847-4882, www.virginia.org) can send you information on almost anything having to do with visiting the state. The **state government** (804/786-4718 or 877/482-3468, www.virginia.gov) is also a good resource.

STUDENT TRAVEL

STA Travel (800/781-4040, www.statravel.com) issues the International Student Identity Card (ISIC) and under-26 Youth Cards that can secure cheap flights and the occasional admission deal. Canadian students should contact a local branch of **Travel CUTS** (866/246-9762, www.travelcuts.com) for rail passes and discounted flights.

GAY AND LESBIAN TRAVELERS

South of the D.C. suburbs, Virginia as a whole tends to lean toward the conservative end of the moral spectrum, so discretion is advised, although you will find that Charlottesville, Richmond, and the Norfolk–Virginia Beach area have a number of gay-friendly businesses and sizeable gay communities. The **Dulles Triangles** (www.dullestriangles.com) is a gay social club in the northern Virginia area. In Richmond, **GayRVA** (www.gayrva.com) is the capital city's online magazine for the LGBT community, and in Washington it's the **DC Agenda** (www.dcagenda.com). The travel section at **PlanetOut.com**) is another good general resource covering resorts, hotels, cruise lines, and airlines.

TRAVELERS WITH DISABILITIES

Wheelchair access varies statewide, so it's always best to call ahead and check. Upscale hotels are usually accessible, but bed-and-breakfasts—often in old houses—may not be. Some theaters and restaurants have ramps and elevators, and some caverns and Civil War sites feature paved trails. All National Park Service visitors centers are wheelchair accessible. Most restrooms and buildings in Shenandoah National Park are accessible, along with some picnic grounds and campgrounds.

The Virginia Tourism Corporation provides special numbers (800/742-3935, TDD 804/371-0327) for questions regarding special-needs travel. The **Opening Door** (804/633-6752, www.travelguides.org) is a local nonprofit organization that publishes the free ***Virginia Travel Guide for Persons with Disabilities*** (www.travelguides.org/vaguide.html), with tons of information on accessible Virginia hotels, restaurants, shops, and attractions.

For more information on traveling with a disability, contact **Mobility International USA** (541/343-1284, www.miusa.org) or the **Society for Accessible Travel and Hospitality** (212/447-7284, www.sath.org).

TRAVELING WITH CHILDREN

From amusement parks and museums to hiking trails and caves, Virginia is overflowing with fun stuff to do with kids. Local baby-sitting agencies can be found through hotel desks. **Family Travel Times** (212/477-5524, www.familytraveltimes) publishes a bimonthly newsletter with articles like "Country Inns That Really Like Kids" and "Mountains of Fun" ($39 for a one-year subscription, $49 for two). Numerous websites such as TravelforKids.com have more ideas.

SENIOR TRAVELERS

Many hotels and attractions offer discounts for seniors: Ask when making reservations or at the gate. The **American Association of Retired Persons (AARP)** (888/687-2277, www.aarp.org) is the country's largest seniors' organization, with discounts for members ($16 per year) on hotels, car rentals, air travel, and tours worldwide. **Exploritas** (800/454-5768, www.exploritas.org) organizes worldwide "extraordinary learning adventures" for people 55 and over.

TRAVEL INSURANCE

Several agencies offer specialized travelers' insurance in various combinations of health, accident, trip-cancellation and trip-interruption, and lost-luggage protection. Two dependable choices are **Travel Guard International** (715/345-0505 or 800/826-4919, www.travelguard.com) and **Access America** (800/284-8300, www.accessamerica.com).

INTERNET ACCESS

As the Internet has nudged its way into nearly every corner of our lives, it's good to know that it's getting easier to hop aboard every day. If you haven't joined the iPhone and BlackBerry thumb-warriors yet, there are still some old-school options for getting wired. Many **public libraries** offer free Internet access, even for non-cardholders, although you may have to wait for a time slot to open. If you have a laptop with you, many hotel chains offer free **wireless high-speed Internet access** in rooms, allowing anyone with a Wi-Fi-enabled laptop to simply log on and start surfing. Plenty of bed-and-breakfasts and private hotels do the same. Many coffee shops offer this service to attract customers, and some entire cities are even going wireless (downtown Roanoke is one big free Wi-Fi hot spot, and so is the Charlottesville pedestrian mall). Pay services such as T-Mobile's HotSpot (http://hotspot.t-mobile.com), available in Starbucks coffee shops and Barnes & Noble bookstores, are still around as well. Many websites list free wireless Internet hot spots; try www.wi-fihotspotlist.com and www.wififreespot.com.

TIME ZONES

Virginia is in the Eastern Standard Time Zone, five hours behind Greenwich mean time.

Daylight saving time sets clocks one hour ahead on the first Sunday in March ("spring forward") and one hour back on the first Sunday in November ("fall back").

BUSINESS HOURS

Stores are generally open 9 A.M.–6 P.M. Monday–Saturday, and occasionally on Sunday. Shopping centers can be open daily, late on weeknights, and noon–5 or 6 P.M. Sunday. Public and private office hours run 9 A.M.–5 P.M. Monday–Friday, and banks are open 9 A.M.–5 P.M. Monday–Friday, sometimes with extended hours on Friday evenings and Saturday mornings. Post office doors open at 9 A.M. Monday–Saturday and stay open until 5 P.M. on weekdays and 1 or 2 P.M. on Saturday. Museum and gallery hours vary, but many are closed on Monday; the same goes for restaurants. Just about everything closes on Thanksgiving, Christmas, and New Year's Day (even sites listed as open daily), and other national holidays may mean closings as well.

TIPPING

As any former restaurant server will tell you (and there are plenty of us out there), a 15 percent tip on bills is standard, since some waitstaff make less than minimum wage before tips. Leave 20 percent or more to reward superior service, and consider talking with the waiter or a manager if there's a problem, instead of leaving a smaller tip. Other service providers, such as taxi drivers and hairstylists, typically receive 10–15 percent, and airport porters and bellhops should get about $1–2 per bag.

RESOURCES

Suggested Reading

BACKGROUND

Barbour, Philip, and Thad Tate, eds. *The Complete Works of Captain John Smith, 1580–1631.* Chapel Hill: University of North Carolina Press, 1986. Three volumes, including *A True Relation of Such Occurrences and Accidents of Note as Hath Happened in Virginia* (1608), and *A Generall Historie of Virginia* (1624).

Dabney, Virginius. *Richmond: Story of a City.* Charlottesville, VA: University Press of Virginia, 1990. The story of the state capital.

Dabney, Virginius. *Virginia: The New Dominion.* Charlottesville, VA: University of Virginia Press, 1989. The consummate state history.

Jefferson, Thomas. *Notes on the State of Virginia.* Chapel Hill: University of North Carolina Press, 1996. Jefferson's only full-length book, an American classic, opens a vivid window into the author's personality and life in the 18th century.

McGraw, Mary Tyler. *At the Falls: Richmond, Virginia, and Its People.* Chapel Hill: University of North Carolina Press, 1994. Beautiful photos, prints, and engravings enhance this comprehensive history of the state capital.

Civil War History

Catton, Bruce. *America Goes to War: The Civil War and Its Meaning in American Culture.* Middletown, CT: Wesleyan University Press, 1992. Catton also wrote a compelling three-volume account of the war, consisting of *The Coming Fury, Terrible Swift Sword,* and *Never Call Retreat.*

McPherson, James. *Battle Cry of Freedom: The Civil War Era.* New York: Ballantine Books, 1988. Dense (900 pages), but probably the best single-volume history of the war.

Ward, Geoffrey C., Ric Burns, and Ken Burns. *The Civil War: An Illustrated History.* New York: Alfred A. Knopf, 1990. The lavishly illustrated companion volume to Ken Burns's award-winning PBS series.

RECREATION

Civil War Touring

Braselton, Susan, ed. *The Civil War Trust's Official Guide to the Civil War Discovery Trail.* New York: Frommer's, 1998. A handy guide that covers the entire theater.

General Outdoor Recreation

Carrol, Steven, and Mark Miller. *Wild Virginia.* Helena, MT: Falcon Press, 2002. If you want to get away from the internal-combustion engine, this is your book: a guide to 30 roadless, wilderness, and special management areas throughout the state (but mostly in the Shenandoah and southwest). Includes trail descriptions and suggestions for day and overnight hikes and cross-country ski routes.

Molloy, Johnny. *Mount Rogers Outdoor Recreation Handbook.* Birmingham, AL: Menasha Ridge Press, 2001. Everything you could possibly want to do around Virginia's highest peak, from hiking and camping to fishing and horseback riding. Even includes information on swimming holes and the Virginia Creeper and New River Trails. This one is comprehensive.

Hiking

Adkins, Leonard. *50 Hikes in Northern Virginia.* Woodstock, VT: The Countryman Press, 2000. For rambles near D.C., from the mountains to the bay.

Adkins, Leonard. *Walking the Blue Ridge.* Chapel Hill: University of North Carolina Press, 1996. Details every trail that touches the Blue Ridge Parkway, 122 in all. Plus descriptions of flora, fauna, history, and geology, and a roadside bloom calendar.

Clauson-Wicker, Su. *Inn to Inn Walking Guide: Virginia and West Virginia.* Birmingham, AL: Menasha Ridge Press, 2001. If you like to hike but aren't a fan of backpacks, consider this: details for 20 day hikes from one bed-and-breakfast to another.

de Hart, Allen. *The Trails of Virginia: Hiking the Old Dominion.* Chapel Hill: University of North Carolina Press, 1995. The authoritative work, covering every trail in the state from Civil War battlefields to backcountry.

Gildart, Bert, and Jane Gildart. *Best Easy Day Hikes Shenandoah.* Helena, MT: Falcon Press, 1998. Pocket-sized version of the Gildarts' larger guide to the park. Twenty-six hikes with maps and pertinent details.

Gildart, Bert, and Jane Gildart. *Hiking Shenandoah National Park.* Helena, MT: Falcon Press, 2000. Fifty-nine hikes from one end of the park to the other, from easy day hikes with children to overnight ventures. Detailed descriptions and maps.

Johnson, Randy. *Hiking Virginia.* Helena, MT: Falcon Press, 1992. A slim but functional guide to a selection (52) of the state's trails, including history hikes, beach rambles, and Shenandoah National Park.

Manning, Russ. *75 Hikes in Virginia's Shenandoah National Park.* Seattle: The Mountaineers Books, 2000. Includes maps, photos, and information on history, plants, animals, and geology.

Potomac Appalachian Trail Club. *Circuit Hikes in Virginia, West Virginia, Maryland, and Pennsylvania.* Vienna, VA: PATC, 1994. This pocket-sized guide includes 15 loop trails in Virginia ranging from day hikes to overnighters, with topographical maps and mile-by-mile descriptions.

Wuertz-Schaefer, Karin. *Hiking Virginia's National Forests.* Guildford, CT: Globe Pequot, 2001. Another pocket-sized guide, now in its seventh printing, that lists more than 50 trails in the George Washington and Jefferson National Forests. Includes parts of the AT.

Bicycling

Adams, Scott. *Mountain Bike America: Virginia.* Guilford, CT: Globe Pequot, 2000. With close to 50 choice trails (and 19 more "honorable mentions") described in detail, this guidebook also throws in GPS-quality topo maps, elevation profiles, and plenty of other tidbits. Highly recommended.

Porter, Randy. *Mountain Bike! Virginia.* Birmingham, AL: Menasha Ridge Press, 2001. Exhaustive guide to 91 bike trails from the coast to the Blue Ridge. Maps and detailed descriptions provided for each one.

Skinner, Elizabeth, and Charlie Skinner. *Bicycling the Blue Ridge.* Birmingham, AL: Menasha Ridge Press, 1990. Point-by-point description of both the Skyline Drive in Shenandoah National Park and the Blue Ridge Parkway in Virginia and North Carolina, all from a cyclist's perspective. Includes elevation profile, maps, and info on restaurants, accommodations, and stores along the way.

Rafting

Sehlinger, Bob, Dave Denner, and Ed Grove. *Appalachian Whitewater: The Southern States.* Birmingham, AL: Menasha Ridge Press, 2000. Covers class I–IV white water in Alabama, Georgia, South Carolina, North Carolina, Tennessee, Kentucky, Virginia, Maryland, and West Virginia. In the Old Dominion, it lists paddling details for the South Fork of the Shenandoah, the Potomac at Great Falls, Whitetop Laurel Creek near Mount Rogers, and the Rappahannock, Tye, Maury, James, and Appomattox Rivers, among others.

Fishing

Camuto, Christopher. *A Fly Fisherman's Blue Ridge.* Athens: University of Georgia Press, 2001. The author, an angler and naturalist, traces one year of fly-fishing in the Blue Ridge in 11 essays. A good read for anyone interested in fishing or the natural history of streams.

Gooch, Bob. *Virginia Fishing Guide.* Charlottesville: University Press of Virginia, 1998. Revised edition.

Ingram, Bruce. *The James River Guide.* Corvallis, OR: Ecopress, 2000. An intimate portrait of the James above Richmond, useful to floaters, anglers, and naturalists.

Miller, Skip. *Tidewater Fishing: The Complete Guide to Eastern Virginia Waters.* Lincolnwood, IL: NTC/Contemporary Publishing, 1996. Focuses on the shore and the Chesapeake Bay.

Murray, Harry. *Virginia Blue Ribbon Fly Fishing Guide.* Portland, OR: Frank Amato Publications, 2000. Fly-fishing spots and advice for streams and rivers statewide.

Climbing

Hörst, Eric. *Rock Climbing Virginia, West Virginia, and Maryland.* Helena, MT: Falcon Press, 2001. Details ascents at Old Rag, Great Falls, Skyline Drive, and other crags, as well as quality climbing spots nearby such as Carderock, Maryland, and Nelson Rocks, West Virginia.

Watson, Jeff. *Virginia Climber's Guide.* Mechanicsburg, PA: Stackpole Books, 1998. The most comprehensive guide to rock climbing throughout the state.

Natural History

Experienced naturalists know it's hard to beat the illustrated Peterson Field Guides series, published by Houghton Mifflin (Boston), the straightforward standard for amateurs and professionals alike. Covering the mid-Atlantic are *A Field Guide to the Mammals* (William H. Burt, 1998), *A Field Guide to Animal Tracks* (J. Murie, 1998), *A Field Guide to the Birds* (Roger Tory Peterson, 1998), and *A Field Guide to Reptiles & Amphibians: Eastern & Central North America* (Roger Conant and Joseph Collins, 1998).

Badger, Curtis. *A Naturalist's Guide to the Virginia Coast.* Mechanicsburg, PA: Stackpole Books, 1996. Great beach reading, divided between background and visiting information. Heavy on bird-watching.

Duda, Mark Damian. *Virginia Wildlife Viewing Guide.* Helena, MT: Falcon Press, 1994. Produced in partnership with a host of state and federal resource agencies and private organizations, this guide points the way to 80 of the state's best viewing areas, with information on who and what you'll see. Color maps and photos.

Frye, Keith. *Roadside Geology of Virginia.* Missoula, MT: Mountain Press, 2003. Includes general information on the state's geologic history, plus guides to those parts visible along major highways throughout the sate.

Gupton, Oscar. *Wildflowers of the Shenandoah Valley and Blue Ridge Mountains.* Charlottesville: University of Virginia Press, 2002. Gupton also wrote *Trees and Shrubs of*

Virginia (UVaP, 2002), *Wildflowers of Tidewater Virginia* (UVaP, 1989), *Wild Orchids of the Middle Atlantic States* (University of Tennessee Press, 1987), *Fall Wildflowers of the Blue Ridge and Great Smoky Mountains* (UVaP, 1987), and *Wildflowers of the Shenandoah Valley and Blue Ridge Mountains* (UVaP, 2002).

Nock, Anne. *Child of the Bay: Past, Present, and Future.* Charlottesville, VA: Hampton Roads Publishing, 1993. Natural history of the Eastern Shore.

Williams, John Page, Jr. *Chesapeake Almanac: Following the Bay Through the Seasons.* Centreville, MD: Tidewater, 1993. A collection of the author's columns from *Chesapeake Bay* magazine that traces the life in and around the bay for a year.

Other Recreation

Cavileer, Sharon. *Virginia Curiosities.* Guilford, CT: Globe Pequot, 2002. I dig guides like this: a compendium of offbeat attractions throughout the Old Dominion, from the Egg Lady in Culpeper to the ghosts that haunt the Chamberlin Hotel in Hampton. Fun to leaf through even if you're not visiting.

Colbert, Judy. *Virginia Off the Beaten Path.* Guilford, CT: Globe Pequot, 2002. Another compendium of unusual attractions—not as wacky as *Virginia Curiosities,* but some interesting finds nonetheless.

Logue, Victoria, Frank Logue, and Nicole Blouin. *Guide to the Blue Ridge Parkway.* Birmingham, AL: Menasha Ridge Press, 1997. A milepost-by-milepost guide to the parkway in Virginia and North Carolina, with interesting historical sidebars and information on geography, plants, animals, culture, and attractions.

Noe, Barabara. *The Official Rails-to-Trails Conservancy Guidebook: Maryland, Delaware, Virginia, and West Virginia.* Guilford, CT: Globe Pequot, 2000. A state-by-state guide to walking, jogging, biking, and skiing 32 of the area's rail-trails.

Sloane, Bruce. *Scenic Driving Virginia.* Helena, MT: Falcon Press, 1999. A former park ranger details 22 day-long drives across the state, from Mount Rogers to the Potomac, including information on history and geology.

FICTION

Brooks, Geraldine. *March.* New York: Penguin, 2006. Civil War as experienced by Mr. March, the absent father in Louisa May Alcott's *Little Women.*

Crane, Stephen. *Red Badge of Courage.* New York: HarperCollins, 1996. The battle of Chancellorsville as seen by an idealistic, frightened young Union recruit. A classroom classic for a reason.

Kingsolver, Barbara. *Prodigal Summer.* New York: HarperCollins, 2001. Three interwoven stories in an isolated pocket of southern Appalachia.

Styron, William. *The Confessions of Nat Turner.* New York: Random House, 1993. Pulitzer Prize–winning account of the abortive 1831 slave uprising in Southampton County.

Trigiani, Adriana. *Big Stone Gap.* New York: Ballantine, 2001. A middle-aged spinster finds love in a small Virginia coal town.

FOLKLORE

Barden, Thomas, ed. *Virginia Folk Legends.* Charlottesville: University of Virginia Press, 1991.

Garrison, Webb. *A Treasury of Virginia Tales.* Nashville, TN: Rutledge Hill Press, 1996. Subtitled "Unusual, Interesting, and Little-Known Stories of Virginia."

Jameson, W. C. *Buried Treasures of the Appalachians: Legends of Homestead Caches, Indian Mines and Loot from Civil War Raids.* Little Rock, AR: August House, 1991. Subtitled "Forty tales of lost wealth, gathered from interviews with those who have searched for it." Even includes maps.

Jameson, W. C. *Buried Treasures of the South: Legends of Lost, Buried, and Forgotten Treasures—From Tidewater Virginia and Coastal Carolina to Cajun Louisiana.* Little Rock, AR: August House, 1992.

NONFICTION

Blake, Allison. *The Chesapeake Bay Book: A Complete Guide.* Lee, MA: Berkshire House, 2002. A great book for those interested in exploring the bay up into Maryland.

Dillard, Annie. *Pilgrim at Tinker Creek.* Hightstown, NJ: McGraw-Hill, 2000. Metaphysical, beautifully written observations on life and the universe set in the Roanoke valley.

Mariner, Kirk. *Off 13: The Eastern Shore of Virginia Guidebook.* New Church, VA: Miona Publications, 2000. Available locally and full of native nuggets.

Rowe, Elliott Walker. *Wandering Through Virginia's Wineries.* Baltimore, MD: Apprentice House, 2005.

Warner, William. *Beautiful Swimmers: Watermen, Crabs and the Chesapeake Bay.* New York: Little, Brown & Co., 1994. Pulitzer Prize–winning account of life on the bay.

Washington, Booker T. *Up From Slavery.* New York: Signet Classic, 2000. A vivid account of the struggle faced by African Americans at the turn of the 20th century.

Whitehead, John Hurt, III. *The Watermen of the Chesapeake Bay.* Centerville, MD: Tidewater Publishing, 1987. Photographic account of watermen in the 1980s, interspersed with colorful quotations.

Internet Resources

A quick—or long—look at the Internet before you travel in Virginia can make your journey both easier and more rewarding. You can do practically anything online except actually set foot on Old Dominion soil, from booking hotel reservations and reserving theater tickets to finding out when the fall colors are their brightest.

Civil War Traveler: Virginia
www.civilwar-va.com/virginia

This great resource for planning Civil War–based sightseeing trips throughout the state includes information on regional attractions and events, with maps and more details available by mail.

Great Outdoor Resource Page (GORP): Virginia
http://gorp.away.com/gorp/location/va/va.htm

Details on all the state's outdoor glory, from hiking and camping to mountain biking and winery tours.

Hiking Upward
www.hikingupward.com

An easy-to-use interactive map of Virginia hiking trail descriptions, directions, maps, and photos. Great source for new adventures.

HomeTownFreePress
www.hometownfreepress.com/va.htm

A list of local Virginia newspapers.

The Mountain Laurel
www.mtnlaurel.com

This "journal of mountain life" focuses on Virginia's Blue Ridge. Online issues include interviews with old-timers, tall tales, crafts, recipes, back-road tours, and genealogy.

The Official Commonwealth of Virginia Home Page
www.state.va.us
Virginia's state government home page offers links to information on government, education, business, and other practical matters.

Virginia.com
www.virginia.com
This general state travel website includes city guides, white and yellow pages, and a hotel reservation service.

Virginia Department of Conservation and Recreation
www.dcr.state.va.us
Everything you ever wanted to know about Virginia's natural world, including parks and recreation areas.

Virginia Is for Lovers
www.virginia.org
Virginia Tourism Corporation's main website provides a wide variety of resources, including information on wineries, outdoor sports, and seasonal events.

Yahoo! Virginia
http://dir.yahoo.com/Regional/U_S__States/Virginia
The Yahoo! web directory's Virginia portal is the best place to start if you're browsing or don't know exactly what you're trying to find.

Index

D

E

H

M

N

O

P

QR

S

T

W

XYZ

List of Maps

Acknowledgments

First off, I owe thanks to my parents for their continued encouragement from afar. Book projects have a way of snowballing, and my mom and dad have a calming way of nudging me forward to keep up with the momentum. Likewise to my husband Mike and dog Denali; I love you both dearly.

Morgana Wingard, thanks for the work dates and the photography tips. I hope to glean only a fraction of your talent behind a camera lens. Kathleen Brady and Liz Klimas, thanks for holding down the fort at the office while I traipsed across the Virginia countryside on my part-time schedule.

Many thanks to the Van Dyke family for generously sharing their favorite places in Virginia and allowing me to show up nearly unannounced on their doorsteps in Richmond (Emilie) and Williamsburg (Jan and Dave). The fifth edition of *Moon Virginia* would not have been possible without you.

I'm especially grateful to the helpful staff at the Virginia Tourism Corporation, as well as countless smaller visitors centers and tourism agencies from Reedville to Staunton. At Avalon Travel, thank you to editor Kathryn Ettinger, production coordinator Elizabeth Jang, and map editor Albert Angulo for deftly moving this edition through to publication. To original author Julian Smith, it was fascinating to follow your footsteps while updating this guidebook, and I'm obliged for your legwork in the previous four editions.

And to the kind man with the West Virginia license plates who winched my Toyota 4Runner out of a snowy ditch near Middleburg, I'm especially indebted. Winter 2009 to 2010 was a doozy.

www.moon.com

DESTINATIONS | ACTIVITIES | BLOGS | MAPS | BOOKS

MOON.COM is ready to help plan your next trip! Filled with fresh trip ideas and strategies, author interviews, informative travel blogs, a detailed map library, and descriptions of all the Moon guidebooks, Moon.com is all you need to get out and explore the world—or even places in your own backyard. While at Moon.com, sign up for our monthly e-newsletter for updates on new releases, travel tips, and expert advice from our on-the-go Moon authors. As always, when you travel with Moon, expect an experience that is uncommon and truly unique.

MOON IS ON FACEBOOK—BECOME A FAN!

JOIN THE MOON PHOTO GROUP ON FLICKR

MAP SYMBOLS

	Expressway		Highlight		Airport		Metro
	Primary Road		City/Town		Airfield		Parking Area
	Secondary Road		State Capital		Mountain		Golf Course
	Unpaved Road		National Capital		Unique Natural Feature		Church
	Trail		Point of Interest		Waterfall		Gas Station
	Ferry		Accommodation		Park		Glacier
	Railroad		Restaurant/Bar		Trailhead		Mangrove
	Pedestrian Walkway		Other Location		Skiing Area		Reef
	Stairs		Campground		Battlefield		Swamp

CONVERSION TABLES

°C = (°F - 32) / 1.8
°F = (°C x 1.8) + 32
1 inch = 2.54 centimeters (cm)
1 foot = 0.304 meters (m)
1 yard = 0.914 meters
1 mile = 1.6093 kilometers (km)
1 km = 0.6214 miles
1 fathom = 1.8288 m
1 chain = 20.1168 m
1 furlong = 201.168 m
1 acre = 0.4047 hectares
1 sq km = 100 hectares
1 sq mile = 2.59 square km
1 ounce = 28.35 grams
1 pound = 0.4536 kilograms
1 short ton = 0.90718 metric ton
1 short ton = 2,000 pounds
1 long ton = 1.016 metric tons
1 long ton = 2,240 pounds
1 metric ton = 1,000 kilograms
1 quart = 0.94635 liters
1 US gallon = 3.7854 liters
1 Imperial gallon = 4.5459 liters
1 nautical mile = 1.852 km

MOON VIRGINIA
Avalon Travel
a member of the Perseus Books Group
1700 Fourth Street
Berkeley, CA 94710, USA
www.moon.com

Editor and Series Manager: Kathryn Ettinger
Copy Editor: Amy Scott
Graphics Coordinator: Elizabeth Jang
Production Coordinator: Elizabeth Jang
Cover Designer: Elizabeth Jang
Map Editor: Albert Angulo
Cartographers: Kat Bennett, Allison Rawley
Indexer: Greg Jewett

ISBN: 978-1-59880-355-6
ISSN: 1537-5803

Printing History
1st Edition – 1999
5th Edition – October 2010
5 4 3 2 1

Front cover photo: Arlington National Cemetery © Katie Githens
Title page photo: emblem on the gate to the Ball's Bluff National Cemetery © Katie Githens

Interior color photos: p. 4 a red barn along Route 662 en route to Waterford; p. 5 (left) the historic Stonewall Jackson Hotel in Staunton, (middle) the Rotunda at the University of Virginia in Charlottesville, (right) the dome of the U.S. Capitol; p. 6 (inset) wildflowers on a fence post in Leesburg, (bottom) flag of the 11th Alabama Infantry at the Museum of the Confederacy in Richmond, © Museum of the Confederacy; p. 7 (top left) the Lincoln Memorial in Washington, D.C., (top right) cannon at Manassas National Battlefield Park, (lower left) stained-glass window detail at the Washington National Cathedral in Washington, D.C., (lower right) the famous Chincoteague wild ponies; p. 10 (top left) portraits on display at the Museum of the Confederacy, © Museum of the Confederacy. All photos © Katie Githens unless otherwise indicated.

Printed in Canada by Friesens

KEEPING CURRENT

If you have a favorite gem you'd like to see included in the next edition, or see anything that needs updating, clarification, or correction, please drop us a line. Send your comments via email to feedback@moon.com, or use the address above.